F# for C# Developers

Tao Liu

PUBLISHED BY
Microsoft Press
A Division of Microsoft Corporation
One Microsoft Way
Redmond, Washington 98052-6399

Library of Congress Control Number: 2013935410
ISBN: 978-0-7356-7026-6

Printed and bound in the United States of America.

First Printing

Microsoft Press books are available through booksellers and distributors worldwide. If you need support related to this book, email Microsoft Press Book Support at mspinput@microsoft.com. Please tell us what you think of this book at http://www.microsoft.com/learning/booksurvey.

Acquisitions Editor: Devon Musgrave
Developmental Editor: Devon Musgrave
Project Editor: Rosemary Caperton
Editorial Production: Waypoint Press
Technical Reviewer: Daniel Mohl; Technical Review services provided by Content Master, a member of CM Group, Ltd.
Indexer: Christina Yeager
Cover: Twist Creative • Seattle and Joel Panchot

Contents at a Glance

Table of Contents

What do you think of this book? We want to hear from you!

Microsoft is interested in hearing your feedback so we can continually improve our
books and learning resources for you. To participate in a brief online survey, please visit:

microsoft.com/learning/booksurvey

PART II   F#'S UNIQUE FEATURES

Chapter 4   Type Providers   163

What do you think of this book? We want to hear from you!

Microsoft is interested in hearing your feedback so we can continually improve our
books and learning resources for you. To participate in a brief online survey, please visit:

microsoft.com/learning/booksurvey

Foreword

People often ask, "What can F# do that C# cannot?" In this book, you will discover much of what F# can do! You will see familiar things such as object programming and design patterns. Further, you will also see powerful new things like pattern matching, piping, first-class events, object expressions, options, tuples, records, discriminated unions, active patterns, agents, computation expressions and, perhaps most distinctively, type providers.

However, we also need to ask the other question: "What can C# do that F# cannot?" There is one important part to this answer that I will focus on here: C# can cause *NullReferenceExceptions*. "What?" I hear you ask. "Does F# not have nulls?" Right! Perhaps the most important thing the C# programmer needs to know about F# is that F# does not use nulls in routine programming.

Let's look at some evidence. People using F# at a major UK energy company did a study of two similar ETL (Extract, Transform, Load) applications.[1] Broadly speaking, the applications were in the same zone in terms of functionality or, if anything, the F# application implemented more features. The F# project had a very low bug rate, and its code was 26 times smaller. The size difference is not only the result of language differences; there are also differences in design methodology. The C# project is characterized by the inappropriate overuse of elaborate object abstractions often seen in Java projects—for example, elaborate and unnecessary class hierarchies.

Interestingly, the comparison records that the C# project had 3036 explicit null checks, where a functionally similar F# project had 27, a reduction of 112 times in the total number of null checks. The other statistics in the comparison shown are also compelling, particularly the "defects since go live": the F# code had zero defects since "go live," and the C# code had "too many." These are not unrelated: nulls cause defects. In my opinion, the lack of nulls in routine coding alone makes it worth switching your programming teams to F# where possible.

In this book, you will learn many wonderful things about F#. But don't lose sight of the big picture: F# is about writing accurate, correct, efficient, interoperable code that gets deployed on time in enterprise scenarios. It does this partly by removing the most pernicious of evils: nulls. If you and your team embrace it, then, all else being equal, your life will be simpler, happy, and more productive.

—Don Syme
F# Community Contributor

[1] *http://www.simontylercousins.net/journal/2013/2/22/does-the-language-you-choose-make-a-difference.html*

Introduction

F# is a functional programming language from Microsoft. It is the first class language shipped in Visual Studio. It has been applied successfully in several areas, such as in the areas of financial software and web development. If you are a C# developer and want to use functional programming to write concise code with fewer bugs, F# is the right tool for you.

F# for C# Developers introduces, in an organized way, the F# language and several applications. It starts from how F# can perform imperative and object-oriented programming tasks and then moves on to covering unique F# features, such as type providers. By introducing F# design patterns with a large number of samples, this book not only delivers a basic introduction but also helps you apply F# in your daily programming work.

In addition to covering core F# core features, I also discuss F# HTML5 development, F# Azure development, and using general-purpose graphics processing units (GPGPUs) with F#. Beyond the explanatory content, each chapter includes examples and downloadable sample projects you can explore for yourself.

Who Should Read This Book

I wrote this book to help existing C# developers understand the core concepts of F# and help C# developers use F# in their daily work. It is especially useful for C# programmers looking to write concise code for algorithm design, web development, and cloud development. Although most readers will have no prior experience with F#, the book is also useful for those familiar with earlier versions of F# and who are interested in learning about the newest features.

You should have at least a minimal understanding of .NET development and object-oriented programming concepts to get the most benefit from this book. You also should have a basic understanding of data structures and generic algorithms. Experience in using C# is required as well.

Who Should Not Read This Book

This book is aimed at both experienced .NET C# developers who interested in extending their knowledge in functional programming and beginners in F# who want to understand F# and apply F# to their daily programming work. If you have no C# programming experience, this book might be difficult for you.

Organization of This Book

This book is divided into three sections, each of which focuses on a different aspect. Part I, "C# and F#," introduce how to port your C# knowledge to F#. This section introduces basic data structures and performing object-oriented implementations using F#. Part II, "F#'s Unique Features," introduces unique F# features and explains how to use them in your daily programming work. Part III, "Real-World Applications," introduces several real-world applications, including web development, Azure cloud development, and GPGPU.

Finding Your Best Starting Point in This Book

The various sections of *F# for C# Developers* cover a wide range of technologies. Depending on your needs and your existing understanding, you might want to focus on specific areas of the book. Use the following table to determine how best to proceed through the book.

If you are	Follow these steps
New to F# but experienced with C#	Focus on Part I to understand the basics and Part II for some unique F# features
Familiar with earlier versions of F#	Briefly read Parts I and II if you need a refresher on the core concepts, but also want to focus on type providers.

Most of the book's chapters include hands-on samples that let you try out the concepts just learned. No matter which sections you choose to focus on, be sure to download and install the sample applications on your system.

Conventions and Features in This Book

This book presents information using conventions designed to make the information readable and easy to follow:

- Boxed elements with labels such as "Note" provide additional information or alternative methods for completing a step successfully.

- Text that you type (apart from code blocks) appears in bold. A plus sign (+) between two key names means that you must press those keys at the same time. For example, "Press Alt+Tab" means that you hold down the Alt key while you press the Tab key.

System Requirements

You will need the following hardware and software to complete the practice exercises in this book:

- Windows 7 or Windows 8

- Visual Studio 2012, any edition (multiple downloads might be required if you're using Express Edition products)

- 1 GB (32 Bit) or 2 GBs (64 Bit) RAM

- 3.5 GBs of available hard disk space

- DirectX 9 capable video card running at 1024 x 768 or higher-resolution display

- DVD-ROM drive (if installing Visual Studio from DVD)

- Internet connection to download software or chapter examples

- If you want to run the GPU code, you need an NVIDIA graphics card and you need to download CUDA SDK from the NVIDIA web site.

Depending on your Windows configuration, you might require Local Administrator rights to install or configure Visual Studio 2012.

Code Samples

Most of the chapters in this book include exercises that let you interactively try out new material learned in the main text. All sample projects, in both their pre-exercise and post-exercise formats, can be downloaded from F# sample pack site (*http://fsharp3sample.codeplex.com/*)

Follow the instructions to download the 670266_FSharp4CSharp_ CompanionContent.zip file.

> **Note** In addition to the code samples, your system should have Visual Studio 2012.

Installing the Code Samples

Follow these steps to install the code samples on your computer so that you can use them with the exercises in this book:

1. Unzip file that you downloaded.

2. If prompted, review the displayed end user license agreement. If you accept the terms, select the accept option, and then click Next.

> **Note** If the license agreement doesn't appear, you can access it from the same webpage from which you downloaded the zip file.

Using the Code Samples

The sample code is organized by chapters. You can look at the folder that has the chapter name to look at the sample code.

Acknowledgments

First I'd like to thank Don Syme, who invented this fantastic language. I had a great time working with the Visual F# Core team, including Brian McNamara, Wonseok Chae, Vladimir Matveev, Matteo Taveggia, Jack Hu, Andrew Xiao, and Zack Zhang. Also, I would like to thank F# MVPs Daniel Mohl, Kit Eason, Zach Bray, Dave Thomas, and Don Syme for reviewing my book and providing valuable suggestions. It was a great experience exchanging ideas with so many talented software professionals. Devon Musgrave and Rosemary Caperton from Microsoft Press put a lot of work into editing this book. This book could never have been published without their efforts.

Finally, I would like to thank my wife, Rui Zhang, and my daughter, Zoey Liu, for their understanding and for sacrificing their time to support me in finishing this book. Without them, this book would never have become a reality.

Errata & book support

We've made every effort to ensure the accuracy of this book and its companion content. Any errors that have been reported since this book was published are listed on our Microsoft Press site at oreilly.com:

http://aka.ms/FsharpCsharpDev/errata

If you find an error that is not already listed, you can report it to us through the same page.

If you need additional support, email Microsoft Press Book Support at *mspinput@microsoft.com.*

Please note that product support for Microsoft software is not offered through the addresses above.

We want to hear from you

At Microsoft Press, your satisfaction is our top priority, and your feedback our most valuable asset. Please tell us what you think of this book at:

http://aka.ms/tellpress

The survey is short, and we read every one of your comments and ideas. Thanks in advance for your input!

Stay in touch

Let's keep the conversation going! We're on Twitter: *http://twitter.com/MicrosoftPress*

C# and F#

CHAPTER 1

C# and F# Data Structures

In this chapter, I'll compare and contrast various data structures from F# and C# programming languages. F# is a powerful multiparadigm language that supports imperative, object-oriented, and functional programming. C# is a multiparadigm language with more of a focus on imperative and object-oriented programming. A C# program usually consists of statements to change the program's state. An imperative language describes how to finish a task with exact steps. A functional-first language, like F#, is more declarative, describing what the program should accomplish.

One example of a programming language adopting functional programming is the C# version 3.0 introduction of LINQ (Language INtegrated Query). The growing popularity of Scala and Closure shows functional programming is growing. In addition, F# is another tool Microsoft ships with Microsoft Visual Studio to solve ever-changing programming challenges. Which language you choose to use depends on your experience and environment, but keep in mind you do not need to make an exclusive selection. I hope this book provides some information that helps you make appropriate decisions.

Any programming language is designed to perform some computation and to process data. The way that data is organized and stored is referred to as the *data structure*. This chapter introduces basic data structures for F#, explains how they relate to C#, and details how you can apply them to create imperative programs. I will follow the tradition in programming books of presenting a Hello-World-like application to introduce a new language. I will provide simple C# code along with the F# imperative equivalent.

Listing 1-1 shows an imperative approach that simply adds up the odd numbers from 0 to 100. C# supports functional programming (such as a LINQ feature), and there is a more concise way to implement the same functionality, which I'll show later in this chapter.

LISTING 1-1 A C# snippet that adds odd numbers from 0 to 100

Imperative C# implementation

```
// add all odd numbers from 0 to 100 and print out the result in the console
int sum = 0;
for (int i = 0; i<=100; i++)
{
    if (i%2 != 0)
        sum += i;
}

Console.WriteLine("the sum of odd numbers from 0 to 100 is {0}", sum);
```

F# implementation

```
let mutable sum = 0
for i = 0 to 100 do
    if i%2 <> 0 then sum <- sum + i
printfn "the sum of odd numbers from 0 to 100 is %A" sum
```

By porting this C# code to the F# equivalent, I'll cover the follow topics:

- The basic data type (such as primitive type literals). See the "Basic Data Types" section.

- The *if*, *while*, and *for* syntax. See the "Flow Control" section.

After implementing the same functionality in F#, I'll cover some F# data structures, such as Seq and *tuple*. Although this particular sample does not require Microsoft Visual Studio 2012, it is highly recommended that you install it, which is the minimum requirement for various samples in this book. I'll also introduce F# Interactive and some other useful add-ins to improve your overall F# programming experience.

Note Because Visual Studio IDE features are not the focus of this book, I encourage you to look at the MSDN website (*www.msdn.com*) or *Coding Faster: Getting More Productive with Microsoft Visual Studio* (Microsoft Press, 2011) to explore the topic by yourself.

Now it's time to start our journey!

Basic Data Types

F# is a .NET family language; therefore, the basic type definition and reference are similar to C#. Table 1-1 lists the C# and F# data types as well as the way to define a variable with each type. F# is a strongly typed language. Any errors related to type conversion are reported at compile time. These errors can be detected at an early stage of development and checked, which enables them to be fixed at compile time.

One big difference between the C# and F# definitions is that the F# examples do not need an explicitly defined type. This is because F# is often able to infer a type from the assigned value. To most C# developers, this feature is a lot like the *var* keyword in C#. There are some fundamental differences between *var* and *let*, but you can think of them as equals for now.

TABLE 1-1 Basic data types

Data Type	C# Representation	F# Representation
Int	int i = 0;	let i = 0 or let i = 0l
Uint	uint i = 1U;	let i = 1u or let i = 1ul
Decimal	decimal d = 1m;	let d = 1m or let d = 1M
Short	short c = 2;	let c = 2s
Long	long l = 5L;	let l = 5L
unsigned short	ushort c = 6;	let c = 6us
unsigned long	ulong d = 7UL;	let d = 7UL
byte	byte by = 86;	let by = 86y let by = 0b00000101y let by = 'a'B
signed byte	sbyte sby = 86;	let sby = 86uy let sby = 0b00000101uy
bool	bool b = true;	let b = true

double	double d = 0.2;
	double d = 0.2d;
	double d = 2e-1;
	double d = 2;
	double d0 = 0;
		let d = 0.2 or
		let d = 2e-1 or
		let d = 2.
		let d0 = 0x0000000000000000LF

float	float f = 0.3; or
	foat f = 0.3f;
	float f = 2;
	float f0 = 0.0f;
		let f = 0.3f or
		let f = 0.3F or
		let f = 2.f
		let f0 = 0x0000000000000000lf

native int	IntPtr n = new IntPtr(4);	let n = 4n
unsigned native int	UIntPtr n = new UIntPtr(4);	let n = 4un

Data Type	C# Representation	F# Representation
char	char c = 'c';	let c = 'a'
string	string str = "abc";	let str = "abc"
big int	BigInteger i = new BigInteger(9);	let i = 9I

One particular F# feature I'd like to call out is the syntax for creating an array of bytes to represent an ASCII string. Instead of asking you to constantly call into the *Encoding.ASCII.GetBytes* function, F# provides the "B" suffix to define an ASCII string. The string in .NET is Unicode-based. If you are mainly programming an ASCII string, you will not like this. In the following code, the representation for *asciiString* is a *byte[]* type internally:

```
let asciiString = "abc"B  // F# code
byte[] asciiBytes = Encoding.ASCII.GetBytes(value);  // C# code
```

Unlike C#, *float* in F# is a double-precision floating point number, which is equivalent to a C# *double*. The float type in C# is a single-precision numerical type, which can be defined in F# via the *float32* type. The .NET 32-bit and 64-bit floating numbers can be positive infinite or a NaN value. F# uses shortcut functions to represent these values:

- **Positive Infinity**   infinity is System.Double. PositiveInfinity and infinityf is System.Single. PositiveInfinity

- **NaN**   nan is System.Double.NaN and nanf is System.Single.NaN

The F# compiler does not allow any implicit type conversion. For a C# developer, an integer can be converted to a float implicitly, and this gives the impression that *29* is the same as *29.0*. Because implicit conversion is not allowed in F#, the explicit conversion *float 29* is needed to convert the integer *29* to a float type. The explicit conversion can eliminate the possibility of lose precision when the conversion is implicit.

F# 2.0 had two syntaxes for strings: normal strings, and verbatim strings, which are prefixed by the at sign (@). F# 3.0 introduces a new feature to define strings using a triple-quoted string.

Triple-Quoted Strings

F# supports normal strings and verbatim strings. This is equivalent to the options that C# provides. Examples of normal and verbatim string definitions are shown in Listing 1-2. The execution result shown in the listing is an example of a normal string and verbatim string being bound to specific values within the F# Interactive window (which I'll introduce shortly in the "Using F# Interactive" section). The result shows the variable name, type, and value.

LISTING 1-2 Normal and verbatim strings

```
let a = "the last character is tab\t"
let b = @"the last character is tab\t"
```

```
val a : string = "the last character is tab         "
val b : string = "the last character is tab\t"
```

Normal and verbatim strings are useful for a variety of tasks. However, scenarios that require included characters, such as double quotes, are still difficult to implement because of the need to escape these characters. Listing 1-3 shows examples of this.

LISTING 1-3 The escape double quote (")

```
// use backslash (\) to escape double quote
let a = "this is \"good\"."

// use two double quote to escape
let b = @"this is ""good""."
```

F# 3.0 introduces a new string format—a triple-quoted string—that alleviates this pain. Everything between the triple quotes (""") is kept verbatim; however, there is no need to escape characters such as double quotes. Triple-quoted strings have a number of use cases. A few examples include the creation of XML strings within your program and the passing of parameters into a type provider. Listing 1-4 shows an example.

LISTING 1-4 A triple-quoted string

```
let tripleQuotedString = """this is "good"."""

// quote in the string can be at the beginning of the string
let a = """"good" dog"""

// quote in the string cannot be at the end of the string
// let a = """this is "good""""
```

 Note Quotes in the triple-quoted string cannot end with a double-quote ("), but it can begin with one.

Variable Names

How to define a variable name is a much-discussed topic. One design goal for F# is to make variable names resemble more normal human language. Almost every developer knows that using a more readable variable name is a good practice. With F#, you can use double-backticks to include nonalphabet characters in the variable name and eventually improve the readability of your code. Examples are shown in Listing 1-5.

LISTING 1-5 Defining a variable

```
// variable with a space
let ``my variable`` = 4

// variable using a keyword
let ``let`` = 4

// apostrophe (') in a variable name
let mySon's = "Feb 1, 2010"
let x' = 3

// include # in the variable name
let ``F#`` = "this is an F# program."
```

Flow Control

To write F# applications in an imperative style, you need to know how to define flow-control statements. F# supports several types of flow control to accomplish this, including the *for* loop, *while* loop, and *if* expression. These statements segment the program into different scopes. C# uses "{" and "}" to segment code into different scopes, while F# does not use those items. Instead, F# uses the space indent to identify different program scopes. This section discusses these three statements in detail.

> **Note** Visual Studio can automatically convert the Tab key to a space. If you edit F# code in another editor that does not support this conversion, you might have to do it manually.

for Loop

There are two forms of the *for* loop: *for...to/downto* and *for...in*. The *for...to/downto* expression is used to iterate from a start value inclusively to or down to an end value inclusively. It is similar to the *for* statement in C#.

FOR...IN is used to iterate over the matches of a pattern in an enumerable collection—for example, a range expression, sequence, list, array, or other construct that supports enumeration. It is like *foreach* in C#. Looking back at the C# code that began this chapter, you see that you can use two F# options (as shown in Listing 1-6) to accomplish the loop of code for each number between 0 and 100. The first approach uses FOR...TO, and the second approach uses *for...in*.

LISTING 1-6 A *for* loop

```
C# version
for (int i=0; i<=100; i++)
```

```
F# versions
// for loop with i from 0 to 100
for i=0 to 100 do ...

// for iterate the element in list 0 to 100
for i in [0..100] do ...
```

```
for...downto sample
// downto go from 100 to 0
for i=100 downto 0 do ...
```

 Note The *[0..100]* defines a list with elements from 0 to 100. The details about how to define a list are discussed later in this book.

Some readers might immediately ask how to make the *for...to/downto* to increase or decrease by 2. *for...to/downto* does not support this, so you have to use *for...in* with a sequence or list. And I can assure you, you will not use *for* loop that often when you understand how to use a sequence or list.

while Loops

Another approach that could be used to accomplish the goal of this example is to use a *while* loop. F# and C# approach the *while* loop in the same way. Listing 1-7 shows an example.

LISTING 1-7 A *while* loop

```
C# version
int i = 0;
while (i<=100)
{
    // your operations
    i++;
}
```

F# version

```
let mutable i = 0
while i <=100 do
    <your operations>
    i <- i + 1
```

> **Note** It's optional to use a semicolon to end a statement. The semicolon is needed only when multiple statements are placed on the same line.

The definition for variable *i* in the previous code snippet has the *mutable* keyword in the definition. The *mutable* keyword indicates *i* is a mutable variable, so its content can be modified by using the <– operator. This brings up an interesting and crucial concept in F#: a variable without the *mutable* keyword is an immutable variable, and therefore its value cannot be changed. The C# code `int i = 0` is equivalent to the F# code `let mutable i = 0`. This looks like a small change, but it is a fundamental change. In C#, the variable is mutable by default. In F#, the variable is immutable by default. One major advantage to using immutable variables is multi-thread programming. The variable value cannot be changed and it is very easy and safe to write multi-thread program.

Although F# does not provide *do...while* loop, it won't be a problem for an experienced C# developer if he is still willing to use the C# imperative programming model after learning about F#. Actually, the more you learn about F#, the less important the *do...while* loop becomes.

if Expressions

At this point, the only part left is the *if* expression. In the earlier example, you need *if* to check whether the value is an odd number. Note that in F# *if* is an expression that returns a value. Each *if/else* branch must return the same type value. The *else* branch is optional as long as the *if* branch does not return any value. The *else* must be present if the *if* branch returns a value. It is similar to the "?:" operator in C#. Although a value must be returned, that returned value can be an indicator of no value. In this case, F# uses *"unit"* to represent the result. Unlike C#'s *if...else*, F# uses *elif* to embed another *if* expression inside. Listing 1-8 shows an example of this. In Listing 1-9, you can see a comparison between the C# and F# code required to check that a value is odd or even.

LISTING 1-8 An *if* expression

```
if x>y then "greater"
elif x<y then "smaller"
else "equal"
```

LISTING 1-9 An *if* expression

```
C# version
if (i%2 != 0) ...


F# version
if i%2 <> 0 then ...
```

Match

In addition to the *if* statement, C# and F# have another way to branch the execution of code. C#
provides a *switch* statement, and F# provides a *match* expression. F# developers can use a *match*
expression to achieve the same functionality as the *switch* statement in C#, but the power of *match*
expressions does not stop there. I will discuss the additional features that *match* provides in Chapter 6,
"Other Unique Features." An example of a simple implementation of *match* that is similar in concept
to a C# *switch* statement is shown in Listing 1-10.

LISTING 1-10 A *match* and *switch* sample

```
C# switch statement
int i = 1;
switch (i)
{
    case 1:
        Console.WriteLine("this is one");
        break;
    case 2:
        Console.WriteLine("this is two");
        break;
    case 3:
        Console.WriteLine("this is three");
        break;
    default:
        Console.WriteLine("this is something else");
        break;
}


F# match statement

let intNumber = 1

match intNumber with
    | 1 -> printfn "this is one"
    | 2 -> printfn "this is two"
    | 3 -> printfn "this is three"
    | _ -> printfn "this is anything else"
```

Console Output

Now you have almost everything to make the functionality work. The last missing piece is to let the computer tell you what was achieved by using console output. In the C# code, you use the *Console.WriteLine* method. Because F# is a .NET language, you can use *Console.WriteLine* from it as well. However, F# also provides a function called *printfn* that provides a more succinct and powerful option. Listing 1-11 shows an example of both of these approaches.

LISTING 1-11 The console output

```
C# version
Console.WriteLine("the sum of odd numbers from 0 to 100 is {0}", sum);
```

```
F# version
// use printfn to output result
printfn "the sum of odd numbers from 0 to 100 is %A" sum

// use Console.WriteLine to output result
System.Console.WriteLine("the sum of odd numbers from 0 to 100 is {0}", sum)
```

F#'s *printfn* is stricter than C#'s *Console.WriteLine*. In C#, *{<number>}* can take anything and you do not have to worry about the type of variable. But F# requires that the placeholder have a format specification indicator. This F# feature minimizes the chance to make errors. Listing 1-12 demonstrates how to use different type-specification indicators to print out the appropriate values. If you really miss the C# way of doing this, you can use %A, which can take any type. The way to execute the code will be explained later in this chapter.

LISTING 1-12 The *printfn* function and data types

```
let int = 42
let string = "This is a string"
let char = 'c'
let bool = true
let bytearray = "This is a byte string"B

let hexint = 0x34
let octalint = 0o42
let binaryinteger = 0b101010
let signedbyte = 68y
let unsignedbyte = 102uy

let smallint = 16s
let smalluint = 16us
let integer = 345l
let usignedint = 345ul
let nativeint = 765n
```

```
let unsignednativeint = 765un
let long = 12345678912345789L
let unsignedlong = 12345678912345UL
let float32 = 42.8F
let float = 42.8

printfn "int = %d or %A" int int
printfn "string = %s or %A" string string
printfn "char = %c or %A" char char
printfn "bool = %b or %A" bool bool
printfn "bytearray = %A" bytearray

printfn "hex int = %x or %A" hexint hexint
printfn "HEX INT = %X or %A" hexint hexint
printfn "oct int = %o or %A" octalint octalint
printfn "bin int = %d or %A" binaryinteger binaryinteger
printfn "signed byte = %A" signedbyte
printfn "unsigned byte = %A" unsignedbyte

printfn "small int = %A" smallint
printfn "small uint = %A" smalluint
printfn "int = %i or %A" integer integer
printfn "uint = %i or %A" usignedint usignedint
printfn "native int = %A" nativeint

printfn "unsigned native int = %A" unsignednativeint
printfn "long = %d or %A" long long
printfn "unsigned long = %A" unsignedlong
printfn "float = %f or %A" float32 float32
printfn "double = %f or %A" float float
```

Execution result

```
int = 42 or 42
string = This is a string or "This is a string"
char = c or 'c'
bool = true or true
bytearray = [|84uy; 104uy; 105uy; 115uy; 32uy; 105uy; 115uy; 32uy; 97uy; 32uy; 98uy;
121uy; 116uy; 101uy; 32uy; 115uy; 116uy; 114uy; 105uy; 110uy; 103uy|]
hex int = 34 or 52
HEX INT = 34 or 52
oct int = 42 or 34
bin int = 42 or 42
signed byte = 68y
unsigned byte = 102uy
small int = 16s
small uint = 16us
int = 345 or 345
uint = 345 or 345u
native int = 765n
unsigned native int = 765un
long = 12345678912345789 or 12345678912345789L
unsigned long = 12345678912345UL
float = 42.800000 or 42.7999992f
double = 42.800000 or 42.8
```

The Console has *In*, *Out*, and *Error* standard streams. F# provides *stdin*, *stdout*, *stderr*, which correspond to these three standard streams. For the conversion task, you already have all the building blocks. So let's give it a try in Listing 1-13.

LISTING 1-13 The C# and F# versions of adding odd numbers from 0 to 100

C# version
```
// add all odd numbers from 0 to 100 and print out the result in the console
int sum = 0;
for (int i = 0; i<=100; i++)
{
    if (i%2 != 0)
        sum += i;
}

Console.WriteLine("the sum of odd numbers from 0 to 100 is {0}", sum);
```

F# version
```
let mutable sum = 0
for i = 0 to 100 do
    if i%2 <> 0 then sum <- sum + i
printfn "the sum of odd numbers from 0 to 100 is %A" sum
```

Listing 1-14 shows how to use a list and a *for...in* loop to solve the same problem. Compared to Listing 1-13, this version has the following changes:

- Uses *for...in* to iterate through 0 to 100, where *[1..100]* is an F# list definition

- Uses the *printf* function, which does not output the "\n"

- Replaces *%A* with *%d*, which tells the compiler that the *sum* variable must be an integer

LISTING 1-14 Using the F# list in the *for* loop

```
let mutable sum = 0
for i in [0..100] do
    if i%2 <> 0 then sum <- sum + i
printf "the sum of odd numbers from 0 to 100 is %d \n" sum
```

Run Your Program

You can run your program from Visual Studio in two ways: create an F# project, much like you would a C# project, or use the F# Interactive window. F# supports the following project types in Visual Studio 2012:

- *F# Application* is a console-application project template.

- *F# Library* is a class-library template.

- *F# Tutorial* is a console application that contains F# samples. I highly recommend going through all of these samples.

- *F# Portable Library* is a class library for F# libraries that can be executed on Microsoft Silverlight, Windows Phone, and Windows platforms, including Windows 8.

- *F# Silverlight Library* is a Silverlight class-library template.

If you want to execute the sample code shown in this chapter up to this point, the F# application project is a good choice.

Note Microsoft Visual Studio Express 2012 for Web is free. Although its name suggests it is for web development and does not support a portable library, you can use it to create a console application by using the F# tutorial template.

Creating a Console Application

Figure 1-1 shows the project template list. You can select F# Application and accept the default name. This F# console-application template creates a solution with a console-application project that includes a default Program.fs file, as you can see in Figure 1-2. To run the simple summing application we've been referring to throughout this chapter, simply replace the content of Program.fs with the F# code from Listing 1-13. The steps are primarily the same for the creation of other project types, so I'll leave this to you to explore.

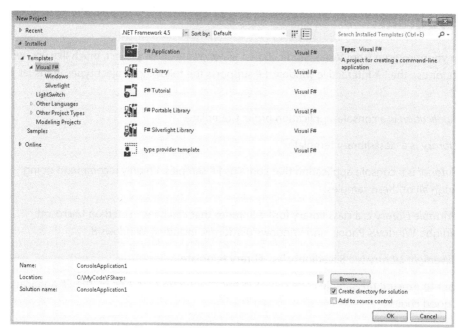

FIGURE 1-1 Creating an F# project

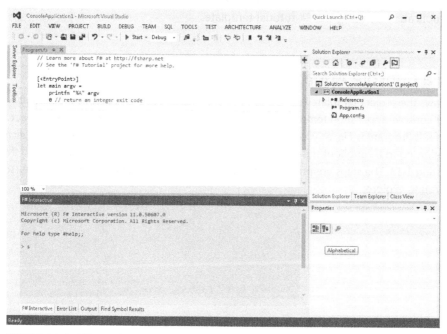

FIGURE 1-2 An F# console application with Program.fs

Using F# Interactive

For simple programs like the one in Listing 1-13, F# ships with an F# Interactive feature (FSI). You can use this to test small F# code snippets. In Visual Studio, the F# Interactive window can be found in the View menu. Depending on the development profile you're using, you can find the F# Interactive window under View, Other Windows, or you can access it directly in the View menu, as shown in Figure 1-3. An example of the FSI window is shown in Figure 1-4.

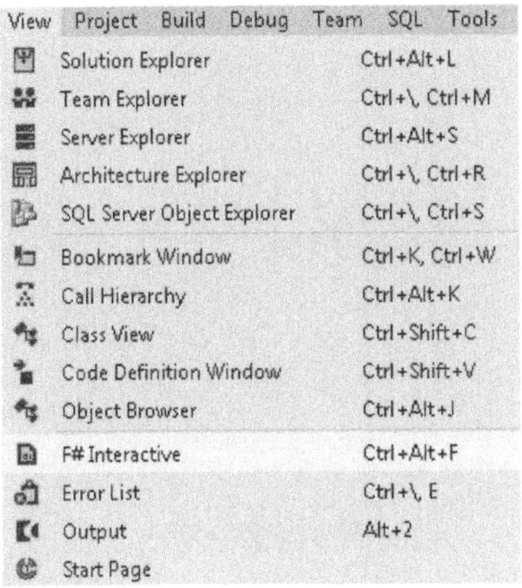

View	Project	Build	Debug	Team	SQL	Tools

Solution Explorer	Ctrl+Alt+L	
Team Explorer	Ctrl+\, Ctrl+M	
Server Explorer	Ctrl+Alt+S	
Architecture Explorer	Ctrl+\, Ctrl+R	
SQL Server Object Explorer	Ctrl+\, Ctrl+S	
Bookmark Window	Ctrl+K, Ctrl+W	
Call Hierarchy	Ctrl+Alt+K	
Class View	Ctrl+Shift+C	
Code Definition Window	Ctrl+Shift+V	
Object Browser	Ctrl+Alt+J	
F# Interactive	Ctrl+Alt+F	
Error List	Ctrl+\, E	
Output	Alt+2	
Start Page		

FIGURE 1-3 Accessing F# Interactive from the View menu

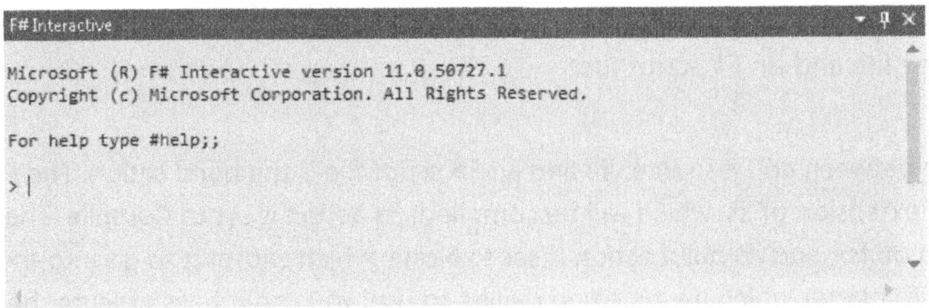

```
F# Interactive                                                    ▼ ⃗ ✕

Microsoft (R) F# Interactive version 11.0.50727.1
Copyright (c) Microsoft Corporation. All Rights Reserved.

For help type #help;;

> |
```

FIGURE 1-4 An F# Interactive window

The FSI window accepts user input, so you can execute your code directly in it. You can use two semicolons (;;) to let FSI know that the statement is finished and can be executed. One major limitation for FSI is that the FSI window does not provide Microsoft IntelliSense. If you don't want to create a full project and still want to use IntelliSense, the F# script file is your best option. You can go to File, New to create a new script file, as shown in Figure 1-5.

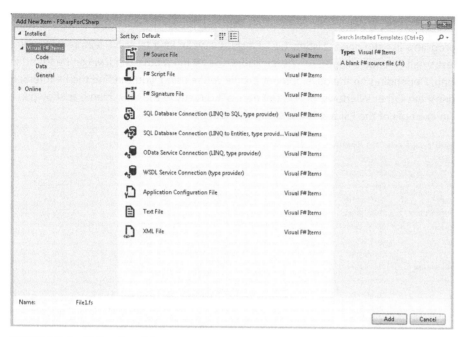

FIGURE 1-5 An F# item template

 Note Many item templates are listed in Figure 1-5. I'll introduce them later. For now, you need only an F# source file and an F# script file.

The primary difference between an F# source file and an F# script file is the build action. The F# source file is a file with an extension of .fs, which will be compiled. Its action is set to Compile. The F# script file has an extension of .fsx, and its build action is set to None, which causes it to go into the build process by default. No matter which file type you decide to use, you can always execute the code by selecting it and using the context (that is, right-click) menu option Execute In Interactive. If you prefer using the keyboard, Alt+Enter is the keyboard shortcut as long as the development profile is set to F#. This command sends the selected code to be executed in FSI, as shown in Figure 1-6. There is also another menu option labeled Execute Line In Interactive. As its name suggests, this option is used to send one line of code to the FSI. The shortcut key for Execute Line In Interactive is Alt + '.

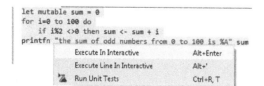

FIGURE 1-6 Executing code in FSI via the context menu

OK, let's put the code in the Program.fs. After that, you can select the code and send it to FSI. The execution result is shown in the FSI window, which then displays the expected result of "the sum of odd numbers from 0 to 100 is 2500," as shown in Figure 1-7. Congratulations! You've got your first F# program running.

```
let mutable sum = 0
for i=0 to 100 do
    if i%2 <>0 then sum <- sum + i
printfn "the sum of odd numbers from 0 to 100 is %A" sum
```

```
100 %   ▾ ◂

F# INTERACTIVE

Microsoft (R) F# 3.0 Interactive build 11.0.50214.1
Copyright (c) Microsoft Corporation. All Rights Reserved.

For help type #help;;

>
the sum of odd numbers from 0 to 100 is 2500

val mutable sum : int = 2500
val it : unit = ()
```

FIGURE 1-7 The execution result in the FSI window

> **Tip** FSI provides a *#time* switch you can use to measure the execution time of your code and Gen 0/1/2 collection numbers. An example of the *#time* switch usage is shown in Listing 1-15. Interested users can perform a long run computation and see how this option works. Other directives can be found in the "FSI Directives" section later in the chapter.
>
> **LISTING 1-15** Switching the timing on and off
>
> ```
> > #time "on";;
>
> --> Timing now on
>
> > #time "off";;
>
> --> Timing now off
> ```

After executing the program, FSI's state is changed causing it to become *polluted*. If you need a clean environment, you can use Reset Interactive Session. If you want to clear only the current output, you should select Clear All. The context menu (shown in Figure 1-8) shows all the available options. You can bring it up by right-clicking in the FSI window.

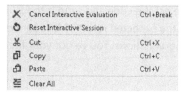

✕	Cancel Interactive Evaluation	Ctrl+Break
↻	Reset Interactive Session	
✂	Cut	Ctrl+X
⧉	Copy	Ctrl+C
⧉	Paste	Ctrl+V
≝	Clear All	

FIGURE 1-8 The FSI context menu

The full list and a description of each command provided in the FSI context menu is shown in Table 1-2.

TABLE 1-2 FSI commands

FSI Command	Description
Cancel Interactive Evaluation	Cancels the current FSI execution.
Reset Interactive Session	Resets the current FSI execution session.
Cut	Cuts the selection in the current editing line to the clipboard. The result from a previous execution or banner cannot be cut.
Copy	Copies the selection to the clipboard.
Paste	Pastes the clipboard text content to the current editing line.
Clear All	Clears all content in the FSI window, including the copyright banner.

FSIAnyCPU

The FSIAnyCPU feature was added with Visual Studio 2012. FSI will be executed as a 64-bit process as long as the current operating system is a 64-bit system. The FSIAnyCPU feature can be enabled by clicking Option, F# Tools, F# Interactive, as shown in Figure 1-9.

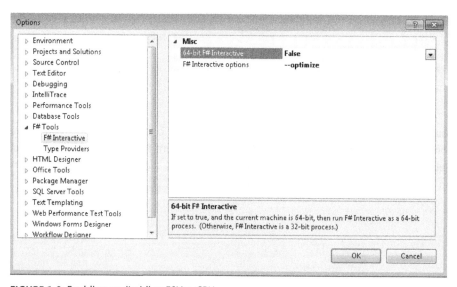

FIGURE 1-9 Enabling or disabling FSIAnyCPU

You can use Process Manager to check whether the FSIAnyCPU process is running, or you can use the *sizeof* operator to check the current *IntPtr* size. The 32-bit machine's *IntPtr* is 32-bit, so the *sizeof* operator returns *4* while the 64-bit machine will return *8*. Listing 1-16 shows the execution result from my 32-bit laptop.

LISTING 1-16 The *sizeof IntPtr* operator in FSI

```
> sizeof<System.IntPtr>;;
val it : int = 4
```

FSI Directives

In addition to the *#time* directive, FSI offers several others:

- *#help* is used to display the help information about available directives.

- *#I* is used to add an assembly search path.

- *#load* is used to load a file, compile it, and run it.

- *#quit* is used to quit the current session. You will be prompted to press Enter to restart. This is how to restart a session from the keyboard.

- *#r* is used to reference an assembly.

The FSI is a great tool that can be used to run small F# snippets of your code for test purposes. If your code is used to perform file I/O operations, the FSI's default directory is the temp folder. Listing 1-17 shows how to get the current FSI folder and change its default folder.

LISTING 1-17 Changing FSI's current folder

```
> System.Environment.CurrentDirectory;;
val it : string = "C:\Users\User\AppData\Local\Temp"

> System.Environment.CurrentDirectory <- "c:\\MyCode";;
val it : unit = ()

> System.Environment.CurrentDirectory;;
val it : string = "c:\MyCode"
```

 Note After you reset the FSI session, the current folder will be set back to the temp folder.

Compiler Directives

FSI is a nice feature to have when you want to execute small programs. However, it is not a good choice for building executable binaries. To build binaries, you need to use Visual Studio. We'll use it to create one of the projects previously mentioned in this chapter. The build and execution process and experience is largely the same for both F# and C# applications, though they have different compilers. I already presented the FSI directives, and I will now list the F# compiler directives. The following five directives are supported by F#:

- *if* is used for conditional compilation. Its syntax is *if <symbol>*. If the symbol is defined by the compiler, the code after the *if* directive is included in the compilation, as shown in Listing 1-18.

- *else* is used for conditional compilation. If the symbol is not defined, the code after *else* is included in the compilation, as shown in Listing 1-18.

- *endif* is used for conditional compilation, and it marks the end of the conditional compilation. This is also shown in Listing 1-18.

- *line* indicates the original source code line and file name.

- *nowarning* is used to disable one or more warnings. F# tends to be more restrictive and gives more warnings than C# does. If your organization has a zero-warning policy, you can ignore specific warnings by using the *nowarning* directive. Only a number is needed as a suffix to a *nowarning* directive, and you can put multiple warning numbers in one line, as in the following example:

```
nowarning "1" "2" "3"
```

LISTING 1-18 A conditional compilation

```
#if VERSION1

let f1 x y =
    printfn "x: %d y: %d" x y
    x + y

#else

let f1 x y =
    printfn "x: %d y: %d" x y
    x - y

#endif
```

> **Note** There is no *#define* directive. You have to either use a compiler option to define a symbol or define that symbol in the project properties. An example is shown in Figure 1-10.

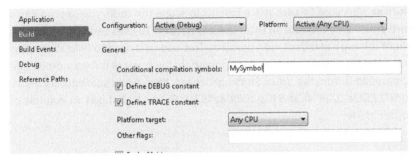

FIGURE 1-10 Defining a compile symbol

The INTERACTIVE compile symbol is a build-in compile symbol. The code wrapped by this symbol will be included in the FSI execution but not in the project build process. Listing 1-19 provides an example. If you are trying to include code only during the project build, the COMPILED symbol can be used, as shown in Listing 1-20.

LISTING 1-19 The INTERACTIVE symbol

```
#if INTERACTIVE

#r "System.Data"
#r "System.Data.Linq"
#r "FSharp.Data.TypeProviders"

#endif
```

LISTING 1-20 The COMPILED symbol

```
#if COMPILED

printfn "this is included in the binary"

#endif
```

Some Useful Add-ins

Visual Studio is a powerful editor with a rich set of editing features. However, some Visual Studio add-ins designed for F# are still recommended as a way to improve your coding experience.

- **F# depth colorizer**   Because F# uses space indents to scope the code, you can run into some seemingly weird errors only because an extra space is needed 10 lines earlier. This extension can highlight this type of indentation problem. This add-in is used to help align code blocks by using different colors. I strongly recommend that you install it if your project gets big. You can download it from the Visual Studio gallery at *http://visualstudiogallery.msdn. microsoft.com/0713522e-27e6-463f-830a-cb8f08e467c4*. Figure 1-11 shows an example of the F# depth colorizer in use.

```
type Blah() =
    let bar() = ()
    member this.Bar() =
        let x = 4
        if true then
            bar()
            if true then
                bar()
```

FIGURE 1-11 The F# depth colorizer

- **F# code snippet**   The code snippet add-in brings the common code—for example, the class definition—to your fingertips. Unlike the C# snippet, the F# snippet also adds any needed dynamic-link library (DLL) references into the project. You can download the add-in and snippet files from *http://visualstudiogallery.msdn.microsoft.com/d19080ad-d44c-46ae-b65c-55cede5f708b*. An example of the extension in use is shown in Figure 1-12. The configuration options that the tool provides are shown in Figure 1-13.

FIGURE 1-12 The F# code snippet

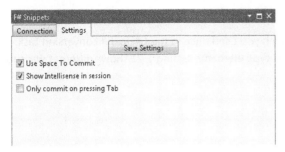

FIGURE 1-13 Configuring the F# code snippet add-in

■ **Add reference add-in** Visual Studio's project system provides a nice UI to manage the reference DLLs. This add-in sends reference statements to FSI and adds reference scripts to the Script folder in the current project. Take a look at Figure 1-14.

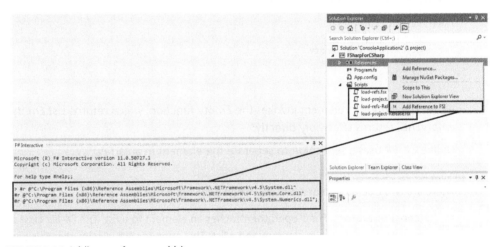

FIGURE 1-14 Adding a reference add-in

List, Sequence, and Array Data Structures

We successfully finished our first task: converting a simple C# program to F#. These days, many C# developers might choose to use LINQ to solve this problem. As I mentioned in this chapter's introduction, long before C# had this LINQ feature, F# had it as a functional programming feature. In this section, you'll learn how to define and use collection data, including the following items: list, sequence, and array. After introducing the list, sequence, and array structures, I'll show you how to use a functional programming style to convert simple C# programs to F#.

Lists

First, we start with the list structure, which you used once in the C#-to-F# conversion task. An F# list is an ordered, immutable series of same-type elements. Listing 1-21 shows different ways to define a list.

LISTING 1-21 Defining an F# list

```
//defines a list with elements from 1 to 10.
let list0 = [1..10]

//defines a list with element 1, 2, and 3.
let list1 = [1;2;3]

//defines a list with elements 0, 1, 4, 9, and 16.
let list2 = [for i=0 to 4 do yield i*i]

//defines an empty list
let emptyList = [ ]
let emptyList2 = List.empty
```

> **Note** The *emptyList* element invokes the *Empty* function, which returns *List.Empty*, while *emptyList2* returns *List.empty* directly.
>
> Unlike C#, F# uses a semicolon to separate the element in an array.

There are two operators that are useful when working with a list:

- **:: (cons) operator** The :: operator attaches an element to a list. The F# *list* class has a constructor that takes an element and a list. This operator actually invokes this constructor and returns a new F# list. Its time complexity is O(1).

  ```
  let list1With4 = 4::list4
  ```

  Here, *list1With4* is a list defined as = [4;1,2;3].

- **@ operator** The @ operator concatenates two lists and returns a new instance of F# list It time complexity is O(min(M, N)) where M is list0's length and N is list1's length.

  ```
  let list0And1 = list0 @ list1
  ```

  Here, *list0And1* is a list defined as = [1;2;3;4;5;6;7;8;9;10;1;2;3], where *1, 2,* and *3* are from *list1*.

Lists support indexing. Unlike C#, if you want to use an indexer in F#, you need to use dot notation. This means that you need to put an extra dot between the list variable and the indexer. Listing 1-22 shows this in action. F# list is a linked list and the time complexity is O(i), where *i* is index passed in the statement.

LISTING 1-22 An indexer in an F# list

```
list0[0]  //won't compile
list0.[0] // correct. Using a dot notation
```

F# lists support something called *structural equality*. Structural equality is to check equivalent identity. Listing 1-23 shows that the list can be equal if elements in both lists are equal. Comparisons between incongruous lists (apples-to-oranges comparisons) are not allowed. As an example, Listing 1-24 will not compile because the comparison between *TextBox* and *Button* doesn't make sense. Additionally, comparisons can be performed only if the elements support equality comparisons. Structural comparison is to provide an ordering of values.

LISTING 1-23 A list comparison

```
List comparison code
let l1 : int list = [ 1; 2; 3 ]
let l2 : int list = [ 2; 3; 1 ]

printfn "l1 = l2? %A" (l1 = l2)
printfn "l1 < l2? %A" (l1 < l2)



Execution result
l1 = l2? False
l1 < l2? True
```

LISTING 1-24 An example of how elements in a list cannot be compared

```
// the following code compiles
open System.Windows.Forms

let l1 = [ new TextBox(); new Button(); new CheckBox() ]
let l2 = [ new Button(); new CheckBox(); new TextBox() ]

// the following code does not compile
// printfn "%A" (l1 < l2) // not compile
```

Note If you want to use the F# list type in a C# project, you need to add a reference to *Microsoft.FSharp.Core.dll*.

The F# list might suggest it has some relationship with the *List<T>* type. Actually, the list type is a *Microsoft.FSharp.Collections.FSharpList<T>* type. It does implement the *IEnumerable<T>* interface, but it is not very similar to the *List<T>* type.

Sequences

According to MSDN documentation, a *sequence* is a logical series of elements of one type. Sequences are particularly useful when you have a large, ordered collection of data but do not necessarily expect to use all the elements. Individual sequence elements are computed only as required, so a sequence can provide better performance than a list in situations in which not all of the elements are needed. Any type that implements the *System.IEnumerable* interface can be used as a sequence. Defining a sequence is similar to defining a list. Listing 1-25 shows a few examples of how to define a sequence.

LISTING 1-25 Defining a sequence in F#

```
// defines a sequence with elements from 1 to 10.
let seq0 = seq { 1..10 }

// defines a sequence with elements 0, 1, 4, 9, and 16.
let seq2 = seq { for i=0 to 4 do yield i*i }

// defines a sequence using for...in
let seq1 = seq {
    for i in [1..10] do i * 2
}

// defines an empty sequence
let emptySeq = Seq.empty
```

> **Note** Be aware that seq { 1; 2; 3 } is not a valid way to define a sequence. However, you can use the *yield* keyword to define a sequence as shown here: seq { yield 1; yield 2; yield 3 }.

A sequence is shown as an *IEnumerable<T>* type when viewed in C#. When you expose a sequence to a C# project, you do not need to add *Microsoft.FSharp.Core.dll*.

Arrays

The definition from MSDN says that *arrays* are fixed-size, zero-based, mutable collections of consecutive data elements that are all of the same type. Listing 1-26 shows how to define an array.

LISTING 1-26 Defining an F# array

```
// defines an array with elements from 1 to 10.
let array0 = [| 1..10 |]

// defines an array with elements 1, 2, and 3.
let array1 = [| 1;2;3 |]

// defines an array with elements 0, 1, 4, 9, and 16.
let array2 = [| for i=0 to 4 do yield i*i |]

// defines an empty array
let emptyArray = [| |]
let emptyArray2 = Array.empty
```

 Note Like the empty case in *Seq*, both *emptyArray* and *emptyArray2* invoke a function that returns *Array.empty*.

Arrays support indexing. Unlike C#, when you use an indexer in F#, you need to use dot notation. Therefore, an extra space is needed between the variable name and indexer. Listing 1-27 shows an example of this.

LISTING 1-27 An indexer in an F# array

```
array0[0]  //won't compile
array0.[0] // correct. Using a dot notation
```

Arrays also have the comparison feature, as shown in Listing 1-23. By changing the list syntax to an array syntax, you can get the same code to perform the structural equality comparison. Listing 1-28 shows an example.

LISTING 1-28 An array comparison

```
let l1 = [| 1; 2; 3 |]
let l2 = [| 2; 3; 1 |]
printfn "l1 = l2? %A" (l1 = l2)
printfn "l1 < l2? %A" (l1 < l2)
```

Another interesting feature provided for working with arrays in F# is *slicing*. You use slicing to take a continuous segment of data from an array. The syntax for slicing is straightforward: myArray.[lowerBound .. upperBound]. Listing 1-29 shows how to use slicing.

LISTING 1-29 Slicing an F# array

```
// define an array with elements 1 to 10
let array0 = [| 1 .. 10 |]

// get slice from element 2 through 6
array0.[2..6]

// get slice from element 4 to the end
array0.[4..]

// get the slice from the start to element 6
array0.[..6]

// get all the elements (copy the whole array)
array0.[*]
```

Arrays are the same in both F# and C#. You do not have to reference to *Microsoft.FSharp.Core.dll* to expose an array from an F# library.

Pipe-Forward Operator

Before presenting the F# code used to rewrite the example from the beginning of this chapter in a functional style, I must first explain the pipe-forward operator (|>). If you're familiar with UNIX's pipeline, you can think of this operator as something similar. It gets the output from one function and pipes that output in as input to the next function. For example, if you have the functions *g(x)* and *f(x)*, the *f(g(x))* function can be written by using a pipe-forward operator, as shown in Listing 1-30.

LISTING 1-30 An F# pipe-forward operator

```
x |> g |> f    // equals to f(g(x))
```

The C# program at the beginning of this chapter focused on how to process each single element from 0 to 100 by iterating through the elements. If the element was an odd number, it was added to a predefined variable. Do we really have to think like this?

F# provides a way to think differently. Instead of thinking about how to process each single element, you can think about how to process the whole data set as a single element—a collection of data. The whole process can instead be thought about like this: after being given data from 0 to 100, I get a subset of the given data that contains only odd numbers, sum them up, and print out the result. The C# code to implement this logic is shown in Listing 1-31, as is the equivalent F# code. The use of the pipe-forward operator allows the F# code to become even more succinct and beautiful than the already beautiful LINQ code. The pipe-forward operator brings the result from *Seq.sum* to *printfn*. Isn't that simple?

LISTING 1-31 A functional approach to solve the odd-number summary problem

```
C# code
var sum = dataFrom0to100
    .Where(n=>n%2!=0)      //filter out the odd number
    .Sum()                 //sum up

//output the result
Console.WriteLine("the sum of the odd number from 0 to 100 is {0}", sum);
```

```
F# code
seq { 0..100 }                            //given data from 0 to 100
|> Seq.filter (fun n -> n%2<>0)      //data subset contains only odd number
|> Seq.sum                                //sum them up
|> printfn "the sum of odd number from 0 to 100 is %A"    //print out the result
```

When the F# code is shown side by side with the C# equivalent, it's easy to tell that *Seq.filter* is a built-in function used to filter data and *Seq.sum* is a function used to sum up the elements in a provided sequence. Because *printfn*, which originally needs two parameters, gets its second parameter from the pipe-forward operator (|>), it takes only one explicitly provided parameter. *Seq* module functions are discussed in more detail in the *"Seq/List/Array* Module Functions" section.

From a coding experience and readability perspective, the functional way is much better than the imperative way. F#, as a functional-first language, shows this advantage very clearly. It can chain the functions together more naturally.

One headache for LINQ developers is the debugging of LINQ code. This would also be a headache for F# if FSI was not present. The FSI lets you execute some code to set up the test environment and then send the code that needs to be tested. In the previous example, if you are not sure if the filter gives you the right result, you can select the first two lines and send them to the FSI. After finishing one test, *Reset Interactive Session* is a convenient way to reset your environment. Isn't that nice!

If you're still digesting the pipe-forward operator, you can think of the parameter on the left side of the operator as the suffix to the end of the right part. The two statements shown next in Listing 1-32 are basically the same.

LISTING 1-32 Using the pipe-forward operator

```
mySeq |> Seq.length      // get the length of the sequence
Seq.length mySeq         // the same as the expression above with |>
```

Tip FSI is not only a good approach for debugging a program and running unit tests, it's also a quick way to check a function's definition. For example, you can type **Seq.filter** into the FSI window. FSI then shows you the function definition, which saves you the two seconds of going to the MSDN documentation.

The Sequence, List, and Array Module Functions

Now you must be wondering where someone can find functions like *Seq.filter* and *Seq.sum*. They are located inside three modules: Seq, List, and Array module. Module is a special way for organizing F# code that will be discussed later in this chapter. For the convenience of later discussion, we denote seq, list, and array as *collections*. The functions listed next are the most commonly used ones. Refer to MSDN document *http://msdn.microsoft.com/en-us/library/ee353413* for a complete function list.

length

It is easy to get the length of a list or an array by using the *length* function. The LINQ *Count* extension method provides the same functionality. An example is shown in Listing 1-33.

LISTING 1-33 The *length* function

```
let myList = [1..10]
let listLength = myList |> List.length  // listLength is 10
let myArray = [| 1..10 |]
let arrayLength = myArray |> Array.length //arrayLength is 10
let mySeq = seq { 1..10 }
let seqLength = mySeq |> Seq.length //seqLength is 10
```

Note Seq does have a length function, but keep in mind that a sequence can be of an infinite length. An infinite-length sequence can make many functions not applicable, unsafe, or both.

exists and exists2

Seq, list, and array all provide the same functions to check whether an element exists and to see whether two collections contain the same element at the same location. The *exists* function is used to check for a single element, and *exists2* is used for checking two collections. Listing 1-34 shows how to use *Seq.exists* and *Seq.exists2*.

LISTING 1-34 The *exists* and *exists2* functions

```
let mySeq = seq { 1..10 }
let mySeq2 = seq { 10..-1..1 }

// check if mySeq contains 3, which will make "fun n -> n = 3" return TRUE
if mySeq |> Seq.exists (fun n -> n = 3) then printfn "mySeq contains 3"

// more concise version to check if it contains number 3
if mySeq |> Seq.exists ((=) 3) then printfn "mySeq contains 3"

// check if two sequences contain the same element at the same location
if Seq.exists2 (fun n1 n2 -> n1 = n2) mySeq mySeq2 then printfn "two sequences contain
same element"
```

You might have trouble understanding the ((=) 3) in the code from the previous example. Everything in F# is a function, and the equal sign (=) is no exception. If you want to see the equal sign definition, you can run the FSI code shown in Listing 1-35. The definition is as follows:

('a -> 'a -> bool)

This definition is a function function that takes an 'a and returns a function ('a -> bool). 'a is something not familiar. It is a type and will be determined by type inference which will be introduced later in this chapter. When an argument is provided to this function, it returns a new function. Back to our sample code of ((=) 3): the code generates a function that takes one argument and checks whether the passed-in argument is equal to 3.

LISTING 1-35 An equal function definition

```
let f = (=);;

val f : ('a -> 'a -> bool) when 'a : equality
```

You might be wondering, "What about ((>) 3)? Does it equal x > 3 or 3 > x?" Good question! Again, let us ask FSI. Listing 1-36 shows the result. The first statement defines the function, and the second one passes *4* to the statement. If the parameter *4* is going to the left side of the equation, the final result should be 4>3 = TRUE. Because the final result is FALSE, the *4* must be on the right side.

LISTING 1-36 An equal function with a fixed parameter

```
> let f = (>) 3;;          // define the function (>) 3
val f : (int -> bool)

> f 4;;                     // pass 4 into the function
val it : bool = false   // result is FALSE
```

> **Note** Using = or > can make your code shorter. However, overuse can make your code less readable.

forall and *forall2*

The *forall* function can be used to check whether all of the elements in a collection meet certain criteria. The LINQ *All* extension method provides the same functionality. Listing 1-37 shows an example of how to use *Seq.forall*.

LISTING 1-37 The *forall* function

```
let myEvenNumberSeq = { 2..2..10 }

// check if all of the elements in the seq are even
myEvenNumberSeq |> Seq.forall (fun n -> n % 2 = 0)
```

Like the *exists2*, *forall2* provides functionality similar to *forall*, but it provides the functionality across two collections. If and only if the user function returns TRUE for the two-element pairs, *forall2* returns TRUE. Listing 1-38 shows this in action.

LISTING 1-38 The *forall2* function

```
let myEvenNumberSeq = { 2..2..10 }
let myEvenNumberSeq2 = { 12..2..20 }

if Seq.forall2 (fun n n2 -> n+10=n2) myEvenNumberSeq myEvenNumberSeq2 then printfn
"forall2 // returns TRUE"
```

find

The *find* function is more like the *First* extension method on *IEnumerable*. It raises *KeyNotFoundException* if no such element exists. See Listing 1-39.

LISTING 1-39 The *find* function

```
// use let to define a function
let isDivisibleBy number elem = elem % number = 0

let result = Seq.find (fun n -> isDivisibleBy 5 n)[ 1 .. 100 ]
printfn "%d " result    //result is 5
```

The *findIndex* function is designed to allow for a quick lookup of an element's index. You can find sample code in the MSDN documentation (*http://msdn.microsoft.com/en-us/library/ee353685*).

map

The *map* function is used to create a new collection based on a given collection by applying a specified function to each element in the provided collection. The LINQ *Select* extension method provides the same functionality. See Listing 1-40.

LISTING 1-40 The *map* function

```
let mySeq = seq { 1..10 }
let result = mySeq |> Seq.map (fun n -> n * 2)  // map each element by multiplying by 2
Seq.forall2 (=) result (seq { 2..2..20 })               // check result
```

filter

The *filter* function returns a new collection containing only the elements of the collection for which the given predicate returns TRUE. The LINQ *Where* extension method provides the same functionality. See Listing 1-41.

LISTING 1-41 The *filter* function

```
let mySeq = { 1..10 }
let result = mySeq |> Seq.filter (fun n -> n % 2 = 0)   //filter out odd numbers
printfn "%A" result
```

fold

The *fold* function aggregates the collection into a single value. Its definition from MSDN shows that *fold* applies a function to each element of the collection and threads an accumulator argument through the computation. The LINQ *Aggregate* extension methods perform the same functionality. Listing 1-42 shows an example that sums all elements in the given sequence.

LISTING 1-42 The *fold* function

```
let mySeq = { 1..10 }
let result = Seq.fold (fun acc n -> acc + n) 0 mySeq
printfn "the sum of 1..10 is %d" result                  //sum = 55
```

One application of the *fold* function is to get the length of a collection. The built-in function *length* supports only 32-bit integers. If the sequence length is a very big number, such as *int64* or even *bigint*, the *fold* function can be used to get the length. The following sample gets the sequence length in *bigint*. See Listing 1-43, which shows the code to accomplish this.

LISTING 1-43 The *fold* function to get a *bigint* length of a sequence

```
let mySeq = { 1..10 }
let length = Seq.fold (fun acc n -> acc + 1I) 0I mySeq
printfn "the bigint length of seq is %A" length
```

collect

The *collect* function applies a user-defined function to each element in the collection and joins results. One good application of this function is the LINQ *SelectMany* extension method. The *Select-Many* method flattens the hierarchy and returns all the elements in the second-level collection. The following sample first generates a list of lists and then combines all the lists. See Listing 1-44.

LISTING 1-44 The *collect* function

```
let generateListTo x = [0..x]

// generates lists [ [0;1]; [0;1;2]; [0;1;2;3] ]
let listOfLists = [1..3] |> List.map generateListTo

// concatenate the result
// seq [0; 1; 0; 1; 2; 0; 1; 2; 3]
let result = listOfLists |> Seq.collect (fun n -> n)
```

> **Tip** If you can use the built-in *id* function, the last line can be rewritten as Seq.collect id.

append

This method takes two collections and returns a new collection where the first collection's elements are followed by the second collection's elements. The LINQ *Concat* function provides the same functionality. See Listing 1-45.

LISTING 1-45 The *append* function

```
// the following concatenates two arrays and generates
// a new array that contains 1;2;3;4;5;6
printfn "%A" (Array.append [| 1; 2; 3|] [| 4; 5; 6|])
```

Math Operations

In addition to the transformation functions, F# provides a rich set of functions that perform mathematical operations on collections:

- **min and max**   The *min* and *max* functions are used to find the minimum or maximum value in a collection. These functions are just like the LINQ *min* and *max* functions. See Listing 1-46.

  LISTING 1-46 The *min* and *max* functions

  ```
  let myList = [1..10]
  let min = myList |> List.min    // min is 1
  let max = myList |> List.max     // max is 10
  ```

- **average**   The *average* function is used to get the mean of all elements in a collection. Because F# does not have implicit type conversion from integer to float, the following code generates an *int* and does not support *DivideByInt* operator, which means the operand has to be transformed to a data type that supports divide, such as *float* or *float32*. See Listing 1-47.

  LISTING 1-47 The *average* function used with integer

  ```
  let myList = [1..10]

  // does not compile because int does not support "DivideByInt"
  let myListAverage = myList |> List.average
  ```

  You can use *map* to change the integer element into a *float* element. Again, the *float* is also a function that converts an integer to a *System.Double*. See Listing 1-48.

  LISTING 1-48 The *average* function in a float sequence

  ```
  let myList = [1..10]

  // the average is float type 5.5
  let myListAverage = myList
                  |> List.map float
                  |> List.average
  ```

- **sum**   The *sum* function returns the sum of elements in a collection. The *sum* result type depends on the input sequence element type. The example in Listing 1-49 showcases this.

  LISTING 1-49 The *sum* function

  ```
  let mySeq = seq { 1..10 }

  // sum is 55
  let result = mySeq |> Seq.sum
  ```

zip and zip3

The *zip* function combines two sequences into a sequence of pairs. The *zip3* function, as its name suggests, combines three sequences into triples. The *zip* sample is shown in Listing 1-50. You can find a *zip3* sample on MSDN (*http://msdn.microsoft.com/en-us/library/ee370585.aspx*).

LISTING 1-50 The *zip* function

```
let myList = [ 1 .. 3 ]
let myList2 = [ "a"; "b"; "c" ]

// the zip result is [(1, "a"); (2, "b"); (3, "c")]
let result = List.zip myList myList2
```

rev

The *rev* function reverses the elements in a list or array. The sample code is shown in Listing 1-51.

LISTING 1-51 The *rev* function

```
let reverseList = List.rev [ 1 .. 4 ]

// print the reversed list, which is [4;3;2;1]
printfn "%A" reverseList
```

> **Note** Seq does not have a *rev* function implemented.

sort

The *sort* function sorts the given list using *Operators.compare*. If the original element's order is preserved, this is called a *stable sort*. The *sort* function on Seq and List are stable sorts, while *Array.sort* is not a stable sort. See Listing 1-52.

LISTING 1-52 The *sort* function

```
let sortedList1 = List.sort [1; 4; 8; -2]

// print out the sorted list, which is [-2; 1; 4; 8]
printfn "%A" sortedList1
```

Convert to Seq/List/Array

Each type of collection has its unique usage. It is common to convert one type to the other type. It is easy to tell how to convert to a new type by looking at the functions. The sample code is shown in Listing 1-53.

- *Seq.toList* is used to convert a seq to a list.

- *Seq.toArray* is used to convert a seq to an array.

- *List.toSeq* is used to convert a list to a seq.

- *List.toArray* is used to convert a list to an array.

- *Array.toSeq* is used to convert an array to a seq.

- *Array.toList* is used to convert an array to a list.

LISTING 1-53 Some seq, list, and array conversion examples

```
// define a sequence
let mySeq = { 1..5 }

// define a list
let myList = [ 1.. 5 ]

// define an array
let myArray = [| 1..5 |]

// convert seq to a list
let myListFromSeq = mySeq |> Seq.toList

// convert seq to an array
let myArrayFromSeq = mySeq |> Seq.toArray

// convert list to an array
let myArrayFromList = myList |> List.toArray

// convert list to an seq
let mySeqFromList = myList |> List.toSeq

// convert array to a list
let myListFromArray = myArray |> Array.toList

// convert array to a seq
let mySeqFromArray = myArray |> Array.toSeq
```

Convert from Seq/List/Array

Unlike C#, which uses a *from* prefix, F# uses an *of* prefix to represent a function that converts from one collection type to another. See Listing 1-54 for examples.

- *Seq.ofList* is used to convert from a list to a seq.

- *Seq.ofArray* is used to convert from an array to a seq.

- *List.ofSeq* is used to convert from a seq to a list.

- *List.ofArray* is used to convert from an array to a list.

- *Array.ofSeq* is used to convert from a seq to an array.

- *Array.ofList* is used to convert from a list to an array.

LISTING 1-54 Some seq, list, and array examples of conversion

```
let mySeq = { 1..5 }
let myList = [ 1.. 5 ]
let myArray = [| 1..5 |]

// convert from list to a seq
let mySeqFromList = myList |> Seq.ofList

// convert from an array to a seq
let mySeqFromArray = myArray |> Seq.ofArray

// convert from a seq to a list
let myListFromSeq = mySeq |> List.ofSeq

// convert from an array to a list
let myListFromArray = myArray |> List.ofArray

// convert from a seq to an array
let myArrayFromSeq = mySeq |> Array.ofSeq

// convert from a list to an array
let myArrayFromList = myList |> Array.ofList
```

Of the three collection-related data structures discussed so far, sequence is likely the most interesting. A function that takes *seq<'T>* as an input parameter always works with list, array, set, and map in F#. Additionally, if you expose seq to a C# project, a reference to *Microsoft.FSharp.Core.dll* will not be required. Last, C#'s LINQ operations will work on sequences.

Table 1-3 lists all of the functions supported and a description of the performance of each.

TABLE 1-3 The collection of functions

Function	Array	List	Seq	Map	Set	Description
append	O(m+n)	O(min(m,n))	O(1)			Concatenates two collections.
add				O(lgN)	O(lgN)	Adds a new element, and returns a new collection.
average /averageBy	O(n)	O(n)	O(n)			Gets an average of all elements.
blit	O(n)					Returns a slice of the array.
cache			O(n)			Caches elements.
cast			O(n)			Converts an element to a specified type.
choose	O(n)	O(n)	O(n)			Chooses the element if not return None.
collect	O(n)	O(n)	O(n)			Applies a function to each element, and concatenates the results.
compareWith			O(n)			Compares element by element using a given function.
concat	O(n)	O(n)	O(n)			Concatenates two collections.
contains					O(logN)	Tests whether contains the specified element.
containsKey				O(logN)		Tests whether an element is in the domain of the map.
count					O(n)	Counts the number of elements in the set.
countBy			O(n)			Counts the generated key numbers. The key is generated from a function.
copy	O(n)		O(n)			Creates a copy of the collection.
create	O(n)					Creates an array.
delay			O(1)			Returns a sequence that is built from the given delayed specification of a sequence.
difference					O(m*lgN)	Returns a new set with an element in *set1* but not in *set2*.
distinct/ distinctBy			O(1)			Returns a new seq with removing duplicated elements.
empty	O(1)	O(1)	O(1)	O(1)	O(1)	Creates an empty collection.
exists	O(n)	O(n)	O(n)	O(logN)	O(logN)	Tests if any element satisfies the condition.
exists2	O(min(n,m))		O(min(n,m))			Tests whether any pair of corresponding elements of the input sequences satisfies the given predicate.
fill	O(n)					Sets the range of element to a specified value.

Function	Array	List	Seq	Map	Set	Description
filter	O(n)	O(n)	O(n)	O(n)	O(n)	Returns a new collection of elements satisfying the given criteria.
find	O(n)	O(n)	O(n)	O(lgN)		Returns the first element satisfying the given criteria.
findIndex	O(n)	O(n)	O(n)			Returns the first element index satisfying the given criteria.
findKey				O(lgN)		Evaluates the function on each mapping in the collection, and returns the key for the first mapping where the function returns TRUE.
fold	O(n)	O(n)	O(n)	O(n)	O(n)	Applies a function to each element of the collection, threading an accumulator argument through the computation.
fold2	O(n)	O(n)				Applies a function to corresponding elements of two collections, threading an accumulator argument through the computation.
foldBack	O(n)	O(n)		O(n)	O(n)	Applies a function to each element of the collection, threading an accumulator argument through the computation.
foldBack2	O(n)	O(n)				Applies a function to corresponding elements of two collections, threading an accumulator argument through the computation.
forall	O(n)	O(n)	O(n)	O(n)	O(n)	Tests whether all elements meet a condition.
forall2	O(n)	O(n)	O(n)			Tests whether all corresponding elements of the collection satisfy the given predicate pairwise.
get/nth	O(1)	O(n)	O(n)			Returns elements by a given index.
head		O(1)	O(1)			Returns the first element.
init	O(n)	O(n)	O(1)			Initializes the collection.
initInfinite			O(1)			Generates a new sequence which, when iterated, will return successive elements by calling the given function.
isProperSubset/ isProperSuperset					O(M * log N)	Tests whether the first set is a proper subset/superset of the second set.
isSubset/ isSuperset					O(M * log N)	Tests whether the first set is a subset/superset of the second set.
iter	O(n)	O(n)	O(n)	O(n)	O(n)	Applies a function to elements in the collection.
iter2	O(n)	O(n)	O(n)			Applies a function to a collection pairwise.

Function	Array	List	Seq	Map	Set	Description
length	O(n)	O(n)	O(n)			Returns the number of elements.
map	O(n)	O(n)	O(1)			Applies the function to each element.
map2	O(n)	O(n)	O(1)			Applies the function to a collection pairwise.
map3		O(n)				Creates a new collection whose elements are the results of applying the given function to the corresponding elements of the three collections simultaneously.
mapi	O(n)	O(n)	O(n)			Builds a new collection from a collection with the index passed in.
mapi2	O(n)	O(n)				Builds a new collection from two collections pairwise with an index passed in.
max/maxBy min/minBy	O(n)	O(n)	O(n)			Finds the max/min element.
maxElement/ minElement					O(log N)	Finds the max/min element in the set.
ofArray		O(n)	O(1)	O(n)	O(n)	Gets a collection from an array.
ofList	O(n)		O(1)	O(n)	O(n)	Gets a collection from a list.
ofSeq	O(n)	O(n)		O(n)	O(n)	Gets a collection from a seq.
pairwise			O(n)			Returns a sequence of each element in the input sequence and its predecessor, with the exception of the first element, which is only returned as the predecessor of the second element.
partition	O(n)	O(n)		O(n)	O(n)	Splits the collection into two collections, containing the elements for which the given predicate returns *true* and *false*, respectively
permutate	O(n)	O(n)				Makes a permutation of the collection.
pick	O(n)	O(n)	O(n)	O(lg N)		Applies the given function to successive elements, returning the first result where the function returns *Some*.
readonly			O(n)			Creates a new sequence object that delegates to the given sequence object.
reduce	O(n)	O(n)	O(n)			Applies a function to each element of the collection, threading an accumulator argument through the computation.
reduceBack	O(n)	O(n)				Applies a function to each element of the collection, threading an accumulator argument through the computation.

Function	Array	List	Seq	Map	Set	Description
remove				O(lg N)	O(lg N)	Removes the element.
replicate		O(n)				Creates a list of a specified length with every element set to the given value.
rev	O(n)	O(n)				Reverses the collection.
scan	O(n)	O(n)	O(n)			Applies a function to each element of the collection, threading an accumulator argument through the computation.
scanBack	O(n)	O(n)				Similar to *foldBack*, but returns both the intermediate and final results.
singleton			O(1)		O(1)	Returns a collection that contains only one element.
set	O(1)					Sets the element value.
skip			O(n)			Skips *n* elements.
skipWhile			O(n)			Skips an element when it meets the condition.
sort/sortBy	O(N log N) Worst is O(N^2)	O(N lg N)	O(N lg N)			Sorts the collection.
sortInPlace/ sortInPlaceBy	O(N log N) Worst is O(N^2)					Sorts the collection by mutating the collection in place.
sortWith	O(N log N) Worst is O(N^2)	O(N lg N)				Sorts the collection by the given function.
sub	O(n)					Gets a sub array.
sum/sumBy	O(n)	O(n)	O(n)			Gets the sum of a collection.
tail		O(n)				Returns collection without the first element.
take			O(n)			Takes *n* elements from the collection.
takeWhile			O(1)			Returns a sequence that, when iterated, yields elements of the underlying sequence while the given predicate returns *true*.
toArray		O(n)	O(1)	O(n)	O(n)	Returns an array from the collection.
toList	O(n)		O(1)	O(n)	O(n)	Returns a list from the collection.
toSeq	O(n)	O(n)		O(n)	O(n)	Returns a seq from the collection.
truncate			O(1)			Truncates the collection.
tryFind	O(n)	O(n)	O(n)	O(lg N)		Tries to find the element by the given function.

Function	Array	List	Seq	Map	Set	Description
tryFindIndex	O(n)	O(n)	O(n)			Tries to find the element index by the given function.
tryFindKey				O(lg N)		Tries to find the key by the given function.
tryPick	O(n)	O(n)	O(n)	O(lg N)		Returns the first result when the function returns *Some*.
unfold			O(n)			Returns a seq from a given computation.
union					O(m * lg N)	Returns a union of two collections.
unionMany					O(n1 * n2...)	Returns a union of collections.
unzip/unzip3	O(n)	O(n)	O(n)			Splits the collection into two collections.
windowed			O(n)			Returns a sequence that yields sliding windows of containing elements drawn from the input sequence.
zip / zip3	O(n)	O(n)	O(n)			Makes collections into a pair/triple collection.

There are two other primary collection data structures: map and set. *Map* is an immutable dictionary of elements; elements are accessed by key. *Set* is an immutable set based on binary trees; the comparison is the F# structural comparison function. For detailed information on these, refer to MSDN at *http://msdn.microsoft.com/en-us/library/ee353686.aspx* and *http://msdn.microsoft.com/en-us/library/ee353619.aspx*.

What Changed

The sequence operation is very much like the LINQ operation, and these operations will be used often in the rest of this book.

The functional style is very different from the imperative style. Imagine presenting the problem of adding all odd numbers between 0 and 100 to a person without any formal computer background. Most likely, that person would go about solving the problem in the same way that the functional approach presented. They would start by finding all of the odd numbers and then adding them up. This is simply a more straightforward approach that more closely resembles how people think about problems.

On the other hand, a person with a deeply rooted imperative software background will likely lean toward a solution with a *sum* variable, IF statement, and FOR loop. If you look at the history of programming languages—from binary coding to assembly language to modern-day programming languages such as C#—the trend is that the programming language is more and more like a human language. The more the programming language resembles the human language, the more programmers will adopt it in their daily work and, consequently, make the language successful.

Other F# Types

Our next task is to refactor the F# code. During the refactoring process, more F# types are explored. These types are the foundation on which you will build when I introduce F# classes in Chapter 2, "Using F# for Object-Oriented Programming."

Defining Constants by Using Attributes

C# supports constants through the use of the *const* keyword. The designers of F# decided not to introduce many keywords and thus left them open for use as variable names. Instead, F# uses an attribute to define constant values. In F#, an attribute needs to be put between *[<* and *>]*. When I present more F# features, you will find F# uses more attributes than keywords when defining a data type. See Listing 1-55. In this example, *Literal* is an attribute that indicates to the F# compiler that *myConstant* is a constant.

LISTING 1-55 Defining a constant

```
[<Literal>]
let MyConstant = 99
```

F# uses some compiler tricks to replace a variable with the constant value, as you can see in Listing 1-56.

LISTING 1-56 Defining a constant for an upper limit

```
[<Literal>]
let upperLimit = 100

seq { 0..upperLimit }                //given data from 0 to 100
|> Seq.filter (fun n -> n%2<>0)      //data subset contains only odd numbers
|> Seq.sum                                    //sum them up
|> printfn "the sum of odd number from 0 to 100 is %A"  //print out the result
```

Enumerations

The enumeration type provides a way to define a set of named integral constants. Listing 1-57 shows how to define an enumeration type. Each field must be a unique value. Listing 1-58 shows how to use the enumeration value once it is defined.

LISTING 1-57 An F# enumeration definition

```
Enumeration definition using integers
type Card =
    |   Jack = 11
    |   Queen = 12
    |   King = 13
    |   Ace = 14



Enumeration definition using a binary integer format
type OptionEnum =
    | DefaultOption = 0b0000
    | Option1 = 0b0001
    | Option2 = 0b0010
    | Option3 = 0b0100
    | Option4 = 0b1000
```

> **Note** Each item in the enumeration must have an integral value assigned to it; you cannot specify only a starting value.

LISTING 1-58 An access enumeration value

```
let option1 = OptionEnum.Option1
let opton1Value = int OptionEnum.Option1     //option1 value is integer 1
```

Like C#, F# does not allow integral type values to be directly set to an enumeration variable. Instead, a conversion with type is needed, as shown in Listing 1-59.

LISTING 1-59 Converting an integer to *OptionEnum*

```
let option1 = enum<OptionEnum>(0b0001)
```

The bitwise operation can use the optimized algorithm to check the odd number. You can use enumeration and a bit operation, as shown in Listing 1-60. F# supports five bitwise operators, which are listed in Table 1-4.

LISTING 1-60 Using a bitwise operation

```
type EvenOddFlagEnum =
    | Odd = 0x1
    | Even = 0x0

seq { 0..100 }                              //given data from 0 to 100
|> Seq.filter (fun n -> n &&& (int EvenOddFlagEnum.Odd) <> 0 ) //data subset contains only
odd numbers
|> Seq.sum                          //sum them up
|> printfn "the sum of odd number from 0 to 100 is %A"    //print out the result
```

TABLE 1-4 F# bitwise operators

Bitwise operation	C# operation	F# operation	Expected result
bitwise AND	0x1 & 0x1	0x1 &&& 0x1	0x1
bitwise OR	0x1 | 0x2	0x1 ||| 0x2	0x3
bitwise XOR	0x1 ^ 0x1	0x1 ^^^ 0x1	0
left shift	0x2 << 1	0x2 <<< 1	0x4
right shift	0x2 >> 1	0x2 >>> 1	0x1

Tuples

A *tuple* is a grouping of unnamed but ordered items. The items in a tuple can have different types. Listing 1-61 demonstrates how to define a tuple.

LISTING 1-61 A tuple definition

```
// Tuple of two integers: int * int
( 1, 5 )

// Tuple with three strings: string * string * string
( "one", "two", "three" )

// mixed type tuple: string * int * float
( "one", 1, 2.0 )

// Tuple can contain non-primitive type values
( a + 1, b + 1)

//tuple which contains tuples: (int * int) * string
((1,2), "good")
```

The tuple introduces an interesting phenomenon. How many parameters are there in the function *F(1,2,3)*? *Three* is the wrong answer. The function *F* takes only one parameter, whose type is a tuple, and the tuple is of type *int*int*int*. A function that takes three parameters is defined as *F 1 2 3*. A tuple can be used to group parameters together to make sure that related parameters are always passed into a function. For example, if you always need to pass the first name and last name together into a function named *g*, it is better to declare *g* like this:

```
// indicate first name and last name be provided together
g (firstName, lastName)
```

That way is better than the following approach:

```
// indicate first name and last name can be passed separately
g firstName lastName
```

The tuple supports structural equality. This means that the code shown in Listing 1-62 returns *true*. This concise syntax can make your code more readable.

LISTING 1-62 The tuple structural equality

```
(1,2) = (1,2)
(1,2) = (1, 1+1)
(1,2) < (2, 4)
```

Forming a tuple can be as simple as putting all elements between a pair of parentheses, although parentheses are optional if omitting them does not introduce confusion. Retrieving the elements requires two functions: the *fst* and *snd* functions are used to retrieve the first and the second elements, respectively, from a tuple. See Listing 1-63.

LISTING 1-63 The *fst* and *snd* functions in a tuple

```
// define tuple without parentheses
let a = 1, 2
let b = 1, "two"

// get first element in a tuple
let isOne = fst a

// get second element in a tuple
let isTwo = snd b
```

If the third or fourth element is needed, the functions defined in Listing 1-64 can be used. The underscore (_) stands for a placeholder where the value can be ignored. You'll find the underscore used in other places as well. It's a way to tell the F# compiler that this is something you don't care about.

LISTING 1-64 The third and fourth functions in a tuple

```
// get the third value of the triple
let third (_,_,c) = c

// get the fourth value of the quadruple
let fourth (_,_,_,d) = d

third (1,2,3) // return 3
fourth (1,2,3,4) //return 4
```

There is another way to retrieve the embedded elements without using these functions. Listing 1-65 shows that the F# compiler can figure out that the element in *l* is a triple. The variables *a*, *b*, and *c* are used to hold the element values in the triple.

LISTING 1-65 Use let and iterating through a triple list and

```
let tripleVariable = 1, "two", "three"
let a, b, c = tripleVariable

let l = [(1,2,3); (2,3,4); (3,4,5)]
for a,b,c in l do
    printfn "triple is (%d,%d,%d)" a b c
```

Functions

If you want to refactor the F# code in the conversion task, one possible way is to define a function that checks whether a given number is odd. Defining a function is a simple task for an experienced C# developer. Most likely, you already figured out how to write an F# function. One thing I want to point out is that F# does not have a *return* keyword. As a result, the value from the last expression is always the returned value. The following function defines an operation that increments a given integer by one:

```
let increaseOne x = x + 1
```

If you run the code in FSI, the result shows that the function takes an integer as input and returns an integer as output. The result might look strange, but it's still understandable:

```
val increaseOne : int -> int
```

Things start to get more interesting when you try to define a *sum* function that takes two parameters. Listing 1-66 shows the code definition and its execution result in FSI.

LISTING 1-66 Defining a *sum* function that takes two parameters

```
// define a sum function that takes two parameters
let sum x y = x + y

// FSI execution result
val sum : int -> int -> int
```

sum is a curried function. You can envision this function as something that takes *x* as a parameter and returns a new function that takes a parameter called *y*. The beauty of this approach is that it enables you to define a new function based on an existing partially applied function. For example, the *increaseOne* function is really a *sum* function where *y* is always *1*. So you can rewrite the *increaseOne* function as follows:

```
let increaseOne2 = sum 1
```

If you give *4* to this *increaseOne2* function, the return value will be *5*. It's like passing *4* and *1* into the *sum* function.

```
increaseOne2 4      // returns 5
sum 4 1                 // pass 4 and 1 into the sum function and yield 5
```

> **Note** You might be tempted to invoke this *sum* function with the following syntax: sum(4,1). If you do this, an error message will point out that the expression expects a type of *int*int*. However, *(4,1)* is an F# type called a *tuple*. The code *sum(4,1)* is trying to pass a *tuple* type into *sum*, which confuses the F# compiler.

Now you can define your own function and refactor the conversion-task F# code, as shown in Listing 1-67.

LISTING 1-67 Defining an F# function in the odd-number sum program

```
// define an enum
type EvenOddFlagEnum =
        |  Odd = 0x1
        |  Even = 0x0

// define a function to check if the given number is odd or not
let checkOdd n = n &&& (int EvenOddFlagEnum.Odd) <> 0
```

```
seq { 0..100 }                        //given data from 0 to 100
|> Seq.filter checkOdd                //data subset contains only odd numbers
|> Seq.sum                            //sum them up
|> printfn "the sum of odd number from 0 to 100 is %A"   //print out the result
```

As the code is getting cleaner, somebody might notice the *Seq.filter* function takes a function as input. Yes, F# treats values and functions the same. If a function takes a function as input or returns a function, that function is called a *higher-order function*. In Listing 1-67, *Seq.filter* is a higher-order function. The *Seq.filter* function provides the skeleton of a filter algorithm. You can then implement your special filter mechanism and pass your function into the skeleton function. Higher-order functions provide an extremely elegant way to reuse code. The higher-order function is a light-weight Strategy design pattern.

We have finished our refactoring work. You might already be eager to see the class definition in F#, but before I start introducing how F# handles object-oriented concepts such as classes, we need to spend a little more time on some basics.

Recursive Functions

The keyword *rec* is needed when defining a recursive function. Listing 1-68 shows how to use the *rec* keyword to define a function to compute Fibonacci numbers.

LISTING 1-68 Using the *rec* keyword to define a recursive function

```
let rec fib n =
    if n <= 2 then 1
    else fib (n - 1) + fib (n - 2)
```

> **Note** This recursive version does not use a tail call (which is defined later in this section), so this version can generate a stack overflow error.

Sometimes a function is *mutually recursive* because the calls form a circle. Listing 1-69 shows the mutually recursive *Even* and *Odd* functions. The F# variable and function resolution is from top to bottom and from left to right. All the functions and variables must be declared first before they can be referenced. In this case, you have to use the *and* keyword to let the compiler know.

LISTING 1-69 A mutually recursive function definition

```
let rec Even x =                //Even calls Odd
    if x = 0 then true
    elif x = 1 then false
    else Odd (x - 1)
and Odd x =                     //Odd calls Even
    if x = 1 then true
    elif x = 0 then false
    else Even (x - 1)
```

In C# code, the stack overflow exception can happen when you use a recursive function. A small amount of memory is allocated when doing each recursive function call, and this allocation can lead to a stack overflow exception when a large amount of recursion is needed. A *tail call* is a function call whose result is immediately treated as the output of the function. Thanks to the tail call in F#, the F# compiler generates a tail-call instruction to eliminate the stack overflow problem when possible. Figure 1-15 shows the project setting's Build tab, which is where you can select (or deselect) the Generate Tail Calls check box.

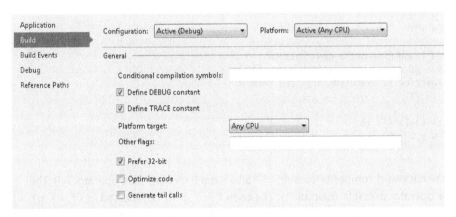

FIGURE 1-15 The Generate Tail Calls check box on the project setting's Build tab

Pipe/Composite Operators

Because functional programming languages see no difference between data and functions, you might be wondering if there are any operators specifically for functions. The pipe-forward operator was introduced already. The real function operators are forward and backward composite operators. See Listing 1-70.

LISTING 1-70 Composing two functions into a new function using the forward composite operator

```
let f0 x = x * 2
let f1 x = x + 7

//composite f and g to get a new function
// g(x) = x + 11
// the f0 function is executed first and then f1
let g = f0 >> f1

// result is 2*2+7 = 11
let result = g 2
```

The forward composite operator executes the function from left to right. The backward composition operator executes the function in the opposite direction, from right to left. Listing 1-71 demonstrates these two operators.

LISTING 1-71 Composing two functions into a new function using the backward composite operator

```
let f0 x = x * 2
let f1 x = x + 7

// composite f and g to get a new function
// g(x) = x + 11
// the f1 function is executed first and then f0
let g = f0 << f1

// result is (2+7)*2 = 18
let result = g 2
```

Similar to the backward composite operator, F# also has a backward pipe operator (<|). The backward pipe operator uses left associativity. The code f <| g <| x is parsed as (f <| g) <| x. It is not parsed as f <| (g <| x), which is equivalent to x |> g |> f. See Listing 1-72.

LISTING 1-72 Comparing forward and backward pipe operators

Pipe-forward operator
```
let f x = x * 2
let g x = x + 5

// forwardPipeResult is 3*2 + 5 = 11
let forwardPipeResult = 3 |> f |> g
```

Pipe-backward operator

```
let f x = x * 2
let g x = x + 5

// forwardPipeResult is 2*(3 + 5) = 16
let forwardPipeResult = f <| (g <| 3)
```

 Note Pipe operators and composite operators do not affect function execution performance. You can choose either of them according to your preference.

If you are curious about how to allow a C# method to hook into the pipe operation, Listing 1-73 shows an example. The code takes an integer list as input, converts each item into a string, and joins them by using "*" as a separator. Because *String.Join* has many overloaded functions, you have to tell the compiler which overload format you prefer. We use *FuncConvert.FuncFromTupled* to convert the .NET function to a curried format, which is easier to work with when using the pipe operator.

LISTING 1-73 Assigning a function and converting function to a curried format

```
let input = [ 1..10 ]

// assign String.Join to join with the string*string list as function signature
let join : string*string list -> string = System.String.Join

// convert join to curry format
let curryFormatJoin = FuncConvert.FuncFromTupled join

input
|> List.map (fun number -> string(number))  //convert int to string
|> curryFormatJoin "*"      // join the string list to a string string using "*"
```

In functional programming, the function is a first-class citizen. Some readers might try to explore mathematical operations with functions. The pipeline operator and the composite operator can be viewed as the *add* operation, which combines two functions. Listing 1-74 does not compile because you cannot compare two functions.

LISTING 1-74 A function does not support the equality comparison

```
let f1 = fun () -> ()
let f2 = fun () -> ()
f1 = f2  //does not compile
```

Unit Types

If a C# method does not have a return value, you use *void* to tell the compiler. In F#, the *unit* keyword is used to accomplish this. There are two ways to tell the compiler that a function returns *void*:

- Specify the return type in the function. See Listing 1-75.

    LISTING 1-75 A function with return unit type and input parameter type specified

    ```
    //define a function return unit
    let f (x) : unit = ()

    //define a function with int parameter and unit return type
    let f (x:int) : unit = ()
    ```

- Make the "()" be the last statement. As I mentioned earlier in this chapter, F# functions do not use the *return* keyword. Instead, F# takes the type from the last statement that the function returns. So the following function returns *unit* as well. You can use the *ignore* operator to throw away the computation result, which makes the function return nothing.

    ```
    // define a function returns unit
    let f x = () // f : 'a -> unit

    // use ignore to throw away the keyboard input and f2 returns unit
    let f2 () = System.Console.ReadKey() |> ignore
    ```

> **Note** When a function can be passed in as a parameter to another function, the passed-in function is of type *Microsoft.FSharp.Core.FSharpFunc*. The function, which is passed in as a parameter, can be called by calling the *Microsoft.FSharp.Core.FSharpFunc.Invoke* method. When this is the case, the Invoke a function returning *unit* actually returns the *Microsoft.FSharp.Core.Unit* type, which is not void at all. Fortunately, the F# Compiler handles this so that you do not have to be aware of the subtle difference when coding.

Type Aliases

Another nice F# feature allows you to give a type an alias. Listing 1-76 shows how to give the built-in system type *int* a different name. This feature is more like *typedef* in C++. From the execution result, you can see that the *int* type can now be referenced by using *I*.

LISTING 1-76 A type alias and the FSI execution result

```
> type I = int
let f (a:I) = a + 1;;

type I = int
val f : I -> I
```

Type Inferences

At this point, you might still be wondering why you don't have to specify type information when writing the F# code shown in Listing 1-13. You might get the wrong impression that F# is a scripting language or a dynamic language, which usually do not emphasize the type. Actually, this is not true; F# is a strongly typed language. F# provides the ability to leave off type definitions through a feature called *type inference*, which can identify type information based on how code is used. Listing 1-77 shows the function *f* and how its definition is shown in FSI. The type for *s* can be determined by the function call *System.String.IsNullOrEmpty*, which takes a string and returns a Boolean. This is how F# identifies the type information.

LISTING 1-77 A type inference sample

```
> let f s = System.String.IsNullOrEmpty s;;

val f : string -> bool
```

Type inference works great, but it will need help sometimes, such as when processing overloaded methods, because overloaded methods distinguish themselves from each other by parameter types. For the example, in Listing 1-78, the *LastIndexOf* method can get both *char* and *string* as input. You did not expect that the compiler could read your mind, did you? Because the variable *ch* can be either the *string* or *char* type, you have to specify the type for the variable *ch*. If you do not tell the compiler the parameter type, there is no way for F# to figure out which overloaded method to use. The correct code is shown in Listing 1-79.

LISTING 1-78 The type inference when using overloaded methods

```
> let f ch = "abc".LastIndexOf(ch);;

  let f ch = "abc".LastIndexOf(ch);;
  ----------^^^^^^^^^^^^^^^^^^^^^^^

stdin(10,12): error FS0041: A unique overload for method 'LastIndexOf' could not be
determined based on type information prior to this program point. A type annotation may
be needed. Candidates: System.String.LastIndexOf(value: char) : int, System.String.
LastIndexOf(value: string) : int
```

LISTING 1-79 The type inference with a type specified

```
> let f (ch:string) = "abc".LastIndexOf(ch);;

val f : string -> int
```

It's good to understand how type inference process work. It is performed from top to bottom and from left to right. It does not start from the program's *main* function. So the code in Listing 1-80 does not compile. The string type cannot be inferred from the *str.Length* because there are tons of types in .NET that have a *Length* property.

LISTING 1-80 The type inference from top to bottom

```
let f str = str.Length  // str type cannot be determined

[<EntryPoint>]
let main argv =
    let result = f "abc"
    0 // return an integer exit code
```

> **Note** It's a best practice to write the code as you go and let the F# compiler figure out the type for you. If there is an error, look at the code above the line that the error is pointing to. Those errors can often be easily fixed by providing type information. Type inference is processed from top to bottom, which could not be the order of how code is executed. The program entry point is usually located at the end of the file, but decorating the variable at entry point does not help.
>
> IntelliSense uses a different way to provide type information for users. Therefore, sometimes IntelliSense shows the type information but the code will not compile. A simple code example is shown next. The type for *str* on the second line is unknown, although IntelliSense shows that *str* is of the *System.String* type.
>
> ```
> let f str =
>     let len = str.Length // str type is unknown
>     str + "aa"
> ```

Type inference tends to make code more general. This simplicity not only saves you typing time, it also improves the readability by making the code more intuitive and friendly, as I think you can see in Listing 1-81.

LISTING 1-81 F# and C# side by side

F# code

```
let printAll aSeq =
    for n in aSeq do
        <your function call>
```

```
C# equivalent
public static void printAll<a>(IEnumerable<a> aSeq)
{
    foreach (a i in aSeq)
    {
        <your function call>
    }
}
```

If you're not convinced yet, Listing 1-82 demonstrates how to use type inference and a tuple to create a general *swap* function. The function can handle any data type. If you try to use C# to implement the same function, you'll find the F# code is more clean and elegant. If you use Visual Studio or MonoDevelop, type information can be shown when hovering over the function.

LISTING 1-82 A tuple and *swap* function

```
// swap a and b
let swap(a,b) = (b,a)
```

Interop and *Function* Parameters

Some F# users start to use F# as a library authoring tool. The F# library is then referenced and invoked from some C# library or application. Because F# is a .NET language, using *interop* with other .NET languages is seamless. Adding a reference to an F# project is exactly same as adding one to a C# project. The only thing that needs to be explained here is how to add a reference to FSI:

1. Use #*r* to reference a DLL.

2. Open the namespace.

Listing 1-83 shows how to reference *System.Core.dll*, open the *System.Collections.Generic* namespace, and use the *HashSet<T>* type.

LISTING 1-83 Creating a *HashSet* in an F# script file or in FSI

```
#r "System.Core.dll"
open System.Collections.Generic
let a = HashSet<int>()
```

Note F# does not need *new* to instantiate an object. However, the *new* keyword is recommended when the class type implements the *IDisposable* interface.

Compared to C#, there is little difference in the approach for invoking a .NET method in F#. Here's how to use a .NET method to convert a string to an integer:

```
System.Convert.ToInt32("234")
```

Passing a tuple to a C# function seems to work well until you have a function that requires an *out* parameter. Tuples do not provide a way to say that a value is *ref* or *out*, but a tuple does help to solve this problem. If you have a C# function like the following

```
public int CSharpFunction(int k, out int n)
```

the function actually returns two values to the invoker. So the solution is to declare a tuple to hold the returned values:

```
let returnValue, nValue = CSharpFunction(1)
```

This approach works for the method, which is not externally declared. A call to an externally declared method requires the & operator. Listing 1-84 shows how to handle an *out* parameter in an *extern* function.

LISTING 1-84 Using F# to invoke a C# *extern* function that has an *out* parameter

```
C# function definition
[DllImport("MyDLL.dll")]
public static extern int ASystemFunction(IntPtr inRef, out IntPtr outPtr);


Define and invoke the function in F#
[<System.Runtime.InteropServices.DllImport("something.dll")>]
extern int ASystemFunction(System.IntPtr inRef, System.IntPtr& outPtr);

let mutable myOutPtr = nativeint 1
let n = ASystemFunction (nativeint 0, &myOutPtr)
```

If you want to expose an *out* parameter to a C# project, you need a special attribute named *System.Runtime.InteropServices.Out*. By decorating a parameter with this attribute in F#, the C# invoker can see that the parameter is intended to be an *out* parameter. See the sample in Listing 1-85. The *byref* keyword is used to declare the variable as being passed in as a reference type.

LISTING 1-85 Using F# to expose an *out* parameter to C#

```
let f ([<System.Runtime.InteropServices.Out>]a: int byref) =  a <- 9
```

I covered the *out* parameter, so now let's shift our attention to *ref*. It's easy to handle the C# *ref* definition as well. Listing 1-86 shows how to handle *ref* parameters in F#. There is a *ref* keyword in the sample code, which I'll introduce in Chapter 6, "Other Unique Features." For now, think of it as a reference variable.

LISTING 1-86 Using F# to invoke a C# function that has a *ref* parameter

```
C# function definition
namespace CSharpProject
{
    public class Chapter1Class
    {
        public static int ParameterFunction(int inValue, ref int refValue)
        {
            refValue += 3;
            return inValue + 7;
        }

        public static void ReturnSample(out int x)
        {
            x = 8;
        }
    }
}


F# code invoking the C# function
//declare a mutable variable
let mutable mutableValue = 2

// declare a reference cell
let refValue = ref 2

// pass mutable variable into the function
let refFunctionValue = CSharpProject.Chapter1Class.ParameterFunction(1, &mutableValue)

// pass reference cell into the function
let refFunctionValue2 = CSharpProject.Chapter1Class.ParameterFunction(1, refValue)

// out parameter
let mutable x = Unchecked.defaultof<_>
CSharpProject.Chapter1Class.ReturnSample(&x)
```

If you want to expose a *ref* parameter from an F# function to a C# project, removing the *Out* attribute from the function definition will do the trick. The use of the *byref* keyword indicates that this is a reference parameter. The code is shown in Listing 1-87.

LISTING 1-87 Exposing a *ref* parameter to a C# project

```
let f (a: int byref) =  a <- 9
```

Module, Namespace, and Program Entry Points

Now that the small F# program is clean, you might want to build an executable. Listing 1-1 is a code snippet, and you need to use Visual Studio to write, debug, and publish a product. This section will cover how to create an F# console application using Visual Studio. Figure 1-16 shows how to create an F# console application.

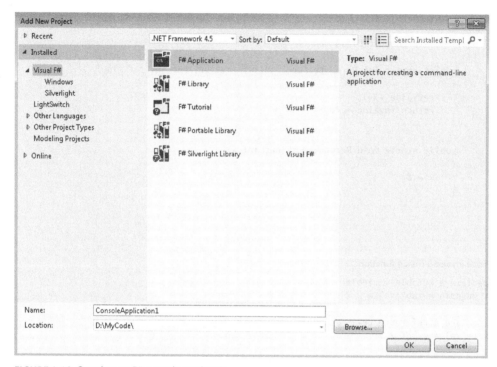

FIGURE 1-16 Creating an F# console application

The default Program.fs file contains a *main* function with an *EntryPoint* attribute; see Figure 1-17. Actually, F# does not need an *entry* function to be defined. For a single file project, the content is executed from the first line to the last.

```
// Learn more about F# at http://fsharp.net
// See the 'F# Tutorial' project for more help.

[<EntryPoint>]
let main argv =
    printfn "%A" argv
    0 // return an integer exit code
```

FIGURE 1-17 The default *main* function for an F# console application

If using the *EntryPoint* attribute is the preferred way, the function must meet the following criteria:

- The function must be decorated with the *[<EntryPoint>]* attribute.

- The function must be in the last file in the project.

- The function must return an integer as exit code.

- The function must take a string array, *string[]*, as input.

> **Tip** In an F# DLL, modules are initialized by a static constructor. This guarantees the initialization occurs before any of the module's values are referenced. On the other hand, in an F# executable, the initialization is performed in the application's entry point, which is defined by the *EntryPoint* attribute. It is recommended that you explicitly define an entry point for an F# executable by using *EntryPoint*.

When you add the F# item in your console project, it can immediately make your code unable to compile. The newly added item is the last item in the project system. This breaks the second requirement in the preceding list. You can use the context menu—see Figure 1-18—or Alt+Up/Down Arrow keys, if the development profile is set to F#, to move your item up and down the project system.

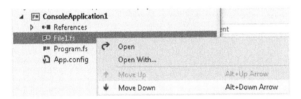

FIGURE 1-18 The context menu for moving an item up and down

It's always a good coding practice to divide the code into different units when the project has multiple files. F# provides the *module* or *namespace* to divide the code into small units. They have subtle differences, which I will discuss later in this chapter.

If you delete all content in the Program.fs file and paste the code shown in Listing 1-33, which does not have a module definition, the F# compiler will create an anonymous module. Its name is the file name with the first letter capitalized. For example, if your code is in file1.fs, the module name will be File1. You can also explicitly provide module names at the first line of the file, as shown in Listing 1-88.

LISTING 1-88 Module definition

```
module MyModule

printfn "Hello World!"
```

A module can contain other modules, type definitions, expressions, values, or any combination of those, but namespaces cannot be inside a module. The nested module needs to be indented and must have an equal sign (=) as a suffix. See Listing 1-89.

LISTING 1-89 Defining a nested module

```
module Print

// general print function
let print x = printf "%A" x

// define sub module NumberPrint
module NumberPrint =
    // function to print int
    let printInt = printf "%d"

    // function to print float
    let printFloat = printf "%f"

// define sub module StringPrint
module StringPrint =
    // function to print string
    let printString = printf "%s"

    // function to print char
    let printChar = printf "%c"

// define sub module with new type
module NewTypes =
    // define a 2D point
    type Point2D = float32*float32

// invoke print functions
NumberPrint.printFloat 4.5
NumberPrint.printInt 2
StringPrint.printChar 'c'
StringPrint.printString "abc"
```

If you want a scope to hold the functions and variables, the namespace and module are the same from F#'s point of view. If the F# project is going to be a library opened from a C# project, the namespace is a better choice. The module is a static class when it's viewed from the C# side. By using a module name and function name together, you can reference a function defined in a different module. If you want to reference a function inside a module, you can use the *open* keyword to open that module or decorate the module with the *AutoOpen* attribute, which can open the module automatically, essentially causing the function to be placed in the global namespace. See Listing 1-90.

LISTING 1-90 Opening a module

```
module Print

// general print function
let print x = printf "%A" x

// auto open  NumberPrint module
[<AutoOpen>]
module NumberPrint =
    // function to print int
    let printInt = printf "%d"

    // function to print float
    let printFloat = printf "%f"

module StringPrint =
    // function to print string
    let printString = printf "%s"

    // function to print char
    let printChar = printf "%c"

// invoke print functions
printFloat 4.5
printInt 2

// use module name to reference the function defined in the module
StringPrint.printChar 'c'
StringPrint.printString "abc"

// open StringPrint module
open StringPrint

printChar 'c'
printString "abc"
```

Note The *open* statement must be located somewhere after the module is defined.

The *RequireQualifiedAccess* attribute indicates that a reference to an element in that module must specify the module name. Listing 1-91 shows how to decorate the attribute on a module and reference a function within.

LISTING 1-91 Using the *RequireQualifiedAccess* attribute

```
[<RequireQualifiedAccessAttribute>]
module MyModule =
    let f() = printfn "f inside MyModule"

//reference to f must use MyModule
MyModule.f()
```

Modules can be extended by creating a new module with the same name. All the items—such as functions, types, expressions, and values—will be accessible as long as the new module is opened. See Listing 1-92. To invoke the extended method, you can open the namespace *MyCollectionExtensions*. Listing 1-93 opens the namespace, and the extension method is shown.

LISTING 1-92 Extending a module

```
Namespace MyCollectionExtensions

open System.Collection.Generic

// extend the array module by adding a lengthBy function
module Array =
    let lengthBy filterFunction array =
        array |> Array.filter fiterFunction |> Array.length
```

> **Note** A module inside a namespace also needs an equal sign (=) as a suffix.

LISTING 1-93 Invoking the function in the extended module

```
open MyCollectionExtensions

let array = [| 1..10 |]
let evenNumber = array |> Array.lengthBy (fun n -> n % 2 = 0 )
```

As mentioned previously, if the F# code needs to be referenced from other .NET languages, a namespace is the preferred way to organize the code. Namespaces can contain only modules and type definitions. You cannot put namespaces, expressions, or values inside of a namespace. See Listing 1-94.

LISTING 1-94 Using a namespace

```
namespace MySpace

// define a 3D point
type Point3D = Point of float32 * float32 * float32

// define module inside namespace
module HelloWorld =
    let msg = @"Hello world"
    printfn "%s" msg

// the following line won't compile because a namespace cannot contain value or expression
// let a = 2
```

Note Namespaces are not supported in FSI because it's difficult to find out where the namespace ends in FSI.

Empty files do not compile in a multifile project. Source code must have either a namespace or a module at the beginning if the project contains multiple files.

CHAPTER 2

Using F# for Object-Oriented Programming

Object-oriented programming (OOP) has been a great success. Many modern business systems are designed and implemented by applying OOP concepts. I will not discuss the benefit of using OOP because, as a C# developer, you probably already have hundreds of such benefits in mind.

F# is a multiparadigm language that supports OOP. Practically everything you can do with C# can be done with F#, and usually with less code. I will follow the approach from the first chapter, converting C# code to F#. Listing 2-1 shows a C# *Point2D* class, which represents a point on a two-dimensional (2D) surface. It shows properties, static and nonstatic fields, an attribute, and member methods. The conversion task will not only do the straightforward translation, but also perform some extra work to demonstrate related F# concepts.

LISTING 2-1 C# Point2D class definition

```
// define a 2D point
[DebuggerDisplay("({X}, {Y})")]
public class Point2D
{
    // define a counter
    private static int count = 0;

    // define the original point
    public readonly Point2D OriginalPoint = new Point2D(0, 0);

    // define an X property with explicit back-end field x
    private double x;
    public double X
    {
        get { return this.x; }
        set { this.x = value; }
    }

    // define a Y property
    public double Y { get; set; }
```

```csharp
//length to original point (0,0)
public double LengthToOriginal
{
    get { return this.GetDistance(this.OriginalPoint); }
}

// default constructor
public Point2D()
    : this(0,0)
{}

// constructor with parameters x and y
public Point2D(double x, double y)
{
    this.X = x;
    this.Y = y;
    count++;            // increase the counter when created a new instance
}

// static method convert (x,y) to Point2D
public static Point2D FromXY(double x, double y)
{
    return new Point2D(x, y);
}

// compute the distance to a given point
public virtual double GetDistance(Point2D point)
{
    var xDif = this.X - point.X;
    var yDif = this.Y - point.Y;
    var distance = Math.Sqrt(xDif * xDif + yDif * yDif);
    return distance;
}

//override the ToString function
public override string ToString()
{
    return String.Format("Point2D({0}, {1})", this.X, this.Y);
}
}
```

Using Classes

When defining a class, C# always needs the *class* keyword. In F#, this keyword is optional. Listing 2-2 demonstrates a class definition in F#.

LISTING 2-2 A class definition

Class definition without a default accessibility modifier
```
// define a public Point2D class
type Point2D() = class

  end
```

Class definition with an explicit accessibility modifier
```
// define an internal Point2D class
type internal Point2D() = class

  end

// define a class without the class keyword
type MyClass() =
  // class fields, methods, and properties, such as the following field definition
  let myField = 9
```

 Note If the class does not contain any member or operation, you have to use *class* keyword; otherwise, *class* keyword is optional.

You might be wondering where the *public* keyword is. Unlike class in C#, which is *internal* by default, the F# class is *public* by default. Ignoring the *public* keyword can save some typing. F# also supports using modules to group code. Table 2-1 lists all of the accessibility modifiers that F# supports.

TABLE 2-1 Accessibility modifier definitions

Accessibility Modifier	Description
public	The *public* modifier indicates that the type, value, and function are accessible anywhere.
private	The *private* access modifier is the least-permissive access level. Private members are accessible only within the body of the class or the struct in which they are declared. The *class* field is private by default.
internal	The *internal* modifier is same as *public* if there is only one assembly. The *internal* types are not accessible from another assembly. It is *public* when accessed from the same assembly and *private* when accessed from a different assembly.

 Note F# does not support the *protected* keyword. F# honors protected visibility when the type is defined in a language that supports protected-level visibility. F# intends to use less protected level members in a class than in C#; instead, it uses interfaces, object expressions, and higher order functions.

In Listing 1-69, we introduced the mutually recursive function definition. You can use the same approach to define mutually recursive types. In Listing 2-3, we define a mutually recursive type.

LISTING 2-3 Mutually recursive type definition without using the *class* keyword

```
type A() =
    let b = B()
and B() =
    let a = A()
```

Unlike C#, F# does not support partial classes, so you have to put all the class code in a single file. F# provides a type-extension feature, which I'll introduce later in this chapter, to provide similar functionality.

Adding Fields

We need to put something in the empty class definition, and a logical place to start is by adding a field. The way F# defines a class field is not much different than defining a value in a module. Listing 2-4 demonstrates how to define a field, named *x*, in the *Point2D* class. Once the class is not empty, we can ignore the *class...end* keywords. The initial value for *x* is set to *0.0*, and its type is inferred to an F# float type.

LISTING 2-4 Defining field *x* in class *Point2D*

```
// define a Point2D class
type Point2D() =
    // define field x
    let mutable x = 0.0
```

 Note The *let* keyword can define only a private field or function when used in a class.

Another way to define an explicit field is to use the *val* keyword. Listing 2-5 defines an explicit field *x* using the *val* keyword. When an explicit field is defined, the type information must be provided explicitly in the field definition. The explicit field definition can have accessibility modifiers such as *public*. The field named *y* in Listing 2-5 is a public field.

LISTING 2-5 Defining an explicit field in a class

```
// define a Point2D class
type Point2D() =
    // define a field x using explicit field
    [<DefaultValue>] val mutable x : float

    // define a field y with public accessibility modifier
    [<DefaultValue>] val mutable public y : float
```

Note The *DefaultValue* attribute is mandatory if the class has a primary constructor. I will explain this later in the "Using Constructors" section.

There is no way to define a public static field.

The *DefaultValue* attribute specifies that fields *x* and *y* are initialized to zero because both fields support zero-initialization. We can say that the type supports zero-initialization if the type meets one of the following conditions:

- A primitive type that has a zero value, such as integer.

- A type that supports a null value, either as a normal value, as an abnormal value, or as a representation of a value, such as a class.

- A .NET value type, such as integer or DateTime. The full list is available at *http://msdn.microsoft.com/en-us/library/hfa3fa08(v=vs.110).aspx.*

- A structure and all its fields support a default zero value.

Like C#, there are several ways to represent any one thing. Another way to set the default value is to use the *Unchecked.defaultof* operator. The function takes a *type* parameter and returns the default value for that type. It is like the default(T) operator in C#. Listing 2-6 shows a sample of how to define a default value.

LISTING 2-6 Using *Unchecked.default* to set a default value

```
// define a Point2D class
type Point2D() =
    // define int field x with Unchecked.defaultof operator
    let mutable x = Unchecked.defaultof<int>
```

Defining a Property

Next we will define a property using the *member* keyword. The property name is always prefixed with a self-identifier. The code in Listing 2-7 also uses *this* keyword as a self-identifier. F# supports user-defined self-identifiers, so you can use any valid identifier name as a self-identifier. This feature can improve the program readability. The self-identifier feature will be discussed later in this chapter. In C#, we can specify a different accessibility level for a property's *getter* and *setter* functions. We can also do this in F# by adding *private*, *public*, or *internal* before the *set* or *get*. Listing 2-7 shows a sample of a property definition.

LISTING 2-7 Defining a property

```
Defining a property with the same accessibility modifier

// define a Point2D class
type Point2D() =
    // define field x
    let mutable x = 0.0

    // define X property
    member this.X with get() = x
                  and set(v) = x <- v


Defining a property with a different accessibility modifier

// define a Point2D class
type Point2D() =
    // define field x
    let mutable x = 0.0

    // define an X property
    member this.X with get() = x
                  and private set(v) = x <- v
```

C# has a shortcut definition for a property. In C# 3.0 and later, the auto-implemented property was introduced. The property *Y* uses the auto-implemented property syntax. F# 3.0 also has this feature, as shown in Listing 2-8. The *0* in the line member val Y = 0 with get, set is the initial value for the *Y* property, and this initial value also is responsible for indicating the variable type. When the initial value is *0*, the value type is automatically inferred to be integer. The F# compiler generates a back-end field *Y@*, and it is decorated with the *CompilerGenerateAttribute* attribute.

LISTING 2-8 An auto-implemented property

```
// define a Point2D class
type Point2D() =
    // define field x
    let mutable x = 0.0
```

```
// define an X property
member this.X with get() = x
            and set(v) = x <- v

// define a Y property using an auto-implemented property
member val Y = 0.0 with get, set
```

Note The auto-implemented property does not support getters or setters with different levels of accessibility. As a result, you cannot define a private setter function when using an auto-implemented property.

An indexed property is nothing but a property with some input parameters. Listing 2-9 shows a sample of an indexed property. It defines a *Screen* type and is used to retrieve the point by using an index. The *Item* property is a special property that can be used in two ways: `screen.[0]` or `screen.Item(0)`.

LISTING 2-9 An indexed property

```
// define a Screen class with a point list
type Screen() =
    let points = System.Collections.Generic.List<Point2D>()

    // the item property
    member this.Item with get(x) = points.[x]
                    and set x v = points.[x] <- v
```

Note The *setter* function does not take an *(x, v)* tuple. It has two parameters, *x* and *v.*

C# provides an object-initializer feature for setting property values. F# has a similar feature that can be used to initialize property values. Listing 2-10 provides an example. In this example, *p* is initialized with *x* and *y* set to *1*.

LISTING 2-10 Setting a property value when creating the object

```
type Point2D() =
    member val X = 0. with get, set
    member val Y = 0. with get, set

let p = Point2D(X = 1., Y = 1.)
```

Defining a Method

A *method* is a function associated with a type. It can be called by a member method or a member function. If you can define a property, you will not have any problem defining a method. In Listing 2-11, we define a *GetDistance* method. The *GetDistance* method definition needs to tell the compiler that the input parameter point is a *Point2D* type. Type inference doesn't work in this case, we first access the property. The C# version of this method is marked as virtual, but the code in Listing 2-11 is not a virtual method. I will discuss how to define a virtual method in a later section.

LISTING 2-11 Defining a member function

```
// define a Point2D class
type Point2D() =
    // define field x
    let mutable x = 0.0

    // define X property
    member this.X with get() = x
                  and set(v) = x <- v

    // define Y property using an auto-implemented property
    member val Y = 0.0 with get, set

    // define a function to get the distance from the current point
    member this.GetDistance (point:Point2D) =
        let xDif = this.X - point.X
        let yDif = this.Y - point.Y
        let distance = sqrt (xDif**2. + yDif**2.)
        distance
```

Note The double star (**) operator is used to compute the exponential value of a given number, and the *sqrt* function is equivalent to *Math.Sqrt*.

Shipped with Microsoft Visual Studio 2010, C# introduced optional parameters and named parameter features. These two types of features are also available in F#. Listing 2-12 shows a C# version of *GetDistance* with optional parameters defined and its F# equivalent. F# does not allow using default values after the parameter name; instead, it uses the *defaultArg* function. The *defaultArg* function takes the optional parameter as the first argument and the default value as a fallback value.

LISTING 2-12 Using optional parameters

C# GetDistance with an optional parameter

```csharp
// compute the distance to a given point
public double GetDistance(double x = 0, double y = 0)
{
    var xDif = this.X - x;
    var yDif = this.Y - y;
    var distance = Math.Sqrt(xDif * xDif + yDif * yDif);
    return distance;
}
```

F# GetDistance with an optional parameter

```fsharp
// define a function to get the distance from the current point
member this.GetDistance(?xValue, ?yValue) =
    // take the (xValue, yValue) tuple and decide whether to use the default value
    let x, y = (defaultArg xValue 0., defaultArg yValue 0.)

    let xDif = this.X - x
    let yDif = this.Y - y
    let distance = sqrt (xDif**2. + yDif**2.)
    distance
```

When the optional parameter is exposed to a C# project, the C# project needs to reference *Microsoft.FSharp.Core.dll*, which you can use to create the F# option types. See Listing 2-13.

LISTING 2-13 Referencing the F# method with an optional parameter

F# code defining a method with an optional parameter

```fsharp
namespace MyClassNamespace

type MyClass() =
    member this.PrintValue(?value:int) =
        match value with
            | Some(n) -> printfn "value is %A" n
            | None -> printfn "sorry, no value"
```

C# code invoking an F# method with an optional parameter

```csharp
static void Main(string[] args)
{
    var myValue = new MyClassNamespace.MyClass();

    myValue.PrintValue(Microsoft.FSharp.Core.FSharpOption<int>.None);
    myValue.PrintValue(new Microsoft.FSharp.Core.FSharpOption<int>(1));
}
```

```
sorry, no value
value is 1
```

If adding a reference to *FSharp.Core.dll* is not the preferred way of doing this, you can use the *System.Runtime.InteropServices.DefaultParameterValueAttribute* to expose the optional parameter. Listing 2-14 shows a sample.

LISTING 2-14 Exposing an F# optional parameter without reference to *FSharp.Core.dll*

F# code exposing an optional parameter

```
namespace MyClassNamespace

open System.Runtime.InteropServices

type MyClass() =
    member this.PrintValue(?value:int) =
        match value with
            | Some(n) -> printfn "value is %A" n
            | None -> printfn "sorry, no value"

    member this.PrintValue2([<Optional;DefaultParameterValue(0)>]value:int,
                            [<Optional;DefaultParameterValue(null)>]str:string) =
        let defaultStr = if str = null then "null value" else str
        printfn "(%A, %A)" value defaultStr
```

C# code invoking the method with an optional parameter

```
static void Main(string[] args)
{
    var myValue = new MyClassNamespace.MyClass();

    myValue.PrintValue2(2);
    myValue.PrintValue2();
    myValue.PrintValue2(3, "three");
}
```

Execution result from the C# code

```
(2, "null value")
(0, "null value")
(3, "three")
```

Note The code segment [<Optional;DefaultParameterValue(0)>] contains two attributes. One is *OptionalAttribute*, and the other is *DefaultParameterValue*.

It's easy to invoke a C# method with an optional parameter from the F# side. Listing 2-15 shows how to invoke a C# method with an optional parameter.

LISTING 2-15 Invoking a C# method with an optional parameter from F#

```
C# code defining a method with an optional parameter
public class CSharpClass
{
    public void MyMethod(int a = 11)
    {
        Console.WriteLine("a = {0}", a);
    }
}


F# code invoking a C# method with an optional parameter
let c = ConsoleApplication1.CSharpClass()

c.MyMethod()
c.MyMethod(100)
c.MyMethod(a=199)


Execution result from F# code
a = 11
a = 100
a = 199
```

Defining a Static Method

We have converted the *field*, *property*, and *member* methods from C# to F#. We can now convert the static method *FromXY*. As in C#, the *static* keyword is needed to define a static method. One approach to accomplishing this is to use a tuple, and another is to define two independent parameters. If you recall the design principle mentioned in the "Defining Tuples" section in Chapter 1, "C# and F# Data Structures," the tuple approach is a better choice because it requires that both *x* and *y* be passed together. The F# code is shown in Listing 2-16.

LISTING 2-16 Defining a static method

```
// define a Point2D class
type Point2D() =
    // define field x
    let mutable x = 0.0

    // define the X property
    member this.X with get() = x
                  and set(v) = x <- v

    // define the Y property using an auto-implemented property
    member val Y = 0.0 with get, set

    // define a function to get the distance from the current point
    member this.GetDistance (point:Point2D) =
        let xDif = this.X - point.X
        let yDif = this.Y - point.Y
        let distance = sqrt (xDif**2. + yDif**2.)
        distance

    // define a static method to return a Point2D from (x,y) tuple
    static member FromXY (x:double, y:double) =
        let point = Point2D()
        point.X <- x
        point.Y <- y
        point
```

Using Constructors

As a C# developer, you might be thinking that a constructor is nothing more than another function. If so, be prepared for something different. F# has two different kinds of constructors. One type is the *primary constructor*, whose parameters appear in parentheses just after the type name. Whether or not you are surprised, realize that the set of parentheses after the type name is the parameter to the primary constructor! Another kind of constructor is an *optional constructor*, which starts with the *new* keyword. Any such additional constructors must call the primary constructor.

That is a lot of information. Let's use the code in Listing 2-16 as a sample. F# treats all the code between the class name and first class member as initialization code. In the sample code, the `let mutable x = 0.0` line of code is initialized when the class is created. If you put a *printf* statement after *let* and before any member function, you will see that the message is printed out.

There are two constructors in the C# code. The one that takes two parameters is more general. Please note that primary constructor is always being called first. In the sample, you use the two-parameter constructor as the primary constructor. The code is shown in Listing 2-17. The fields *x* and *y* take *xValue* and *yValue*, respectively, as their initial value. The code in Listing 2-18 defines an additional parameterless constructor, which calls into the primary constructor and passes an initial value of *0*. Note that F# does not generate a default constructor as C# does. If a class is defined without a constructor, it can be compiled, but there is no way to instantiate it.

LISTING 2-17 Using a parameterized constructor as the primary constructor

```
// define a Point2D class with a parameterized primary constructor
type Point2D(xValue:double, yValue:double) =
    // define field x
    let mutable x = xValue

    // define an X property
    member this.X with get() = x
                  and set(v) = x <- v

    // define a Y property using an auto-implemented property
    member val Y = yValue with get, set

    // define a function to get the distance from the current point
    member this.GetDistance (point:Point2D) =
        let xDif = this.X - point.X
        let yDif = this.Y - point.Y
        let distance = sqrt (xDif**2. + yDif**2.)
        distance

    // define a static method to return a Point2D from (x,y) tuple
    static member FromXY (x, y) =
        Point2D(x,y)
```

Note The member function cannot be invoked in the constructor code.

In some cases, you need a different way to initialize an object. C# allows multiple constructors. The sample in Listing 2-18 shows how to define an additional constructor in F#.

LISTING 2-18 An additional constructor

```
// define a Point2D class with a parameterized primary constructor
type Point2D(xValue:double, yValue:double) =
    // define field x
    let mutable x = xValue

    //additional constructor
    new() = Point2D(0.,0.)

    // define an X property
    member this.X with get() = x
                  and set(v) = x <- v

    // define a Y property using an auto-implemented property
    member val Y = yValue with get, set

    // define a function to get the distance from the current point
    member this.GetDistance (point:Point2D) =
```

```
        let xDif = this.X - point.X
        let yDif = this.Y - point.Y
        let distance = sqrt (xDif**2. + yDif**2.)
        distance

    // define a static method to return a Point2D from (x,y) tuple
    static member FromXY (x, y) =
        Point2D(x,y)
```

Although the constructor definition (xValue:double, yValue:double) is right after the type name, you can still squeeze in the accessibility modifier *public, internal,* or *private.* Listing 2-19 defines a private parameterless constructor and an internal parameterized primary constructor. The *internal* keyword before Point2D is for the class and the second *internal* after Point2D is for the primary constructor

LISTING 2-19 Using accessibility modifiers on constructors

Point2D definition with an accessibility modifier

```
// define a Point2D class with a parameterized primary constructor
type internal Point2D internal (xValue:double, yValue:double) =
    // define field x
    let mutable x = xValue

    //additional constructor
    private new() = Point2D(0.,0.)

    // define an X property
    member this.X with get() = x
                  and set(v) = x <- v

    // define a Y property using an auto-implemented property
    member val Y = yValue with get, set

    // define a function to get the distance from the current point
    member this.GetDistance (point:Point2D) =
        let xDif = this.X - point.X
        let yDif = this.Y - point.Y
        let distance = sqrt (xDif**2. + yDif**2.)
        distance

    // define a static method to return a Point2D from (x,y) tuple
    static member FromXY (x, y) =
        Point2D(x,y)
```

Invoke the Point2D

```
// let internal p = Point2D(X = 1., Y = 1.)
//won't compile because private constructor
let internal p = Point2D(1., 1.)
```

Let's stop for a moment to clean up some basic concepts. The code `let mutable x = 0.0` in Listing 2-16 is called a *let binding*. The variable defined in a let binding can be accessed at the class level. Actually, the let binding creates a private field or private function. You can think of the let binding as a private function library for the class. As long as a *static* keyword is present in the definition, a let binding can be a static let binding. The let binding is executed when the instance is created and the static let binding code will be executed before the type is first used.

The let binding can be used in a primary constructor to set an initial value. But what if you want to perform some operations? You can use a *do binding* during the object-creation phase to perform some extra operations. Like the let binding, the do binding also supports static binding. The nonstatic do binding is executed when the instance is created and the static let binding code will be executed before the type is first used. Listing 2-20 demonstrates how to use a let binding and a do binding to implement the count feature that was shown in the C# code.

LISTING 2-20 An example of let binding and do binding

```
// define a Point2D class with a parameterized primary constructor
type Point2D(xValue:double, yValue:double) =
    // define field x
    let mutable x = xValue

    // define a static field named count
    static let mutable count = 0

    // perform a do binding to increase the count each time a new instance is created
    do
        count <- count + 1

    //additional constructor
    new() = Point2D(0.,0.)

    // define an X property
    member this.X with get() = x
                  and set(v) = x <- v

    // define a Y property using an auto-implemented property
    member val Y = yValue with get, set

    // define a function to get the distance from the current point
    member this.GetDistance (point:Point2D) =
        let xDif = this.X - point.X
        let yDif = this.Y - point.Y
        let distance = sqrt (xDif**2. + yDif**2.)
        distance

    // define a static method to return a Point2D from (x,y) tuple
    static member FromXY (x, y) =
        Point2D(x,y)
```

> **Note** A let binding and do binding cannot have attributes or an accessibility modifier in class definition. A let binding in module can have attribute and accessibility modifiers.

The primary constructor can use a do binding to perform additional initialization code. The *then* keyword can be used to help a nonprimary constructor execute additional code. See Listing 2-21.

LISTING 2-21 Using the *then* keyword with a nonprimary constructor

```
type Student(nameIn : string, idIn : int) =
    let mutable name = nameIn
    let mutable id = idIn

    do printfn "Created a student object"

    member this.Name with get() = name and set(v) = name <- v
    member this.ID with get() = id and set(v) = id <- v

    new() =
        Student("Invalid studnet name", -1)
        then
            printfn "Created an invalid student object. Please input student name."
```

F# strictly follows a "define first and reference later" approach. As an example, auto-implemented properties insert a back-end field after the do binding. Because of the "define first and reference later" principle, this back-end field is inaccessible in the do binding section of the code. Because of this hidden field insertion, the code in Listing 2-22 is invalid. When you perform the do binding, the back-end *Y@* field has not been initialized, so the code generates an *InvalidOperationException* error. Because of this , we will not use an auto-implemented property; instead, we'll stick to the old way of defining a property. You can still use an auto-implemented property if the constructor logic is simple.

LISTING 2-22 An auto-implemented property that affects do binding

The following code won't compile

```
// An auto-implemented property that causes the following code to not compile
type A() as this =
    do this.F()
    // let Y@ = 0      //hidden backend field
    member this.F() = printfn "aaa"  // InvalidOperationException error!
    member val Y = 0 with get,set

let a = A()
```

There's one more topic I want to cover before I finish talking about F# constructors: *static constructors*. Listing 2-23 shows how to define a static constructor code and its execution result.

LISTING 2-23 Static *let/do* code

```
// define a Point2D class with a parameterized primary constructor
type Point2D(xValue:double, yValue:double) =
    // define a static field named count
    static let mutable count = 0
    static do printfn "point2D constructor"

// define a screen class
type Screen() =
    let points = System.Collections.Generic.List<Point2D>()
    static do printfn "screen constructor"
    member this.ShowPoint() = printf "inside ShowPoint"

// define a test module
module TestModule =
    let screen = Screen()
    screen.ShowPoint()



Execution result

point2D constructor
screen constructor
inside ShowPoint
```

Note XML document for primary constructor is not supported. The workaround is to define another constructor with a dummy parameter, as in this example:

```
/// my xml doc
type A(args) =
            <your code>

// change to the following code with a dummy parameter
type A private(args, _dummyParameter:unit) =
            /// docs
            new(args) = A(args, ())
```

Creating an Indexer

If you want to create an indexer in F#, you need to define a special property named *Item*. The *Item* property will be evaluated whenever the *.[...]* is invoked. Listing 2-24 demonstrates how to define an indexer with one parameter and an indexer with two parameters.

Defining the indexer

```
// define a Screen class
type Screen() =
    let points = System.Collections.Generic.List<Point2D>()
    let width = 800
    let height = 600
    // <some code to initialize the points list to 800>
    do
        points.AddRange(Seq.init (width*height) (fun _ ->Point2D()))

    // an indexer that takes one parameter
    member this.Item with get(x:int) = points.[x]
                     and set(x:int) (v) = points.[x] <- v

    // an indexer that takes two parameters
    member this.Item with get(x:int, y:int) = points.[x + width*y]
                     and set(x:int, y:int) v = points.[x + width*y] <- v
```

Invoking the indexer

```
let s = Screen()
s.[1,1] <- Point2D()
```

Using a Self-Identifier

Everything seems to be working perfectly until you try to assign a value to your property in the do binding section in Listing 2-24. If you put this.Y <- 0 in the do binding section, the F# compiler spits out an error message complaining that *this* is not defined. This error can throw most C# developers off their chairs. Why does the keyword need to be defined?

A *self-identifier* is a reference to the current instance. The *this* in C# and *Me* in Microsoft Visual Basic are self-identifiers. Interestingly, F# does not require that the self-identifier be any particular word. You can use any word as the self-identifier for the whole class definition or just for an individual method:

- To define a self-identifier for the whole class, use the *as* keyword after the closing parentheses of the primary constructor and specify the identifier name.

- To define a self-identifier for just one method, provide the self-identifier in the *member* declaration before the method name and use a period (.) as a separator in between.

Listing 2-25 shows these two ways of creating a self-identifier. The scope for *self* is established for the whole class and the self-identifier is only in the *Print* method. So *Print* is prefixed with *this*, and you can still use *self* to invoke *Print* in the default constructor. Keep in mind that the self-identifier is decorated on the primary constructor. It is required to have a self-identifier on the other constructors if the constructor code needs to access the resource from the current class instance.

LISTING 2-25 Using a self-identifier

```
type MyClass(v) as self =
    let data = v
    do
        self.Print()
    member this.Print() =
        printf "MyClass print"
```

Now the error about *this* not being defined is explained. To get the property working in the do binding section, you have to define the self-identifier at the class level. See Listing 2-26 for the solution.

LISTING 2-26 The self-identifier and access property in the do binding section

```
// define a Point2D class with a parameterized primary constructor
type Point2D(xValue:double, yValue:double) as this=
    // define field x
    let mutable x = xValue

    // define a static field named count
    static let mutable count = 0

    // perform a do binding to increase the count
    do
        count <- count + 1
        this.Print("in constructor")

    //additional constructor
    new() = Point2D(0.,0.)

    // print out message
    member this.Print(msg) = printfn "%s" msg

    // define an X property
    member this.X with get() = x
                  and set(v) = x <- v

    // define a Y property using an auto-implemented property
    member val Y = yValue with get, set

    // define a function to get the distance from the current point
    member this.GetDistance (point:Point2D) =
        let xDif = this.X - point.X
        let yDif = this.Y - point.Y
        let distance = sqrt (xDif**2. + yDif**2.)
        distance

    // define a static method to return a Point2D from (x,y) tuple
    static member FromXY (x, y) =
        Point2D(x,y)
```

The C# class has its *ToString* method overridden. To do this in F#, you can use the *override* keyword. Listing 2-27 shows how to override the *ToString* function in F#. Inside the *ToString* implementation, you use *sprintf* as an alternative to *String.Format*. The *sprintf* function can be viewed as a strongly typed version of *String.Format*. You pretty much have the conversion work done, but let's continue using *Point2D* as a sample to explore more OOP concepts in F#.

LISTING 2-27 Function override

```
// define a Point2D class with a parameterized primary constructor
type Point2D(xValue:double, yValue:double) as this=
    // define field x
    let mutable x = xValue

    // define a static field named count
    static let mutable count = 0

    // perform a do binding to increase the count
    do
        count <- count + 1
        this.Y <- 0.

    //additional constructor
    new() = Point2D(0.,0.)

    // define an X property
    member this.X with get() = x
                  and set(v) = x <- v

    // define a Y property using an auto-implemented property
    member val Y = yValue with get, set

    // define a function to get the distance from the current point
    member this.GetDistance (point:Point2D) =
        let xDif = this.X - point.X
        let yDif = this.Y - point.Y
        let distance = sqrt (xDif**2. + yDif**2.)
        distance

    // define a static method to return a Point2D from (x,y) tuple
    static member FromXY (x, y) =
        Point2D(x,y)

    // override the ToString function
    override this.ToString() =
        // String.Format("Point2D({0}, {1})", this.X, this.Y)
        sprintf "Point2D(%f, %f)" this.X this.Y
```

> **Note** In C#, you can use the *new* modifier to explicitly hide a member inherited from a base class. F# does not need to use the *new* keyword. F# by default hides members from base class unless the *override* keyword is used.
>
> Also, *sprintf* provides the same functionality as *String.Format*. *sprintf* requires the pattern string specify the data type, such as *%d* for integer ,and it also supports *%O* and *%A*, which accept any data type and they convert values to string as *String.Format* does. Additionally, *sprintfn* does not support a pass-pattern string as parameter, such as `sprintfn myPattern 1 2`.

Another concept in object-oriented programming is *inheritance*. In a moment, I'll describe how to implement inheritance in F#.

Using a Special/Reserved Member Name

The variable name in F# can be a keyword and supports space and other special characters. You can use these special strings or characters to define the class member name as well. Listing 2-28 shows a sample.

LISTING 2-28 Using special characters and keywords in a class member definition

```
let f() =
    let ``else`` = 99
    let ``end`` = 100
    let ``F#`` = 101
    let ``my value`` = 102
    let ``let`` = 103
    ()
f()

type MyClass() = class
    member val ``else`` = 0 with get, set
    member val ``end`` = 0 with get, set
    member val ``F#`` = 0 with get, set
    member val ``My Value`` = 0 with get, set
    member val ``let`` = 0 with get, set
end

let myValue = MyClass()

printfn "put break point here"
```

Note The Watch window in Microsoft Visual Studio does not support all these characters and keywords. It does not show C# keywords and special character variable names, but it does support *view* if these special characters and keywords are class members. The following two screen shots show how it works:

Using Inheritance

F# uses the *inherit* keyword to represent the inheritance relationship. Listing 2-29 shows the C# code and its equivalent F# code.

LISTING 2-29 Particle class using inheritance

```
C# Particle class code
public class Particle : Point2D
{
    public double Mass { get; set; }
}



F# code
type Particle() =
    inherit Point2D()
    member val Mass = 0. with get, set
```

You might not have fully recovered yet from the shock of the F# self-identifier. Does F# allow a user to define any identifier for referring to a base class instance? The answer is no. Like C#, the *base* keyword is used to refer to the base class instance, and a user cannot define her own identifier.

Listing 2-30 shows that the *inherit* keyword can be used to invoke a base class constructor. When the base class has multiple constructors, the *inherit* keyword can indicate which constructor to use.

LISTING 2-30 Using the *inherit* keyword to invoke different base class constructors

```
// define BaseClass
type BaseClass =
    val x : int
    new () = BaseClass(0)
    new (a) = { x = a }

// define a derived class inherited from BaseClass
type DerivedClass =
    inherit BaseClass
    val y : int

    // invoke the base constructor with one parameter
    new (a, b) = { inherit BaseClass(a); y = b }

    // invoke the base constructor without a parameter
    new (b) = { inherit BaseClass(); y = b }
```

If the inherit declaration appears in the primary constructor, it is called *implicit class construction*. The code in Listing 2-31 is a sample. It is always a good practice to use an implicit constructor and provide an explicit constructor (or constructors) to overload. However, the code in Listing 2-30 does not include a primary constructor and instead explicitly specifies the desired base class constructor. We refer to this as *explicit class construction*. It is a recommended way to use implicit constructors.

LISTING 2-31 Example of a keyword base

```
type Particle() =
    inherit Point2D()
    member val Mass = 0. with get, set
    override this.ToString() =
        sprintf "Particle_%s with Mass=%f" (base.ToString()) this.Mass
```

Using Abstract and Sealed Classes

The class hierarchies that are formed from inheritance make a tree structure. Sometimes the root of the tree can be an abstract class. C# uses an *abstract* keyword to define an abstract class. Unlike C#, F# requires the *AbstractClass* attribute to be used to define an abstract class when no default implementations are provided. See the code in Listing 2-32.

LISTING 2-32 Defining an abstract class

```
[<AbstractClass>]
type MyAbstractClass() =
    member this.F() = 1

    // define an abstract member function
    abstract member FunctionNotImplemented : unit -> int
```

Tip If you cannot remember how to write the function definition for an abstract member method, you can always use FSI. For example, if you want to define a function with an *int* parameter as input and an *int* as output, you can type **let f (i:int) = 1;;** in FSI and the `val f : int -> int` will display the function definition, which is `int->int`.

In C#, a method can be overridden if it is a virtual method. F# does not have a *virtual* keyword to define a virtual method. Instead, F# uses the *abstract* keyword and the *default* keyword to define a virtual method. In Listing 2-33, the *GetDistance* method is defined as a virtual method, and then a default implementation of that method is defined.

```fsharp
// define a Point2D class with a parameterized primary constructor
type Point2D(xValue:double, yValue:double) as this=
    // define field x
    let mutable x = xValue

    // define a static field named count
    static let mutable count = 0

    // perform a do binding to increase the count
    do
        count <- count + 1

    //additional constructor
    new() = Point2D(0.,0.)

    // print out message
    member this.Print() = printfn "In class Point2D"

    // define an X property
    member this.X with get() = x
                  and set(v) = x <- v

    // define a Y property using an auto-implemented property
    member val Y = yValue with get, set

    // define a virtual function to get the distance from the current point
    abstract GetDistance : point:Point2D -> double
    default this.GetDistance(point) =
        let xDif = this.X - point.X
        let yDif = this.Y - point.Y
        let distance = sqrt (xDif**2. + yDif**2.)
        distance

    // define a static method to return a Point2D from (x,y) tuple
    static member FromXY (x, y) =
        Point2D(x,y)

    override this.ToString() = sprintf "Point2D(%f, %f)" this.X this.Y
```

C# provides the *new* keyword to provide different implementations for a nonvirtual method. Overriding a nonvirtual method is not a good practice, although it is a necessary approach under certain circumstances. F# does not support the *new* keyword like C# does, but it still allows users to do it. If you override a nonvirtual method, there will be a warning. Listing 2-34 shows a sample.

LISTING 2-34 Overriding a nonvirtual method

C# code using the *new* keyword

```
public class MyClass : List<int>
{
    public new void Add(int n)
    {
        base.Add(n);
        // <additional operations>
    }
}
```

F# code overriding a nonvirtual method

```
type MyList () =
    inherit System.Collections.Generic.List<int>()      //inherit List

    //add element
    member this.Add(n) =  // yield a warning 864
        base.Add(n)
        // <additional operations>
```

Note You can use #nowarn "864" to disable the warning.

I'm going to change direction slightly and introduce attributes. They are used to define F# features such as an abstract class and sealed classes. An attribute in F# is used in a way that is very similar to C#. Listing 2-35 shows how to decorate the *Point2D* class with *DebuggerDisplayAttribute*.

LISTING 2-35 Adding the *DebuggerDisplay* attribute to a class

```
// define a Point2D class with a parameterized primary constructor
[<System.Diagnostics.DebuggerDisplay("({X}, {Y})")>]
type Point2D(xValue:double, yValue:double) as this=
    // define field x
    let mutable x = xValue

    // define a static field named count
    static let mutable count = 0

    // perform a do binding to increase the count
    do
        count <- count + 1

    //additional constructor
    new() = Point2D(0.,0.)

    // print out message
    member this.Print() = printfn "In class Point2D"
```

```
    // define an X property
    member this.X with get() = x
                  and set(v) = x <- v

    // define a Y property using an auto-implemented property
    member val Y = yValue with get, set
```

The *AbstractClass* attribute is used to define an abstract class, and the *Sealed* attribute is for defining a sealed class. See Listing 2-36.

LISTING 2-36 A *Sealed* class definition

```
[<Sealed>]
type MySealedClass() =
    member this.F() = 1
```

Creating an Instance

F# has the *new* keyword to create an object. The *new* keyword is optional when creating a new object unless the class implements the *IDisposable* interface. If the *new* keyword is not used, there will be a compile-time warning indicating the *new* keyword should be used and the class will implement the *IDisposable* interface. See Listing 2-37.

LISTING 2-37 Using the *new* keyword when creating an object that implements *IDisposable*

```
// create object with the new keyword for a class implementing the IDisposable interface
let myObj = new System.Data.SqlClient.SqlConnection()

// Warning: It is recommended that objects that support the
// IDisposable interface are created using 'new Type(args)'
// rather than 'Type(args)' to indicate that resources may
// be owned by the generated value
let myObj2 = System.Data.SqlClient.SqlConnection()
```

Note When the class implements the *IDisposable* interface, *use* can replace *let* in a nonmodule context. Keep in mind that *use* is treated like *let* in a module and *use* in C# is different from in F#.

As a C# developer, you might use the *new* keyword everywhere through force of habit. If that is the case, you should be aware of one small catch when using the *new* keyword. When using the *new* keyword with generic types, the *type* parameter is automatically set to *System.Object* in Listing 2-38 to narrow the scope of the code shown below. Also, the *type* parameter cannot be ignored if you use the *new* keyword, even if your *type* parameter is *System.Object*. See Listing 2-38.

LISTING 2-38 Using the *new* keyword with a generic type

```
let f ()=
    let myDictionary = System.Collections.Generic.List()
    printfn "my type is %A" (myDictionary.GetType())

// following code does not compile because it needs the type parameter
//     let myDictionary2 = new System.Collections.Generic.List()
//     printfn "my type is %A" (myDictionary.GetType())

    let myDictionary2 = new System.Collections.Generic.List<int>()
    printfn "my type is %A" (myDictionary2.GetType())

f()
```

Execution result

```
my type is System.Collections.Generic.List'1[System.Object]
my type is System.Collections.Generic.List'1[System.Int32]
```

> **Note** Creating a generic type without specifying the *type* parameter does not always work at the top level.

Using Type Casting

I've already introduced many data types, including both basic types and complex class types. Let me now leave the C# code conversion task and introduce type casting. In a real-world application, you might need to do casting, which could involve not only basic data types, from *int* to *float*, but also object casting up and down the class hierarchy.

Converting Numbers and Using *enum*

Let's start with a basic type of conversion: *number conversion*. The way F# converts a number is similar to the way that C# does it. See Listing 2-39.

LISTING 2-39 Converting a number

```
C# conversion
int i = 5;
double d = (double)i
```

```
F# conversion
let i:int = 5
let d:double = double(i)
```

Note C# supports *implicit conversion*, which means that in C# you can assign an integer to a *double* without having to explicitly do the casting. The ability to deduce type and implicitly convert type can make development easier at earlier stages, but it introduces more chances to generate runtime errors. F# statically resolves the type and minimizes the runtime error by allowing only explicit type conversion.

The F# *enum* conversion is shown in Listing 2-40.

LISTING 2-40 An *enum* conversion

```
type PixelColor =
    | R = 0
    | G = 1
    | B = 2

// convert number to enum
let colorR : PixelColor = enum 0
let colorB = enum<PixelColor> 2
```

Upcasting and Downcasting

Casting an object up the hierarchy is the act of casting a derived object to its base object. You can use the :> operator or the *upcast* keyword to convert a derived class instance to a base class instance. Listing 2-41 shows a sample of how to use :> and *upcast*.

LISTING 2-41 Upcasting conversion

```
// define a base class
type Base() = class end

// define a derived class
type Derived() = inherit Base()

let myDerived = Derived()

// upcasting
let cast = myDerived :> Base

// use upcast
let cast2 : Base = upcast myDerived
```

 Note Casting to a base class (by using *:>* or *upcast*) is always safe and can be verified at compile time.

Casting an object down the hierarchy happens when you need to cast from a base object to a derived object. The *:?>* operator or the *downcast* keyword is used to accomplish this. The *downcast* operator does some sanity checks; for example, the type casting down needs to have an inheritance relationship with current type, but most of the checking still has to be verified at runtime. If the cast fails, an *InvalidCastException* will be raised. Listing 2-42 casts the base class to a derived class.

LISTING 2-42 An example of downcasting

```
// define a base class
type Base() = class end

// define a derived class
type Derived() = inherit Base()

let myDerived = Derived()

// upcasting
let upCastResult = myDerived :> Base

// use upcast
let cast2 : Base = upcast myDerived

// downcasting
let downCastResult = upCastResult :?> Derived

//use downcast
let case3 : Derived = downcast cast
```

Note The *upcast* and *downcast* keywords are alternatives to the *:>* and *:?>* operators.

Boxing and Unboxing

Like C#, F# also supports the concept of boxing and unboxing. When the common language runtime (CLR) boxes a value type, it wraps the value inside of a *System.Object* and stores it on the managed heap. Unboxing is the opposite process; it extracts the value type from the object. Because F# does not support implicit type conversion, an extra step is needed. See Listing 2-43.

LISTING 2-43 Boxing and unboxing

```
let intValue = 4
let o = box(intValue)
// let r = o + 2    //does not compile because o is an obj type
let i : int = unbox(o)
let r = i + 2
```

Note F# uses *obj* as a type abbreviation for *System.Object*.

Defining an Interface

An interface is just a collection of properties and methods, and its implementation is finished in the class that implements the interface. The interface provides an is-a relationship to the type. Once the type implements the interface, it is basically broadcasting that it can perform the operations described in the interface definition. The typical interface declaration in F# is like the code in Listing 2-44. Listing 2-45 shows how to define an interface with a property and how the lightweight F# syntax allows the *interface...end* keywords to be optional.

LISTING 2-44 Defining an interface

```
type IInterface =
    // a method that takes int and returns int
    abstract member InterfaceMethod : int -> int


type IInterface2 = interface
    // a method that takes int and returns int
    abstract member InterfaceMethod : int -> int
end
```

LISTING 2-45 Defining an interface with properties

Interface definition with *interface...end*

```
type I2DLocation = interface
    abstract member X : float with get, set
    abstract member Y : float with get, set
end
```

Lightweight interface definition

```
type I2DLocation =
    abstract member X : float with get, set
    abstract member Y : float with get, set
```

 Note Unlike C#, an F# interface does not support a partial keyword. Therefore, an interface has to be in one file.

F# requires that interfaces be explicitly implemented; as a result, the code needs some extra work. See Listing 2-46. Adding an interface seems to not add much value to this code; however, the interface can make code easy to expand and testing frameworks such as Fakes in Visual Studio requires an interface.

LISTING 2-46 Implementing an interface

```
// 2D location interface
type I2DLocation =
    abstract member X : float with get, set
    abstract member Y : float with get, set


// define a Point2D class with a parameterized primary constructor
type Point2D(xValue:double, yValue:double) as this=
    // <other Point2D members such as property X and Y>
        // define field x
    let mutable x = xValue

    // define an X property
    member this.X with get() = x
                  and set(v) = x <- v

    // define a Y property using an auto-implemented property
    member val Y = yValue with get, set
```

```
// implement the I2DLocation interface
interface I2DLocation with
    member this.X with get() = this.X and set(v) = this.X <- v
    member this.Y with get() = this.Y and set(v) = this.Y <- v

override this.ToString() = sprintf "Point2D(%f, %f)" this.X this.Y
```

When looking at the code in Listing 2-46, some people will be scared because of a possible stack overflow exception. It seems that the code is calling the *get()* function of property *X* inside a *get()* function. After you run the code, there is no stack overflow. When stepping into the code, you will find that the execution is going into the property defined in the class rather than the property in the interface. The *this* identifier represents the *Point2D* type, which can be proved by positioning your pointer over the *this* identify—as you can see in Figure 2-1—so there won't be a stack overflow exception. If you really want to see a stack overflow, cast this to *I2DLocation* by using `this :> I2DLocation`.

The code in Listing 2-47 and Listing 2-48 shows how to access class methods and how to use a type casting operator to access interface methods.

LISTING 2-47 Accessing the class property without type conversion

```
// invoke the Point2D defined in Listing 2-46

let c = Point2D()
let x = c.X
```

LISTING 2-48 Accessing the property defined in the interface

```
let c = Point2D()

//cast c to I2DLocation type
let c2 = c :> I2DLocation

let x = c2.X
```

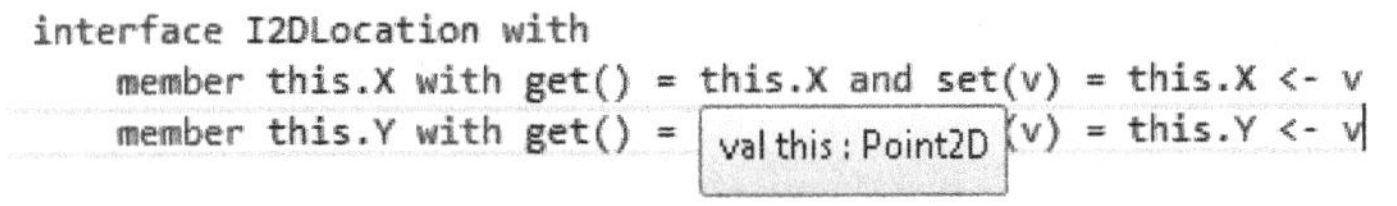

```
interface I2DLocation with
    member this.X with get() = this.X and set(v) = this.X <- v
    member this.Y with get() =  [ val this : Point2D ] (v) = this.Y <- v
```

FIGURE 2-1 Self-identifier in the interface implementation code

The explicit interface implementation does introduce some extra work for a developer; however, it provides a clear vision so that you can make sure that the right function can be invoked. For example, there are two interfaces that have defined the same property, and the implementation of one of those properties was accidently forgotten. The discovery of this kind of bug will most likely be delayed to runtime.

Interfaces in F# also support inheritance. The next task is to define a new interface, inherit from *I2DLocation*, and add an extra method called *GetDistance*. Listing 2-49 shows the sample code.

LISTING 2-49 Defining an interface and inheritance

```
// define a base interface
type I2DLocation =
    abstract member X : float with get, set
    abstract member Y : float with get, set

// define an interface that inherits from I2DLocation
type IPoint2D =
    inherit I2DLocation
    abstract member GetDistance : Point2D -> float
```

Compared with the code in Listing 2-49, the code in the Listing 2-50 reverses the order of *IPoint2D* and *I2DLocation*. This is not a problem for C#, but in F# you have to use the *and* keyword to resolve the type reference problem. The *IPoint2D* interface has a function that takes *Point2D* as a parameter, while the *Point2D* interface is defined next. Because F# resolves the type and symbols from top to bottom and from left to right, there will be a compile error unless the *and* keyword is applied.

LISTING 2-50 Implementing interfaces with an inheritance relationship

```
// define an IPoint2D interface
// need the and keyword to resolve the type-resolution problem
type IPoint2D =
    inherit I2DLocation

    // this function takes I2DLocation as a parameter, which is defined below
    abstract member GetDistance : I2DLocation -> float

// define a 2D location interface
and I2DLocation =     abstract member X : float with get, set
    abstract member Y : float with get, set



// define a Point2D class with a parameterized primary constructor
type Point2D(xValue:double, yValue:double) as this=
    // define field x
    let mutable x = xValue
```

```
// define a static field named count
static let mutable count = 0

// perform a do binding to increase the count
do
    count <- count + 1


//additional constructor
new() = Point2D(0.,0.)


// define an X property
member this.X with get() = x
            and set(v) = x <- v

// define a Y property using an auto-implemented property
member val Y = yValue with get, set

// define a function to get the distance from the current point
abstract GetDistance : point: I2DLocation -> double
default this.GetDistance(point) =
    let xDif = this.X - point.X
    let yDif = this.Y - point.Y
    let distance = sqrt (xDif**2. + yDif**2.)
    distance

// define a static method to return a Point2D from (x,y) tuple
static member FromXY (x, y) =
    Point2D(x,y)

interface I2DLocation with
    member this.X with get() = this.X and set(v) = this.X <- v
    member this.Y with get() = this.Y and set(v) = this.Y <- v
interface IPoint2D with
    member this.GetDistance(p) = this.GetDistance(p)

override this.ToString() = sprintf "Point2D(%f, %f)" this.X this.Y
```

Using the *IDisposable* Interface

The *IDisposable* interface is used mainly for releasing unmanaged resources. The garbage collector can automatically reclaim the memory for managed objects. However, garbage collection lacks key knowledge about the unmanaged resources, such as opened files or streams. By invoking the *Dispose* method, you have control over when to release the unmanaged resources.

In C#, you have the *using* keyword to implicitly invoke the *dispose* method when exiting the code scope. F# also provides the same functionality with the *use* keyword and *using* function. Listing 2-51 shows the *Database* class implementing the *IDisposable* interface, as well as how to instantiate the class by applying the *use* keyword and the *using* function. There is only a slight difference between the functionality of *use* and *using*: the determination of when the *Dispose* method is going to be invoked. The *use* keyword invokes the *Dispose* function at the end of the containing code block, and the *using* function calls the *Dispose* method at the end of the lambda. In the sample code, the *Dispose* method is invoked when *testIDisposable* exits, and the *using* function invokes the *Dispose* method when *testUsing* exits. In general, you should choose *use* over *using*.

LISTING 2-51 Using the *IDisposable* interface

Define a class with the *IDisposable* interface

```
type Database(conString) =
    let con = new SqlConnection(conString)
    member this.ConnectionString = conString
    member this.Connect() =
        con.Open()
    member this.Close() = con.Close()
    interface IDisposable with
        member this.Dispose() = this.Close()
```

Instantiate an object with the *use* keyword

```
let testIDisposable() =
    use db = new Database("my connection String")
    db.Connect()
```

The *using* keyword used for the *IDisposable* interface

```
let testUsing(db:Database) = db.Connect()
using (new Database("my connection string")) testUsing
```

> **Note** The *use* keyword cannot be put into a module directly because it will be treated as a let binding. The *using* function can be used in a module.

Using F# Generic Types and Constraints

Although F# can provide very good generalized code, it still needs generic types and constraints. Table 2-2 lists C# and F# constraints. From the table, you can see that F# provides more choices.

TABLE 2-2 C# and F# constraints

C# Constraint	F# Constraint	Description
where T: struct	*when 'T : struct*	The type must be a *value* type.
where T : class	*when 'T : not struct*	The provided type must be a *reference* type.
where T : new()	*when 'T : (new : unit -> 'a)*	C# constraints requires the *type* argument to have a public parameterless constructor and the *new()* constraint must be specified last if there is another constraint. F# requires that the provided type to have a default constructor.
where T : <base type name>	*when 'T :> type*	The *type* argument must be derived from the specified base type. The base type can be an interface.
where T : U	**Not supported**	The *type* argument supplied for *T* must be derived from the argument supplied for *U*.
Not supported	*when 'T : null*	The type needs to support the NULL value.
Not supported	*when 'T or 'U : (member-signature)*	At least one of the *type* arguments should have a member that has the specified signature.
Not supported	*when 'T : enum<underlying-type>*	The provided type must be an *enum* type that has the specified underlying type.
Not supported	*when 'T : delegate<tuple-parameter-type,return-type>*	The provided type must be a *delegate* type that has the specified arguments and return value.
Not supported	*when 'T : comparison*	The provided type must support *comparison*.
Not supported	*when 'T: equality*	The provided type must support *equality*.
Not supported	*when 'T : unmanaged*	The provided type must be an unmanaged type. Unmanaged types are either certain primitive types (such as *sbyte, byte, char, nativeint, unativeint, float32, float, int16, uint16, int32, uint32, int64, uint64,* or *decimal*), enumeration types, *nativeptr<_>,* or a nongeneric structure whose fields are all unmanaged types.

> **Note** Unlike in C#, new : unit -> a does not need to be the last constraint.

F# handles the NULL value in a different manner, which will be discussed later. Therefore, the F# list, F# tuple, function, F# class, *union* type, and *record* type cannot be NULL. I will introduce the *union* and *record* types later. Listing 2-52 is the sample code that shows how NULL constraints are used. The general rule is if the type is from the Microsoft .NET Framework, the type always supports NULL. F# types do not support NULL unless otherwise specified.

LISTING 2-52 NULL constraints on some F# types

```
// generic type with NULL constraint
type MyClass<'T when 'T : null> () =
    let a:'T = Unchecked.defaultof<'T>

// string array that can have NULL as a proper value
let b = MyClass<string []>()

// string sequence that can have NULL as a proper value
let b3 = MyClass<string seq>()

// string list that CANNOT have NULL as a proper value
// let b2 = MyClass<string list>()

type MyRecord = { X : int; Y : string }
// record that CANNOT have NULL as a proper value
// let b4 = MyClass<MyRecord>()

// use .NET tuple as a constraint that can take NULL
let b5 = MyClass< System.Tuple<string,string> >()

// string*string tuple CANNOT have NULL
// let b6 = MyClass< string*string > ()

// function int->int CANNOT have NULL
// let b7 = MyClass< int->int > ()

type MyClass2() = class

    end

// class MyClass2 cannot be NULL
//let b8 = MyClass< MyClass2 >()
```

Listing 2-53 shows how to change the Point2D code to use generic constraints. Listing 2-54 shows how to define two type parameters in the generic type definition and how to use the *and* keyword to chain multiple constraints.

LISTING 2-53 Generic constraints

```
// define a 2D location interface
type I2DLocation =
    abstract member X : float with get, set
    abstract member Y : float with get, set

// define a IPoint2D interface
and IPoint2D =
    inherit I2DLocation
    abstract member GetDistance<'T when 'T :> I2DLocation> : I2DLocation -> float
```

```
// define a Point2D class with a parameterized primary constructor
type Point2D(xValue:double, yValue:double) =
    // define field x
    let mutable x = xValue

    // define a static field named count
    static let mutable count = 0

    // perform a do binding to increase the count
    do
        count <- count + 1

    //additional constructor
    new() = Point2D(0.,0.)

    // define an X property
    member this.X with get() = x
                  and set(v) = x <- v

    // define a Y property using an auto-implemented property
    member val Y = yValue with get, set

    // define a function to get the distance from the current point
    abstract GetDistance<'T when 'T :> I2DLocation > : point:'T -> double
    default this.GetDistance<'T when 'T :> I2DLocation >(point:'T) =
        let xDif = this.X - point.X
        let yDif = this.Y - point.Y
        let distance = sqrt (xDif**2. + yDif**2.)
        distance

    // define a static method to return a Point2D from (x,y) tuple
    static member FromXY (x, y) =
        Point2D(x,y)

    interface I2DLocation with
        member this.X with get() = this.X and set(v) = this.X <- v
        member this.Y with get() = this.Y and set(v) = this.Y <- v
    interface IPoint2D with
        member this.GetDistance<'T when 'T :> I2DLocation > (p) = this.GetDistance(p)

    override this.ToString() = sprintf "Point2D(%f, %f)" this.X this.Y
```

Note If you position your pointer over the definition of *GetDistance*, it shows override Point2D.GetDistance : point #IPoint2D -> float. The # indicates that the function accepts the object derived from *IPoint2D*. This is called a *flexible type*. You can use the "#*<type name>*" in a class member definition to save yourself some typing.

LISTING 2-54 Two type parameters with constraints

```
// two type parameters with constraints
type MyGenericType2<'T when 'T : (new : unit -> 'T) and 'T :> Point2D > () = class
    end

// two type parameters with constraints
type MyGenericType3<'T, 'U when 'T :> Point2D and 'U :> Point2D> () = class
    end
```

Defining Structure

You might be wondering if a class is really needed when designing such a simple data structure. It is a very good question. For simple data structures like *Point*, a struct is actually a better choice. A struct is a value type, which means that it can be put on the stack. Struct instances, if allocated on the stack, consume less memory and do not need garbage collection. So let's go ahead and define a *Point2D* struct, as shown in Listing 2-55.

LISTING 2-55 Defining a struct for *Point2D*

```
Struct definition with struct...end

type Point2D_Struct(xValue:double, yValue:double) = struct
    member this.X = xValue
    member this.Y = yValue
end


Struct definition with a struct attribute

[<Struct>]
type Point2D_Struct(xValue:double, yValue:double) =
    member this.X = xValue
    member this.Y = yValue
```

There are some restrictions for struct types, though. The struct is, by default, sealed with a *[<Sealed>]* attribute. It is impossible to override the default constructor, which always exists. All fields in the struct are set to their default values. In Listing 2-56, the parameterless constructor is always invoked even if it is not explicitly declared. Another restriction is that a struct cannot use a let binding.

LISTING 2-56 Creating a struct instance in FSI

```
> let a = Point2D_Struct()
a.X;;

val a : Point2D_Struct = FSI_0003+Point2D_Struct
val it : double = 0.0
```

The *val* binding can be used to define a mutable field, as shown in Listing 2-57.

LISTING 2-57 Defining mutable fields in a struct

```
[<Struct>]
type Point2D_Struct =
    val mutable X : double
    val mutable Y : double
```

The struct can have a *StructLayout* attribute, which lets you control the physical layout of the struct data fields. However, when you apply the attribute, a "warning 9" message is generated:

> *Uses of this construct may result in the generation of unverifiable .NET IL code. This warning can be disabled using '--nowarn:9' or '#nowarn "9"'.*

This message warns you of the side effect shown in Listing 2-58. Even if the struct is initialized with *1* and *2*, fields *X* and *Y* are both set to *2*. This side effect leads to subtle bugs, and this is why F# chooses to generate a warning.

LISTING 2-58 Struct with *StructLayoutAttribute*

```
[< StructLayout(LayoutKind.Explicit) >]
type D =
    [< FieldOffset 0 >] val mutable X : int
    [< FieldOffset 0 >] val mutable Y : int
    new(a,b) = { X = a; Y = b }

let d = D(1, 2)  // two fields X and Y are both 2
```

Using Extension Methods

C# introduces a very useful feature called *extension methods*, which allow for the easy extension of a class without requiring modification of the existing class. When using the type, these extension methods appear to be additional members on the existing type. F# actually provides the same functionality. Listing 2-59 shows how F# can extend the built-in system integer type.

LISTING 2-59 Extension method to the integer type

```
// extend built-in system type
type System.Int32 with
    member this.ToBinaryString() = sprintf "0x%X" this
```

> **Note** The *type* extension needs to reside in a module. It is invalid to define a type extension in a namespace.

F# can extend built-in system types and customized types. Listing 2-60 shows how to extend a user-defined class. The basic syntax is similar to the previous sample. F# extension methods have the same restrictions as C# extension methods. They cannot define a field. Also, they cannot access any fields defined in the *main* class. In the sample code, it is not possible to access *fileName* or *myField*.

LISTING 2-60 Extending your own types

```
type File(fileName:string) =
    let myField = 0
    member this.MyFunction() = myField
    member this.FileName with get() = fileName

// extend a user-defined class
type File with
    // let myField2 = 0      //cannot define new field
    member this.GetFileName() = this.FileName
```

The preceding extension method can be recognized only within the F# world. If you want to expose the extension methods to a C# project, you need to use the *System.Runtime.CompilerServices.Extension* attribute, as shown in Listing 2-61. You have to put the attribute on both the method name and module.

LISTING 2-61 Extension method for a C# project

```
[<System.Runtime.CompilerServices.Extension>]
module MyExtensionMethods =

    // extension methods can be invoked from a C# project
    [<System.Runtime.CompilerServices.Extension>]
    let ToBinaryString i = sprintf "0x%X" i

    // F# way to extend a type
    type System.Int32 with
        member this.ToBinaryString() = ToBinaryString this
```

Note If the code will be invoked by a C# project, always consider putting the code inside a namespace.

Using Operator Overloading

Operator overloading is used to add new meaning to an operator. The operator that needs to be overloaded has to be in parentheses. If the operator is a unary operator, you have to add a tilde (~) as a prefix. Listing 2-62 shows how to add an operator overload in the *Point2D* class.

LISTING 2-62 Operator overloading

```
Defining an operator in a class
// define a 2D location interface
type I2DLocation =
    abstract member X : float with get, set
    abstract member Y : float with get, set

// define a IPoint2D interface
type IPoint2D =
    inherit I2DLocation
    abstract member GetDistance<'T when 'T :> IPoint2D> : IPoint2D -> float

// define a Point2D class with a parameterized primary constructor
and Point2D(xValue:double, yValue:double) =
    // define field x
    let mutable x = xValue

    // define a static field named count
    static let mutable count = 0

    // perform a do binding to increase the count
    do
        count <- count + 1
```

```
//additional constructor
new() = Point2D(0.,0.)

// define an X property
member this.X with get() = x
             and set(v) = x <- v

// define a Y property using an auto-implemented property
member val Y = yValue with get, set

// define a function to get the distance from the current point
abstract GetDistance<'T when 'T :> IPoint2D > : point:'T -> double
default this.GetDistance<'T when 'T :> IPoint2D>(point:'T) =
    let xDif = this.X - point.X
    let yDif = this.Y - point.Y
    let distance = sqrt (xDif**2. + yDif**2.)
    distance

// define a static method to return a Point2D from (x,y) tuple
static member FromXY (x, y) =
    Point2D(x,y)

// overload the + operator
static member (+) (point:Point2D, offset:double) =
    Point2D(point.X + offset, point.Y + offset)

// unary - operator
static member (~-) (point:Point2D) =
    Point2D(-point.X, -point.Y)

interface I2DLocation with
    member this.X with get() = this.X and set(v) = this.X <- v
    member this.Y with get() = this.Y and set(v) = this.Y <- v
interface IPoint2D with
    member this.GetDistance<'T when 'T :> IPoint2D > (p) = this.GetDistance(p)

override this.ToString() = sprintf "Point2D(%f, %f)" this.X this.Y
```

Using the operators defined

```
let c =Point2D(2., 2.)
let d = -c
let originalPoint = d + 2.    // the result is original point (0,0)
```

When the F# compiler compiles an operator, it generates a method that has a compiler-generated name. If you use reflection, or Microsoft IntelliSense, the generated method name is what you will see. Table 2-3 shows the standard operators and corresponding names.

TABLE 2-3 Standard operators and generated names

Operator	Generated Name
[]	op_Nil
::	op_Cons
+	op_Addition
−	op_Subtraction
*	op_Multiply
/	op_Division
@	op_Append
^	op_Concatenate
%	op_Modulus
&&&	op_BitwiseAnd
|||	op_BitwiseOr
^^^	op_ExclusiveOr
<<<	op_LeftShift
~~	op_LogicalNot
>>>	op_RightShift
~+	op_UnaryPlus
~−	op_UnaryNegation
=	op_Equality
<=	op_LessThanOrEqual
>=	op_GreaterThanOrEqual
<	op_LessThan
>	op_GreaterThan
?	op_Dynamic
?<−	op_DynamicAssignment
|>	op_PipeRight
<|	op_PipeLeft
!	op_Dereference
>>	op_ComposeRight
<<	op_ComposeLeft
<@ @>	op_Quotation
<@@ @@>	op_QuotationUntyped
+=	op_AdditionAssignment
−=	op_SubtractionAssignment

Operator	Generated Name
*=	op_MultiplyAssignment
/=	op_DivisionAssignment
..	op_Range
.. ..	op_RangeStep

Other operators not listed are the combination of operator names. For example, +– will be *op_PlusMinus*. The operator characters and corresponding names are listed in Table 2-4.

TABLE 2-4 Operator characters and names

Operator Character	Name
>	Greater
<	Less
+	Plus
–	Minus
*	Multiply
/	Divide
=	Equals
~	Twiddle
%	Percent
.	Dot
&	Amp
|	Bar
@	At
^	Hat
!	Bang
?	Qmark
(	LParen
,	Comma
)	RParen
[	LBrack
]	RBrack

F# provides a broad range of operators, not all of which are supported in C#. Only the following operators are recognized in F#:

- **Binary operators**   +, –, *, /, &, %, |, >>, <<, +=, –=, /=, %=

- **Unary operators**   ~+, ~–, ~!, ~++, ~––

You can also define operators at the global level. Listing 2-63 defines an operator –?.

LISTING 2-63 Global-level operator

```
let inline (-?) (x: int) (y: int) = x - 3*y
printf "%d" (10 -? 1)     // result is 7

let (!++) (seq:int seq) = seq |> Seq.sum
let result = !++ [1..4]
```

Note Global operators can decrease the readability of the code. If that is the case, you can download the math symbol add-on for F# from *http://visualstudiogallery.msdn.microsoft. com/fe627c2a-5d09-4252-bcc7-300821ae707c*. After setting the mapping file to show *!++* as ∑, the code in the Visual Studio editor windows will be much cleaner. A sample screen shot is shown here:

```
let ( ∑ ) (seq:int seq) = seq |> Seq.sum
let result =  ∑ [1..4]
```

Using Delegates and Events

According to the definition in MSDN (*http://msdn.microsoft.com/en-us/library/ms173171(v=vs.80). aspx*), a *delegate* is a type-safe way to reference a method. A delegate is similar to a C++ function pointer, but it is type safe. A C++ function pointer can point to any function, but a delegate can point only to the function with the same function signature. The introduction of a delegate-enabled function can be treated like a variable and passed as a parameter. One of the major applications for a delegate is to define an event. Listing 2-64 shows how to define a delegate in F#.

LISTING 2-64 Defining and invoking a delegate type

```
let f a b = a + b

// define a delegate type
type MyDelegateType = delegate of int * int -> int
let delegateValue = new MyDelegateType(f)

// invoking the function and delegate returns the same result
let fResult = f 1 2
let fromDelegate = delegateValue.Invoke(1,2)
```

If a class member takes a delegate as a parameter, you can pass in a lambda expression and F# will create a delegate behind the scenes. See Listing 2-65.

LISTING 2-65 Passing a lambda to a class member that takes a delegate type

```
// define a delegate type
type IntDelegate = delegate of int -> unit

//define a class that takes a delegate parameter
type MyType =
    static member Apply (i:int, d:IntDelegate) =
        d.Invoke(i)

// pass lambda to the function that takes a delegate type
MyType.Apply (0, (fun x -> printfn "%d" x))
```

> **Note** The implicit conversion works only on a class member. It will not work on a let binding.

A delegate is similar to an F# function. A delegate provides an extra interesting feature called *delegate combination*. Combining multiple delegates allows a user to invoke combined functions with a single *Invoke* call. In Listing 2-66, a *Combine* function and *Remove* function can be used to edit the coalesced function set.

LISTING 2-66 Delegate combination

```
//define a delegate type
type PrintDelegate = delegate of string -> unit

// create delegates
let printOne = PrintDelegate(fun s -> printfn "One %s" s)
let printTwo = PrintDelegate(fun s -> printfn "Two %s" s)

// combine delegates
let printBoth = PrintDelegate.Combine(printOne, printTwo)

// invoke the combined delegates
printBoth.DynamicInvoke("aaa")
```

> **Note** A delegate created in F# does not have *BeginInvoke* and *EndInvoke*; therefore, you cannot invoke the delegate asynchronously.

An *event* is just a delegate property on a class. Invoking an event is nothing more than invoking a combined delegate. An event is defined in the *Microsoft.FSharp.Control* namespace in *FSharp.Core.dll*.

If you take a closer look at the namespace, there are two *Event* types defined. Both of them provide identical class members. You can use either of them to define your event:

- **Event<'Delegate,'Args>** Event implementations for a delegate type following the standard .NET Framework convention of a first-sender argument

- **Event<'T>** Event implementations for the *IEvent<_>* type

> **Note** If you do not remove the event from the object, the reference to the object will prevent garbage collection from reclaiming the memory.

If you look at Listing 2-67, the process to define an event in F# is similar to the one in C#. First define a delegate, and then define the event using the delegate. In the example, *myEvent* is created as an *Event<'D, 'T>* type. The *Event* type supports two methods, *Publish* and *Trigger*. *Publish* is used to publish an event so that the event can be subscribed to, and *Trigger* is used to raise the event. The *CLIEvent* attribute is used to make the event type compile as a CLI event, so that you can use += and −= to subscribe to this event from C# code.

LISTING 2-67 *Event<'D, 'T> sample*

Defining a class in F#

```
// define a delegate
type Delegate = delegate of obj * System.EventArgs -> unit

// define a class with event
type MyClassWithEvent() =
    let myEvent = new Event<Delegate, System.EventArgs>()
    [<CLIEvent>]
    member this.Event = myEvent.Publish
    member this.RaiseEvent (args) = myEvent.Trigger(this, args)

let classWithEvent2 = new MyClassWithEvent()
classWithEvent2.Event.Add(fun (e) -> printfn "message is %A" e)
classWithEvent2.RaiseEvent(System.EventArgs())
```

C# code using F#

```
static void Main(string[] args)
{
    var myEventClass2 = new Chapter2.MyClassWithEvent();
    myEventClass2.Event += MyHandler2;
    myEventClass2.RaiseEvent(new EventArgs());
}

private static void MyHandler2(object sender, EventArgs e)
{
    // sender is myEventClass2
}
```

Listing 2-68 provides code that demonstrates how to use *Event<'T>*, which is a simpler format. The underscore in the *Event<'T>* definition is a placeholder that is used to inform the F# compiler to figure out the type information. If you compare these two *Event* implementations, they are different in the following way:

- The *Event<'T>* version is simpler.

- The *Event<'D, 'T>* version is closer to C#'s event-definition process.

- *Event<'T>* requires adding *FSharp.Core.dll* as a reference. Otherwise, the compiler complains about not finding the type `'Microsoft.FSharp.Control.FSharpHandler'1<T0>'`. *Event<'D, 'T>* does not need to reference to *FSharp.Core.dll*.

- The *sender* value in *MyHandler2* holds the *sender* instance, but *MyHandler* hides the sender information in the first element of the tuple.

LISTING 2-68 *Event<'T>* sample

Defining a class in F#

```
// define a class with event
type MyClassWithCLIEvent() =
    let myEvent = new Event<_>()
    [<CLIEvent>]
    member this.MyEvent = myEvent.Publish
    member this.RaiseEvent(arg) = myEvent.Trigger(this, arg)

let classWithEvent = MyClassWithCLIEvent()

// subscribe the event by using Add
classWithEvent.MyEvent.Add(fun (sender, arg) -> printfn "message is %A" arg)

// raise event
classWithEvent.RaiseEvent("hello world")
```

Using an F# event from C#

```
class Program
{
    static void Main(string[] args)
    {
        var myEventClass = new Chapter2.MyClassWithCLIEvent();
        myEventClass.MyEvent += MyHandler;
        myEventClass.RaiseEvent("Hello word");
    }

    private static void MyHandler(object sender, Tuple<MyClassWithCLIEvent,object> args)
    {
        // sender is NULL
        // args.Item1 is the sender
        // args.Item2 is the raised message
    }
}
```

Note In C# code, the sender is NULL, and the sender is the first element of tuple. If you have an event on an interface and you want to interoperate with C#, you need to define the CLIEvent attribute on the interface and all implementations.

Interoperating with a C# Project

C# is the *de facto* standard OOP language on the .NET platform, and thousands of applications have been developed using C#. It is inevitable to have F# code interacting with C#. In this section, I'll cover how to add a reference and add *AssemblyInfo*.

Adding a Reference

Adding a reference to C# from F# (or vice versa) can be accomplished by using the Add Reference dialog box. See Figure 2-2.

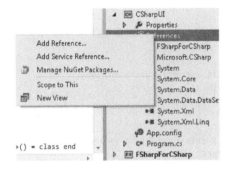

FIGURE 2-2 The Add Reference dialog box

Note There are two ways to add a reference to a project in a solution. One is to add a reference to the generated binary file located in \bin\Debug folder. The other way is to add a reference to the project, and Visual Studio can resolve the binary file path. F# supports both approaches, but the project reference cannot be viewed by using Object Browser. To address this limitation, you can directly add a reference to the binary file. If you decide to reference to the DLL directly, please remember to change it back when you build the release binary.

Using AssemblyInfo

AssemblyInfo consists of all of the build options for the project, including the version, company name, GUID, compilers options, and other such information. For a commercial application, this information is very important. Most of the file content consists of assembly-level attributes. The assembly-level attributes must be placed above a do binding. See Listing 2-69. You can use \169 to represent the ©. Additionally, because Visual Studio supports Unicode, you can actually put © in the string.

LISTING 2-69 AssemblyInfo file

```
open System.Reflection
open System.Runtime.CompilerServices
open System.Runtime.InteropServices

// General information about an assembly is controlled through the following
// set of attributes. Change these attribute values to modify the information
// associated with an assembly.
[<assembly: AssemblyTitle("myApp from © XYZ Company")>]
[<assembly: AssemblyDescription("myApp")>]
[<assembly: AssemblyConfiguration("")>]
[<assembly: AssemblyCompany("XYZ Company")>]
[<assembly: AssemblyProduct("myApp")>]
[<assembly: AssemblyCopyright("© XYZ Company 2012. All rights reserved.")>]
[<assembly: AssemblyCulture("")>]


// Setting ComVisible to false makes the types in this assembly not visible
// to COM components.  If you need to access a type in this assembly from
// COM, set the ComVisible attribute to true on that type.
[<assembly: ComVisible(false)>]


// The following GUID is for the ID of the typelib if this project is exposed to COM
[<assembly: Guid("c95f0dd1-9182-4d48-8bc2-b6cc2bca17bc5")>]


// Version information for an assembly consists of the following four values:
//
//      Major Version
//      Minor Version
//      Build Number
//      Revision
//
// You can specify all the values or you can default the Build and Revision Numbers
// by using the '*' as shown below:
[<assembly: AssemblyVersion("1.0.0325.0003")>]
[<assembly: AssemblyFileVersion("1.0.0325.0003")>]
do ()
```

Real-World Samples

I'll finish this chapter with two samples. The first one is a Windows Presentation Foundation (WPF) converter that can pipe the converter function. The other one implements the *INotifyCollection-Changed* interface, which can substitute the *ObservableCollection*.

Using the WPF Converter

The WPF converter is a nice feature you can use to convert data before presenting it to the UI. When you have several of these converters, you can start thinking about how to combine them to reduce redundancy. There are some open source frameworks trying to chain the converters. The converter itself is a function. So it is perfect place to use function composition and pipelining to solve the problem. See Listing 2-70. The string-to-visibility conversion is performed by using function composition and a pipeline. Compared to other object-oriented implementations, this approach is much simpler.

LISTING 2-70 WPF converter

```
namespace FSharp.Converters

open System
open System.Windows
open System.Windows.Data
open Microsoft.FSharp.Reflection

[<AutoOpen>]
module FunctionLibrary =
    let nullFunction = fun value _ _ _ -> value

    let stringToInt (a:Object) = Convert.ToInt32(a)
    let intToBool = fun i -> i = 0
    let boolToVisibility = fun b ->
        if b then Visibility.Visible
        else Visibility.Collapsed

    let convert<'T> f (obj:System.Object) (t:Type) (para:System.Object)
        (culture:Globalization.CultureInfo)  = (obj :?> 'T) |> f |> box

/// abstract class for converter
[<AbstractClass>]
type ConverterBase(convertFunction, convertBackFunction) =
    /// constructor take nullFunction as inputs
    new() = ConverterBase(nullFunction, nullFunction)

    // implement the IValueConverter
    interface IValueConverter with
        /// convert a value to new value
        override this.Convert(value, targetType, parameter, culture) =
            this.Convert value targetType parameter culture
```

```
            /// convert a value back
            override this.ConvertBack(value, targetType, parameter, culture) =
                this.ConvertBack value targetType parameter culture

        abstract member Convert : (obj -> Type -> obj -> Globalization.CultureInfo->obj)
        default this.Convert = convertFunction

        abstract member ConvertBack : (obj -> Type -> obj -> Globalization.CultureInfo->obj)
        default this.ConvertBack = convertBackFunction

    /// Sample concrete implementation
    type StringToVisiblityConverter() =
        inherit ConverterBase(stringToInt >> intToBool >> boolToVisibility |> convert,
    nullFunction)

    /// debugger converter used to debug the data binding problem(s)
    type DebuggerConverter() =
        inherit ConverterBase(nullFunction, nullFunction)
```

Using *ObservableCollection* with List Features

If you have been frustrated because *ObservableCollection* lacks some basic *List* functionality and does
not work well with LINQ, then *ObservableList* is a solution you might be interested in. In Listing 2-71,
ObservableList<'T> is derived from a *List<'T>* type. Additionally, it provides a *CollectionChanged*
event. The *CollectionChanged* event is fired when an element in the collection changes. It behaves like
ObservableCollection<T> but provides LINQ and other *List<>* specific features.

The code seems lengthy, but it's actually simple. *ObservableCollection<T>* notifies the WPF
framework of different changes by firing events with different parameters:

- *NotifyCollectionChangedAction.Add* generates a notification that one or more items were
  added to the collection.

- *NotifyCollectionChangedAction.Remove* generates a notification that one or more items were
  removed from the collection.

- *NotifyCollectionChangedAction.Replace* generates a notification that one or more items were
  replaced in the collection.

- *NotifyCollectionChangedAction.Move* generates a notification that one or more items were
  moved in the collection.

- *NotifyCollectionChangedAction.Reset* generates a notification that the collection experienced
  dramatic changes.

LISTING 2-71 *INotifyCollectionChanged* implementation

```
#nowarn "864"

namespace Chapter2RealWorldSample

open System.Collections.Generic
open System.Collections.Specialized

// define ObservableList<'T> class
type ObservableList<'T> () =
    inherit System.Collections.Generic.List<'T>()        //inherit List

    let collectionChanged = Event< _ , _ > ( )

    let mutable isTriggerEvent = false    //mutable variable

    // additional constructor to initialize the instance with given items
    new(items) = ObservableList<'T>() then base.AddRange(items)

    // implement the INotifyCollectionChanged interface
    interface INotifyCollectionChanged with
        [< CLIEvent >]
        member this.CollectionChanged = collectionChanged.Publish

    // property to control if any of the events should be triggered
    member this.IsTriggerEvent
        with get() = isTriggerEvent
        and set(v) = isTriggerEvent <- v

    //add element
    member this.Add(n:'T) =
        base.Add(n)
        this.TriggerAdd(n, base.Count)

    // remove element
    member this.Remove(n:'T) =
        let index = this.IndexOf(n)
        if index <> -1 then
            let r = base.Remove(n)
            this.TriggerRemove(n, index)
            r
        else
            false

    member this.Remove(n:'T seq) =
        n |> Seq.iter (this.Remove >> ignore)
    member this.RemoveAt(index) =
        if this.Count > 0 then
            if index >=0 && index < this.Count then
                let item = base.[index]
                base.RemoveAt(index)
```

```
            this.TriggerRemove(item, index)
    member this.RemoveRange(index, count) =
        [0..count-1] |> Seq.iter (fun i -> this.RemoveAt(index))

    // sort elements
    member this.Sort()=
        base.Sort()
        this.TriggerReset()
    member this.Sort(comparer:IComparer<'T>) =
        base.Sort(comparer)
        this.TriggerReset()
    member this.Sort(index, count, comparer) =
        base.Sort(index, count, comparer)
        this.TriggerReset()

    // reverse elements in the list
    member this.Reverse() =
        base.Reverse()
        this.TriggerReset()
    member this.Reverse(index, count) =
        base.Reverse(index, count)
        this.TriggerReset()

    // add items
    member this.AddRange(items) =
        items |> Seq.iter this.Add

    // clear current list
    member this.Clear() =
        base.Clear()
        this.TriggerReset()

    // insert element at the index location
    member this.Insert(index, item) =
        base.Insert(index, item)
        this.TriggerAdd(item, index)

    // insert multiple elements at the index location
    member this.InsertRange(index, items) =
        items |> Seq.iteri (fun i item -> this.Insert(index+i, item))

    // define an indexer
    member this.Item
        with get(i) = base.[i]
        and set i v =
            let old = base.[i]
            base.[i] <- v
            this.TriggerReplace(v, old, i)

    // trigger add, remove, replace, and reset events
    member private this.TriggerAdd(item, index) =
        if this.IsTriggerEvent then
            collectionChanged.Trigger(this,
                NotifyCollectionChangedEventArgs(NotifyCollectionChangedAction.Add, item,
index))
```

```
    member private this.TriggerRemove(item, index) =
        if this.IsTriggerEvent then
            collectionChanged.Trigger(this,
                NotifyCollectionChangedEventArgs(NotifyCollectionChangedAction.Remove,
item, index))
    member private this.TriggerReplace(item, oldItem, index) =
        if this.IsTriggerEvent then
            collectionChanged.Trigger(this,    NotifyCollectionChangedEventArgs(NotifyColl
ectionChangedAction.Replace, item, oldItem, index))
    member public this.TriggerReset() =
        if this.IsTriggerEvent then
            collectionChanged.Trigger(this,
                NotifyCollectionChangedEventArgs(NotifyCollectionChangedAction.Reset,
null, -1))

    // static function to convert any IEnumerable variable
    static member FromList(items) = ObservableList(items)
```

 Note If the preceding code is pasted into an empty Program.fs file. You might get the warning, "Main module of program is empty: nothing will happen when it is run."

From these two samples, F# shows that it can implement the same functionality as C#. You also saw that F# is especially good at function processing. Do not stop here. You've seen only the tip of the iceberg! F# has a compelling story awaiting you...

CHAPTER 3

F# and Design Patterns

I constantly hear people say that F# is a cool cutting-edge technology, but they do not know how to use it. In previous chapters, I showed how C# developers can pretty much map their existing imperative, LINQ, and data-structure knowledge to F#. However, this is not enough know-how to design or implement a component or a system. In this chapter, I use well-known design patterns to introduce performing system design by using F#. The samples in this chapter use unique F# language features to implement well-known design patterns. These samples will help you start to think of F# as something other than a niche language.

I do not see a huge difference between computer language and human language. Both languages are used to convey human thinking, only the audiences are different. One is the computer, and the other is a human. If you want to master a language and use it to write a beautiful article, having knowledge of only the basic words of that language would definitely not be enough. Likewise, if people really want to use F# fluently in their daily programming work, they need to know more than how to write a float type and a FOR loop.

In this chapter, a number of design patterns are implemented in F#. These implementations should help you gain more insight about how our team designed the language and, consequently, how to use these features to solve system-design problems. Ultimately, my goal is to help you start to really think in F# terms.

There are some design patterns that are easily implemented with more advanced F# language features, such as F# object expressions. I am not going to discuss every aspect of these features. More detailed information about these special language features will be presented in Chapter 5, "Write Your Own Type Provider." If any aspects of this chapter are not clear, I encourage you to refer to Chapter 5, where F# unique features are introduced in detail.

Using Object-Oriented Programming and Design Patterns

Like many well-studied concepts, *design pattern* has many definitions. In this book, I borrow the definition from the Wikipedia page on the topic (*http://en.wikipedia.org/wiki/Software_design_pattern*). My quick definitions of the design patterns in this chapter are also largely based on Wikipedia.

The design pattern is the reusable solution template for a problem. It can speed up the development process by providing tested, proven development paradigms. The effective software design requires considering problems that may not become obvious until later in the implementation. Reusing design patterns helps to prevent subtle issues that can cause major problems, and it also improves code readability for coders and architects who are familiar with the patterns.

From the preceding statements, you can see that design patterns are not necessarily tied to specific languages or programming paradigms. Given that the object-oriented programming (OOP) paradigm is the most used, most design-pattern implementations and discussions are based on languages that target OOP—for example, C#. Some people from the functional programming community have suggested that design patterns are merely a means to address flaws in OOP languages. I will not go into the details of this topic; instead, I will cover how to use F# to implement design patterns.

First, I'll cover three basic concepts in programming languages that primarily target OOP:

■ *Encapsulation* is a construct that facilitates the bundling of data with methods (or other functions) that operate on that data.

■ *Inheritance* is a way to compartmentalize and reuse code. It creates a subtype based on an existing type.

■ *Polymorphism: subtype polymorphism*, which is almost universally called just *polymorphism* in the context of object-oriented programming, is the ability to create a variable, a function, or an object that has more than one form.

The typical C# implementations of design patterns often use all three of these concepts. In the rest of the chapter, you will see how F# can use both OOP and functional features to implement most common design patterns.

Before demonstrating these design patterns, I'd like to remind you that a design pattern can have more than one implementation. Each of the implementations in the following examples show different F# language features in practice. Additionally, they provide a better way to apply F# in component or system design than what would be achieved by simply porting over a C# implementation.

Working with F# and Design Patterns

Let's start by looking at some of the design patterns that will be discussed in this chapter along with the definitions of each. Note that the following definitions are from an OOP perspective, so the definitions occasionally still use object-oriented terminology:

■ The *chain of responsibility pattern* avoids coupling the sender of a request to its receiver by giving more than one object a chance to handle the request. It chains the receiving objects and passes the request along the chain until an object handles it.

- The *decorator pattern* attaches additional responsibilities to an object dynamically. Decorators provide a flexible alternative to subclassing for extending functionality.

- The *observer pattern* defines a one-to-many dependency between objects so that when one object changes state, all its dependents are notified and updated automatically.

- The *proxy pattern* provides a surrogate or placeholder for another object to control access to it.

- The *strategy pattern* defines a family of algorithms, encapsulates each one, and makes them interchangeable. This pattern lets the algorithm vary independently from clients that use it.

- The *state pattern* allows an object to alter its behavior when its internal state changes.

- The *factory pattern* lets a class defer instantiation to subclasses.

- The *adapter pattern* and *bridge pattern* are both used to convert the interface of a class into another interface. The adapter pattern lets classes work together that couldn't otherwise because of incompatible interfaces. If we don't focus on interfaces or classes, we can rephrase the definition to a shorter one: These are patterns that provide a way to allow incompatible types to interact.

- The *singleton pattern* ensures a class has only one instance and provides a global point of access to it.

- The *command pattern* is used to allow an object to store the information needed to execute some other functionality at a later time. For example it can help implement a redo-undo scenario.

- The *composite pattern* describes a group of objects that are to be treated in the same way as a single instance of an object. The intent of a composite is to *compose* objects into tree structures to represent part-whole hierarchies. Implementing the composite pattern lets clients treat individual objects and compositions uniformly. The *visitor pattern* separates the algorithm implementation from the data structure. These two patterns can work together. The composite pattern forms a tree structure, and the visitor pattern applies a function to the tree structure and brings the result back.

- The *template pattern* is, as its name suggests, a program or algorithm skeleton.

- The *private data class pattern* is used to encapsulate fields and methods that can be used to manipulate the class instance.

- The *builder pattern* provides abstract steps of building objects. Using this pattern allows a developer to pass different implementations of abstract steps.

- The *façade pattern* allows you to create a higher level interface that can be used to make it easier to invoke underlying class libraries.

- The *memento pattern* saves an object's internal state for later use.

Working with the Chain of Responsibility Pattern

The chain of responsibility pattern is a design pattern consisting of a source of command objects and a series of processing objects. Each processing object contains a set of logic that describes the types of command objects it can handle and how to pass off those it cannot handle to the next processing object in the chain. The sample in Listing 3-2 shows a physical check process that needs to make sure that a person's age is between 18 and 65, that their weight is no more than 200 kilograms, and that they are taller than 120 centimeters.

The type in Listing 3-2 is called a *Record*. Listing 3-2 uses a *Record* to store a patient's medical data. It has several named fields that are used to hold the patient's data. It is very much like a database record. Listing 3-1 shows how to define a *Record* type and create a *record* object. The sample code creates a point record that has its *X* and *Y* fields set to *(1, 1)*.

LISTING 3-1 Defining a record type and creating a *Record* object

```
// define a point record
type Point2D = {
    X : float
    Y : float
}

// create original point record
let originalPoint = { X = 0.0; Y = 0.0 }

// create (1,1) point record
let onePoint = { X = 1.0; Y = 1.0 }
```

The record object implicitly forces data initialization; therefore, initial values are not optional when creating a *Record* type. The invoker must define the patient with some data, and this eliminates any possible initialization problems.

LISTING 3-2 Chain of responsibility pattern

```
// define a record to hold a person's age and weight
type Record = {
    Name : string;
    Age : int
    Weight: float
    Height: float
}

// Chain of responsibility pattern
let chainOfResponsibility() =
```

```
// function to check that the age is between 18 and 65
let validAge record =
    record.Age < 65 && record.Age > 18

// function to check that the weight is less than 200
let validWeight record =
    record.Weight < 200.

// function to check that the height is greater than 120
let validHeight record =
    record.Height > 120.

// function to perform the check according to parameter f
let check f (record, result) =
    if not result then record, false
    else record, f(record)

// create chain function
let chainOfResponsibility = check validAge >> check validWeight >> check validHeight

// define two patients' records
let john = { Name = "John"; Age = 80; Weight = 180.; Height = 180. }
let dan = { Name = "Dan"; Age = 20; Weight = 160.; Height = 190. }

printfn "John's result = %b" (chainOfResponsibility (john, true) |> snd)
printfn "Dan's result = %b" (chainOfResponsibility (dan, true) |> snd)
```

Execution result from the chain of responsibility sample

```
John's result = false
Dan's result = true
```

 Note You have to execute the *chainOfResponsibility* function to get the result shown.

In the implementation in Listing 3-2, three functions (responsibilities) are composed into a chain and the data is passed along the chain when it is being processed. The parameter passed in contains a Boolean variable that decides whether the data can be processed. In Listing 3-2, all the functions are in effect AND-ed together. The parameter passed into the first function contains a Boolean value. The successive function can be invoked only if the Boolean value is *true*.

The other implementation is used for pipelining, as shown in Listing 3-3, rather than function composition. The *chainTemplate* higher-order function takes a process and *canContinue* function. The *canContinue* function always returns true, and the process function is a simple "increase one" function. The execution result is *2*.

LISTING 3-3 Chain of responsibility sample using pipelining

```
// chain template function
let chainTemplate processFunction canContinue s =
    if canContinue s then
        processFunction s
    else s

let canContinueF _ = true
let processF x = x + 1

//combine two functions to get a chainFunction
let chainFunction = chainTemplate processF canContinueF

// use pipeline to form a chain
let s = 1 |> chainFunction |> chainFunction

printfn "%A" s
```

The other chain of responsibility implementation uses the partial pattern feature in F#. I introduced the unit of measure to make the code readable. The process goes from the first case and stops when the condition is met. The sample code is listed in Listing 3-2. The sample code checks the height and weight value for some predefined criteria. The person's data is checked against *NotPassHeight* and then *NotPassWeight* if his height passes the validation criteria. The code also demonstrates how to use the F# unit-of-measure feature, which avoids possible confusion because of the unit of measure used. The parameter for *makeCheck* is #*Person*, which means that any object of type *Person* or derived from a *Person* type can be passed in.

Listing 3-4 uses units-of-measure language constructs within a calculation. Only the number with the same unit of measure can be involved in the same calculation. Listing 3-4 shows how to define a kilogram (*kg*) unit and decorate it with a number.

LISTING 3-4 Defining and using a *kg* unit of measure

```
// define unit-of-measure kg
[<Measure>] type kg

// define 1kg and 2kg variables
let oneKilo = 1<kg>
let twoKilo = 1<kg> + 1<kg>
```

The *None* and *Some(person)* syntax in the sample code in Listing 3-6 represents a *Nullable*-type-like data structure called an *option*. You can think of *None* as NULL. The special function let (| NotPassHeight | _ |) is called an *active pattern*. It takes a *person* parameter and decides whether the person meets certain criteria. If the person meets the criteria, the function returns *Some(person)* and triggers the match statement. Listing 3-5 shows how to use the *Some()/None* syntax to check for an odd number. This sample introduced several new concepts. I will come back to these concepts in detail in Chapter 5.

LISTING 3-5 Using active pattern, *option*, and *match* to check for an odd number

```
// define an active pattern function to check for an odd number
let (| Odd | _ |) x = if x % 2 = 0 then None else Some(x)

// define a function to check for an odd number
let findOdd x =
    match x with
    | Odd x -> printfn "x is odd number"
    | _ -> printfn "x is not odd number"

// check odd number
findOdd 3
findOdd 4
```

Execution result

```
x is odd number
x is not odd number
```

LISTING 3-6 Chain of responsibility pattern using partial pattern matching

```
// define two units of measure: cm and kg
[<Measure>] type cm
[<Measure>] type kg

// define a person class with its height and weight set to 0cm and 0kg
type Person() =
    member val Height = 0.<cm> with get, set
    member val Weight = 0.<kg> with get, set

// define a higher order function that takes a person record as a parameter
let makeCheck passingCriterion (person: #Person) =
    if passingCriterion person then None  //if passing, say nothing, just let it pass
    else Some(person)    //if not passing, return Some(person)

// define NotPassHeight when the height does not meet 170cm
let (| NotPassHeight | _ |) person = makeCheck (fun p -> p.Height > 170.<cm>) person

// define the NotPassWeight when weight does not fall into 100kg and 50kg range
let (| NotPassWeight | _ |) person =
    makeCheck (fun p -> p.Weight < 100.<kg> && p.Weight > 50.<kg>) person

// check incoming variable x
let check x =
    match x with
    | NotPassHeight x -> printfn "this person is not tall enough"
    | NotPassWeight x -> printfn "this person is out of weight range"
    | _ -> printfn "good, this person passes"
```

```
// create a person with 180cm and 75kg
let p = Person(Height = 180.<cm>, Weight = 75.<kg>)

// perform the chain check
check p
```

Execution result

```
good, this person passes
```

Working with the Adapter Pattern

The adapter pattern is a design pattern that translates one interface for a type into an interface that is compatible with some other type. An adapter allows classes to work together that normally could not because of incompatible types. In Listing 3-8, we use the *Generic Invoke(GI)* function as an adapter or bridge to invoke two methods of incompatible types. By using the GI function, a common interface is no longer needed and the function can still be invoked. The GI function is a static type *constraint* function, it requires that type *T* define a certain member function. For example, in Listing 3-7, it requires that the type *T* has a *canConnect* function that takes *void (unit)* and returns a Boolean. (Note that F# requires you to declare a function as "inline" when arguments of the function are *statically resolved type parameters* such as those in the following code listing.)

LISTING 3-7 GI function

```
// define a GI function
let inline canConnect (x : ^T) = (^T : (member CanConnect : unit->bool) x)
```

The interesting thing about the design pattern implementation in Listing 3-8 is that *Cat* and *Dog* do not have any common base class or interface. However, they can still be processed in a unified function. This implementation can be used to invoke the legacy code, which does not share any common interface or base class. (You should note, by the way, that this is a sloppy way of solving the problem and should be considered only when no other option is available.)

Imagine that you have two legacy systems that need to be integrated and that you do not have access to the source code. It would be difficult to integrate the systems in other languages, but it's possible and even easy in F# using the *generic invoke* technique.

LISTING 3-8 The adapter pattern (bridge pattern)

```
//define a cat class
type Cat() =
    member this.Walk() = printfn "cat walks"

// define a dog class
type Dog() =
    member this.Walk() = printfn "dog walks"

// adapter pattern
let adapterExample() =
    let cat = Cat()
    let dog = Dog()

    // define the GI function to invoke the Walk function
    let inline walk (x : ^T) = (^T : (member Walk : unit->unit) x)

    // invoke GI and both Cat and Dog
    walk(cat)
    walk(dog)
```

Execution result from adapter pattern sample

```
cat walks
dog walks
```

Note The implementation in Listing 3-8 can also be viewed as a bridge pattern.

Working with the Command Pattern

The command pattern is a design pattern in which an object is used to represent and encapsulate all the information needed to call a method at a later time. Listing 3-10 shows how to use the command pattern to implement a redo-undo framework. This is an example of typical usage of the command pattern in the OOP world.

Listing 3-9 defines a result using the *ref* keyword. The *ref* keyword defines a reference type that points to the value *7*. The result is a reference cell. You can think of the *ref* keyword as a way to define a mutable variable.

LISTING 3-9 Reference cell

```
// define a reference cell to value 0
let a = ref 0

// define a function to increase a's value by 1
let increaseA() =
    a := !a + 1

// increase a's value and print out result
increaseA()
printfn "a = %A" !a
```

Execution result

```
a = 1
```

Note F# provides *incr* and *decr* to increase or decrease reference cell values by 1. When using the *incr* function, the *increaseA* function becomes `let increaseA() = incr a`.

Note The *:=* operator is used to assign a new value to the content of the reference cell. The *!* (pronounced *bang*) operator is used to retrieve the reference cell content.

LISTING 3-10 Command pattern

```
// define a command record
type Command = { Redo: unit->unit; Undo: unit->unit }

let commandPatternSample() =

    // define a mutable storage
    let result = ref 7

    // define the add command
    let add n = {
        Redo = (fun _ -> result := !result + n)
        Undo = (fun _ -> result := !result - n) }

    // define the minus command
    let minus n = {
        Redo = (fun _ -> result := !result - n)
        Undo = (fun _ -> result := !result + n) }

    // define an add 3 command
    let cmd = add 3
    printfn "current state = %d" !result
```

```
// perform add 3 redo operation
cmd.Redo()
printfn "after redo: %d" !result

// perform an undo operation
cmd.Undo()
printfn "after undo: %d" !result
```

Execution result from the command pattern sample obtained by invoking the
commandPatternSample **function**

```
current state = 7
after redo: 10
after undo: 7
```

Note There is no storage structure for command history; however, adding such a storage structure is trivial.

Note According to the MSDN documentation (*http://msdn.microsoft.com/en-us/library/ dd233186.aspx*), a mutable variable should be used instead of a reference cell whenever possible. The preceding code uses a reference cell just for demo purposes. You can convert this code to use a mutable variable.

There is another implementation that emphasizes that the command can be treated like data. The code defines two types of commands: *deposit* and *withdraw*. The *Do* and *Undo* functions are used to perform the do and undo actions. See Listing 3-12.

To implement this *Do* and *Undo* functionality, it is helpful to understand the F# discriminated union (DU) feature. Listing 3-11 demonstrates how to use a DU to check whether or not the given time is a working hour. Note how the first DU, *DayOfAWeek*, looks a lot like an enum, but without the default numeric value. In the second example, *TWorkingHour*, the DU case *Hour* has a tuple value, where the first element of the tuple is a *DayOfAWeek* and the second element is an integer.

LISTING 3-11 Using DU to check whether the given time is a working hour

```
// define day of the week
type DayOfAWeek =
    | Sunday
    | Monday
    | Tuesday
    | Wednesday
    | Thursday
    | Friday
    | Saturday
```

```
// define working hour
type TWorkingHour =
    | Hour of DayOfAWeek * int

// check that the working hour is Monday to Friday 9:00 to 17:00
let isWorkingHour day =
    match day with
    | Hour(Sunday, _) -> false
    | Hour(Saturday, _) -> false
    | Hour(_, time) -> time >= 9 && time <= 17

// check if Sunday is working hour
let sunday = Hour(Sunday, 9)
printfn "%A is working hour? %A" sunday (isWorkingHour sunday)

// check if Monday 10:00 is working hour
let monday = Hour(Monday, 10)
printfn "%A is working hour? %A" monday (isWorkingHour monday)
```

Execution result

```
Hour (Sunday,9) is working hour? false
Hour (Monday,10) is working hour? true
```

Now that you understand discriminated unions, you can apply them to the command pattern.

LISTING 3-12 Command pattern implementation II

```
// define two command types
type CommandType =
    | Deposit
    | Withdraw

// define the command format, which has a command type and an integer
type TCommand =
    | Command of CommandType * int

// mutable variable result
let result = ref 7

// define a deposit function
let deposit x = result := !result + x

// define a withdraw function
let withdraw x = result := !result - x

// do function to perform a do action based on command type
let Do = fun cmd ->
    match cmd with
    | Command(CommandType.Deposit, n) -> deposit n
    | Command(CommandType.Withdraw,n) -> withdraw n
```

```
// undo function to perform an undo action based on command type
let Undo = fun cmd ->
    match cmd with
    | Command(CommandType.Deposit, n) -> withdraw n
    | Command(CommandType.Withdraw,n) -> deposit n

// print the current balance
printfn "current balance %d" !result

// deposit 3 into the account and print the balance
let depositCmd = Command(Deposit, 3)
Do depositCmd
printfn "after deposit: %d" !result

// undo the deposit command and print the balance
Undo depositCmd
printfn "after undo: %d" !result
```

Execution result

```
current balance 7
after deposit: 10
after undo: 7
```

Working with the Observer Pattern

The observer pattern is a pattern in which a *subject* object maintains a list of its observer dependents.
The *subject* automatically notifies its dependents of any changes by calling one of the dependent's
methods. The implementation in Listing 3-13 passes the function into the *subject,* and the *subject*
notifies its changes by calling this function along with some parameters.

LISTING 3-13 Observer pattern

```
// define a subject
type Subject() =
    // define a default notify function
    let mutable notify = fun _ -> ()

    // subscribe to a notification function
    member this.Subscribe notifyFunction =
        let wrap f i = f i; i
        notify <- wrap notifyFunction >> notify

    // reset notification function
    member this.Reset() = notify <- fun _ -> ()

    // notify when something happens
    member this.SomethingHappen k =
        notify k
```

```
// define observer A
type ObserverA() =
    member this.NotifyMe i = printfn "notified A %A" i

// define observer B
type ObserverB() =
    member this.NotifyMeB i = printfn "notified B %A" i

// observer pattern
let observer() =
    // create two observers
    let a = ObserverA()
    let b = ObserverB()

    // create a subject
    let subject = Subject()

    // let observer subscribe to subject
    subject.Subscribe a.NotifyMe
    subject.Subscribe b.NotifyMeB

    // something happens to the subject
    subject.SomethingHappen "good"
```

Execution result from the observer pattern sample obtained by invoking the *observer* function

```
notified B "good"
notified A "good"
```

F#'s *Observable* module can be used to implement this pattern as well. In Listing 3-14, an event is defined along with three observers of the event. Compared to the version in Listing 3-13, this version is much more lightweight. The *myEvent* value is bound to an instance of the F# *event* type. For the *Observable* module to subscribe to the event, you have to publish the event. After the event is published, the *Observable.add* function is used to add the event-handler function to this event. When the event is fired by using *Trigger*, all the event-handler functions will be notified.

LISTING 3-14 Using the *Observable* module to implement the observer pattern

```
// define an event
let myEvent = Event<_>()

// define three observers
let observerA = fun i -> printfn "observer A noticed something, its value is %A" i
let observerB = fun i -> printfn "observer B noticed something, its value is %A" i
let observerC = fun i -> printfn "observer C noticed something, its value is %A" i

// publish the event and add observerA
myEvent.Publish
|> Observable.add observerA
```

```
// publish the event and add observerA
myEvent.Publish
|> Observable.add observerB

// publish the event and add observerA
myEvent.Publish
|> Observable.add observerC

//fire event with value 1
myEvent.Trigger 1
```

Execution result

```
observer A noticed something, its value is 1
observer B noticed something, its value is 1
observer C noticed something, its value is 1
```

Working with the Decorator Pattern

The decorator pattern can be used to extend (a.k.a. *decorate*) the functionality of an object at
run-time. In Listing 3-15, the decorator pattern is used along with the composite operator to add new
logic to the existing function. As the function is passed dynamically into a structure, the run-time
behavior can be easily changed. The sample code defines a property that exposes a function. This
function can then be changed at runtime.

LISTING 3-15 Decorator pattern

```
// define the Divide class
type Divide() =
    // define basic divide function
    let mutable divide = fun (a,b) -> a / b

    // define a property to expose the function
    member this.Function
        with get() = divide
        and set(v) = divide <- v

    // method to invoke the function
    member this.Invoke(a,b) = divide (a,b)

// decorator pattern
let decorate() =

    // create a divide instance
    let d = Divide()

    // set the check zero function
    let checkZero (a,b) = if b = 0 then failwith "a/b and b is 0" else (a,b)
```

```
// invoke the function without check zero
try
    d.Invoke(1, 0) |> ignore
with e -> printfn "without check, the error is = %s" e.Message

// add the check zero function and then invoke the divide instance
d.Function <- checkZero >> d.Function
try
    d.Invoke(1, 0) |> ignore
with e -> printfn "after add check, error is = %s" e.Message
```

Execution result from the decorator pattern sample obtained by invoking the *decorate* function

```
without check, the error is = Attempted to divide by zero.
after add check, error is = a/b and b is 0
```

Working with the Proxy Pattern

The proxy pattern uses a class that acts as a placeholder or interface for another object or function. It's often used for caching, to control access, or to delay the execution or creation of an object that is costly in the form of time or resources. See Listing 3-16. The *CoreComputation* class hosts two calcula-tion functions, named *Add* and *Sub*. The class also exposes a proxy class from which a user can get access to the computation.

LISTING 3-16 Proxy pattern

```
// define core computation
type CoreComputation() =
    member this.Add(x) = x + 1
    member this.Sub(x) = x - 1
    member this.GetProxy name =
        match name with
        | "Add" -> this.Add, "add"
        | "Sub" -> this.Sub, "sub"
        | _ -> failwith "not supported"

// proxy implementation
let proxy() =
    let core = CoreComputation()

    // get the proxy for the add function
    let proxy = core.GetProxy "Add"

    // get the compute from proxy
    let coreFunction = fst proxy

    // get the core function name
    let coreFunctionName = snd proxy
```

```
    // perform the core function calculation
    printfn "performed calculation %s and get result = %A" coreFunctionName (coreFunction 1)
```

Execution result from the proxy pattern sample obtained by invoking the *proxy* function

```
performed calculation add and get result = 2
```

Working with the Strategy Pattern

The strategy pattern is a software design pattern whereby algorithms can be selected and used at runtime. Listing 3-17 uses a function to hold different strategies. During runtime, the strategy can be modified.

LISTING 3-17 Strategy pattern

```
// quick sort algorithm
let quicksort l =
    printfn "quick sort"

// shell short algorithm
let shellsort l =
    printfn "shell short"

// bubble short algorithm
let bubblesort l =
    printfn "bubble sort"

// define the strategy class
type Strategy() =
    let mutable sortFunction = fun _ -> ()
    member this.SetStrategy f = sortFunction <- f
    member this.Execute n = sortFunction n

let strategy() =
    let s = Strategy()

    // set strategy to be quick sort
    s.SetStrategy quicksort
    s.Execute [1..6]

    // set strategy to be bubble sort
    s.SetStrategy bubblesort
    s.Execute [1..6]
```

Execution result from the strategy pattern sample obtained by invoking the *strategy* function

```
quick sort
bubble sort
```

Note The sample code does not really implement three sorting algorithms. Instead, the code simply outputs the name of the algorithm that would be used.

Listing 3-17 shows how to implement this pattern using the OOP paradigm. However, the strategy pattern can be implemented more succinctly with a functional approach. Listing 3-18 shows how to use the higher-order function named *executeStrategy* to implement this pattern using a functional paradigm.

LISTING 3-18 Strategy pattern using a higher-order function

```
// quick sort algorithm
let quicksort l =
    printfn "quick sort"

// shell short algorithm
let shellsort l =
    printfn "shell short"

// bubble short algorithm
let bubblesort l =
    printfn "bubble sort"

let executeStrategy f n = f n

let strategy() =
    // set strategy to be quick sort
    let s = executeStrategy quicksort
    // execute the strategy against a list of integers
    [1..6] |> s

    // set strategy to be bubble sort
    let s2 = executeStrategy bubblesort
    // execute the strategy against a list of integers
    [1..6] |> s2
```

Working with the State Pattern

The state pattern is used to represent the ability to vary the behavior of a routine depending on the state of an object. This is a clean way for an object to partially change its type at runtime. Listing 3-19 shows that the interest rate is decided by the internal state: account balance. The higher the balance is, the higher the interest is that a customer will receive. In the sample, I also demonstrate how to use the unit-of-measure feature.

LISTING 3-19 State pattern

```fsharp
// define account state
type AccountState =
    | Overdrawn
    | Silver
    | Gold

// define unit of measure as US dollar
[<Measure>] type USD

// define an account that takes the unit of measure
type Account<[<Measure>] 'u>() =
    // field to hold the account balance
    let mutable balance = 0.0<_>

    // property for account state
    member this.State
        with get() =
            match balance with
            | _ when balance <= 0.0<_> -> Overdrawn
            | _ when balance > 0.0<_> && balance < 10000.0<_> -> Silver
            | _ -> Gold

    // method to pay the interest
    member this.PayInterest() =
        let interest =
            match this.State with
                | Overdrawn -> 0.
                | Silver -> 0.01
                | Gold -> 0.02
        interest * balance

    // deposit into the account
    member this.Deposit x =
        let a = x
        balance <- balance + a

    // withdraw from account
    member this.Withdraw x =
        balance <- balance - x

// implement the state pattern
let state() =
    let account = Account()

    // deposit 10000 USD
    account.Deposit 10000.<USD>

    // pay interest according to current balance
    printfn "account state = %A, interest = %A" account.State (account.PayInterest())

    // deposit another 2000 USD
    account.Withdraw 2000.<USD>
```

```
// pay interest according to current balance
printfn "account state = %A, interest = %A" account.State (account.PayInterest())
```

Execution result from the state pattern sample obtained by invoking the *state* function

```
account state = Gold, interest = 200.0
account state = Silver, interest = 80.0
```

In F#, one way to implement a state machine is with a *MailboxProcessor*. The F# *MailboxProcessor* can be viewed as a message queue. It takes an asynchronous workflow as the processing logic. The asynchronous workflow will be introduced in the next chapter, and it can be thought of as a simple function being executed on a background thread. The *Post* method is used to insert a message into the queue, and the *Receive* method is used to get the message out of the queue. In Listing 3-20, the variable *inbox* represents the message queue. When the state machine starts, it goes to *state0*, which is represented by the *state0()* function, and waits for user input. The state machine will transition to another state according to the user's input.

LISTING 3-20 State pattern with F# *MailBoxProcessor*

```
open Microsoft.FSharp.Control

type States =
    | State1
    | State2
    | State3

type StateMachine() =
    let stateMachine = new MailboxProcessor<States>(fun inbox ->
                let rec state1 () = async {
                    printfn "current state is State1"
                    // <your operations>

                    //get another message and perform state transition
                    let! msg = inbox.Receive()
                    match msg with
                        | State1 -> return! (state1())
                        | State2 -> return! (state2())
                        | State3 -> return! (state3())
                }
            and state2() = async {
                    printfn "current state is state2"
                    // <your operations>

                    //get another message and perform state transition
                    let! msg = inbox.Receive()
                    match msg with
                        | State1 -> return! (state1())
                        | State2 -> return! (state2())
                        | State3 -> return! (state3())
                }
```

```
               and state3() = async {
                   printfn "current state is state3"
                   // <your operations>

                   //get another message and perform state transition
                   let! msg = inbox.Receive()
                   match msg with
                       | State1 -> return! (state1())
                       | State2 -> return! (state2())
                       | State3 -> return! (state3())
                   }
               and state0 () =
                   async {

                       //get initial message and perform state transition
                       let! msg = inbox.Receive()
                       match msg with
                           | State1 -> return! (state1())
                           | State2 -> return! (state2())
                           | State3 -> return! (state3())
                       }
               state0 ())

        //start the state machine and set it to state0
        do
             stateMachine.Start()

        member this.ChangeState(state) = stateMachine.Post(state)

let stateMachine = StateMachine()
stateMachine.ChangeState(States.State2)
stateMachine.ChangeState(States.State1)
```

Execution result in FSI

```
current state is state2
current state is State1
```

 Note If the preceding code is executed in Microsoft Visual Studio debug mode, *Thread.Sleep* is needed because the main process (thread) needs to give CPU cycles to the background execution.

Working with the Factory Pattern

The factory pattern in Listing 3-21 is an object-oriented design pattern used to implement the concept of *factories*. It uses the *function* keyword as shortcut to the *match* statement. It can create an object without specifying the exact class of object that will be created. Listing 3-22 shows an example that uses the *object* expression to implement the factory pattern.

LISTING 3-21 Using the *function* keyword

```
// define two types
type Type =
    | TypeA
    | TypeB

// check with function keyword
let checkWithFunction = function
    | TypeA -> printfn "type A"
    | TypeB -> printfn "type B"

// check with match keyword
let checkWithMatch x =
    match x with
    | TypeA -> printfn "type A"
    | TypeB -> printfn "type B"
```

In Listing 3-22, the *factory* inside *factoryPattern* is actually a function. It is a shortcut for a *match* statement. The *checkWithFunction* and *checkWithMatch* functions in Listing 3-21 are equivalent.

LISTING 3-22 Example of the factory pattern

```
// define the interface
type IA =
    abstract Action : unit -> unit

// define two types
type Type =
    | TypeA
    | TypeB

let factoryPattern() =
    // factory pattern to create the object according to the input object type
    let factory = function
        | TypeA -> { new IA with
                        member this.Action() = printfn "I am type A" }
        | TypeB -> { new IA with
                        member this.Action() = printfn "I am type B" }

    // create type A object
    let obj1 = factory TypeA
    obj1.Action()

    // create type B object
    let obj2 = factory TypeB
    obj2.Action()
```

Execution result from the factory pattern sample obtained by invoking the *factoryPattern* function

```
I am type A
I am type B
```

The *factory* function returns an object that is not familiar. Actually, the return type is something called an *object expression*, and this lightweight syntax can simplify your code significantly. If the object is not involved in inheritance, you can pretty much use an object expression to replace a class definition completely. Listing 3-23 shows how to create an instance of interface *IA* using object expression syntax.

LISTING 3-23 Using object expression

```
// define the interface
type IA =
   abstract Action : unit -> unit

let a = { new IA with
          member this.Action() =
             printfn "this is from object expression" }
```

Working with the Singleton Pattern

The singleton pattern is a design pattern used to implement the mathematical concept of a *singleton*. It restricts the instantiation of a class to a single instance. This is useful when exactly one object is needed to coordinate actions across the system. One example of a singleton in F# is a *value*. An F# value is immutable by default, and this guarantees there is only one instance. Listing 3-24 shows how to make sure that an F# class instance is a singleton. The sample declares a private constructor and ensures that the class has only one instance in memory.

LISTING 3-24 An example of the singleton pattern

```
// define a singleton pattern class
type A private () =
    static let instance = A()
    static member Instance = instance
    member this.Action() = printfn "action from type A"

// singleton pattern
let singletonPattern() =
    let a = A.Instance
    a.Action()
```

Working with the Composite Pattern

The composite pattern is a partitioning design pattern. The composite pattern describes a group of objects that are to be treated in the same way as a single instance of that object. The typical application is a tree structure representation. Listing 3-25 demonstrates a tree structure. The sample focuses more on how to access this tree structure and bring back the result.

The dynamically generated wrapper object can be treated like a visitor to the tree. The visitor accesses the node and brings the result back to the invoker. In the sample code, the *CompositeNode* structure not only defines the tree but also defines three common ways to traverse the tree. It does the heavy lifting by encapsulating the tree traversal algorithm. The visitor defines how to process the single node and is responsible for bringing the result back to the invoker. In this sample, the visitor adds the value in the tree nodes and brings back the sum.

LISTING 3-25 An example of the composite pattern

```
// define visitor interface
type IVisitor<'T> =
    abstract member Do : 'T -> unit

// define a composite node
type CompositeNode<'T> =
    | Node of 'T
    | Tree of 'T * CompositeNode<'T> * CompositeNode<'T>
    with
        // define in-order traverse
        member this.InOrder f =
            match this with
            | Tree(n, left, right) ->
                left.InOrder f
                f n
                right.InOrder(f)
            | Node(n) -> f n

        // define pre-order traverse
        member this.PreOrder f =
            match this with
            | Tree(n, left, right) ->
                f n
                left.PreOrder f
                right.PreOrder f
            | Node(n) -> f n

        // define post order traverse
        member this.PostOrder f =
            match this with
            | Tree(n, left, right) ->
                left.PostOrder f
                right.PostOrder f
                f n
            | Node(n) -> f n

let invoke() =
    // define a tree structure
    let tree = Tree(1, Tree(11, Node(12), Node(13)), Node(2))
```

```
// define a visitor, it gets the summary of the node values
let wrapper =
    let result = ref 0
    ({ new IVisitor<int> with
            member this.Do n =
                result := !result + n
    }, result)

// pre-order iterates the tree and prints out the result
tree.PreOrder (fst wrapper).Do
printfn "result = %d" !(snd wrapper)
```

Execution result from the composite pattern sample obtained by calling the *invoke* function

```
result = 39
```

Working with the Template Pattern

The template pattern is, as its name suggests, a program or algorithm skeleton. It is a behavior-based pattern. In F#, we have higher-order functions that can serve as a template to generate other functions. It is natural to use higher-order functions to implement this pattern. Listing 3-26 defines a three-stage database operation function named *TemplateF*. The actual implementation is provided outside of this skeleton function. I do not assume the database connection and query are all the same, so three functions are left outside of the class definition, and the user can define and pass in their own version of each.

LISTING 3-26 An example of the template pattern

```
// the template pattern takes three functions and forms a skeleton function named
TemplateF
type Template(connF, queryF, disconnF) =
    member this.Execute(conStr, queryStr) =
        this.TemplateF conStr queryStr
    member this.TemplateF =
            let f conStr queryStr =
                connF conStr
                queryF queryStr
                disconnF ()
            f

// connect to the database
let connect conStr =
    printfn "connect to database: %s" conStr

// query the database with the SQL query string
let query queryStr =
    printfn "query database %s" queryStr
```

```
// disconnect from the database
let disconnect () =
    printfn "disconnect"

let template() =
    let s = Template(connect, query, disconnect)
    s.Execute("<connection string>", "select * from tableA")

template()
```

Execution result from the template pattern sample obtained by invoking the *template* function

```
connect to database: <connection string>
query database select * from tableA
disconnect
```

 Note The *connect*, *query*, and *disconnect* functions can be implemented as private functions in a class.

The class definition is convenient for C# projects that need to reference the implementation of this design pattern in an F# project. However, the class is not necessary in an F#-only solution. Listing 3-27 shows how to use higher-order functions to implement the template pattern.

LISTING 3-27 Template pattern with a higher-order function

```
// connection, query, and disconnect functions
let connect(conStr ) = printfn "connect using %s" conStr
let query(queryStr) = printfn "query with %s" queryStr
let disconnect() = printfn "disconnect"

// template pattern
let template(connect, query, disconnect) (conStr:string) (queryStr:string)=
    connect(conStr)
    query(queryStr)
    disconnect()

// concrete query
let queryFunction = template(connect, query, disconnect)

// execute the query
do queryFunction "<connection string>" "select * from tableA"
```

Working with the Private Data Class Pattern

The private data class pattern is a design pattern that encapsulates class properties and associated data manipulation. The purpose of the private accessibility is to prevent the modification of these values. C# uses the *readonly* property, which does not have a *setter* function, to solve this problem. F# values are immutable by default, so implementing this *readonly* type of behavior is supported inherently. In the following example, I use an F# record type to implement the pattern by extending the record type. The *with* keyword in the code shown in Listing 3-28 is a way to tell the compiler that some property, method, or both will be added to the *record* type. In the sample code, the circle data remains the same once it is created. Some object-oriented implementations even implement another class so that there is little chance to modify the values. The immutability of *record* types eliminates the needs of a second class, as well as the need for explicitly defining *getter*-only properties with a keyword.

LISTING 3-28 An example of the private data class pattern

```
type Circle = {
    Radius : float;
    X : float;
    Y : float }



with
    member this.Area = this.Radius**2. * System.Math.PI
    member this.Diameter = this.Radius * 2.
let myCircle = {Radius = 10.0; X = 5.0; Y = 4.5}
printfn "Area: %f Diameter: %f" myCircle.Area myCircle.Diameter
```

Working with the Builder Pattern

The builder pattern provides abstract steps of building objects. This allows you to pass different implementations of specific abstract steps. Listing 3-29 demonstrates the abstract steps of making a pizza. The invoker can pass in different implementation steps to the *cook* function to generate different pizzas.

LISTING 3-29 An example of the builder pattern sample

```
// pizza interface
type IPizza =
    abstract Name : string with get
    abstract MakeDough : unit->unit
    abstract MakeSauce : unit->unit
    abstract MakeTopping: unit->unit
```

```
// pizza module that defines all recipes
[<AutoOpen>]
module PizzaModule =
    let makeNormalDough() = printfn "make normal dough"
    let makePanBakedDough() = printfn "make pan baked dough"
    let makeCrossDough() = printfn "make cross dough"

    let makeHotSauce() = printfn "make hot sauce"
    let makeMildSauce() = printfn "make mild sauce"
    let makeLightSauce() = printfn "make light sauce"

    let makePepperoniTopping() = printfn "make pepperoni topping"
    let makeFiveCheeseTopping() = printfn "make five cheese topping"
    let makeBaconHamTopping() = printfn "make bacon ham topping"

// define a pepperoni pizza recipe
let pepperoniPizza =
        {   new IPizza with
                member this.Name = "Pepperoni Pizza"
                member this.MakeDough() = makeNormalDough()
                member this.MakeSauce() = makeHotSauce()
                member this.MakeTopping() = makePepperoniTopping() }

// cook takes pizza recipe and makes the pizza
let cook(pizza:IPizza) =
    printfn "making pizza %s" pizza.Name
    pizza.MakeDough()
    pizza.MakeSauce()
    pizza.MakeTopping()

// cook pepperoni pizza
cook pepperoniPizza
```

Execution result from the builder pattern sample

```
making pizza Pepperoni Pizza
make normal dough
make hot sauce
make pepperoni topping
```

The pizza interface and object expression give the program a good structure, but it makes things unnecessarily complicated. The builder pattern requires the actual processing function or functions be passed in, which is a perfect use of higher-order functions. Listing 3-30 uses a higher-order function to eliminate the interface and object expression.

```
// pizza module that defines all recipes
[<AutoOpen>]
module PizzaModule =
    let makeNormalDough () = printfn "make normal dough"
    let makePanBakedDough () = printfn "make pan baked dough"
    let makeCrossDough() = printfn "make cross dough"

    let makeHotSauce() = printfn "make hot sauce"
    let makeMildSauce() = printfn "make mild sauce"
    let makeLightSauce() = printfn "make light sauce"

    let makePepperoniTopping() = printfn "make pepperoni topping"
    let makeFiveCheeseTopping() = printfn "make five cheese topping"
    let makeBaconHamTopping() = printfn "make bacon ham topping"

// cook takes the recipe and ingredients and makes the pizza

let cook pizza recipeSteps =
    printfn "making pizza %s" pizza
    recipeSteps
    |> List.iter(fun f -> f())

[ makeNormalDough; makeMildSauce
  makePepperoniTopping ]
|> cook "pepperoni pizza"
```

Working with the Façade Pattern

The façade pattern provides a higher-level interface that makes invoking an underlying class library easier, more readable, or both. Listing 3-31 shows how to perform an employment background check.

LISTING 3-31 An example of the façade pattern

```
// define Applicant record
type Applicant = { Name : string }

// library to perform various checks
[<AutoOpen>]
module SubOperationModule =
    let checkCriminalRecord (applicant) =
        printfn "checking %s criminal record..." applicant.Name
        true

    let checkPastEmployment (applicant) =
        printfn "checking %s past employment..." applicant.Name
        true

    let securityClearance (applicant, securityLevel) =
        printfn "security clearance for %s ..." applicant.Name
        true
```

```
// façade function to perform the background check
let isBackgroundCheckPassed(applicant, securityLevel) =
    checkCriminalRecord applicant
    && checkPastEmployment applicant
    && securityClearance(applicant, securityLevel)

// create an applicant
let jenny = { Name = "Jenny" }

// print out background check result
if isBackgroundCheckPassed(jenny, 2) then printfn "%s passed background check" jenny.Name
else printfn "%s failed background check" jenny.Name
```

Execution result from the façade pattern sample

```
checking Jenny criminal record...
checking Jenny past employment...
security clearance for Jenny ...
Jenny passed background check
```

Working with the Memento Pattern

The memento pattern saves an object's internal state so that it can be used later. In Listing 3-32, the *particle* class saves its location information and later restores that information back to the saved location. If the state data is relatively small, a list storage can easily turn the memento pattern into a redo-undo framework.

LISTING 3-32 An example of the memento pattern

```
// define location record
type Location = { X : float; Y : float }

// define a particle class with a location property
type Particle() =
    let mutable loc = {X = 0.; Y = 0.}
    member this.Loc
        with get() = loc
        and private set v = loc <- v
    member this.GetMemento() = this.Loc
    member this.Restore v = this.Loc <- v
    member this.MoveXY(newX, newY) = loc <- { X = newX; Y = newY }


// create a particle
let particle = Particle()
```

```
// save current state
let currentState = particle.GetMemento()
printfn "current location is %A" particle.Loc

// move particle to new location
particle.MoveXY(2., 3.)
printfn "current location is %A" particle.Loc

// restore particle to previous saved location
particle.Restore currentState
printfn "current location is %A" particle.Loc
```

Writing Design Patterns: Additional Notes

As I mentioned in the beginning of this chapter, design patterns have been criticized since their birth. Many functional programmers believe that design patterns are not needed when programming in a functional style. Peter Norvig, in his paper "Design Patterns in Dynamic Languages," claims that design patterns are just missing language features and demonstrates that design patterns can be simplified or eliminated completely when using a different language. I am not planning to be part of these discussions. Design patterns are a way to represent a system or idea. It is really a de facto and concise way for many computer professionals to describe system design. If the program is simple and small, design patterns are often unnecessary. For these scenarios, the use of basic data and flow-control structure is enough. However, when a program becomes large and complicated, a tested approach is needed to organize thinking and avoid possible design flaws or bugs. If the basic data structure is analogous to a word in a sentence, design patterns can be viewed as the idea to organize an article.

As a functional-first programming language, F# is adept at creating code with a functional style. For example, the *pipeline* and *function* composition operators make function operation much easier. Instead of being confined to a class, the function can be freely passed and processed like data in F#. If the design pattern is mainly about how to pass an action/operation or coordinate the flow of an operation, the pipeline and function composition operators can definitely simplify the implementation. The chain of responsibility pattern is an example. The biggest change from C# is that a function in F# is no longer auxiliary to the data; instead, it can be encapsulated, stored, and manipulated in a class. The data (field and property) in a class can actually be provided as a function or as method parameters and remain auxiliary to the function. Additionally, the presence of a class is optional if the class only serves as an operation container. The builder pattern demonstrates a way to eliminate the class while still implementing the same functionality.

Functional programming can still have a structure to encapsulate logic into a unit. Functions, which can be treated like data, can be encapsulated in a class or inside a closure and, more importantly, the application of object expressions provides an even simpler way to organize the code. Listing 3-33 shows different ways to encapsulate the data.

LISTING 3-33 Data encapsulation

F# closure

```
let myFunction () =
    let constValue = 100
    let f () = [1..constValue] |> Seq.iter (printfn "%d")
    f()
```

Object expression

```
let obj =
    let ctor = printfn "constructor code"
    let field = ref 8
    { new IA with
        member this.F() = printfn "%A" (!field)
      interface System.IDisposable with
        member this.Dispose() = ()}
```

Object expressions are great, because the type is created on the fly by the compiler. Instead of inventing a permanent boilerplate class to hold the function and data, you can use object expressions to quickly organize functions and data into a unit and get the job done. Imagine an investment bank with a bunch of mathematicians who lack a computer background: object expressions can let them quickly transform their knowledge into code without worrying about programmers complaining about their inability to implement complex inheritance hierarchies. The flattened structure from the object expression is a straightforward and suitable approach for quick prototyping and agile development. The command pattern is a good sample for demonstrating how to use object expressions to simplify the design.

Both functional programming and object-oriented programming have their own way of reusing the code. Object-oriented programming uses inheritance, while functional programming uses higher-order functions. Both approaches have loyal followers, and you might already be convinced that one is superior to the other. I say that both approaches have their own advantages under certain circumstances. Unfortunately, neither is a silver bullet that can be used to solve all problems. Using the right tool for the right job is the key. F#, which supports both OO and functional programming, provides both approaches, and this gives the developer the liberty to use the best way to perform the system design.

F# provides the alternative to encapsulation (object expressions) and inheritance (higher order functions): polymorphism. It can also be implemented by higher-order functions when given different parameters. This is yet another example of how F# provides a wide set of tools for developers to implement their components and systems.

In addition, the adapter pattern introduces the GI function, which breaks class encapsulation and makes possible communication between objects that do not share a common base class. It is not a recommended way to use the original object-oriented design; however, it is a feasible approach to wrap legacy code because of inaccessibility to the source code. It is not fair to blame a gun for causing crime and not blame the criminal. Likewise, F# provides this approach, but I'll leave the decision to you regarding when and how to use it.

It is totally fine to copy a standard object-oriented approach when doing system design, especially when someone is new to a language. If you are motivated to use F# to write design patterns, here are some principles that I used to implement the design patterns in this chapter. If the design pattern is a behavior design pattern, its main focus is on how to organize the function, so consider using the function composition and pipeline operators. If the function needs to be organized into a unit, put the function into a module and use object expressions to organize the function. If the design pattern is a structural design pattern, I always question why extra structure is needed. If the extra structure is a placeholder for functionality, higher-order functions most likely will do the same job. If the extra structure is needed to make two unrelated objects work together, the GI function could be a good candidate to simplify the design.

F# is a young language and how to properly apply its language feature into the system design is still a new topic. Keep in mind that F# provides the OOP way of implementing class encapsulation, inheritance, and polymorphism. This chapter is only a small step to explore how to use F# in system design.

F#'s Unique Features

Type Providers

F# 3.0 introduces a new feature called *type providers*. The major application of a type provider is to provide language features for working within a data-rich environment. One example of a data-rich environment is the database. One major problem when programming against a database is how to generate code for database tables, stored procedures, and other database objects. Not every developer prefers to write database-access code manually, and nice tooling support is something developers always desire. Ideally, you could interact with a rich data environment such as a database using Microsoft Visual Studio features such as IntelliSense. Using IntelliSense would make it easier to write the necessary code, and it would save the time it would otherwise take to continually go back to check the database schema via the database management console.

The SQL Server type provider is designed to solve this problem, and it is shipped with Visual Studio 2012. One of the benefits you get with type providers is that they bring the database or web service schema information to your fingertips in the form of IntelliSense. As a result, when you type, the remote data structure is retrieved, which helps you finish your coding much more quickly. For a data-rich environment, this feature can improve your productivity significantly. If you're familiar with code-generation tools such as SqlMetal.exe, you can think of a type provider as a wrapper around these tools. At first glance, the type provider seems like something similar to tools that are currently integrated into the Visual Studio integrated development environment (IDE). Actually, an F# type provider does not rely on the IDE. You can use your favorite code editor, and the F# compiler and type provider assembly will bring all of the generated types to you. Note that this process does not involve any IDE work. In addition to being independent of the Visual Studio IDE, a type provider is an open framework compared to other tools, such as svcutil.exe. This means that developers can write their own type provider or providers. I'll cover how to write a custom type provider in Chapter 5, "Write Your Own Type Provider."

The following four built-in type providers can be used to access data from databases and web services:

- LINQ-to-SQL
- SQL Entity
- Web Services Description Language (WSDL)
- Open Data Protocol (OData)

This chapter focuses on how to use these type providers and F# queries. It also shows how to use type providers to access the Microsoft Windows Azure Marketplace.

Using the LINQ-to-SQL Type Provider

The first obvious data-rich environment is a database. Assume you have a local SQL database, and the database schema is like the one shown in Figure 4-1. This is a simple student-course system. The Student table stores information about all the students. The Course table stores all the course information, and the CourseSelection table is where course-selection information for all students is stored.

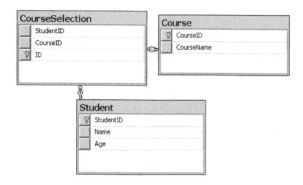

FIGURE 4-1 Test database diagram

Like any new programming feature, type providers require a certain syntax. Visual Studio ships with a number of item templates to generate the majority of the code. The only thing left for the user to do is fill out connection information. For a SQL type provider, it is the database connection string. Figure 4-2 shows item templates for four built-in type providers. The LINQ-to-SQL type provider is the first one. In this chapter, I use the term *SQL type provider* to represent the LINQ-to-SQL type provider.

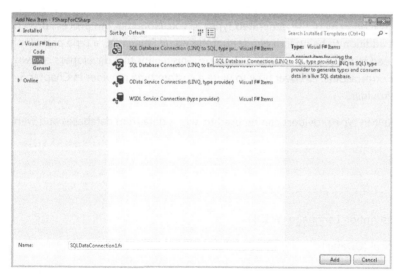

FIGURE 4-2 The Add New Item dialog box in Visual Studio, where you can select a LINQ-to-SQL data type provider

After clicking the Add button, the SQL type provider code is added. Along with the code, a reference to a crucial assembly named *FSharp.Data.TypeProviders* is also added. This is where the type provider resides. The generated code is shown in Listing 4-1. The connection string is highlighted, and that is all you need to change to make this type provider work. The most convenient way to try a new feature is to use F# Interactive (FSI). Most of the samples in this chapter will use FSI as the default way to execute.

LISTING 4-1 SQL type provider code

```
// The SqlDataConnection (LINQ-to-SQL) TypeProvider allows you to write code that
// uses a live connection to a database. For more information, please go to
//    http://go.microsoft.com/fwlink/?LinkId=229209

module SQLDataConnection1

#if INTERACTIVE
#r "System.Data"
#r "System.Data.Linq"
#r "FSharp.Data.TypeProviders"
#endif

open System.Data
open System.Data.Linq
open Microsoft.FSharp.Data.TypeProviders

// You can use Server Explorer to build your ConnectionString.

type SqlConnection = Microsoft.FSharp.Data.TypeProviders.SqlDataConnection<ConnectionStri
ng =
    @"Data Source=(LocalDB)\v11.0;Initial Catalog=tempdb;Integrated Security=True">

let db = SqlConnection.GetDataContext()

//let table = query {
//    for r in db.Table do
//    select r
//    }
//

//for p in table do
//    printfn "%s" p.Property
```

> **Note** The #if INTERACTIVE section allows the code in Listing 4-1 to be executed in FSI. In other words, you can select the code segment and test it in FSI when desired.
>
> When the code needs to be executed in FSI, module SqlDataConnection1 should not be selected.

The type provider accepts a string value for its connection string. The value can be accessed only at run time, and it is very difficult to use a run-time value to generate design time logic. One way to work around this is to use the *Literal* attribute and conditional compile symbols. The sample code is shown in Listing 4-2. This trick can work for all type providers. The other way to specify the connection string is to use a configuration file, which I will leave for you to explore.

LISTING 4-2 Using the conditional symbol and constant with type providers

```
#if DEVELOPMENT

[<Literal>]
let conStr = "< my development environment connection string> "

#else

[<Literal>]
let conStr = "< production environment connection string> "

#endif

// define a type provider with constant value
type T = Microsoft.FSharp.Data.TypeProviders.SqlDataConnection<ConnectionString=conStr>
let db = T.GetDataContext()
```

> **Note** If you're not using integrated authorization, the user password is stored in the binary. The *GetDataContext* method has an overloaded version that takes the connection string at run time. The schema of the database accessed at run time, which is specified by the connection string provided at run time, must match the one used at compile time. If it does not match exactly, at least the schema accessed by your code should be same.
>
> Using conditional compilation symbols is not a best practice when creating assemblies, but it is totally fine when writing an F# script.

The compilation process displays a warning message box like the one shown in Figure 4-3. To retrieve the database schema information, the type provider needs to access the database specified by the connection string. To ensure that you are always aware of this external access, you will be asked if this access should be granted. Once you feel comfortable, you can click Enable to allow the type provider to do its thing.

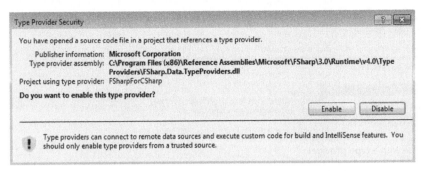

FIGURE 4-3 The Type Provider Security dialog box, which asks you whether you want to enable the specified type provider

Note For other third-party type providers, to which you later decide to revoke trust, you can go to Tools, Option, F# Tools and press the Delete key to remove the trusted type providers. Figure 4-4 provides an example.

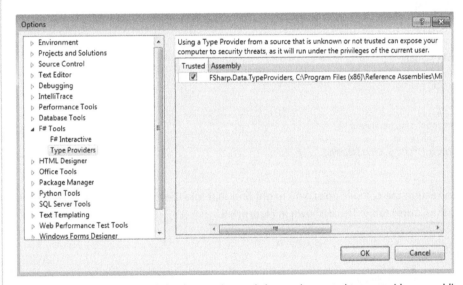

FIGURE 4-4 Use the Options dialog box to view and change the trusted type provider assemblies

Depending on the network and database server speed, it can take a few seconds for the type provider to gather all the schema information locally. IntelliSense will be shown when you try to access the database context instance named *db*. IntelliSense shows the table names and stored procedure names. You do not have to open Server Explorer or Notepad; the schema information from the database is just at your fingertips. See Figure 4-5.

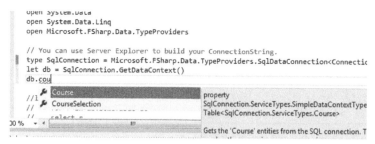

FIGURE 4-5 IntelliSense with a type provider

When you uncomment the query and FOR loop with *printfn* inside, you will receive an error because the query targets a fake database. Fortunately, IntelliSense guides you so that you can easily fix those errors and get the executable code looking like what's shown in Listing 4-3. The code prints all of the course names in the table. The F# query feature is a large topic, and I'll explain it further in the "Query" section later in the chapter. For now, we can use a simple query syntax to verify that our type provider is working correctly.

LISTING 4-3 The query code

```
// query the course table
let table = query {
    for r in db.Course do
    select r
    }

// print out course names
for p in table do
    printfn "%s" p.CourseName
```

After correcting the compile error, you might find that IntelliSense can also show all the column names for the Course table. This is shown in Figure 4-6.

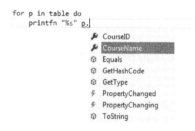

FIGURE 4-6 IntelliSense prompts for column names

Note IntelliSense shows up only within an F# project. When referenced from a C# project, the provided type and the *db* variable are visible but no column names are shown. This is also true for other type providers. IntelliSense information is provided only by the F# language service.

The stored procedure is common in SQL databases. By default, the LINQ-TO-SQL type provider allows stored procedures to also be visible. You can set the *storedProcedures* parameter to *false* to disable it, as shown in Listing 4-4.

LISTING 4-4 Disabling a stored procedure

```
type SqlConnection = Microsoft.FSharp.Data.TypeProviders.SqlDataConnection<ConnectionStri
ng =
    @"Data Source=taliu0;Initial Catalog=TestDataBase;Integrated Security=True",
    StoredProcedures=false>
let db = SqlConnection.GetDataContext()
```

The *SqlConnection* type also contains a class definition representing tables. The generated table class is nested under *SqlConnection.ServiceTypes*. These types make it possible for you to delete, insert, or update records in a database, as shown in Listing 4-5.

LISTING 4-5 Updating a database

```
Add a new item
let newRecord = new  SqlConnection.ServiceTypes.Course(CourseName = "aa", CourseID = 100)
db.Course.InsertOnSubmit(newRecord)

try
    db.DataContext.SubmitChanges()
    printfn "record added"
with _ -> printfn "update failed"


Delete an item
db.Course.DeleteOnSubmit(newRecord)

try
    db.DataContext.SubmitChanges()
    printfn "record deleted"
with _ -> printfn "update failed"
```

More generally, you can execute any SQL command by using the *ExecuteCommand* method in the *DataContext*. See Listing 4-6.

LISTING 4-6 Executing a SQL command

```
try
    let numOfRecord = db.DataContext.ExecuteCommand("select * from Course")
    printfn "%d records affected" numOfRecord
with _ -> printfn "failed"
```

SQL Type Provider Parameters

The SQL type provider uses SQLMetal.exe as the underlying code-generation tool. The SQL type provider has many parameters that can be configured to specify how SQLMetal will generate the code. Table 4-1 lists all the parameters the SQL type provider supports. Although all the parameters are optional, you have to specify either *ConnectionString* or *ConnectionStringName* at the very least.

TABLE 4-1 SQL type provider parameters

Parameter Name	Description
ConfigFile	The name of the configuration file used for connection strings. Its default value is either *app.config* or *web.config*.
ConnectionString	The connection string for the database connection.
ConnectionStringName	The name of the connection string for the database connection in the configuration file.
ContextTypeName	The name of the data context class. The name is derived from the database name by default.
DataDirectory	The name of the data directory; it's used to replace *DataDirectory* in the connection strings. The project or script directory is the default value.
ForceUpdate	Requires that a direct connection to the database be availabe at design-time, and forces the refresh of the local schema file. The default value is TRUE.
Functions	Extracts database functions. The default value is TRUE.
LocalSchemaFile	The local .dbml file for the database schema. There is no local schema file by default.
Pluralize	Automatically pluralizes or singularizes class and member names using English language rules. The default value is FALSE.
ResolutionFolder	The folder used to resolve relative file paths at compile time. The default value is the project or script folder.
Serializable	Generates uni-directional serializable classes. The default behavior is to have no serialization.
StoredProcedure	Extracts a stored procedure. The default value is TRUE.
TimeOut	The timeout value is specified in seconds which is used when SqlMetal accesses the database. The default value is 0, which means an infinite amount of time.
Views	Extracts database views. The default value is TRUE.

SQL Entity Type Provider

If you are not satisfied with the code generated by the SQL type provider, which is primarily provided by LINQ-to-SQL, the SQL Entity type provider is another way for you to access a database. According to the MSDN document at *http://msdn.microsoft.com/en-us/library/bb386976*, LINQ-to-SQL is a SQL access technology that works only with Microsoft SQL Server. The ADO.NET Entity Framework provides a more flexible way to handle not only the SQL Server database but also other relational databases. If you are not familiar with ADO.NET Entity Framework, the following is the definition from MSDN (*http://msdn.microsoft.com/en-us/library/bb386876.aspx*):

> The ADO.NET Entity Framework supports data-centric applications and services, and provides a platform for programming against data that raises the level of abstraction from the logical relational level to the conceptual level. By enabling developers to work with data at a greater level of abstraction, the Entity Framework supports code that is independent of any particular data storage engine or relational schema.

If you try to access an Azure SQL database by using the SQL type provider introduced in the "LINQ-to-SQL Type Provider" section, you'll get an error. The right way to access the data in an Azure SQL database is to use the SQL Entity type provider. Overall, creating a SQL Entity type provider is similar to creating the SQL type provider shown earlier. Figure 4-7 shows how to add an Entity Framework–based type provider by using the Add New Item dialog box.

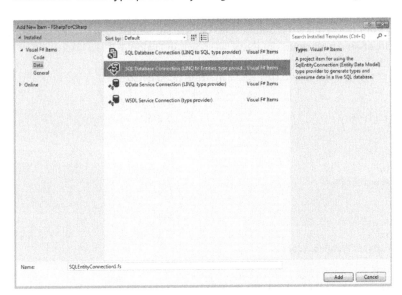

FIGURE 4-7 Using the Add New Item dialog box to add a SQL Entity type provider

The actual code for the SQL Entity type provider is quite similar to the SQL type provider. The only difference is the type name. The SQL type provider's type name is *SqlDataConnection*; the SQL Entity type provider's type name is *SqlEntityConnection*. The sample code is shown in Listing 4-7.

LISTING 4-7 SQL Entity type provider

```
#if INTERACTIVE
#r "System.Data"
#r "System.Data.Entity"
#r "System.Data.Linq"
#r "FSharp.Data.TypeProviders"
#endif

open System.Data
open System.Data.Entity
open Microsoft.FSharp.Data.TypeProviders

// You can use Server Explorer to build your ConnectionString.

type internal SqlConnection =
    Microsoft.FSharp.Data.TypeProviders.SqlEntityConnection<ConnectionString =
        @"Data Source=(LocalDB)\v11.0;Initial Catalog=tempdb;Integrated Security=True">

let internal db = SqlConnection.GetDataContext()
```

Note Because the SQL Entity type provider cannot be used across assemblies, its type can be only private or internal. This restriction prevents an F# assembly from exposing the type provider to a C# project.

The Entity Framework does not require the database to be SQL Server database. You can use SQL Entity type provider to target an Azure cloud database, as shown in Listing 4-8.

LISTING 4-8 Using the SQL Entity type provider to connect to an Azure cloud database

```
module SQLEntityConnection1

#if INTERACTIVE
#r "System.Data"
#r "System.Data.Entity"
#r "FSharp.Data.TypeProviders"
#endif

open System.Data
open System.Data.Entity
open Microsoft.FSharp.Data.TypeProviders

[<Literal>]
let con = """Server=tcp:<your server>.database.windows.net,1433;
    Database=<your database>;User ID=<user name>;Password=<your
    password>;Trusted_Connection=False;Encrypt=True;Connection Timeout=30"""
```

```
// You can use Server Explorer to build your ConnectionString.
type internal SqlConnectionT =
    Microsoft.FSharp.Data.TypeProviders.SqlEntityConnection<ConnectionString = con>

let internal db = SqlConnectionT.GetDataContext()
```

The way to add and delete commands for the SQL Entity type provider is different; the type provider uses *AddObject* and *DeleteObject* to add and remove a record or records from a database. Listing 4-9 shows how to use these two methods.

LISTING 4-9 Adding and removing records from an Azure cloud database by using the SQL Entity type provider

```
module SQLEntityConnection1

#if INTERACTIVE
#r "System.Data"
#r "System.Data.Entity"
#r "FSharp.Data.TypeProviders"
#endif

open System.Data
open System.Data.Entity
open Microsoft.FSharp.Data.TypeProviders

[<Literal>]
let con = """Server=tcp:<your server>.database.windows.net,1433;
    Database=<your database>;User ID=<user name>;Password=<your
    password>;Trusted_Connection=False;Encrypt=True;Connection Timeout=30"""

// You can use Server Explorer to build your ConnectionString.
type internal SqlConnectionT =
    Microsoft.FSharp.Data.TypeProviders.SqlEntityConnection<ConnectionString = con>

let internal db = SqlConnectionT.GetDataContext()

let internal newRecord = new SqlConnectionT.ServiceTypes.Course(CourseName = "aa",
CourseID = 100)
db.Course.AddObject(newRecord);
try
    let recordNumber = db.DataContext.SaveChanges()
    printfn "%d record(s) affected" recordNumber
with _ -> printfn "update failed"

db.Course.DeleteObject(newRecord);
try
    let recordNumber = db.DataContext.SaveChanges()
    printfn "%d record(s) affected" recordNumber
with _ -> printfn "update failed"
```

```
1 record(s) affected
1 record(s) affected
```

If you want to execute your own SQL query, you can use the *ExecuteStoreQuery* method. Listing 4-10 shows how to use this method to check the total number of courses in the database.

LISTING 4-10 Executing your own query by using the SQL Entity type provider

```
let result = db.DataContext.ExecuteStoreQuery("select count(*) from Course")
printfn "%d course(s) in the database" (result |> Seq.head)
```

SQL Entity Type Provider Parameters

Like the SQL type provider, the SQL Entity type provider needs either *ConnectionString* or *ConnectionStringName* as a parameter. The full list of parameters is shown in Table 4-2.

TABLE 4-2 SQL Entity type provider parameters

Parameter Name	Description
ConfigFile	The name of the configuration file used for connection strings. The default value is either *app.config* or *web.config*.
ConnectionString	The connection string to the database.
ConnectionStringName	The name of the connection string for the database connection in the configuration file.
DataDirectory	The name of the data directory, used to replace *DataDirectory* in the connection string. The default value is the project folder or script folder.
EntityContainer	The name to use for the *EntityContainer* in the conceptual model.
ForceUpdate	Requires that a direct connection to the database be available at design time, and forces the refresh of the local schema file. The default value is TRUE.
LocalSchemaFile	The local file for the database schema.
Pluralize	Automatically pluralizes or singularizes class and member names using English language rules. The default value is FALSE.
Provider	The name of the ADO.NET data provider to be used for Store Schema Definition Language (SSDL) generation. If you are interested in SSDL, please refer to MSDN document at *http://msdn.microsoft.com/en-US/data/jj652016*. The default provider is *System.Data.SqlClient*.
ResolutionFolder	The folder used to resolve relative file paths at compile time. The default value is the project folder or script folder.
SuppressForeignKeyProperties	Excludes foreign key properties in entity type definitions. The default value is FALSE.

WSDL Type Provider

The web is another area that is rich with data. The public application programming interfaces (APIs) exposed by companies around the world is increasing exponentially year by year. If the data schema can be automatically accessed and shown with IntelliSense, this will make your coding significantly easier and boost productivity.

Web Services Description Language (WSDL) is an XML-based language which is used to describe the functionality provided by a web service. A WSDL file offers a machine-readable XML document that explains how the service can be called, what operations are available, what parameters are required, and the values that can be returned.

The easiest way to add a WSDL type provider is to use the Add New Item dialog box in Visual Studio, which is shown in Figure 4-8. The code generated is shown in Listing 4-11. When you connect to your favorite data source, you get not only IntelliSense about data names but also comments to help you understand what the data is for. Isn't that nice!

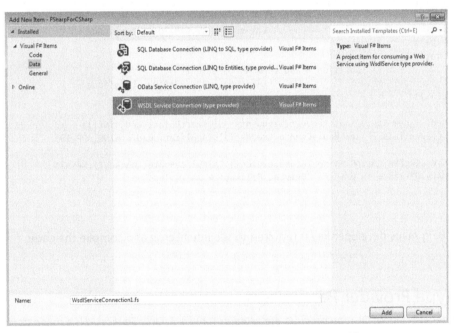

FIGURE 4-8 Using the Add New Item dialog box to add a WSDL type provider

LISTING 4-11 WSDL type provider

```
open System.Runtime.Serialization
open System.ServiceModel
open Microsoft.FSharp.Data.TypeProviders

// You can sign up for a Bing service developer account at http://msdn.microsoft.com/en-
us/library/gg605201.aspx
let BING_APP_ID = "<your Bing Maps Developer Key>"

// Using Bing Map API routing service to calculate the driving distance between two
Geolocations. http://www.microsoft.com/maps/developers/mapapps.aspx

type RouteService = Microsoft.FSharp.Data.TypeProviders.WsdlService<ServiceUri =
    "http://dev.virtualearth.net/webservices/v1/routeservice/routeservice.svc?wsdl">
    type RouteCommon = RouteService.ServiceTypes.dev.virtualearth.net.webservices.
v1.common
    type Route = RouteService.ServiceTypes.dev.virtualearth.net.webservices.v1.route

let startPoint = Route.Waypoint(
                    Location = RouteCommon.Location(
                                Latitude = 47.64012046, Longitude =
-122.1297104))
let endPoint = Route.Waypoint(
                    Location = RouteCommon.Location(
                                Latitude = 47.62049103, Longitude =
-122.3492355))

let routReq1 = new Route.RouteRequest(Waypoints = [|startPoint; endPoint|])
routReq1.Credentials <- new RouteCommon.Credentials(ApplicationId = BING_APP_ID)

RouteService.GetBasicHttpBinding_IRouteService().CalculateRoute(routReq1).Result
    .Summary.Distance |> printfn "Driving Distance = %A (miles)"
```

 Note A Bing maps developer key is required to see IntelliSense and compile the code.

WSDL Type Provider Parameters

The parameters for the WSDL type provider are listed in Table 4-3. Only *ServiceUri* is a mandatory parameter; the other parameters are optional.

TABLE 4-3 WSDL type provider parameters

Parameter Name	Description
Async	Indicates if whether both synchronous and asynchronous method signatures should be generated. The default value is FALSE, which means that only synchronous method signatures will be generated.
CollectionType	A fully-qualified or assembly-qualified name of the type to use as a collection data type when code is generated from the schema.

Parameter Name	Description
EnableDataBinding	Indicates whether the INotifyPropertyChanged interface should be added on all data contract types to enable data binding. The default value is FALSE.
ForceUpdate	Requires that a direct connection to the service be available at design time, and forces the refresh of the local schema file. The default value is TRUE.
LocalSchemaFile	The .wsdl schema file to store locally cached service schema.
MessageContract	Indicates whether message contract types should be generated. The default value is FALSE.
ResolutionFolder	The folder used to resolve relative file paths at compile time. The default value is the folder that contains the project or script.
Serializable	Indicates whether the generated classes should be marked with the Serializable attribute. The default value is FALSE.
ServiceUri	The URI for the WSDL service. This is a mandatory parameter.

OData Type Provider

Another way to access remote services or data is to use the Open Data Protocol (OData) type provider. OData is an open web protocol for querying and updating data over the HTTP transport protocol. You can use it to retrieve results in formats like Atom, JSON, or plain XML. Figure 4-9 shows how to use Visual Studio to create an OData type provider, and the generated sample code is shown in Listing 4-12. The OData type provider does not support fixed queries. You have to download the fixed query schema file to work with the OData type provider.

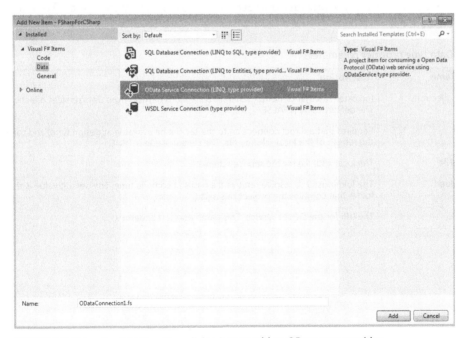

FIGURE 4-9 Using the Add New Item dialog box to add an OData type provider

LISTING 4-12 OData type provider

```
open System.Data.Services.Client
open Microsoft.FSharp.Data.TypeProviders

// Access demographic info such as population and income from the OData service at
// Azure Marketplace. For more information, go to https://datamarket.azure.com/dataset/
// c7154924-7cab-47ac-97fb-7671376ff656

type Demographics = Microsoft.FSharp.Data.TypeProviders.ODataService<ServiceUri =
    "https://api.datamarket.azure.com/Esri/KeyUSDemographicsTrial/">
let ctx = Demographics.GetDataContext()

//To sign up for an Azure Marketplace account at https://datamarket.azure.com/
account/infoctx.Credentials <- System.Net.NetworkCredential("<your liveID>",
"<your Azure Marketplace Key>")
```

 Note You need a Windows Live ID and an Windows Azure Marketplace key to show IntelliSense and compile the code from the previous example.

OData Type Provider Parameters

Compared to the WSDL type provider, the OData type provider's parameter list (shown in Table 4-4) is much shorter. Like the WSDL type provider, only *ServiceUri* is a mandatory parameter; the other parameters are optional.

TABLE 4-4 OData type provider parameters

Parameter Name	Description
DataServiceCollection	Indicates whether or not to generate collections derived from DataServiceCollection. The default value is FALSE.
ForceUpdate	Requires that a direct connection to the service be available at design time, and forces the refresh of the local schema file. The default value is TRUE.
LocalSchemaFile	The local .csdl file for the service schema.
ResolutionFolder	The folder used to resolve relative file paths at compile time. The default value is the folder that contains the project or script.
ServiceUri	The URI for the OData service. This parameter is mandatory.

Other Type Providers

As I mentioned at the beginning of this chapter, the type provider is extensible. Because the type provider concept is public, many type providers have been developed by the community. Many of these type providers are provided by the FSharpX project on GitHub. I'm not going to present a detailed introduction to these type providers, but you can find out more about them at *https://github.com/fsharp/fsharpx*. This website provides information on type providers such as these:

- **File System**   Used to provide type information taken from a file system. The type provider provides types for directories and files on the computer.

- **Xml File**   Used to provide type information for an XML file. The XML type provider can infer a schema from the loaded data and generate types with properties.

- **JSON**   Used to provide type information for JSON data. The JSON type provider provides strongly typed access to data provided in the JavaScript Object Notation (JSON) data-interchange format.

- **Registry**   Used for the registry. The registry key and value are generated from the type provider.

- **Xaml**   Provides type information for a WPF XAML file, which is essentially in XML format. The generated types are WPF UI elements.

The other way to get these type providers is to use the NuGet packages. Figure 4-10 shows how to access the management options for NuGet packages from a project reference. The FSharpX type provider for NuGet packages can be located by typing **TypeProviders** in the Search box in the upper-right corner of the Manage NuGet Packages dialog box, as shown in Figure 4-11.

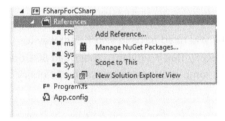

FIGURE 4-10 Selecting the NuGet packages management options from a reference listing

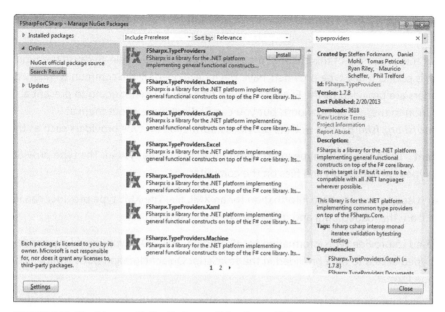

FIGURE 4-11 The Manage NuGet Packages dialog box, which you use to configure settings for the NuGet Packages type provider

The type provider provides a way for F# programmers to interpret the data from the outside world. You are not given an *XmlElement* when parsing an XML file; instead, you are given a more meaningful data type, such as *StudentInfo*. You'll have an opportunity to write your own custom type provider in Chapter 5.

Query

When a type provider brings back a large amount of data, you need to have a sufficient way to process that data. Luckily, F# offers *query* to help. The query syntax is similar to that of an SQL query or LINQ query. I use the SQL data or entity provider in the sample, but you can use the F# query syntax to interact with any other type providers as well.

To see the query syntax work with one of the previously shown SQL type providers, you need to first set up an SQL database. The database is a basic student-course database with Student, Course, and CourseSelection tables. The SQL script in Listing 4-13 is used to create the student-course database and some sample data.

The query is independent of a specific type provider, which means it can be applied to any type provider and even to a memory data structure. In the sample code, one person's age is set to NULL. This is not a bug. This NULL value will demonstrate how to use F# nullable operators.

LISTING 4-13 SQL script for creating database tables and inserting data

```
CREATE TABLE Student(
    StudentID int not null
        constraint PrimaryKey primary key,
    Name nvarchar(50) null,
    Age int null,);

CREATE TABLE Course(
    CourseID int not null
        constraint PrimaryKey2 primary key,
    CourseName varchar(max) null);

CREATE TABLE AnotherStudentTable (
    StudentID int not null
        constraint PrimaryKey3 primary key,
    Name nvarchar(50) null,
    Age int null,);

go

CREATE TABLE CourseSelection(
    StudentID int not null
        constraint foreignKey references dbo.Student(StudentID),
    CourseID int null
        constraint foreignKey2 references dbo.Course(CourseID),
    ID int null);

go

INSERT Student VALUES (1, 'Lisa', 21)
INSERT Student VALUES (2, 'Brent', 22)
INSERT Student VALUES (3, 'Anita', 20)
INSERT Student VALUES (4, 'Ken', 22)
INSERT Student VALUES (5, 'Cathy', 22)
INSERT Student VALUES (6, 'Tom', 20)
INSERT Student VALUES (7, 'Zeoy', 21)
INSERT Student VALUES (8, 'Mark', 23)
INSERT Student VALUES (9, 'John', null)
go

INSERT Course VALUES (1, 'Math')
INSERT Course VALUES (2, 'Physics')
INSERT Course VALUES (3, 'Biology')
INSERT Course VALUES (4, 'English')
go

INSERT CourseSelection VALUES(1, 1, null)
INSERT CourseSelection VALUES(2, 1, null)
INSERT CourseSelection VALUES(3, 1, null)
INSERT CourseSelection VALUES(2, 2, null)
INSERT CourseSelection VALUES(2, 3, null)
INSERT CourseSelection VALUES(3, 3, null)
INSERT CourseSelection VALUES(3, 2, null)
go
```

I'll use the SQL Entity type provider in the sample code. All the sample code is written on the assumption you already created a SQL Entity type provider and assigned it to a value named *db*. Because some query operations are not supported in the SQL Entity type provider, I'll use *AsEnumerable* or *array* to create an in-memory data structure. The code is shown in Listing 4-14.

LISTING 4-14 Creating an in-memory student table

```
open System
open System.Linq
open Microsoft.FSharp.Linq.NullableOperators

// define a student class
type Student() =
    member val ID = 0 with get, set
    member val Name = "" with get, set
    member val Age = Nullable(0) with get, set

// define the general show result function
let showResult query = query |> Seq.iter (printfn "%A")

// set the in-memory student table
let studentTable = [
        Student(ID = 1, Name = "Anita", Age = Nullable(22));
        Student(ID = 1, Name = "Kate", Age = Nullable(22))
        Student(ID = 1, Name = "Brent", Age = Nullable(23))
        Student(ID = 1, Name = "Lisa", Age = Nullable(23))
        Student(ID = 1, Name = "Mark", Age = Nullable(24)) ].AsQueryable()
```

Using the *select* Operator

The code in Listing 4-15 is a simple *select* example. You can think of the *select* operator as being like the *yield* keyword in sequence generation or the *select extension* method in LINQ. It tells the compiler to return the value. The *for...in...do* code iterates through the data, and the *select* operator specifies what needs to be inserted into the final result. I'll use the code `let showResult query = query |> Seq.iter (printfn "%A")` to show the query result.

LISTING 4-15 Simple *select* example

Code for the *select* example

```
// simple select
let internal q0 = query {
    for n in db.Course do
    select n.CourseName }

// general function to show the query result
let showResult query = query |> Seq.iter (printfn "%A")
showResult q0
```

Execution result

```
"Math"
"Physics"
"Biology"
"English"
```

If the query can be translated to the server-side code, it will be executed on the server side. Unfortunately, not all computations can be translated to the server-side code. Listing 4-16 uses *AsEnumerable()* to specify that the computation should be performed on the client side, because *sprintf* cannot be translated to server-side code. Once the data is local, you are free to use any .NET function or pipeline operator.

LISTING 4-16 Selection code with transform code

Code for *select* with transform

```
let internal q1 = query {
    for n in db.Course.AsEnumerable() do
    select (sprintf "course name = %s" n.CourseName) }

showResult q1
```

Execution result

```
"course name = Math"
"course name = Physics"
"course name = Biology"
"course name = English"
```

You can also create more complex queries that involve multiple *select* statements. Listing 4-17 shows how to print out all the value pairs where the first value is less than the second value. For this example, a value pair is formed from two data sources.

LISTING 4-17 Selecting from different sources

```
let A = [0; 2; 4; 5; 6; 8; 9]
let B = [1; 3; 5; 7; 8]

query {
        for a in A do
        for b in B do
        where (a < b)
        select (a, b)
}
|> Seq.iter(fun (n, e) -> printfn "%d is less than %d" n e)
```

```
0 is less than 1
0 is less than 3
0 is less than 5
0 is less than 7
0 is less than 8
2 is less than 3
2 is less than 5
2 is less than 7
2 is less than 8
4 is less than 5
4 is less than 7
4 is less than 8
5 is less than 7
5 is less than 8
6 is less than 7
6 is less than 8
```

Using the *where* Operator

The *where* operator is used to filter data according to given conditions. Like the *select* operator, the computation can be executed either on the server side or client side. Listing 4-18 shows how to filter the student names whose length is greater than 4 characters long. Because the result is filtered on the server side, only three items are transferred over the wire.

LISTING 4-18 A *where* example

Code for the *where* example

```
let internal q2 = query {
    for n in db.Student do
    where (n.Name.Length > 4)
    select n.Name }

showResult q2
```

Execution result

```
"Brent"
"Anita"
"Cathy"
```

Although performing the filter action on the client side is not a recommended approach, especially if the resulting data set is large, I still list the sample code here in case complex filtering is needed on the client side. See Listing 4-19.

LISTING 4-19 The *where* filter function performed on the client side

The *where* filter function performed on the client side

```
let internal q3 = query {
    for n in db.Student do
    select n.Name }

// filter on client side
let q3_2 = q3 |> Seq.filter (fun n -> n.Length > 4)

showResult q3_2
```

Execution result

```
"Brent"
"Anita"
"Cathy"
```

Listing 4-20 is another example of filtering data on the client side. The code gives each element an ID value and filters the results later according to this client-side-generated ID.

LISTING 4-20 Filter based on a client-side-generated value

```
let internal myQuery = query {
    for n in db.Student do
    select n.Name }

// filter on client side based on ID
let result =
    myQuery
    |> Seq.mapi (fun i n -> (i, n))
    |> Seq.filter (fun (i, n) -> i % 2 = 0)
    |> showResult
```

Execution result

```
(0, "Lisa")
(2, "Anita")
(4, "Cathy")
(6, "Zeoy")
(8, "John")
```

Note The actual result you get might be different, depending on the targeted data storage.

Using the *join* Operator

The *join* example in Listing 4-21 shows how to join data that is scattered across different tables. In the *join* statement, the order of the keys is significant. The outside table db.Student, which is the main table, must be present first in the *on condition* part. The example lists the course ID and student name as a result.

LISTING 4-21 A *join* example

Code for the *join* example

```
let internal q5 = query {
    for student in db.Student do
    join course in db.CourseSelection on (student.StudentID = course.StudentID)
    select (course.CourseID, student.Name) }

showResult q5
```

Execution result

```
(3, "Anita")
(1, "Lisa")
(2, "Anita")
(2, "Brent")
(3, "Brent")
(1, "Anita")
(1, "Brent")
```

The *CourseID* in the result from Listing 4-21 is far from user friendly. If the student name can be shown, that will be great. In Listing 4-22, a *groupJoin* operator is used to show a more user-friendly result. Because *CourseID* is a nullable integer type, you can use *"?="* in the *Microsoft.FSharp.Linq. NullableOperators* module to perform the comparison.

LISTING 4-22 Using a group join

```
let q6 = query {
    for student in db.Student do
    groupJoin courseSelection in db.CourseSelection
        on (student.StudentID = courseSelection.StudentID) into g
    for courseSelection in g do
    join course in db.Course on (courseSelection.CourseID ?= course.CourseID)
    select (student.Name, course.CourseName) }

showResult q6
```

("Anita", "Biology")
("Lisa", "Math")
("Anita", "Physics")
("Brent", "Physics")
("Brent", "Biology")
("Anita", "Math")
("Brent", "Math")

There is another join scenario called an *outer join*. The F# outer join operator is similar to SQL's outer join, but it supports only the left outer join. The right outer join functionality can be achieved by switching the two tables. Listing 4-23 shows how to use *leftOuterJoin* to show the course selection information.

LISTING 4-23 Using the left outer join

```
let internal q5 = query {
    for student in db.Student do
    leftOuterJoin selection in db.CourseSelection on
                (student.StudentID =? selection.CourseID) into result
    for selection in result do
    select (student.Name, selection.Course.CourseName)
    }

showResult q5
```

Execution result

("Lisa", "Math")
("Lisa", "Math")
("Lisa", "Math")
("Brent", "Physics")
("Brent", "Physics")
("Anita", "Biology")
("Anita", "Biology")
("Ken", null)
("Cathy", null)
("Tom", null)
("Zeoy", null)
("Mark", null)
("John", null)

Note Because *CourseID* is a *Nullable<int>*, you need to use *=?* to perform the equality operation. You need to use open `Microsoft.FSharp.Linq.NullableOperators`. Both *=?* and *?=* are valid operators. If the nullable value is on left side of the operator, *?=* is applied; however, *=?* is used if the nullable value is on right side.

Using the *Value* property in a *Nullable<T>* type does not work in the query. This is by design, because using it in this way can lead to a NULL exception when the *Nullable<T>* value is NULL.

Using the *sortBy* Operator

Listing 4-24 shows how to use the *sortBy* operator to show the sorted names whose name length is greater than 4 characters. By default, *sortBy* sorts the result in ascending order. The *sortByDescending* operator serves the purpose of sorting the results in a descending manner.

LISTING 4-24 Using the *sort* code

Sort code

```
let internal q4 = query {
    for n in db.Student do
    sortBy n.Name
    where (n.Name.Length > 4)
    select n.Name }

showResult q4
```

Execution result

```
"Anita"
"Brent"
"Cathy"
```

You can sort by a second criterion by using *thenBy* or *thenByDescending*. Listing 4-25 sorts the result first by a student's name and then by the student's age.

LISTING 4-25 Using the *thenBy* keyword

```
let internal q4_2 = query {
    for student in db.Student do
    sortBy student.Age.Value
    thenBy student.Name
    select (student.Name, student.Age) }

showResult q4_2
```

```
("John", null)
("Anita", 20)
("Tom", 20)
("Lisa", 21)
("Zeoy", 21)
("Brent", 22)
("Cathy", 22)
("Ken", 22)
("Mark", 23)
```

In Listing 4-25, *Age* is a nullable value, so you have to reference the *Value* property in order to sort. The F# query feature provides a set of operators that can handle nullable values. Listing 4-26 shows how to use *sortByNullableDescending*.

- **sortByNullable**   Sorts elements in ascending order by a given nullable key

- **sortByNullableDescending**   Sorts elements in descending order by a given nullable key

- **thenByNullable**   Like the *thenBy* operator, performs subsequent ordering of the elements in ascending order by a given nullable key

- **thenByNullableDescending**   Like the *thenByDescending* operator, performs subsequent ordering of the elements in descending order by a given nullable key

LISTING 4-26 Using *sortByNullableDescending*

```
let internal q4_3 = query {
    for student in db.Student do
    sortByNullableDescending student.Age
    thenBy student.Name
    select (student.Name, student.Age) }

showResult q4_3
```

Execution result

```
("Mark", 23)
("Brent", 22)
("Cathy", 22)
("Ken", 22)
("Lisa", 21)
("Zeoy", 21)
("Anita", 20)
("Tom", 20)
("John", null)
```

Using the *group* Operator

The *group* operator is often used with an aggregate function. Listing 4-27 counts the number of students in each age group.

LISTING 4-27 A *groupBy* example

The code for a *groupBy* query

```
let internal q7 = query {
    for student in db.Student do
    groupBy student.Age into g
    select (g.Key, g.Count()) }

showResult q7
```

Execution result

```
(null, 1)
(20, 2)
(21, 2)
(22, 3)
(23, 1)
```

Again, the result is not user friendly because the result does not show the student names in the result. To show the student names, you can use *groupValBy* to select a value with the group. The full code is shown in Listing 4-28. It shows a student name sequence in each age group.

LISTING 4-28 A *groupValBy* example

Code for using *groupValBy*

```
let internal q8 = query {
    for student in db.Student do
    groupValBy student.Name student.Age into g
    select (g, g.Key, g.Count()) }

showResult q8
```

Execution result

```
(seq ["John"], null, 1)
(seq ["Anita"; "Tom"], 20, 2)
(seq ["Lisa"; "Zeoy"], 21, 2)
(seq ["Brent"; "Ken"; "Cathy"], 22, 3)
(seq ["Mark"], 23, 1)
```

Using the *take* and *skip* Operators

The *take* and *skip* operators are used when you are interested only in a certain range of the query results. Listing 4-29 sorts the students by age and skips the first student. This can be very useful in an OData service, which often returns the results in pages.

LISTING 4-29 Using *skip* to ignore the first element

The code for the *skip* example

```
let internal q9 = query {
    for student in db.Student do
    sortByNullable student.Age
    skip 1
    select student.Name }

showResult q9
```

Execution result

```
"Tom"
"Anita"
"Lisa"
"Zeoy"
"Brent"
"Ken"
"Cathy"
"Mark"
```

The *skip* and *take* operators are similar when used in the query. The *take* example is shown in Listing 4-30. The sample code sorts the students by age and returns only the first three student names.

LISTING 4-30 An example that uses *take* on the first three elements

The code for the *take* example

```
let internal q9 = query {
    for student in db.Student do
    sortByNullable student.Age
    take 3
    select student.Name }

showResult q9
```

Execution result

```
"John"
"Anita"
"Tom"
```

The *skip* operation also can be used with a condition statement rather than just a given number. Listing 4-31 shows how to skip the results for people in the database who have an age value less than 23.

LISTING 4-31 A *skipWhile* example

The code for the *skipWhile* example
```
open System
open System.Linq
open Microsoft.FSharp.Linq.NullableOperators

type Student() =
    member val ID = 0 with get, set
    member val Name = "" with get, set
    member val Age = Nullable(0) with get, set

let showResult query = query |> Seq.iter (printfn "%A")

let studentTable = [
        Student(ID = 1, Name = "Anita", Age = Nullable(22));
        Student(ID = 1, Name = "Kate", Age = Nullable(22))
        Student(ID = 1, Name = "Brent", Age = Nullable(23))
        Student(ID = 1, Name = "Lisa", Age = Nullable(23))
        Student(ID = 1, Name = "Mark", Age = Nullable(24)) ].AsQueryable()

// skip student whose age is less than 23
let internal q10 = query {
    for student in studentTable do
    sortByNullable student.Age
    skipWhile (student.Age ?< 23)
    select student.Name }

showResult q10
```

Execution result
```
"Brent"
"Lisa"
"Mark"
```

> **Note** Because one student's age is NULL, you have to use the *?<* operator in the *Microsoft.FSharp.Linq.NullableOperators* module to compare the nullable value.
>
> Because the underlying SQL data source does not support a *skipWhile* operator, we use the in-memory structure that was shown in Listing 4-14.

Using the *min/max*, *average*, and *sum* Operators

There is not much to explain about these operations; their names describe their functionalities. Because you have to handle the nullable value, each operator has a twin to handle the nullable value. I present them using a nullable operator in this section. Listing 4-32 shows how to get the maximum, minimum, and average ages of the student group, as well as the sum of their ages.

LISTING 4-32 Finding the minimum, maximum, average, and sum of the students' ages

```
let internal q11 = query {
    for student in db.Student do
    sumByNullable student.Age }

printf "sum of student age = "
showResult [ q11 ]

let internal q12 = query {
    for student in db.Student do
    minByNullable student.Age }

printf "youngest student age = "
showResult [ q12 ]

let internal q13 = query {
    for student in db.Student do
    maxByNullable student.Age }

printf "oldest student age = "
showResult [ q13 ]

let internal q14 = query {
    for student in db.Student do
    averageByNullable (Microsoft.FSharp.Linq.Nullable.float student.Age) }

printf "average student age = "
showResult [ q14 ]


Execution result

sum of student age = 171
youngest student age = 20
oldest student age = 23
average student age = 21.375
```

> **Note** The *average* operation cannot be performed on an integer type. Instead, you need to use the *Nullable.float* type that is located in the *Microsoft.FSharp.Linq* module, which converts the *Nullable<int>* to *Nullable<float>*.

Using the *head*, *last*, and *nth* Operators

Sometimes you need only one element in the sequence. The *head, last,* and *nth* operators are designed for this purpose. You use the *head* operator on the SQL storage and the other operators with the in-memory structure. Listing 4-33 shows the first student's name. Listing 4-34 shows how to get the *last* and *nth* elements.

LISTING 4-33 A *head* example

```
// return first element
let internal q15 = query {
    for student in db.Student do
    select student.Name
    head }

showResult [ q15 ]

// get the first element; if there is no first element returned, returns default
value let internal q16 = query {
    for student in db.Student do
    select student.Name
    headOrDefault }

showResult [ q16 ]
```

LISTING 4-34 Example that uses *last* and *nth*

```
open System
open System.Linq
open Microsoft.FSharp.Linq.NullableOperators

type Student() =
    member val ID = 0 with get, set
    member val Name = "" with get, set
    member val Age = Nullable(0) with get, set

let showResult query = query |> Seq.iter (printfn "%A")

let studentTable = [
        Student(ID = 1, Name = "Anita", Age = Nullable(22));
        Student(ID = 1, Name = "Kate", Age = Nullable(22))
        Student(ID = 1, Name = "Brent", Age = Nullable(23))
        Student(ID = 1, Name = "Lisa", Age = Nullable(23))
        Student(ID = 1, Name = "Mark", Age = Nullable(24)) ].AsQueryable()

// take the last student
let internal q15 = query {
    for student in studentTable do
    select student.Name
    last }
```

```
showResult [ q15 ]

// take the last student; if there is no last student, use default value
let internal q16 = query {
    for student in studentTable do
    select student.Name
    lastOrDefault }

showResult [ q16 ]

// return the 4th student in the list
let internal q17 = query {
    for student in studentTable do
    select student.Name
    nth 3 }

showResult [ q17 ]



Execution result
"Mark"
"Mark"
"Lisa"
```

Using the *count* and *distinct* Operators

The *count* operator is used to count the number of elements. Listing 4-35 shows how many students are in the Student table.

LISTING 4-35 A *count* example

```
let internal q17 = query {
    for student in db.Student do
    count }

showResult [ q17 ]
```

You might have noticed in the results from Listing 4-21 that some of the student names were repeated. The *distinct* operator is used to get the distinct elements in the result set, as shown in Listing 4-36.

LISTING 4-36 A *distinct* example

```
let internal q18 = query {
    for student in db.Student do
    join selection in db.CourseSelection on
        (student.StudentID = selection.StudentID)
    select student.Name
    distinct }

showResult q18
```

Execution result

```
"Anita"
"Brent"
"Lisa"
```

Using the *contains*, *exists*, and *find* Operators

The *contains* and *exists* operators are used to determine whether the set contains elements that meet a given condition. Listing 4-37 checks whether there is a student named Lisa.

LISTING 4-37 An example that uses *contains* and *exists*

```
let internal q19 = query {
    for student in db.Student do
    select student.Name
    contains "Lisa" }

showResult [ q19 ]

let internal q20 = query {
    for student in db.Student do
    exists (student.Name = "Lisa") }

showResult [ q20 ]
```

The *contains* and *exists* operators return only a Boolean value. If you need to see whether the first element meets certain criteria, you can use *find* as shown in Listing 4-38. If there is no student who meets the criteria, a *System.InvalidOperationException* will be thrown.

LISTING 4-38 A *find* example

```
let internal q21 = query {
    for student in db.Student do
    find (student.Age ?> 20) }

showResult [ q21.Name ]
```

Execution result

"Lisa"

Using the *exactlyOne* and *all* Operators

The *all* operator is used to test whether all the elements meet the criterion. Listing 4-39 is used to check whether all the students' names start with the letter *L*.

LISTING 4-39 An *all* example

```
let internal q22 = query {
    for student in db.Student do
    all (SqlClient.SqlMethods.Like(student.Name, "L%")) }

showResult [ q22 ]
```

Note The sample does not work with SqlEntityConnection but will work with SqlDataConnection.

To check whether a class has only one student with the name *Lisa* and return her information, you can use *exactlyOne* or *exactlyOneOrDefault*. The *exactlyOne* operation yields a *System.InvalidOperationException* if there is not exactly one match. See Listing 4-40.

LISTING 4-40 An *exactlyOne* example

```
let internal q23 = query {
    for student in db.Student do
    where (student.Name = "Lisa")
    exactlyOne }

showResult [ q23.Name ]
```

SQL Query and F# Query

The previous section provided a number of query operators. For some readers, the list might be too long, while others might still be waiting for more. If you are looking for more, you might be trying to map your existing T-SQL knowledge to F# query. If so, this section is the right place to be. I won't repeat my explanations of *select* or *where* here because they are easy to map to your existing T-SQL knowledge. If you are familiar with T-SQL, the following list can help you easily transfer your T-SQL knowledge to F# query:

- The *in* keyword in T-SQL is used to check whether a value is in the specified list of values, as shown in Listing 4-41. The equivalent of this T-SQL code in F# query is shown in Listing 4-42.

  LISTING 4-41 SQL *in* example

  ```
  SELECT * FROM Student
  WHERE Student.StudentID IN (1, 2, 3)
  ```

  LISTING 4-42 F# syntax for *in*

  ```
  let ids = query { for id in [1; 2; 3] do select id }

  query {
      for student in db.Student do
      where (ids.Contains(student.StudentID))
      select student }
  ```

- The *top* T-SQL keyword is used to return a number of elements on the top of the return list. At first glimpse, it might appear that F# query does not have an *equivalent* operator. However, closer examination will reveal that the *take* operator can do exactly the same thing.

- The *like* T-SQL keyword is a character-mapping operator in SQL. Although *like* is not a keyword in F# query, you can use *SqlMethods.Like*, as shown in Listing 4-39. *SQLMethods* also contains other methods that can be used to handle date and time differences. See Table 4-5 for more details.

TABLE 4-5 The *SQLMethods* member list

Function Name	Corresponding SQL Operator	Description
DateDiffDay	DATEDIFF	Counts the date difference in days
DateDiffHour	DATEDIFF	Counts the date difference in hours
DateDiffMicrosecond	DATEDIFF	Counts the date difference in microseconds
DateDiffMillisecond	DATEDIFF	Counts the date difference in milliseconds.
DateDiffMinute	DATEDIFF	Counts the date difference in minutes
DateDiffMonth	DATEDIFF	Counts the date difference in months

Function Name	Corresponding SQL Operator	Description
DateDiffNanosecond	DATEDIFF	Counts the date difference in nanoseconds
DateDiffSecond	DATEDIFF	Counts the date difference in seconds
DateDiffYear	DATEDIFF	Counts the date difference in years
Like	LIKE	Decides whether the input matches the specific pattern

- The *between* T-SQL keyword is not a keyword in F# query, but you can use the comparison operators combined with *&&* to achieve the same result.

- The functionality provided by the *union* and *intersection* T-SQL keywords can be achieved with F# query, as shown in Listing 4-43 and Listing 4-44.

LISTING 4-43 SQL *union* and *intersection*

```
SELECT * from Student
UNION
SELECT * from AnotherStudentTable

SELECT * from Student
INTERSECT
SELECT * from AnotherStudentTable
```

LISTING 4-44 F# query *union*

```
let q0 = query { for student in db.Student do select student.Name }
let q1 = query { for student in db.AnotherStudentTable do select student.Name }

// union two query results
q1.Union(q0)

// intersect two query results
q1.Intersect(q0)
```

- The *case* T-SQL keyword is supported in F# query by using an *if* statement. See Listing 4-45 and Listing 4-46.

LISTING 4-45 SQL *case* example

```
SELECT student.Name,
    CASE student.Age
    WHEN 0 then 1000
    ELSE student.Age
    END
FROM Student
```

LISTING 4-46 F# query using an *if* statement

```
let q = query {
    for student in db.Student do
    select ( if student.Age ?= -1 then (student.Name, Nullable<int>(1000))
                    else (student.Name, student.Age)  )  }
```

Other F# Operators

In this section, I will present some F# operators that can be used as shortcut to make the query code more readable. As mentioned in the previous section, you will inevitably find scenarios that require bringing data to the client to perform certain computations. F# provides a few shortcuts for some of the more widely used .NET functions associated with these scenarios. These functions can be used in queries and in other data processing:

- **|||>, ||>, <|||, and <|| operators**   These operators are used to break triple and tuple to a function. After reviewing the sample in Listing 4-47, it is not difficult to find the similarity between these operators and the pipeline operator. For example, |||> takes a triple, breaks the triple into three elements, and feeds the elements into a function that takes three parameters in curried format.

  LISTING 4-47 The |||>, ||>, <|||, and <|| operators

  ```
  // define a function taking 3 parameters in curried format
  let f3 a b c = a + b + c + 1

  // define a function taking 2 parameters in curried format
  let f2 a b = a + b + 1

  // define a function taking a parameter
  let f a = a + 1

  let print x = printfn "value = %A" x

  print ( (1, 2, 3) |||> f3 )
  print ( (1, 2) ||> f2 )
  print ( 1 |> f )

  print ( f3 <||| (1, 2, 3) )
  print ( f2 <|| (1, 2) )
  print ( f <| 1 )
  ```

Execution result

```
value = 7
value = 4
value = 2
value = 7
value = 4
value = 2
```

- **sin, cos, tan, sinh, cosh, and tanh** The first three functions—*sin*, *cos*, and *tan*—are the trigonometric functions. sine, cosine, and tangent. The *sinh*, *cosh*, and *tanh* functions are the hyperbolic functions hyperbolic sine, hyperbolic cosine, and hyperbolic tangent.

- **log and log10** The *log* function is the natural logarithm function, while the *log10* function is a logarithm function with base equal to 10.

- **min and max** These function names are used to get the minimum or maximum value of two given values.

- **floor, ceil, and round** The *floor* and *ceil* functions are designed to find the floor and ceil of a given number, while the *round* function is used to find the rounded value of a given number.

- **abs** The *abs* function is used to find the absolute value of a given number.

- **asin, acos, and atan** The *asin*, *acos*, and *atan* functions are inverse sine, inverse cosine, and inverse tangent functions.

Using a Type Provider to Connect to the Windows Azure Marketplace

In this chapter, you used type providers to query a database and an in-memory structure. Another source of data is the Windows Azure Marketplace (*https://datamarket.azure.com/*). Hundreds of data sources and APIs are available in the Marketplace, and the number is increasing every day. Many innovations and applications are enabled by using these data and web APIs. In this section, I'll show how to use a type provider to access the free UK Foreign and Commonwealth Office Travel Advisory Service at the Windows Azure Marketplace. To use this free service, go to Windows Azure Marketplace and search for **UK Foreign and Commonwealth Office Travel Advisory Service**, the service is located at *https://datamarket.azure.com/dataset/uk.gov/traveladvisoryservice*. You can sign in with your Windows Live ID. Figure 4-12 shows the Details tab, which describes the service URL and service schema information.

As programmers, we are interested in the Details tab because it lists the connection string and all of the data schemas, including the data names and types. We will need the service root URI for this example.

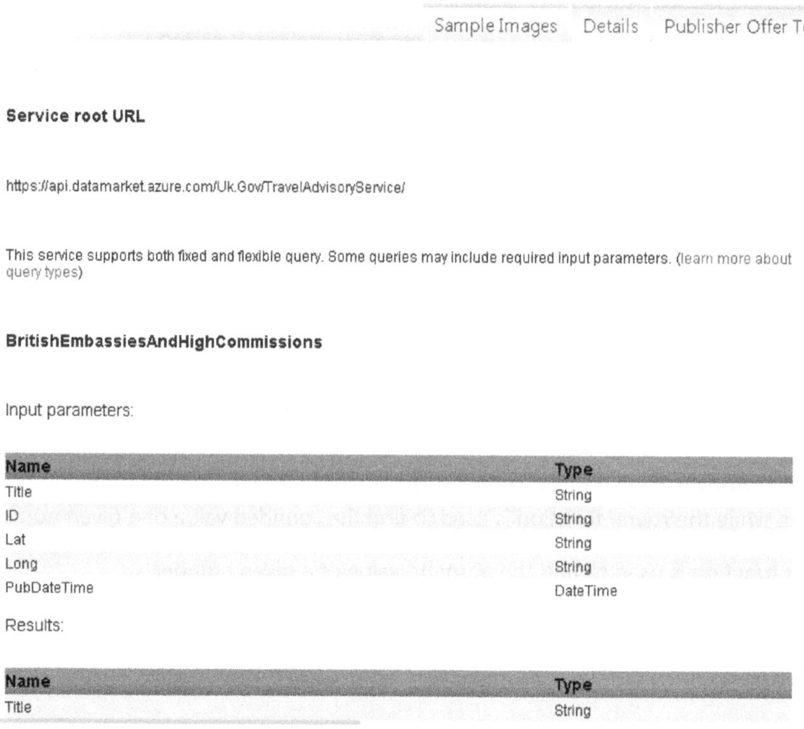

Sample Images   Details   Publisher Offer Terms

Service root URL

https://api.datamarket.azure.com/Uk.Gov/TravelAdvisoryService/

This service supports both fixed and flexible query. Some queries may include required input parameters. (learn more about query types)

BritishEmbassiesAndHighCommissions

Input parameters:

Name	Type
Title	String
ID	String
Lat	String
Long	String
PubDateTime	DateTime

Results:

Name	Type
Title	String

FIGURE 4-12 Data source detailed information found on the Details tab

Setting Up the Azure Account

To access the data in the Windows Azure Marketplace, you need an account. Account registration is free (again, at *https://datamarket.azure.com/*). (To register for an account, you first need a Windows Live ID.) Figure 4-13 shows the My Account page; take note of the Customer ID and Primary Account Key on your My Account page because you will need these in the future.

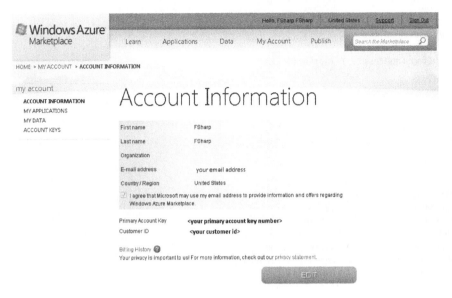

FIGURE 4-13 My Account page in the Windows Azure Marketplace

Connecting To and Consuming Data

You can use OData to connect to the data source. The OData type provider needs three parameters:

- Service URI API address: *https://api.datamarket.azure.com/Uk.Gov/TravelAdvisoryService/*

- Windows Live ID

- Primary Account Key from the Windows Azure Marketplace My Account page

The query code and partial execution result are shown in Listing 4-48.

LISTING 4-48 Connecting to the Windows Azure Marketplace by using OData

```
// define the type provider
type Demographics = Microsoft.FSharp.Data.TypeProviders.ODataService<ServiceUri =
    "https://api.datamarket.azure.com/Uk.Gov/TravelAdvisoryService/">

let ctx = Demographics.GetDataContext()

// set the credentials
ctx.Credentials <- System.Net.NetworkCredential(<liveID>, <id>)

// query the data source
let q = query {
    for n in ctx.BritishEmbassiesAndHighCommissions do
    select (n.Title, n.OfficeHours) }
```

```
// print out the result
q
|> Seq.iter (fun (address, _)-> printfn "%s" address)
```

Partial execution result

```
Australia, Hobart, British Honorary Consul
Australia, Adelaide, British Honorary Consul
Afghanistan, Kabul, British Embassy
Vietnam, Hanoi, British Council
Taiwan, Kaohsiung, British Council
Japan, Tokyo, British Council
Burma, Rangoon (Yangon), British Embassy
Australia, Canberra, Consular Section
New Zealand, Auckland, British Consulate-General
China, Guangzhou, British Consulate-General
Australia, Melbourne, British Consulate-General
Japan, Osaka, British Consulate-General
China, Shanghai, British Consulate-General
Australia, Brisbane, British Consulate
Australia, Perth, British Consulate
...
```

Good! The connection is working well, and the first query returns data. Now, let's find out about all
the UK embassies or consulates in China. You might be tempted to try to achieve this goal by placing
the *where* operator in the query. Unfortunately, the *where* keyword is not supported when executed
on the server side. Instead, the filter operation has to be done on the client. See Listing 4-49.

LISTING 4-49 Finding all UK embassies or consulates in China

```
// define the type provider
type Demographics = Microsoft.FSharp.Data.TypeProviders.ODataService<ServiceUri =
    "https://api.datamarket.azure.com/Uk.Gov/TravelAdvisoryService/">

let ctx = Demographics.GetDataContext()

// set the credentials
ctx.Credentials <- System.Net.NetworkCredential(<liveID>, <id>)

// query the data source
let q = query {
    for n in ctx.BritishEmbassiesAndHighCommissions do
    //where (n.Title.Contains("United States"))  // where is not supported on server side
    select (n.Title, n.OfficeHours) }

// print out the result
q
|> Seq.filter (fun (title, _) -> title.Contains("China"))
|> Seq.iter (fun (title, _)-> printfn "%s" title)
```

Execution result

```
China, Guangzhou, British Consulate-General
China, Shanghai, British Consulate-General
China, Chongqing, British Consulate-General
China, Beijing, British Embassy
China, Beijing, British Embassy, Cultural &amp; Education Section
```

You get a surprise when you use the same code to query for UK embassies in the United States. The query does not return any results. It is hard to believe that the UK does not have at least one embassy in the country. The reason is that this query returns only part of all the results. For performance reasons, it would not be a wise decision to return all the results at once. The query returns only one page of data for each query execution. The results shown in Listing 4-49 include only those from the first page of the total results. This is a good time to use the *skip* operator to ignore the previously retrieved data and return the next page of the query results, as shown in Listing 4-50.

LISTING 4-50 Finding all UK embassies or consulates in the United States by using *skip*

```
// define the type provider
type Demographics = Microsoft.FSharp.Data.TypeProviders.ODataService<ServiceUri =
    "https://api.datamarket.azure.com/Uk.Gov/TravelAdvisoryService/">

let ctx = Demographics.GetDataContext()

// set the credentials
ctx.Credentials <- System.Net.NetworkCredential(<liveID>, <id>)

// query pages
let rec queryFunction (startPoint) =
    seq {
        // query the data source
        let q = query {
            for n in ctx.BritishEmbassiesAndHighCommissions do
            skip startPoint
            select (n.Title, n.OfficeHours) }
        let count = Seq.length q
        if count <> 0 then
            for item in q do
                yield item
            for item in queryFunction(startPoint + count) do
                yield item
    }

// print out the result
queryFunction(0)
|> Seq.filter (fun (title, _) -> title.Contains("United States"))
|> Seq.iter (fun (title, _)-> printfn "%s" title)
```

Execution result

```
United States, Denver, British Consulate-General
United States, Atlanta, British Consulate-General
United States, Boston, British Consulate-General
United States, Chicago, British Consulate-General
United States, Houston, British Consulate-General
United States, Los Angeles, British Consulate-General
United States, New York, British Consulate-General
United States, San Francisco, British Consulate-General
United States, Miami, British Consulate-General
United States, Orlando, British Consulate
United States, Washington, British Embassy
United States, Anchorage, British Honorary Consulate
United States, Nashville, British Honorary Consulate
United States, New Orleans, British Honorary Consulate
United States, Philadelphia, British Honorary Consulate
United States, Phoenix, British Honorary Consulate
United States, Pittsburgh, British Honorary Consulate
United States, Salt Lake City, British Honorary Consulate
United States, Charlotte, British Honorary Consulate
United States, Michigan, British Honorary Consulate
United States, Minnesota, British Honorary Consulate
United States, Ohio, British Honorary Consulate
```

Performing Translations with Microsoft Translator

As mentioned in the previous section, the OData type provider does not work with "fixed query" datasets. Although the number of datasets that support only fixed queries is insignificant, it's good to know how to interact with them when needed. In this section, I'll use the Microsoft Translator, which supports only a fixed-query dataset, to demonstrate how to use F# to work with fixed-query datasets.

Any dataset that supports a fixed query provides a pre-created proxy class for the dataset. The proxy class file is available on the dataset Details page after you make a purchase from Azure Marketplace. In Figure 4-14, the C# proxy class file is shown in the upper-right portion of the page. You need to download this file and make a C# class library for the main F# project to reference. I am not going to go through how to create and reference a C# project. The F# code in Listing 4-51 shows how to invoke the proxy class.

Thank You

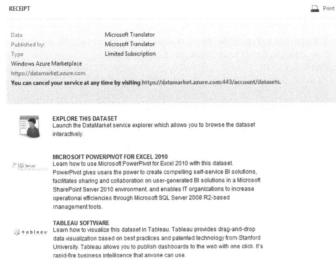

RECEIPT

🖨 Print

Data	Microsoft Translator
Published by:	Microsoft Translator
Type	Limited Subscription

Windows Azure Marketplace
https://datamarket.azure.com

You can cancel your service at any time by visiting https://datamarket.azure.com:443/account/datasets.

EXPLORE THIS DATASET
Launch the DataMarket service explorer which allows you to browse the dataset interactively.

MICROSOFT POWERPIVOT FOR EXCEL 2010
Learn how to use Microsoft PowerPivot for Excel 2010 with this dataset. PowerPivot gives users the power to create compelling self-service BI solutions, facilitates sharing and collaboration on user-generated BI solutions in a Microsoft SharePoint Server 2010 environment, and enables IT organizations to increase operational efficiencies through Microsoft SQL Server 2008 R2-based management tools.

TABLEAU SOFTWARE
Learn how to visualize this dataset in Tableau. Tableau provides drag-and-drop data visualization based on best practices and patented technology from Stanford University. Tableau allows you to publish dashboards to the web with one click. It's rapid-fire business intelligence that anyone can use.

🔲 .NET C# Class Library ❓

🔲 Language codes for Microsoft Translator (ISO 693-1)
This page provides a listing of language codes for use with Microsoft Translator/Bing Translator.

🔲 Microsoft Translator - Developer Offerings
Microsoft Translator offers developers a wide spectrum of translation and language APIs for integration into applications and services.

FIGURE 4-14 Proxy class file for fixed-query dataset

LISTING 4-51 Invoking the C# proxy class from F#

```
open System.Linq

// define a translate function by taking an English sentence and translating it to
Chinese let translate txt =
    let serviceRootUri =
        new System.Uri("https://api.datamarket.azure.com/Bing/MicrosoftTranslator/")

    // the account key is the same as in the previous section
    let accountKey = <id>

    // create a translator container that is defined in the proxy class
    let tc = Microsoft.TranslatorContainer(serviceRootUri)
    tc.Credentials <- new System.Net.NetworkCredential(accountKey, accountKey)

    //translate from English(en) to Chinese (zh-CHS)
    let translationQuery = tc.Translate(txt, "zh-CHS", "en")
    let translationResult = translationQuery.Execute().ToList().FirstOrDefault()

    // if there is no translation result, something went wrong so return empty string
    if (translationResult = null) then
        System.String.Empty
    else
        translationResult.Text
```

You can use this translation service to translate recent news from English to Chinese, as shown in Listing 4-52.

LISTING 4-52 Translating the latest news from English to Chinese with Microsoft Translator

```
// define the type provider
type Demographics = Microsoft.FSharp.Data.TypeProviders.ODataService<ServiceUri =
    "https://api.datamarket.azure.com/Uk.Gov/TravelAdvisoryService/">
let ctx = Demographics.GetDataContext()

// set the credentials
ctx.Credentials <- System.Net.NetworkCredential(<liveID>, <id>)

//get latest news
let latestNews = query {
    for n in ctx.LatestTravelNewsFromFco do
    select (n.Title, n.Summary)
}

latestNews
|> Seq.map fst            // only leave title to translate
|> Seq.map translate      //translate from English to Chinese
|> Seq.iter (fun n -> printfn "%s" n)


Execution result
恶劣天气影响整个欧洲的旅行
下个星期为欧洲足球赛事旅游忠告
西班牙机场中断
象牙海岸的旅游建议的变化
玻利维亚旅游忠告-鲁雷纳瓦克在封锁
在欧洲旅行的中断
澳大利亚旅游忠告-东澳大利亚的水浸
美国旅游忠告-暴雪条件
旅游忠告-尤文图斯 v 曼城
希腊旅游忠告-工业行动
. . .
```

 Note You need to install Chinese locally on your computer to see Chinese characters in the console output.

The actual execution result is pretty long; the result shown is only part of the result set.

Storing Data Locally

You might be wondering how to serialize or deserialize the data from Windows Azure Marketplace. I cover two approaches in this section. One shows you how to do the serialization programmatically, and the other shows you how to save the content to a Microsoft Excel file.

Performing Serialization

The topic of .NET serialization could be expanded into a 50-page chapter, so I'll leave that for you to explore on your own. In this section, I present the JSON and XML serializers. The first example in Listing 4-53 shows how to use the JSON serializer. The example demonstrates how to serialize and deserialize a tuple instance.

LISTING 4-53 Use JSON serialization

```
open System.Runtime.Serialization.Json
open System.Runtime.Serialization

let serializeAndDeserialize (originalValue:'T) =

    // Create a serializer to serialize the data
    let serializer = DataContractJsonSerializer(typeof<'T>)
    use out = new System.IO.MemoryStream()
    printfn "input data is %A" originalValue
    serializer.WriteObject(out, originalValue)

    // Get the serialized text
    let text = out.ToArray() |> System.Text.Encoding.UTF8.GetString
    out.Seek(0L, System.IO.SeekOrigin.Begin) |> ignore
    printfn "serialized data as: %s" text

    let deserializedValue = serializer.ReadObject out
    printfn "deserialized the data as: %A" deserializedValue

serializeAndDeserialize (1,2)
```

Execution result
```
input data is (1, 2)
serialized data as: {"m_Item1":1,"m_Item2":2}
deserialized the data as: (1, 2)
```

If the XML serializer is your favorite, Listing 4-54 shows you how to serialize the data to an XML file by using it. The sample demonstrates how to serialize and deserialize data from the UK government Travel Advisory Service to and from a local XML file.

LISTING 4-54 Serializing and deserializing data from Windows Azure Marketplace by using XML serialization

```
// declare a NewsRecord class
type NewsRecord() =
    member val Title = System.String.Empty with get, set
    member val Summary = System.String.Empty with get, set
```

```
// define the type provider
type Demographics = Microsoft.FSharp.Data.TypeProviders.ODataService<ServiceUri =
    "https://api.datamarket.azure.com/Uk.Gov/TravelAdvisoryService/">
let ctx = Demographics.GetDataContext()

// set the credentials
ctx.Credentials <- System.Net.NetworkCredential(<liveID>, <id>)

// query the latest news
let latestNews = query {
    for n in ctx.LatestTravelNewsFromFco do
    select (NewsRecord(Title = n.Title, Summary = n.Summary))
}

// query the latest news
let latestNews = query {
    for n in ctx.LatestTravelNewsFromFco do
    select { NewsRecord.Title = n.Title; NewsRecord.Summary = n.Summary}
}

let news = latestNews |> Seq.toArray

// deserialize from xml
let deserialize<'T> (fileName:string) =
    let reader = System.Xml.Serialization.XmlSerializer(typeof<'T>)
    use file = new System.IO.StreamReader(fileName)
    let fileData = reader.Deserialize(file) :?> 'T
    fileData

// serialize data
let serialize data (fileName:string)=
    let writer = System.Xml.Serialization.XmlSerializer(data.GetType());
    use file = new System.IO.StreamWriter(fileName)
    writer.Serialize(file, data);

//serialize the data
serialize news "myLocalNews.xml"

// deserialize the file
let data = deserialize<NewsRecord array> "myLocalNews.xml"
```

Serialized XML file

```
<?xml version="1.0" encoding="utf-8"?>
<ArrayOfNewsRecord xmlns:xsi="http://www.w3.org/2001/XMLSchema-instance"
xmlns:xsd="http://www.w3.org/2001/XMLSchema">
  <NewsRecord>
    <Title>Severe weather affecting travel across Europe</Title>
    <Summary>Adverse weather conditions are affecting travel across Europe, and
there are airport
 closures and flight cancellations in the UK.</Summary>
  </NewsRecord>
```

```
<NewsRecord>
  <Title>Travel advice for European football matches next week</Title>
  <Summary>Chelsea, Rangers and Spurs are playing in Europe next week. Check our
travel advice
for fans if you're going to the matches.</Summary>
</NewsRecord>
...
```

Note Only part of the execution result is shown.

Exporting to Microsoft Excel

XML and JSON serialization are very useful to a programmer, but the result is definitely not for the average user. In Listing 4-55, I'll you show how to use F# to write the cloud data into an Excel file. The sample retrieves the data from Azure, opens the Excel file, and inserts the title from cells B1 to B100 and the summary from cells C1 to C100.

LISTING 4-55 Inserting the title and summary from Azure to Excel

```
open Microsoft.Office.Interop.Excel

// Run Excel
let app = new ApplicationClass(Visible = true)

// Create a new file, and get the 1st worksheet
let workbook = app.Workbooks.Add(XlWBATemplate.xlWBATWorksheet)

// Note that worksheets are started from 1 not 0
let worksheet = (workbook.Worksheets.[1] :?> Worksheet)

// define the type provider
type Demographics = Microsoft.FSharp.Data.TypeProviders.ODataService<ServiceUri =
    "https://api.datamarket.azure.com/Uk.Gov/TravelAdvisoryService/">
let ctx = Demographics.GetDataContext()

// set the credentials
ctx.Credentials <- System.Net.NetworkCredential(<liveID>, <id>)

// declare a NewsRecord class
type NewsRecord() =
    member val Title = System.String.Empty with get, set
    member val Summary = System.String.Empty with get, set

// query the latest news
let latestNews = query {
    for n in ctx.LatestTravelNewsFromFco do
    select (NewsRecord(Title = n.Title, Summary = n.Summary))
}
```

```
let news = latestNews |> Seq.toArray

// get the range tuple such as "A1", "A10"
let getRangeStrings columnName news =
    let start = sprintf "%c%d" columnName 1
    let ''end'' = sprintf "%c%d" columnName (news |> Seq.length)
    start, ''end''

let len = news.Length

// get range tuple, which contains start and end
let range0 = (getRangeStrings 'B' news)
let range1 = (getRangeStrings 'C' news)

// insert title to B column
(worksheet.Range (fst range0, snd range0)).Value2 <- Array2D.init len 1 (fun x _ ->
news.[x].Title)

// insert summary to C column
(worksheet.Range (fst range1, snd range1)).Value2 <- Array2D.init len 1 (fun x _ ->
news.[x].Summary)
```

 Note A reference to the *Microsoft.Excel.Interop.dll* is needed to invoke the Excel function.

Generating a Word Document

In addition to an Excel file, you can also export data to a Microsoft Word file by using the Office OpenXML SDK, which can be downloaded from *http://www.microsoft.com/en-us/download/details.aspx?id=5124*. The sample presented in this section is used to generate a notification letter for students who pass an exam. The pass/fail information is stored in the database. The type provider queries the database and filters out the students who have passed the exam. The students' information is then passed to various OpenXML methods to generate the Word documents. Listing 4-56 creates the table in a SQL Server database. The table has three columns:

- **Name**   Student name, which is also the keyword

- **Course**   Course name

- **Passed**   Boolean value to indicate whether the student passed the exam

```
CREATE TABLE [dbo].[StudentScoreTable](
    [Name] [nvarchar](50) NOT NULL,
    [Course] [nchar](64) NULL,
    [Passed] [bit] NULL,
 CONSTRAINT [PK_StudentScoreTable] PRIMARY KEY CLUSTERED
(
    [Name] ASC
)WITH (PAD_INDEX  = OFF, STATISTICS_NORECOMPUTE  = OFF,
    IGNORE_DUP_KEY = OFF, ALLOW_ROW_LOCKS  = ON, ALLOW_PAGE_LOCKS  = ON) ON [PRIMARY]
) ON [PRIMARY]


Insert test record data
insert into StudentScoreTable(Name,Course, Passed)
Values('Brent', 'History', 1)

insert into StudentScoreTable(Name,Course, Passed)
Values('Chris', 'Math', 1)

insert into StudentScoreTable(Name,Course, Passed)
Values('Anita', 'History', 1)

insert into StudentScoreTable(Name,Course, Passed)
Values('Andy', 'Math', 0)
```

The code in Listing 4-57 is F# code. It retrieves data from the database by using the SQL type provider. The *generatePassLetter* function is used to generate the Word document for students who pass the exam. The execution for this sample code generates three files, for the students named Anita, Chris, and Brent. Andy did not pass the exam, so there is no file for him.

LISTING 4-57 Generating Word documents from the type provider query results

```
open System
open System.Linq
open DocumentFormat.OpenXml
open DocumentFormat.OpenXml.Packaging
open DocumentFormat.OpenXml.Wordprocessing
open Microsoft.FSharp.Data.TypeProviders
open Microsoft.FSharp.Linq.NullableOperators

type T = SqlDataConnection<"<your connection to the database>">
let t = T.GetDataContext()

let passedCandidates = query {
    for student in t.StudentScoreTable do
    where (student.Passed ?= true)
    select (student.Name, student.Course) }
```

```fsharp
// generate pass letter using OpenXML SDK
let generatePassLetter record =
    let name, course = record
    let filePath = sprintf @".\%s.docx" name
    let myDoc = WordprocessingDocument.Create(filePath, WordprocessingDocumentType.
Document)

    // Add a new main document part.
    let mainPart = myDoc.AddMainDocumentPart()

    //Create Document tree
    mainPart.Document <- Document()

    //Create Body
    let body = Body()

    //Create paragraph
    let createParagraph text =
        let paragraph = Paragraph()
        let run_paragraph = Run()

        // put text
        let text_paragraph = Text text

        //Append elements.
        ignore <| run_paragraph.AppendChild(text_paragraph)
        ignore <| paragraph.AppendChild(run_paragraph)

        // return paragraph
        paragraph

    //create a paragraph with text
    let paragraph0 =
            createParagraph
                (sprintf "Dear %s" name)
    let paragraph1 =
            createParagraph
                (sprintf "Congratulations! You passed %s" course)

    [paragraph0; paragraph1]
    |> List.iter (body.AppendChild>>ignore)

    ignore <| mainPart.Document.AppendChild(body)

    // Save changes
    mainPart.Document.Save()

    // close the document and save all changes
    myDoc.Close()

// generate letters for all passing students
passedCandidates
|> Seq.iter generatePassLetter
```

Note You need to add a reference to *DocumentFormat.OpenXml.dll*, *FSharp.Data.TypeProviders.dll*, *System.Data.dll*, *System.Data.Linq.dll*, *System.Xml.dll*, and *WindowsBase.dll* to make the project compile.

List.iter requires that the provided function returns *unit*. *AppendChild* returns a non-unit type. By using >> and the *ignore* function, you can get a new function that returns *unit*. If you forget how to use the |>, <|, <<, and >> operators, you can refer to the "Pipeline-Forward Operator" section in Chapter 1.

CHAPTER 5

Write Your Own Type Provider

There are four built-in type providers in F# 3.0. If you've wondered how to make a type provider that can be used to interpret data—such as the data in a database, in the cloud, or in an XML file—this chapter will show you how to do it.

What Is a Type Provider?

As I mentioned at the beginning of Chapter 4, "Type Providers," the type provider is an adapter component that reads the underlying information schema and converts it to types in .NET. The information can be from data stores, services, or any other source of structured data. The type-generation process is known as the provided type. The type generated from a type provider can be picked up by Microsoft IntelliSense. In addition to the class type and members, the type provider can provide metadata such as a description of each column in a database table. These descriptions appear as tooltips. The type provider provides compile-time meta-programming support. This definition might seem heavy and difficult to digest. If that is the case, don't worry. As more and more type provider samples are presented, different aspects of the type provider will be examined and things will become clear.

You need to understand that the type provider types and methods are generated in a lazy way. The lazy generation decreases the code size. Imagine you have a complex database schema and your code accesses only one table in the database. The erased type provider generates only the code for that particular table. This allows the provided type space to be large and even infinite. The built-in type providers use *type generation*, which involves wrapping existing code-generation tools. This chapter focuses on how to write the erased type provider and the generated type provider. The *erased type provider* provides types that will be erased to other types, such as *System.Object*. The following statement is from MSDN (*http://msdn.microsoft.com/en-us/library/hh361034.aspx#BK_Erased*):

> Each provided type is erased to type **obj**, and all uses of the type will appear as type **obj** in compiled code. In fact, the underlying objects in these examples are strings, but the type will appear as **Object** in .NET compiled code. As with all uses of type erasure, you can use explicit boxing, unboxing, and casting to subvert erased types. In this case, a cast exception that isn't valid may result when the object is used. A provider runtime can define its own private representation type to help protect against false representations. You can't define erased types in F# itself. Only provided types may be erased. You must understand the ramifications,

both practical and semantic, of using either erased types for your type provider or a provider that provides erased types. An erased type has no real .NET type. Therefore, you cannot do accurate reflection over the type, and you might subvert erased types if you use runtime casts and other techniques that rely on exact runtime type semantics. Subversion of erased types frequently results in type cast exceptions at runtime.

The erased type provider generates types that exist only at design time, whereas the generated type provider generates a real type that is compiled in the assembly.

Setting Up the Development Environment

F# provides an API that you can use to write your own type providers. The type-provider author requires several files. A type-provider template is available to help make the type-provider authoring process easier. The type-provider template contains several API files that are also published on the F# Sample Pack site (*http://fsharp3sample.codeplex.com/*). The type-provider feature is new in F# 3.0 and, as such, will not work with previous versions of F#.

> **Note** It is highly recommended that you use Microsoft Visual Studio 2012 to author type providers.

As an alternative to performing a manual setup of the Visual Studio solution and project, you can use a Visual Studio template package published at the Visual Studio Gallery, which can be downloaded from *http://visualstudiogallery.msdn.microsoft.com/43d00ffd-1b9a-4581-a942-da85b6a83b9c*. After the package is installed, the type-provider project can be created via the New Project dialog box, as shown in Figure 5-1.

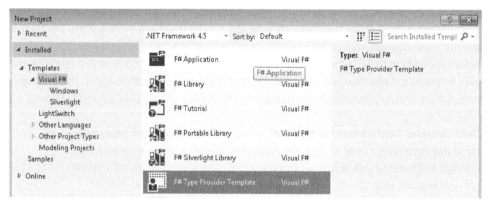

FIGURE 5-1 Type-provider project template

The type-provider project is a class library project, and it contains four files. The type-provider class, which is named *TypeProvider1.fs*, is the backbone of the project. It contains the type-provider code. *TestScript.fsx* is a script file that can be used to test the type provider. The generated project is shown in Figure 5-2.

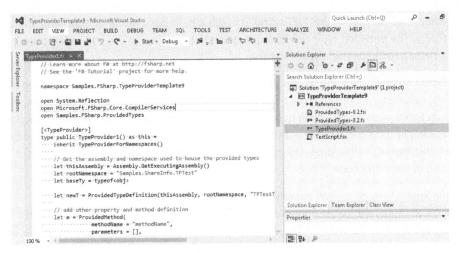

FIGURE 5-2 Generated files from the Type Provider template

Listing 5-1 contains the code needed to reference a type provider. The type-provider type is denoted as the provided type, and the method and property is denoted as a provided method and provided property. The first line adds a reference to the Type Provider dynamic-link library (DLL). After the reference is ready, the second and third lines create the provided type and assign it to the value named *t*.

It is a good practice to first design how an end user will invoke the type provider. For example, *TPTestType* should have a parameterless constructor that does not require any special initialization code. Also, it has a property called *Property1*.

LISTING 5-1 Type-provider test file

```
#r @".\bin\Debug\TypeProviderTemplate9.dll"

type T = Samples.ShareInfo.TPTest.TPTestType
let t = T()

let c = t.Property1
t.Property1 <- "aa"
printfn "methodName() = %A" (t.methodName())


Execution result
setter code
methodName() = 2
```

The type-provider class code is shown in Listing 5-2. As you saw in Listing 5-1, the class should have a parameterless constructor and one property. The type-provider class should inherit from the *TypeProviderFromNamespaces* class and be decorated with the *TypeProvider* attribute. The type-provider type is created by the *ProvidedTypeDefinition* class. There are four parameters and, for now, only two of them are of interest to us. The namespace is specified when the *ProvidedTypeDefinition* instance is created. Like all types in the .NET world, it needs a base class. In the sample code, the base type is *typeof<obj>*. The provided type definition, named *newT*, is added at the end of the code, by calling *AddNamespace* with the namespace variable.

Once the type is created, the method and property are easy to understand. *ProvidedMethod* takes a method name, parameters, a return type, a Boolean that indicates whether or not the property is static, and a function that contains a code quotation that will be executed whenever the method is invoked. In the sample code, *InvokeCode* is 1+1, so it will always return *2*. The property is added by creating a *ProvidedProperty* with a property name, a property type, an indication of whether it is static or not, and *getter/setter* code.

The function logic has to be a code quotation. The code quotation is a tree structure that represents F# code. There is no direct equivalent in C#. You can think of it as being like C# LINQ. There are two ways to generate an F# code quotation. One is to use <@@ and @@> operators, and the other way is to use *Expr* functions. Both approaches can generates the same code quotation, so you can choose either way. The sample code in this chapter demonstrates both ways to generate code quotation.

The F# class cannot be instantiated without a constructor; therefore, the constructor is mandatory for a type-provider type, although in most cases it does nothing. *ProvidedConstructor* takes no parameters, and the constructor code does nothing. The provided method, property, and constructor are finally added to the *ProvidedTypeDefinition* variable *newT* by invoking the *AddMember* function.

LISTING 5-2 Generated type-provider code

```
namespace Samples.FSharp.HelloWorldTypeProvider

open System.Reflection
open Microsoft.FSharp.Core.CompilerServices
open Samples.FSharp.ProvidedTypes

[<TypeProvider>]
type public TypeProvider1() as this =
    inherit TypeProviderForNamespaces()

    // Get the assembly and namespace used to house the provided types
    let thisAssembly = Assembly.GetExecutingAssembly()
    let rootNamespace = "Samples.ShareInfo.TPTest"
    let baseTy = typeof<obj>

    let newT = ProvidedTypeDefinition(thisAssembly, rootNamespace, "TPTestType", Some
baseTy)
```

```
// add other property and method definition
let m = ProvidedMethod(
            methodName = "methodName",
            parameters = [],
            returnType = typeof<int>,
            IsStaticMethod = false,
            InvokeCode = fun args ->
                <@@ 1 + 1 @@>
            )

let ctor = ProvidedConstructor(parameters = [], InvokeCode = fun args -> <@@ (* base
class
initialization or null*) () @@>)

let prop2 = ProvidedProperty(propertyName = "Property1",
                             propertyType = typeof<string>,
                             IsStatic=false,
                             GetterCode= (fun args -> <@@ "Hello!" @@>),
                             SetterCode = (fun args -> <@@ printfn "setter code" @@>))

do prop2.AddXmlDocDelayed(fun () -> "xml comment")
do
    newT.AddMember(m)
    newT.AddMember(prop2)
    newT.AddMember(ctor)

do this.AddNamespace(rootNamespace, [newT])

[<TypeProviderAssembly>]
do ()
```

Note Other functions and attributes will be covered in later sections.

The test script is lightweight and good for testing and debugging a small type provider, but it is not the only way to do that. For complex type providers, using two instances of Visual Studio is a better choice. Use one instance of Visual Studio to develop the type provider and refer to that instance as *Developing Visual Studio*. Use the other instance of Visual Studio to host the testing project, and refer to it as *Testing Visual Studio*. *Developing Visual Studio* needs to attach to the testing Visual Studio.

Tip Because the type-provider DLL is locked by Visual Studio, restarting Visual Studio is unavoidable. If the test script is used, make sure that the script file is not the current file when you are closing the project; otherwise, it will be opened automatically and consequently lock the DLL the next time that the project is opened.

Exploring the HelloWorld Type Provider

If you understood the F# type-provider template code from the prior section, the HelloWorld type-provider example in this section will be easy for you to follow. However, if any of the code presented in the last section is not clear, the HelloWorld type provider example will provide some clarity. This type-provider example has five methods and five properties. Listing 5-3, which defines how users invoke the HelloWorld type provider, can be used to design and test the type provider.

LISTING 5-3 HelloWorld type-provider test script

```
#r @".\bin\Debug\HelloWorldTypeProvider.dll"

let assertFunction x =
    if not x then failwith "expression is false"

type T = Samples.ShareInfo.TPTest.HelloTypeProvider
let t = T()
assertFunction( t.Method1() = 1 )
assertFunction( t.Method2() = 2 )
assertFunction( t.Method3() = 3 )
assertFunction( t.Method4() = 4 )
assertFunction( t.Method5() = 5 )
assertFunction( t.Property6 = "Property 6")
assertFunction( t.Property7 = "Property 7")
assertFunction( t.Property8 = "Property 8")
assertFunction( t.Property9 = "Property 9")
assertFunction( t.Property10 = "Property 10")
```

Note In Listing 5-3, *assert* is the F# keyword used to check for a TRUE/FALSE value, but it works only when the DEBUG symbol is defined. In the sample, a user-defined function named *assert* is used instead.

First create the Type Provider project using the Type Provider template with **HelloWorldTypeProvider** as the project name. (See Figure 5-3.) The template, which can be downloaded from *http://visualstudiogallery.msdn.microsoft.com/43d00ffd-1b9a-4581-a942-da85b6a83b9c*, has four files created by default. The *TypeProvider1.fs* file is where the type-provider code will be placed.

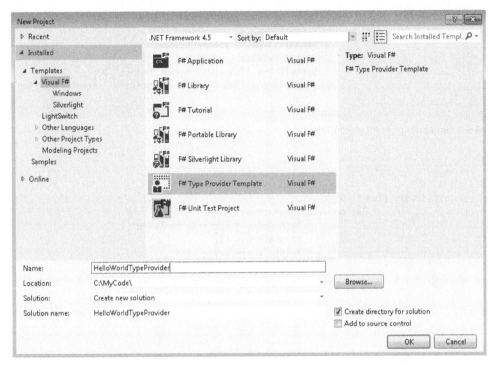

FIGURE 5-3 Create the HelloWorld type-provider project

Because the type provider generates a type named *HelloWorldTypeProvider*, *ProvidedTypeDefinition* needs *"HelloWorldTypeProvider"* to be provided as the third parameter in the constructor:

```
let newT = ProvidedTypeDefinition(thisAssembly, rootNamespace, "HelloWorldTypeProvider", Some
baseTy)
```

As mentioned previously, the type provider has five methods and five properties. The template adds the code to generate a single method and property (as shown in Listing 5-4) by creating *ProvidedMethod* and *ProvidedProperty*. As a result, it is not difficult to add a *List.map* to the generated code so that five methods and five properties (which you can see in Listing 5-5) are generated by the type provider.

LISTING 5-4 *ProvidedMethod* and *ProvidedProperty*

```
let m = ProvidedMethod(
        methodName = "methodName",
        parameters = [],
        returnType = typeof<int>,
        IsStaticMethod = false,
        InvokeCode = fun args ->
            <@@ 1 + 1 @@>
        )
```

```
let prop2 = ProvidedProperty(propertyName = "Property1",
                             propertyType = typeof<string>,
                             IsStatic=false,
                             GetterCode= (fun args -> <@@ "Hello!" @@>),
                             SetterCode = (fun args -> <@@ printfn "setter code" @@>))
```

LISTING 5-5 Generating five *ProvidedMethod* and *ProvidedProperty* instances

```
let ms =
    [ 1..5 ]
    |> List.map (fun i ->
                    let m = ProvidedMethod(
                                methodName = sprintf "Method%d" i,
                                parameters = [],
                                returnType = typeof<int>,
                                IsStaticMethod = false,
                                InvokeCode = fun args ->
                                <@@ i @@>)
                    m)

let props =
    [ 6..10 ]
    |> List.map (fun i ->
                    let prop2 = ProvidedProperty(propertyName = sprintf "Property%d"
i,
                                propertyType = typeof<string>,
                                IsStatic=false,
                                GetterCode= (fun args -> <@@ sprintf "Property %d" i
@@>),
                                SetterCode = (fun args -> <@@ () @@>))
                    prop2.AddXmlDocDelayed(fun () -> sprintf "xml comment for
Property%d" i)
                    prop2)
```

Because the default constructor is good enough for the HelloWorldTypeProvider project, you can now add a *ProvidedMethod* list, a *ProvidedProperty* list, and a constructor to the *ProvidedTypeDefinition*. (See Listing 5-6.) The code for the type provider after these changes are made is shown in Listing 5-7.

LISTING 5-6 Adding *ProvidedMethod*, *ProvidedProperty*, and constructor instances

```
do
    ms |> Seq.iter newT.AddMember
    props |> Seq.iter newT.AddMember
    newT.AddMember(ctor)
```

LISTING 5-7 HelloWorldTypeProvider code

```fsharp
// Learn more about F# at http://fsharp.net
// See the 'F# Tutorial' project for more help.

namespace Samples.FSharp.HelloWorldTypeProvider


open System.Reflection
open Microsoft.FSharp.Core.CompilerServices
open Samples.FSharp.ProvidedTypes

[<TypeProvider>]
type public TypeProvider1() as this =
    inherit TypeProviderForNamespaces()

    // Get the assembly and namespace used to house the provided types
    let thisAssembly = Assembly.GetExecutingAssembly()
    let rootNamespace = "Samples.ShareInfo.TPTest"
    let baseTy = typeof<obj>

    let newT = ProvidedTypeDefinition(thisAssembly, rootNamespace,
"HelloWorldTypeProvider",
                                        Some baseTy)


    // add other property and method definition
    let ms =
        [ 1..5 ]
        |> List.map (fun i ->
                    let m = ProvidedMethod(
                                methodName = sprintf "Method%d" i,
                                parameters = [],
                                returnType = typeof<int>,
                                IsStaticMethod = false,
                                InvokeCode = fun args ->
                                <@@ i @@>
                    m)

    let ctor = ProvidedConstructor(parameters = [],
                                InvokeCode = fun args ->
                                            <@@ (* base class initialization or
null*) () @@>)

    let props =
        [ 6..10 ]
        |> List.map (fun i ->
                    let prop2 =
                        ProvidedProperty(
                            propertyName = sprintf "Property%d" i,
                            propertyType = typeof<string>,
                            IsStatic=false,
```

```
                              GetterCode= (fun args -> <@@ sprintf "Property %d" i
@@>),

                              SetterCode = (fun args -> <@@ () @@>))
                     prop2.AddXmlDocDelayed(fun () -> sprintf "xml comment for
Property%d" i)
                     prop2)

    do
        ms |> Seq.iter newT.AddMember
        props |> Seq.iter newT.AddMember
        newT.AddMember(ctor)

    do this.AddNamespace(rootNamespace, [newT])

[<TypeProviderAssembly>]
do ()
```

Because most of the work is done by the template, the basic rules to write a simple type provider are as follows:

- The type-provider type is defined by *ProvidedTypeDefinition*.

- If a method is needed, create an instance of the *ProvidedMethod* type and add it to the *ProvidedTypeDefinition* instance.

- If a property is needed, create an instance of the *ProvidedProperty* type and add it to the *ProvidedTypeDefinition* instance.

- You will always need a constructor, and it also needs to be added to the *ProvidedTypeDefinition* instance. The default constructor that is generated by the template is good for most cases.

As long as the F# snippet add-on and latest snippet-file Visual Studio extensions are installed, the snippet to generate *ProvidedMethod*, *ProvidedProperty*, and *ProvidedConstructor* is under Type Providers And Query, Write Type Provider, as shown in Figure 5-4. The F# code snippet add-on can be downloaded from *http://visualstudiogallery.msdn.microsoft.com/d19080ad-d44c-46ae-b65c-55cede5f708b*, and the latest snippet file is located as an open source project at *http://fsharpcodesnippet.codeplex.com/*.

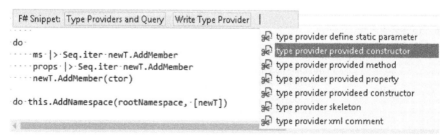

FIGURE 5-4 Code snippet to generate *ProvidedConstructor*, *ProvidedProperty*, and *ProvidedMethod*

Using the Regular-Expression Type Provider

As you know, the type provider is used to generate a new type with class members, such as methods and properties. HelloWorldTypeProvider generates class members from a predefined data schema. The predefined data schema in this case requires five methods and five properties. As software developers, we always look for something that can be created programmatically. Is there any way to create the class members from some variable passed in by a user? The answer is "Yes." The regular-expression type provider dynamically generates class members based on a regular-expression parameter passed in by a user, as shown in Listing 5-8.

LISTING 5-8 Invoking a regular-expression type provider

```
type T = Samples.ShareInfo.TPTest.RegularExpressionTypeProvider<
            @"(?<AreaCode>^\d{3})-(?<PhoneNumber>\d{3}-\d{4}$)" >
let reg = T()
let result = T.IsMatch("425-555-2345")
let r = reg.Match("425-555-2345").AreaCode.Value
```

The first line in the listing shows how the type provider takes the parameters between < and >. This is the most common way for a type provider to get parameters. The third line shows a static method, but this is not a problem because *ProvidedMethod* can take `IsStaticMethod = true`. The last line is the most interesting part. The *Match* function returns a variable that has an *AreaCode* property. But the *AreaCode* property does not look like any standard .NET property. It is a generated property from the regular-expression group *AreaCode*. From the preceding analysis, something is needed to take and interpret the regular-expression pattern string and the type provider needs at least two types. One is the type-provider type, and the other one is a type with an *AreaCode* property.

First you need to get the regular-expression pattern string. To parameterize the type provider, you pass a list of *ProvidedStaticParameters* containing the name and type of each parameter to the *DefineStaticParameter* method, along with an instantiation callback function, as shown in Listing 5-9. At runtime, values the user supplies for each static parameter will be passed into the second argument of the callback function in the same order that they were defined.

LISTING 5-9 Getting the type-provider static parameter

```
let staticParams = [ProvidedStaticParameter("pattern", typeof<string>)]

do newT.DefineStaticParameters(
        parameters=staticParams,
        instantiationFunction=(fun typeName parameterValues ->
          ... .
          ))
```

Therefore, when using static parameters, the creation of additional types and members must be performed inside the callback function. Consequently, the type provider's code structure changes as shown in Listing 5-10. The only change from HelloWorldTypeProvider is that now the operation must be performed on the *ty* variable defined inside the instantiation function. The instantiation function must return a new type. If *RegexTypeProvider* can be viewed as a generic type and the regular-expression pattern string as a type parameter, the type returned from the instantiation function is a new type after applying the type parameter. In Listing 5-8, the type *T* was the new type returned from the instantiation function. This new type is the target to which you attach properties and methods.

LISTING 5-10 Type with a static parameter

```
let staticParams = [ProvidedStaticParameter("pattern", typeof<string>)]

do newT.DefineStaticParameters(
       parameters=staticParams,
       instantiationFunction=(fun typeName parameterValues ->
          match parameterValues with
          | [| :? string as pattern|] ->
             let ty = ProvidedTypeDefinition(
                thisAssembly,
                rootNamespace,
                typeName,
                Some baseTy,
                HideObjectMethods = true)

             let ctor = ProvidedConstructor(
                             parameters = [],
                             InvokeCode = fun args ->
                                <@@ (* base class initialization or null*)
() @@>)

                 ty.AddMember(ctor)

                 ty
       ))
```

> **Note** The *HideObjectMethods* property determines whether the object method, such as *ToString*, can be shown in IntelliSense.

To make the *IsMatch* static method work, a few problems need to be solved:

- How to define a provided function with a parameter
- How to get parameter values inside of the provided method

In Listing 5-11, function parameters are defined using *ProvidedParameter*, which requires a parameter name and parameter type. The parameter passed into the function is named *args*, and it is of type *Expr* list. The way to get the value out of the *Expr* list is to use a quotation splicing operator (%%) and specify its type. Because the function is a static method, the first element in the *args* list is the parameter you want. If the method is not a static method, %%args.[0] is the pointer to the instance.

LISTING 5-11 The *IsMatch* method

```
let m = ProvidedMethod(
                methodName = "IsMatch",
                parameters = [ ProvidedParameter("input", typeof<string>) ],
                returnType = typeof<bool>,
                IsStaticMethod = true,
                InvokeCode = fun args ->
                <@@
                    System.Text.RegularExpressions.Regex.IsMatch((%%args.[0]:string),
pattern)
                @@>)

ty.AddMember(m)
```

> **Note** Both % and %% are quotation splicing operators. Their job is to enable a user to insert a code expression object into a quotation. The difference between % and %% is that % inserts a typed expression but %% inserts an untyped expression. In the code sample just shown, *args* is an F# expression, and the %% operator converts the expression into a quotation.

The last line in Listing 5-8 returns a type that has an *AreaCode* property, which is a group name defined in the regular-expression pattern string. As a result, a new type is needed to host this property, and it can be returned from the *Match* method. (See Listing 5-12.) The new type is named *matchTy*. It is created and used as the return type for *matchMethod*. The group names are retrieved, and the *AreaCode* property is added to *matchTy*. The property assumes its parent object is *System. Text.RegularExpressions.Match* type.

LISTING 5-12 Implementing the *Match* method

```
let matchTy = ProvidedTypeDefinition("Match",
                                baseType = Some baseTy,
                                HideObjectMethods = true)

for group in r.GetGroupNames() do
    // ignore the group named 0, which represents all input
    if group <> "0" then
        let prop = ProvidedProperty(
                    propertyName = group,
```

```
                    propertyType = typeof<System.Text.RegularExpressions.Group>,
                    GetterCode =
                      fun args ->
                      <@@
                      ((%%args.[0]:obj):?>System.Text.RegularExpressions.Match).Groups.
        [group]
                      @@>)

            matchTy.AddMember prop

    let matchMethod =
        ProvidedMethod(
            methodName = "Match",
            parameters = [ProvidedParameter("input", typeof<string>)],
            returnType = matchTy,
            InvokeCode =
              fun args ->
              <@@
              ((%%args.[0]:obj):?>System.Text.RegularExpressions.Regex).Match(%%args.
        [1]):>obj
              @@>)

    ty.AddMember(matchMethod)

    ty.AddMember(matchTy)
```

A little extra code is needed in the *matchTy* constructor, because the *AreaCode* property needs its calling object to be a *Match* type. Listing 5-13 shows the necessary code additions.

LISTING 5-13 Constructor for *ty*

```
    let ctor = ProvidedConstructor(
                parameters = [],
                InvokeCode = fun args -> <@@ System.Text.RegularExpressions.Regex(pattern)
    :> obj @@>)

    ty.AddMember(ctor)
```

Before presenting the complete code for the regular expression type provider, there is one thing I need to clarify. The code `((%%args.[0]:obj) :?> System.Text.RegularExpressions.Match)` in Listing 5-12 might seem odd when you review the value type that is then converted to a *Match* type. The reason this is needed is that the *matchTy* type needs to have a base type of *System.Object*. Although you could use a base type of *System.Text.RegularExpression.Match*, and consequently avoid the conversion, the end-user experience would be diminished by this. The problem with using *System. Text.RegularExpression* is that viewing *Match* via IntelliSense shows all the built-in members from the *Match* type. This makes the generated *AreaCode* property more difficult to find. Figure 5-5 shows a side-by-side comparison that illustrates this issue. The complete code for the regular-expression type provider is shown in Listing 5-14.

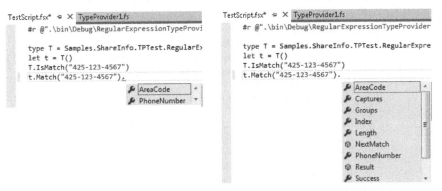

FIGURE 5-5 IntelliSense affected by the base type; *Match* is used as the base type in the image on the right

LISTING 5-14 Completing the regular-expression type-provider code

```
// Learn more about F# at http://fsharp.net
// See the 'F# Tutorial' project for more help.

namespace Samples.FSharp.RegularExpressionTypeProvider

open System.Reflection
open Microsoft.FSharp.Core.CompilerServices
open Samples.FSharp.ProvidedTypes

[<TypeProvider>]
type public TypeProvider1() as this =
    inherit TypeProviderForNamespaces()

    // Get the assembly and namespace used to house the provided types
    let thisAssembly = Assembly.GetExecutingAssembly()
    let rootNamespace = "Samples.ShareInfo.TPTest"
    let baseTy = typeof<obj>

    let newT = ProvidedTypeDefinition(thisAssembly, rootNamespace,
                    "RegularExpressionTypeProvider", Some baseTy)

    let staticParams = [ProvidedStaticParameter("pattern", typeof<string>)]
    do newT.DefineStaticParameters(
            parameters=staticParams,
            instantiationFunction=(fun typeName parameterValues ->
                match parameterValues with
                | [| :? string as pattern|] ->
                    let ty = ProvidedTypeDefinition(
                                thisAssembly,
                                rootNamespace,
                                typeName,
                                Some baseTy,
                                HideObjectMethods = true)
                    let r = System.Text.RegularExpressions.Regex(pattern)
```

```
let m = ProvidedMethod(
        methodName = "IsMatch",
        parameters = [ProvidedParameter("input", typeof<string>)],
        returnType = typeof<bool>,
        IsStaticMethod = true,
        InvokeCode = fun args ->
            <@@
              System.Text.RegularExpressions.Regex.IsMatch(
                (%%args.[0]:string),
                pattern)
            @@>
        )
ty.AddMember(m)

let ctor = ProvidedConstructor(
            parameters = [],
            InvokeCode =
              fun args ->
                <@@
                  System.Text.RegularExpressions.Regex(pattern) :>
obj
                @@>)
ty.AddMember(ctor)

let matchTy = ProvidedTypeDefinition("Match",
              baseType = Some baseTy,
              HideObjectMethods = true)

for group in r.GetGroupNames() do
    // ignore the group named 0, which represents all input
    if group <> "0" then
        let prop =
          ProvidedProperty(
            propertyName = group,
            propertyType = typeof<System.Text.RegularExpressions.
Group>,
            GetterCode =
              fun args ->
                <@@
                  ((%%args.[0]:obj)
                   :?>System.Text.RegularExpressions.Match).Groups.
[group]
                @@>)

        matchTy.AddMember prop

let matchMethod =
      ProvidedMethod(
        methodName = "Match",
        parameters = [ProvidedParameter("input", typeof<string>)],
        returnType = matchTy,
        InvokeCode =
```

```
                          fun args ->
                              <@@
                                      ((%%args.[0]:obj)
                                      :?>System.Text.RegularExpressions.Regex)
                                          .Match(%%args.[1])
                                      :>obj
                                      @@>)

                  ty.AddMember(matchMethod)

                  ty.AddMember(matchTy)

                  ty
              ))

      do this.AddNamespace(rootNamespace, [newT])

[<TypeProviderAssembly>]
do ()
```

Using the CSV Type Provider

The regular-expression type provider uses a static parameter to provide the type information. The static parameter can also point to a file that contains the type information. The current implementation allows a user to generate only .NET 1.x-compatible types. One exception is unit-of-measure types. Type providers do support the generation of unit-of-measure types. The CSV type provider demonstrates how to get type information from a local CSV file and how to generate unit-of-measure types.

As with the previous examples, the first step is to design how the API should look for the end user. (See Listing 5-15.) The sample CSV file is shown in Listing 5-16.

LISTING 5-15 CSV type-provider test script

```
#r @".\bin\Debug\CSVTypeProvider.dll"

type T = Samples.ShareInfo.TPTest.CSVTypeProvider<"TextFile1.csv">
let t = T()
for row in t.Data do
    let time = row.Time
    printfn "%f" (float time)
```

LISTING 5-16 Sample CSV file

```
Distance (metre),Time (second)
50,3.73
100,4.22
150,7.3
```

The type information is stored in the first line of the CSV file. Each row, except the first row, also needs a type to hold all of the fields. *ProvidedMeasureBuilder* is needed when creating unit-of-measure types. Listing 5-17 shows how to create *kg*, *meter*, and *kg/m²*.

LISTING 5-17 Creating unit-of-measure types in type provider

```
let measures = ProvidedMeasureBuilder.Default

// make the kilogram and meter
let kg = measures.SI "Kilogram"
let m = measures.SI "Meter"

// make float<kg> type
let float_kg = measures.AnnotateType(typeof<float>,[kg])

// make float<m²> type
let kgpm2 = measures.Ratio(kg, measures.Square m)

// make float<kg/m²> type
let dkgpm2 = measures.AnnotateType(typeof<float>,[kgpm2])

// make Nullable<float< kg/m²>> type
let nullableDecimal_kgpm2 = typedefof<System.Nullable<_>>.MakeGenericType [|dkgpm2 |]
```

Referencing a local file is an easy task as long as the user gives the correct file path. If a relative path is preferred, *TypeProviderConfig* can be used. The instance of a type provider can take an instance of a type named *TypeProviderConfig* during construction, which contains the *resolution folder* for the type provider, the list of referenced assemblies, and other information. Listing 5-18 shows how to use the *TypeProviderConfig* value.

LISTING 5-18 Using the *TypeProviderConfig* value to get a resolution path

```
[<TypeProvider>]
type public CsvProvider(cfg:TypeProviderConfig) as this =
    inherit TypeProviderForNamespaces()
    ...

    // Resolve the filename relative to the resolution folder.
    let resolvedFilename = System.IO.Path.Combine(cfg.ResolutionFolder, filename)
```

Now that the two problems are solved, the CSV type provider can be implemented as shown in Listing 5-19. The structure of the code for the CSV type provider is similar to that of the regular-expression type provider. The *Data* property returns a CSV file line, which is represented as a *Row*.

LISTING 5-19 CSV type provider

```
// Learn more about F# at http://fsharp.net
// See the 'F# Tutorial' project for more help.

namespace Samples.FSharp.CSVTypeProvider

open System.Reflection
open Microsoft.FSharp.Core.CompilerServices
open Samples.FSharp.ProvidedTypes
open System.IO
open System.Text.RegularExpressions

module CsvFileModule =
    let data filename =
        [| for line in File.ReadAllLines(filename) |> Seq.skip 1 do
                yield line.Split(',') |> Array.map float |]

[<TypeProvider>]
type public CsvProvider(cfg:TypeProviderConfig) as this =
    inherit TypeProviderForNamespaces()

    // Get the assembly and namespace used to house the provided types.
    let asm = System.Reflection.Assembly.GetExecutingAssembly()
    let ns = "Samples.ShareInfo.TPTest"

    // Create the main provided type.
    let csvTy = ProvidedTypeDefinition(asm, ns, "CSVTypeProvider", Some(typeof<obj>))

    // Parameterize the type by the file to use as a template.
    let filename = ProvidedStaticParameter("filename", typeof<string>)
    do csvTy.DefineStaticParameters([filename], fun tyName [| :? string as filename |] ->

        // Resolve the filename relative to the resolution folder.
        let resolvedFilename = Path.Combine(cfg.ResolutionFolder, filename)

        // Get the first line from the file.
        let headerLine = File.ReadLines(resolvedFilename) |> Seq.head

        // Define a provided type for each row, erasing to a float[].
        let rowTy = ProvidedTypeDefinition("Row", Some(typeof<float[]>))

        // Extract header names from the file, splitting on commas.
        // use Regex matching to get the position in the row at which the field occurs
        let headers = Regex.Matches(headerLine, "[^,]+")

        // Add one property per CSV field.
        for i in 0 .. headers.Count - 1 do
            let headerText = headers.[i].Value
```

```
                // Try to decompose this header into a name and unit.
                let fieldName, fieldTy =
                    let m = Regex.Match(headerText, @"(?<field>.+) \((?<unit>.+)\)")
                    if m.Success then
                        let fieldName = m.Groups.["field"].Value
                        let unitName = m.Groups.["unit"].Value
                        let units = ProvidedMeasureBuilder.Default.SI unitName
                        let fieldType =
                            ProvidedMeasureBuilder.Default.AnnotateType(typeof<float>,[uni
ts])
                        (fieldName, fieldType)
                    else
                        // no units, just treat it as a normal float
                        headerText, typeof<float>

                let fieldProp = ProvidedProperty(fieldName, fieldTy,
                                                GetterCode = fun [row] -> <@@
(%%row:float[]).[i] @@>)

                // Add metadata that defines the property's location in the referenced file.
                fieldProp.AddDefinitionLocation(1, headers.[i].Index + 1, filename)
                rowTy.AddMember fieldProp

            // Define the provided type
            let ty = ProvidedTypeDefinition(asm, ns, tyName, Some(typeof<obj>))

            // Add a parameterless constructor that loads the file that was used to define the
schema.
            let ctor0 = ProvidedConstructor([],
                                            InvokeCode = fun _ -> <@@ () @@>)

            // Add a more strongly typed Data property, which uses the existing property at
runtime.
            let prop = ProvidedProperty("Data", typedefof<seq<_>>.MakeGenericType(rowTy),
                                        GetterCode = fun _ -> <@@ CsvFileModule.data
resolvedFilename @@>)

            ty.AddMember prop
            ty.AddMember ctor0

            // Add the row type as a nested type.
            ty.AddMember rowTy
            ty)

        // Add the type to the namespace.
        do this.AddNamespace(ns, [csvTy])

[<TypeProviderAssembly>]
do ()
```

Note Wrapping the functions in modules helps make the type provider tidy.

Another approach is to use a user-defined CSV class to process the file and return a list of data. The type provider's job is to provide unit-of-measure types and extra class members to the design-time IntelliSense. The CSV class and type provider code are shown in Listing 5-20. The CSV file's first line is parsed by using a regular expression; the column name, which also contains the unit-of-measure types, is retrieved and generated. The CSV class returns the *Data* property, and its content is passed into the generated type *rowTy*. The *rowTy* type provides the unit-of-measure type and named property for each data item.

LISTING 5-20 CSV file class

```
// Learn more about F# at http://fsharp.net
// See the 'F# Tutorial' project for more help.

namespace Samples.FSharp.CSVTypeProvider

open System.Reflection
open Microsoft.FSharp.Core.CompilerServices
open Samples.FSharp.ProvidedTypes
open System.IO
open System.Text.RegularExpressions

// CSV file class
type CsvFile(filename) =
    let data =
        [| for line in File.ReadAllLines(filename) |> Seq.skip 1 do
                yield line.Split(',') |> Array.map float |]
    member __.Data = data

// CSV file type provider code with unit-of-measure support
[<TypeProvider>]
type public CsvProvider(cfg:TypeProviderConfig) as this =
    inherit TypeProviderForNamespaces()

    // Get the assembly and namespace used to house the provided types.
    let asm = System.Reflection.Assembly.GetExecutingAssembly()
    let ns = "Samples.ShareInfo.TPTest"

    // Create the main provided type.
    let csvTy = ProvidedTypeDefinition(asm, ns, "CSVTypeProvider", Some(typeof<obj>))

    // Parameterize the type by the file to use as a template.
    let filename = ProvidedStaticParameter("filename", typeof<string>)

    do csvTy.DefineStaticParameters([filename], fun tyName [| :? string as filename |] ->

        // Resolve the filename relative to the resolution folder.
        let resolvedFilename = Path.Combine(cfg.ResolutionFolder, filename)

        // Get the first line from the file.
        let headerLine = File.ReadLines(resolvedFilename) |> Seq.head
```

```
// Define a provided type for each row, erasing to a float[].
let rowTy = ProvidedTypeDefinition("Row", Some(typeof<float[]>))

// Extract header names from the file and use
// Regex to get the position in the row at which the field occurs
let headers = Regex.Matches(headerLine, "[^,]+")

// One property per CSV field.
for i in 0 .. headers.Count - 1 do
    let headerText = headers.[i].Value

    // Try to decompose this header into a name and unit.
    let fieldName, fieldTy =
        let m = Regex.Match(headerText, @"(?<field>.+) \((?<unit>.+)\)")
        if m.Success then
            let fieldName = m.Groups.["field"].Value
            let unitName = m.Groups.["unit"].Value
            let units = ProvidedMeasureBuilder.Default.SI unitName
            let fieldType =
              ProvidedMeasureBuilder.Default.AnnotateType(typeof<float>,[units])
            (fieldName, fieldType)
        else
            // no units, just treat it as a normal float
            headerText, typeof<float>

    let fieldProp = ProvidedProperty(fieldName, fieldTy,
                                    GetterCode = fun [row] -> <@@
(%%row:float[]).[i] @@>)

    // Add metadata that defines the property's location in the referenced file.
    fieldProp.AddDefinitionLocation(1, headers.[i].Index + 1, filename)
    rowTy.AddMember fieldProp

// Define the provided type
let ty = ProvidedTypeDefinition(asm, ns, tyName, Some(typeof<CsvFile>))

// Add a parameterless constructor that loads the file that was used to define the
schema.
let ctor0 = ProvidedConstructor([],
                                 InvokeCode = fun [] -> <@@
CsvFile(resolvedFilename) @@>)

// Add a more strongly typed Data property, which uses the existing property at
runtime.
let prop = ProvidedProperty("Data", typedefof<seq<_>>.MakeGenericType(rowTy),
                            GetterCode = fun [csvFile] -> <@@ (%%csvFile:CsvFile).
Data @@>)

ty.AddMember prop
ty.AddMember ctor0
```

```
        // Add the row type as a nested type.
        ty.AddMember rowTy
        ty)

    // Add the type to the namespace.
    do this.AddNamespace(ns, [csvTy])

[<TypeProviderAssembly>]
do ()
```

> **Note** The csvFile value in the fun [csvFile] -> <@@ (%%csvFile:CsvFile).Data @@>)
> uses an active pattern to decompose the arguments into a single element list. This code
> could also be written as fun args -> <@@ ((%%args.[0]):CsvFile).Data @@>.

Two interesting concepts have been introduced in the implementation of this type provider. The
type-provider type and provided class members are derived from the schema information, which
defines the meaning of the data. The regular-expression pattern and CSV file header in the schema
defines how the data is presented. Any schematized data can potentially have a type provider that
helps to interpret and process the data. A few examples include image data and network transmission
data.

Using the Excel-File Type Provider

Starting with Excel 2007, a new file format with extension XLSX was introduced. This file format is the
Office Open XML File format, which is an open international, ECMA-376, Second Edition, and ISO/IEC
29500 standard. This new format is an XML-format file that can be accessed by using the Open XML
SDK. The Open XML SDK can be downloaded from *http://www.microsoft.com/en-us/download/details.
aspx?id=5124*. After the SDK is installed successfully, *DocumentFormat.OpenXml.dll* is installed under
the C:\Program Files\Open XML SDK folder.

The sample Excel file Book1.xlsx has three cells. The C1 cell value is computed by adding the values
in A1 and B1. The screen shot is shown in Figure 5-6. This file needs to be put in the project folder
where the type-provider project file is located.

Clipboard			Font	
	A2	▼		
	A	B	C	
1	1	2	3	
2				
3				

FIGURE 5-6 Excel file content

Listing 5-21 creates an *ExcelFile* class to access the XLSX file using the Open XML SDK. To run this code, *DocumentFormat.OpenXml.dll*, *System.Xml.dll*, and *WindowsBase.dll* have to be added to the project reference.

LISTING 5-21 Accessing the Excel XLSX file using the OpenXML SDK

```
module ExcelClass

open DocumentFormat.OpenXml.Packaging
open DocumentFormat.OpenXml.Spreadsheet
open DocumentFormat.OpenXml

type CellContent = { Name: string* string; Value : string; Formula : string; Cell : Cell}
    with
        override this.ToString() = sprintf "%s%s(%s, %s)" (fst this.Name) (snd this.Name)
                                           this.Value this.Formula

let (|CellName|) (name:string) =
    let filterBy f =
        name
        |> f System.Char.IsLetter
        |> Seq.toArray
        |> fun l -> System.String l
    let col = filterBy Seq.takeWhile
    let row = filterBy Seq.skipWhile
    (col, row)

type ExcelFile(filename:string, editable:bool) =
    let myWorkbook = SpreadsheetDocument.Open(filename, editable)
    let part = myWorkbook.WorkbookPart

    let cells = part.Workbook.Descendants<Sheet>()
                |> Seq.map (fun sheet ->
                                let a = part.GetPartById sheet.Id.Value
                                let c =
                                    match a with
                                    | :? WorksheetPart as part ->
                                        let rows = part.Worksheet.Descendants<Row>()
                                        [ for row in rows do
                                            for cell in row.Descendants<Cell>() do
                                                let formula =
                                                    if cell.CellFormula = null then
                                                        ""
                                                    else
                                                        cell.CellFormula.Text
                                                match cell.CellReference.Value with
                                                | CellName(col,row) ->
                                                    yield
                                                        {  Cell = cell
                                                           Name = col, row
                                                           Formula = formula
                                                           Value = cell.CellValue.
Text } ]
```

```
                                    | _ -> [ ]
                            (sheet.Name.Value, c))
                |> Seq.map snd
                |> Seq.collect id
                |> Seq.toList

    member this.Cells = cells
    member this.Cell(col,row) =
        cells |> Seq.tryFind (fun cell->cell.Name=(col,row))
    member this.Cell(col,row, v) =
        let cell = this.Cell(col,row)
        match cell with
        | Some c ->
            if c.Cell.CellFormula = null then
                c.Cell.CellValue.Text <- v
        | None -> ()
    member this.Close() = myWorkbook.Close()
```

 Note The *Close* method saves and closes the XLSX file.

The type-provider script, presented in Listing 5-22, shows what class members are exposed to the end user. The code opens Book1.xlsx and reads the A1 cell content first. Then the A1 content is changed to *99*.

LISTING 5-22 *ExcelTypeProvider* script file

```
#r @".\bin\Debug\TypeProviderTemplate2.dll"

type T = Samples.Excel.ExcelTypeProvider<"Book1.xlsx">

let t = T()
let (Some(cell)) = t.GetCell(t.A, t.''1'')
printfn "%A" cell.Value

t.SetCell(t.A, t.''1'', "99")
t.Close()

let t2 = T()

let (Some(cell2)) = t2.GetCell(t2.A, t2.''1'')
printfn "%A" cell2.Value

t2.Close()
```

Note The *Close* method needs to be invoked; otherwise, the script will generate an error after it is executed once. The error message is "Cannot access Book1.xlsx because it is opened by another process."

The type provider code, shown in Listing 5-23, provides several methods. It uses *System.Object* as a base class to hide the ExcelFile members. It also provides Excel columns and row names as read-only properties.

LISTING 5-23 *ExcelTypeProvider* implementation code

```
// Learn more about F# at http://fsharp.net
// See the 'F# Tutorial' project for more help.

namespace Samples.FSharp.TypeProviderTemplate2

open System.Reflection
open Microsoft.FSharp.Core.CompilerServices
open Samples.FSharp.ProvidedTypes
open ExcelClass

[<TypeProvider>]
type public TypeProvider1(cfg:TypeProviderConfig) as this =
    inherit TypeProviderForNamespaces()

    // Get the assembly and namespace used to house the provided types
    let thisAssembly = Assembly.GetExecutingAssembly()
    let rootNamespace = "Samples.Excel"
    let baseTy = typeof<obj>

    let newT = ProvidedTypeDefinition(
                    thisAssembly,
                    rootNamespace,
                    "ExcelTypeProvider",
                    Some baseTy)

    let filename = ProvidedStaticParameter("filename", typeof<string>)
    do newT.DefineStaticParameters(
            [filename],
            fun tyName [| :? string as filename |] ->
                let path = System.IO.Path.Combine (cfg.ResolutionFolder, filename)
                let ty = ProvidedTypeDefinition(
                            thisAssembly, rootNamespace, tyName, Some(typeof<obj>))
                ty.AddMember(
                    ProvidedConstructor([], InvokeCode = fun _ -> <@@ ExcelFile(path,
true) @@>))

                let file = ExcelFile(path, false)
                let rows = file.Cells
                        |> Seq.map (fun cell -> cell.Name)
                        |> Seq.map (fun (col,row) -> row)
                        |> Seq.distinct
                let cols = file.Cells
```

```
                           |> Seq.map (fun cell -> cell.Name)
                           |> Seq.map (fun (col,row) -> col)
                           |> Seq.distinct
                    rows
                    |> Seq.append cols
                    |> Seq.iter (fun n ->
                            ty.AddMember(
                                ProvidedProperty(
                                    n,
                                    typeof<string>,
                                    GetterCode= fun _ -> <@@ n @@>)))

                    file.Close()

                    let mi = ProvidedMethod(
                                "GetCell",
                                [ProvidedParameter("row", typeof<string>);
                                 ProvidedParameter("col", typeof<string>)],
                                typeof<CellContent option>,
                                InvokeCode =
                                    fun [me; row; col] ->
                                        <@@
                                          ((%%me:obj):?>ExcelFile).Cell((%%row:string),
                                                                         (%%col:string))
                                        @@>)

                    let close = ProvidedMethod(
                                    "Close", [], typeof<unit>,
                                    InvokeCode =
                                        fun [me] -> <@@ ((%%me:obj) :?> ExcelFile).Close()
@@>)

                    let save = ProvidedMethod(
                                "SetCell",
                                [ProvidedParameter("row", typeof<string>)
                                 ProvidedParameter("col", typeof<string>)
                                 ProvidedParameter("value", typeof<string>)],
                                typeof<unit>,
                                InvokeCode =
                                    fun [me; row; col; v] ->
                                        <@@ ((%%me:obj) :?> ExcelFile).
Cell((%%row:string),

(%%col:string),

(%%v:string)) @@>)

                    ty.AddMember(mi)
                    ty.AddMember(save)
                    ty.AddMember(close)
                    ty)

        do this.AddNamespace(rootNamespace, [newT])

[<TypeProviderAssembly>]
do ()
```

Note The "Incomplete pattern matches on this expression" warnings are expected and can be ignored.

Using the Type-Provider Base Class

Until now, there has been no way to share information or coordinate the actions between class methods within a type provider. The type-provider methods do not show relationships when invoked. The interesting part about Listing 5-24 is that it stores the file name in the base class and enables methods to share that information between method calls.

Sharing Information Among Members

A simple example is shown in Listing 5-24. The type-provider base provides a non-object-based property that can be used to store information that can be shared between method calls. The type provider defines two methods, and these two provided methods provide a wrapper around this existing property. The code is very close to the HelloWorld type provider except for the base class.

One thing that needs to be called out is the constructor. Because the provided type is erased to the base type, the constructor needs to return the base type instance instead of nothing. Listing 5-25 shows how to invoke the type provider. The F1 function sets the underlying base class value and the F2 function can retrieve it. This code seems to do nothing, but it opens the door to a more interesting scenario, which will be presented in the next section.

LISTING 5-24 Type provider sharing information between members

```
namespace Samples.FSharp.ShareInfoProvider

open System.Reflection
open Microsoft.FSharp.Core.CompilerServices
open Samples.FSharp.ProvidedTypes
open System.IO
open System.Collections.Generic

// base class the type provider erased to
type BaseType2() =
    member val X = "" with get, set

[<TypeProvider>]
type public CheckedRegexProvider() as this =
    inherit TypeProviderForNamespaces()

    // Get the assembly and namespace used to house the provided types
    let thisAssembly = Assembly.GetExecutingAssembly()
    let rootNamespace = "Samples.ShareInfo.TPTest"
    let baseTy = typeof<BaseType2>
```

```
let regexTy = ProvidedTypeDefinition(thisAssembly, rootNamespace, "TPTestType", Some
baseTy)

    let f1 = ProvidedMethod(
                        methodName = "F1",
                        parameters = [ProvidedParameter("input", typeof<string>)],
                        returnType = typeof<unit>,
                        IsStaticMethod = false,
                        InvokeCode = fun args -> <@@ (%%args.[0]:BaseType2).X <-
(%%args.[1]) @@>)

    let f2 = ProvidedMethod(
                        methodName = "F2",
                        parameters = [],
                        returnType = typeof<string>,
                        IsStaticMethod = false,
                        InvokeCode = fun args -> <@@ (%%args.[0]:BaseType2).X @@>)

    // constructor needs to return the BaseType2 instance
    let ctor = ProvidedConstructor(
                        parameters = [],
                        InvokeCode = fun args -> <@@ BaseType2() @@>)

    do
        regexTy.AddMember ctor
        regexTy.AddMember f1
        regexTy.AddMember f2

    do this.AddNamespace(rootNamespace, [regexTy])

[<TypeProviderAssembly>]
do ()
```

LISTING 5-25 Test script for the *TPTestType* provider sharing information between methods

```
#r @".\bin\Debug\ShareInfoSampleTypeProvider.dll"

type T = Samples.ShareInfo.TPTest.TPTestType
let t = T()
t.F1("hello")
let a = t.F2()

printfn "%A" a // the print result is hello
```

Because the provided type is based on *BaseType2* and because the constructor returns an instance of *BaseType2*, the variable *t* in the test script is of type *BaseType2*.

Using a Wrapper Type Provider

Imagine that you have a sealed class and need to add some logic for each member function, such as logging the function usage. The most common technique for a C# developer is to write a wrapper class with the sealed class instance as a variable, as shown in Listing 5-26. It would be a tedious and boring task to refactor the sealed class. Reflection can be an option, but the performance impact of this approach is something that cannot be ignored.

LISTING 5-26 Wrapper class used to expand a sealed class

```
// sealed class A
public sealed class A
{
    public void F1() { ... }
}

// new class to add logging function around the F1 defined in sealed class A
public class MyClass
{
    private A a = new A();
    public void F1()
    {
        LogBefore();
        a.F1();
        LogAfter();
    }
}
```

A custom type provider is another way to perform meta-programming, and it has a performance advantage over reflection. The type provider logic is simple:

- Generate the same provided method with the same function name and signature.

- In the function implementation, first invoke the *LogBefore* method, then invoke the base class' method, and finally invoke the *LogAfter* method.

As usual, the way to invoke the type provider is defined first, as you can see in Listing 5-27. The sealed class and the logging function are defined in Listing 5-28.

LISTING 5-27 Invoking the wrapper type provider and the expected result

```
#r @".\bin\Debug\ShareInfoSampleTypeProvider.dll"

type T = Samples.ShareInfo.TPTest.TPTestType
let t = T()

//invoke F1 and also output logging info
t.F1("hello")
```

```
//invoke F2 and also output logging info
t.F2(2)
```

```
log before Samples.FSharp.ShareInfoProvider.BaseType2 "F1"
hello
log after Samples.FSharp.ShareInfoProvider.BaseType2 "F1"

log before Samples.FSharp.ShareInfoProvider.BaseType2 "F2"
2
log after Samples.FSharp.ShareInfoProvider.BaseType2 "F2"
```

LISTING 5-28 Sealed class for the wrapper type provider

```
[< Sealed >]
type BaseType2() =
    member this.F1(s) = printfn "%s" s
    member this.F2(i) = printfn "%d" i

// logging functions
type LoggingFunctions =
    static member LogBeforeExecution(obj:BaseType2, methodName:string) =
        printfn "log before %A %A" obj methodName
    static member LogAfterExecution(obj:BaseType2, methodName:string) =
        printfn "log after %A %A" obj methodName
```

The next task is determining how to invoke the logging functions and base class method by using a quotation. The following two problems need to be solved, and the code that provides the solutions is shown in Listing 5-29:

- **Invoke a method** The method call is performed by *Expr.Call*, which takes three parameters if the method is not a static method and only two parameters if it is a static method. The parameter to *Expr.Call* is created by using *Expr.Value*.

- **Invoke a sequence of statements** Invoking statements is handled by *Expr.Sequential*. It might seem like a problem that this only takes two elements, especially when more than two statements need to be invoked. Actually, this is not a problem at all. If the second parameter is an *Expr.Sequential*, it has an extra space to hold the following statement.

LISTING 5-29 Quotation code to invoke the base class method and logging function

```
let baseTExpression = <@@ (%%args.[0]:BaseType2) @@>
let mi = baseTy.GetMethod(methodName)
```

```
// get LogBefore function code quotation
let logExpr = Expr.Call(typeof<LoggingFunctions>.GetMethod("LogBeforeExecution"),
                        [ baseTExpression; Expr.Value(methodName) ])

// invoke the base class's method
let invokeExpr = Expr.Call(baseTExpression, mi, args.Tail)

// get logAfter function code quotation
let logAfterExpr = Expr.Call(typeof< LoggingFunctions >.GetMethod("LogAfterExecution"),
                             [ baseTExpression; Expr.Value(methodName) ])

// invoke logBefore, base method, and logAfter
Expr.Sequential(logExpr, Expr.Sequential(invokeExpr, logAfterExpr))
```

The complete code is presented in Listing 5-30. Reflection is used to get the method names from the base class and to generate the provided methods. Because the reflection code is only executed at compile time (design time), the generated *IL* (which is shown in Listing 5-31) does not contain any reflection code. This wrapper class has visibility to the base class' public methods and properties, and the cost to generate and maintain it is significantly lower than the manual way shown in Listing 5-26.

The wrapper type provider can work for cases in which source code is not available. The *Activator. CreateInstance* method is not something new for C# developers. The DLL path and type name can be passed in as a string, and *CreateInstance* can be used to create the sealed class instance.

LISTING 5-30 The complete type-provider code

```
namespace Samples.FSharp.ShareInfoProvider

open System.Reflection
open Microsoft.FSharp.Core.CompilerServices
open Samples.FSharp.ProvidedTypes
open System.IO
open System.Collections.Generic
open Microsoft.FSharp.Quotations

[<Sealed>]
type BaseType2() =
    member this.F1(s) = printfn "%s" s
    member this.F2(i) = printfn "%d" i

type LoggingFunctions =
    static member LogBeforeExecution(obj:BaseType2, methodName:string) =
        printfn "log before %A %A" obj methodName
    static member LogAfterExecution(obj:BaseType2, methodName:string) =
        printfn "log after %A %A" obj methodName
```

```fsharp
[<TypeProvider>]
type public CheckedRegexProvider() as this =
    inherit TypeProviderForNamespaces()

    // Get the assembly and namespace used to house the provided types
    let thisAssembly = Assembly.GetExecutingAssembly()
    let rootNamespace = "Samples.ShareInfo.TPTest"
    let baseTy = typeof<BaseType2>

    let regexTy = ProvidedTypeDefinition(thisAssembly, rootNamespace, "TPTestType", Some
baseTy)

    let methods = baseTy.GetMethods()
    let getParameters (mi:MethodInfo) =
        let parameters = mi.GetParameters()
        parameters
        |> Seq.map (fun p -> ProvidedParameter(p.Name, p.ParameterType))
        |> Seq.toList

    let providedMethods =
        methods
        |> Seq.map (fun m ->let methodName = m.Name
                            ProvidedMethod(
                                methodName = methodName,
                                parameters = (getParameters m),
                                returnType = m.ReturnType,
                                IsStaticMethod = false,
                                InvokeCode = fun args ->
                                    let baseTExpression = <@@ (%%args.[0]:BaseType2) @@>
                                    let mi = baseTy.GetMethod(methodName)
                                    let logExpr = Expr.Call(
                                                    typeof<LoggingFunctions>
                                                        .GetMethod("LogBeforeExecution"),
                                                        [baseTExpression; Expr.
Value(methodName) ])
                                    let invokeExpr = Expr.Call(baseTExpression, mi, args.
Tail)
                                    let logAfterExpr = Expr.Call(
                                                        typeof<LoggingFunctions>
                                                            .GetMethod("LogAfterExecuti
on"),
                                                        [baseTExpression;Expr.
Value(methodName)]
                                                        )
                                    Expr.Sequential(
                                            logExpr,
                                            Expr.Sequential(invokeExpr, logAfterExpr))
                                    ))

    let ctor = ProvidedConstructor(
                    parameters = [],
                    InvokeCode = fun args -> <@@ BaseType2() @@>)
```

```
        do
            regexTy.AddMember ctor
            providedMethods |> Seq.iter regexTy.AddMember

        do this.AddNamespace(rootNamespace, [regexTy])

[<TypeProviderAssembly>]
do ()
```

LISTING 5-31 IL code from the compiled binary reference to the type provider

```
IL_0000: nop
IL_0001: newobj instance void
[ShareInfoSampleTypeProvider]Samples.FSharp.ShareInfoProvider.BaseType2::.ctor()
IL_0006: box [ShareInfoSampleTypeProvider]Samples.FSharp.ShareInfoProvider.BaseType2
IL_000b: unbox.any [ShareInfoSampleTypeProvider]Samples.FSharp.ShareInfoProvider.BaseType2
IL_0010: dup
IL_0011: stsfld class
[ShareInfoSampleTypeProvider]Samples.FSharp.ShareInfoProvider.BaseType2 '<StartupCode$Cons
oleApplication1>.$Program'::t@5
IL_0016: stloc.0
IL_0017: call class [ShareInfoSampleTypeProvider]Samples.FSharp.ShareInfoProvider.
BaseType2
Program::get_t()
IL_001c: ldstr "F1"
IL_0021: call void
[ShareInfoSampleTypeProvider]Samples.FSharp.ShareInfoProvider.InsertFunctions::LogBeforeEx
ecution(class [ShareInfoSampleTypeProvider]Samples.FSharp.ShareInfoProvider.BaseType2,
string)
IL_0026: call class [ShareInfoSampleTypeProvider]Samples.FSharp.ShareInfoProvider.
BaseType2
Program::get_t()
IL_002b: ldstr "hello"
IL_0030: callvirt instance void
[ShareInfoSampleTypeProvider]Samples.FSharp.ShareInfoProvider.BaseType2::F1(string)
IL_0035: call class [ShareInfoSampleTypeProvider]Samples.FSharp.ShareInfoProvider.
BaseType2
Program::get_t()
IL_003a: ldstr "F1"
IL_003f: call void
[ShareInfoSampleTypeProvider]Samples.FSharp.ShareInfoProvider.InsertFunctions::LogAfterExe
cution(class [ShareInfoSampleTypeProvider]Samples.FSharp.ShareInfoProvider.BaseType2,
string)
IL_0044: call class [ShareInfoSampleTypeProvider]Samples.FSharp.ShareInfoProvider.
BaseType2
Program::get_t()
IL_0049: ldstr "F2"
```

```
IL_004e: call void
[ShareInfoSampleTypeProvider]Samples.FSharp.ShareInfoProvider.InsertFunctions::LogBeforeEx
ecution(class [ShareInfoSampleTypeProvider]Samples.FSharp.ShareInfoProvider.BaseType2,
string)
IL_0053: call class [ShareInfoSampleTypeProvider]Samples.FSharp.ShareInfoProvider.
BaseType2
Program::get_t()
IL_0058: ldc.i4.2
IL_0059: callvirt instance void
[ShareInfoSampleTypeProvider]Samples.FSharp.ShareInfoProvider.BaseType2::F2(int32)
IL_005e: call class [ShareInfoSampleTypeProvider]Samples.FSharp.ShareInfoProvider.
BaseType2
Program::get_t()
IL_0063: ldstr "F2"
IL_0068: call void
[ShareInfoSampleTypeProvider]Samples.FSharp.ShareInfoProvider.InsertFunctions::LogAfterExe
cution(class [ShareInfoSampleTypeProvider]Samples.FSharp.ShareInfoProvider.BaseType2,
string)
IL_006d: ret
```

At first glance, the wrapper type provider does not appear to derive its type and members from a schema. In this case, the schema is being defined by the data returned from *TypeInfo* and *MethodInfo* via reflection. From this sample, I can say that the base class is another way to get schema data in addition to static type parameters and local files. The type provider has the ability to rearrange the data, which are methods and properties, to its new inheritance location and insert customized code during the relocation. The next sample shows how to make an inheritance structure with a type provider.

Using the Multi-Inheritance Type Provider

With C#, the decision was made not to support multi-inheritance. Discussions about the advantages or disadvantages of multi-inheritance often open a can of worms. I am not going to pick a side in this discussion. Instead, this example attempts to demonstrate that a type provider can create a new inheritance hierarchy. Because the user has full control over how to generate the class members, she can decide how to handle any duplicated function names or other nasty problems. This example uses only unique function names and leaves the duplicated-function-name problem to the reader.

First assume C# classes need to be handled by the type provider. The C# class definition is presented in Listing 5-32. The C# classes that are sealed make the traditional inheritance more difficult. Note that if the class is located in another assembly, you to make sure that the assembly can be found (as shown in Listing 5-33) if the DLL is located next to the type provider DLL.

LISTING 5-32 C# classes

```
namespace ClassLibrary1
{
    public sealed class Class1
    {
        public void F1()
        {
            Console.WriteLine("from Class1.F1");
        }

        public void F2()
        {
            Console.WriteLine("from Class1.F2");
        }
    }

    public sealed class Class2
    {
        public void F11()
        {
            Console.WriteLine("from Class2.F11");
        }

        public void F12()
        {
            Console.WriteLine("from Class2.F12");
        }
    }
}
```

LISTING 5-33 Code to resolve the reference assembly

```
[<TypeProvider>]
type public CheckedRegexProvider(tpc :
Microsoft.FSharp.Core.CompilerServices.TypeProviderConfig) as this =
    inherit TypeProviderForNamespaces()

    let handler = System.ResolveEventHandler(fun _ args ->
        let asmName = AssemblyName(args.Name)
        // assuming that we reference only dll files
        let expectedName = asmName.Name + ".dll"
        let expectedLocation =
            // we expect to find this assembly near the dll with type provider
            let d = System.IO.Path.GetDirectoryName(tpc.RuntimeAssembly)
            System.IO.Path.Combine(d, expectedName)
        if System.IO.File.Exists expectedLocation then
            Assembly.LoadFrom expectedLocation
        else
            null
        )
```

```
      do System.AppDomain.CurrentDomain.add_AssemblyResolve handler

      interface System.IDisposable with
            member this.Dispose() = System.AppDomain.CurrentDomain.remove_AssemblyResolve
handler
```

Listing 5-34 shows how to use the type provider to generate the provided method whenever the user wants to. The straightforward way is to use a module to hold instances of C# classes and then create provided methods. From the test script, the inheritance is not obvious, but compared to the next example, this approach is more straightforward.

LISTING 5-34 Multi-inheritance type provider with a test script

```
namespace Samples.FSharp.ShareInfoProvider

open System.Reflection
open Microsoft.FSharp.Core.CompilerServices
open Samples.FSharp.ProvidedTypes
open System.IO
open System.Collections.Generic
open Microsoft.FSharp.Quotations
open ClassLibrary1

[<AutoOpen>]
module Module =
    let c1 = Class1()
    let c2 = Class2()

[<TypeProvider>]
type public CheckedRegexProvider(tpc :
Microsoft.FSharp.Core.CompilerServices.TypeProviderConfig) as this =
    inherit TypeProviderForNamespaces()

    let handler = System.ResolveEventHandler(fun _ args ->
        let asmName = AssemblyName(args.Name)
        // assuming that we reference only dll files
        let expectedName = asmName.Name + ".dll"
        let expectedLocation =
            // we expect to find this assembly near the dll with type provider
            let d = System.IO.Path.GetDirectoryName(tpc.RuntimeAssembly)
            System.IO.Path.Combine(d, expectedName)
        if System.IO.File.Exists expectedLocation then Assembly.LoadFrom expectedLocation
else null
        )
    do System.AppDomain.CurrentDomain.add_AssemblyResolve handler

    // Get the assembly and namespace used to house the provided types
    let thisAssembly = Assembly.GetExecutingAssembly()
    let rootNamespace = "Samples.ShareInfo.TPTest"
    let baseTy = typeof<obj>
```

```
let regexTy = ProvidedTypeDefinition(
                    thisAssembly,
                    rootNamespace,
                    "MultiInheritanceTypeProvider",
                    Some baseTy)

let getParameters (mi:MethodInfo) =
    let parameters = mi.GetParameters()
    parameters
    |> Seq.map (fun p -> ProvidedParameter(p.Name, p.ParameterType))
    |> Seq.toList

let methodsFromC1 = c1.GetType().GetMethods()
let providedMethodsFromC1 =
    methodsFromC1
    |> Seq.map (fun m ->let methodName = m.Name
                        ProvidedMethod(
                            methodName = methodName,
                            parameters = (getParameters m),
                            returnType = m.ReturnType,
                            IsStaticMethod = false,
                            InvokeCode = fun args ->
                                let baseTExpression = <@@ c1 @@>
                                let mi = c1.GetType().GetMethod(methodName)
                                let invokeExpr = Expr.Call(baseTExpression, mi,
args.Tail)

                                invokeExpr
                        ))

let methodsFromC2 = c2.GetType().GetMethods()
let providedMethodsFromC2 =
    methodsFromC2
    |> Seq.map (fun m ->let methodName = m.Name
                        ProvidedMethod(
                            methodName = methodName,
                            parameters = (getParameters m),
                            returnType = m.ReturnType,
                            IsStaticMethod = false,
                            InvokeCode = fun args ->
                                let baseTExpression = <@@ c2 @@>
                                let mi = c2.GetType().GetMethod(methodName)
                                let invokeExpr = Expr.Call(baseTExpression, mi,
args.Tail)

                                invokeExpr
                        ))

let ctor = ProvidedConstructor(
                    parameters = [],
                    InvokeCode = fun args -> <@@ System.Object() @@>)

do
    regexTy.AddMember ctor
    providedMethodsFromC1 |> Seq.iter regexTy.AddMember
    providedMethodsFromC2 |> Seq.iter regexTy.AddMember
```

```
    do this.AddNamespace(rootNamespace, [regexTy])

    interface System.IDisposable with
        member this.Dispose() = System.AppDomain.CurrentDomain.remove_AssemblyResolve
handler

[<TypeProviderAssembly>]
do ()
```

Test script
```
#r @".\bin\Debug\ShareInfoSampleTypeProvider.dll"
#r @".\bin\Debug\ClassLibrary1.dll"

type T = Samples.ShareInfo.TPTest.MultiInheritanceTypeProvider
let t = T()
t.F1()
t.F2()
t.F11()
t.F12()
```

If the class does not have complex constructors and creating an object is straightforward, you can use the static parameter and *Activator.CreateInstance* to create the instance and host it in the base class. Because the static parameter passed into the type provider can only be a basic type such as *int* and *string*, this approach is not the best choice for the object that needs a non-basic type parameter. The base class uses a dictionary that creates a relationship between the type name and type instance, as shown in Listing 5-35. This version of a type provider takes a DLL file path and two type names, which are used to create the instance for that type. This version is more general, but it requires that the instance creation be simple.

LISTING 5-35 Base class for a multi-inheritance type provider

```
type MyBase(dll:string, names:string array) =
    let assembly = Assembly.LoadFile(dll)
    let myDict =
        names
        |> Array.map (fun name -> name, System.Activator.CreateInstance(System.Type.
GetType(name)))
        |> dict
    member this.GetObj(name:string) = myDict.[name]
    member this.GetMethods(name) =
        myDict.[name].GetType().GetMethods()
    member this.GetMethod(name, methodName) =
        myDict.[name].GetType().GetMethod(methodName)
```

```fsharp
namespace Samples.FSharp.ShareInfoProvider

open System.Reflection
open Microsoft.FSharp.Core.CompilerServices
open Samples.FSharp.ProvidedTypes
open System.IO
open System.Collections.Generic
open Microsoft.FSharp.Quotations
open ClassLibrary1

type MyBase(dll:string, names:string array) =
    let assembly = Assembly.LoadFile(dll)
    let myDict =
        names
        |> Array.map (fun name -> name, System.Activator.CreateInstance(System.Type.
GetType(name)))
        |> dict
    member this.GetObj(name:string) = myDict.[name]
    member this.GetMethods(name) =
        myDict.[name].GetType().GetMethods()
    member this.GetMethod(name, methodName) =
        myDict.[name].GetType().GetMethod(methodName)


[<TypeProvider>]
type public CheckedRegexProvider(tpc :
Microsoft.FSharp.Core.CompilerServices.TypeProviderConfig) as this =
    inherit TypeProviderForNamespaces()

    let handler = System.ResolveEventHandler(fun _ args ->
        let asmName = AssemblyName(args.Name)
        // assuming that we reference only dll files
        let expectedName = asmName.Name + ".dll"
        let expectedLocation =
            // we expect to find this assembly near the dll with type provider
            let d = System.IO.Path.GetDirectoryName(tpc.RuntimeAssembly)
            System.IO.Path.Combine(d, expectedName)
        if System.IO.File.Exists expectedLocation then
            Assembly.LoadFrom expectedLocation
        else
            null
    )
    do System.AppDomain.CurrentDomain.add_AssemblyResolve handler

    // Get the assembly and namespace used to house the provided types
    let thisAssembly = Assembly.GetExecutingAssembly()
    let rootNamespace = "Samples.ShareInfo.TPTest"
    let baseTy = typeof<obj>

    let regexTy = ProvidedTypeDefinition(thisAssembly,
                                         rootNamespace,
                                         "MultiInheritanceTypeProvider",
                                         Some baseTy)
```

```
let getParameters (mi:MethodInfo) =
    let parameters = mi.GetParameters()
    parameters
    |> Seq.map (fun p -> ProvidedParameter(p.Name, p.ParameterType))
    |> Seq.toList


let staticParams = [ProvidedStaticParameter("dll", typeof<string>);
                    ProvidedStaticParameter("type", typeof<string>);
                    ProvidedStaticParameter("type2", typeof<string>)]
do regexTy.DefineStaticParameters(
        parameters=staticParams,
        instantiationFunction=(fun typeName parameterValues ->

            let name = parameterValues.[1] :?> string;
            let name2 = parameterValues.[2] :?> string;
            let dll = System.IO.Path.Combine(
                        System.IO.Path.GetDirectoryName(tpc.RuntimeAssembly),
                        parameterValues.[0] :?> string)
            let r = MyBase(dll, [| name; name2 |])

            let ty = ProvidedTypeDefinition(
                        thisAssembly,
                        rootNamespace,
                        typeName,
                        Some typeof<obj>,
                        HideObjectMethods = true)
        [| name; name2 |]
        |> Seq.iter (fun n ->
            let methods = r.GetMethods(n)
            let providedMethods =
                methods
                |> Seq.map (fun m ->let methodName = m.Name
                                    ProvidedMethod(
                                        methodName = methodName,
                                        parameters = (getParameters m),
                                        returnType = m.ReturnType,
                                        IsStaticMethod = false,
                                        InvokeCode = fun args ->
                                          let baseValue = r
                                          let baseTExpression = <@@
                                            ((%%args.[0]:obj) :?> MyBase).
GetObj(n) @@>

                                          let mi = baseValue.GetObj(n)
                                                        .GetType()


.GetMethod(methodName)

                                          let t = System.Type.GetType(n)
                                          let invokeExpr =
                                            Expr.Call(Expr.
Coerce(baseTExpression, t),

                                                      mi,
                                                      args.Tail)
                                          invokeExpr
                                    ))
                providedMethods |> Seq.iter ty.AddMember)
```

```
            let ctor =
                ProvidedConstructor(
                    parameters = [],
                    InvokeCode = fun args -> <@@ MyBase(dll, [| name; name2 |]) :> obj
@@>)

            ty.AddMember(ctor)

            ty
            ))

    let ctor = ProvidedConstructor(parameters = [],
                                   InvokeCode = fun args -> <@@ System.Object() @@>)

    do
        regexTy.AddMember ctor

    do this.AddNamespace(rootNamespace, [regexTy])

    interface System.IDisposable with
        member this.Dispose() = System.AppDomain.CurrentDomain.remove_AssemblyResolve
handler

[<TypeProviderAssembly>]
do ()
```

Test script

```
#r @".\bin\Debug\ShareInfoSampleTypeProvider.dll"
#r @".\bin\Debug\ClassLibrary1.dll"

type T = Samples.ShareInfo.TPTest.MultiInheritanceTypeProvider<
    "ClassLibrary1.dll",
    "ClassLibrary1.Class1, ClassLibrary1, Version=1.0.0.0, Culture=neutral,
PublicKeyToken=null",
    "ClassLibrary1.Class2, ClassLibrary1, Version=1.0.0.0, Culture=neutral,
PublicKeyToken=null">

let t = T()
t.F1()
t.F2()
t.F11()
t.F12()
```

 Note Because the dictionary returns a *System.Object* type, and because it needs to be converted to the correct type, the conversion code Expr.Coerce(baseTExpression, t) is required.

The wrapper and multi-inheritance type provider sample shows how a type provider can be used for meta-programming. The data passed into the type provider can originate from a base class or module inside the type-provider code in addition to the static parameter, local files, or both.

Using the XML Type Provider

This section shows you how to use the XML type provider's design-time feature. The definition of the type provider shows that it is a design-time adapter component. The example I present in this section explores the design-time part of the definition. Many applications use XML files as feeders of input data. The problem with this approach is that XML can become complicated and errors in this text file can be checked only at run time. The XML type provider moves validation that is typically done during run time to design time.

InvokeCode in *ProvidedMethod* returns a code quotation, and it can also contain other code. The quotation will be executed at run time, whereas the other code is executed at design time. This is where the validation code can be inserted and executed.

The production code and the sample XML file are shown in Listing 5-37 and Listing 5-38, respectively. Both listings require that the XML file meet certain criteria: the start value must be equal or smaller than the end value. If the validation can happen only at run time, that could be a disaster. Another approach is to use a validation tool, such as a check-in gate validation. None of these approaches can provide a comparable coding experience if this validation can be performed at design time. Ideally, when a user invokes the method, he will see the error right away.

LISTING 5-37 Production code to be invoked by the type provider

```
type MyProductionCode() =
    member this.Work() =
        let xml = XDocument.Load("XmlFile1.xml")
        let start = xml.Descendants(XName.Get("Start")) |> Seq.head
        let end' = xml.Descendants(XName.Get("End")) |> Seq.head

        // if start > end, something bad will happen
        if Convert.ToInt32(start.Value) > Convert.ToInt32(end'.Value) then
            failwith "report illegal parameter from runtime"
```

LISTING 5-38 Sample XML file

```
<?xml version="1.0" encoding="utf-8" ?>

<Config>
  <Start>6</Start>
  <End>5</End>
</Config>
```

As usual, the test script is defined first. (See Listing 5-39.) If the XML file is invalid, the error will be shown in Visual Studio, as you can see in Figure 5-7. The developer will know immediately that the configuration file is invalid.

LISTING 5-39 Test script for XMLTypeProvider

```
#r @".\bin\Debug\XMLTypeProvider.dll"

type T = Samples.ShareInfo.TPTest.XMLTypeProvider<"XmlFile1.xml">
let t = T()
let a = t.Work()
```

```
#r @".\bin\Debug\XMLTypeProvider.dll"

type T = Samples.ShareInfo.TPTest.XMLTypeProvider<"XmlFile1.xml">
let t = T()
let a = t.Work()
```

FIGURE 5-7 Design-time error from the type provider

The beauty of this type provider is that the validation code will be executed only at design time. Unlike the test case that executed regardless of whether the function was invoked, the final binary allows the function to be invoked only if the validation passes. To recap, the type provider moves the run-time failure check to design time. The completed code is shown in Listing 5-40.

LISTING 5-40 XMLTypeProvider code

```
// Learn more about F# at http://fsharp.net
// See the 'F# Tutorial' project for more help.

namespace Samples.FSharp.XMLTypeProvider

open System.Reflection
open Microsoft.FSharp.Core.CompilerServices
open Samples.FSharp.ProvidedTypes
open System.Xml.Linq
open Microsoft.FSharp.Quotations
open System

type MyProductionCode() =
    member this.Work() =
        let xml = XDocument.Load("XmlFile1.xml")
        let start = xml.Descendants(XName.Get("Start")) |> Seq.head
        let end' = xml.Descendants(XName.Get("End")) |> Seq.head

        // if start > end, something bad will happen
        if Convert.ToInt32(start.Value) > Convert.ToInt32(end'.Value) then
            failwith "report illegal parameter from runtime"
```

```fsharp
type MyTest() =
    member this.Test1(xml:string) =
        let xml = XDocument.Load(xml)
        let start = xml.Descendants(XName.Get("Start")) |> Seq.head
        let end' = xml.Descendants(XName.Get("End")) |> Seq.head
        if Convert.ToInt32(start.Value) > Convert.ToInt32(end'.Value) then
            failwith "report illegal parameter from design-time"


[<AutoOpen>]
module TestModule =
    let test = MyTest()


[<TypeProvider>]
type public TypeProvider1(cfg : Microsoft.FSharp.Core.CompilerServices.TypeProviderConfig)
    as this =
    inherit TypeProviderForNamespaces()

    // Get the assembly and namespace used to house the provided types
    let thisAssembly = Assembly.GetExecutingAssembly()
    let rootNamespace = "Samples.ShareInfo.TPTest"
    let baseTy = typeof<obj>

    let newT = ProvidedTypeDefinition(thisAssembly, rootNamespace,
                                      "XMLTypeProvider", Some baseTy)

    let ctor = ProvidedConstructor(
                    parameters = [],
                    InvokeCode = fun args -> <@@ (* base class initialization or null*) ()
@@>)

    let staticParams = [ProvidedStaticParameter("xml file name", typeof<string>)]
    do newT.DefineStaticParameters(
        parameters = staticParams,
        instantiationFunction=(fun typeName parameterValues ->
            let baseTy = typeof<MyProductionCode>

            let ty = ProvidedTypeDefinition(
                        thisAssembly,
                        rootNamespace,
                        typeName,
                        baseType = Some baseTy)

            let xmlFileName = System.IO.Path.Combine(
                                cfg.ResolutionFolder,
                                parameterValues.[0] :?> string)
            let m = ProvidedMethod(
                        methodName = "Work",
                        parameters = [],
                        returnType = typeof<unit>,
                        IsStaticMethod = false,
                        InvokeCode = fun args ->
                            test.Test1(xmlFileName)
                            <@@ (%%args.[0]:MyProductionCode).Work() @@>
                        )
```

```
                let ctor = ProvidedConstructor(
                                    parameters = [],
                                    InvokeCode = fun args -> <@@ MyProductionCode()
@@>)
                ty.AddMember(ctor)
                ty.AddMember(m)

                ty.AddXmlDoc "xml comment"
                ty))

        do
            newT.AddMember(ctor)

        do this.AddNamespace(rootNamespace, [newT])

[<TypeProviderAssembly>]
do ()
```

 Note This code requires a reference to *System.Xml* and *System.Xml.Linq*.

The type provider gives the user a place to design his own design-time logic. You can use type providers to better take advantage of the editing power of Visual Studio without getting into the details of the Visual Studio SDK.

Using the DGML-File Type Provider

Directed Graph Markup Language (DGML) is supported in Visual Studio. DGML is used to draw a diagram representing a graph structure that contains nodes and edges. You can use DGML to represent a state machine, where the node is the state and the edge is the possible transition between states. Figure 5-8 illustrates how the DGML is shown in Visual Studio. It represents a state machine with four states: State0 to State3. The DGML file is actually an XML file. Listing 5-41 shows the content of the DGML file that is shown in Figure 5-8. The Nodes section defines all the nodes in the graph, and the Links section defines all the edges.

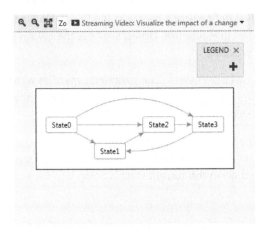

FIGURE 5-8 DGML file that represents a state machine with four states

LISTING 5-41 DGML file content

```xml
<?xml version="1.0" encoding="utf-8"?>
<DirectedGraph GraphDirection="LeftToRight" Layout="Sugiyama"
xmlns="http://schemas.microsoft.com/vs/2009/dgml">
  <Nodes>
    <Node Id="State0" Bounds="0,19.02,53.36,25.96" />
    <Node Id="State1" Bounds="170.095,93.0200000000001,53.36,25.96" />
    <Node Id="State2" Bounds="85.0474999999999,93.02,53.36,25.96" />
    <Node Id="State3" Bounds="255.1425,93.02,53.3600000000001,25.96" />
  </Nodes>

  <Links>
    <Link Source="State0" Target="State1"
Bounds="53.3600006103516,32,131.471939086914,53.2166442871094" />
    <Link Source="State0" Target="State2"
Bounds="41.5977897644043,44.9799995422363,48.4222755432129,42.1323204040527" />
    <Link Source="State0" Target="State3"
Bounds="43.9286956787109,1.24344978758018E-14,229.335739135742,84.6670761108398" />
    <Link Source="State1" Target="State2"
Bounds="132.513122558594,118.980003356934,50.1091003417969,16.2699966430664" />
    <Link Source="State2" Target="State3"
Bounds="138.407501220703,82.2404556274414,108.355163574219,16.3045043945313" />
    <Link Source="State3" Target="State1"
Bounds="217.560623168945,118.980003356934,50.1091156005859,16.2699966430664" />
  </Links>

  <Properties>
    <Property Id="Bounds" DataType="System.Windows.Rect" />
    <Property Id="GraphDirection"
DataType="Microsoft.VisualStudio.Diagrams.Layout.LayoutOrientation" />
    <Property Id="Layout" DataType="System.String" />
  </Properties>

</DirectedGraph>
```

As I did with the other type-provider samples, I first define how a user uses the DGML-file type provider. The DGML file defines a state machine shown in Figure 5-8. Listing 5-42 has the following three parts and shows how a user can use the type provider:

- Part I creates the type provider, which takes two parameters. One parameter specifies where the DGML file is. The other parameter specifies the initial state of the state machine. At this point, the state machine is created from the DGML file.

- Part II defines a set of transition functions. The transition is encapsulated in an object expression that implements the *IState* interface, which is defined in the following code sample. *EnterFunction* and *ExitFunction* will be invoked when the current state is going into the enter or exit state.

```
type IState =
    // function which will be invoked when entering a state
    abstract member EnterFunction : unit -> unit

    // function which will be invoked when exiting a state
    abstract member ExitFunction : unit->unit
```

- Part III performs a series of transition operations. From the DGML definition, you can see that the first three transitions are valid. The last transition, which is from the current state of State3 to State2, is invalid and thus the transition function is not executed.

LISTING 5-42 Test script for the DGML-file type provider

```
// Part I
#r @".\bin\Debug\TypeProviderTemplate1.dll"

type T =
  Samples.ShareInfo.TPTest.TPTestType<
    """C:\MyCode\TypeProviderTemplate1\TypeProviderTemplate1\Graph1.dgml""", "State0">
let t = T()

// Part II
// define print function
let syncRoot = ref 0
let print str = lock(syncRoot) (fun _ -> printfn "%s" str)

// object expression for transition
let printObj = { new StateMachineTypeProvider.IState with
                        member this.EnterFunction() = print ("Enter " +
t.CurrentState)
                        member this.ExitFunction() = print ("Exit " + t.CurrentState)
}

// set the transition functions
t.SetFunction(t.State0, printObj)
t.SetFunction(t.State1, printObj)
t.SetFunction(t.State2, printObj)
t.SetFunction(t.State3, printObj)
```

```
// Part III
// valid transitions
t.TransitTo_State1()
t.TransitTo_State2()
t.TransitTo_State3()

// invalid transition
t.TransitTo_State2()
```

The state machine reads the DGML file and generates a graph structure. *MailboxProcessor* is applied to process the message in an asynchronous way. The actual implementation defines two classes, as shown in Listing 5-43. The *DGMLClass* type represents the DGML file with a list of nodes and links defined in the file. The *StateMachine* class inherits from *DGMLClass*. It adds *MailboxProcessor* to process the transition asynchronously and several member methods to set the transition functions. These two classes can be treated like a library that can process any DGML file.

LISTING 5-43 DGML-file type provider state machine implementation

DGMLClass **representing the DGML file**

```
namespace StateMachineTypeProvider

open System.Xml
open System.Xml.Linq

// define the state interface
type IState =
    // function which will be invoked when entering a state
    abstract member EnterFunction : unit -> unit

    // function which will be invoked when exiting a state
    abstract member ExitFunction : unit->unit

// define a node record
type Node = { Name : string; NextNodes : Node list}

// define DGML DU
type DGML =
    | Node of string
    | Link of string * string

// define DGML class
type DGMLClass() =

    let mutable nodes = Unchecked.defaultof<Node list>
    let mutable links = Unchecked.defaultof<DGML list>
    let mutable currentState = System.String.Empty

    // current state
    member this.CurrentState
        with get() = currentState
        and private set(v) = currentState <- v
```

```
// all links in the DGML file
member this.Links
    with get() = links
    and private set(v) = links <- v

// all nodes in the DGML file
member this.Nodes
    with get() = nodes
    and private set(v) = nodes <- v

// initialize the state machine from fileName and set the initial state to initState
member this.Init(fileName:string, initState) =
    let file = XDocument.Load(fileName, LoadOptions.None)
    this.Links <-
        file.Descendants()
        |> Seq.filter (fun node -> node.Name.LocalName = "Link")
        |> Seq.map (fun node ->
                        let sourceName = node.Attribute(XName.Get("Source")).Value
                        let targetName = node.Attribute(XName.Get("Target")).Value
                        DGML.Link(sourceName, targetName))
        |> Seq.toList

    let getNextNodes fromNodeName=
            this.Links
            |> Seq.filter (fun (Link(a, b)) -> a = fromNodeName)
            |> Seq.map (fun (Link(a,b)) -> this.FindNode(b))
            |> Seq.filter (fun n -> match n with Some(x) -> true | None -> false)
            |> Seq.map (fun (Some(n)) -> n)
            |> Seq.toList

    this.Nodes <-
        file.Descendants()
        |> Seq.filter (fun node -> node.Name.LocalName = "Node")
        |> Seq.map (fun node -> DGML.Node( node.Attribute(XName.Get("Id")).Value) )
        |> Seq.map (fun (Node(n)) -> { Node.Name=n; NextNodes = [] })
        |> Seq.toList

    this.Nodes <-
        this.Nodes
        |> Seq.map (fun n -> { n with NextNodes = (getNextNodes n.Name) } )
        |> Seq.toList

    this.CurrentState <- initState

// find the node by the given nodeName
member this.FindNode(nodeName) : Node option=
    let result =
        this.Nodes
        |> Seq.filter (fun n -> n.Name = nodeName)
    if result |> Seq.isEmpty then None
    else result |> Seq.head |> Some
```

```
// current node
member this.CurrentNode
    with get() =
        this.Nodes
        |> Seq.filter (fun n -> n.Name = this.CurrentState)
        |> Seq.head

// determine if one node can transit to another one represented by the nodeName
member this.CanTransitTo(nodeName:string) =
    this.CurrentNode.NextNodes |> Seq.exists (fun n -> n.Name = nodeName)

// force current state to a new state
member this.ForceStateTo(args) =
    this.CurrentState <- args

// assert function used for debugging
member this.Assert(state) =
    if this.CurrentState <> state then
        failwith "assertion failed"
```

StateMachine class inheriting from DGMLClass

```
// state machine class which inherits the DGML class
// and uses a MailboxProcessor to perform asynchronous message processing
type StateMachine() as this =
    inherit DGMLClass()

    let functions = System.Collections.Generic.Dictionary<string, IState>()
    let processor = new MailboxProcessor<string>(fun inbox ->
                    let rec loop () =
                        async {
                            let! msg = inbox.Receive()
                            if this.CanTransitTo(msg) then
                                this.InvokeExit(this.CurrentNode.Name)
                                this.ForceStateTo(msg)
                                this.InvokeEnter(msg)
                            return! loop ()
                        }
                    loop ())

do
    processor.Start()

// define the second constructor taking the file name and initial state name
new(fileName, initState) as secondCtor=
    new StateMachine()
    then
        secondCtor.Init(fileName, initState)

// asynchronously transit to a new state
member this.TransitTo(state) =
    processor.Post(state)
```

```
    // set the transition function
    member this.SetFunction(name:string, state:IState) =
        if functions.ContainsKey(name) then
            functions.[name] <- state
        else
            functions.Add(name, state)

    // invoke the Exit function
    member private this.InvokeExit(name:string) =
        if functions.ContainsKey(name) then
            functions.[name].ExitFunction()

    // invoke the Enter function
    member private this.InvokeEnter(name:string) =
        if functions.ContainsKey(name) then
            functions.[name].EnterFunction()
```

The type-provider implementation uses the *StateMachine* type as a base class. It generates the transition function *TransitTo_<target node name>* and the assert function *Assert_<node name>*. Because it is easy to make a typo when specifying the state name, I chose to generate the state name as a read-only property. *SetFunction* is not generated from the type provider; it is a function defined on the *StateMachine* class. The code is shown in Listing 5-44.

LISTING 5-44 DGML-file type provider code

```
namespace Samples.FSharp.TypeProviderTemplate1

open System.Reflection
open Microsoft.FSharp.Core.CompilerServices
open Samples.FSharp.ProvidedTypes

open StateMahcineTypeProvider

[<TypeProvider>]
type public TypeProvider1() as this =
    inherit TypeProviderForNamespaces()

    // Get the assembly and namespace used to house the provided types
    let thisAssembly = Assembly.GetExecutingAssembly()
    let rootNamespace = "Samples.ShareInfo.TPTest"
    let baseTy = typeof<StateMachine>

    let newT = ProvidedTypeDefinition(thisAssembly, rootNamespace, "TPTestType", Some
baseTy)

    // define two static parameters: one is the DGML file name and
    // the other is the initial state
    let staticParams = [ProvidedStaticParameter("dgml file name", typeof<string>);
                        ProvidedStaticParameter("init state", typeof<string>)]
```

```
    do newT.DefineStaticParameters(
        parameters=staticParams,
        instantiationFunction=(fun typeName parameterValues ->
                let ty = ProvidedTypeDefinition(
                            thisAssembly,
                            rootNamespace,
                            typeName,
                            baseType = Some baseTy)

                let dgml, initState = parameterValues.[0] :?> string, parameterValues.[1]
:?> string

                // generate a new StateMachine instance to generate the read-only state
properties
                let stateMachine = StateMachine()
                stateMachine.Init(dgml, initState)

                let stateProperties =
                    stateMachine.Nodes
                    |> Seq.map (fun n ->
                                let name = n.Name
                                let prop1 = ProvidedProperty(propertyName = n.Name,
                                        propertyType = typeof<string>,
                                        IsStatic=false,
                                        GetterCode= (fun args -> <@@ name @@>))
                                prop1
                                )

                stateProperties
                |> Seq.iter ty.AddMember

                // generate the assert functions
                let asserts =
                    stateMachine.Nodes
                    |> Seq.map (fun n ->
                                    let name = n.Name
                                    let assertFunction =
                                        ProvidedMethod(
                                            methodName = sprintf "Assert_%s" name,
                                            parameters = [],
                                            returnType = typeof<unit>,
                                            IsStaticMethod = false,
                                            InvokeCode = fun args ->
                                                <@@ (%%args.[0] :> StateMachine).
Assert(name)   @@>
                                            )
                                    assertFunction)
                asserts
                |> Seq.iter ty.AddMember

                // generate the transition functions
                let transits =
                    stateMachine.Nodes
                    |> Seq.map (fun node ->
                                    let name = node.Name
```

```
                                    let m = ProvidedMethod(
                                            methodName = sprintf "TransitTo_%s" name,
                                            parameters = [],
                                            returnType = typeof<unit>,
                                            IsStaticMethod = false,
                                            InvokeCode = fun args ->
                                                <@@
                                                    (%%args.[0] :> StateMachine).
TransitTo(name)

                                                @@>
                                            )
                                m)
                    transits
                    |> Seq.iter ty.AddMember

                    let setFunction =
                            ProvidedMethod(
                                methodName = "SetFunction",
                                parameters = [ProvidedParameter("name", typeof<string>);
                                            ProvidedParameter("state
class",typeof<IState>)],
                                returnType = typeof<unit>,
                                IsStaticMethod = false,
                                InvokeCode = fun args ->
                                                <@@ (%%args.[0] :> StateMachine)
                                                        .SetFunction(%%args.[1] :>
string,

                                                                    %%args.[2] :>
IState)
                                                @@>
                                            )
                    ty.AddMember(setFunction)

                    // define the constructor
                    let ctor = ProvidedConstructor(
                                    parameters = [],
                                    InvokeCode = fun args -> <@@ StateMachine(dgml,
initState) @@>)
                    ty.AddMember(ctor)

                    ty.AddXmlDoc "xml comment"
                    ty))

        do this.AddNamespace(rootNamespace, [newT])

[<TypeProviderAssembly>]
do ()
```

Note The type provider does not erase the type to *System.Object* anymore; therefore, IntelliSense shows a full list of class members from the base class. In the sample, *SetFunction* is visible in the IntelliSense drop-down list.

This sample shows a way to enhance the experience of working with a DGML file using a general-purpose library. The type provider can customize the property according to a specific DGML file, and any breaking change on the file will be reflected at compile time.

Separating Run Time and Design Time

The XML type provider shows how type providers handle design-time logic and run-time logic. Actually, design-time logic and run-time logic can be separated into different assemblies. The design-time DLL not only provides the design-time logic, it also inserts extra logic to change the final assembly's logic. Listing 5-45 shows the run-time DLL. The *TypeProvider* attribute is the key that indicates which DLL is the type-provider assembly.

> **Note** The run-time DLL and type-provider DLL should be located in the same folder.

The sample solution has two projects. One is for the run-time assembly, and the other is the design-time type-provider code. The structure of the solution is shown in Figure 5-9.

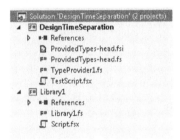

FIGURE 5-9 Type-provider solution separating run time and design time into two assemblies

LISTING 5-45 Run-time logic for the type provider in the Library1 project

```
namespace Samples.MiniTypeSpace.Runtime

type ObjectBase() =
    member x.Kind = "I'm an object"

type ObjectRepresentation(contents:string) =
    inherit ObjectBase()
    member x.Contents = contents

type RuntimeMethods() =
    static member Create(s:string) = ObjectRepresentation(s + " - hello!") :> ObjectBase
    static member GetContents(s:ObjectBase) = (s :?> ObjectRepresentation).Contents

// This declaration points the compiler to the right design-time DLL for the selected
```

```
runtime DLL.
open Microsoft.FSharp.Core.CompilerServices
[<assembly:TypeProviderAssembly("DesignTimeSeparation")>]

do()
```

> **Note** The type provider project will generate an assembly named *DesignTimeSeparation*.

The design-time type-provider code is listed in Listing 5-46. It generates class members to invoke the functions present in Listing 5-45.

LISTING 5-46 Type-provider code in the DesignTimeSeparation project associated with the run-time DLL in Listing 5-45

```
// Learn more about F# at http://fsharp.net
// See the 'F# Tutorial' project for more help.

namespace Samples.FSharp.DesignTimeSeparation

open System.Reflection
open Microsoft.FSharp.Core.CompilerServices
open Samples.FSharp.ProvidedTypes
open Microsoft.FSharp.Quotations

[<TypeProvider>]
type public TypeProvider1(config: TypeProviderConfig) as this =
    inherit TypeProviderForNamespaces()
    let assem = config.RuntimeAssembly
    let runtimeAssembly = System.Reflection.Assembly.ReflectionOnlyLoadFrom(assem)

    let objectBase = runtimeAssembly.GetType("Samples.MiniTypeSpace.Runtime.ObjectBase")
    let runtimeMethods = runtimeAssembly.GetType("Samples.MiniTypeSpace.Runtime.
RuntimeMethods")
    let createMethod = runtimeMethods.GetMethod("Create")
    let getContentsMethod = runtimeMethods.GetMethod("GetContents")

    // Get the assembly and namespace used to house the provided types
    let rootNamespace = "Samples.ShareInfo.TPTest"
    let baseTy = objectBase

    let newT = ProvidedTypeDefinition(runtimeAssembly, rootNamespace, "TPTestType", Some
baseTy)

    let ctor = ProvidedConstructor([ProvidedParameter("Contents",typeof<string>)],
                            InvokeCode = (fun args -> Expr.Call(createMethod, [
args.[0] ])))
```

```
            // This is a property. At runtime, the property just gets the string value
            let prop2 = ProvidedProperty(
                            "Property2",
                            typeof<string>,
                            GetterCode= (fun args -> Expr.Call(getContentsMethod, [ args.[0] ])))

            do prop2.AddXmlDocDelayed(fun () -> "xml comment")
            do
                newT.AddMember(prop2)
                newT.AddMember(ctor)

            do this.AddNamespace(rootNamespace, [newT])

[<TypeProviderAssembly>]
do ()
```

Invoking the type provider, as shown in Listing 5-47, is similar to the other example. The reference part is the main difference. In the other examples, there is only one assembly, but now there are two assemblies. The run-time DLL is what our test code needs to reference in order to use this type provider.

LISTING 5-47 Invoking the type provider

```
#r @".\bin\Debug\Library1.dll"

type T = Samples.ShareInfo.TPTest.TPTestType
let t = T("AA")
let c = t.Kind
let d = t.Property2
```

Generated Type Provider

The last example in this chapter is a generated type provider. The generated type provider behaves like a code generator. It does not support lazy type generation like an erased type provider does. However, there are several advantages to using a generated type provider versus an erased type provider. The generated type provider generates an assembly that can be used from other language. Because the generated assembly is present, you can use .NET reflection to retrieve type information. I'll start by showing you how to write a generated type provider. The code needed to create a generated type provider, which is shown in Listing 5-48, is similar to the erased version except that a new *ProvidedAssembly* class is needed. Let's start from a simple HelloWorld type-provider project, TypeProviderTemplate3, which is created from the TypeProvider template. If you compare Listing 5-48 and Listing 5-7, there are a few differences. There is an assembly variable whose type is *ProvidedAssembly*. The *ProvidedType newT* needs to set its *IsErased* and *SuppressRelocation* properties to *false* before it can be added to *ProvidedAssembly*.

LISTING 5-48 HelloWorld generated type provider

```
namespace Samples.FSharp.TypeProviderTemplate3

open System.Reflection
open Microsoft.FSharp.Core.CompilerServices
open Samples.FSharp.ProvidedTypes

[<TypeProvider>]
type public TypeProvider1() as this =
    inherit TypeProviderForNamespaces()

    // Get the assembly and namespace used to house the provided types
    let assembly = ProvidedAssembly(@"c:\mycode\tt.dll")
    let thisAssembly = Assembly.GetExecutingAssembly()
    let rootNamespace = "Samples.ShareInfo.TPTest"
    let baseTy = typeof<obj>

    let newT = ProvidedTypeDefinition(thisAssembly, rootNamespace, "TPTestType", Some
baseTy)

    // add other property and method definition
    let m = ProvidedMethod(
                methodName = "methodName",
                parameters = [],
                returnType = typeof<int>,
                IsStaticMethod = false,
                InvokeCode = fun args ->
                    <@@ 1 + 1 @@>
                )

    let ctor = ProvidedConstructor(parameters = [], InvokeCode = fun args -> <@@ obj()
@@>)

    let prop2 = ProvidedProperty(propertyName = "Property1",
                                 propertyType = typeof<string>,
                                 IsStatic=false,
                                 GetterCode= (fun args -> <@@ "Hello!" @@>),
                                 SetterCode = (fun args -> <@@ printfn "setter code" @@>))

    do prop2.AddXmlDocDelayed(fun () -> "xml comment")
    do
        newT.AddMember(m)
        newT.AddMember(prop2)
        newT.AddMember(ctor)
        newT.IsErased <- false
        newT.SuppressRelocation <- false
        assembly.AddTypes [newT]

    do this.AddNamespace(rootNamespace, [newT])

[<TypeProviderAssembly>]
do ()
```

Note Be sure that the C:\MyCode folder is created because the DLL will be generated there.

The constructor needs to return obj(). If the default <@@ () @@> is used, the constructor will return a NULL value and generate a runtime error.

You need to create another project to consume the generated type or types, so you create an F# console project for that purpose. Instead of adding a reference to the generated *tt.dll* under C:\MyCode, you need to add a reference to the output of the type-provider project TypeProviderTemplate3. Figure 5-10 shows the Console project references.

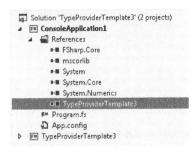

FIGURE 5-10 Project reference in a generated type-provider solution

Listing 5-49 shows *Program.fs*, which creates the generated type and prints out the property value.

LISTING 5-49 *Program.fs*, which accesses the generated types

```
type T = Samples.ShareInfo.TPTest.TPTestType
let t = T()
let p = t.Property1

printfn "t.Property1 value is %A" p

ignore <| System.Console.ReadKey()
```

For a generated type provider, you can create fields to hold values by using *ProvidedField*. Listing 5-50 shows how to create a field and expose it.

LISTING 5-50 Using *ProvidedField* to create a field in a generated type provider

```
namespace Samples.FSharp.TypeProviderTemplate3

open System.Reflection
open Microsoft.FSharp.Core.CompilerServices
open Samples.FSharp.ProvidedTypes
```

```fsharp
[<TypeProvider>]
type public TypeProvider1() as this =
    inherit TypeProviderForNamespaces()

    // Get the assembly and namespace used to house the provided types
    let assembly = ProvidedAssembly(@"c:\mycode\tt.dll")
    let thisAssembly = Assembly.GetExecutingAssembly()
    let rootNamespace = "Samples.ShareInfo.TPTest"
    let baseTy = typeof<obj>

    let newT = ProvidedTypeDefinition(thisAssembly, rootNamespace, "TPTestType", Some
baseTy)

    // add other property and method definition
    let m = ProvidedMethod(
                methodName = "methodName",
                parameters = [],
                returnType = typeof<int>,
                IsStaticMethod = false,
                InvokeCode = fun args ->
                    <@@ 1 + 1 @@>
                )

    let ctor = ProvidedConstructor(parameters = [], InvokeCode = fun args -> <@@ obj()
@@>)

    let prop2 = ProvidedProperty(propertyName = "Property1",
                                 propertyType = typeof<string>,
                                 IsStatic=false,
                                 GetterCode= (fun args -> <@@ "Hello!" @@>),
                                 SetterCode = (fun args -> <@@ printfn "setter code" @@>))

    let field1 = ProvidedField("myField", typeof<string>)
    let prop3 = ProvidedProperty(
                propertyName = "Property2",
                propertyType = typeof<string>,
                IsStatic=false,
                GetterCode= (fun [me] -> Microsoft.FSharp.Quotations.Expr.
FieldGet(me,field1)),
                SetterCode = (fun [me;v] -> Microsoft.FSharp.Quotations.Expr.
FieldSet(me,field1, v)))

    do prop2.AddXmlDocDelayed(fun () -> "xml comment")
    do
        newT.AddMember(m)
        newT.AddMember(prop2)
        newT.AddMember(field1)
        newT.AddMember(prop3)
        newT.AddMember(ctor)

        newT.IsErased <- false
```

```
            newT.SuppressRelocation <- false
            assembly.AddTypes [newT]


    do this.AddNamespace(rootNamespace, [newT])

[<TypeProviderAssembly>]
do ()
```

 Note Assigning *SuppressRelocation* generates a warning, which you can ignore.

The test code is presented in Listing 5-51. From the execution result, you can see the field is created in the assembly and that you can use *Property2* to access the field.

LISTING 5-51 Test code for a generated type provider with a generated field

```
type T = Samples.ShareInfo.TPTest.TPTestType
let t = T()
let p = t.Property1

printfn "t.Property1 value is %A" p

let b = t.GetType().GetField(
            "myField",
            System.Reflection.BindingFlags.Instance |||
            System.Reflection.BindingFlags.NonPublic)

printfn "found myField? %A" ( b<>null )

printfn "t.Property2 value is %A" t.Property2
t.Property2 <- "aa"
printfn "t.Property2 value is %A" t.Property2

ignore <| System.Console.ReadKey()



Execution result

t.Property1 value is "Hello!"
found myField? True
t.Property2 value is <null>
t.Property2 value is "aa"
```

The type-provider API also provides a way to decorate a property with an attribute. Listing 5-52 shows how to add an attribute to a property and how to generate the type that is returned from the *DefineStaticParameters* function.

LISTING 5-52 Adding an attribute to a generated property

```
namespace Samples.FSharp.TypeProviderTemplate4

open System.Reflection
open Microsoft.FSharp.Core.CompilerServices
open Samples.FSharp.ProvidedTypes

type MyAttribute() =
    inherit System.Attribute()

[<TypeProvider>]
type public TypeProvider1() as this =
    inherit TypeProviderForNamespaces()

    // Get the assembly and namespace used to house the provided types
    let thisAssembly = Assembly.GetExecutingAssembly()
    let rootNamespace = "Samples.ShareInfo.TPTest"
    let baseTy = typeof<obj>

    let newT = ProvidedTypeDefinition(thisAssembly, rootNamespace, "TPTestType", Some
baseTy)
    let assembly = ProvidedAssembly(@"c:\Mycode\tt.dll")
    let data = ProvidedStaticParameter("filename", typeof<string>)
    do newT.DefineStaticParameters(
            [data],
            fun tyName [| :? string as data |] ->
                let ty = ProvidedTypeDefinition(
                            thisAssembly,
                            rootNamespace,
                            tyName,
                            Some(typeof<obj>))
                ty.AddMember(ProvidedConstructor([], InvokeCode = fun _ -> <@@ obj() @@>))
                let p = ProvidedProperty(data, typeof<string>,
                                            GetterCode = fun [me] -> <@@ data @@>)
                p.AddAttribute(typeof<MyAttribute>)
                ty.AddMember(p)

                ty.IsErased <- false
                ty.SuppressRelocation <- false
                assembly.AddTypes [ty]
                ty)
```

```
    do
        newT.IsErased <- false
        newT.SuppressRelocation <- false
        this.AddNamespace(rootNamespace, [newT])
        assembly.AddTypes [newT]


[<TypeProviderAssembly>]
do ()
```

Listing 5-53 shows the attribute is correctly added to the property.

LISTING 5-53 A test-provided property that has an attribute

```
type T = Samples.ShareInfo.TPTest.TPTestType<"PropertyA">
let t = T()
printfn "propertyA value is %A" t.PropertyA
let pi = t.GetType().GetProperty("PropertyA")
printfn "propertyA has attribute %s"
    ( pi.GetCustomAttributes(typeof<Samples.FSharp.TypeProviderTemplate4.MyAttribute>,
true)
        |> Seq.head
        |> fun attribute -> attribute.ToString() )

ignore <| System.Console.ReadKey()
```

Execution result

```
propertyA value is "PropertyA"
propertyA has attribute Samples.FSharp.TypeProviderTemplate4.MyAttribute
```

Using Type-Provider Snippets

The F# snippets are designed to make the act of authoring a type provider even easier. The snippet project is published at *http://fsharpcodesnippet.codeplex.com/* as an open source project. Each type provider snippet does not have shortcut support; however, you can press Ctrl+K,X to bring up a list of all snippets, as shown in Figure 5-11. Table 5-1 lists the commonly used code snippets for type-provider authoring.

FIGURE 5-11 Code snippets for type-provider writing

TABLE 5-1 Code snippets for type-provider writing

Snippet Name	Description

Type provider define static parameter	Generates skeleton code for the DefineStaticParameters function that takes the static parameter. Here is the default code generated:
	
	``fsharp
	let staticParams = [ProvidedStaticParameter("pattern", typeof<string>)]
	    do regexTy.DefineStaticParameters(
	        parameters=staticParams,
	        instantiationFunction=(fun typeName parameterValues ->
	            let ty = ProvidedTypeDefinition(
	                thisAssembly,
	                rootNamespace,
	                typeName,
	                baseType = Some baseTy)
	
	            ty.AddXmlDoc "xml comment"
	            ty))
	``

Type provider provided constructor	Generates the type-provider constructor. Here is the default code generated:
	
	``fsharp
	let ctor = ProvidedConstructor(
	        parameters = [],
	        InvokeCode = fun args ->
	                <@@
	                    (* base class initialization or null*) ()
	                @@>)
	``

Type provider provided method	Generates the type-provider method. Here is the default code generated:
	
	``fsharp
	let m = ProvidedMethod(
	        methodName = "methodName",
	        parameters = [],
	        returnType = typeof<int>,
	        IsStaticMethod = false,
	        InvokeCode = fun args ->
	            <@@ 1 + 1 @@>
	        )
	``

Type provider provided property	Generates the type-provider property. Here is the default code generated:
	
	``fsharp
	let prop1 = ProvidedProperty(
	            propertyName = "Property1",
	            propertyType = typeof<string>,
	            IsStatic=false,
	            GetterCode= (fun args -> <@@ "Hello!" @@>),
	            SetterCode = (fun args -> <@@ printfn "setter code" @@>))
	``

Snippet Name	Description

Type provider skeleton	Generates the skeleton for a type provider. This is the default code generated:
	
	`namespace Samples.FSharp.ShareInfoProvider`
	
	`open System.Reflection`
	`open Microsoft.FSharp.Core.CompilerServices`
	`open Samples.FSharp.ProvidedTypes`
	
	`[<TypeProvider>]`
	`type public CheckedRegexProvider() as this =`
	`    inherit TypeProviderForNamespaces()`
	
	`    // Get the assembly and namespace used to house the provided types`
	`    let thisAssembly = Assembly.GetExecutingAssembly()`
	`    let rootNamespace = "Samples.ShareInfo.TPTest"`
	`    let baseTy = typeof<obj>`
	
	`    let regexTy = ProvidedTypeDefinition(thisAssembly, rootNamespace,`
	`                                          "TPTestType", Some baseTy)`
	
	`    // add other property and method definition`
	
	`    do this.AddNamespace(rootNamespace, [regexTy])`
	
	`[<TypeProviderAssembly>]`
	`do ()`

Type provider xml comment	Generates the XML comment. This is the default code generated: `ctor.AddXmlDocDelayed(fun () -> "xml comment")`

Provided measure builder	Generates the unit of measure for the type-provider type. Here is the default code generated:
	`let units = ProvidedMeasureBuilder.Default.SI "metre"`
	`let unitType = ProvidedMeasureBuilder.Default.AnnotateType(typeof<float>, [units] )`

Type provider provided parameter	Generates the type-provider function parameter. This is the default code generated: `ProvidedParameter("var", typeof<string>)`

Type-Provider Limitations

The type-provider mechanism that shipped with F# 3.0 has some limitations. The first limitation that a reader might have already noticed is that the static parameter can only take basic types, such as integer and string. The other limitation is that the type provider can only generate .NET 1.x types. Most of the F# specific types such as record are not supported. The only exception is the units of measure types, which are supported in this release. These limitations will be eliminated in a future release, but for now we have to live with them.

CHAPTER 6

Other Unique Features

In previous chapters, I showed you exciting things you can do in F# as well as various F# data structures. This chapter itemizes the F# data structures and describes them in detail. This chapter is crucial to starting your F# development in full swing.

Working with Reference Cells

You already used the reference cell in Listing 1-86 from Chapter 1, "C# and F# Data Structures." In that code, a reference cell was used to wrap a *ref* parameter. According to the MSDN documentation, a *reference cell* is a storage structure used to create mutable data. The reference cell definition is shown in Listing 6-1, which is actually a record type containing a mutable variable.

LISTING 6-1 Reference cell definition

```
type Ref<'a> =
    { mutable contents: 'a }
```

This is another way to define mutable data, which you can see in Listing 6-2. You can think of the reference cell as a pointer. The *ref* operator is used to get the *pointer*, the := is used to set the underlying value, and the exclamation point (!) is used to return the underlying value. Listing 6-2 provides an example.

LISTING 6-2 Reference cell example

```
// make a reference.
let refVar = ref 1

// Change the value pointed by the reference.
refVar := 5

// Dereference by using ! operator.
printfn "%d" !refVar
```

As mentioned previously in this book, F# provides two shortcut functions, *incr* and *decr*, to increase or decrease the reference value. Listing 6-3 demonstrates how to use these two functions.

LISTING 6-3 Reference cell functions *incr* and *decr*

```
let a = ref 0

// increase a by 1
incr a
printfn "a = %A" !a

// decrease a by 1
decr a
printfn "a = %A" !a
```

Execution result

```
a = 1
a = 0
```

The reference cell might seem like a redundant design. As you explore more F# features, you will soon realize that under certain circumstances the reference cell is the only way to define mutable values.

Working with Object Expressions

C# has anonymous functions you can use so that making function definitions is faster. As a functional-first language, F# already solves this problem, but F# needs a better way to define classes and implement interfaces. Well, you have object expressions to solve this problem. One advantage of object expressions is that less code is needed to create an instance of an object because you don't need to declare a full type definition. You will see the advantage of this shortly with several of the examples in this section. You might be familiar with the SOLID (Single responsibility, Open-closed, Liskov substitution, Interface segregation, and Dependency inversion) design principles, which are described at *http://en.wikipedia.org/wiki/SOLID_(object-oriented_design)*. The last principle referred to in the acronym requires that the program rely on abstractions rather than concrete implementations. The object expression is a way for F# developers to provide concrete implementations of interfaces with less code.

The object expression can create an instance of a dynamically created, anonymous object type based on an existing type. In Listing 6-4 and Listing 6-7, the types for *objExpression* and *objExpression2* are created on the fly. Listing 6-4 shows how to implement an interface with an object expression. The *objExpression* variable type is based on *IMyInterface* and can be passed in any function that needs an *IMyInterface* parameter.

LISTING 6-4 Use mutable-variable data storage in the object expression

```
// define interface IA
type IA =
    abstract member F : int with get, set


// object expression
let objectExpression =
    let dataStorage = ref 9  //actual data storage
    {
        new IA with
            member this.F
                with get() = !dataStorage
                and set(v) = dataStorage :=  v
    }
```

The object expression is very powerful. It can be used to implement multiple interfaces or create objects based on a class. However, the object expression cannot extend base classes by adding new methods or properties. It can override only virtual or abstract methods. An object expression, like *objExpression2*, is not a type, so it is not possible to create object expressions based on other object expressions.

LISTING 6-5 Implementing an object expression interface

```
// first interface
type IMyInterface =
    abstract F : unit -> unit

// second interface
type IMyInterface2 =
    abstract F2 : unit -> unit

// implement one interface using object expression
let objExpression =
    {
        new IMyInterface with
            member this.F() = printfn "hello object expression"
    }

// object expression implementing two interfaces
let objExpression2 =
    {
        new IMyInterface with
            member this.F() = printfn "from interface"
        interface IMyInterface2 with
            member this.F2() = printfn "from interface2"
    }
```

> **Note** Auto-implemented properties are not supported in an object expression. Properties in object expressions can be declared only by using the old syntax.

If the field needs to be mutable, another approach is to use a reference cell. Listing 6-6 shows how to define a reference cell inside and outside of the object expression. And Listing 6-7 shows how to extend a base class.

LISTING 6-6 Object expression with a property

```
// first interface
type IMyInterface =
    abstract F : unit -> unit
    abstract Prop0 : string with get, set
    abstract Prop1 : string with get, set

// define a reference cell outside of objExpression
let myData = ref ""

// implement one interface using object expression
let objExpression =
    // define a reference cell inside the objExpression
    let x = ref ""
    {
        new IMyInterface with
            member this.F() = printfn "hello object expression"
            member this.Prop0 with get() = !x and set(v) = x:=v
            member this.Prop1 with get() = !myData and set(v) = myData:=v
    }

// set the Prop0 and print out the result
objExpression.Prop0 <- "set Prop0"
printfn "%s" objExpression.Prop0

// set the Prop1 and print out the result
objExpression.Prop1 <- "set Prop1"
printfn "%s" objExpression.Prop1
```

LISTING 6-7 Object expression based on class

```
// define an interface
type IMyInterface2 =
    abstract F2 : unit -> unit

// abstract class definition
[<AbstractClass>]
type MyAbstractClass() =
    abstract F : unit -> unit
    member this.F2() = printfn "my abstract class"
```

```
// object expression with abstract class and interface
let objExpressionInterfaceAbstract =
    {
        new MyAbstractClass() with
            override this.F() = printfn "implement the abstract class"
        interface IMyInterface2 with
            member this.F2() = printfn "from interface2"
    }

// override the object's ToString method using object expression
let objExpressionExtendObject =
    {
        new System.Object() with
            override this.ToString() = "hello from object expression"
    }
```

Note As in C#, the base class (which contains some concrete class member implementations) must come before all interfaces in the derived class definition. In an F# object expression, an abstract class must be present before any interface. In other words, the code will not compile if *MyAbstractClass* is put after *IMyInterface2* in the *objExpressionInterfaceAbstract*.

Listing 6-8 is a real-world example that implements a WPF command. WPF commands usually do not involve the construction of a class hierarchy. So it is a perfect place to use an object expression. From the sample code, you can see the object expression can have fields that cannot be accessed directly from outside. The variable *event1* can be viewed as a private field being implemented in the object expression. This example also shows that an object expression with parameters, like *action* in *createCommand*, can serve as a class factory to create objects based on passed-in functions.

LISTING 6-8 WPF command using an object expression

```
open System.Windows.Input

// class factory to generate the WPF command object
let createCommand action canExecute=
        let event1 = Event<_, _>()
        {
            new ICommand with
                member this.CanExecute(obj) = canExecute(obj)
                member this.Execute(obj) = action(obj)
                member this.add_CanExecuteChanged(handler) =
                    event1.Publish.AddHandler(handler)
                member this.remove_CanExecuteChanged(handler) =
                    event1.Publish.AddHandler(handler)
        }
```

```
// create a dummy command that does nothing and can always be executed
let myDummyCommand = createCommand
                            (fun _ -> ())    // execution function does nothing
                            (fun _ -> true) // this command can always be executed
```

 Note *PresentationCore.dll* and *WindowsBase.dll* need to be referenced for this example to compile.

Imagine a scenario where you have functions and variables in your module and need a way to provide the functionality to a C# method. The quickest way to organize the code inside a module and pass it to a C# method is to use an object expression. Listing 6-9 shows a sample solution with three projects. The object expression provides a convenient way to put individual functions defined in a module into a unit. If the development team has some domain-knowledge experts whose background is not in computer software, these domain experts can write the function in the module and a software developer can use the object expression to quickly organize the functions into a unit. The following list shows how to use F# object expression to organize code:

- First, a C# project is created in which an interface named *IMyInterface* is defined. This project will be referenced by other C# projects and the F# project.

- Second, a C# project is created and defines a class method named *MyFunction*, which takes *IMyInterface* as a parameter.

- And finally, an F# project creates an object expression and passes the object expression to the *MyFunction* class.

LISTING 6-9 Using object expressions to organize code

IMyInterface definition in the first C# project
```
public interface IMyInterface
{
    void MyFunction();
    int MyProperty { get; set; }
}
```

MyFunction definition in the second C# project
```
public class MyClass
{
    public void MyFunction(IMyInterface myObj)
    {
        // <my operations>
    }
}
```

Using an object expression to organize code and invoke a C# function

```
// function library module
module MyFunctionLibrary =
    let myFunction () = () //< other operations >

// use object expression to organize code from module
let myData =
        let myData = ref 9
        { new ClassLibrary1.IMyInterface with
                member this.MyFunction() = MyFunctionLibrary.myFunction()
                member this.MyProperty
                    with get() = !myData
                    and set(v) = myData := v
        }

// invoke the C# method using an object expression
let myClass = ConsoleApplication1.MyClass()
myClass.MyFunction(myData)
```

There are some restrictions for object expressions. The type information for the object is generated by the compiler; therefore, the type name is not user friendly. The type that backs up the object expression is sealed, so the back-end type does not help you a lot when you really need a complex inheritance hierarchy.

Working with Options

Listing 6-10 defines a function that returns an *int* option. According to the MSDN documentation, options have the following characteristics:

> *The option type in F# is used when an actual value might not exist for a named value or variable. An option has an underlying type and can hold a value of that type, or it might not have a value.*

For a C# developer, Listing 6-10 is similar to Listing 6-11, which uses *Nullable<T>*. Both functions filter out odd numbers. The C# function returns NULL, while the F# function returns *None*. Table 6-1 shows the members in the option.

TABLE 6-1 Option property and method

Property or Method	Type	Description
None	'T option	The option None value. This is a static property.
IsNone	Boolean	If the option is None, it returns TRUE.
IsSome	Boolean	If the option has some value, it returns TRUEs.
Some	'T option	Like None, but it returns a Some value.
Value	'T	Retrieves the underlying value. If there is no value (None), a NullReferenceException is thrown.

There is a subtle difference between NULL and *None*. First, F# classes and other reference objects do not accept NULL as a valid value. For example, the *GetDistance* function in Listing 2-16 cannot be passed NULL.

LISTING 6-10 Function that returns an *int* option

```
// function only returns even-number option
let filterOutOddNumber a =
    if a % 2 = 0 then Some(a)
    else None
```

LISTING 6-11 C# function that filters out odd numbers

```
static Nullable<int> FilterOutOddNumber(int a)
{
    if (a % 2 == 0)
    {
        return a;
    }
    else
    {
        return null;
    }
}
```

The fact that the F# function *GetDistance* cannot accept NULL as a parameter is not a bug. Actually, this is a carefully thought-out F# feature. Listing 6-12 shows how to check the user input string in C# and F#. The C# code seems perfect until you realize that *str* can be *null*! So you have to first check that `str != null` and then perform the real work. And this kind of error can be caught only at runtime. Many developers think about this kind of error, but the errors are often missed. The person who implements *read_string* often assumes that the invoker should handle the NULL, and the compiler does not say anything if the NULL value is not being considered.

LISTING 6-12 Reading an input string using C# and F#

```
C# code
//a function that returns a string type value
var str = read_string();

if (str.Length < 10) Console.WriteLine("less than 10");
else Console.WriteLine"long string...";
```

```
// return a string option to indicate the return value can be an uninitialized value
let str = read_string()
match str with
    | Some data -> printfn "good, we got value and we can process..."
    | None -> printfn "what happened, call IT right now!"
```

Note A simple implementation of *read_string()* is *Console.ReadLine()*. When Ctrl+Z is pressed, the *Console.ReadLine()* method returns NULL.

For the F# programmer, the situation is different. The user can give invalid input, so the code must represent the invalid input. An option type is used to explicitly indicate the invalid state. When an F# programmer invokes the *read_string* function, the returned option type reminds (or even forces) the programmer to handle this invalid situation. The design of F# helps the developer avoid many bugs. One typical example is how F# introduces an option rather than using a NULL value to represent multiple states. If you count how many NULL exceptions you received in the last month, it is not difficult to understand why F# programmers report fewer bugs in their code.

Let's look at a customized class sample in C#. If you have a *Person* type object, what is the meaning of an assigned value of NULL? It can mean either the object is in an unassigned state or the object is in a special-case state (that is, it has an invalid value). This ambiguity breaks the single-responsibility principle, the first principle in SOLID. If two different developers on the same team have a different view about what NULL means for the object, there will likely be many null-reference flaws in the application. If you compare this to the F# option approach, *None* is used to represent no value and *Some(...)* is used to represent any valid value. This clarifies the definition.

When we designed the language, we knew that not everyone agreed with the preceding argument. This is totally fine because you can use the *AllowNullLiteral* attribute to make a class nullable. Listing 6-13 shows an example of how to use the *AllowNullLiteral* attribute.

LISTING 6-13 Using *AllowNullLiteral* on a type

```
[<AllowNullLiteral>]
type NullableType() =
    member this.TestNullable(condition) =
        if condition then NullableType()
        else null
```

> **Note** This code does not compile if the type is not decorated with the *AllowNullLiteral* attribute.

After reading through Listing 6-13, you might wonder why F# still allows null values. This is because F# is living in a world full of objects and methods that accept NULL as an input value. If there were no support for NULL in F#, a number of .NET calls would be impossible. Also, NULL is needed when a variable needs to be bound to a function. See Listing 6-14.

LISTING 6-14 Checking the function initialization

```
type A() =
    [<DefaultValue>]
    val mutable MyFunction : unit -> int
    member this.IsMyFunctionInitialized
        with get() = box this.MyFunction = null
```

In summary, the NULL restriction exists only in F#. If you reference an F# project from a C# project, you can still pass NULL into an F# function. If a C# function returns a NULL value inside of F# code, it is also still acceptable.

Before finishing this section, I will list some helper functions and tricks you can use to handle NULL and options. Listing 6-15 provides a way to convert the NULL value to an option and convert it back to NULL if it is *None*. In addition to using *AllowNullLiteral*, this code provides an alternative to handle the NULL problem. The *Unchecked.defaultof<T>* operator returns the default value for *T*, such as *0* for *int* and NULL for any reference type.

LISTING 6-15 Converting NULL to or from an option when interacting with C#

```
type A() =
    let mutable a:option<A> = None
    member this.Value
        with get() =
            match a with
            | Some n -> n
            | None -> Unchecked.defaultof<A>
        and set v =
            if v = Unchecked.defaultof<A> then a <- None
            else a <- Some v
```

Working with Units of Measure

When I drove from freezing Toronto, Ontario to the NASA space center in Florida, I was shocked to see an LED screen showing that the current temperature was 28. I had just crossed the Niagara Falls a few minutes prior and could not believe that the warm Florida weather was so close! People from the US will giggle because they know that the temperature on the LED was expressed in Fahrenheit. Because Canada uses Celsius, the difference between metric and English units of measure confused me. Believe it or not, the first story I heard from NASA was about the Mars Climate Orbiter accident in 1999, whose root cause was the use of an incorrect unit of measure.

If a programming language supports units, as F# does, these problems are totally avoidable. Listing 6-16 shows how to define a unit of measure. The value *x* is bound to 3 cm, and the value *c* is bound to 27 ml. If you try to set a float number of 2.8 to the value *c*, it will not work because *c* is a *float<ml>* type, which cannot take a *float*. Similarly, the value *c* cannot take x^2 because the milliliter is a cube of centimeter.

LISTING 6-16 Defining and using a unit-of-measure type

```
Defining the units

//define centimeter
[<Measure>] type cm

// define milliliter which is cm2
[<Measure>] type ml = cm^3

let x = 3.<cm>
let c = x * x * x
// let c:float<ml> = x * x   //does not compile, because ml is a cube of cm
// let c:float<ml> = 2.8     //does not compile, cannot assign float to float<ml>


Execution result

[<Measure>]
type cm
[<Measure>]
type ml = cm ^ 3
val x : float<cm> = 3.0
val c : float<ml> = 27.0
```

> **Note** Spaces are not allowed between a number and a unit of measure.

> **Note** F# supports the (**) operator, which is equivalent to *Math.Pow*. However, the ** does not support *unit*, so the code let d:float<ml> = x ** 3 does not compile. This is because ** yields a *float*, which is not compatible with a *float<ml>* type.

The unit of measure can be presented in different but equivalent ways. F# can convert these different representations to a consistent format. From the execution result in Listing 6-17, you can see that the variables *kgm21* to *kgm24* show the same result *kg/m²*.

LISTING 6-17 Different definition formats convert to consistent format

```
Define unit of measure
[<Measure>] type kg
[<Measure>] type m

[<Measure>] type kgm21 = kg/m ^ -2
[<Measure>] type kgm22 = kg/m/m
[<Measure>] type kgm23 = kg/(m * m)
[<Measure>] type kgm24 = kg/(m ^ 2)


Execution result
[<Measure>]
type kg
[<Measure>]
type m
[<Measure>]
type kgm21 = kg m ^ 2
[<Measure>]
type kgm22 = kg/m ^ 2
[<Measure>]
type kgm23 = kg/m ^ 2
[<Measure>]
type kgm24 = kg/m ^ 2
```

Units of measure can be converted as well. Listing 6-18 shows a function that converts *gram* to *kilogram*.

LISTING 6-18 Converting units from *gram* to *kilogram*

```
// define gram
[<Measure>] type g

// define kilogram
[<Measure>] type kg

// define a conversion function that converts gram to kilogram
let convertGramToKilogram (x : float<g>) = x / 1000.0<g/kg>
```

> **Note** Because the unit of measure exists only at F#'s compile time, C# code is not able to access the unit of measure. The *float<'measureUnit>* can be viewed only as a double in C# code.

> **Note** As mentioned in the previous note, a unit of measure is a compile-time feature that cannot be accessed at runtime. Any attempt to access the unit at runtime will not work. For example, *ToString()* cannot print out any unit information.

A unit of measure can have static members, as shown in Listing 6-19.

LISTING 6-19 Adding static members to unit-of-measure types

```
[<Measure>]
type m =
        static member C = 3.28<foot/m>
        static member FromFoot (x:float<foot>) = x / m.C
        static member ToFoot(x:float<m>) = x * m.C

and [<Measure>] foot =
        static member FromMeter = m.ToFoot
        static member ToMeter = m.FromFoot

m.FromFoot(3.28<foot>)
```

Execution result

```
val it : float<m> = 1.0
```

A unit of measure is defined as a type, so it can be used in generic functions. Listing 6-20 defines a generic unit function that can add any two numbers. The function makes sure that numbers with different units of measure cannot be processed together. The execution result is `result1 = 10.0`, `result2 = 5.0`.

LISTING 6-20 A generic function using a unit of measure

```
// define units of measure
[<Measure>] type lb
[<Measure>] type inch

// generic function
let add ( x : float<'u>) (y : float<'u>)= x + y * 2.

let result1 = add 4.<lb> 3.<lb>
let result2 = add 1.<inch> 2.<inch>

printfn "result1 = %A, result2 = %A" result1 result2
```

Note In the printfn statement, you have to use *%A* as the type identifier. The variable *result1* is a *float* at runtime, but it is *float<lb>* type at compile time. The *%f* is not compatible with the unit of measure, so it will not compile.

F# also supports the ability to create a float value with units of measure by using *LanguagePrimitives.FloatWithMeasure* and *LanguagePrimitives.Float32WithMeasure*. Additionally, you can remove a unit of measure by converting it to a number. See Listing 6-21.

LISTING 6-21 Converting a number to and from a unit of measure

```
// remove unit and return float
let removeUnit<[<Measure>]'u> x = float x

let result = removeUnit 4.<lb>

// give a unit of measure to a float
let fourlb : float<lb> = LanguagePrimitives.FloatWithMeasure result
```

Units of measure can be applied only to float and signed-integer types. If you want to use a unit with a customized type, you need to use the generic type definition. The unit of measure is a special type, so it can be used in the generic type definition without any problem. Listing 6-22 defines a bank account class. By applying different units of measure, you generate bank accounts for different currencies.

LISTING 6-22 Bank account using a unit of measure

```
// account state enum
type AccountState =
    | Overdrawn
    | Silver
    | Gold

// units of measure: US and Canadian dollars
[<Measure>] type USD
[<Measure>] type CND

// bank account class
type Account<[<Measure>] 'u>() =
    let mutable balance = 0.0<_>
    member this.State
        with get() =
            match balance with
            | _ when balance <= 0.0<_> -> Overdrawn
            | _ when balance > 0.0<_> && balance < 10000.0<_> -> Silver
            | _ -> Gold
```

```
    member this.PayInterest() =
        let interest =
            match this.State with
                | Overdrawn -> 0.
                | Silver -> 0.01
                | Gold -> 0.02
        interest * balance
    member this.Deposit x =  balance <- balance + x
    member this.Withdraw x = balance <- balance - x

let measureSample() =
    // make US dollar account
    let account = Account<USD>()
    let USDAmount = LanguagePrimitives.FloatWithMeasure 10000.
    account.Deposit USDAmount
    printfn "US interest = %A" (account.PayInterest())

    // make Canadian dollar account
    let canadaAccount = Account<CND>()
    let CADAmount : float<CND> = LanguagePrimitives.FloatWithMeasure 10000.
    canadaAccount.Deposit CADAmount
    printfn "Canadian interest = %A" (canadaAccount.PayInterest())

measureSample()
```

For some C# developers, type is something they encounter every day but pay little attention to. A large number of test cases are brought up each day to check the correctness of the program. Have you ever thought about the compiler that actually checks your code on every branch before you run the program? If an error can be caught at compile time, it can be fixed much easier. The unit of measure is one example that uses the type system to reduce the possibility of making mistakes. Later in this section, you will see more examples of using the type system to reduce the possibility of making errors.

Working with Records

As previously mentioned, a tuple is a set of values. You can think of a record as an enhanced version of a tuple. A record is a set of named values, and it provides more features than a tuple does. Listing 6-23 shows how to define and create a record. If the label in the record definition is unique, the record name is optional when you create the record instance; otherwise, you have to specify the record type name. For example, both *Point2D* and *Point* have *x* and *y* labels. Because of this, the type name is needed when you create a record instance of *Point2D* or *Point*.

LISTING 6-23 Defining a record and creating a record

```
// define record
type Point2D = { x : float; y: float }
type Point = { x : float; y: float }
type Student = { Name: string; Age : decimal; }
type Person = { First : string
                Last: string }

// create record

// the record name is mandatory because the label is not unique
let point2DRecord = { Point2D.x = 1.; Point2D.y = 2. }
let pointRecord = { Point.x = 1.; Point.y = 2. }

// record name is optional because the label is unique
let studentRecord = { Name = "John"; Age = 18m; }
let personRecord = { First = "Chris"
                     Last = "Root" }
```

 Note When you place each label on a new line, the semicolon (;) is optional. Also, the last semicolon is always optional.

The fields in a record are immutable by default. Listing 6-24 shows how to use the *with* keyword to make a copy of an existing record.

LISTING 6-24 Record copying

```
type Person = { First : string
                Last: string }

let personRecord = { First = "Chris"
                     Last = "Root" }

let personRecord2 = { personRecord with First = "Matt" }
```

Execution result

```
type Person =
  {First: string;
   Last: string;}
val personRecord : Person = {First = "Chris";
                             Last = "Root";}
val personRecord2 : Person = {First = "Matt";
                              Last = "Root";}
```

Note To avoid odd compile errors, make sure *First* and *Last* are aligned correctly. I highly recommend installing and using the F# depth colorizer to assist with this.

The record fields can be mutable if they are decorated with the *mutable* keyword. Also, records can define member functions or properties to extend their functionality. See Listing 6-25.

LISTING 6-25 A record with a mutable field and members

```
type Car =

    {
    Make : string
    Model : string
    mutable Odometer : int
    }
    member this.Drive(mile) =
        printfn "you drove another %d miles" mile
        this.Odometer <- this.Odometer + mile
    member this.CurrentMileage with get() = this.Odometer

let myCar = { Make = "Plymouth"; Model = "Neon"; Odometer = 100892 }
myCar.Drive(20)
printfn "current mileage = %d" myCar.CurrentMileage
```

Execution result

```
you drove another 20 miles
current mileage = 100912
```

Note F# uses space indents to distinguish between language elements. If the *member* keyword in the record definition is not aligned correctly, you will get a compile error.

The record does not support default values on its fields. However, you can declare a static member with a default value and mutate its value by using the *with* keyword. Listing 6-26 shows how to do this.

LISTING 6-26 Using a static member as a base template record

```
// define a Point2D record with originalPoint = (0,0)
type Point2D =
    { x : float; y : float }
    static member OriginalPoint =
                { x = 0.; y = 0.}
```

```
let original = Point2D.OriginalPoint
let onePoint = { Point2D.OriginalPoint with x = 1.; y = 1.}

printfn "original point = %A \r\nand one point = %A" original onePoint
```

Execution result

```
original point = {x = 0.0;
 y = 0.0;}
and one point = {x = 1.0;
 y = 1.0;}
```

Record equality is performed by using a structural comparison. Listing 6-27 shows a record-equality comparison.

LISTING 6-27 Record structural comparison

```
// define record type
type MyRecord = { X : int; mutable Y : int }

// create two record instances
let r0 = { X = 0; Y = 1 }
let r1 = { X = 0; Y = 1 }

printfn "r0 = r1 ? %A" (r0 = r1)

r1.Y <- 2
printfn "r0 = r1 ? %A" (r0 = r1)
```

Execution result

```
r0 = r1 ? true
r0 = r1 ? false
```

Using the *CLIMutable* Attribute

The default constructor is needed for many of these scenarios. By default, a record type does not generate a default constructor. If you ever try to data bind to a record, you will be blocked by this behavior. The requirement for a default constructor is not limited to XAML; it also is a requirement with serialization, WCF, and other scenarios. The *CLIMutable* attribute was introduced in F# 3.0 to generate a default constructor for a record. Listing 6-28 shows a type named *R* that is decorated with the *CLIMutable* attribute, which will cause a default constructor and property setters to be generated, although those features are not exposed to the F# side.

LISTING 6-28 *CLIMutable* attribute

Defining a *CLIMutable* attribute in F# code

```
[<CLIMutable>]
type R =
  { X : int; Y : int }

// R2 does not have default constructor
type R2 =
  { X : int; Y : int }
```

C# code invoking the *CLIMutable* record

```
var x = new R();
var x2 = new R(0, 2);
var y = new R2(0, 2);
// var y2 = new R2();     //does not compile
```

Adding the default constructor not only enables support for XAML, but also makes the record serialization story much easier. The Azure marketplace serialization example (shown in Listing 4-54) can be rewritten to use a record as shown in Listing 6-29. The last line of the code uses structural comparison to make sure that the data is the same before and after the serialization.

LISTING 6-29 Using a record type in serialization

```
// define the type provider
type Demographics = Microsoft.FSharp.Data.TypeProviders.ODataService<ServiceUri =
    "https://api.datamarket.azure.com/Uk.Gov/TravelAdvisoryService/">
let ctx = Demographics.GetDataContext()

// set the credentials
ctx.Credentials <- System.Net.NetworkCredential(<liveID>, <id>)

// define a serializable record
[<CLIMutable>]
type NewsRecord = { Title : string; Summary : string }

// query the latest news
let latestNews = query {
    for n in ctx.LatestTravelNewsFromFco do
    select { NewsRecord.Title = n.Title; NewsRecord.Summary = n.Summary}
}

let news = latestNews |> Seq.toArray
```

```
// deserialize from xml
let deserialize<'T> (fileName:string) =
    let reader = System.Xml.Serialization.XmlSerializer(typeof<'T>)
    use file = new System.IO.StreamReader(fileName)
    let fileData = reader.Deserialize(file) :?> 'T
    fileData

// serialize data
let serialize data (fileName:string) =
    let writer = System.Xml.Serialization.XmlSerializer(data.GetType())
    use file = new System.IO.StreamWriter(fileName)
    writer.Serialize(file, data)

//serialize the data
serialize news "myLocalNews.xml"

// deserialize the file
let data = deserialize<NewsRecord array> "myLocalNews.xml"

// structural comparison to make sure the data is the same
let isEqual = news = data
```

Comparing a Record with Other Data Structures

It might be confusing as to when to choose a record type over other data types, such as struct or
class. The record type is still a class, while the struct is a lightweight data structure. If you have a large
number of objects allocating memory on the heap, a struct is a better choice. This is because a struct
does not trigger garbage collection. Instead, a struct is allocated on the stack, which will be cleared
when the function returns. In other words, if there is a place where a struct can bring more benefit,
you should use a struct. Otherwise, a record is your best choice. If you need more functionality than a
record provides, use a full-fledged class.

If a record is more like a class, what is the difference between a record and a class? One main
difference is in how you set the initial values. The creation of a record needs an initial value to be
present, and it forces the invoker to give a meaningful value explicitly. So when explicit value initialization is mandatory, a record is preferred. The class equality and record equality are different. The
class uses reference equality, while the record uses structural equality. The class provides more flexible
ways of initialization by making it possible to specify multiple constructors, while the record does not
provide a way to add more constructors.

Working with Discriminated Unions

If the record can be viewed as a tuple with labels, the *discriminated union* (DU) can be viewed as a union of different types. Listing 6-30 shows how to define a shape union that contains a circle, triangle, and rectangle. The possible value in the union is called a *union case*. The shape union has three union cases, and each case has a different type. For example, the triangle case has three double tuples.

LISTING 6-30 Defining a discriminated union

DU with type
```
type Shape =
    | Circle of double
    | Triangle of double * double * double
    | Rectangle of double * double
```

DU without type
```
type Number = OddNumber | EvenNumber
```

> **Note** If the union case is on the same line, the first pipe (|) is not mandatory.

The DU can be recursive. Just like with other recursive types, you can define one in a DU with the *and* keyword. A typical application of the DU recursive feature is to define a tree structure. See Listing 6-31.

LISTING 6-31 Defining a tree structure using a DU

Defining a tree using DU
```
type Tree =
    | Tip of int
    | Node of int * Tree * Tree
```

Defining a tree with a recursive type
```
type Tree =
    | Tip of NodeType
    | Node of int * Tree * Tree
and NodeType =
    | NodeContent of int
```

As with record, the DU supports member methods and properties. Listing 6-32 shows how to override the *ToString* method so that it shows the current type name.

LISTING 6-32 DU with a method

```
type Tree =
    | Tip of NodeType
    | Node of int * Tree * Tree
    override this.ToString() = "this is a Tree DU"

and NodeType =
    | NodeContent of int
    override this.ToString() = "this is NodeType DU"
```

> **Note** A class hierarchy can be extended at will by adding new subclasses; however, the discriminated union structure is closed and cannot be extended.

The DU introduces an interesting feature that is comparable to the class hierarchy. The *Shape* type shown in Listing 6-30 can be viewed as an abstract base class, and the three union cases are three subclasses derived from the base class.

Listing 6-33 shows how to use an interface with the DU. One interesting point in this example is that the different union case types are now unified by the interface. Different DU instances now can be passed into a function that requires the *IShape* interface.

LISTING 6-33 DU with an interface

```
// define an interface
type IShape =
    abstract Area : double with get

// DU with interface
type ShapeWithInterface =
    | Circle of double
    | Triangle of double * double * double
    | Rectangle of double * double
    interface IShape
        with member this.Area =
                match this with
                | Circle(r) -> r*r* System.Math.PI
                | Triangle(a, b, c) ->
                    let s = (a + b + c)/2.
                    sqrt(s * (s - a) * (s - b) * (s - c))
                | Rectangle(a, b) -> a * b
    override this.ToString() = "This is a ShapeWithInterface type"

let getArea2 (shape:IShape) = shape.Area
getArea2 (Circle(4.))
```

Listing 6-34 uses DU implement a binary tree structure and traverses it with *Seq.unfold*. The algorithm uses a queue to hold the unvisited node.

LISTING 6-34 Defining a binary tree using DU and performing a layer traversal

```
type NodeType = int

type BinaryTree =
    | Nil
    | Node of NodeType * BinaryTree * BinaryTree

let tree = Node(5,
              Node(42,
                  Node(3, Nil, Nil),
                  Node(2, Nil, Nil)),
              Node(4,
                  Node(13,
                      Node(14, Nil, Nil),
                      Node(16, Nil, Nil)),
                  Node(12,
                      Node(15, Nil, Nil),
                      Node(21,
                          Node(22, Nil, Nil),
                          Nil))))

let layerTraverse state =
    match state with
    | [] -> None
    | h::t ->
        match h with
        | Nil -> None
        | Node(v, Nil, Nil) -> Some (v, t)
        | Node(v, subTree, Nil)
        | Node(v, Nil, subTree) -> Some (v, t@[subTree])
        | Node(v, l, r) -> Some (v, t@[l;r])

[tree]
|> Seq.unfold layerTraverse
|> Seq.toList
```

Note If you replace t@[subTree] and t@[l;r] with [subTree]@t and [l;r]@t, the algorithm becomes a pre-order traversal.

Working with Comparison Operations for a Record, Tuple, and DU

If I ask you to tell me the result of comparing two tuples such as (1,1) < (2,1), you might think this comparison does not make sense because these two tuples are two different physical objects. The comparison should not be allowed. Actually, this comparison returns TRUE. The code and execution result from F# Interactive (FSI) is shown in Listing 6-35.

LISTING 6-35 Comparing two tuples

```
> (1, 1) < (2, 1);;
val it : bool = true
```

F# uses structural comparison, structural hashing, and structural equality on records, tuples, and DUs. Listing 6-36 shows that (1+2, 1) is equal to (3, 1) and that they have the same hash value.

LISTING 6-36 Compare (1+2,1) and (3,1)

```
> (1 + 2, 1) = (3, 1);;
val it : bool = true
> hash (1+2,1) = hash (3,1);;
val it : bool = true
```

> **Note** The hash function in the preceding example is used to get the hash value of the tuple.

Listing 6-37 shows the record, tuple, and DU comparison. Records are compared on each pair of fields in declaration order and then return the first non-zero result. DU compares first on the index of the union cases according to the declaration order and then compares the union value. The last comparison, which compares *Case4* and *Case3*, returns Case4 < Case3 because *Case3* is declared before *Case4*.

LISTING 6-37 Compare a record, tuple, and DU

Record, tuple, and DU comparison code

```
//define a record
type MyRecord = { X : int; Y : string }

// define a tuple type
type MyTuple = int*string
```

```
// define a DU type
type MyDU =
    | Case1 of int
    | Case2 of string
    | Case3 of MyRecord
    | Case4 of MyTuple

// define a comparison function
let inline compare x y =
    if x > y then
        printfn "%A > %A" x y
    elif x=y then
        printfn "%A = %A" x y
    else
        printfn "%A < %A" x y

// create records
let record1 = { X = 1; Y = "1" }
let record2 = { X = 1; Y = "2" }
let record3 = { X = 2; Y = "1" }
let record4 = { X = 1; Y = "1" }

compare record1 record2
compare record1 record3
compare record2 record3
compare record1 record4

// create tuples
let tuple1 : MyTuple = 1, "1"
let tuple2 : MyTuple = 1, "2"
let tuple3 : MyTuple = 2, "1"
let tuple4 : MyTuple = 1, "1"

compare tuple1 tuple2
compare tuple1 tuple3
compare tuple2 tuple3
compare tuple1 tuple4

// create DU Case1 instances
let du1 = Case1(1)
let du2 = Case1(2)
let du3 = Case1(1)

compare du1 du2
compare du1 du3
compare du2 du3

// create DU Case3 instances
let duRecord1 = Case3(record1)
let duRecord2 = Case3(record2)
let duRecord3 = Case3(record3)
let duRecord4 = Case3(record4)
```

```
compare duRecord1 duRecord2
compare duRecord1 duRecord3
compare duRecord2 duRecord3
compare duRecord1 duRecord4

// create DU Case4 instances
let duTuple1 = Case4(tuple1)
let duTuple2 = Case4(tuple2)
let duTuple3 = Case4(tuple3)
let duTuple4 = Case4(tuple4)

compare duTuple1 duTuple2
compare duTuple1 duTuple3
compare duTuple2 duTuple3
compare duTuple1 duTuple4

// compare Case4 with Case3
compare duTuple1 duRecord1
```

Execution result from the record, tuple, and DU comparison code

```
{X = 1; Y = "1";} < {X = 1; Y = "2";}
{X = 1; Y = "1";} < {X = 2; Y = "1";}
{X = 1; Y = "2";} < {X = 2; Y = "1";}
{X = 1; Y = "1";} = {X = 1; Y = "1";}

(1, "1") < (1, "2")
(1, "1") < (2, "1")
(1, "2") < (2, "1")
(1, "1") = (1, "1")

Case1 1 < Case1 2
Case1 1 = Case1 1
Case1 2 > Case1 1

Case3 {X = 1; Y = "1";} < Case3 {X = 1; Y = "2";}
Case3 {X = 1; Y = "1";} < Case3 {X = 2; Y = "1";}
Case3 {X = 1; Y = "2";} < Case3 {X = 2; Y = "1";}
Case3 {X = 1; Y = "1";} = Case3 {X = 1; Y = "1";}

Case4 (1, "1") < Case4 (1, "2")
Case4 (1, "1") < Case4 (2, "1")
Case4 (1, "2") < Case4 (2, "1")
Case4 (1, "1") = Case4 (1, "1")
Case4 (1, "1") > Case3 {X = 1; Y = "1";}
```

 Note Some returns and extra spaces are removed to increase the readability.

Using Pattern Matching

We used pattern matching in various examples in Chapter 1, such as in Listing 1-10. At that time, your understanding of pattern matching was that it is something similar to a C# *switch* statement. Although this is true, pattern matching is much more powerful.

Let's start by defining patterns. Patterns are simply rules used to transform data. According to this definition, you can use pattern matching to match input data with some patterns and trigger corresponding actions, such as actions that transform data. What's more, the pattern also provides a way to decompose input data. Listing 6-38 uses pattern matching to rewrite the odd-number program from Chapter 1. The transform function *transformEvenToZero* converts all even numbers to zero and then sums up the elements in the transformed sequence.

Pattern matching comes in several flavors. Listing 6-38 is the simplest pattern-matching example; it matches the input data against a constant value. This is called a *constant pattern*.

LISTING 6-38 Pattern-matching sample

```
let isEvenNumber x = x % 2 = 0
let transformEvenToZero x =
    match isEvenNumber x with
    | true -> 0
    | false -> x

// sum of odd number from 0 to 100
let r = seq {0..100} |> Seq.sumBy transformEvenToZero
```

Before I introduce more complex patterns, I should briefly introduce the *function* keyword. Listing 6-39 shows how to use the *function* keyword to simplify the match expression, which is the match x with in the sample code. The *function* keyword implicitly appends a parameter to the containing function.

LISTING 6-39 Using the *function* keyword

```
Using match in a function
let matchSample x =
    match x with
        | 1 -> printfn "this is one"
        | 2 -> printfn "this is two"
        | 3 -> printfn "this is three"
        | _ -> printfn "other value"
```

Using *function* to represent a match

```
let functionSample =
    function
        | 1 -> printfn "this is one"
        | 2 -> printfn "this is two"
        | 3 -> printfn "this is three"
        | _ -> printfn "other value"
```

Using the Tuple Pattern

A more complex pattern is the tuple pattern, which is used to match a value pair. Listing 6-40 implements the logical OR function. The first version lists all the values in the form of a tuple. The OR function returns FALSE only when the two inputs are both FALSE. The simplified version implements this idea by using underscore (_), which can match anything. Note that the tuple can have more than two values. Listing 1-65 uses tuple matching to decompose a triple element in the list.

LISTING 6-40 Tuple pattern

OR function with tuple pattern matching

```
let orFunction (x, y) =
    match x, y with
        | true, true -> true
        | true, false -> true
        | false, true -> true
        | false, false -> false
```

Simplified OR function with tuple pattern matching

```
let orFunction2 (x, y) =
    match x, y with
        | false, false -> false
        | _, _ -> true
```

Note The _, _ can be further simplified as _. The _, _ is used to match any tuple value, while _ is used to match any value.

Listing 6-41 shows how to use pattern matching to work with a tuple that is returned from the *TryGetValue* function.

```
let f x =
    let dict = System.Collections.Generic.Dictionary()
    dict.[0] <- "0"
    dict.[1] <- "1"

    match dict.TryGetValue x with
    | true, v -> sprintf "found %A mapped to %A" x v
    | false, _ -> "cannot find"

printfn "%A" (f 0)
printfn "%A" (f 1)
printfn "%A" (f 2)
```

Execution result

```
"found 0 mapped to "0""
"found 1 mapped to "1""
"cannot find"
```

One nice feature about pattern matching is that F# can generate a warning if one possible pattern is missing in the match expression. For example, when sending the code in Listing 6-42 to FSI, F# warns the user about this problem.

LISTING 6-42 Missing one pattern in the pattern-matching expression

```
>   let orFunction (x, y) =
        match x, y with
        | true, true -> true
        //| true, false -> true // miss one pattern
        | false, true -> true
        | false, false -> false;;

        match x, y with
--------------^^^^

stdin(2,15): warning FS0025: Incomplete pattern matches on this expression. For example,
the
  value '(_,false)' may indicate a case not covered by the pattern(s).
```

Using the List and Array Patterns

Like a tuple, patterns can also decompose a list or array into values. Listing 6-43 decomposes an array and gets the array length.

LISTING 6-43 An array pattern

```
let arrayLength array =
    match array with
    | [| |] -> 0
    | [| _ |] -> 1
    | [| _; _ |] -> 2
    | [| _; _; _ |] -> 3
    | _ -> Array.length array
```

Listing 6-44 shows how to use a recursive function to decompose a list into a head and tail and get the length of that list. The con operator (::) decomposes the list into a head part and a tail part.

LISTING 6-44 An example of the con operator pattern

```
let rec listLength list =
    match list with
    | head :: tail -> 1 + (listLength tail)
    | [] -> 0
```

Note The preceding code can cause a stack overflow because it is not tail recursive. The following code provides a version that is tail recursive:

```
let rec listLength acc list =
    match list with
    | head :: tail ->
        listLength (acc + 1) tail
    | [] -> acc
```

There are some interesting examples in Listing 6-45 for the list pattern matching. The first code snippet matches the list and decomposes it into two elements, and it contains a list that represents the tail. The second code snippet checks the element type and converts the element back to the type, as it was prior to being boxed.

LISTING 6-45 Pattern matching for list

```
let list = [1;2;3;4;]
match list with
| h0::h1::t -> printfn "two elements %A %A and tail %A" h0 h1 t
| _ -> ()

let objList = [box(1); box("a"); box('c')]
match objList with
```

```
| [:? int as i;
  :? string as str;
  :? char as ch] ->
      printfn "values are %A %A %A" i str ch
| _ -> ()
```

 Note The code `:? Int as i` is a type of pattern match that will be discussed later in this section.

Using the NULL Pattern

As I mentioned in the "Working with Options" section earlier in the chapter, an option is generally a better choice than using a NULL value. The first code snippet shown in Listing 6-46 shows a match expression that uses the option type.

Another option is to match against a NULL. This is known as the NULL pattern, and an example of this is shown in the second code snippet in Listing 6-46. An important application of the NULL pattern is to convert to a NULL from an option or vice versa.

LISTING 6-46 NULL pattern

Using an identifier pattern to test and extract an option value

```
let extractOption x =
    match x with
    | Some a -> printfn "option has value %A" a
    | None -> printfn "option has no value"
```

Using a NULL pattern to convert a nullable .NET value to an F# option

```
let toOption x =
    match x with
    | null -> None
    | _ -> Some x
```

Using the Record and Identifier Patterns

Listing 6-47 shows how to use the identifier pattern to decompose a discriminated union. The second code snippet shows how to use the record pattern to decompose a record.

LISTING 6-47 Record and identifier patterns

Using an identifier pattern for a discriminated union

```
type Shape =
    | Circle of double
    | Triangle of double * double * double
    | Rectangle of double * double

let getArea shape =
    match shape with
    | Circle(r) -> r * r * System.Math.PI
    | Triangle(a, b, c) ->
        let s = (a + b + c) / 2.
        sqrt s * (s - a) * (s - b) * (s - c)
    | Rectangle(a, b) -> a * b
```

Using a record pattern

```
type Point2D = { x : float; y: float }

let isOnXAxis p =
    match p with
    | { Point2D.x = 0.; Point2D.y = _ } -> true
    | _ -> false
```

F# uses the type system to help prevent bugs and improve readability. Listing 6-48 uses the
Currency DU type to convert the decimal type to either the USD or CAD type. The sample extends the
Currency DU type by adding two operators.

LISTING 6-48 Using DU and pattern matching in a currency calculation

```
type Currency =
    | USD of decimal
    | CAD of decimal

    // extend the DU type with the + and - operators
    with
        static member (+) (x:Currency, y:Currency) =
            match x, y with
                | USD(a), USD(b) -> USD(a+b)
                | CAD(a), CAD(b) -> CAD(a+b)
                | _ -> failwith "cannot add different unit value"

        static member (-) (x:Currency, y:Currency) =
            match x,y with
                | USD(a), USD(b) -> USD(a - b)
                | CAD(a), CAD(b) -> CAD(a - b)
                | _ -> failwith "cannot add different unit value"
```

```
// perform currency add and minus operations
try
    printfn "result = %A" (USD(1m) + USD(11m))
    printfn "result = %A" (CAD(1m) - CAD(11m))

    // this line generates an exception
    printfn "result = %A" (USD(100m) - CAD(10m))
with
    | _ as e -> printfn "%A" e
```

Execution result

```
result = USD 12M
result = CAD -10M
System.Exception: cannot add different unit value
```

> **Note** Unlike the unit-of-measure approach, this approach adds runtime overhead.

The pattern matching for a record needs to make sure the record is decomposed when performing the match. The *match* statement in Listing 6-49 matches any record with the listed records even when the type differs. The correct way to match the record is shown in Listing 6-50.

LISTING 6-49 Match Record Sample I

```
type MyRecord = { X : int list; Y : string }
type MyRecord2 = { XX : int; YY : string; Z : int }

let rr = { X = [100; 200; 300]; Y = "aa" }
let r0 = { X = [100; 200; 3]; Y = "aa" }
let r1 = { XX = 1; YY = "bb"; Z = 9 }

match r1 with
    | rr -> "a"
    | _ -> "b"
```

> **Note** A warning "This rule will never be matched" will be generated on the last line.

LISTING 6-50 Match Record Sample II

```
type MyRecord = { X : int list; Y : string }
type MyRecord2 = { XX : int; YY : string; Z : int }

let r1 = { XX = 1; YY = "bb"; Z = 9 }
let r2 = { XX = 2; YY = "r2"; Z = 10 }

match r2 with
    | {YY = "bb"} -> """r1 is matched with YY="bb" """
    | _ -> "others"
```

Working with the And/Or Pattern and Pattern Grouping

The And/Or pattern combines two patterns with an AND/OR relationship. Listing 6-51 tests whether the point is on the axis using the AND pattern. All the patterns in the match list are OR-ed together; therefore, the OR pattern sample can be rewritten using pattern grouping, as shown in Listing 6-52.

LISTING 6-51 And/Or pattern used to test a point

And pattern used to test a point

```
let testPoint2 point =
    match point with
    | x, y & 0, 0 -> "original point"
    | x, y & 0, _ -> "on x axis"
    | x, y & _, 0 -> "on y axis"
    | _ -> "other"
```

Or pattern

```
let testPoint3 point =
    match point with
    | x, y & (0, 0) -> "original point"
    | x, y & (0, _ | _, 0) -> "on axis"
    | _ -> "other"
```

LISTING 6-52 Pattern grouping

```
let testPoint4 point =
    match point with
    | (x, y) & (0, 0) -> "original point"
    | (x, y) & (0, _) | (x, y) & (_, 0) -> "on axis"
    | _ -> "other"
```

Using Variable Patterns and the *when* Guard

Up until now, the patterns you've looked at have not handled relationships among decomposed data items. If you want to know whether the decomposed data meets certain criteria, you can use the *when* guard. Listing 6-53 decides whether or not the (x,y) point is on the line f(x) = x.

LISTING 6-53 Point relative to line f(x) = x

```
let testPoint tuple =
    match tuple with
    | x, y when x = y -> "on the line"
    | x, y when x > y -> "below the line"
    | _ -> "up the line"
```

Note F# does not consider the *when* guard's result to decide whether the match expression is complete. Therefore, even if you changed the last pattern in Listing 6-53 to x, y when x < y, the compiler would still think that the match expression was not complete and generate a warning message.

Note Another option is to use active patterns, which will be introduced in the next section.

Using the Type Pattern and *as pattern*

When the input parameter is decomposed to different parts, the different parts might need a name for future reference. The *as pattern* is introduced for this purpose. Listing 6-54 shows how to write a type check. Instead of using an *is* operator, as you might do in C#, F# uses *:?* operator to check the type.

LISTING 6-54 Type pattern example

```
let testType (x:obj) =
    match x with
    | :? float as f -> printfn "float value %f" f
    | :? int as i -> printfn "int value %d" i
    | _ -> printfn "type cannot process"
```

Note The input parameter must be the superclass of the type in the pattern. In Listing 6-54, *float* and *int* are derived from *obj*.

Using the Choice Helper Type

There is a helper type used to encapsulating several choices called Choice. You can use Choice when you have between 2 and 7 choices. Listing 6-55 shows how to initialize a dual-choice structure and how to match against the structure.

LISTING 6-55 Choice example

```
open System

// initialize a Choice<int,int>
let a : Choice<int, int> = Choice2Of2 1

// match against the choice
let f x =
    match x with
        | Choice1Of2 e -> printfn "value is %A" e
        | Choice2Of2 e -> printfn "value is %A" e

f a
```

Execution result

```
value is 1
```

Note Unlike the C++ union, Choice does not share the same memory. Setting *Choice2of2* makes the execution go to the second pattern.

Working with Active Patterns

As you've already seen, pattern matching introduces a way to decompose data into small pieces. However, the decomposition process cracks the data only by its structure. For example, a tuple is decomposed only into a value pair. If instead you need to check the data, a *when* guard is needed. But when the checking logic gets complex, the *when* guard can have piles of conditions and, as a consequence, make the code hard to maintain.

You can use the active pattern to resolve this issue. It is a special function in itself. By evaluating this function, the data is decomposed, segmented by an active pattern function, and associated with the active pattern name. In other words, the active pattern is a customized way to decompose and label data.

Using Single-Case Active Patterns

The simplest form of an active pattern is the single-case active pattern. Listing 6-56 defines an active pattern named *Reminder2*. When using the active pattern, the expected value must be passed in. For example, the *0* in `Remainder2 0` is the expected value. If the input value can make the active pattern yield the expected value, this union case is matched to the pattern *Remainder2*.

LISTING 6-56 Defining a single-case active pattern

```
// define a single-case active pattern
let (| Remainder2 |) x = x % 2

// use Remainder pattern to check even/odd number
let checkNumber x =
    match x with
        | Remainder2 0 -> "even number"
        | Remainder2 1 -> "odd number"
```

Note Active patterns are not used in completeness evaluations. Although the preceding pattern does cover all the cases, a warning will still be generated. The following code uses a wildcard to eliminate the warning:

```
// define a single-case active pattern
let (| Remainder2 |) x = x%2

// use Remainder pattern to check even/odd number
let checkNumber x =
    match x with
        | Remainder2 0 -> "even number"
        | Remainder2 1 -> "odd number"
        | _ -> "other number"
```

In the final analysis, the active pattern is a special function. Listing 6-57 shows that a single-case active pattern can be used to make a safe *Dictionary* object.

LISTING 6-57 Using a single-case active pattern as a function

```
open System.Collections.Generic

let (|SafeDict|) (d : Dictionary<_, _>) =
    if d = null then Dictionary<_, _>()
    else d
```

```
let tryFind (SafeDict dic) key =
    if dic.ContainsKey key then
        Some dic.[key]
    else None
```

You can use the single-case active pattern to categorize the data and clean up the code, but the value that it provides falls short in more complex scenarios.

Using Partial-Case Active Patterns

The partial-case active pattern is an enhanced version of the single-case active pattern. Partial-case active patterns identify only part of the incoming data and leave the rest of data untouched (or unlabeled). The partial-case active pattern must return an option type. The pattern will be ignored when *None* is returned. Listing 6-58 defines two partial-case active patterns. If the variable *x* is less than *10*, the first pattern is triggered.

LISTING 6-58 Partial-case active pattern

```
// define partial active patterns
let (|LessThan10|_|) x = if x < 10 then Some x else None
let (|Btw10And20|_|) x = if x >= 10 && x < 20 then Some x else None

let checkNumber2 x =
    match x with
    | LessThan10 a -> printfn "less than 10, the value is %d" a
    | Btw10And20 a -> printfn "between 10 and 20, the value is %d" a
    | _ -> printfn "that's a big number %d " x
```

Unlike the single-case active pattern, the variable succeeding the active pattern is bound to the function's return value. For example, the *a* in LessThan10 a is used to hold the values smaller than *10*.

Using Multicase Active Patterns

If you view the partial-case active pattern as something used for decomposing the input data into two portions, you can consider the multicase active pattern as a pattern used to decompose data into multiple portions. Listing 6-59 is used to determine the quarter of the year in which the provided date falls.

LISTING 6-59 Multicase active pattern example

```
let (|FirstQuarter|SecondQuarter|ThirdQuarter|FourthQuarter|) (date:System.DateTime) =
    let month = date.Month
    match month with
    | 1 | 2 | 3 -> FirstQuarter month
    | 4 | 5 | 6 -> SecondQuarter month
    | 7 | 8 | 9  -> ThirdQuarter month
    | _ -> FourthQuarter month

let newYearResolution date =
    match date with
    | FirstQuarter _-> printfn "New Year resolution: lose 10 lbs this year!"
    | SecondQuarter _-> printfn "beef is good for summer BBQ?"
    | ThirdQuarter _ -> printfn "maybe I should diet?"
    | FourthQuarter _-> printfn "Mom's apple pie is wonderful!"
```

Note The underscore (_) in the second pattern match instructs the F# compiler to ignore the returned value from the active pattern.

Note Active patterns cannot return more than seven possibilities. So the code let (|A|B|C|D|E|F|G|H|I|J|K|) x = x will generate a compile error.

Using Parameterized Active Patterns

The active pattern is a special function. If it is a function, can it accept parameters? The answer is yes. Parameters for an active pattern can be included immediately after the active pattern label, but they must appear before the active pattern return value. Listing 6-60 shows how to parse a phone number and return all numbers in that phone number. The pattern string is the parameter and the *out* variable is used to store the return value from the active pattern.

LISTING 6-60 Parameterized active pattern example

```
open System.Text.RegularExpressions

// define the parameterized active pattern
let (|RegexMatch|_|) (pattern:string) (input:string) =
    let regex = Regex(pattern).Match(input)
    if regex.Success then Some(List.tail [ for x in regex.Groups -> x.Value])
    else None

let parsePhoneNumber str =
    match str with
```

```
    | RegexMatch "(\d{3})-(\d{3})-(\d{4})" out -> System.String.Join("", out)
    | RegexMatch "(\d{3})-(\d{3})(\d{4})" out ->  System.String.Join("", out)
    | _ -> "Not supported format"

// two statements below show 4251231234
parsePhoneNumber "425-123-1234"
parsePhoneNumber "425-1231234"

// this format does not parse and shows "Not supported format"
parsePhoneNumber "(425)123-1234"
```

Tip The active pattern is a special function you can use to create a higher order function and use it in a match expression. The *parsePhoneNumber* function can be rewritten as follows:

```
let (|RegexMath2|_|) = (|RegexMatch|_|) "(\d{3})-(\d{3})-(\d{4})"
let parsePhoneNumber str =
    match str with
    | RegexMath2 out -> System.String.Join("", out)
    | RegexMath2 out ->  System.String.Join("", out)
    | _ -> "Not supported format"
```

Listing 6-61 shows how to use the AND pattern with the parameterized active pattern. The sample code is checked if the number is divisible by 6.

LISTING 6-61 Parameterized active pattern with AND pattern example

```
let (|Divisible|_|) x y=
    if y % x = 0 then
        Some Divisible
    else
        None

let f2 = function
    | Divisible 2 & Divisible 3 -> "divisible by 6"
    | _ -> "other"

f2 6
```

You might be wondering why I am introducing the active pattern if it is just a function in itself. If you combine the active pattern and pattern matching, the value of active pattern can be seen. When the active patterns are put into the *match* statement, the *match* statement can make sure all the cases (data segments) are processes. If there is one case missing, there will be a compile-time warning generated.

Working with Exceptions

As a C# developer, you're probably familiar with exceptions. In C#, exceptions can be found all over the place. The normal execution will be interrupted when an exception happens. This feature is used as a way to notify you that something is wrong. If you find that typing **System.Exception** is overly repetitive, you are not alone. F# actually introduces an abbreviation named *exn* for the *System.Exception* type. Listing 6-62 shows how *exn* is defined.

LISTING 6-62 The *exn* abbreviation for *System.Exception*

```
type exn = System.Exception
```

Catching Exceptions

Listing 6-63 shows how to catch an exception in F#.

LISTING 6-63 Using *try...with* to handle an exception

```
open System

let exceptionCatch() =
    try
        let a = 3 / 0       //divide by zero exception
        printfn "%d" a
    with
    | :? DivideByZeroException -> printfn "divided by zero"

exceptionCatch()
```

> **Note** Although the *try...with* statement is similar to the *match* statement, it does not check for pattern completeness. As with C#, if the exception is not caught, it will bubble up.

In addition to *try...with*, F# also supports *try...finally*. See Listing 6-64. F# does not provide *try...with...finally*. If *finally* is used to release resources, the *use* statement can solve this without involving *finally*. If you require functionality similar to the *try...catch...finally* functionality in C#, you can nest *try...with* within a *try...finally* to achieve the same functionality, as shown in Listing 6-65.

LISTING 6-64 Using *try...finally*

```
// try...finally sample
try
    <some exception thrown>
finally
    printfn "ignore the exception and perform some clean up"
```

LISTING 6-65 Implementing *try...with...finally*

```
// try...catch...finally
try
    try
        <some exception thrown>
    with _ -> printfn "catch the exception"
finally
    printfn "finally section executing..."
```

Throwing Exceptions

F# provides a shortcut to throw exceptions by using *failwith* or *failwithf*. Both of these functions generate a *System.Exception*. The *failwith* function takes a string as a parameter, and *failwithf* takes a string format, like *printf*, to generate a more sophisticated error message. The sample code is shown in Listing 6-66. Note that this listing contains a compile warning that can be ignored.

LISTING 6-66 The *failwith* and *failwithf* examples

```
open System

try
    failwith "this is an exception"
with :? Exception as e -> printfn "the exception msg is %s" e.Message

try
    failwithf "this is an exception generated at %A" DateTime.Now
with _  as e -> printfn "the exception msg is %s" e.Message
```

 Note The last line can also written as *with e -> printfn "the exception msg is %s" e.Message*

C# has a *throw* keyword that is used to throw an exception. What is the equivalent in F#? In F#, the *raise* and *reraise* functions can be used. Listing 6-67 shows how to raise a *System.Exception* and how to throw an exception in the *with* section.

LISTING 6-67 The *raise* exception

```
open System

try
    raise (Exception("raise exception"))
with _ -> printfn "catch exception"

try
    try
        raise (Exception("raise exception"))
    with _ -> printfn "catch exception"; reraise()
with _ -> printfn "catch reraise exception"
```

In addition to the *failwith* and *reraise* functions, F# provides three other shortcut functions to raise common argument exceptions. Listing 6-68 shows how to use these three shortcut functions:

- An invalid argument exception is thrown by using *invalidArg* with two string type parameters.

- An invalid operation exception is thrown by using *invalidOp* with one string type parameter.

- A *Null* argument exception is thrown by using *nullArg* with one string type parameter.

LISTING 6-68 The *nullArg*, *invalidArg*, and *invalidOp* functions

```
let demoInvalidArgumentAndOperation arg0 arg1 =
    if arg0 = null then
        nullArg "arg0 is null"
    if arg1 = System.String.Empty then
        invalidArg "arg1" "arg1 is empty string"
    invalidOp "sorry, this is an invalid operation"
```

Defining Exceptions

F# supports using class and inheritance to define an exception. It also has a shortcut way of defining an exception. Listing 6-69 defines the *MyException* type. If you are curious about how to access the customized fields defined in the *MyException* type, Listing 6-70 provides an example.

LISTING 6-69 Defining an exception

```
//define an exception type with int*int tuple
exception MyException of int * int

try
    raise (MyException(1, 2))
with _ as e -> printfn "%A" e
```

LISTING 6-70 Accessing customized fields in the exception

```
//define an exception type with int*int tuple
exception MyException of int * int

try
    raise (MyException(1, 2))
with :? MyException as e -> printfn "exception data is %d and %d" e.Data0 e.Data1
```

Working with a Generic Invoke Function

The generic invoke (GI) function is a static member constraint function. It is used to invoke a member function on a type that has a specific signature. A sample GI function is shown in Listing 6-71. The *functionA* function requires that the parameter be a type with a member method whose name is *MyMethod* and that has a function signature of unit->int. The GI function takes at least one parameter, which is the object *x*. The other several samples in Listing 6-71 demonstrate how to pass additional parameters into the GI function, such as a tuple. In the sample code, there is type information for the parameter, which is optional. This type information can help you identify what parameters should be passed into the GI function. There is an interesting keyword named *inline* in the function, which makes the restriction happen. I will discuss it in the "Using the *inline* Function" section.

LISTING 6-71 Generic invoke (GI) function example

```
// GI function takes one parameter
let inline functionA (x : ^T) = (^T : (member MyMethod : unit -> int) x)

// GI function takes two parameters
let inline functionB (x : ^T) str =
  (^T : (member CanConnectWithConnectString : string -> int)
    (x, str))

// GI function takes three parameters
let inline functionC (x : ^T) a b = (^T : (member Add : int -> int -> int) (x, a, b))

// GI function takes a tuple as a parameter
let inline functionD (x : ^T) a b = (^T : (member Add : int * int -> int) (x, a, b))

// GI function takes a tuple and another value as parameters
// c is float type that will go into MyFunction's second parameter
let inline functionE (x : ^T) a b (c:float) =
  (^T : (member MyFunction : int * int -> float -> int)
    (x, a, b, c))
```

The GI function is a powerful weapon you can use to crack the boundary of encapsulation formed by a class. It requires only that the signature of the methods match. If you ponder this feature more, you can see how this could be something significant. And you are right. The GI function is the fundamental building block for one of our design patterns that was discussed in Chapter 3. The other application is to use this function in the library with the *inline* keyword, which will be discussed in the next section.

Using the *inline* function

The *inline* keyword changes the type resolution. Listing 6-72 shows how to use the *inline* keyword to change variable *x*'s inferred type to any type. This makes it so that *x* can be a *float* as well as an *int*.

LISTING 6-72 The *inline* keyword affects the type infererence

```
let F x = float x + 1.0
let inline F_inline x = float x + 1.0
```

```
Execution result in FSI
```

```
val F : int -> float
val inline F_inline :
    ^a -> float when  ^a : (static member op_Explicit :  ^a -> float)
```

The *inline* keyword can be applied to functions at the top level, at the module level, or to the method in the class. See Listing 6-73.

LISTING 6-73 The *inline* keyword

```
let inline f x = x + 1
type InlineSample() =
    member inline this.F x = x + 1
    static member inline F x = x + 1
```

The *inline* keyword optimizes the code, but this should be the last item on your optimization to-do list.

Working with Asynchronous and Parallel Workflows

Modern computers are shipped with multiple cores. This means they contain multiple, independent processing units, which enable them to process several tasks at the same time. As a developer, this seems attractive, but creating programs that use these cores actually increases complexity and the risk of introducing bugs. In this section, I first cover the basic concept of threads and how to program with threads in F#. I then move to another one of F#'s unique features, named *asynchronous workflows*, which makes working with multiple cores much easier and safer.

Using Threads

According to the definition at Wikipedia—*http://en.wikipedia.org/wiki/Thread_(computing)*—a *thread* is the smallest unit of processing that can be scheduled by an operating system. Different operating systems can have different thread and process implementations, but usually a thread is contained inside a process. Threads share the memory heap. So the spawned threads in a process can communicate by writing to this shared memory.

Listing 6-74 demonstrates how to create a thread and print out the current time and managed thread ID. The thread uses the *Sleep* method to pause the execution for a certain time—in the sample code, it is 1000 milliseconds. During this pause time, the operating system can schedule other threads to execute.

LISTING 6-74 Spawning a thread

```
open System.Threading
open System

// define a thread function body
let thread() =
    [1..5]
    |> Seq.iter (fun _ -> Thread.Sleep 1000;
                          printfn "%A from thread %d"
                              DateTime.Now
                              Thread.CurrentThread.ManagedThreadId)

// create a new thread
let spawn() =
    let thread = Thread thread
    thread.Start()

spawn()
spawn()
```

 Note The spawn function uses the variable shadowing feature. Look at the first line of code in the spawn function: `let thread = Thread(thread)`. The first thread is a *System.Threading.Thread* type, while the second thread in `Thread(thread)` is a function.

When dealing with multiple threads in C#, the most commonly used keyword is *lock*. It marks a code block with a mutually-exclusive lock. F# also provides a lock feature, but it is in the form of a function, as shown in Listing 6-75.

LISTING 6-75 The *lock* function

```
C# lock
lock (o)
{
    myCode();
}


F# lock
lock o (fun () ->
            SomeCode()
        )
```

Note The *lock* function can take only a reference type, which means you cannot use a struct or int. In C#, you can use an object as a *syncRoot*, while a reference cell in F# can serve this purpose without any problem. See Listing 6-76.

Listing 6-76 demonstrates how to lock a long-running thread execution and make sure that it does not get interrupted during the execution.

LISTING 6-76 Using *lock* in a long thread execution

```
open System
open System.Threading

let synRoot = ref 0
let presenterFunction() =
    let id = Thread.CurrentThread.ManagedThreadId
    printfn "I (%d) starting, please do not interrupt..." id
    Thread.Sleep 1000
    printfn "I (%d) finished, thank you!" id

let longTalk () =
    lock(synRoot) (fun () -> presenterFunction())

ThreadPool.QueueUserWorkItem(fun _ -> longTalk()) |> ignore
ThreadPool.QueueUserWorkItem(fun _ -> longTalk()) |> ignore
ThreadPool.QueueUserWorkItem(fun _ -> longTalk()) |> ignore
```

Note In F#, the *printfn* function's printout result can be interleaving in a multithreaded environment. You can either use the *lock* function to make it thread-safe or use *Console.WriteLine* instead.

Using Asynchronous Workflows

If you ever read an article about the advantages of F#, you likely found some information about the ease of parallel programming and usually some association to the *Async.Parallel* method. If you want to do parallel/asynchronous programming, F# asynchronous workflows provide the cleanest way to do it.

Let's start by solving a simple problem with an asynchronous workflow: checking whether a given sequence is in an increasing order. The algorithm is simple. Multiple threads are launched to cut the incoming sequence into a number of two-element small lists. If the first element is smaller than the second element, you increase a shared variable by one. At end of the execution, if the shared variable value is the sequence length minus one, the sequence is in an increasing order. The code is shown in Listing 6-77. Note that this algorithm and code serve only as a sample for demonstrating the asynchronous workflow. I do not intend to use this code to discuss the performance between single-threaded and multithreaded programming.

According to the algorithm, the first problem that needs to be solved is how to lock a variable so that the write operation is thread-safe. You can use the *lock* function presented in Listing 6-75 to solve this problem. The real interesting part starts with the use of *async*, which specifies that an asynchronous workflow can be executed in parallel. The function takes a two-element array. If the first element *x* is smaller than the second element *y*, the shared variable is increased by one.

You use the *Seq.windowed* function to create the two-element sequences that will be used as input. *Async.Parallel* is then used to make sure that these threads execute in parallel and wait to join the result when executing *Async.RunSynchronously*. This is known as the Fork/Join pattern.

LISTING 6-77 An asynchronous workflow sample that is used to check an increasing sequence

```
type AsyncSample(l:seq<int>) =
    member this.IsIncreasing() =
        // declare a reference cell to hold the shared variable
        let num = ref 0

        // safely increase the shared variable
        let inc () = lock(num) ( fun _ -> num := (!num) + 1 )

        // make the sequence into a sequence containing a number of small two-element
sequences
        let windowedList = l |> Seq.windowed 2
```

```
// the compare function
let compare s =
    async {
        let list = List.ofSeq s
        let [ x; y ] = list   // the two-element list can be assigned to x and y

        // if x < y, then increase the shared variable; otherwise, do nothing
        if x < y then inc()
        else ()
        }

// split the sequence into small two-element sequences and execute
// the function in parallel
let compute =
    windowedList
    |> Seq.map compare  // can think as map seq of data into seq of functions
    |> Async.Parallel
    |> Async.RunSynchronously

// compare the shared variable with sequence length
(!num) + 1 = Seq.length l
```

 Note The segment let [x; y] = list generates a warning message. The pattern matching at compile time does not know that the list is a two-element list, so the F# compiler generates a warning. This warning can be ignored in this scenario.

When debugging a multithreaded program, one of the common techniques you resort to using for assistance is the *printfn* function. F# *printfn* uses a different technique than *Console.WriteLine*. As previously mentioned, it does not lock the output stream. As a consequence, a call to *printfn* without using the *lock* function yields interleaving information. Listing 6-78 demonstrates how to write a *printfn* with a *lock*.

LISTING 6-78 Using *printfn* with the *lock* function

```
let syncRoot = ref 0
lock(syncRoot) ( fun _ ->  printfn "not interleaving printfn" )
```

You might be wondering how this sample can be made general enough so that it can test both decreasing and increasing cases. The answer is in Listing 6-79. Some readers might still be surprised to see that "<" can be passed in as an argument to a function. This implies two important points that distinguish F# from C#. The "<" is a function that takes two parameters and returns a Boolean result. Because F# is a functional-first language, this function can be passed into another function. By taking the function as a parameter, the *IsAll* function becomes a higher-order function.

```
type AsyncSample(l:seq<int>) =
    member this.AreAll(compareFunction) =
        // declare a reference cell to hold the shared variable
        let num = ref 0

        // safely increase the shared variable
        let inc () = lock(num) ( fun _ -> num := (!num) + 1 )

        // make the sequence into a sequence containing a number of small two-element
sequences
        let windowedList = l |> Seq.windowed 2

        // the compare function
        let compare s =
            async {
                let list = List.ofSeq s
                let [ x; y ] = list    // the two-element list can be assigned to x and y
                if compareFunction x y then inc()
                else ()
                }

        // split the sequence into small two-element sequences and execute
        // the function in parallel
        let compute =
            windowedList
            |> Seq.map compare  // can think as map seq of data into seq of functions
            |> Async.Parallel
            |> Async.RunSynchronously

        // compare the shared variable with sequence length
        (!num) + 1 = Seq.length l

// create an object with sequence 1 to 10
let asyncObj = AsyncSample(seq { 1..10 })

// pass function "<" to perform the comparison
asyncObj.AreAll(<)
```

> **Note** Passing an operator to a higher-order function can save you some typing. However, overusing this technique can make the code as easy to read as a World War II encrypted telegram, meaning that it can decrease the readability significantly.

Working with the Asynchronous Programming Model

Even though multithreaded programming can solve a number of problems, asynchronous programming is often a better choice. .NET provides support for asynchronous programming via a pattern called the *Asynchronous Programming Model (APM)*. The typical APM has two parts. One is a method called *Begin\<Operation>*—where *Operation* is the desired name of the asynchronous action—which initializes the operation asynchronously. The other is a method called *End<Operation>*, which is invoked when the operation finishes. The problem with APM is that it makes the code difficult to understand and maintain because related code is scattered in multiple places.

Asynchronous workflows are designed to solve this problem and simplify asynchronous programming tasks. Listing 6-80 shows how to read a file and write the processed result into a new file asynchronously with an F# asynchronous workflow. If you have a file named tt.txt in c:\MyCode that contains the text "A", the content will become "B" after the execution.

LISTING 6-80 File process with an asynchronous workflow

```
open System.IO

let encryptFile fn =
    let operation =
        async {
            use fs = new FileStream(fn, FileMode.Open)

            // read the file content
            let! data = fs.AsyncRead(int fs.Length)
            let data' = data |> Array.map (fun n -> n+1uy)
            use encryptedFile = new FileStream(fn + ".out", FileMode.Create)

            // write the new content to the new file
            do! encryptedFile.AsyncWrite(data')
        }

    // start the operation with a three-scenario handler function
    Async.StartWithContinuations (operation,
        (fun _ -> printfn "finished"),       // print out when finished successfully
        (fun e -> printfn "something bad happened, %A" e),  //print when exception thrown
        (fun _ -> printfn "user gives up"))  // print when operation is cancelled

encryptFile @"c:\mycode\tt.txt"
```

There is something unfamiliar in Listing 6-80—the *let!* (pronounced *let-bang*) and *do!* (pronounced *do-bang*). The *let!* extracts the underlying result out of the *Async<'T>*. If you position your pointer over the *AsyncRead* function, you see that its return type is *Async<byte[]>*, while the variable data's type is *byte[]*. The *do!* is a special case of *let!*. It is used to handle the *Async<unit>* type where the return type is *unit*. The *do!* is used to start the asynchronous operation. The real computation is started when the *operation* variable is passed into the *Async.StartWithContinuation* function. The *Async.StartWithContinuation* function takes four parameters. The first one is the asynchronous operation, and the other three are used to specify the normal completion callback function, exception-handler function, and user-cancellation handler function, respectively.

The scattered code no longer exists thanks to *let!* and *do!*. You might be thinking that this sounds a lot like the Async and Await features in C# 5.0. If so, you are absolutely correct. F# has provided this functionality for many years, and the success of F# asynchronous workflows is the reason why C# 5.0 introduces these same features.

Handling Exceptions

The *aysnc* keyword seems to work nicely with the APM, but how about exception handling? Is it possible to handle the exception as you would in code that is executed sequentially? The answer is "Yes." Listing 6-81 shows how to handle an exception inside of an asynchronous workflow.

LISTING 6-81 Asynchronous workflow exception handler

```
open System

let asyncOperationWithException =
    async {
        try
            /// some operations could throw an exception
        with
            | :? DivideByZeroException as e -> printfn "divided by zero"
            | :? ArgumentException as e -> printfn "this is an argument exception"
    }
```

You might have noticed immediately that this code is not safe. If *failwith* is put into the *try* section, the process can be brought down. Nice catch! The most obvious solution is to add an extra handler function in Listing 6-81. Another approach is to use the *Async.StartWithContinuation* function, as shown in Listing 6-80. If you like a more F#-oriented approach, examine Listing 6-82, which uses *Async.Catch* to solve the problem. The FSI execution result shows that a *System.Exception* with a "my error" message is caught.

LISTING 6-82 Handling an exception using *Async.Catch*

```
open System

let asyncOperationWithException =
    async {
        try
            failwith "my error"
        with
            | :? DivideByZeroException as e -> printfn "divided by zero"
            | :? ArgumentException as e -> printfn "this is a argument exception"
    }

asyncOperationWithException
|> Async.Catch
|> Async.RunSynchronously
|> function
    | Choice1Of2 _ -> printfn "everything is good. No exception"
    | Choice2Of2 ex -> printfn "caught error: %A" ex
```

```
caught error: System.Exception: my error
   at FSI_0002.asyncOperationWithExcpetion@10-2.Invoke(Exception _arg1)
   at Microsoft.FSharp.Control.AsyncBuilderImpl.callA@769.Invoke(AsyncParams`1 args)
```

Using Cancellation

If everything could be done in the blink of an eye, you might never need *async*. The reality is that users lose patience after a few blinks, and once their patience is lost they are likely to start searching for a cancel button. Asynchronous workflows can be cancelled when the execution is on *let!* or *do!*. After the cancellation, a handling function will be invoked to give the developer a chance to run some customized code. Other than using the *Async.StartWithContinuation* function, Listing 6-83 shows how to use a *Cancel* token to interrupt and cancel the execution.

LISTING 6-83 Cancelling an asynchronous workflow

```
open System.Threading

let syncRoot = ref 0

// define printfn with lock
let lockedProcessingPrintf () =
    lock(syncRoot)
        (fun _ -> printfn "processing... reported from %d"
                      Thread.CurrentThread.ManagedThreadId)
let cancelPrintf() = lock(syncRoot) (fun _ -> printfn "cancelling operation...")
let lockPrintf str = lock(syncRoot) (fun _ -> printfn str)

let computation (tokenSource:System.Threading.CancellationTokenSource) =
    async {
        use! cancelHandler = Async.OnCancel(fun _ -> cancelPrintf())
        while true do
            lockedProcessingPrintf()
            do! Async.Sleep 100
    }

// a warning will be generated here if used inside a module
use ts1 = new CancellationTokenSource()
use ts2 = new CancellationTokenSource()

printfn "Starting..."

//start the computation with a cancellation token
Async.Start(computation ts1, ts1.Token)
Async.Start(computation ts2, ts2.Token)

Thread.Sleep(1 * 1000)
```

```
lockPrintf "Cancelling..."
ts1.Cancel()
ts2.Cancel()

// give some time for thread to finish
Thread.Sleep(1 * 1000)

System.Console.ReadLine() |> ignoreExamining Some Asynchronous Workflow Samples
```

Before proceeding with real-world examples, I first need to present a sample that demonstrates callback and cancellation within an asynchronous workflow. Listing 6-84 presents back-end, callback, and cancellation processes.

LISTING 6-84 Asynchronous workflow example using back-end, callback, and cancellation processes

```
open System.Threading

let sleep : int -> unit = Thread.Sleep
let print : string -> unit = System.Console.WriteLine

// back-end process
let proc x =
    async {
        print "processing"
        sleep 5000
        print "processed"
        return x + 7
    }

// callback function
let callBack i =
    print "in call function function"
    print (sprintf "call back value = %A" i)

// aysnc using a back-end process and callback function
let myProcess callBackFunction x =
    async {
        let! v = proc x
        callBackFunction v
    }

// function print timer message with cancellation
let timer cancelCallBack =
    async {
        use! cancel = cancelCallBack
        while true do
            print "time..."
            sleep 1000
    }
```

```
// set up cancellation
let cancelToken = new CancellationTokenSource()
let cancelCallBack = Async.OnCancel (fun _ -> print "cancelling")
Async.Start(timer cancelCallBack, cancelToken.Token)

// start the back-end process
4
|> myProcess callBack
|> Async.RunSynchronously

// cancel timer
cancelToken.Cancel()
```

Note Because *System.Console.WriteLine* has multiple overloaded versions, the type definition `string->unit` is necessary.

In this section, there are two samples using asynchronous workflows as well as other previously introduced data structures. Listing 6-85 uses an asynchronous workflow to compute the Fibonacci number. The notable point for this sample is the *Async.StartChild*, which starts another workflow.

LISTING 6-85 Using asynchronous workflows to compute a Fibonacci number

```
let rec fibonacci = function
    | 0 -> async { return 0 }
    | 1 -> async { return 1 }
    | n -> async { let! n2Async = fibonacci(n - 2) |> Async.StartChild
                   let! n1 = fibonacci(n - 1)
                   let! n2 = n2Async
                   return n1 + n2 }

printfn "fibonacci(20) = %A"
    (Async.RunSynchronously <| (fibonacci 20 ))
```

Execution result
```
fibonacci(20) = 6765
```

Note .NET 4+ uses the Task Parallel Library (TPL) to execute the asynchronous workflow.

The second example, presented in Listing 6-86, is a quick sort implementation. It uses not only the asynchronous workflow, but also pattern matching and active patterns.

LISTING 6-86 A quick sort using an asynchronous workflow

```fsharp
// partial-case active pattern
let (|Empty|_|) l = if l |> Array.isEmpty then Some l else None
let (|SingleValue|_|) l = if l |> Array.length = 1 then Some l else None

// quick sort function
let rec quickSort (intArray : int array )=
    // pattern matching
    match intArray with
    | Empty empty ->
            async {return [||]}

    | SingleValue singleValue ->
            async {return singleValue}

    | multValues ->
            async {
                        //pivot
                        let p = ref 0
                        //headFlag, tailFlag
                        let h, t = ref 0, ref (multValues.Length - 1)
                        //tail active -- compare from tail to head ,by default
                        let tA = ref true

                        while (!h <= !t) do
                            if(!t - !h = 1) then
                                if(multValues.[!t] < multValues.[!h]) then
                                    let temp = multValues.[!h]
                                    multValues.[!h] <- multValues.[!t]
                                    multValues.[!t] <- temp
                            if (!tA = true) then
                                if (multValues.[!t] >= multValues.[!p]) then
                                    t := !t - 1
                                else
                                    let temp = multValues.[!t]
                                    multValues.[!t] <- multValues.[!p]
                                    multValues.[!p] <- temp
                                    p := !t
                                    h := !h + 1
                                    tA := false
                            else
                                if(multValues.[!h] <= multValues.[!p]) then
                                    h := !h + 1
                                else
                                    let temp = multValues.[!h]
                                    multValues.[!h] <- multValues.[!p]
                                    multValues.[!p] <- temp
                                    p := !h
                                    t := !t - 1
                                    tA := true

                        let leftArray = Array.sub multValues 0 (!p + 1)
                        let rigthArray = Array.sub multValues (!p + 1) (multValues.Length-
!p-1)
```

```
            let! leftAsync = quickSort(leftArray) |> Async.StartChild
            let! rightAsync = quickSort(rigthArray) |> Async.StartChild

            let! left = leftAsync
            let! right = rightAsync

            return (Array.append left right) }

printfn " %A" (Async.RunSynchronously <| quickSort [|3; 7; 8; 5; 2; 1; 9; 5; 4|])
```

Execution result

```
[|1; 2; 3; 4; 5; 5; 7; 8; 9|]
```

Building Your Own Asynchronous Primitives

For some legacy code that provides only the APM *Begin<Operation>* and *End<Operation>* methods,
you need to write a simple function to allow them to be used in an asynchronous workflow. The
Async.FromBeginEnd function is designed to assist in this scenario. Listing 6-87 takes a delegate's
BeginInvoke and *EndInvoke* to form an asynchronous workflow.

LISTING 6-87 Building an asynchronous primitive

```
open System
open System.IO

type MyAsyncPrimitive() =
    static member AsyncCopy(source, target) =
        // create a delegate
        let copyDelegate = new Func<_*_, _>(File.Copy)

        // convert delegate to asynchronous workflow
        Async.FromBeginEnd((source,target), copyDelegate.BeginInvoke, copyDelegate.
EndInvoke)

let asyncCopy source target =
    async { do! MyAsyncPrimitive.AsyncCopy(source, target) }
```

> **Note** The code in Listing 6-87 is for demo purposes. Changing a delegate to an
> asynchronous operation does not always improve the performance.

Debugging Multithreaded Applications

Debugging a multithreaded application is always tricky. In addition to using the traditional console output technique shown in Listing 6-78, you can use Microsoft Visual Studio to view different threads. If the thread is spawned by *FSharp.Core* and cannot be viewed, you can try to enable or disable the Just My Code option under Tools, Options to see the call stack. (See Figure 6-1.)

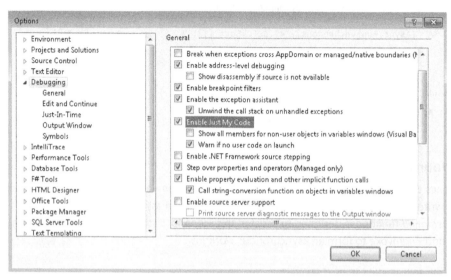

FIGURE 6-1 Changing the Just My Code debug setting

Using Agents

In additional to asynchronous workflows, F# provides another great feature known as the *mailbox processor*, which can be used to perform asynchronous programming tasks. Listing 6-88 shows how to use a mailbox processor to implement a simple agent. The only function for this simple agent is printing the received message. The agent is started by using the *MailBoxProcessor.Start* method. The posted message is retrieved by calling *Receive()*. The post action is done by the *Post* method. You can think of an agent as a monitored message queue that executes the code only after the call to *Receive()* when a message arrives in that queue.

LISTING 6-88 Mailbox processor agent

```
// rename the mailbox processor to Agent
type Agent<'T> = MailboxProcessor<'T>

// create the agent with async
let agent =
    Agent.Start(fun mailbox ->
        async { while true do
                    let! msg = mailbox.Receive()
                    printfn "got message '%s'" msg } )
```

```
// post the message
agent.Post "hello"
agent.Post "world"
```

At this point, you might be thinking that an agent is directly mapped to a thread. Luckily, this is not true. The mailbox processor is backed up by the *ThreadPool*. A mailbox processor is logically single threaded at the back end, For example, to send 100 messages to 1 box, only one thread is needed to process them serially. Sending 100 threads to 100 mailboxes will use *X* threads, where *X* is a number chosen by the *ThreadPool*. Listing 6-89 creates 100,000 agents. A 32-bit machine can barely create several hundred threads, so this shows that the agent is not directly mapped to a thread. The execution result shows the execution time in FSI with the time switch set to ON. The mailbox processor can handle 100,000 messages in just two to three seconds!

LISTING 6-89 Creating 100,000 agents

```
// rename the mailbox processor to Agent
type Agent<'T> = MailboxProcessor<'T>

// create agents
let agents =
    [1 .. 100 * 1000]
    |> List.map  (fun i->
       Agent.Start(fun n ->
         async {
            while true do
               let! msg = n.Receive()
               if i % 20000 = 0 then
                   printfn "agent %d got message '%s'" i msg } ))

// post message to all agents
for agent in agents do
    agent.Post "hello"


Execution time
Real: 00:00:02.665, CPU: 00:00:03.375, GC gen0: 26, gen1: 24, gen2: 1
```

It's rare for an agent to exist in isolation. Often, you need to interact with other aspects of your code from within the body of an agent. One approach for accomplishing this is to publish an event from within an agent to communicate with the outside world. Listing 6-90 fires an event for every 30,000 messages that are received.

LISTING 6-90 An agent that fires an event

```
// rename the mailbox processor to Agent
type Agent<'T> = MailboxProcessor<'T>

// event to be raised
let myEvent = new Event<int>()

// current sync context
let syncContext = System.Threading.SynchronizationContext.Current

// create agents
let agents =
    [1 .. 100 * 1000]
    |> List.map  (fun i->
        Agent.Start(fun n ->
            async {
                while true do
                    let! msg = n.Receive()
                    if i % 30000 = 0 then
                        syncContext.Post( (fun _ -> myEvent.Trigger i), null) } ))

// added event handler
Event.add (fun n-> printfn "%A messages received" n) myEvent.Publish

// post message to all agents
for agent in agents do
    agent.Post "hello"
```

We live in an imperfect world—inevitably, our beautiful code will run across something unexpected and have to handle an exception. Listing 6-91 shows how to handle an exception within the agent code. There will be one "something is wrong" message printed out when 100 is divided by 0.

LISTING 6-91 Handling an exception in the agent

```
// rename the mailbox processor to Agent
type Agent<'T> = MailboxProcessor<'T>

// event to be raised
let myEvent = new Event<int>()

let syncContext = System.Threading.SynchronizationContext.Current

// create agents
let agents =
    [-100 * 1000 .. 100 * 1000]
    |> List.map  (fun i->
        use a = new Agent<_>(fun n ->
                async {
                    while true do
                        let! msg = n.Receive()
                        let result = 100 / i;
```

```
                        if i % 30000 = 0 then
                            syncContext.Post( (fun _ -> myEvent.Trigger i), null) } )
        a.Error.Add(fun _ -> printfn "something is wrong")
        a.Start()
        a)


// added event handler
Event.add (fun n-> printfn "%A message received" n) myEvent.Publish


// post message to all agents
for agent in agents do
    agent.Post "hello"
```

You can use *MailboxProcessor* to simulate a message-box banking account system where the deposit and withdrawal operations are performed asynchronously. The sample code is shown in Listing 6-92.

LISTING 6-92 Banking account using *MailboxProcessor*

```
open Microsoft.FSharp.Control

[<Measure>] type USD

// define account state
type AccountState =
    | Overdrawn
    | Silver
    | Gold

// define operations: deposit and withdraw
type Operation =
    | Deposit of decimal<USD>
    | Withdraw of decimal<USD>

// define the account class
type Account() =
    let mutable balance = 0.m<USD>

    // define a MailboxProcessor
    let bank = new MailboxProcessor<Operation>(fun inbox ->
            let rec loop () =
                async {
                    let! msg = inbox.Receive()
                    match msg with
                        | Deposit n -> balance <- balance + n
                        | Withdraw n -> balance <- balance - n
                    return! loop ()
                }

            loop ())
```

```
          // start the MailboxProcessor instance
          do
              bank.Start()

          // define operations which post the message to MailboxProcessor
          member this.Deposit(args) =
              bank.Post(Deposit(args))
          member this.Withdraw(args) =
              bank.Post(Withdraw(args))

          member this.State
              with get() =
                  match balance with
                      | _ when balance <= 0.m<USD> -> AccountState.Overdrawn
                      | _ when balance > 0.m<USD> && balance < 10000.m<USD> -> AccountState.
Silver
                      | _ -> AccountState.Gold
          member this.PayInterest() =
              while bank.CurrentQueueLength > 0 do
                  System.Threading.Thread.Sleep (100)
              printfn "current state is %A" this.State
              match this.State with
                  | AccountState.Overdrawn -> ()
                  | AccountState.Silver -> this.Deposit(balance * 0.01m)
                  | AccountState.Gold -> this.Deposit(balance * 0.02m)
          member this.ShowBalance() =
              while bank.CurrentQueueLength > 0 do
                  System.Threading.Thread.Sleep (100)
              printfn "current balance is %A" balance

let account = Account()
account.Deposit(1000.m<USD>)
account.Deposit(10000.m<USD>)
account.PayInterest()
account.ShowBalance()
```

Execution result in FSI

```
current state is Gold
current balance is 11220.00M
```

Working with Computation Expressions

I introduced *query* and *async* in Chapter 4 in the "Asynchronous Workflows" section. When you look at the blue-color *async* and *query* syntax in the Visual Studio editor window, you might think they are keywords, like the *this* keyword in C#. However, if that were the case, these keywords couldn't be used as variable names. For example, how does the code in Listing 6-93 compile?

LISTING 6-93 Using *async, seq,* and *query* as variables

```
let async = 0
let seq = 1
let query = 2
```

Actually, the code compiles because *async, seq,* and *query* are not keywords. Instead, they are a special F# feature called *computation expressions.* The MSDN documentation (*http://msdn.microsoft.com/en-us/library/dd233182.aspx*) provides a good definition of computation expressions:

> *Computation expressions in F# provide a convenient syntax for writing computations that can be sequenced and combined using control flow constructs and bindings. They can be used to provide a convenient syntax for monads, a functional programming feature that can be used to manage data, control, and side effects in functional programs.*

F# provides computation expressions so that the language can be expanded. The reason you can put your code inside a *seq* is because it is a computation expression. Listing 6-94 revisits the sequence-generation code that was discussed in Chapter 1.

LISTING 6-94 Sequence generation using a reference cell

Sequence generation code
```
let indices = [1, 2; 3, 4; 5, 6 ]

let newIndices = seq {
    let currentCell = ref 0
    for a, b in indices do
        yield !currentCell, a
        yield a, b
        currentCell := b
    yield !currentCell, 100
    }
```

Execution result
```
> newIndices;;
val it : seq<int * int> = seq [(0, 1); (1, 2); (2, 3); (3, 4); ...]
```

Note This sample code also demonstrates how to use a reference cell. It is invalid to use a mutable variable in the computation expression. The only way to define a mutable variable in this scenario is to use a reference cell.

In addition to the mutable-variable restriction, there is another restriction for computation expressions. It is invalid to use *base* in the computation expression. (See Listing 6-95.) The workaround is simple, just use *this*.

LISTING 6-95 Using *this* in a *seq* computation expression

```
type BaseClass() =
    member val X = 0 with get, set

type ClassA() =
    inherit BaseClass()
    member this.F() =
        let r = seq {
            let a = 0

            // use base here to generate a compile error
            let b = this.X //base.X
            yield a }
        r
```

Expanding a .NET language seems like an exciting possibility. OK, let's do it now. The first sample is a bank system in which the decimal number is rounded when calculating a customer's interest, as shown in Listing 6-96.

LISTING 6-96 Rounding computation expression

```
// define a rounded computation expression
type RoundComputationBuilder(digits:int) =
    let round (x:decimal) = System.Math.Round(x, digits)
    member this.Bind(result, restComputation ) =
        restComputation (round result)
    member this.Return x = round x

// calculate the bank interests
let bankInterest = RoundComputationBuilder 2

bankInterest {
    let! x = 23231.34m * 0.002m
    return x
}
```

The *RoundComputationBuilder* defines two special methods: *Bind* and *Return*. These two methods correspond to *let!* and *return* if you debug into the code. Table 6-2 shows a full list of method names and corresponding statements. In most cases, the method name suggests its usage.

TABLE 6-2 Computation expression methods

Method	Description
For seq<'a> * ('a -> Result<unit>) -> Result<unit>	Enables the FOR loop
Zero unit -> Result<unit>	Enables the execute unit expression, which returns "void" in C#
Combine Result<unit> -> Result<'a> -> Result<'a>	Links the computation expression parts
While (unit -> bool) * Result<unit> -> Result<unit>	Enables the WHILE loop
Return 'a -> Result<'a>	Enables the return keyword
ReturnFrom 'a -> Result<'a>	Enables the return! keyword
Yield 'a -> Result<'a>	Enables the yield keyword
YieldFrom seq<'a> -> Result<'a>	Enables the yield! keyword
Delay (unit -> Result<'a>) -> Result<'a>	Used along with the Combine method to ensure the correct order of statement execution
Run Result<'a> -> Result<'a>	Executes before the execution of a computation expression—like the C# Before<Operation>
Using 'a * ('a -> Result<'b>) -> Result<'b> when 'a :> System.IDisposable	Enables the use and use! keywords
Bind Result<'a> * ('a -> Result<'b>) -> Result<'b>	Enables the let! and do! keywords
TryFinally Result<'a> * (unit -> unit) -> Result<'a>	Enables the try...finally expression
TryWith Result<'a> * (e -> Result<'a>) -> Result<'a>	Enables the try...with expression

With the full table listed, you can expand Listing 6-96 by adding two more members, as shown in Listing 6-97. The *return!* keyword returns the value without going through the rounding process. The *Run* method prints a message before any execution starts. Note that *let* (not *let!*) does not invoke any computation expression method.

LISTING 6-97 Computation expression example with more methods implemented

Computation expression code

```
type RoundComputationBuilder(digits:int) =
    let round (x:decimal) = System.Math.Round(x, digits)
    member this.Bind(result, restComputation ) =
        restComputation (round result)
    member this.Return x = round x
    member this.ReturnFrom x = x  //keep the original value
```

```
        member this.Run f =
            printfn "now start to run.."
            f

    let bankInterest = RoundComputationBuilder 2

    let roundedResult =
        bankInterest {
            let! x = 23231.34m * 0.002m    //invoke the Bind method
            return x          //invoke the Return
        }

    let result =
        bankInterest {
            let y = 23231.34m * 0.002m    // do not invoke the Bind method
            return! y         //invoke the ReturnFrom
        }

    printfn "roundResult = %A, unroundedResult = %A" roundedResult result
```

Execution result

```
now start to run..
now start to run..
roundResult = 46.46M, unroundedResult = 46.46268M
```

A more practical example is the *retry* computation expression, shown in Listing 6-98. It performs the retry logic a given number of times before giving up.

LISTING 6-98 The *retry* computation expression

Retry computation expression code

```
// define a retry computation expression
type Retry (retryTimes:int) = class
    let mutable success = false
    member public this.Bind(value, restFunction:unit -> _) =
        success <- false
        let mutable n = retryTimes
        while not success && n > 0 do
            n <- n - 1
            try
                value()
                success <- true
            with _ as e -> printfn "failed with %s, %d times" e.Message (retryTimes - n)
        restFunction ()
    member public this.Return args =
        success
end
```

```
module TestModule =
    // set the retry limit to 4
    let retry = Retry 4

    // computation expression returns a Boolean value
    let a = retry {
        do! (fun () -> printfn "let us try";
                        failwith "test failure")  // fail the process on purpose
    }

    printfn "result is %A" a
```

Execution result

```
let us try
failed with test failure, 1 times
let us try
failed with test failure, 2 times
let us try
failed with test failure, 3 times
let us try
failed with test failure, 4 times
result is false
```

The computation expression creates a small region with its own language and maybe its own way of performing the computation. If you repeatedly write the same code, a computation expression is something that can be of great assistance.

Using Computation Expression Attributes

If *query* and *seq* are both computation expressions, you might be wondering how other keywords such as *where* are defined. They are defined by using attributes. Let's start from a simple example, *SimpleSequenceBuilder*. Listing 6-99 shows a simple sequence builder and the code to which it will be translated. This is the starting point to show how to add customer operators such as *where*.

LISTING 6-99 Simple sequence builder

```
// define the sequence builder class
type SimpleSequence() = class
    member this.For(source:seq<'a>, f:'a -> seq<'b>) =
        seq { for n in source do yield! f n }
    member this.Yield(n) = seq { yield n }
end

let mySeq = SimpleSequence()
let r = mySeq { for i in 1..10 do yield i * i }
```

Translation result

```
let b = mySeq
b.For ( [1..10] , fun i -> b.Yield(i * i))
```

The *where* operation is introduced by the *CustomOperation* attribute, which is shown in Listing 6-100. The *ProjectionParameter* on the second parameter is useful to simplify the function definition. Lacking this attribute, the *where* part in the computation expression has to be written as fun i -> ... explicitly. The *ProjectionParameter* is also useful when there is a let binding between the customer operator and *ForEach* operation, like the one shown in Listing 6-101.

LISTING 6-100 Using *CustomOperation* and *ProjectionParameter* attributes

```
type SimpleSequence2() =
    member this.For(source:seq<'a>, f:'a -> seq<'b>) =
        seq { for n in source do yield! f n }
    member this.Yield(n) = seq { yield n }
    [<CustomOperation("where")>]
    member this.Where(source:seq<'a>, [<ProjectionParameter>]f:'a -> bool) =
        source |> Seq.filter f

let mySeq2 = SimpleSequence2()
let r2 = mySeq2 {
            for i in 1..10 do
            where (i > 3)
        }
```

Translation result

```
let b2 = mySeq2
b2.Where ( b.For([1..10] , fun i -> b.Yield(i)), fun i-> i > 3)
```

LISTING 6-101 *ProjectParameter* and *let* binding

```
let r3 = mySeq2 {
            for i in 1..10 do
            let j = i + 3
            where (i > 5 && j < 10)
        }
```

Translation result

```
let b3 = mySeq2
b3.Where(b.For([1..10], fun i ->
                    let j = i + 3
                    b.Yield(i, j)),
        fun (i, j) -> i > 5 && j < 10)
```

There are two properties in the *CustomOperation* attribute. The *MaintainsVariableSpace* property supports writing statements such as `where i>5 && j<10`, like the one shown here:

```
where (i>5)
where (j<10)
```

The sample code is shown in Listing 6-102. The other property is the *AllowIntoPattern*. Like its name suggests, it supports the *into* syntax, as shown in Listing 6-103.

LISTING 6-102 *MaintainsVariableSpace* in the *CustomOperation* attribute

```
type SimpleSequence3() =
    member this.For(source:seq<'a>, f:'a -> seq<'b>) =
        seq { for n in source do yield! f n }
    member this.Yield(n) = seq { yield n }
    [<CustomOperation("where", MaintainsVariableSpace=true)>]
    member this.Where(source:seq<'a>, [<ProjectionParameter>]f:'a -> bool) =
        source |> Seq.filter f

let mySeq3 = SimpleSequence3()
let r4 = mySeq3 {
            for i in 1..10 do
            let j = i + 3
            where (i > 5)
            where (j < 10)
            }
```

Translation result

```
let b4 = mySeq3
b4.Where(
    b4.Where(
    b4.For([1..10], fun i ->
                    let j = i + 3
                    b4.Yield(i, j)),
        fun (i, j) -> i > 5),
    fun (i, j) -> j < 10)
```

 Note the above code generate a warning, the warning can be eliminated by adding `|> ignore` in the end.

LISTING 6-103 *AllowIntoPattern* in the *CustomerOperation* attribute

```
type SimpleSequence4() =
    member this.For(source:seq<'a>, f:'a -> seq<'b>) =
        seq { for n in source do yield! f n }
    member this.Yield(n) = seq { yield n }
    [<CustomOperation("where", AllowIntoPattern=true)>]
    member this.Where(source:seq<'a>, [<ProjectionParameter>]f:'a -> bool) =
        source |> Seq.filter f

let mySeq4 = SimpleSequence4()
let r5 = mySeq4 {
            for i in 1..10 do
            where (i > 5) into j
            where (j < 10)
            }
```

Translation result

```
let b5 = mySeq4
b5.Where(
    b5.For(
        b5.Where(
            b5.For([1..10], fun i-> b5.Yield(i)),
            fun i -> i > 5),
        fun j -> b5.Yield(j)),
fun j -> j < 10)
```

 Note the above code generate a warning, the warning can be eliminated by adding |> *ignore* in the end.

Other than the *MaintainsVariableSpace* property, there is another property named *MaintainsVariableSpaceUsingBind*, which can be used to pass the variable down the chain, but in a different way. The sample is shown in Listing 6-104.

LISTING 6-104 *MaintainsVariableSpaceUsingBind* in the *CustomerOperation* attribute

```
type SimpleSequence5() =
    member this.For(source:seq<'a>, f:'a -> seq<'b>) =
        seq { for n in source do yield! f n }
    member this.Return(n) = seq { yield n }
    [<CustomOperation("where",AllowIntoPattern=true,MaintainsVariableSpaceUsingBind=tr
ue)>]
    member this.Where(source:seq<'a>, [<ProjectionParameter>]f:'a -> bool) =
        source |> Seq.filter f
    member this.Bind(value, cont) = cont value
```

```
let mySeq5 = SimpleSequence5()

let r6 = mySeq5 {
        for i in 1..10 do
        where (i > 5 && i + 3 < 10) into j
        return j
    }
```

Translation result

```
let b6 = mySeq5

b6.Bind(
    b6.Where(
        b6.For([1..10], fun i -> b6.Return(i)),
            fun i -> i > 5 && i + 3 < 10),
        fun j -> b6.Return(j))
```

Certain properties on the *CustomOperationAttribute* introduce *join-like* operators. Listing 6-105 shows how to use the *IsLikeJoin* property.

LISTING 6-105 Using *IsLikeJoin* in a computation expression

```
type SimpleSequenceBuilder() =
    member __.For (source : seq<'a>, body : 'a -> seq<'b>) =
        seq { for v in source do yield! body v }
    member __.Yield (item:'a) : seq<'a> = seq { yield item }

    [<CustomOperation("merge", IsLikeJoin = true, JoinConditionWord = "whenever")>]
    member __.Merge (src1:seq<'a>, src2:seq<'a>, ks1, ks2, ret) =
        seq { for a in src1 do
                  for b in src2 do
                      if ks1 a = ks2 b then yield((ret a ) b)
            }

let myseq = SimpleSequenceBuilder()
```

IsLikeJoin indicates that the custom operation is similar to a join in a sequence computation, supporting two inputs and a correlation constraint. The expression in Listing 6-106 is translated into Listing 6-107.

LISTING 6-106 Query code related to *LikeJoin*

```
myseq {
    for i in 1 .. 10 do
    merge j in [5 .. 15] whenever (i = j)
    yield j
    }
```

LISTING 6-107 Translated code from Listing 6-106

```
let b = myseq

b.For(
    b.Merge([1..10], [5..15],
            (fun i -> i), (fun j -> j),
            (fun i -> fun j -> (i, j))),
    fun j -> b.Yield (j))
```

The computation expression is a big and advanced topic. Interested readers can refer to the latest F# language specification (*http://research.microsoft.com/en-us/um/cambridge/projects/fsharp/manual/spec.html*) for more information.

Using Computation Expression Sample

Listing 6-108 demonstrates a bank system that makes deposits to and withdrawals from an account. The computation expression creates a transaction with multiple deposit and withdrawal operations. The operation starts from the *Yield* method, which provides the account object for succeeding operations, such as deposit. The *Deposit* and *Withdraw* methods take two parameters. The first parameter is the *account* parameter, and the second one is the *amount* parameter, which is passed by the user. The *Run* method is the last one to be invoked. It returns a function `unit->Account<'u>` type.

LISTING 6-108 Bank-system computation expression example

```
type Account<[<Measure>]'u>() =
    member val Balance = 0.0<_> with get, set
    member val PendingAmount = 0.0<_> with get, set

type Bank<[<Measure>]'u>(account:Account<'u>) =
    member this.Yield (()) =
        account

    [<CustomOperation("deposit")>]
    member this.Deposit (account:Account<'u>, v:float<'u>) : Account<'u> =
        account.PendingAmount <- account.PendingAmount + v
        account

    [<CustomOperation("withdraw")>]
    member this.Withdraw (account:Account<'u>, v:float<'u>) : Account<'u> =
        account.PendingAmount <- account.PendingAmount - v
        account

    member this.Run (account:Account<'u>) =
        fun () ->
            let finalBalance = account.Balance + account.PendingAmount
```

```
        if finalBalance > 0.<_> then
            account.Balance <- finalBalance
            account
        else
            printfn "not enough found"
            account

[<Measure>] type USD
let account = Account<USD>()
let bank = Bank<USD>(account)

let transaction =
    bank {
        deposit 100.<USD>
        withdraw 50.<USD>
    }

printfn "balance after one transaction = %A" (transaction().Balance)
```

```
balance after one transation = 50.0
```

FIGURE 6-2 Computation expression execution result

Using Reflection

As a C# developer, reflection is not likely a new concept for you. Usually, reflection in C# involves defining or applying attributes and getting type or method information.

Defining Attributes

Listing 6-109 shows how to define a customized attribute.

LISTING 6-109 Defining an attribute

```
// define attribute with a property
type MyAttribute() =
    inherit System.Attribute()
    member val MyAttributeProperty = System.String.Empty with get, set
```

You can apply one or more attributes to modules, or smaller program elements, such as classes and properties, by putting the attribute name between [< and >]. The assembly-level attribute is different, because it can be applied only by using the *do* keyword. The attribute can be applied separately as is done in C#. Additionally, multiple attributes can be applied in a group format, where multiple attributes are put into one [< >] and separated by semi-colons. Listing 6-110 shows how to apply one or more attributes to a class definition. There is little difference between applying attributes to a class and to an interface/struct. I will leave this exercise to you.

LISTING 6-110 Applying an attribute to a class and class members

```
// define an attribute
type MyAttribute() =
    inherit System.Attribute()

// define an attribute
type MyAttribute2() =
    inherit System.Attribute()
// define a class with one attribute
[<MyAttribute>]
type MyClassWithOneAttribute() = class

    end

// define a class with two attributes applied separately
[<MyAttribute>]
[<MyAttribute2>]
type MyClassWithTwoAttributes() = class

    end

// define a class with two attributes applied as a group
[<MyAttribute; MyAttribute2>]
type MyClassWithGroupedAttribute() = class

    end

// apply an attribute to a method, property, and field
type MyClass3() =
    [<MyAttribute>]
    let mutable MyVariable = 0




    [<MyAttribute>]
    member this.MyMethod([<MyAttribute2; MyAttribute>] x0, [<MyAttribute>] x1) = ()

    member this.MyProperty
        with [<MyAttribute2>] get() = MyVariable
        and set(v) = MyVariable <- v

    [<MyAttribute>]
    member val MyProperty2 = 0 with get, set
// apply attribute to mutual reference class
type MyClass4() =
    let a:MyClass5 = MyClass5()
and [<MyAttribute>] MyClass5() = class

    end
```

Listing 6-111 shows how to apply attributes to F#-specific structures, such as a *let* binding and a record. Also, it shows how to apply attributes on the special structures in F# class definitions, such as the primary constructor.

LISTING 6-111 An attribute on F#-specific data structures

```
// define an attribute
type MyAttribute() =
    inherit System.Attribute()

[<MyAttribute>]
let myValue = 0

[<MyAttribute>]
let myFunction x = x + 1

// the functionality from the following two statements are the same
let [<MyAttribute>] a, b = 1, 2

[<MyAttribute>]
let c, d = 1, 2

// apply an attribute to a function
let rec [<MyAttribute>] f() = g()

// apply an attribute to mutual reference functions
and [<MyAttribute>] g() = printfn "hello"

//apply an attribute to a record
[<MyAttribute>]
type Point = {
    [<MyAttribute>] x : float;
    [<MyAttribute>] y: float;
    z: float; }

// apply an attribute to a DU
[<MyAttribute>]
type DU =
| [<MyAttribute>] Case1 of float
| Case2 of double
| [<MyAttribute>] Case3 of double

// apply an attribute to a unit of measure
[<Measure; MyAttribute>] type km

// apply an attribute to an enumeration
[<MyAttribute>]
type Color =
    | [<MyAttribute>] Red = 0
    | Green = 1
    | [<MyAttribute>] Blue = 2
```

```
// apply an attribute to an exception type
[<MyAttribute>]
exception MyError of string

// apply an attribute to a tuple parameter
let f3 ([<MyAttribute>] a, [<MyAttribute>] b) = a + b
let f4 ([<MyAttribute>] a, [<MyAttribute>] b) c = a + b + c

[<MyAttribute>]
module MyModule =
    let myTest = 0

// apply an attribute to a primary constructor
type MyClass2[<MyAttribute>]() = class

    end

// apply an attribute to the parameter of a constructor
type MyClass([<MyAttribute>] xValue:double, yValue:double)=

    // define a static field named count
    [<MyAttribute>]
    static let mutable count = 0

    //additional constructor
    [<MyAttribute>]
    new() = MyClass(0., 0.)
```

Some F# structures do not accept attributes. The pattern matching `expression`
`let ([<MyAttribute>] myValue2, myValue3)` segment in the following example does not
support attributes. Also, attributes cannot be applied to the exception parameters in an F# exception
definition. You can use an exception class definition to solve this problem. Also, curried functions do
not accept attributes on parameters. The auto-implemented property's *getter* and *setter* functions
cannot have attributes. If the attribute is needed, you have to use the old syntax.

```
// pattern does not allow attribute
let ([<MyAttribute>] myValue2, myValue3) = (2, 3)

// attribute cannot be applied to exception parameter
exception MyError2 of [<MyAttribute>] string

//apply attribute to curried function
let f2 [<MyAttribute>]a [<MyAttribute>]b = a + 1

//apply attribute to auto-implemented property's getter or setter function
type MyClass() =
    member val MyProperty = 0 with [<MyAttribute >] get, set
```

> **Note** The sample code does not compile.

Working with Type and Member Info

F# supports the *typeof* operator similar to C#. For example, *typeof<int>* returns a *System.Int32* type. Because *typeof* always takes the *type* parameter as a type of object, F# introduces the *typedefof* function to work with generic types. Listing 6-112 shows the difference between *typeof* and *typedefof*.

LISTING 6-112 The *typeof* and *typedefof* operators

```
Typeof and typedefof code
typeof<System.Collections.Generic.IEnumerable<_>>

typedefof<System.Collections.Generic.IEnumerable<_>>


Execution result
val it : System.Type =
    System.Collections.Generic.IEnumerable'1[System.Object]

val it : System.Type =
    System.Collections.Generic.IEnumerable'1[T]
```

Getting the type info enables you to invoke methods or access the properties of an object. Listing 6-113 shows how to use reflection to retrieve *MethodInfo* and invoke the method on a *Student* class. The output from the code shows that the student variable's content is changed from *("John", 16)* to *("Brent", 18)*.

LISTING 6-113 Reflection by using F#

```
// define student class
type Student(nameIn : string, idIn : int) =
    let mutable name = nameIn
    let mutable id = idIn

    do printfn "Created a student object"
    member this.Name with get() = name and set v = name <- v
    member this.ID with get() = id and set v = id <- v
    member public this.SetStudentInfo(name, id) =
        this.Name <- name
        this.ID <- id

module TestModule =

    let student = Student("John", 16)
    let studentType = typeof<Student>
```

```
    //use reflection to invoke SetStudentInfo method
    let result = studentType.GetMethod("SetStudentInfo").Invoke(student, [| "Brent"; 18 |]
)

    printfn "new student info: name = %s, id = %d" student.Name student.ID
```

Execution result

```
Created a student object
new student info: name = Brent, id = 18
```

Using Reflection on F# Types

Reflection was introduced before F# came into production, so F# needed a way to provide reflection on its specific types, such as a tuple. You can find all of these F# specific reflection functions in the *Microsoft.FSharp.Reflection* namespace.

Using Tuples

Listing 6-114 shows how to use reflection to get the element types in a tuple, get element values, and make a tuple from an object array.

LISTING 6-114 F# reflection on a tuple

```
Source code
open Microsoft.FSharp.Reflection

let tuple = ("John", 18, "Canada")

// get element types in a tuple
FSharpType.GetTupleElements(tuple.GetType())

// retrieve given tuple field value
FSharpValue.GetTupleField(tuple, 2)

// retrieve all fields in a tuple
FSharpValue.GetTupleFields tuple

// make a tuple from an array array
FSharpValue.MakeTuple([| "Lisa"; 20; "USA" |], tuple.GetType())

// check if a type is a tuple
FSharpType.IsTuple (tuple.GetType())

// make a tuple type
let t = FSharpType.MakeTupleType([| typeof<int>; typeof<string> |])
FSharpValue.MakeTuple([| 1; "One" |], t)
```

```
val tuple : string * int * string = ("John", 18, "Canada")
val it : System.Type [] = [|System.String; System.Int32; System.String|]

>
val it : obj = "Canada"
>
val it : obj [] = [|"John"; 18; "Canada"|]
>
val it : obj = ("Lisa", 20, "USA")
>
val it : bool = true
>

val t : System.Type = System.Tuple'2[System.Int32,System.String]
val it : obj = (1, "One")
```

Using Functions Related to Discriminated Unions

Listing 6-115 shows the discriminated union–related functions. The sample code shows how to use reflection to check the type, get union case info, get a union field, and create a union value.

LISTING 6-115 F# reflection on discriminated unions

Source code

```
open Microsoft.FSharp.Reflection

// define a shape discriminated union
type Shape =
    | Circle of double
    | Triangle of double * double * double
    | Rectangle of double * double

let du = Shape.Rectangle(2., 3.)

// check if the type is a discriminated union
FSharpType.IsUnion(du.GetType())

// get union case type info
FSharpType.GetUnionCases(du.GetType())

// get union field
FSharpValue.GetUnionFields(du, du.GetType())

// create new discriminated union value
let caseInfo = fst <| FSharpValue.GetUnionFields(du, du.GetType())
FSharpValue.MakeUnion(caseInfo, [| 10.; 20. |])
```

```
val it : bool = true
>


val it : UnionCaseInfo [] =
  [|Shape.Circle {DeclaringType = FSI_0033+Shape;
                  Name = "Circle";
                  Tag = 0;}; Shape.Triangle {DeclaringType = FSI_0033+Shape;
                                             Name = "Triangle";
                                             Tag = 1;};
    Shape.Rectangle {DeclaringType = FSI_0033+Shape;
                     Name = "Rectangle";
                     Tag = 2;}|]
>

val it : UnionCaseInfo * obj [] =
  (Shape.Rectangle {DeclaringType = FSI_0033+Shape;
                    Name = "Rectangle";
                    Tag = 2;}, [|2.0; 3.0|])
>

val caseInfo : UnionCaseInfo = Shape.Rectangle
val it : obj = Rectangle (10.0,20.0)
```

Using Functions Related to Records

The F# record-related functions are shown in Listing 6-116. The sample code shows how to use reflection to check the type, get a record's fields, get a particular field, and make a record from an array.

LISTING 6-116 F# reflection on a record

Source code

```
open Microsoft.FSharp.Reflection

type Point2D = { x : float; y: float }
let point2DRecord = { Point2D.x = 1.; Point2D.y = 2. }

// check if it is a record type
FSharpType.IsRecord(point2DRecord.GetType())

// get record fields
FSharpType.GetRecordFields(point2DRecord.GetType())

// get a record field
let fields = FSharpType.GetRecordFields(point2DRecord.GetType())
FSharpValue.GetRecordField(point2DRecord, fields.[1])

// make a record from an array
FSharpValue.MakeRecord(point2DRecord.GetType(), [| 4.; 5. |])
```

```
val it : bool = true
>

val it : System.Reflection.PropertyInfo [] =
  [|Double x
      {Attributes = None;
       CanRead = true;
       CanWrite = false;
       CustomAttributes = seq
                         [[Microsoft.FSharp.Core.CompilationMappingAttribute((Microso
ft.FSharp.Core.SourceConstruct
Flags)4, (Int32)0)]];
       DeclaringType = FSI_0038+Point2D;
       GetMethod = Double get_x();
       IsSpecialName = false;
       MemberType = Property;
       MetadataToken = 385876070;
       Module = FSI-ASSEMBLY;
       Name = "x";
       PropertyType = System.Double;
       ReflectedType = FSI_0038+Point2D;
       SetMethod = null;};

    Double y
      {Attributes = None;
       CanRead = true;
       CanWrite = false;
       CustomAttributes = seq
                         [[Microsoft.FSharp.Core.CompilationMappingAttribute((Microso
ft.FSharp.Core.SourceConstruct
Flags)4, (Int32)1)]];
       DeclaringType = FSI_0038+Point2D;
       GetMethod = Double get_y();
       IsSpecialName = false;
       MemberType = Property;
       MetadataToken = 385876071;
       Module = FSI-ASSEMBLY;
       Name = "y";
       PropertyType = System.Double;
       ReflectedType = FSI_0038+Point2D;
       SetMethod = null;};|]
>

val fields : System.Reflection.PropertyInfo [] = [|Double x; Double y|]
val it : obj = 2.0

val it : obj = {x = 4.0;
               y = 5.0;}
```

Using Exceptions with F#

Although the exception is not an F# specific type, F#'s exception definition can be very different from a C# exception definition. Listing 6-117 shows how to use F# reflection on exceptions—specifically, how to check the exception, get exception fields, and get exception field values.

LISTING 6-117 Using F# reflection on an exception

Source code
```
open Microsoft.FSharp.Reflection

exception MyException of int * int

let ex = MyException(1, 2)

// check if it is an exception representation
FSharpType.IsExceptionRepresentation(ex.GetType())

// get exception fields
FSharpType.GetExceptionFields(ex.GetType())

// get exception field values
FSharpValue.GetExceptionFields(ex)
```

Execution result
```
val it : bool = true
>

val it : System.Reflection.PropertyInfo [] =
  [|Int32 Data0
      {Attributes = None;
       CanRead = true;
       CanWrite = false;
       CustomAttributes = seq
                           [[Microsoft.FSharp.Core.CompilationMappingAttribute((Microso
ft.FSharp.Core.SourceConstruct
Flags)4, (Int32)0)]];
       DeclaringType = FSI_0046+MyException;
       GetMethod = Int32 get_Data0();
       IsSpecialName = false;
       MemberType = Property;
       MetadataToken = 385876082;
       Module = FSI-ASSEMBLY;
       Name = "Data0";
       PropertyType = System.Int32;
       ReflectedType = FSI_0046+MyException;
       SetMethod = null;};
    Int32 Data1
      {Attributes = None;
       CanRead = true;
```

```
        CanWrite = false;
        CustomAttributes = seq
                            [[Microsoft.FSharp.Core.CompilationMappingAttribute((Microso
ft.FSharp.Core.SourceConstruct
Flags)4, (Int32)1)]];
        DeclaringType = FSI_0046+MyException;
        GetMethod = Int32 get_Data1();
        IsSpecialName = false;
        MemberType = Property;
        MetadataToken = 385876083;
        Module = FSI-ASSEMBLY;
        Name = "Data1";
        PropertyType = System.Int32;
        ReflectedType = FSI_0046+MyException;
        SetMethod = null;}|]
>
val it : obj [] = [|1; 2|]
```

Function

F# provides a way to make a function by using reflection. Listing 6-118 shows how to implement *printfn*.

LISTING 6-118 Using reflection to implement an F# function

```
open System

type FSV = Microsoft.FSharp.Reflection.FSharpValue
type FST = Microsoft.FSharp.Reflection.FSharpType

let notImpl<'T> : 'T = raise (NotImplementedException())
let printfn (fmt : Printf.TextWriterFormat<'T>) : 'T =
    let rec chain (ty : System.Type) : obj =
        if FST.IsFunction ty then
            let argTy, retTy = FST.GetFunctionElements ty
            FSV.MakeFunction(ty, (fun _ -> chain retTy))
        else
            if ty.IsValueType then Activator.CreateInstance(ty) else null

    chain typeof<'T> :?> 'T

let printf fmt = printfn fmt
```

Checking F# Types

This section presents a sample that returns the F# type using *Microsoft.FSharp.Reflection* functions and an active pattern. Listing 6-119 detects the function, tuple, record, DU, and other types, such as .NET types.

LISTING 6-119 Checking F# types

```
// define the DU
type 'T ty =
    | Abbreviation of 'T list * string
    | Function of 'T ty * 'T ty
    | Record of string * (string * 'T) list
    | Tuple of 'T ty list
    | DU of string * (string * 'T list) list

// define the active patterns
let (| Fun | _ |) ty = if Reflection.FSharpType.IsFunction ty then Some ty else None
let (| Tup | _ |) ty = if Reflection.FSharpType.IsTuple ty then Some ty else None
let (| Rec | _ |) ty = if Reflection.FSharpType.IsRecord ty then Some ty else None
let (| Union | _ |) ty = if Reflection.FSharpType.IsUnion ty then Some ty else None

// function to get F# types
let rec typeofFun (myFunction) = function
    | Fun ty ->
        let arg, ret = Reflection.FSharpType.GetFunctionElements ty
        Function(typeofFun myFunction arg, typeofFun myFunction ret)
    | Tup ty ->
        Tuple ((Reflection.FSharpType.GetTupleElements ty )
                |> List.ofArray
                |> List.map (fun ty -> typeofFun myFunction ty ))
    | Rec ty ->
        Record(ty.Name,
                (Reflection.FSharpType.GetRecordFields ty)
                |> List.ofArray
                |> List.map (fun n -> (n.GetAccessors())
                                        |> List.ofArray
                                        |> List.map (fun acc -> (n.Name, acc)))
                |> List.collect id
                |> List.map (fun (n, acc) -> n, myFunction acc.ReturnType))
    | Union ty ->
        DU(ty.Name,
                (Reflection.FSharpType.GetUnionCases ty)
                |> List.ofArray
                |> List.map (fun n ->
                            let args = (n.GetFields())
                                        |> List.ofArray
                                        |> List.map (fun field -> myFunction field.
PropertyType)
                            n.Name, args))
    | ty ->
        Abbreviation(
                (ty.GetGenericArguments())
                |> List.ofArray
                |> List.map (fun ty -> myFunction ty),
                ty.FullName)
```

```
// function to be passed in the typeofFun
let f = fun (t:System.Type) -> t.Name

// code to get the types
let intType = typeof<int> |> typeofFun f
let tupleType = typeof<int*float> |> typeofFun f
let funType = typeof<int->string> |> typeofFun f
let funType2 = typeof<int->string->float32> |> typeofFun f
let intOption = typeof<int option> |> typeofFun f
let stringList = typeof<string list> |> typeofFun f

// print out result
[ intType; tupleType; funType; funType2; intOption; stringList; ]
|> Seq.iter (printfn "%A")
```

Execution result

```
Abbreviation ([],"System.Int32")
Tuple [Abbreviation ([],"System.Int32"); Abbreviation ([],"System.Double")]
Function (Abbreviation ([],"System.Int32"),Abbreviation ([],"System.String"))
Function
  (Abbreviation ([],"System.Int32"),
    Function (Abbreviation ([],"System.String"),Abbreviation ([],"System.Single")))
DU ("FSharpOption'1",[("None", []); ("Some", ["Int32"])])
DU ("FSharpList'1",[("Empty", []); ("Cons", ["String"; "FSharpList'1"])])
```

Working with Code Quotation

F# code quotation, which can be shortened to just *quotation*, is another way to expose source code information—even more information than reflection can provide. Reflection can give only the surface information of a function, such as return type or parameter type. However, the tree structure provided by a quotation can show the implementation details of a function.

You can choose whether or not to have the result of a quotation include type information. Listing 6-120 shows how to declare a quotation with and without type information. The <@ @> is used to get the typed code quotation and the <@@ @@> is used to get the untyped code quotation. The result shows that *expr* is an *Expr<int>* type and that *expr2* is an *Expr* (without a type).

LISTING 6-120 Defining a quotation

Source code

```
open Microsoft.FSharp.Quotations

// A typed code quotation.
let expr : Expr<float> = <@ 1.2  + 2.4 @>

// An untyped code quotation.
let expr2 : Expr = <@@ 1.2 + 2.4 @@>
```

Execution result

```
val expr : Quotations.Expr<int> =
  Call (None, op_Addition, [Value (1), Value (1)])

val expr2 : Quotations.Expr = Call (None, op_Addition, [Value (1), Value (1)])
```

For a complex function, the <@ @> and <@@ @@> are not the most convenient way to get the quotation. If that is the case, you can use the *ReflectedDefinition* attribute as shown in Listing 6-121. Before F# 3.0, *ReflectedDefinition* could be applied only on a function. F# 3.0 now also supports this attribute on the module. If a module is decorated with this attribute, it works as though all functions within the module have this attribute.

LISTING 6-121 Using the *ReflectedDefinition* attribute

Source code

```
[<ReflectedDefinition>]
let ff a b =
    if a then b + 1 else b + 3

let q = <@ ff @>
```

Execution result

```
val ff : a:bool -> b:int -> int

val q : Expr<(bool -> int -> int)> =
  Lambda (a, Lambda (b, Call (None, ff, [a, b])))
```

The quotation is a tree structure, and you can iterate through it by using a recursive function. The function in Listing 6-122 is a skeleton that can be used to go over the quotation tree. You can replace the () in each case to iterate through the expression tree. This function is a good starting point if you want to convert the F# code to another language, such as .NET IL code.

LISTING 6-122 Recursive function to access a quotation

```
let rec iterate exp
  match exp with
          | DerivedPatterns.Applications (e, ell) -> ()
          | DerivedPatterns.AndAlso (e0, e1) -> ()
          | DerivedPatterns.Bool e -> ()
          | DerivedPatterns.Byte e -> ()
          | DerivedPatterns.Char e -> ()
          | DerivedPatterns.Double e -> ()
          | DerivedPatterns.Int16 e-> ()
          | DerivedPatterns.Int32 e-> ()
          | DerivedPatterns.Int64 e -> ()
          | DerivedPatterns.OrElse (e0, e1)-> ()
          | DerivedPatterns.SByte e -> ()
          | DerivedPatterns.Single e -> ()
          | DerivedPatterns.String e -> ()
          | DerivedPatterns.UInt16 e -> ()
          | DerivedPatterns.UInt32 e -> ()
          | DerivedPatterns.UInt64 e -> ()
          | DerivedPatterns.Unit e -> ()
          | Patterns.AddressOf address -> ()
          | Patterns.AddressSet (exp0, exp1) -> ()
          | Patterns.Application (exp0, exp1) -> ()
          | Patterns.Call (expOption, mi, expList) -> ()
          | Patterns.Coerce (exp, t)-> ()
          | Patterns.DefaultValue exp -> ()
          | Patterns.FieldGet (expOption, fi) -> ()
          | Patterns.FieldSet (expOption, fi, e) -> ()
          | Patterns.ForIntegerRangeLoop (v, e0, e1, e2) -> ()
          | Patterns.IfThenElse (con, exp0, exp1) -> ()
          | Patterns.Lambda (var,body) -> ()
          | Patterns.Let (var, exp0, exp1) -> ()
          | Patterns.LetRecursive (tupList, exp) -> ()
          | Patterns.NewArray (t, expList) -> ()
          | Patterns.NewDelegate (t, varList, exp) -> ()
          | Patterns.NewObject (t, expList) -> ()
          | Patterns.NewRecord (t, expList) -> ()
          | Patterns.NewObject (t, expList) -> ()
          | Patterns.NewRecord (t, expList) -> ()
          | Patterns.NewTuple expList -> ()
          | Patterns.NewUnionCase (t, expList) -> ()
          | Patterns.PropertyGet (expOption, pi, expList) -> ()
          | Patterns.PropertySet (expOption, pi, expList, e) -> ()
          | Patterns.Quote e -> ()
          | Patterns.Sequential (e0, e1) -> ()
          | Patterns.TryFinally (e0, e1) -> ()
          | Patterns.TryWith (e0, v0, e1, v1, e2) -> ()
          | Patterns.TupleGet (e, i) -> ()
          | Patterns.TypeTest (e, t) -> ()
          | Patterns.UnionCaseTest (e, ui) -> ()
          | Patterns.Value (obj, t) -> ()
          | Patterns.Var v -> ()
          | Patterns.VarSet (v, e) -> ()
          | Patterns.WhileLoop (e0, e1) -> ()
          | _ -> failwith "not supported pattern"
```

Working with the Observable Module

The event is a nice feature that can be used to notify others about something that happens elsewhere in the application. The .NET event is a delegate, which is similar to a function. According to the description on MSDN (*http://msdn.microsoft.com/en-us/library/ee370313.aspx*), the Observable module introduces a number of functions that make an event a first-class citizen. If you are not quite sure what I mean when I call it a *first class citizen*, Table 6-3 might give you a better idea. If you see the similarity between an event and data, you get the point.

TABLE 6-3 Comparison of the Observable module and the Seq module

Observable module	Seq module

`// define an event`
`let myEvent = Event<int>()`
 	
`myEvent.Publish`
`|> Observable.map (fun n -> n.ToString())`
`|> Observable.filter (fun n -> n<>"")`
`|> Observable.choose (fun n -> Some n)`
	`// define a sequence`
	`let myData = seq { 1.. 10 }`
	
	`myData`
	`|> Seq.map (fun n -> n.ToString())`
	`|> Seq.filter (fun n -> n<>"")`
	`|> Seq.choose (fun n -> Some n)`

So I'll explain more about the Observable module, starting with the partition function. Listing 6-123 fires 10 events with arguments 1 to 10. Depending on the value of the provided argument, the events are partitioned or classified into two kinds of events: *oddNumEvent* and *evenNumEvent*. The event-handler function prints out the number in the end. This sample shows how the Observable module functions can process events as if they were data.

LISTING 6-123 Observable module partition function

```
// define an event
let myEvent = Event<int>()

// depending on the value, the event will be given a different label
let evenNumEvent, oddNumEvent =
        myEvent.Publish
        |> Observable.partition (fun n -> n % 2=0)

//set even-number event handler
evenNumEvent.Add(fun i -> printfn "even number %d triggered event" i)

//set odd-number event handler
oddNumEvent.Add(fun i -> printfn "odd number %d triggered event" i)

//fire 10 events with arguments from 1 to 10
[1..10]
|> Seq.iter myEvent.Trigger


Execution result

odd number 1 triggered event
even number 2 triggered event
```

```
odd number 3 triggered event
even number 4 triggered event
odd number 5 triggered event
even number 6 triggered event
odd number 7 triggered event
even number 8 triggered event
odd number 9 triggered event
even number 10 triggered event
```

Listing 6-124 shows how to filter out the even-number event by using *Observable.filter*. The event can be filtered in much the same way as data is filtered in a list!

LISTING 6-124 Filtering out even numbers from events

```
// define an event
let myEvent = Event<int>()

// depending on the value, the event will be given a different label
let evenNumEvent, oddNumEvent =
        myEvent.Publish
        |> Observable.filter (fun n-> n % 2 = 0)
        |> Observable.partition (fun n -> n % 2 = 0)

//set even-number event handler
evenNumEvent.Add(fun i -> printfn "even number %d triggered event" i)

//set odd-number event handler
oddNumEvent.Add(fun i -> printfn "odd number %d triggered event" i)

//fire 10 events with arguments from 1 to 10
[1..10]
|> Seq.iter myEvent.Trigger


Execution result

even number 2 triggered event
even number 4 triggered event
even number 6 triggered event
even number 8 triggered event
even number 10 triggered event
```

The partitioned events can be merged, and the event arguments can be transformed as well. Listing 6-125 merges the *oddNumEvent* and *evenNumEvent* and converts the integer argument to a float.

LISTING 6-125 Merging and converting the event

```
// define an event
let myEvent = Event<int>()

// depending on the value, the event will be given a different label
let evenNumEvent, oddNumEvent =
    myEvent.Publish
        |> Observable.partition (fun n -> n % 2 = 0)

let merged = Observable.merge evenNumEvent oddNumEvent
merged
|> Observable.map float
|> Observable.add (fun floatValue -> printfn "got value %f" floatValue)

//set even-number event handler
evenNumEvent.Add(fun i -> printfn "even number %d triggered event" i)

//set odd-number event handler
oddNumEvent.Add(fun i -> printfn "odd number %d triggered event" i)

//fire 5 events with arguments from 1 to 5
[1..5]
|> Seq.iter myEvent.Trigger
```

Execution result

```
got value 1.000000
odd number 1 triggered event
got value 2.000000
even number 2 triggered event
got value 3.000000
odd number 3 triggered event
got value 4.000000
even number 4 triggered event
got value 5.000000
odd number 5 triggered event
```

If you compare the sample code here and the code in the seq module, they are very similar. As mentioned a few times in this section, the Observable module makes the event processing pretty much like data processing. The reason I've mentioned it a few times is that this is something that other .NET languages do not provide without help from other libraries.

Using Lazy Evaluation, Partial Functions, and Memoization

One of the functional programming features F# provides is *lazy evaluation* or *lazy computation*. F# ships with a *lazy* keyword and a Lazy module that can be used to define lazy computations. The reason to use lazy evaluation is that the result is computed when it is needed. This can often improve performance.

The quickest way to define a lazy computation is to use the *lazy* keyword. Listing 6-126 shows a sample that demonstrates the syntax of the *lazy* keyword. From the execution result, you can see that the *myLazy* variable has a type of *Lazy<int>*, where the int is the type from the expression (1+1). The actual value *2* is not created immediately.

LISTING 6-126 The *lazy* syntax and sample

```
// lazy syntax : let variable = lazy ( expression )
let myLazy = lazy ( 1 + 1 )

// lazy variable with explicit type info
let a:Lazy<int> = lazy 1



Execution result
val myLazy : Lazy<int> = Value is not created.
val a : Lazy<int> = Value is not created.
```

When the computation value is needed, you can invoke the *Force* method. This causes the computation to be executed a single time. Additional calls to *Force* do not trigger the computation, but simply return the value that was computed during the first execution. Listing 6-127 shows how to use *Force* and how the variable state changes.

LISTING 6-127 Force the computation on *lazy*

```
// define a lazy computation
let myLazy = lazy(1 + 1)
printfn "myLazy is %A" myLazy

// force computation
let computedValue = myLazy.Force()
printfn "computed value = %d" computedValue
printfn "myLazy is %A" myLazy
```

```
myLazy is Value is not created.
computed value = 2
myLazy is 2
```

The *lazy* keyword is good at wrapping a value. For creating a lazy computation from a function, you can use *Lazy.Create*. Listing 6-128 computes the sum from a given number down to 0 by using *Lazy.Create*.

LISTING 6-128 Wrapping a function using *Lazy.Create*

```
// create a lazy computation from a function
let myLazy n = Lazy.Create (fun () ->
    let rec sum n =
        match n with
        | 0 -> 0
        | 1 -> 1
        | n -> n + sum (n - 1)
    sum n)

let lazyVal = myLazy 10
printfn "%d" (lazyVal.Force())
```

> **Note** The preceding code can potentially cause a stack-overflow exception, because it is not tail recursive. The following code is a tail-recursive version, which won't cause a stack overflow.
>
> ```
> let myLazy n = Lazy.Create (fun () ->
>     let rec sum acc n =
>         match n with
>         | 0 -> 0
>         | 1 -> acc + 1
>         | n -> sum (acc + n) (n - 1)
>     sum 0 n)
> ```

The other way to caching the value is to use a partial function. F# automatically caches the value from any function that takes no parameter. Listing 6-129 and Listing 6-130 show a nonpartial function and how to define a partial function. The data in a nonpartial function is created each time the function is invoked, while the partial function caches the data and the data is created only once.

LISTING 6-129 Nonpartial function definition

```
let f x =
    let data =
        printfn "the data is created"
        [1; 2; 3; 4]
    data |> Seq.tryFind ( (=) x )

f 1
f 2
f 3
f 5
```

Execution result

```
the data is created
the data is created
the data is created
the data is created

val f : x:int -> int option
val it : int option = None
```

LISTING 6-130 Partial function definition

```
let f2 =
    let data =
        printfn "the data is created"
        [1; 2; 3; 4]
    fun x -> data |> Seq.tryFind ( (=) x )

f2 1
f2 2
f2 3
f2 5
```

Execution result

```
the data is created

val f2 : (int -> int option)
val it : int option = None
```

Note For a C# developer, the function without a parameter is something like `f()`. However, the function `f()` has one parameter, which is *unit*.

Memoization is way to cache an intermediate result to speed up the computation. Memoization uses a lookup table such as `Dictionary<TKey, TValue>` to cache the intermediate computation result. Listing 6-131 shows the nonmemoization and memoization versions of Fibonacci code. To get the performance data, you need to run "#time" in FSI. From the execution result, the nonmemoization version takes much longer than the memoization version.

LISTING 6-131 Memoization and nonmemoization functions

```
// non-memoization version
let rec fibonacci n =
    match n with
    | 0 | 1 -> 1
    | _ -> ( fibonacci (n - 1) ) + ( fibonacci (n - 2) )

// memoization version
let rec fibonacci2=
    let lookup = System.Collections.Generic.Dictionary<_, _>()
    fun n ->
        match lookup.TryGetValue n with
        | true, v -> v
        | _ ->
            let a =
                match n with
                | 0 | 1 -> 1
                | _ -> ( fibonacci2 (n - 1) ) + ( fibonacci2 (n - 2) )
            lookup.Add(n, a)
            a
```

Execution result in FSI

```
> #time;;

--> Timing now on

> fibonacci 45;;
Real: 00:00:14.697, CPU: 00:00:14.640, GC gen0: 0, gen1: 0, gen2: 0
val it : int = 1836311903

> fibonacci2 45;;
Real: 00:00:00.001, CPU: 00:00:00.000, GC gen0: 0, gen1: 0, gen2: 0
val it : int = 1836311903
```

You can derive a more general function for a memoization function, as shown in Listing 6-132.

LISTING 6-132 A more general memoization function

```
let mem f =
    let lookup = System.Collections.Generic.Dictionary<_, _>()
    fun n ->
        match lookup.TryGetValue n with
        | true, v -> v
        | _ ->
            let a = f n
            lookup.Add(n, a)
            a

let rec fibonacci3 = mem (fun n ->
                        match n with
                        | 0 | 1 -> 1
                        | _ -> (fibonacci3 (n - 1)) + (fibonacci3 (n - 2)))
```

Note Listing 6-132 generates a warning: "This and other recursive references to the object(s) being defined will be checked for initialization-soundness at runtime through the use of a delayed reference. This is because you are defining one or more recursive objects, rather than recursive functions. This warning might be suppressed by using '#nowarn "40"' or '--nowarn:40'." This warning is to prevent the user from writing the following code, which will generate a runtime exception:

```
let init f = f()
let rec foo = init (fun() -> foo : obj)
```

Listing 6-132 is not a template you can pass in any recursive function. Thanks to Uladzimir on our team, a new version is shown in Listing 6-133.

LISTING 6-133 Memoization code template

```
let memorize wrapFunction =
    let cache = System.Collections.Generic.Dictionary()
    let rec f x =
        match cache.TryGetValue x with
        | true, v -> v
        | false, _ ->
            let v = wrapFunction f x
            cache.[x] <- v
            v
    f
```

```
let fib =
    memorize (
        fun f x ->
            if x < 2 then 1
            else f(x - 1) + f(x - 2)
    )

fib 45
```

Summary

For C# developer, the first three chapters introduce the imperative and object-oriented features provided by F#. This chapter introduces unique F# features that are not provided by C#. These new language features make F# development more efficient and allow you to develop applications that contain fewer bugs. A few examples include the unit-of-measure and pattern-matching feature. In the later chapters in this book, you can see more complex samples that use these features.

PART III

Real-World Applications

Portable Library and HTML/ JavaScript

The client-side development experience dramatically changed when Microsoft released Windows 8 and continues to change as HTML5 gains full traction in web development. In this chapter, I will describe how to write F# portable library for Windows Store apps as well as web applications based on HTML/JavaScript.

Developing Windows Store Applications with F#

Windows Store is a platform for distributing Windows Runtime (WinRT) and desktop applications. WinRT is a cross-platform architecture for Windows 8. WinRT supports development in C++/CX, JavaScript, and managed languages such as C# and Visual Basic .NET. The portable library support makes F# another choice for library development for Windows Store apps. The Portable Class Library project was introduced with Microsoft Visual Studio 2012. The MSDN documentation (*http://msdn. microsoft.com/en-us/library/gg597391.aspx*) describes it like this:

> The Portable Class Library project supports a subset of assemblies from the .NET Framework, Silverlight, .NET for Windows Store apps, Windows Phone, and Xbox 360, and provides a Visual Studio template that you can use to build assemblies that run without modification on these platforms. If you don't use a Portable Class Library project, you must target a single app type, and then manually rework the class library for other app types. With the Portable Class Library project, you can reduce the time and costs of developing and testing code by building portable assemblies that are shared across apps for different devices.

There are different .NET frameworks available. The desktop application uses the traditional .NET Framework. Silverlight and Windows Store apps use a different, more limited, version of the .NET Framework. If you create applications for different platforms, the cost to maintain these different code versions is very high. The portable class library (or simply, *portable library*) is the best choice when you are developing an application or library with the intent of targeting multiple platforms. For the core business logic that does not change across platforms, the portable library is a suitable choice. That's also the recommended way to use an F# portable library. The portable library does have a limitation: it cannot contain a reference to a platform-specific project or binary file.

If you're planning to create a Windows Store application using F#, creating an F# portable library is the way to do it. The back-end business logic can be hosted in an F# portable library, and the UI can be built as a C# project.

Creating an F# Portable Library

You can create a portable library with Visual Studio 2012. Start by clicking New Project. The portable library is shown under the Visual F# node, as shown in Figure 7-1. The project creates an F# library (.DLL) that can be executed on Windows and Silverlight.

FIGURE 7-1 Creating an F# portable library

The default for the project is simple: it contains one class with one member. Because the library is most likely invoked by another language, a namespace is used. The default code is shown in Listing 7-1.

LISTING 7-1 Default content for an F# portable library

```
namespace PortableLibrary1

type Class1() =
    member this.X = "F#"
```

After the project is created, you can go to the properties for the project, which offer more detailed information about the supported platform, as shown in Figure 7-2. The F# portable library is supported for .NET for Windows Store apps, .NET Framework 4.5 for desktop applications, and Silverlight 5.

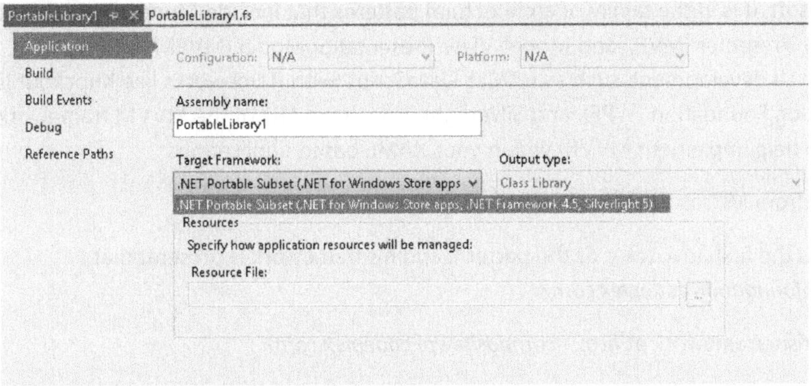

FIGURE 7-2 Project properties for an F# portable library

Once the code is compiled, the generated DLL is a portable library. The portable library project can only reference a smaller number of .NET assemblies. In Visual Studio, adding a reference to a project is performed by using Reference Manager. The Reference Manager dialog box is shown in Figure 7-3.

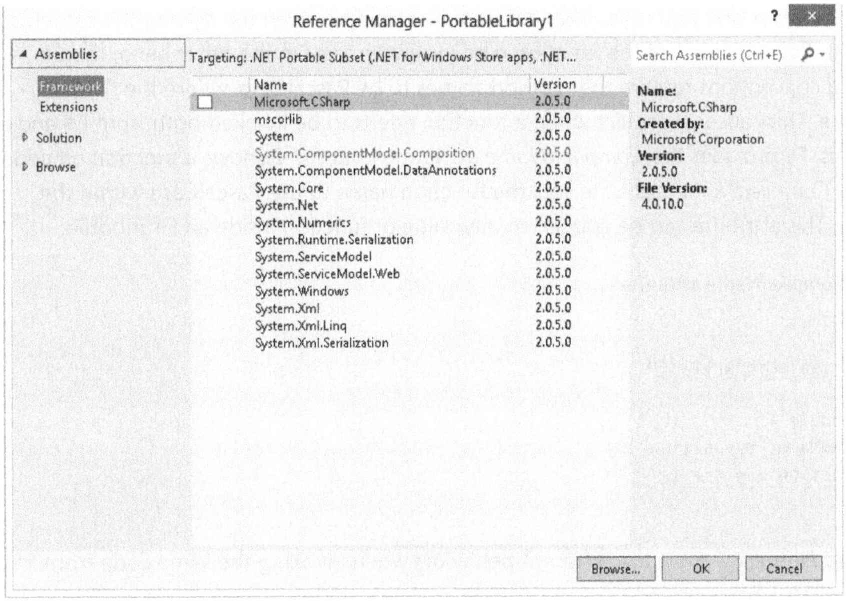

FIGURE 7-3 Reference Manager dialog box for a portable library

Later in this chapter, I'll show you how to use F# to perform HTML5 programming by using WebSharper. For XAML-based application development, the easiest approach for developing the UI aspects is to use tooling provided for other languages, such as C#.

One commonly used pattern to accomplish the separation between the business logic and UI is known as Model-View-ViewModel (MVVM). MVVM is an architectural design pattern that was proposed by Microsoft. It is in the family of architectural patterns that include Model-View-Controller (MVC), Model-View-Presenter (MVP), and Model-View-PresentationModel (MVPM). MVVM is targeted at modern UI development, such as HTML5+JavaScript (with frameworks like Knockout.js), Windows Presentation Foundation (WPF), and Silverlight. Here are a few of the MVVM frameworks that can be used to help implement MVVM within your XAML-based applications:

- WPF toolkit from Microsoft (*http://wpf.codeplex.com/*)

- Josh Smith is the first advocator of the pattern, and his framework is presented at *http://mvvmfoundation.codeplex.com/*.

- Microsoft Prism framework at *http://compositewpf.codeplex.com/*

- MVVM Light Toolkit at *http://www.galasoft.ch/mvvm/*.

Now it's time to show you some code and demonstrate how to write a portable library in F#.

Using the *CompiledName* Attribute

As you've seen, a common way to use F# functions in a Windows Store app is to invoke the F# portable library from a C# project. However, this can cause inconsistencies when it comes to naming conventions for methods and functions. The F# function naming convention follows the camelCase format, where the first character of the function name is lowercase. On the other hand, the C# and .NET naming conventions require the method names to be PascalCase, where the first character is uppercase. This causes a conflict when a function needs to be invoked both from F# and C#. To resolve this, F# provides the *CompiledName* attribute. Listing 7-2 shows a function named *myFunction*. The *CompiledName* attribute sets the function name to use PascalCase within the compiled binary. This attribute can be applied to any value or function inside an F# module.

LISTING 7-2 The *CompiledName* attribute

```
namespace PortableLibrary1

module TestModule =
    [<CompiledName("MyFunction")>]
    let myFunction x = x + 1
```

Figure 7-4 and Figure 7-5 show the different behaviors when invoking the same code from F# and C# in a Portable Class Library project.

```
namespace PortableLibrary1

module TestModule =
    [<CompiledName("MyFunction")>]
    let myFunction x = x + 1


TestModule.|
        myFunction      val myFunction : x:int -> int
```

FIGURE 7-4 Invoking a function decorated with the *CompiledName* attribute from an F# project

```
using System;
using System.Collections.Generic;
using System.Linq;
using System.Text;
using System.Threading.Tasks;

namespace CompiledName
{
    class Program
    {
        static void Main(string[] args)
        {
            var x = PortableLibrary1.TestModule.
        }                    ⊚ Equals
    }                        ⊚ MyFunction
}                            ⊚ ReferenceEquals
```

FIGURE 7-5 Invoking a function decorated with the *CompiledName* attribute from a C# project

Exploring the Portable Library Samples

As previously mentioned, the portable library supports only a subset of the assemblies provided by .NET. This presents a good opportunity for you to apply F# features to some complex problems. In this section, algorithm and data structure samples, which are the foundation to implementing complex business logic, are presented. When solving these complex problems, I will also demonstrate how to use F# features to improve the overall coding experience. I do not believe that code should always be written in the same way. Different strokes for different folks. You should be able to recognize the features that are most useful to you with your existing skill set and apply them to your daily work.

> **Note** This section does not discuss algorithm design. If you are interested in this topic, I encourage you to reference other sources, such as The Algorithmist website at *http://www.algorithmist.com/index.php/Main_Page*.

Let's start with a small number-cracking problem. Imagine that you did not have the modulo operator available to you. How would you check whether a number is divisible by 7? The math required for determining this, as illustrated by Listing 7-3, is a number in the following form:

$10a + b$ is divisible by 7 if and only if $a - 2b$ is divisible by 7

LISTING 7-3 Checking that a number is divisible by 7

```
let rec ``7?`` x =
    match x with
    | 0
    | 7 -> true
    | _ when x > 0 && x < 10 -> false
    | _ when x < 0 -> ``7?`` -x
    | _ ->
        let a = x / 10
```

```
    let b = x - x / 10 * 10
    ``7?`` (a  2 * b)

let data = [-100..100]

let resultData = data |> List.filter ``7?``

// test data
let oracle =
      data
      |> List.filter (fun n -> n % 7 = 0)

let c = resultData = oracle
```

Note This sample shows how to use a special character in the function name. Except for requiring that the active pattern name be started with an uppercase letter, F# does not impose many restrictions on names. You can even use Unicode characters in a function name.

You can use F# Interactive (FSI) to print out a list of characters. You can use Alt+<number key in the number keyboard> to type in the character, and FSI will figure out the characters. A sample is shown here. The first character is Alt + 900, and the last character is Alt + 980. If your keyboard does not have a number keypad, you can use the other software such as Microsoft Word to generate these characters.

```
> ['ä'..'ŀ'];;
val it : char list =
  ['ä'; 'å'; 'æ'; 'ç'; 'è'; 'é'; 'ê'; 'ë'; 'ì'; 'í'; 'î'; 'ï'; 'ð'; 'ñ'; 'ò';
   'ó'; 'ô'; 'õ'; 'ö'; '÷'; 'ø'; 'ù'; 'ú'; 'û'; 'ü'; 'ý'; 'þ'; 'ÿ'; 'Ā'; 'ā';
   'Ă'; 'ă'; 'Ą'; 'ą'; 'Ć'; 'ć'; 'Ĉ'; 'ĉ'; 'Ċ'; 'ċ'; 'Č'; 'č'; 'Ď'; 'ď'; 'Đ';
   'đ'; 'Ē'; 'ē'; 'Ĕ'; 'ĕ'; 'Ė'; 'ė'; 'Ę'; 'ę'; 'Ě'; 'ě'; 'Ĝ'; 'ĝ'; 'Ğ'; 'ğ';
   'Ġ'; 'ġ'; 'Ģ'; 'ģ'; 'Ĥ'; 'ĥ'; 'Ħ'; 'ħ'; 'Ĩ'; 'ĩ'; 'Ī'; 'ī'; 'Ĭ'; 'ĭ'; 'Į';
   'į'; 'İ'; 'ı'; 'Ĳ'; 'ĳ'; 'Ĵ'; 'ĵ'; 'Ķ'; 'ķ'; 'ĸ'; 'Ĺ'; 'ĺ'; 'Ļ'; 'ļ'; 'Ľ';
   'ľ'; 'Ŀ'; 'ŀ'; 'Ł'; 'ł'; 'Ń'; 'ń'; 'Ņ'; 'ņ'; 'Ň'; ...]
```

Developing the WinRT Application

In Visual Studio 2012, F# is shipped with a new template called the F# Portable Library. This template is used for developing the WinRT application. When developing a WinRT application, you can use an F# portable library to host the business logic. C# can provide a UI for the portable library.

The portable library is the intersection of three .NET frameworks: Silverlight, the desktop, and WinRT. Because the portable library is the subset of these .NET frameworks, moving an application from a desktop environment to a portable library does not work in some cases. For example, *System.IO.File* is not present in the portable library because the Silverlight .NET framework does not support *System.IO.File*.

If you want to develop business logic for WinRT applications, F# portable library is a good choice. The F# portable library is designed to be executed from within Windows Store applications, Silverlight applications, and desktop applications. You will now create a Windows Store application that will serve as the test UI container for the examples in the rest of this chapter.

When creating a new project, you can expand the C# node and select the Windows Store node in Visual Studio 2012 on Windows 8. Blank App is the template you are going to use, as shown in Figure 7-6.

> **Note** The initial release of F# 3.0 with Visual Studio 2012 did not include some important settings, which caused the Windows 8 verification process to fail for Windows 8 applications that used F#. This Windows 8 verification bug has been fixed in the Visual Studio Update. If installing the Visual Studio Update is not an option, you can resolve the problem by editing the fsproj file for the portable DLL project and adding the following at the end of the first *PropertyGroup*:

```
<PropertyGroup Condition=" '$(Configuration)|$(Platform)' == 'Release|AnyCPU' ">
   <OtherFlags>--staticlink:FSharp.Core</OtherFlags>
 </PropertyGroup>
 <PropertyGroup>
   <RunPostBuildEvent>OnOutputUpdated</RunPostBuildEvent>
   <PostBuildEvent>if \"$(ConfigurationName)\"==\"Release\" (
"C:\Program Files (x86)\Microsoft SDKs\Windows\v8.0A\bin\NETFX 4.0 Tools\ildasm.exe" /
linenum
/nobar /out="$(TargetName).il" $(TargetFileName)

powershell "$lines = '}','} /*','} */'; $matchCount = 0; $clashCount = 0; filter GetOutput
{ if
($_ -eq '  } // end of method MatchFailureException::.ctor') { $lines[$matchCount++] }
else { if
($_ -eq '  } // end of method Clash::.ctor') { $lines[$clashCount++] } else { $_ } } };
(Get-Content
$(TargetName).il) | GetOutput | Set-Content $(TargetName).il"

"C:\Windows\Microsoft.NET\Framework\v4.0.30319\ilasm.exe" /dll /debug=opt /quiet
$(TargetName).il

copy /y $(TargetName).* ..\..\obj\Release\
)
   </PostBuildEvent>
 </PropertyGroup>
```

FIGURE 7-6 Creating a Windows Store blank app (XAML) project

An example of the generated solution structure is shown in Figure 7-7.

FIGURE 7-7 Windows 8 application generated from the Blank App template

From the project properties page, the F# portable library can be configured to target WinRT, .NET 4.5, and Silverlight 5. See Figure 7-8.

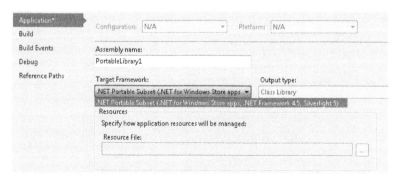

FIGURE 7-8 Portable library project properties page

You can now add a text block to the main form, as shown in Listing 7-4.

LISTING 7-4 XAML code in the main form

```
<Page
    x:Class="Win8UI.MainPage"
    xmlns=http://schemas.microsoft.com/winfx/2006/xaml/presentation
    xmlns:x=http://schemas.microsoft.com/winfx/2006/xaml
    xmlns:local="using:Win8UI"
    xmlns:d=http://schemas.microsoft.com/expression/blend/2008
    xmlns:mc=http://schemas.openxmlformats.org/markup-compatibility/2006
    mc:Ignorable="d">

    <Grid Background="{StaticResource ApplicationPageBackgroundThemeBrush}">
        <TextBlock x:Name="result_box" Text="Result"/>
    </Grid>
</Page>
```

The F# portable library project can now be created in the same solution, as shown in Figure 7-9.

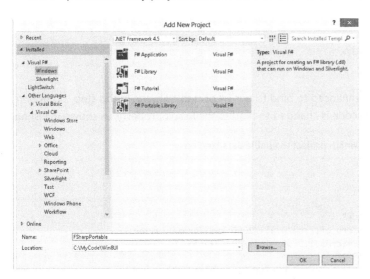

FIGURE 7-9 Creating an F# portable library in the Win8UI solution

The new solution structure with the F# Portable Class Library project is shown in Figure 7-10.

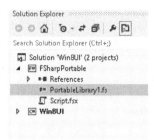

FIGURE 7-10 Solution structure with the F# Portable Class Library project and Win8UI project

For brevity, I am not going to go through a complete MVVM implementation. Instead, I will provide just enough of an implementation to enable data binding to be done. The first modification that is required is to add the *Result* member to *Class1* in the PortableLibrary1.fs file, as shown in Listing 7-5.

LISTING 7-5 Code change in the PortableLibrary1.fs

```
namespace FSharpPortable

type Class1() =
    member this.Result = "F#"
```

The UI project can now be enhanced to bind to our F# portable library. In this step, *DataContext* is set to *Class1* and the UI XAML code is changed to bind to the *Result* property, as shown in Listing 7-6.

LISTING 7-6 Code change in the Win8UI project to enable data binding

XAML code change

```
<Page
    x:Class="Win8UI.MainPage"
    xmlns=http://schemas.microsoft.com/winfx/2006/xaml/presentation
    xmlns:x=http://schemas.microsoft.com/winfx/2006/xaml
    xmlns:local="using:Win8UI"
    xmlns:d=http://schemas.microsoft.com/expression/blend/2008
    xmlns:mc=http://schemas.openxmlformats.org/markup-compatibility/2006
    mc:Ignorable="d">

    <Grid Background="{StaticResource ApplicationPageBackgroundThemeBrush}">
        <TextBlock x:Name="result_box" Text="{Binding Result}"/>
    </Grid>
</Page>
```

C# code change to set *DataContext*

```
using System;
using System.Collections.Generic;
using System.IO;
```

```
using System.Linq;
using Windows.Foundation;
using Windows.Foundation.Collections;
using Windows.UI.Xaml;
using Windows.UI.Xaml.Controls;
using Windows.UI.Xaml.Controls.Primitives;
using Windows.UI.Xaml.Data;
using Windows.UI.Xaml.Input;
using Windows.UI.Xaml.Media;
using Windows.UI.Xaml.Navigation;

// The Blank Page item template is documented at http://go.microsoft.com/
fwlink/?LinkId=234238

namespace Win8UI
{
    /// <summary>
    /// An empty page that can be used on its own or navigated to within a Frame.
    /// </summary>
    public sealed partial class MainPage : Page
    {
        public MainPage()
        {
            this.InitializeComponent();
        }

        /// <summary>
        /// Invoked when this page is about to be displayed in a Frame.
        /// </summary>
        /// <param name="e">Event data that describes how this page was reached.  The
Parameter
        /// property is typically used to configure the page.</param>
        protected override void OnNavigatedTo(NavigationEventArgs e)
        {
            this.DataContext = new FSharpPortable.Class1();
        }
    }
}
```

> **Note** You can also create a Silverlight project and enable data binding. The steps and code are very similar.

Now you have the UI bound to the portable library. The portable F# code in the rest of this chapter can be placed in the *Result* property to allow the result to be shown in the UI.

> **Note** Although the portable library can be referenced from the Windows Store, Silverlight, and desktop applications, a console application is still a convenient way to test small code snippets.

Now that you know what the portable library is. The major application for F# portable library is to implement algorithms.. The next several sections provide samples of common algorithms implemented with F#. These algorithms are perfect examples of what can be put into the back-end library In addition, if you take a second look these familiar algorithms and how to use F# to implement them, you can get a better understanding of F#.

Using an Array, List, and Seq

In this section, I will present several examples related to collection data structures, such as arrays, lists, and sequences. One of the most common problems for processing these collection data structures is sorting.

Sorting data types   The first example demonstrates how to use the built-in sorting functions to do sorting. This is shown in Listing 7-7. The portable library does not support the *printfn* statement, so the testing of this code is performed in a console application.

LISTING 7-7 An example of sorting data structures

```
open System

// type alias for IEnumerable
type IE = System.Collections.IEnumerable

// define record type
type MyRecord = { X : int; Y : string }

// define DU type
type MyDU =
    | Case1 of string
    | Case2 of int

// define a class
type MyClass() =
    member val MyProperty = 0 with get, set
    member val MyProperty2 = String.Empty with get, set
    override this.ToString() =
        sprintf "(%A, %A)" this.MyProperty this.MyProperty2

type DataSource() =
    let random = Random()

    // define data sequence
    let seq0 = [2; 3; 4; 5; 10; 10; 11; 13; 14; 19]
    let seq1 = seq0 |> Seq.map (fun x -> float x)
    let seq2 = seq0 |> Seq.map (fun x -> bigint x)
    let seqTuple = Seq.zip seq0 (seq0 |> Seq.map (sprintf "%A"))
    let seqRecord = seqTuple |> Seq.map (fun (i, s) -> {X = i; Y = s})
    let seqDU = seqTuple |> Seq.map (fun (i, s) -> Case2(i))
    let seqDU2 = seqTuple |> Seq.map (fun (i, s) -> Case1(s))
    let seqClass = seqTuple |> Seq.map (fun (i, s) -> MyClass(MyProperty = i, MyProperty2
= s))
```

```
// define data list; this list is an F# list type
let list0 = seq0 |> Seq.toList
let list2 = seq2 |> Seq.toList
let listTuple = seqTuple |> Seq.toList
let listRecord = seqRecord |> Seq.toList
let listDU = seqDU |> Seq.toList
let listClass = seqClass |> Seq.toList

let toString x =
    let seq =
        x
        |> Seq.toList
        |> List.map (fun n -> sprintf "%A" n)
    String.Join(",", seq)

member this.Seqs : list<IE> =
        [ seq0
          seq1
          seq2
          seqTuple
          seqRecord
          seqDU
          seqDU2
          seqClass ]

member this.Lists : list<IE> =
        [ list0
          list2
          listTuple
          listRecord
          listDU
          listClass ]

member this.TestSeq() =
    let seq0 = seq0 |> Seq.sort |> toString
    let seq1 = seq1 |> Seq.sort |> toString
    let seq2= seq2 |> Seq.sort |> toString

    let seqTuple=seqTuple |> Seq.sort |> toString
    let seqRecord=seqRecord |> Seq.sort |> toString
    let seqDU=seqDU |> Seq.sort |> toString
    let seqDU2=seqDU2 |> Seq.sort |> toString
    let r =
        [ seq0
          seq1
          seq2
          seqTuple
          seqRecord
          seqDU
          seqDU2 ]
    r
    |> Array.ofList

member this.TestList() =
    let list0 =list0 |> Seq.sort   |> toString
```

```
            let list2 =list2 |> Seq.sort |> toString
            let listTuple=listTuple|> Seq.sort |> toString
            let listRecord=listRecord|> Seq.sort |> toString
            let listDU=listDU|> Seq.sort |> toString
            let r =
                [ list0
                  list2
                  listTuple
                  listRecord
                  listDU ]
            r
            |> Array.ofList

    member this.TestSeqSortBy_Tuple() =
        let r = seqTuple |> Seq.sortBy (fun (i, s) -> i) |> toString
        r

    member this.TestSeqSortBy_Record() =
        let r = seqRecord |> Seq.sortBy (fun n -> n.X) |> toString
        r

    member this.TestSeqSortBy_DU() =
        let r = seqDU |> Seq.sortBy (fun (Case2(n)) -> n) |> toString
        r

    member this.TestSeqSortBy_Class() =
        let r = seqClass |> Seq.sortBy (fun n -> n.MyProperty2) |> toString
        r
```

Console application code to test the portable library

```
let data = DataSource()
printfn "test seq"
let join (x:'T array) = System.String.Join("\r\n", x)

[ join (data.TestSeq());
join (data.TestList());
data.TestSeqSortBy_Class();
data.TestSeqSortBy_DU();
data.TestSeqSortBy_Record();
data.TestSeqSortBy_Tuple() ]
|> Seq.iter (printfn "%A")
```

Execution result from console testing

```
test seq
"2,3,4,5,10,10,11,13,14,19
2.0,3.0,4.0,5.0,10.0,10.0,11.0,13.0,14.0,19.0
2,3,4,5,10,10,11,13,14,19
(2, "2"),(3, "3"),(4, "4"),(5, "5"),(10, "10"),(10, "10"),(11, "11"),(13, "13"),(14,
"14"),(19,
"19")
{X = 2;
 Y = "2";},{X = 3;
```

```
     Y = "3";},{X = 4;
     Y = "4";},{X = 5;
     Y = "5";},{X = 10;
     Y = "10";},{X = 10;
     Y = "10";},{X = 11;
     Y = "11";},{X = 13;
     Y = "13";},{X = 14;
     Y = "14";},{X = 19;
     Y = "19";}
Case2 2,Case2 3,Case2 4,Case2 5,Case2 10,Case2 10,Case2 11,Case2 13,Case2 14,Case2 19
Case1 "10",Case1 "10",Case1 "11",Case1 "13",Case1 "14",Case1 "19",Case1 "2",Case1
"3",Case1
"4",Case1 "5""
"2,3,4,5,10,10,11,13,14,19
2,3,4,5,10,10,11,13,14,19
(2, "2"),(3, "3"),(4, "4"),(5, "5"),(10, "10"),(10, "10"),(11, "11"),(13, "13"),(14,
"14"),(19,
"19")
{X = 2;
     Y = "2";},{X = 3;
     Y = "3";},{X = 4;
     Y = "4";},{X = 5;
     Y = "5";},{X = 10;
     Y = "10";},{X = 10;
     Y = "10";},{X = 11;
     Y = "11";},{X = 13;
     Y = "13";},{X = 14;
     Y = "14";},{X = 19;
     Y = "19";}
Case2 2,Case2 3,Case2 4,Case2 5,Case2 10,Case2 10,Case2 11,Case2 13,Case2 14,Case2 19"
"(10, "10"),(10, "10"),(11, "11"),(13, "13"),(14, "14"),(19, "19"),(2, "2"),(3, "3"),(4,
"4"),(5,
"5")"
"Case2 2,Case2 3,Case2 4,Case2 5,Case2 10,Case2 10,Case2 11,Case2 13,Case2 14,Case2 19"
"{X = 2;
     Y = "2";},{X = 3;
     Y = "3";},{X = 4;
     Y = "4";},{X = 5;
     Y = "5";},{X = 10;
     Y = "10";},{X = 10;
     Y = "10";},{X = 11;
     Y = "11";},{X = 13;
     Y = "13";},{X = 14;
     Y = "14";},{X = 19;
     Y = "19";}"
"(2, "2"),(3, "3"),(4, "4"),(5, "5"),(10, "10"),(10, "10"),(11, "11"),(13, "13"),(14,
"14"),(19,
"19")"
```

 Note The preceding execution result is from a console application. Silverlight and Windows Store apps might show small differences, because they have to show the result in a UI element.

Using a quick-sort algorithm   The *quick sort* is a common sorting algorithm. Compared to a C# implementation, the F# code in Listing 7-8 is more concise and readable. This sample uses pattern matching. If the code in Listing 7-3 makes you think the match is nothing but a switch, you will now see that this is far from the truth. Notice the *head::tail* line of code. This pattern causes the data list to be automatically decomposed into a head and a tail. The head is the first element in the list, and the tail is a list that contains all elements from the original list except the *head* element. You do not even have to declare the variable. The type and value are handled by the F# compiler automatically. If you are wondering how to decompose the data into a customized format—such as head, last elements, and a tail collection—I will show you a sample later in this chapter.

The @ operator does almost the opposite of ::. It concatenates two lists. It is used at the end of the function to combine the results of the two branches of recursion.

LISTING 7-8 Quick-sort algorithm implementation

```
let rec quickSort (data:int list) =
    match data with
    | [] -> []
    | [a] -> [a]
    | head::tail ->
        let l0 =
            tail
            |> List.filter ((<=) head)
        let l1 =
            tail
            |> List.filter ((>) head)
        quickSort(l0) @ [head] @ quickSort(l1)

quickSort [-2; -3; 4; -1; 0; 1; 5; 7; -2]
```

Note If the (<=) in the eighth line is replaced with (<), the result will not contain duplicated elements.

When you execute this sample with the Win8UI project provided as the front end, it will not show all the elements on the UI. This can be solved by using the *Seq.fold* function to aggregate the result:

```
quickSort [-2; -3; 4; -1; 0; 1; 5; 7; -2]
|> Seq.fold (fun state t -> (string t) + "," + state) ""
```

The (<=) and (>) in the code shows that the operator in F# is also a function. I am using the higher-order function feature in F# to generate a new function from (<=) by applying a value to it.

Performing a merge sort   The *merge sort* is used to perform sorting in two stages:

- Divide the unsorted list into *n* sublists, each containing only one element.

- Merge repeated sublists into new sublists until there is only one sublist remaining.

Listing 7-10 once again shows pattern matching. Note that in this section of the *merge* function, two cases have the same name but different data.

> | [], list

| list, [] -> list

One case is from *list0*, and the other is from *list1*. The pattern matching not only gives you the ability to decompose the data, but also the ability to unify the data as long as the cases have the same name.

LISTING 7-10 Merging a sort sample

```
open System

// merge two list into one list
let rec merge list0 list1 =
    match list0, list1 with
    | [], [] -> []
    | [], list
    | list, [] -> list
    | h0::t0, h1::t1 ->
        if h0 < h1 then
            [h0] @ merge t0 list1
        else
            [h1] @ merge list0 t1

// merge sort algorithm function
let rec mergeSort list =
    match list with
    | [] -> []
    | [a] -> [a]
    | [a; b] -> [ min a b; max a b ]
    | _ ->
        let firstHalf =
            list
            |> Seq.take (list.Length / 2)
            |> Seq.toList
        let secondHalf =
            list
            |> Seq.skip (list.Length / 2)
            |> Seq.toList

        let sortedFirstHalf = mergeSort firstHalf
        let sortedSecondHalf = mergeSort secondHalf

        merge sortedFirstHalf sortedSecondHalf

mergeSort [1;3;9;2;4;7;6;5]
```

Finding a sum from an array Listing 7-9 finds all elements in an array that add up to a certain number. This sample shows F# code written in an imperative style. The *for* loop iterates through the list and uses the *yield* keyword to output the *list* element.

LISTING 7-9 Finding elements in an array that add up to a given number

```
let findElement (list:int list) start target =
    list
    |> Seq.skip start
    |> Seq.tryFind ((=) target)

let find sum (list:int list)  =
    [ for i in [0..list.Length-4] do
        for j in [i + 1..list.Length-3] do
            for k in [j + 1..list.Length-2] do
                let rest = sum - (list.[i] + list.[j] + list.[k])
                let result = findElement list (k+1) rest
                match result with
                | Some n -> yield (list.[i], list.[j], list.[k], n)
                | None -> ()
    ]

find 23 [10; 2; 3; 4; 5; 9; 7; 8]
```

Execution result

```
val it : (int * int * int * int) list =
  [(10, 2, 3, 8); (10, 2, 4, 7); (2, 4, 9, 8); (2, 5, 9, 7); (3, 4, 9, 7);
   (3, 5, 7, 8)]
```

Merging two sorted arrays You saw how to perform a merge sort on one array. This next algorithm (Listing 7-11) is used to perform a merge operation on two sorted arrays. The merge operation is performed in-place, taking advantage of the fact that in F#, array elements are automatically mutable.

LISTING 7-11 Merging two arrays

```
let (|Exhausted|_|) i =
    if i < 0 then
        Some()
    else
        None

let array1 = [| 1; 3; 4; 6; 9; 0; 0; 0; 0; 0; |]
let array2 = [| 2; 3; 5; 8; 10; |]

let rec merge (i, j, k) =
    match i, j with
    | Exhausted, Exhausted
```

```
    | _, Exhausted ->
        ()
    | Exhausted, _ ->
        array1.[k] <- array2.[i]
        let i, j, k = i, (j - 1), (k - 1)
        merge (i, j, k)
    | _ ->
        if array1.[i] > array2.[j] then
            array1.[k] <- array1.[i]
            let i, j, k = (i - 1), j, (k - 1)
            merge(i, j, k)
        else
            array1.[k] <- array2.[j]
            let i, j, k = i, (j - 1), (k - 1)
            merge(i, j, k)

merge (4, 4, array1.Length - 1)
```

Finding the maximum sum of an array Listing 7-12 finds the largest sum of contiguous subarrays within a one-dimensional array of numbers. The Kadane algorithm is the typical solution for this problem. The execution result is 7. This sample once again shows how to create F# code using the imperative programming style.

LISTING 7-12 Finding the largest sum of a contiguous subarray

```
let kadane data =
    let mutable maxV, max_currentPoint = 0, 0
    for i in data do
        max_currentPoint <- max 0 (max_currentPoint + i)
        maxV <- max maxV max_currentPoint

    maxV

kadane [-2; -3; 4; -1; -2; 1; 5; -3; ]
```

If the source array can be iterated as a circle, you have to consider a second case where the maximum value is achieved through wrapping. Listing 7-13 solves this problem. The second case is used to find the range that affects the array sum the most. The rest of the array is a range that passes the array boundary. If the sum of the range is greater than the range that does not cross the boundary, this is the result you are looking for.

LISTING 7-13 Finding the maximum sum in a circular array

```
let kadane data =
    let mutable maxV, max_currentPoint = 0, 0
    for i in data do
        max_currentPoint <- max 0 (max_currentPoint + i)
```

```
            maxV <- max maxV max_currentPoint

        maxV

    let kadaneCircle data =
        // normal case
        let kadaneValue = kadane data

        // 2nd case
        let sum = Seq.sum data
        let invertMax =
            data
            |> List.map ((*) -1)
            |> kadane
        let ``2ndCase`` = sum + invertMax

        max kadaneValue ``2ndCase``

    kadaneCircle [12; -5; 4; -8; -2; 11]
```

Execution result

```
val kadane : data:seq<int> -> int
val kadaneCircle : data:int list -> int
val it : int = 23
```

Finding the median of two sorted arrays   If the array can be envisioned as a sample data set, the sum is one attribute of the array. The median is another important attribute for a one-dimensional data set. The median is the value at which half of the array values are below and half of the values are above. Listing 7-14 shows how to find the median value from two sorted arrays.

LISTING 7-14 Finding the median value from two sorted arrays

```
    let findMedian (list0:int list) (list1:int list) =
        let totalCount = list0.Length + list1.Length

        let rec findFunction (list0:int list) list1 count =
            if count > 1 then
                match list0, list1 with
                | [], [] -> failwith "not possible, check empty first"
                | head::tail, [] -> findFunction tail [] (count - 1)
                | [], head::tail -> findFunction [] tail (count - 1)
                | h0::t0, h1::t1 ->
                    if h0 < h1 then
                        findFunction t0 list1 (count-1)
                    else
                        findFunction list0 t1 (count-1)
```

```
          else
              match list0, list1 with
              | [], [] -> failwith "not possible, check empty first"
              | head::tail, []
              | [], head::tail ->
                  let pre = head
                  let now = tail.Head
                  if totalCount % 2 = 0 then
                      (float (pre + now)) / 2.
                  else
                      float now
              | h0::t0, h1::t1 ->
                  if totalCount % 2 = 0 then
                      (float (h0 + h1)) / 2.
                  else
                      float (max h0 h1)

      if list0.IsEmpty && list1.IsEmpty then
          failwith "please input valid data"

      findFunction list0 list1 ((list0.Length + list1.Length) / 2)

  findMedian [1] [2; 4; 5; 6; 7; 8; 10]
```

> **Note** This sample uses a recursive function instead of a *for/while* loop. For some people, it is easy to understand, while others do not think it's so easy. The recursive function is very useful if you want to write code that's free from side effects.

Here's another way to get the medians from two arrays. If both medians are the same, you hit the jackpot and the median is the final result. If the median from *array0*, which is called *median0*, is smaller, the final result should be bigger and the search should continue on the elements equal to or greater than *median0*. If *median0* is bigger, the search should continue on the elements equal to or smaller than *median0*, as you can see in Listing 7-15.

So let's get back to the question I posed when I presented the quick-sort sample in Listing 7-8: how do you decompose a data set in a customized way? The Median pattern used in Listing 7-15 decomposes the array into three parts:

- The left part, which contains all elements smaller than the median

- The median value

- The right part, which contains all elements greater than the median

LISTING 7-15 Finding the median value from two sorted arrays (version 2)

```
let getMedian (list:float array) =
    let len = list.Length
    if len % 2 = 0 then
        (list.[len / 2 - 1] + list.[len / 2]) / 2.
    else
        list.[len / 2]

let (|Median|) (list:float array) =
    let median = getMedian list
    let len = list.Length
    if len % 2 = 0 then
        (list.[0..len / 2 - 1], median, list.[len / 2..])
    else
        (list.[0..len / 2], median, list.[len / 2..])

let rec getMedianFromTwo (list0:float array) (list1:float array) =
    match list0, list1 with
    | [||], [||] -> 0.
    | [|a|], [|b|] -> (a + b) / 2.
    | [|a0; a1|], [|b0; b1|] -> ((max a0 b0) + (min a1 b1)) / 2.
    | Median(l0, m0, r0), Median(l1, m1, r1) ->
        if m0 = m1 then
            m0
        elif m0 < m1 then
            getMedianFromTwo r0 l1
        else //m0 > m1
            getMedianFromTwo l0 r1

let list0 = [|1.; 4.; 7.; 8.; 9.; 10.|]
let list1 = [|2.; 4.; 6.; 7.; 9.; 10.|]

let c = getMedianFromTwo list0 list1
```

Dealing with the Dutch national flag problem This is a categorizing problem. Given a (low, high) tuple, you need to arrange the elements in an array into three categories. The first category of elements are smaller than *low*, the second category of elements are between *low* and *high*, and the last category is larger than *high*. See Listing 7-16.

LISTING 7-16 Dutch national flag problem

```
type CompareResult =
    | Higher
    | Lower
    | Middle

let compare = function
    | low,current,_ when current <= low -> Lower
    | _, current,high when current >= high -> Higher
    | _ -> Middle
```

```
let dutchFlag (list: _ array) (low, high) =
    let swap (i,j) =
        let temp = list.[i]
        list.[i] <- list.[j]
        list.[j] <- temp

    let mutable i = 0
    let mutable lowPointer = 0
    let mutable highPointer = list.Length - 1

    while i<highPointer do
        let value = low, list.[i], high
        match compare value with
        | Lower ->
            swap (lowPointer, i)
            lowPointer <- lowPointer + 1
            i <- i + 1
        | Higher ->
            swap (highPointer, i)
            highPointer <- highPointer - 1
        | Middle ->
            i <- i + 1

let arr = [| 1; 9; 8; 2; 4; 3; 6; 7; 5; 0; |]
dutchFlag arr (3, 7)
```

Finding the longest increasing sequence To determine the longest increasing sequence (LIS), you use a array variable (named DP) to hold the current LIS up to the current index. For example, if the value in DP.[10] is *3*, the LIS for array.[0..9] is *3*. The value of DP.[i] is updated only when the new value (DP.[j] + 1) is higher than the current value (DP.[i] < DP.[j] + 1) and the value is still increasing (array.[i] > array.[j]). See Listing 7-17.

LISTING 7-17 Longest increasing sequence code

```
let list = [|10; 22; 9; 33; 21; 50; 41; 60; 80|]
let DP = Array.create list.Length 1

let findMax () =
    let mutable maxLength = 1
    for i = 1 to list.Length - 1 do
        for j = i - 1 downto 0 do
            if list.[i] > list.[j] &&
                DP.[i] < DP.[j] + 1 then
                    DP.[i] <- DP.[j] + 1

        maxLength <- max maxLength DP.[i]

    maxLength

findMax()
```

Creating a Tree Structure

A tree is a basic data structure in computer science. It is a hierarchy indicated by a tree-like structure that has some nodes within it. A typical tree structure is shown in Figure 7-11, and the sections that follow it describe variations in this structure.

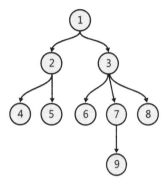

FIGURE 7-11 A tree structure

F# tree representation and traversal   The F# representation of the tree structure in Figure 7-11 is shown in Listing 7-18. This structure is created with the help of a discriminated union (DU).

LISTING 7-18 Tree representation for the tree structure in Figure 7-11

```
type NodeType = int

// DU definition for a tree structure
type Tree =
    | Node of NodeType * Tree list

let createTree() =
    Node(1, [ Node(2, [Node(4, []);
                       Node(5, [])
                      ]);
             Node(3, [Node(6, []);
                      Node(7, [Node(9,[])]);
                      Node(8, [])
                     ])
           ])
```

Pre-order and post-order tree traversal are two basic tree operations. *Pre-order traversal* processes the tree from the current node and then processes subtrees starting from the root node. *Post-order traversal* processes the tree from the subtrees and then processes the current node starting from the root node. Listing 7-19 shows both processes.

LISTING 7-19 Pre-order and post-order traversal

```
let rec preOrder visit tree =
    match tree with
        | Node(value, children) ->
            visit value
            children
            |> Seq.iter (preOrder visit)

let rec postOrder visit tree =
    match tree with
        | Node(value, children) ->
            children
            |> Seq.iter (postOrder visit)
            visit value

let mutable result = []
let sum v =
    result <- result @ [v]
preOrder sum (createTree())

result <- []
postOrder sum (createTree())
```

Execution result for pre-order

```
val it : NodeType list = [4; 5; 2; 6; 9; 7; 8; 3; 1]
```

Execution result for post-order

```
val it : NodeType list = [1; 2; 4; 5; 3; 6; 7; 9; 8]
```

Note As previously stated, the portable library does not support the *printfn* function, but you can always use FSI to evaluate the function.

Note In Listing 7-19, *visit* is the function used to access the tree node.

F# binary tree and in-order traversal The binary tree, shown in Figure 7-12, is a special tree in which each node has a maximum of two child nodes. One child is called the *left child*, and the other is called the *right child*. A binary tree is shown in Figure 7-12. As in the previous example, a DU is applied in Listing 7-20 to implement the binary tree structure.

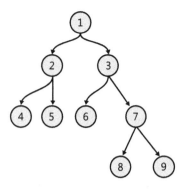

FIGURE 7-12 A binary tree structure

LISTING 7-20 Binary tree and in-order traversal

```
type NodeType = int

type BinaryTree =
    | Nil
    | Node of NodeType * BinaryTree * BinaryTree

let createBinaryTree() =
    Node(1, Node(2, Node(4, Nil, Nil),
                    Node(5,  Nil, Nil)),
            Node(3, Node(6, Nil, Nil),
                    Node(7, Node(9, Nil, Nil),
                            Node(8, Nil, Nil))
        ))

let rec inOrder visit tree =
    match tree with
        | Nil -> ()
        | Node(v, left, right) ->
            inOrder visit left
            visit v
            inOrder visit right

let mutable result = []
let sum v =
    result <- result @ [v]

inOrder sum (createBinaryTree())
```

Execution result for in-order traversal

```
val it : NodeType list = [4; 2; 5; 1; 6; 3; 9; 7; 8]
```

In addition to using pre-order, in-order, and post-order traversals, you can traverse a tree structure by layer. For the tree in Figure 7-12, the result of layer traversal is [1; 2; 3; 4; 5; 8; 6; 7; 9]. Layer traversal uses the queue data structure, as shown in Listing 7-21.

LISTING 7-21 Layer traversal for a binary tree

```
type NodeType = int

type BinaryTree =
    | Nil
    | Node of NodeType * BinaryTree * BinaryTree

let createBinaryTree() =
    Node(1, Node(2, Node(4, Nil, Nil),
                    Node(5,
                            Node(6, Nil, Nil),
                            Node(7, Nil, Nil))),
        Node(3,
                Nil,
                Node(8,
                        Nil,
                        Node(9, Nil, Nil)))
    )

let mutable queue : BinaryTree list = []
let enqueue x = queue <- [x] @ queue
let dequeue() =
    let result = Seq.last queue
    queue <-
        queue
        |> Seq.take (queue.Length - 1)
        |> Seq.toList
    result
let queueEmpty() = queue.Length = 0

let mutable result = []
let visit v = result <- result @ [v]

let layerTree tree =
    enqueue tree
    while not <| queueEmpty() do
        let tree = dequeue()
        match tree with
        | Nil -> ()
        | Node(v, left, right) ->
            visit v
            enqueue left
            enqueue right

layerTree (createBinaryTree())
```

> **Note** The parentheses around *createBinaryTree()* are necessary. If these are not provided, *layerTree* will treat *createBinary* and *()* as two parameters and generate a compile error.
>
> A portable library does support *System.Collections.Generic.Queue*. If you want to, you can replace the queue operation in Listing 7-21 with *System.Collections.Generic.Queue*.

Binary search tree A binary search tree (BST), shown in Figure 7-13, is a special tree that has a node value greater than any value on its left subtree and smaller than any value on its right subtree. Listing 7-22 creates the sample BST.

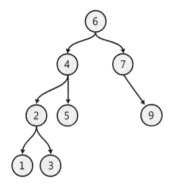

FIGURE 7-13 Binary search tree

LISTING 7-22 Sample binary search tree

```
type NodeType = int

type BinaryTree =
    | Nil
    | Node of NodeType * BinaryTree * BinaryTree

let createBinaryTree() =
    Node(6, Node(4, Node(2,
                            Node(1, Nil, Nil),
                            Node(3, Nil, Nil)),
                    Node(5,  Nil, Nil)),
            Node(7,
                    Nil,
                    Node(9, Nil, Nil))
        )
```

When checking whether a tree is a BST, a common mistake is to check only two child nodes rather than the whole subtree. For example, the child's right tree could contain a node with more than two children. From the definition of a BST, the in-order traversal generates an ordered sequence. You can use this property to validate the BST. The validation function is used to order the result, check whether or not the result is in order, or both. See Listing 7-23.

LISTING 7-23 BST validation

```
type NodeType = int

type BinaryTree =
    | Nil
    | Node of NodeType * BinaryTree * BinaryTree

let createBinaryTree() =
    Node(6, Node(4, Node(2,
                          Node(1, Nil, Nil),
                          Node(3, Nil, Nil)),
                 Node(5,  Nil, Nil)),
          Node(7,
               Nil,
               Node(9, Nil, Nil))
       )

let rec checkInOrder value list =
    match list with
    | [] -> true
    | head::tail ->
        if value<head then
            checkInOrder head tail
        else
            false

let rec inOrder visit tree =
    match tree with
        | Nil -> ()
        | Node(v, left, right) ->
            inOrder visit left
            visit v
            inOrder visit right

let mutable result = []
let sum v =
    result <- result @ [v]

inOrder sum (createBinaryTree())

checkInOrder System.Int32.MinValue result
```

 Note The *match* statement has an interesting advantage over the if statement: it can generate a warning if there are any unhandled paths in your logic.

A tree is a complex structure. In addition to the common tree traversal operations I just described, there are other operations you can perform related to tree structures.

Delete a tree   You can delete a tree without using recursion, as Listing 7-24 demonstrates. After execution, all the nodes are tagged with a 0 (zero).

LISTING 7-24 Removing a tree without using recursion

```
type NodeType = { mutable X: int }

type Tree =
    | Node of NodeType * Tree list

let mutable stack : Tree list = []

let createTree() =
    Node({X=1}, [ Node({X = 2}, [Node({X = 4}, []);
                                 Node({X = 5}, [])
                      ]);
                  Node({X = 3}, [Node({X = 6}, []);
                      Node({X = 7}, [Node({X = 9},[])]);
                      Node({X = 8}, [])
                      ])
            ])

let push x =
    stack <- [x] @ stack
let pop () =
    match stack with
    | [] -> None
    | head::tail ->
        stack <- tail
        Some head
let isEmpty() = Seq.isEmpty stack

let tagAsDelete (x:NodeType) = x.X <- 0

let deleteTree tree =
    push tree
    while not <| isEmpty() do
        let node : Tree option = pop()
        match node with
        | None -> ()
        | Some(Tree.Node(v, list)) ->
            list |> Seq.iter push
            tagAsDelete v

let tree = createTree()
deleteTree tree
```

 Note The portable library supports *System.Collections.Generic.Stack*. You can replace the stack section with this structure.

A recursive version is preferred because it allows mutable variables to be eliminated

Build a tree from pre-order and in-order sequences   The tree-traversal result does not preserve the structure information, but a binary tree can be built from a pre-order and in-order sequence. The pre-order traversal accesses the root first. The in-order traversal yields the root after finishing the left subtree. The root node from pre-order can help divide the in-order traversal sequence into a left subtree and a right subtree. You can easily find these elements in the pre-order sequence. The sequence from pre-order can show the root for a subtree. Repeating this process until all elements in the sequence have been exhausted will eventually build the tree.

The following sequences are generated from the tree in Listing 7-22. Listing 7-25 builds a binary tree from a pre-order sequence and an in-order sequence.

- **Pre-order sequence**   [6; 4; 2; 1; 3; 5; 7; 9]

- **In-order sequence**   [1; 2; 3; 4; 5; 6; 7; 9]

LISTING 7-25 Building binary trees from pre-order and in-order sequences

```
type NodeType = int

type BinaryTree =
    | Nil
    | Node of NodeType * BinaryTree * BinaryTree

let getLeftPart inorder head =
    inorder
    |> Seq.takeWhile(fun n -> n <> head)
    |> Seq.toList

let getRightPart inorder head =
    inorder
    |> Seq.skipWhile(fun n -> n <> head)
    |> Seq.skip 1
    |> Seq.toList

let getPreOrderLeftPart preorder inorderLeft =
    let len = inorderLeft |> Seq.length
    preorder
    |> Seq.skip 1
    |> Seq.take len
    |> Seq.toList

let getPreOrderRightPart preorder inorderLeft =
    let len = inorderLeft |> Seq.length
    preorder
    |> Seq.skip 1
    |> Seq.skip len
    |> Seq.toList
```

```
let rec buildTree inorder preorder =
    match preorder with
    | [] -> Nil
    | head::tail ->
        let inorderLeft = getLeftPart inorder head
        let inorderRight = getRightPart inorder head
        let preorderLeft = getPreOrderLeftPart preorder inorderLeft
        let preorderRight = getPreOrderRightPart preorder inorderLeft
        Node(head,
             buildTree inorderLeft preorderLeft,
             buildTree inorderRight preorderRight)

buildTree [1; 2; 3; 4; 5; 6; 7; 9] [6; 4; 2; 1; 3; 5; 7; 9]
```

Execution result

```
BinaryTree =
  Node
    (6,Node (4,Node (2,Node (1,Nil,Nil),Node (3,Nil,Nil)),Node (5,Nil,Nil)),
     Node (7,Nil,Node (9,Nil,Nil)))
```

Build a BST from a pre-order iteration list   The sample in the previous section shows how to build a binary tree. In this section, I demonstrate how to get a BST from a pre-order iteration list. Building a tree is useful for finding the root, left subtree, and right subtree. Because the left subtrees are all smaller than the root, the pre-order iteration list can be divided into the following three parts (as shown in Listing 7-26):

- The root node is the first element of the iteration list.

- The left subtree list contains elements immediately following the root node. The left subtree nodes are smaller than the root node.

- The right subtree list contains elements listed after the left subtree list. The right subtree nodes are larger than the root node.

LISTING 7-26 Building a BST from a pre-order iteration list

```
type NodeType = int

type BinaryTree =
    | Nil
    | Node of NodeType * BinaryTree * BinaryTree

let rec buildBSTfromPreOrder (l:NodeType list) =
    match l with
    | [] -> Nil
    | [a] -> Node(a, Nil, Nil)
```

```
        | h::t ->
            let smaller =
                t
                |> Seq.takeWhile (fun n -> n < h)
                |> Seq.toList
            let bigger =
                t
                |> Seq.skipWhile (fun n -> n < h)
                |> Seq.toList
            Node(h, buildBSTfromPreOrder(smaller), buildBSTfromPreOrder(bigger))

let input = [10; 5; 1; 7; 40; 50]
buildBSTfromPreOrder input
```

Execution result
```
val it : BinaryTree =
  Node
    (10,Node (5,Node (1,Nil,Nil),Node (7,Nil,Nil)),
     Node (40,Nil,Node (50,Nil,Nil)))
```

Check that a BST has only one child   Usually, one sequence from the traversal is not enough to reveal the binary tree internals. The algorithm in this section is used to determine if every node in the BST has only one child. All of the descendants of a node must either be larger or smaller than the node. The following are steps to check each node in a loop:

1.   Find the next child, and denote it as *A*.

2.   Find the last pre-order node, which is the last element of the pre-order sequence, and denote it as *B*.

3.   If both A and B are larger or smaller than the current node, then continue. Otherwise, return *false*.

The sample code is shown in Listing 7-27; a C# version is also provided. You might notice that the C# version breaks the loop in the middle when certain conditions are met. For F#, it is not possible to break the loop in the middle. Instead, the F# version uses lazy evaluation as well as other seq functions to mimic the return/break functionality in the loop. The F# code can be read as a preparation for all the data for the pre-order sequence, and then you can check whether any data is *Diff*. If the data meets the Diff criteria, the function returns FALSE. The sequence generation can move the code filtering and processing function out of the sequence-generation loop. I find that this can make the code more readable than the C# imperative version.

LISTING 7-27 Checking that each BST node only has one child

```fsharp
let (|Diff|_|) (a, b) =
    if (a * b < 0) || (a * b = 0 && a + b < 0) then Some true
    else None

let checkOneChild (preorder : int list) =

    seq {
        for i=0 to preorder.Length - 2 do
            let a = preorder.[i]-preorder.[i + 1];
            let b = preorder.[i]-preorder.[preorder.Length - 1];
            yield (a, b)
    }
    |> Seq.forall (fun (a, b) -> match a, b with
                                 | Diff _ -> false
                                 | _ -> true)

let list = [20; 10; 11; 13; 12;]

checkOneChild list
```

C# version

```csharp
bool checkOneChild(int[] preorder)
    {
        for (int i = 0; i < preorder.Length - 2; i++)
        {
            int a = preorder[i] - preorder[i + 1];
            int b = preorder[i] - preorder[preorder.Length - 1];
            if ( (a * b < 0) || (a * b == 0 && a + b < 0) )
            {
                return false;
            }
        }

        return true;
    }
```

 Note The partial active pattern is used to categorize data. If (a, b) are different, the function will return *false*.

Find the common elements from two BSTs   The previous sample examines the property of a single BST. Listing 7-28 finds the common elements in two BSTs.

LISTING 7-28 Algorithm for finding the common elements from two BSTs

```
type NodeType = int

type BinaryTree =
    | Nil
    | Node of NodeType * BinaryTree * BinaryTree

let bst1 = Node(10,
                Node(7,
                    Node(5, Nil, Nil),
                    Node(9, Nil, Nil)),
                Node(12,
                    Node(11, Nil, Nil),
                    Nil))

let bst2 = Node(10,
                Node(7,
                    Node(4, Nil, Nil),
                    Node(9, Nil, Nil)),
                Node(12,
                    Node(11, Nil, Nil),
                    Nil))

let result = System.Collections.Generic.List<NodeType>()

let rec findCommon (tree0, tree1) =
    match tree0, tree1 with
    | Nil, Nil
    | Nil, _
    | _, Nil -> ()
    | Node(v0, l0, r0), Node(v1, l1, r1) ->
        if v0 = v1 then
            result.Add(v0)
            findCommon(l0, l1)
            findCommon(r0, r1)
        elif v0 < v1 then
            findCommon(tree0, l1)
        else //v0 > v1
            findCommon(l0, tree1)

findCommon (bst1, bst2)

result |> Array.ofSeq
```

Execution result

```
[| 10; 7; 9; 12; 11 |]
```

Find the tree diameter   The tree is a structure with a shape, and the tree diameter is the maximum value of the following three values:

- The diameter of the left tree.

- The diameter of the right tree.

- The longest path between nodes through the tree root. The longest path value can be computed by the tree height.

A sample tree is shown in Figure 7-14, with code for it shown in Listing 7-29. The diameter for the tree shown in the figure is 7.

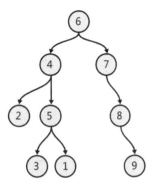

FIGURE 7-14 Tree for measuring the diameter

LISTING 7-29 Tree diameter code

```
type NodeType = int

type BinaryTree =
    | Nil
    | Node of NodeType * BinaryTree * BinaryTree

let createBinaryTree() =
    Node(1, Node(2, Node(4, Nil, Nil),
                    Node(5,
                            Node(6, Nil, Nil),
                            Node(7, Nil, Nil))),
            Node(3,
                    Nil,
                    Node(8,
                            Nil,
                            Node(9, Nil, Nil)))
        )
```

```
let rec treeHeight tree =
    match tree with
    | Nil -> 0
    | Node(v, left, right) ->
        let leftHeight = treeHeight left
        let rightHeight = treeHeight right
        (max leftHeight rightHeight) + 1

let rec treeDiameter tree =
    match tree with
    | Nil -> 0
    | Node(v, left, right) ->
        let leftHeight = treeHeight left
        let rightHeight = treeHeight right
        let leftDiameter = treeDiameter left
        let rightDiameter = treeDiameter right
        max (leftHeight + rightHeight + 1)
            (max leftDiameter rightDiameter)

treeDiameter (createBinaryTree())
```

 Note If the data structure is a DU, it's common to see many *match* statements in the code to decompose the DU.

Find the lowest common ancestor   Given two nodes in a binary tree, one common operation is used to find the lowest common ancestor (LCA) for these two nodes. For example, the ancestors for 2 and 1 in Figure 7-15 are 6 and 4, respectively, but 4 is lower than 6, so the LCA for 2 and 1 is 4. Listing 7-30 takes two nodes and returns the LCA of these two nodes.

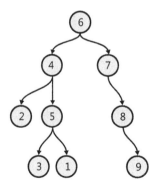

FIGURE 7-15 Finding the LCA in a binary tree

LISTING 7-30 LCA for a binary tree

```
type NodeType = int

type BinaryTree =
    | Nil
    | Node of NodeType * BinaryTree * BinaryTree

let createBinaryTree() =
    Node(1, Node(2, Node(4, Nil, Nil),
                    Node(5,
                        Node(6, Nil, Nil),
                        Node(7, Nil, Nil))),
            Node(3,
                Nil,
                Node(8,
                    Nil,
                    Node(9, Nil, Nil)))
        )

let findLCA (node0, node1) root =
    let rec commonAncestor (node0, node1) root =
        match root with
        | Nil -> None
        | Node(v, left, right) ->
            match left, right with
            | Nil, Nil -> None
            | Node(v, _, _), _ when v = node0 || v = node1 -> Some root
            | _, Node(v, _, _) when v = node0 || v = node1 -> Some root
            | _ ->
                let l = left |> commonAncestor (node0, node1)
                let r = right |> commonAncestor (node0, node1)
                match l, r with
                | None, None -> None
                | Some(_), Some(_) -> Some root
                | Some(_) as n, None -> n
                | None, (Some(_) as n) -> n

    match root with
    | Nil -> None
    | Node(v, left, right) when v=node0 || v=node1 -> Some root
    | Node(v, left, right) -> commonAncestor (node0, node1) root

let tree = createBinaryTree()
type ResultRecord = { Nodes : NodeType*NodeType; Ancestor : NodeType }
let output r pair =
    match r with
    | Some(Node(v, _, _)) -> { Nodes = pair; Ancestor = v }
    | _ -> { Nodes = pair; Ancestor = -1 }

let pairsToFindAncestor = [
    (2, 3)
    (1, 8)
    (1, 2)
```

```
        (3, 8)
        (8, 7)
        (4, 6)
        (4, 7) ]

let r =
    pairsToFindAncestor
    |> List.map (fun pair -> pair, (tree |> findLCA pair))
    |> List.map (fun (pair, result) -> pair |> output result)
```

Execution result

```
[{Nodes = (2, 3); Ancestor = 1;};
 {Nodes = (1, 8); Ancestor = 1;};
 {Nodes = (1, 2); Ancestor = 1;};
 {Nodes = (3, 8); Ancestor = 1;};
 {Nodes = (8, 7); Ancestor = 1;};
 {Nodes = (4, 6); Ancestor = 2;};
 {Nodes = (4, 7); Ancestor = 2;}]
```

 Note The result is copied from the FSI output windows with some reformatting for better readability.

If the tree is a BST, finding LCA will be easier because the LCA is the first node whose value is between two given values. The sample code that creates the tree structure shown in Figure 7-16 and finds the LCA in it is shown in Listing 7-31.

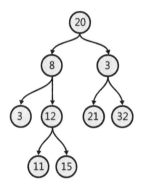

FIGURE 7-16 BST structure for LCA

LISTING 7-31 Finding the LCA in a BST

```
type NodeType = int

type BinaryTree =
    | Nil
    | Node of NodeType * BinaryTree * BinaryTree

let createBinaryTree() =
    Node(20, Node(8, Node(5, Nil, Nil),

                     Node(12,
                          Node(11, Nil, Nil),
                          Node(15, Nil, Nil))),
              Node(30,
                   Node(21, Nil, Nil),
                   Node(32, Nil, Nil))
        )

let tree = createBinaryTree()

let rec findLCAInBST (n0, n1) root =
    match root with
    | Nil -> None
    | Node(v, left, right) ->
        if v >= n0 && v <= n1 then
            Some v
        elif v > n0 && v > n1 then
            findLCAInBST (n0, n1) left
        else
            findLCAInBST (n0, n1) right

tree |> findLCAInBST (3, 15)
```

Validate the sum of all child nodes   If the tree has some value, you can validate whether the value is the sum of all its children. The sample is shown in Listing 7-32.

LISTING 7-32 Checking whether a node's value is the sum of the values of the child nodes

```
type NodeType = int

type BinaryTree =
    | Nil
    | Node of NodeType * BinaryTree * BinaryTree

let createBinaryTree() =
    Node(32, Node(9, Node(4, Nil, Nil),
                     Node(5,  Nil, Nil)),
              Node(23, Node(6, Nil, Nil),
                       Node(17, Node(10, Nil, Nil),
                                Node(7, Nil, Nil))
              ))
```

```
let rec checkTree root =
    match root with
    | Nil -> true, None
    | Node(v, left, right) ->
        let leftResult, leftSum = checkTree left
        let rightResult, rightSum = checkTree right
        match leftSum, rightSum with
        | None, None -> true, Some v
        | _ ->
            let leftS = match leftSum with Some(n) -> n | None -> 0
            let rightS = match rightSum with Some(n) -> n | None -> 0
            let result = leftResult && rightResult && (leftS + rightS = v)
            result, Some v

createBinaryTree() |> checkTree |> fst
```

Calculate the tree boundary The tree's boundary can be calculated with code such as that shown in Listing 7-33 (for the tree structure defined in Figure 7-17). The dashed line shows how the boundary is visited.

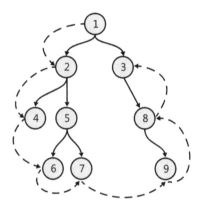

FIGURE 7-17 Tree boundary visit

LISTING 7-33 Calculating the tree boundary

```
type NodeType = int

type BinaryTree =
    | Nil
    | Node of NodeType * BinaryTree * BinaryTree

let createBinaryTree() =
    Node(1, Node(2, Node(4, Nil, Nil),
                    Node(5,
                        Node(6, Nil, Nil),
```

```
                                Node(7, Nil, Nil))),
                Node(3,
                        Nil,
                        Node(8,
                                Nil,
                                Node(9, Nil, Nil)))
        )

let mutable result = []
let add x =
    result <- result @ [x]

let rec visitLeaf root =
    match root with
    | Nil -> ()
    | Node(v, Nil, Nil) -> add v
    | Node(v, left, right) ->
        visitLeaf left
        visitLeaf right

let rec visitLeftBoundary root =
    match root with
    | Nil -> ()
    | Node(v, Nil, Nil) -> ()
    | Node(v, Nil, right) ->
        add v
        visitLeftBoundary right
    | Node(v, left, _) ->
        add v
        visitLeftBoundary left

let rec visitRightBoundary root =
    match root with
    | Nil -> ()
    | Node(v, Nil, Nil) -> ()
    | Node(v, left, Nil) ->
        visitRightBoundary left
        add v
    | Node(v, _, right) ->
        visitRightBoundary right
        add v

let getBoundary root =
    match root with
    | Nil -> ()
    | Node(v, left, right) ->
        add v
        visitLeftBoundary left
        visitLeaf left
        visitLeaf right
        visitRightBoundary right

let tree = createBinaryTree()

getBoundary tree
```

```
> result;;
val it : NodeType list = [1; 2; 4; 6; 7; 9; 8; 3;]
```

Using String Operations

String is probably the most commonly used data type next to integer. Although .NET provides a great many build-in methods for processing strings, you may find it useful to see how string processing algorithms can be expicitly coded in F#.

Substring   Listing 7-34 shows how to decompose a string into substrings consisting of one or more repeats of the same character. If the input is "34445", the function will return "3", "444", and "5".

LISTING 7-34 How to decompose a string into substrings

```
let str = "34445"
let getSub (str:string) =
    [
        let result = ref ""
        for c in str do
            if !result = "" then
                result := string c
            elif (!result).EndsWith(string c) then
                result := !result + string c
            else
                yield !result
                result := string c
        yield !result]

getSub str
```

Palindrome in a string   This sample is used to find the largest palindrome in a string. For example, the palindrome in the string "yabadabadoo" is "abadaba". The straightforward but slowest algorithm is shown in Listing 7-35. (Note the use of double back-quotes to allow us to use *end* as a value name, even though it is an F# keyword.)

LISTING 7-35 Slow algorithm for finding largest palindrome in a string

```
let getPalindrome (str:string) =
    let rec isStringPalindrome (str:string) =
        if str.Length = 0 || str.Length = 1 then true
        else
            let start, ``end`` = 0, str.Length-1
            if str.[start] = str.[``end``] then isStringPalindrome(str.[start+1..``end`` -
1])
            else false
```

```
        let mutable result = System.String.Empty

        for i = 0 to str.Length - 1 do
            let subStr = str.[i..str.Length - 2]
            for explore = i + 1 to str.Length - 1 do
                let strToCheck = str.[i..explore]
                if isStringPalindrome(strToCheck) then
                        result <- if result.Length > strToCheck.Length then result else strToCheck

        sprintf "%s" result

getPalindrome "abab"
getPalindrome "sambabmiv"
getPalindrome "aa"
getPalindrome "aaa"
getPalindrome "yabadabadoo"
```

Execution result

```
bab
mbabm
aa
aaa
abadaba
```

 Note A suffix tree is a more efficient way to solve this problem. You can find related material on the web at *http://en.wikipedia.org/wiki/Suffix_tree*.

Permutations of a string Listing 7-36 shows how to get all permutations of a string. For example, the permutations of the string "abc" will be "abc", "acb", "bca", "bac", "cab", and "cba".

LISTING 7-36 Permutations of a string

```
open System

let rec permute (str:string) =
    let chList =
        str
        |> List.ofSeq
    match chList with
    | [] -> []
    | [ch] -> [ string ch ]
    | head::tail ->
        let ch = head
        let tail = String.Join("", tail)
        let subStringList = permute tail
```

```
            [ for (subString:string) in subStringList do
                for i = 0 to subString.Length do
                    let resultString = subString.Insert(i, string ch)
                    yield resultString]

permute "abcd"
```

Execution result from FSI

```
val it : string list =
  ["abcd"; "bacd"; "bcad"; "bcda"; "acbd"; "cabd"; "cbad"; "cbda"; "acdb";
   "cadb"; "cdab"; "cdba"; "abdc"; "badc"; "bdac"; "bdca"; "adbc"; "dabc";
   "dbac"; "dbca"; "adcb"; "dacb"; "dcab"; "dcba"]
```

String interleaving   String interleaving is a restricted permutation. An interleaved string of two strings keeps the order of the characters in the strings. If two given strings are "a" and "bc", "abc", and "bac" are valid string interleaving results, but "cba" is not because the "cb" is in the wrong order. The code to implement string interleaving is shown in Listing 7-37.

LISTING 7-37 String interleaving

```
open System

let (| AllEmpty | Str0NotEmpty | Str1NotEmpty | Both |) (str0, str1) =
    let b0 = String.IsNullOrEmpty(str0)
    let b1 = String.IsNullOrEmpty(str1)
    match b0, b1 with
    | true, true -> AllEmpty
    | false, true -> Str0NotEmpty
    | true, false -> Str1NotEmpty
    | false, false -> Both

let mutable result = []
let add x =
    result <- result @ [x]

let interLeaving str0 str1 =
    let rec interLeavingStrs str0 str1 current =
        match str0, str1 with
        | AllEmpty _ -> ()
        | Str1NotEmpty -> add (current+str1)
        | Str0NotEmpty -> add (current+str0)
        | Both ->
            interLeavingStrs (str0.Substring(1)) str1 (current + string str0.[0])
            interLeavingStrs str0 (str1.Substring(1)) (current + string str1.[0])

    interLeavingStrs str0 str1 ""

interLeaving "ab" "cd"
```

```
> result;;
val it : string list = ["abcd"; "acbd"; "acdb"; "cabd"; "cadb"; "cdab"]
```

KMP string search algorithm   Imagine that you have two strings and that you want to find all occurrences of a target string. The KMP string search algorithm is an algorithm you can use to do this. The search algorithm complexity is *O(n)*, where *n* is the length of the source string. In addition to demonstrating the algorithm, the code also shows how to use an F# record, a type alias, and extension methods. Also note the use of a match statement in which the branching logic is implemented solely by 'when' guards, all the actual patterns being '_'. The sample code is shown in Listing 7-38.

LISTING 7-38 KMP string search algorithm

```
type List = System.Collections.Generic.List<int>

let kmp ( w: string ) =
    let t = List([1..w.Length])
    let mutable pos = 2
    let mutable cnd = 0
    t.[0] <- -1
    t.[1] <- 0

    while pos < w.Length do
        match pos, cnd with
        | _ when w.[pos - 1] = w.[cnd] ->
            cnd <- cnd + 1
            t.[pos] <- cnd
            pos <- pos + 1
        | _ when cnd > 0 ->
            cnd <- t.[cnd]
        | _ ->
            t.[pos] <- 0
            pos <- pos + 1

    t |> List.ofSeq

type ResultType =
    { mutable Result : int; mutable Found : bool }
        with
        member this.SetFound(b) = this.Found <- b
        member this.SetResult(c) = this.Result<- c
        static member InitialValue = { Result = -1; Found = false }

let kmpSearch (s:string) (w:string) : int =
    let mutable m = 0
    let mutable i = 0
    let t = kmp w
    let v = ResultType.InitialValue
```

```
        while (i + m) < s.Length && not v.Found do
            if w.[i] = s.[m + i] then
                if i = w.Length - 1 then
                    v.SetFound true
                    v.SetResult m
                i <- i + 1
            else
                m <- m + i + t.[i]
                i <- if t.[i] > -1 then t.[i] else 0

        v.Result

let s = "ABCABCDABABCDABCDABDE"
kmpSearch s "ABCDABD"
```

Using the Graph Library

The graph library is used to implement a graph structure that contains nodes and edges. (We are using the formal mathemetical definition of *graph* here: a representation of a set of nodes where some nodes are connected by links (edges). This is nothing to do with graphs in the sense of a graphical chart or plot.) Each node in the library has outgoing edges and an incoming edge collection. The graph operation is performed by the *Graph* class, which also maintains lists of all nodes and edges. (See Listing 7-39.) This library shows how flexible the F# library is. There are no constraints on the node ID's type. The type inference system will make sure everything is assigned the appropriate type.

LISTING 7-39 Graph library

```
open System

type Graph() =
    let mutable nodes = []
    let mutable edges = []

    member this.Nodes = nodes
    member this.Edges = edges

    member this.CreateNode id =
        match this.FindNode id with
            | Some n -> None
            | None ->
                let node = Node(this, ID = id)
                nodes <- nodes @ [ node ]
                Some node
    member this.CreateEdgeFromNode(from:Node, ``to``:Node, id) =
        match this.FindEdge id with
        | Some edge -> None
```

```
        | None ->
            let edge = Edge(this, from, ``to``, ID = id)
            from.AddOutgoingEdge(edge)
            ``to``.AddIncomingEdge(edge)

            edges <- edges @ [edge]
            Some edge

    member this.CreateEdgeFromID(from, ``to``, id) =
        let fromNode = this.FindNode(from)
        let toNode = this.FindNode(``to``)
        match fromNode, toNode with
            | Some n0, Some n1 -> this.CreateEdgeFromNode(n0, n1, id)
            | _ -> None

    member this.FindNode id =
        (nodes:Node list) |> Seq.tryFind(fun n -> n.ID = id)
    member this.FindEdge id =
        (edges:Edge list) |> Seq.tryFind(fun edge -> edge.ID = id)

    member this.RemoveEdge(edge:Edge) =
        (edge.FromNode:Node).RemoveOutgoingEdge(edge)
        (edge.ToNode:Node).RemoveIncomingEdge(edge)
        edges <- edges |> List.filter (fun n -> n <> edge)
    member this.RemoveNode(node:Node) =
        node.OutgoingEdges @ node.IncomingEdges |> List.iter this.RemoveEdge
        nodes <- nodes |> List.filter (fun n -> n<>node)

and Node(g) =
    let mutable incomingEdges = []
    let mutable outgoingEdges = []

    member val ID = Unchecked.defaultof<_> with get, set
    member val Data = Unchecked.defaultof<_> with get, set

    member this.IncomingEdges = incomingEdges
    member this.OutgoingEdges = outgoingEdges

    member this.AddIncomingEdge(edge:Edge) =
        if edge.ToNode = this then
            incomingEdges <- incomingEdges |> List.append [edge]
    member this.AddOutgoingEdge(edge:Edge) =
        if edge.FromNode = this then
            outgoingEdges <- outgoingEdges |> List.append [edge]

    member this.RemoveIncomingEdge(edge:Edge) =
        incomingEdges <- incomingEdges |> List.filter (fun n -> n <> edge)
    member this.RemoveOutgoingEdge(edge:Edge) =
        outgoingEdges <- outgoingEdges |> List.filter (fun n -> n <> edge)

    override this.ToString() =
        sprintf "Node(%A)" this.ID
```

```
and Edge(g, from:Node, ``to``:Node) =
    member val ID = Unchecked.defaultof<_> with get, set
    member val Data = Unchecked.defaultof<_> with get, set

    member this.FromNode = from
    member this.ToNode = ``to``

    override this.ToString() =
        sprintf "Edge(%A, %A -> %A)" this.ID this.FromNode this.ToNode
```

In Visual Studio, a DGML format file supports the representation of a graph. Listing 7-40 shows how to deserialize a graph from a DGML file using portable library functions. The portable library does not support creating a *StreamReader*. The *StreamReader* is passed in from the nonportable project. The sample code needed to invoke the DGMLReader is the following:

```
let g = DGMLGraph.MyClass(new System.IO.StreamReader(@"<your DGML file path>"))
```

LISTING 7-40 Deserializing from a DGML file

```
type DGMLReader(textReader:TextReader) =
    let doc = XDocument.Load(textReader:TextReader)
    let graph = Graph()
    do
        let nodes = doc.Descendants() |> Seq.filter (fun n -> n.Name.LocalName = "Node")
        let graphNodes =
            nodes
            |> Seq.map (fun node -> graph.CreateNode(node.Attribute(XName.Get("Id")).
Value))
            |> Seq.toList
        let edges = doc.Descendants() |> Seq.filter (fun n -> n.Name.LocalName="Link")
        edges
        |> Seq.iteri (fun i edge->
                        let fromNode = edge.Attribute(XName.Get("Source")).Value
                        let toNode = edge.Attribute(XName.Get("Target")).Value
                        ignore <| graph.CreateEdgeFromID(fromNode, toNode, i)
                        ())

    member this.Graph = graph
```

 Note You need to add references to *System.Xml* and *System.Xml.Linq* to the Portable Class Library project to run this sample.

With the graph structure in hand, I can now implement several graph algorithms.

Depth-first search   Depth-first search (DFS) is a search algorithm that traverses the tree down a single branch as far as possible before backtracking. The sample code for the DFS graph is shown in Listing 7-41. The code executed on the graph in Figure 7-18 generates a result such as [Node("1"); Node("2"); Node("3"); Node("4"); Node("5"); Node("6")].

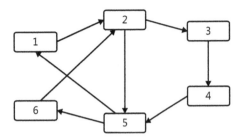

FIGURE 7-18 Sample graph in DGML format

LISTING 7-41 DFS on a graph

```
DFS code in the Portable Class Library project
type NodeStack = System.Collections.Generic.Stack<Node>
type VisitedList = System.Collections.Generic.List<Node>

let stack = NodeStack()
let visited = VisitedList()

let visit node =
    visited.Add(node)

let (| Visited | _ |) node =
    if visited.Contains(node) then
        Some node
    else
        None

let dfsGraph graph (start:Node)=
    stack.Push(start)
    visited.Clear()

    while stack.Count <> 0 do
        let currentNode = stack.Pop()
        match currentNode with
        | Visited(_) -> ()
        | _ ->
            visit currentNode
            let nodes =
                currentNode.OutgoingEdges
                |> Seq.map (fun edge -> edge.ToNode)
```

```
                |> Seq.distinctBy (fun node -> node.ID)
                |> Seq.toList
         nodes
         |> Seq.iter (fun node -> stack.Push node)
```

Invoker code

```
let g = DGMLGraph.DGMLReader(new
System.IO.StreamReader(@"C:\MyCode\ConsoleApplication1\Graph1.dgml"))
let (Some startNode) = g.Graph.FindNode("1")
DGMLGraph.dfsGraph g startNode
printfn "%A" (Seq.toList <| DGMLGraph.visited)
```

Breadth-first search   Breadth-first search (BFS) is different from DFS only in how it stores nodes.
DFS uses a stack, and BFS uses a queue. Listing 7-42 provides a BFS sample.

LISTING 7-42 A BFS graph sample

```
type NodeQueue = System.Collections.Generic.Queue<Node>
type VisitedList = System.Collections.Generic.List<Node>

let queue = NodeQueue()
let visited = VisitedList()

let visit node =
    visited.Add node

let (| Visited | _ |) node =
    if visited.Contains node then
        Some node
    else
        None

let dfsGraph graph (start:Node)=
    queue.Enqueue start
    visited.Clear()

    while queue.Count <> 0 do
        let currentNode = queue.Dequeue()
        match currentNode with
        | Visited(_) -> ()
        | _ ->
            visit currentNode
            let nodes =
                currentNode.OutgoingEdges
                |> Seq.map (fun edge -> edge.ToNode)
                |> Seq.distinctBy (fun node -> node.ID)
                |> Seq.toList
            nodes
            |> Seq.iter (fun node -> queue.Enqueue node)
```

Find all paths in a graph Another way to represent a graph is to use a matrix. Listing 7-43 shows how to access the graph and find all possible paths from one point to another. If the element in the matrix is 1, that is a *passage*. If the element in the matrix is 0, it is a *blocker*. The sample code finds all of the paths from (0,0) to (4,2).

LISTING 7-43 Finding all paths in a graph

```
type Location = { X : int; Y : int }
type Path = Location list

let graph = [
        [1;1;1;1;0]
        [0;1;0;1;0]
        [0;1;0;1;1]
        [0;1;1;1;0]
        [0;1;0;1;0]
        ]

let getNeighbors (point:Location) =
    let getLeft (point:Location) =
        if point.X = 0 then None
        else Some { X = point.X - 1; Y = point.Y }
    let getTop (point:Location) =
        if point.Y = 0 then None
        else Some { X = point.X; Y = point.Y - 1 }
    let getRight (point:Location) =
        if point.X = 4 then None
        else Some { X = point.X + 1; Y = point.Y }
    let getBottom (point:Location) =
        if point.Y=4 then None
        else Some { X = point.X; Y = point.Y + 1 }
    let result =
        [getLeft point;
         getTop point;
         getRight point;
         getBottom point]
    result
    |> List.filter (fun n -> match n with Some _ -> true | None -> false )
    |> List.map (fun (Some n) -> n)
    |> List.filter (fun n -> graph.[n.Y].[n.X] <> 0)

let rec findAllPath (startPoint:Location) (endPoint:Location) (path:Path)=
    if startPoint = endPoint then
        [ path ]
    else
        let neighbours =
            getNeighbors startPoint
            |> List.filter (fun n -> path |> List.exists (fun x -> x=n) |> not)
        [ for n in neighbours do
            for path in findAllPath n endPoint (path@[n]) do
                if path.Length > 0 then
                    yield path
                else
                    () ]
```

```
let start = { X = 0; Y = 0 }
let endPoint = { X = 4; Y = 2 }

let path = [start]
let c = findAllPath start endPoint path
```

 Note In a Portable Class Library project, List<T> is still present. You can replace List<Location> with an F# Location list to take advantage of immutability.

A* algorithm The A* (pronounced *A star*) algorithm is another graph algorithm. The graph is represented in a matrix, where 0 cannot be passed. There is an *openList* and a *closedList*. The *openList* keeps track of the unvisited nodes and the closedList keeps nodes that have already been processed. The *openList* is sorted by the node cost *F*. The node cost *F* is computed from two parts: *H* and *MoveCost*. *MoveCost* is the move cost from previous nodes, while *H* is a heuristic cost that is an estimated cost from the current node. The *H* part is only an estimate. Imagine that you are going from your current location to particular destination. On the way to your destination, you have a feeling of whether next move is closer to or further from the destination. This is how the A* algorithm works. The *H* value is your estimate from your current location to your destination; this value plays a role in your decision when making a move closer to your destination.

The algorithm starts from the *openList* with a starting point, and the *TotalCost* set to *0*. During each iteration in the algorithm, the minimum *TotalCost* node is taken from the *openList* and denoted as the *currentNode*. The neighbor nodes are retrieved and put on the *openList*, as long as they are not visited and on the *closedList*. The *MoveCost* value of neighbor nodes is computed from the current node. If the cost is less than the current value, which means the current node is a better choice, the node's *PreviousNnode* is set to *CurrentNnode* and the *MoveCost* cost is updated accordingly. The whole process is terminated when all of the target nodes are in *closedList* or *openList* is empty, as shown in Listing 7-44.

LISTING 7-44 An A* algorithm sample

```
type Location = { X : int; Y : int }

[<System.Diagnostics.DebuggerDisplay("({Location.X},{Location.Y})")>]
type Node() as this =
    member val IsBlock = false with get, set
    member val PreviousNode = this with get, set
    member val Location = {X = 0; Y = 0} with get, set
    member val H = 0 with get, set
    member val MoveCost = 1000 with get, set
    member this.TotalCost = this.MoveCost + this.H

type Path = Location list
```

```
let graph = [
        [1;1;1;1;1;1;1]
        [1;1;1;0;1;1;1]
        [1;1;1;0;1;1;1]
        [1;1;1;0;1;1;1]
        [1;1;1;0;1;1;1]
        [1;1;1;1;1;1;1]
        [1;1;1;1;1;1;1]
        ]

let nodeGraph =
    graph
    |> List.mapi (fun y row ->
                    row
                    |> List.mapi (fun x n ->
                        let loc = {X = x; Y = y}
                        Node(IsBlock= (if n = 1 then false else true),
                            Location = loc))
                )

let rightMax = 6

let getNeighbors (point:Location) =
    let getLeft (point:Location) =
        if point.X = 0 then None
        else Some { X = point.X - 1; Y = point.Y }
    let getTop (point:Location) =
        if point.Y = 0 then None
        else Some { X = point.X; Y = point.Y - 1 }
    let getRight (point:Location) =
        if point.X = rightMax then None
        else Some { X = point.X + 1; Y = point.Y }
    let getBottom (point:Location) =
        if point.Y=rightMax then None
        else Some { X = point.X; Y = point.Y + 1 }
    let getLeftTop (point:Location) =
        if point.X = 0 || point.Y = 0 then None
        else Some { X = point.X - 1; Y= point.Y - 1 }
    let getRightTop (point:Location) =
        if point.X = rightMax || point.Y = 0 then None
        else Some { X = point.X + 1; Y=point.Y - 1 }
    let getRightBottom (point:Location) =
        if point.X = rightMax || point.Y = rightMax then None
        else Some { X = point.X + 1; Y = point.Y + 1 }
    let getLeftBottom (point:Location) =
        if point.X = 0 || point.Y = rightMax then None
        else Some { X = point.X - 1; Y=point.Y + 1 }
    let result =
        [(10, getLeft point); (10, getTop point); (10, getRight point); (10, getBottom
point);
        (14, getLeftTop point); (14, getRightTop point); (14, getRightBottom point);
```

```
            (14, getLeftBottom point);
        ]
    let result =
        result
        |> List.filter (fun (cost, n) -> match n with Some _ -> true | None -> false )
        |> List.map (fun (cost, (Some n)) -> cost,n)
        |> List.filter (fun (cost, n) -> nodeGraph.[n.Y].[n.X].IsBlock |> not)
        |> List.map (fun (cost, n) -> cost, nodeGraph.[n.Y].[n.X])
    result

let mutable openList : Node list = []
let mutable closedList : Node list = []

let addOpenList node =
    openList <- openList @ [node]

let addClosedList node =
    closedList <- closedList @ [node]

let closedListContain (endPoint:Node) =
    closedList
    |> Seq.exists (fun n -> n.Location = endPoint.Location)

let openListContain (node:Node) =
    openList
    |> Seq.exists (fun n -> n.Location = node.Location)

let ``a*`` start (endPoint:Node) =
    addOpenList start
    nodeGraph
    |> List.iter (fun list ->
                    list
                    |> List.iter (fun n ->
                                    n.H <- 10 * (abs (n.Location.X - endPoint.Location.X)
                                          + abs (n.Location.Y - endPoint.Location.Y))))
    while not <| closedListContain endPoint && openList.Length > 0 do
        let currentNode::tail = openList |> List.sortBy (fun n -> n.TotalCost)
        openList <- tail
        addClosedList currentNode

        let neighbours:(int*Node) list =
                getNeighbors currentNode.Location
                |> List.filter (fun (_, node) -> node |> closedListContain |> not)
        for cost, node in neighbours do
            if node.MoveCost > currentNode.MoveCost + cost then
                node.PreviousNode <- currentNode
                node.MoveCost <- currentNode.MoveCost + cost
            if not <| openListContain node then
                addOpenList node

let start = nodeGraph.[0].[0]
start.MoveCost <- 0
let endPoint = nodeGraph.[2].[5]

``a*`` start endPoint
```

Dijkstra algorithm   The Dijkstra algorithm is another algorithm you can use to find the shortest path from a given point to all other nodes in the graph. In Listing 7-45, the graph library is changed to host the shortest distance from the starting point.

LISTING 7-45 Dijkstra algorithm

```
module DGMLGraph

open System

type Graph() =
    let mutable nodes = []
    let mutable edges = []

    member this.Nodes with get() = nodes
    member this.Edges with get() = edges
    member this.CreateNode (id) =
        match this.FindNode (id) with
        | Some (n) -> None
        | None ->
            let node = Node(this, ID = id)
            nodes <- nodes @ [ node ]
            Some node
    member this.CreateEdgeFromNode(from:Node, ``to``:Node, id) =
        match this.FindEdge id with
        | Some (edge) -> None
        | None ->
        let edge = Edge(this, from, ``to``, ID = id)
        from.AddOutgoingEdge (edge)
        ``to``.AddIncomingEdge (edge)
        edges <- edges @ [edge]
        Some edge
    member this.CreateEdgeFromID(from, ``to``, id) =
        let fromNode = this.FindNode (from)
        let toNode = this.FindNode (``to``)
        match fromNode, toNode with
        | Some(n0), Some(n1) -> this.CreateEdgeFromNode(n0, n1, id)
        | _ -> None
    member this.FindNode (id) =
        (nodes:Node list) |> Seq.tryFind(fun n -> n.ID = id)
    member this.FindEdge (id ) =
        (edges:Edge list) |> Seq.tryFind(fun edge -> edge.ID = id)
    member this.RemoveEdge(edge:Edge) =
        (edge.FromNode:Node).RemoveOutgoingEdge (edge)
        (edge.ToNode:Node).RemoveIncomingEdge (edge)
        edges <- edges |> List.filter (fun n -> n<>edge)
    member this.RemoveNode(node:Node) =
        node.OutgoingEdges @ node.IncomingEdges |> List.iter this.RemoveEdge
        nodes <- nodes |> List.filter (fun n -> n<>node)

and Node(g) =
    let mutable incomingEdges = []
    let mutable outgoingEdges = []
```

```
        member val ID = Unchecked.defaultof<_> with get, set
        member val Data = Unchecked.defaultof<_> with get, set
        member this.IncomingEdges with get() = incomingEdges
        member this.OutgoingEdges with get() = outgoingEdges
        member this.AddIncomingEdge(edge:Edge) =
            if edge.ToNode = this then
            incomingEdges <- incomingEdges |> List.append [edge]
        member this.AddOutgoingEdge(edge:Edge) =
            if edge.FromNode = this then
            outgoingEdges <- outgoingEdges |> List.append [edge]
        member this.RemoveIncomingEdge(edge:Edge) =
            incomingEdges <- incomingEdges |> List.filter (fun n -> n <> edge)
        member this.RemoveOutgoingEdge(edge:Edge) =
            outgoingEdges <- outgoingEdges |> List.filter (fun n -> n <> edge)
        override this.ToString() =
            sprintf "Node(%A)" this.ID

and Edge(g, from:Node, ``to``:Node) =
    member val ID = Unchecked.defaultof<_> with get, set
    member val Data = Unchecked.defaultof<_> with get, set
    member this.FromNode with get() = from
    member this.ToNode with get() = ``to``
    override this.ToString() =
        sprintf "Edge(%A, %A -> %A)" this.ID this.FromNode this.ToNode


open System.IO
open System.Xml.Linq


type DGMLReader(textReader:TextReader) =
    let doc = XDocument.Load(textReader:TextReader)
    let graph = Graph()
    do
        let nodes = doc.Descendants() |> Seq.filter (fun n -> n.Name.LocalName = "Node")
        let graphNodes =
                nodes
                |> Seq.map (fun node ->
                        let (Some graphNode) =
                            graph.CreateNode(node.Attribute(XName.Get("Id")).Value)
                        graphNode.Data <- System.Int32.MaxValue)
                |> Seq.toList
        let edges = doc.Descendants() |> Seq.filter (fun n -> n.Name.LocalName = "Link")
        edges
        |> Seq.iteri (fun i edge->
                let fromNode = edge.Attribute(XName.Get("Source")).Value
                let toNode = edge.Attribute(XName.Get("Target")).Value
                let (Some graphEdge) = graph.CreateEdgeFromID(fromNode, toNode, i)
                graphEdge.Data <- Convert.ToInt32 ( edge.Attribute(XName.Get("Label")).
Value )
                ())
    member this.Graph with get() = graph


type Path = System.Collections.Generic.List<Node>
```

```
let openList = Path()
let closedList = Path()

open System.Collections.Generic
open System.Linq

let getNeighbors (currentNode:Node) =
    currentNode.OutgoingEdges
    |> List.map (fun edge -> edge.ToNode)
    |> List.filter (fun node -> not <| closedList.Contains(node))

let getCost (node:Node, currentNode:Node) =
    let (Some edge) =
        currentNode.OutgoingEdges
        |> List.tryFind (fun edge -> edge.ToNode = node)
    edge.Data

let ``Dijkstra's algorithm`` startPoint =
    openList.Add (startPoint)
    startPoint.Data <- 0
    while openList.Count > 0 do
        let currentNode = openList |> Seq.minBy (fun n -> n.Data)
        let neighbors : Node list = getNeighbors currentNode
        neighbors
        |> List.iter (fun node ->
                let distance = getCost (node, currentNode)
                node.Data <- min (currentNode.Data + distance) node.Data)
        openList.AddRange (neighbors)
        ignore <| openList.Remove (currentNode)
        closedList.Add (currentNode)
```

Note You have to add *System.Xml* and *System.Xml.Linq* to the project references.

Examining Other Samples

This section gives you other useful options to try.

Combination   Combination is an approach used to select several items out of a larger collection. Unlike the permutation approach, combination does not care about the order. Listing 7-46 shows how to get a combination from a collection of elements.

LISTING 7-46 Getting a combination from a list

```
let getCombination (list:int list) elementNeeded =
    let rec getCombinationFunction (list:int list) elementNeeded currentList =
        if elementNeeded = 0 then
            [ currentList ]
        else
            [ for n in list do
```

```
            let newList =
                list
                |> Seq.skipWhile (fun x -> x<>n)
                |> Seq.skip 1
                |> Seq.toList
            let newElementNeeded = elementNeeded - 1
            for l in getCombinationFunction newList newElementNeeded (currentList@[n])
do
                yield l ]

    getCombinationFunction list elementNeeded []

getCombination [1; 2; 3; 4] 3
```

Execution result

```
val getCombination : list:int list -> elementNeeded:int -> int list list
val it : int list list = [[1; 2; 3]; [1; 2; 4]; [1; 3; 4]; [2; 3; 4]]
```

Phone keyboard   The telephone keyboard enables you to input non-numeric characters as well as number characters. Listing 7-47 demonstrates how to get the character sequence from number inputs.

LISTING 7-47 Generating output from digital-character input

```
let letters =
    [
    '0', ['0']
    '1', ['1']
    '2', ['2'; 'A'; 'B'; 'C']
    '3', ['3'; 'D'; 'E'; 'F']
    '4', ['4'; 'G'; 'H'; 'I']
    '5', ['5'; 'J'; 'K'; 'L']
    '6', ['6'; 'M'; 'N'; 'O']
    '7', ['7'; 'P'; 'Q'; 'R'; 'S']
    '8', ['8'; 'T'; 'U'; 'V']
    '9', ['9'; 'W'; 'X'; 'Y'; 'Z']
    ]
    |> Map.ofList

let mutable currentState = ('0', -1)
let mutable result = System.Collections.Generic.List<_>()

let output() =
    let char, times = currentState
    if times >=0 then
        let l = letters.[char]
        let len = l.Length
```

```
        let c = l.[times%len]
        result.Add(c)
    else
        ()

let getInput (chs:char seq) =
    chs
    |> Seq.iter (fun ch ->
                    let char, times = currentState
                    if ch=char then
                        currentState <- (ch, times+1)
                    else
                        output()
                        currentState <- (ch, 0))

    output()

    result |> Seq.toList

getInput "12224444444210"
```

> **Note** The letters variable is converted from a tuple list. The '0' , ['0'] is a tuple whose surrounding brackets are optional.

Shuffle algorithm   The algorithm in Listing 7-48 shuffles a sequence and generates a randomly shuffled list. In the algorithm code, it does not specify the type of the sequence. The use of an underscore (_) indicates that the sequence element type can be inferred from the code usage. For instance, an integer is passed to the algorithm, F# will infer that the data is an integer seq, and the result is a List<int>.

LISTING 7-48 Random shuffle algorithm

```
open System

let rand = Random()
let shuffleYateFisher (data:seq<_>) =
    let result = System.Collections.Generic.List<_> ()
    data
    |> Seq.iter (fun n ->
                    let index = rand.Next(0, result.Count)
                    if index = result.Count then
                        result.Add(n)
                    else
                        result.Add(result.[index])
                        result.[index] <- n)

    result
```

```
let seq = seq { for i = 0 to 10 do yield i }

for i=0 to 5 do
    let l = shuffleYateFisher seq
    l |> Seq.iter (printf "%A ")
    printfn ""
```

Note Randomness and shuffling are complex topics. Don't use any random number generation or shuffling algorithm for mission critical features (encryption, security, gaming engines) without assuring yourself that they are of sufficient quality.

Reservoir sampling Reservoir sampling is related to the processing of large amounts of data. This algorithm is another random-selection algorithm. The algorithm is trying to get N elements from a large data set, which is so big that it is not possible to hold it in memory. In the sample code, I will use a sequence as the incoming data structure.

The algorithm first tries to fill the result set whose size is *resultSize*. Once the elements are successfully retrieved, the rest of the elements are selected randomly based on a uniform distribution from 0 to the current index value. If the generated random number is in the range of *[0, resultSize)*, you can replace the result set's element with the new element, as shown in Listing 7-49.

LISTING 7-49 Reservoir-sampling algorithm

```
let rand = System.Random()

let (|InReservoirRange|_|) i resultSize =
    if i < resultSize then
        Some()
    else
        None

type ResultList<'a> = System.Collections.Generic.List<'a>
let result = ResultList<_>()

let reservoirSampling data resultSize =
    let (|InReservoirRange|_|) i = (|InReservoirRange|_|) i resultSize
    data
    |> Seq.iteri (fun index n ->
            match index with
            | InReservoirRange->
              result.Add(n)
            | _ ->
              let newIndex = rand.Next(index)
              match newIndex with
              | InReservoirRange ->
                result.[newIndex] <- n
              | _ -> ())

let seq = seq { for i = 0 to 100 do yield i }
reservoirSampling seq 5
```

Note This sample shows the parameterized partial active pattern and how to generate a new active pattern from an existing pattern. The active pattern provides a way to give more precise meaning to the data. Like its name suggests, the *InReservoirRange* indicates the value is in the reservoir range.

If the data set is large, a *bigint* number generator and a *Seq.iteri* using *bigint* are needed. A sample *bigint* random-number generator is shown here:

```
open System

let rand = Random()
type Random with
    member this.RandomBigInt() =
        let len = 20
        let getRandByte() =
            let arr = Array.create 1 0uy
            rand.NextBytes arr
            arr.[0]
        let arr = Array.init len (fun _ -> getRandByte())

        let big = bigint arr
        big

printfn "%A" (rand.RandomBigInt())
```

Check intersecting line segments Another common use of an active pattern is to check whether two line segments can intersect. The sample takes two line segments on a two-dimensional (2D) surface. The line segment is represented by two points. In Listing 7-50, a tuple is used to represent the point.

LISTING 7-50 Checking for intersecting line segments

```
let (|Vertical|_|) ((x1, y1), (x2, y2)) = if x1 = x2 then Some() else None
let assertFunction a b = if a <> b then failwith "fail test"

let checkIntersect (p0, p1, p2, p3) =
    let x1, y1 = p0
    let x2, y2 = p1
    let x3, y3 = p2
    let x4, y4 = p3

    match (p0, p1), (p2, p3) with
    | Vertical, Vertical -> x1 = x3
    | Vertical, _ ->
        let delta (x, y) = (y3 - y4) / (x3 - x4) * (x - x3) + y3 - y
        (x1 - x3) * (x1 - x4) <= 0 &&
        delta (x2, y2) * delta (x1, y1) <= 0

    | _, Vertical
    | _ ->
        let delta (x, y) = (y1 - y2) / (x1 - x2) * (x - x1) + y1 - y
        (x3 - x1) * (x3 - x2) <= 0 &&
```

```
        delta (x3, y3) * delta (x4, y4) <= 0

// one line is a normal line from (0, 0) to (5, 5)
assertFunction true <| checkIntersect ( (0, 0), (5, 5), (0, 5), (5, 0) )
assertFunction false <| checkIntersect ( (0, 0), (5, 5), (0, 5), (1, 4) )
assertFunction false <| checkIntersect ( (0, 0), (5, 5), (5, 0), (4, 1) )
assertFunction true <| checkIntersect ( (0, 0), (5, 5), (1, 0), (1, 5) )
assertFunction false <| checkIntersect ( (0, 0), (5, 5), (4, 0), (4, 2) )
assertFunction true <| checkIntersect ( (0, 0), (5, 5), (4, 0), (4, 5) )
assertFunction false <| checkIntersect ( (0, 0), (5, 5), (0, 4), (1, 4) )
assertFunction true <| checkIntersect ( (0, 0), (5, 5), (0, 4), (5, 4) )
assertFunction false <| checkIntersect ( (0, 0), (5, 5), (5, 4), (5, 4) )
assertFunction true <| checkIntersect ( (0, 0), (5, 5), (5, 5), (5, 5) )
```

Find triangles   The last sample presented here, in Listing 7-51, is a combination problem. The problem is to find the number of triangles that can be formed by three different elements in the array. The array contains positive integers. If three numbers can form a triangle, the sum from any two of them should be larger than the third.

LISTING 7-51 Finding triangles in an array

```
let getTriangle (l:_ list) =
    let len = l.Length
    [
        for i = 0 to len - 1 do
            for j = i + 1 to len - 1 do
                for k = j + 1 to len - 1 do
                    if l.[i] + l.[j] > l.[k] &&
                       l.[j] + l.[k] > l.[i] &&
                       l.[k] + l.[i] > l.[j] then yield l.[i], l.[j], l.[k] ]

getTriangle [10; 21; 22; 100; 101; 200; 300]
```

Execution result
```
val it : (int * int * int) list =
  [(10, 21, 22); (10, 100, 101); (21, 100, 101); (22, 100, 101);
   (100, 101, 200); (101, 200, 300)]
```

Neural network   In Chapter 6, "Other Unique Features," I presented a generic algorithm implementation. In computational intelligence research, other than a genetic algorithm, there is another famous algorithm called the *neural network*. If the neural network (NN) is not a familiar concept, the following definition from Wikipedia (*http://en.wikipedia.org/wiki/Neural_network*) can be helpful to understanding neural networks:

> *A neural network is an interconnected group of natural or artificial neurons that uses a mathematical or computational model for information processing based*

on a connectionistic approach to computation. In most cases a NN is an adaptive system that changes its structure based on external or internal information that flows through the network. In more practical terms neural networks are non-linear statistical data modeling or decision making tools. They can be used to model complex relationships between inputs and outputs or to find patterns in data.

Listing 7-52 implements a simple neural network that simulates the XOR operator. Its structure is shown in Figure 7-19. The *Neuron* class in the code represents the neuron node. The edge between the neuron nodes is *NeuralFactor*. The whole neural network has three layers: an input layer, a hidden layer, and an output layer. The input value is set at the top-level nodes, and the output is generated from the bottom node.

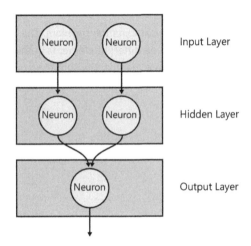

FIGURE 7-19 XOR neural network structure

LISTING 7-52 A simple XOR neural network implementation

```
namespace FSharp.NN

open System
open System.Collections.Generic

// linkage between neurons
type NeuralFactor(weight:float) =
    member val HVector = 0. with get, set
    member val Weight = weight with get, set

    member this.SetWeightChange rate =
        this.Weight <- this.Weight + this.HVector * rate

    member this.Reset() =
        this.HVector <- 0.
```

```
    override this.ToString() =
        sprintf "(HVector=%A, Weight=%A)" this.HVector this.Weight

type Map = Dictionary<Neuron, NeuralFactor>

// neuron in the neural network
and Neuron(bias) =
    let sigmoid v = 1. / (1. + exp(-v))

    member val Bias = NeuralFactor(bias) with get, set
    member val Error = 0. with get, set
    member val Input = Map() with get, set
    member val LastError = 0. with get, set



    member val Output = 0. with get, set

    member this.Pulse() =
        this.Output <- 0.
        for item in this.Input do
            this.Output <- this.Output + item.Key.Output * item.Value.Weight
        this.Output <- this.Output + this.Bias.Weight
        this.Output <- sigmoid this.Output

    member this.ApplyLearning rate =
        for value in this.Input.Values do
            value.SetWeightChange rate

        this.Bias.SetWeightChange rate

    member this.Initialize() =
        this.Input.Values
        |> Seq.iter (fun value -> value.Reset())

        this.Bias.Reset()

    override this.ToString() =
        sprintf "(Bias=%A, Error=%A, Output=%A)" this.Bias this.Error this.Output

// layer in the neural network
type NeuralLayer() =
    inherit List<Neuron>()
    member this.Pulse() =
        this
        |> Seq.iter (fun n->n.Pulse())
    member this.Apply rate =
        this
        |> Seq.iter (fun n->n.ApplyLearning rate)
    member this.Initialize() =
        this
        |> Seq.iter (fun n->n.Initialize())
```

```
// neural network
type NeuralNet()=
    let sigmoidDerivative v = v * ( 1. - v)
    let rand = new Random()

    member val LearningRate = 3.0 with get, set
    member val InputLayer = NeuralLayer() with get, set
    member val HiddenLayer = NeuralLayer() with get, set
    member val OutputLayer = NeuralLayer() with get, set

    member this.Initialize(inputNeuronCount, hiddenNeuronCount, outputNeuronCount) =
        [1..inputNeuronCount] |> Seq.iter (fun _ -> this.InputLayer.Add(Neuron(0.)))
        [1..outputNeuronCount] |> Seq.iter (fun _ -> this.OutputLayer.Add(Neuron(0.)))
        [1..hiddenNeuronCount] |> Seq.iter (fun _ -> this.HiddenLayer.Add(Neuron(0.)))

        for hiddenNode in this.HiddenLayer do
            for inputNode in this.InputLayer do
                hiddenNode.Input.Add(inputNode, new NeuralFactor(rand.NextDouble()))

        for outputNode in this.OutputLayer do
            for hiddenNode in this.HiddenLayer do
                outputNode.Input.Add(hiddenNode, new NeuralFactor(rand.NextDouble()));

    member this.Pulse() =
        [ this.HiddenLayer; this.OutputLayer]
        |> Seq.iter (fun n -> n.Pulse())

    member this.Apply() =
        [ this.HiddenLayer; this.OutputLayer]
        |> Seq.iter (fun n -> n.Apply(this.LearningRate))

    member this.InitializeLearning() =
        [ this.HiddenLayer; this.OutputLayer]
        |> Seq.iter (fun n -> n.Initialize())

    member this.Train(input: float list list, expected: float list list, iteration) =
        [1..iteration]
        |> Seq.iter (fun n ->
                        this.InitializeLearning()
                        for i = 0 to input.Length - 1 do
                            this.BackPropagation(input.[i], expected.[i])
                        this.Apply())

    member this.Prepare(input) =
        Seq.zip this.InputLayer input
        |> Seq.iter (fun (a, b) -> a.Output <- b)

    member this.Calculate() =
        for outputNode in this.OutputLayer do
            for hiddenNode in this.HiddenLayer do
                outputNode.Input.[hiddenNode].HVector <-
                    outputNode.Input.[hiddenNode].HVector + outputNode.Error * hiddenNode.
Output
```

```
            outputNode.Bias.HVector <-
                    outputNode.Bias.HVector + outputNode.Error * outputNode.Bias.Weight

        for hiddenNode in this.HiddenLayer do
            for inputNode in this.InputLayer do
                hiddenNode.Input.[inputNode].HVector <-
                    hiddenNode.Input.[inputNode].HVector + hiddenNode.Error * inputNode.
Output;
                hiddenNode.Bias.HVector <-
                    hiddenNode.Bias.HVector + hiddenNode.Error * hiddenNode.Bias.Weight;

    member this.CalculateErrors desiredResults =
        Seq.zip this.OutputLayer desiredResults
        |> Seq.iter (fun (outputNode, v) ->
                        outputNode.Error <-
                            (v - outputNode.Output) * sigmoidDerivative(outputNode.
Output))

        for hiddenNode in this.HiddenLayer do
            hiddenNode.Error <-
                this.OutputLayer
                |> Seq.sumBy (fun n ->
                                let weight = n.Input.[hiddenNode].Weight
                                (n.Error * weight) * sigmoidDerivative(hiddenNode.
Output))

    member this.BackPropagation(input, expected) =
        this.Prepare(input)
        this.Pulse()
        this.CalculateErrors(expected)
        this.Calculate()

    member this.Inputs with get(i) = this.InputLayer.[i]
    member this.Output with get(i) = this.OutputLayer.[i]

    member this.GetOutputs() =
        [ for output in this.OutputLayer do yield output.Output ]

    member this.PrepareInput(input:float list) =
        Seq.zip this.InputLayer input
        |> Seq.iter (fun (a, b) -> a.Output <- b)
```

Listing 7-53 shows how to create, train, and test the neural network. The test module creates the neural network. The neural network needs to be trained first. The neural network is trained using the input and output data set. The training data helps the neural network build up the relationship between input and output. Once this relationship is established, it can generate correct results even when the input data is not in the training data set.

LISTING 7-53 Training and testing neural network

```
module Test =
    let high = 0.99
    let low = 0.01
    let mid = 0.5
    let rate = 3.4
    let input = [ [high; high]; [low; high]; [high; low]; [low; low] ]
    let output = [ [low]; [high]; [high]; [low] ]
    let mutable cont = true

    let net = NeuralNet()
    net.Initialize(2, 2, 1)
    let mutable count = 0
    while cont do
        count <- count + 1
        net.Train(input, output, 5)

        net.PrepareInput([low; low])
        net.Pulse()
        let [ll] = net.GetOutputs()

        net.PrepareInput([high; low])
        net.Pulse()
        let [hl] = net.GetOutputs()

        net.PrepareInput([low; high])
        net.Pulse()
        let [lh] = net.GetOutputs()

        net.PrepareInput([high; high])
        net.Pulse()
        let [hh] = net.GetOutputs()

        cont <- hh > (mid + low) / 2.
                    || lh < (mid + high) / 2.
                    || hl < (mid + low) / 2.
                    || ll > (mid + high)/2.

    net.PrepareInput([high; low])
    let [v] = net.GetOutputs()
    let result = v < 0.5
```

Using the Continuation Passing Style

Continuation passing style (CPS) is a way to rewrite recursive functions to avoid stack overflow problem. Many samples in this chapter use recursive functions. Recursive functions make the code tidy and easy to understand; however, careless use of them can cause stack overflow problems. A stack overflow occurs when a function call continuously adds elements to the stack until the limited memory that is allocated to the stack is depleted.

One way to solve the stack overflow problem is to make sure the function is a *tail call*. A tail call is a function at the tail position. According to the F# team blog (*http://blogs.msdn.com/b/fsharpteam/ archive/2011/07/08/tail-calls-in-fsharp.aspx*), the tail position is defined recursively as

- The body of a function or method

- The body of an action in a *match* expression, where the *match* expression is in the tail position

- The body of an *if*, *elif*, or *else* branch, where the conditional expression is in the tail position

- The last expression in a sequence, where the sequence is in the tail position

- The body of a *let* or *let rec* binding, where the binding expression is in the tail position

The tail call can be executed without allocating extra function frames on the call stack, and it will not have stack overflow problems at runtime. And it can be optimized by the compiler and converted to a loop. Listing 7-54 shows a few tail-position samples.

LISTING 7-54 Tail-position samples

```
fun x -> tailCallFunction x

fun x -> if <BooleanExpression> then
             tailCallFunction()
         else
             tailCallFunction2()
```

> **Note** The tail position does not imply that the tail call is at the end of the function. The function *sum* in the following sample is not in the tail position. The last operation in the function is + and invoking the sum will create an extra function frame on the call stack (re-sulting in a stack overflow in certain scenarios):
>
> ```
> let rec sum = function
>     | [] -> 0
>     | h::t -> h + sum t
> ```

Another solution is to use continuation passing style (CPS). CPS passes the control explicitly in the form of a continuation. From the definition from Wikipedia (*http://en.wikipedia.org/wiki/- Continuation-passing_style*), a function written in CPS takes an extra argument called a *continuation*. When the CPS function has computed its result value, it returns by invoking the continuation function.

Listing 7-55 shows how to use recursion to find the sum of a list of numbers. It has three modules. The first module is a recursive version that can run into a stack overflow problem. The second module is a tail-call version. The last module, *CPSModule*, is CPS version, which also uses tail calls.

LISTING 7-55 Sum list using recursion, tail calls, and CPS

Recursive version

```
module RecursiveModule =
    let l = [1..1000000]

    let rec sum l =
        match l with
        | [] -> 0
        | h::t -> h + sum t

    sum l
```

Tail call and CPS version

```
module TailCallModule =
    let l = [1..1000000]

    let rec sum l acc =
        match l with
        | [] -> acc
        | h::t -> sum t (acc + h)

    let res() = sum l 0

module CPSModule =
    let l = [1..1000000]

    let rec sum l cont =
        match l with
        | [] -> cont 0
        | h::t ->
            let afterSum v =
                cont (h+v)
            sum t afterSum

    sum l id
```

Note The recursive version generates a stack overflow exception when processing a large list.

The tail-call and CPS versions can be executed in FSI without generating a stack overflow. When the CPS code is compiled in Visual Studio, make sure the Generate Tail Calls check box in the project properties is selected:

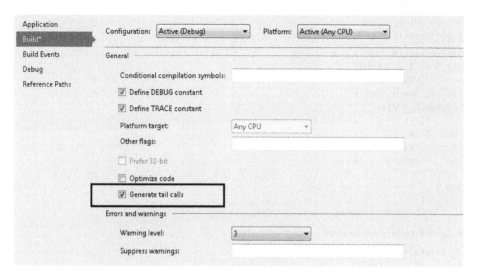

Now I'll demonstrate how to convert from the recursive version to the CPS version. During the conversion process, the intermediate code at some steps might not compile. (See Listing 7-56.)

- Step 1 uses a variable to hold the function return value.

- Step 2 adds the continuation function to the sum function and converts the return statement h+r to cont(h+r).

- Step 3 is used to convert the recursive function call inside. It consists of three substeps:

- Define the *afterSum* function.

- Move cont (h+v) inside the *afterSum* function

- Use sum t afterSum to replace cont(h+v), which has already been moved inside *afterSum*.

LISTING 7-56 Converting the recursive code to CPS

```
Step 1: Introduce a variable
module RecursiveModule =
    let l = [1..1000000]

    let rec sum l =
        match l with
        | [] -> 0
        | h::t ->
            let r = sum t
            h + r

    sum l
```

Step 2: Add the continuation function to the sum

```
module RecursiveModule =
    let l = [1..1000000]

    let rec sum l cont =
        match l with
        | [] -> 0
        | h::t ->
            let r = sum t
            cont (h + r)

    sum l
```

Step 3: Convert the recursive function

```
module RecursiveModule =
    let l = [1..1000000]

    let rec sum l cont =
        match l with
        | [] -> cont 0
        | h::t ->
          let afterSum v =
              cont (h + v)
          sum t afterSum

    sum l id
```

Now you can look at a more complex problem: converting a tree traversal to CPS. In a complex scenario such as this, tail recursion isn't an option, but CPS comes to your rescue. Listing 7-57 is used to get the sum of all the node values in a binary tree. It has both a recursive version and a CPS version. The *deepTree* variable in Listing 7-57 is a tree structure; the tree structure is shown in Figure 7-20. If *N* is set to 1,000,000, the tree is very deep and makes the non-CPS code generate a stack overflow exception.

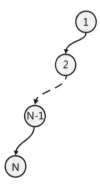

FIGURE 7-20 Deep tree for testing recursive and CPS code

LISTING 7-57 Sum of the tree node values

```
type NodeType = int

type BinaryTree =
    | Nil
    | Node of NodeType * BinaryTree * BinaryTree

let tree n =
    let mutable subTree = Node(1, Nil, Nil)
    for i=0 to n do
        subTree <- Node(1, subTree, Nil)
    subTree

let deepTree = tree 1000000

module TreeModule =
    let rec sum tree =
        match tree with
        | Nil -> 0
        | Node(v, l, r) ->
            let sumL = sum l
            let sumR = sum r
            v + sumL + sumR

    sum deepTree

module TreeCSPModule =
    let rec sum tree cont =
        match tree with
        | Nil -> cont 0
        | Node(v, l, r) ->
            let afterLeft lValue =
                let afterRight rValue =
                    cont (v + lValue + rValue)
                sum r afterRight
            sum l afterLeft

    sum deepTree id
```

Now I'll demonstrate how to convert from the recursive version to the CPS version; see Listing 7-58. During the conversion process, the intermediate code at some steps might not compile.

LISTING 7-58 Converting a tree traversal to CPS

Step 1: Add a continuation function

```
module TreeModule =
    let rec sum tree cont =
        match tree with
        | Nil -> 0
```

```
        | Node(v, l, r) ->
             let sumL = sum l
             let sumR = sum r
             cont (v + sumL + sumR)

    sum deepTree id
```

Step 2: Introduce *afterRight*, and use it as a continuation

```
module TreeModule =
    let rec sum tree cont =
        match tree with
        | Nil -> 0
        | Node(v, l, r) ->
             let sumL = sum l
             // let sumR = sum r
             let afterRight rValue =
                  cont (v + sumL + rValue)
             sum r afterRight

    sum deepTree id
```

Step 3: Introduce *afterLeft*, and use it as a continuation

```
module TreeModule =
    let rec sum tree cont =
        match tree with
        | Nil -> 0
        | Node(v, l, r) ->
             //let sumL = sum l
             let afterLeft lValue =
                  let afterRight rValue =
                       cont (v + lValue + rValue)
                  sum r afterRight
             sum l afterLeft

    sum deepTree id
```

 Note The *id* function is passed in as argument to the function *sum*.

Using the preceding steps, you can convert the recursive Fibonacci function to a CPS version. Both versions are shown in Listing 7-59.

LISTING 7-59 Recursive and CPS Fibonacci functions

```
module FibModule =
    let rec fib x =
        match x with
        | _ when x = 1I -> 1I
        | _ when x = 2I -> 1I
        | _ -> ( fib (x - 1I) ) + (fib (x - 2I) )

    fib 30I

module FibCPSModule =
    let rec fib x cont =
        match x with
        | _ when x = 1I -> cont 1I
        | _ when x = 2I -> cont 1I
        | _ ->
            let after1 a =
                let after2 b =
                    cont(a + b)
                fib (x - 2I) after2
            fib (x - 1I) after1

    fib 30I id
```

Working with HTML5 and WebSharper

In addition to using F# for portable library development, you can use it to build modern web applications. One great option for building web applications with F# is a framework named WebSharper. WebSharper can be downloaded from *http://www.websharper.com/home*. It supports not only web development, but also development of mobile applications. Let's start with a simple ASP.NET web sample.

Creating an ASP.NET Website with WebSharper

After you successfully install WebSharper, a bunch of new project templates appear under the Visual F# node in the New Project dialog box, as shown in Figure 7-21.

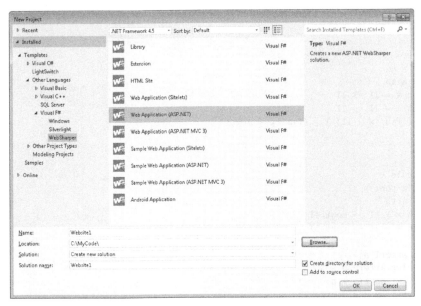

FIGURE 7-21 The WebSharper project options in the New Project dialog box

The generated solution contains two projects. One is the website, and the other is the F# class library where you can define how the webpage will look. The solution structure is shown in Figure 7-22.

FIGURE 7-22 ASP.NET WebSharper solution structure

The first task is to implement an interactive webpage that takes input and generates output. When a user clicks the button, the input string is shown in a label on the page. The code is shown in Listing 7-60. The *Main* function in the *ScriptModule* module defines elements that will be shown on the page. The *input* is a text box that takes the user input, and *output* is where the output should be shown. The *Button*'s *OnClick* event is triggered when a user clicks the button. This event causes the value entered in the text box to be displayed in the output label. The execution result is shown in Figure 7-23.

LISTING 7-60 F# code for WebSharper ASP.NET control

```
namespace Website

open IntelliFactory.WebSharper
open IntelliFactory.WebSharper.Html

module ScriptModule =
    [<JavaScript>]
    let Main() =
        let input = Input [Attr.Type "Text"]
        let output = Label []
        Div [
            input
            Button [Text "Click Me!"]
            |>! OnClick (fun e args ->
                        output.Text <- input.Value)
            output
        ]

type MyControl() =
    inherit Web.Control()

    [<JavaScript>]
    override this.Body = ScriptModule.Main() :> _
```

FIGURE 7-23 Execution result from the ASP.NET site project

It is illusory that F# code is executed in this example. In reality, most of the F# code in Listing 7-61 is translated to JavaScript during the compilation process. This generated JavaScript is placed in a file located under the Web\Scripts folder of the web project. The content of the file WebSite.dll.js that was generated from our example is shown in the listing.

LISTING 7-61 Generated JavaScript code

```
(function()
{
 var Global=this,Runtime=this.IntelliFactory.Runtime,Website,ScriptModule,WebSharper,Html,
Default,List,T,EventsPervasives;
 Runtime.Define(Global,{
  Website:{
   MyControl:Runtime.Class({
    get_Body:function()
    {
```

CHAPTER 7 Portable Library and HTML/JavaScript **457**

```
      return ScriptModule.Main();
    }
  }),
  ScriptModule:{
   Main:function()
   {
    var input,_this,output,x,_this1,x1,f,x2;
    input=Default.Input(List.ofArray([(_this=Default.Attr(),_this.
NewAttr("type","Text"))]));
    output=(x=Runtime.New(T,{
     $:0
    }),(_this1=Default.Tags(),_this1.NewTag("label",x)));
    return Default.Div(List.ofArray([input,(x1=Default.Button(List.ofArray([Default.
Text("Click
Me!")])),(f=(x2=function()
    {
     return function()
     {
      return output.set_Text(input.get_Value());
     };
    },function(arg10)
    {
     return EventsPervasives.Events().OnClick(x2,arg10);
    }),(f(x1),x1))),output]));
   }
  }
 }
});
Runtime.OnInit(function()
{
 Website=Runtime.Safe(Global.Website);
 ScriptModule=Runtime.Safe(Website.ScriptModule);
 WebSharper=Runtime.Safe(Global.IntelliFactory.WebSharper);
 Html=Runtime.Safe(WebSharper.Html);
 Default=Runtime.Safe(Html.Default);
 List=Runtime.Safe(WebSharper.List);
 T=Runtime.Safe(List.T);
 return EventsPervasives=Runtime.Safe(Html.EventsPervasives);
});
Runtime.OnLoad(function()
{
});
}());
```

Using a Formlet Type to Get Input and Generate Output

Listing 7-60 showed how to use basic input and output with WebSharper. In this section, Listing 7-62
shows how to use a formlet. The UI in Figure 7-24 consists of two parts. One part, which is bound
to the value named *formlet*, is a form with a name input and country selection. The other part is
the output, which is used to show the process result. The variable output is the control showing the
result. The formlet can be further broken down to two formlets: *nameF* and *countryF*. Because of the
declarative nature of F# code, *nameF* is a control receiving input and being enhanced with validation

logic, a Validation icon, and a *TextLabel*. The data received by *nameF* and *countryF* are passed into the callback function defined in `Formlet.Yield (fun name data -> {Name = name; Country = data})`. The callback function takes two parameters, which return from *nameF* and *countryF* and form a *Person* record defined at the beginning of the source code.

LISTING 7-62 Using a formlet with WebSharper

```
namespace Website

open IntelliFactory.WebSharper
open IntelliFactory.WebSharper.Html
open IntelliFactory.WebSharper.Formlet
open IntelliFactory.WebSharper.Formlet.Controls

module ScriptModule =
    type Person = {
        Name: string
        Country: string
    }

    [<Rpc>]
    let countries() =
        [ "USA", "From USA"; "Canada", "From Canada"; "UK", "From United Kingdom" ]

    [<JavaScript>]
    let PersonFormlet () : Formlet<Person> =
        let nameF =
            Controls.Input ""
            |> Validator.IsNotEmpty "Empty name not allowed"
            |> Enhance.WithValidationIcon
            |> Enhance.WithTextLabel "Name"
        let countryF =
            Select 0 (countries())
            |> Enhance.WithTextLabel "Country"
        Formlet.Yield (fun name data -> {Name = name; Country = data})
        <*> nameF
        <*> countryF
        |> Enhance.WithSubmitAndResetButtons
        |> Enhance.WithLegend "Add a New Person"
        |> Enhance.WithFormContainer

    [<JavaScript>]
    let Main () =
        let p = PersonFormlet()
        let output = Label []
        let formlet = Formlet.Run (fun data -> output.Text <- string data.Name + ":" +
string
 data.Country) p
        Div [
            formlet
            output :> _
        ]
```

```
type MyControl() =
    inherit Web.Control()

    [<JavaScript>]
    override this.Body = ScriptModule.Main() :> _
```

Note The segment output :> _ is used to convert the output to a Formlet type. The segment :> _ tells the F# type inference system to figure out the type.

Because *sprintf* is not supported in WebSharper, you need to use code such as the following to convert to a string:

```
string data.Name + ":" + string data.Country
```

John:From United Kingdom

FIGURE 7-24 Execution result from the formlet sample in Listing 7-62

Using a Formlet Type as a Wizard

In this section, you will expand the previous sample to get more personal information, such as phone number and ID number. The ID number of a person from the USA is the Social Security Number (SSN), while Canada and UK use the Social Insurance Number (SIN) and National Insurance number (NI). Depending on the input from the user, the UI changes appropriately. The execution results are shown in Figure 7-25 and Figure 7-26. If the user selects Canada, the next page will show SIN as the ID type. The *MorePersonalInfo* formlet takes an ID name and uses it to display the appropriate label on the UI. The *Rpc* attribute in the code provides a seamless way to interact with the server. (See Listing 7-63.)

LISTING 7-63 Using a formlet as a wizard and to create seamless interactions with the server

```
namespace Website

open IntelliFactory.WebSharper
open IntelliFactory.WebSharper.Html
open IntelliFactory.WebSharper.Formlet
open IntelliFactory.WebSharper.Formlet.Controls
```

```
module ScriptModule =

    type Person = {
        Name: string
        Country: string
        Phone: string
        IDNumber: string
    }
    with
        member this.Output() =
            let output = "("
                                + string this.Name + "; "
                                + string this.Country + ";"
                                + string this.Phone + ";"
                                + string this.IDNumber + ";"
                            + ")"
            output


    [<Rpc>]
    let countries() =
        [ "USA", "SSN"; "Canada", "SIN"; "UK", "NI" ]

    [<JavaScript>]
    let PersonFormlet () : Formlet<Person> =
        let nameF =
            Controls.Input ""
            |> Validator.IsNotEmpty "Empty name not allowed"
            |> Enhance.WithValidationIcon
            |> Enhance.WithTextLabel "Name"
        let countryF =
            Select 0 (countries())
            |> Enhance.WithTextLabel "Country"
        Formlet.Yield (fun name data -> {Name = name; Country = data; Phone=""; IDNumber =
""})
        <*> nameF
        <*> countryF
        |> Enhance.WithLegend "Add a New Person"
        |> Enhance.WithFormContainer


    [<JavaScript>]
    let MorePersonalInfo idName : Formlet<Person> =
        let phoneF =
            Controls.Input ""
            |> Validator.IsNotEmpty "Please input phone number"
            |> Enhance.WithValidationIcon
            |> Enhance.WithTextLabel "Phone"

        let idF =
            Controls.Input ""
            |> Validator.IsNotEmpty "Please give your id number"
            |> Enhance.WithValidationIcon
            |> Enhance.WithTextLabel idName
```

```
        Formlet.Yield (fun phone id -> {Name = ""; Country = ""; Phone=phone; IDNumber =
id})
        <*> phoneF
        <*> idF
        |> Enhance.WithLegend "Add a New Person"
        |> Enhance.WithFormContainer


    [<JavaScript>]
    let Main () =
        let output = Label []
        let fc = {
                Enhance.FormContainerConfiguration.Default  with
                    Header = "Sample" |> Enhance.FormPart.Text |> Some
                }

        let personF =
            PersonFormlet()
            |> Enhance.WithSubmitAndResetButtons
            |> Enhance.WithCustomFormContainer {
                    fc with
                        Description = "Step1"
                        |> Enhance.FormPart.Text
                        |> Some
                }

        let idF nationality =
            MorePersonalInfo nationality
            |> Enhance.WithSubmitAndResetButtons
            |> Enhance.WithCustomFormContainer {
                    fc with
                        Description = "Step2"
                        |> Enhance.FormPart.Text
                        |> Some
                }

        Formlet.Do {
                    let! p = personF
                    let! i = idF (p.Country)
                    return!
                        Formlet.OfElement (fun () -> Div [Text "Thank you!"])
                        |> Formlet.Map (fun _ -> {Name = p.Name;
                                                  Country = p.Country;
                                                  Phone = i.Phone;
                                                  IDNumber = i.IDNumber})

                }
        |> Formlet.Flowlet
        |> Formlet.Map ignore

type MyControl() =
    inherit Web.Control()

    [<JavaScript>]
    override this.Body = ScriptModule.Main() :> _
```

FIGURE 7-25 Formlet used for the name and country input

FIGURE 7-26 Formlet used for the phone number and ID

Creating an HTML5 Page

As previously mentioned, WebSharper supports generating HTML5 pages. Listing 7-64 shows how to draw two rectangles on an HTML5 *Canvas* element, as shown in Figure 7-27.

LISTING 7-64 Drawing rectangles on an HTML5 *Canvas* element

```
namespace Website

open IntelliFactory.WebSharper
open IntelliFactory.WebSharper.Html
open IntelliFactory.WebSharper.Html5

module ScriptModule =

    [<JavaScript>]
    let example1 (ctx: CanvasRenderingContext2D) =
            ctx.FillStyle <- "rgb(100, 0, 0)"
            ctx.FillRect(10., 10., 50., 50.)
            ctx.FillStyle <- "rgba(0, 0, 100, 0.5)"
            ctx.FillRect(30., 30., 50., 50.)

    [<JavaScript>]
    let Main() =
        let element = HTML5.Tags.Canvas []
```

```
        let canvas  = As<CanvasElement> element.Dom
        canvas.Height <-100
        canvas.Width <- 100
        example1(canvas.GetContext "2d")
        Div [Attr.Style "float: center"] -< [
            element
        ]

type MyControl() =
    inherit Web.Control()

    [<JavaScript>]
    override this.Body = ScriptModule.Main() :> _
```

FIGURE 7-27 Rectangles on an HTML5 canvas

The combination of WebSharper and F# can provide nice animations. In Listing 7-65, a rectangle is drawn and moved progressively from the left side to the right.

LISTING 7-65 HTML5 animation

```
open System
open IntelliFactory.WebSharper
open IntelliFactory.WebSharper.Html
open IntelliFactory.WebSharper.Html5

module CanvasAnimation =
    [<JavaScript>]
    let AnimatedCanvas draw width height caption =
        let element = Tags.NewTag "Canvas" []
        let canvas  = As<CanvasElement> element.Dom
        canvas.Width  <- width
        canvas.Height <- height
        let ctx = canvas.GetContext "2d"
        let timeStep = ref 0
        let rec loop =
            async {
                do! Async.Sleep 50
                do draw(ctx, !timeStep)
                do timeStep := !timeStep + 1
                do! loop
            }
```

```
        draw(ctx, !timeStep)
        Async.Start loop
        Div [ Width (string width); Attr.Style "float:left" ] -< [
            Div [ Attr.Style "float:center" ] -< [
                element
                P [Align "center"] -< [
                    I [Text <| "Example " + caption]
                ]
            ]
        ]

    [<JavaScript>]
    let Main () =
        let example1 (ctx: CanvasRenderingContext2D, time:int) =
            ctx.Save()
            let previous = time - 1
            ctx.ClearRect(float previous, 20., 20., 20.)
            ctx.Rect(float time, 20., 20., 20.)
            ctx.FillRect(float time, 20., 20., 20.)
            ctx.Restore()

        Div [
            AnimatedCanvas example1 150 150 "1"
            Div [Attr.Style "clear:both"]
        ]

type MyCanvasAnimationViewer() =
    inherit Web.Control()
    [<JavaScript>]
    override this.Body = CanvasAnimation.Main () :> _
```

 Note The .aspx page needs to be updated to reflect the *MyCanvasAnimationViewer* type name.

WebSharper provides a nice way to use F# to build web solutions. However, WebSharper enables complex algorithms designed in F# and renders the result with HTML5. Here are the benefits of using WebSharper:

- It's a single language used for the full web stack. Image you have some existing .NET or F# algorithm implementation. WebSharper can make the development much easier and more efficient.

- The inconsistency between the browsers is taken care of by the framework.

It automatically takes advantage of emerging technologies such as HTML5.

CHAPTER 8

Cloud and Service Programming with F#

Cloud services provide online resources to host a company's business platform. The cloud solution is cost effective because there is no need for a company to maintain and manage the standalone hardware and software associated with hosting a solution. Because the data shared on the cloud can be accessed anywhere in the world, you can easily coordinate work with offshore teams or provide the data to different devices and geographic locations without incurring the capital expenditure that would normally be required.

Cloud computing also provides a scalable framework. Consider, for example, a company in the US that provides tax-preparation services. From March to April is the busiest time of year for the company. During this period, the company needs more computing power than at any other time of the year. A cloud service provider can offer computing power to the business in a more flexible way. Because the cloud lowers a company's computing expenses, the company can focus more on innovation within its core business.

To understand the importance of cloud computing, just look at the investment in it by big companies such as Microsoft and Google—it is clear that cloud computing is the next big thing. For a global company that has data distributed at different locations, the cloud allows computations to span different CPU cores as well as different virtual machines. It is well known that successful distributed or parallel computations need a combination of novel algorithm design, computation abstraction, and programming implementation. This requires a language that can work well on all of these fronts. F# is perfect for this task. Let's start with the basics of Microsoft Windows Azure.

Introducing Windows Azure

Windows Azure is Microsoft's cloud-computing platform. Developers can use Windows Azure to develop, publish, and manage applications. The applications are then hosted at Microsoft datacenters across the world. The application running on Windows Azure can be implemented with different programming languages. This section covers a few key concepts in Windows Azure application development, including cloud queue, WCF service, blob storage, and SQL Azure. More detailed information about Azure can be found at *http://www.windowsazure.com*.

Setting Up Your Environment

To develop a Windows Azure application, you need a Windows Azure account, which can be acquired from the aforementioned website. Figure 8-1 shows the initial page you see when signing up for a Windows Azure account.

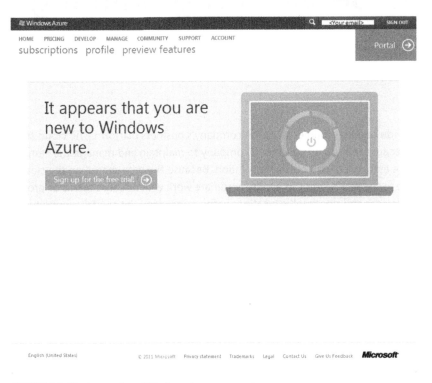

FIGURE 8-1 Signing up for a Windows Azure account

Once you sign in with your Windows LiveID, you can take advantage of the free trial offer, as shown in Figure 8-2.

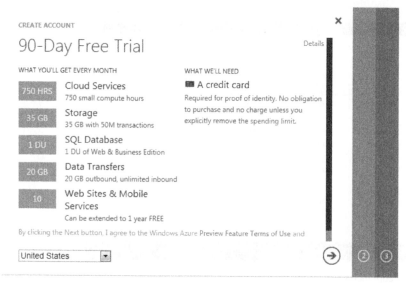

FIGURE 8-2 Free trial offer from Windows Azure

After the account is set up, you can log in to the management portal where most of the configuration and management tasks are performed. The login page is shown in Figure 8-3.

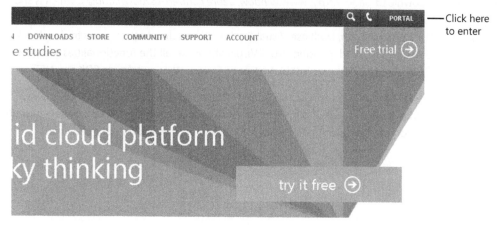

FIGURE 8-3 Logging in to the management portal

From the management portal, shown in Figure 8-4, you can perform management tasks such as configuring a database. Now you have a place to host your application when it is ready.

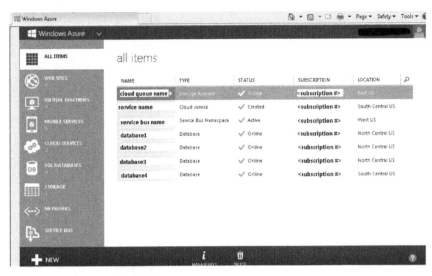

FIGURE 8-4 Windows Azure management portal

You are now ready to start development-related tasks. There are a few options for interacting with Azure through code. The easiest approach for a .NET developer is to use the Windows Azure Software Development Kit (SDK) for .NET. The Windows Azure SDK for .NET can be downloaded from the .NET section download page (*http://www.windowsazure.com/en-us/downloads/*), which is shown in Figure 8-7. The Windows Azure SDK for .NET can work with Microsoft Visual Studio 2010 and Visual Studio 2012. In this chapter, I will use Visual Studio 2012 to demonstrate how to develop Azure applications. The Azure SDK is independent from Visual Studio, so all the functionalities are the same in Visual Studio 2010. Figure 8-5 shows installation page for the Windows Azure SDK for .NET.

Windows Azure SDK for .NET is installed by using Microsoft Web Platform Installer 4.5. If you installed Visual Studio 2012, the Web Platform Installer has already been installed on your computer. The standalone version can be downloaded from *http://www.microsoft.com/web/downloads/platform.aspx*.

FIGURE 8-5 Windows Azure SDK for .NET installation in progress

The installation process adds the following components to your system, as shown in Figure 8-6:

- ASP.NET Web Pages 2

- Microsoft SQL Server 2012 Data-Tier Application Framework (DACFx) for x86

- SQL Server Data Tools - Build Utilities

- Microsoft Web Tooling 1.1 for Visual Studio 2012

- Windows Azure Emulator 1.8

- Windows Azure Tools 1.8 for Microsoft Visual Studio 2012

- Windows Azure Authoring Tools 1.8

- Windows Azure Libraries for .NET 1.8

- LightSwitch Azure Publishing 2.0 add-on for Visual Studio 2012

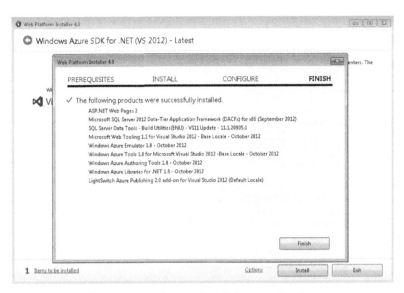

FIGURE 8-6 Window Azure SDK for .NET installation completed

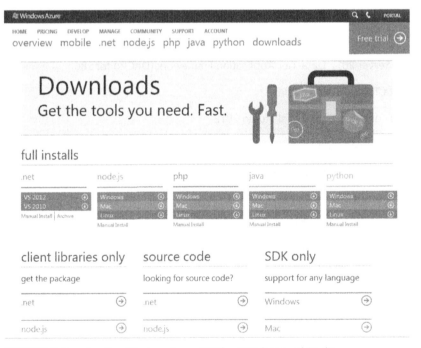

FIGURE 8-7 Downloading Windows Azure SDK for .NET for Visual Studio

Developing a Windows Azure Application

After successfully installing the .NET Azure SDK, you can start to create your first Windows Azure application. The Azure SDK supports creating several types of projects. In this sample, you will create a Windows Azure cloud service. The location to create a Windows Azure Cloud Service project is under the Visual C# language node, as shown in Figure 8-8.

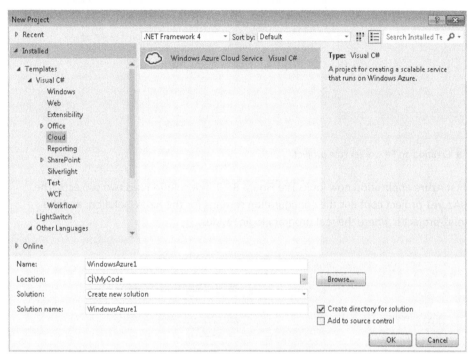

FIGURE 8-8 Creating a Windows Azure Cloud Service project in Visual Studio

After you select the project and click OK, a new dialog box (shown in Figure 8-9) is displayed, which you can use to add information about the Azure Cloud Service project. As part of the Cloud Service project, you need to create a Worker role that performs background processing service. The worker role code is the project hosting the processing code. You need to select the F# Worker Role project in this dialog box. A worker role project is used to create a background processing service. You can change the project name by clicking WorkerRole1 once. For the purpose of this demo, let's use the default name, WorkerRole1.

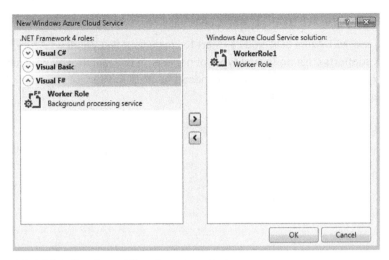

FIGURE 8-9 Creating an F# worker role project

Your first Azure application now looks like Figure 8-10. The solution has two projects. The WindowsAzure1 project contains the configuration settings for the Azure solution, and the WorkerRole1 project is where the real program logic resides.

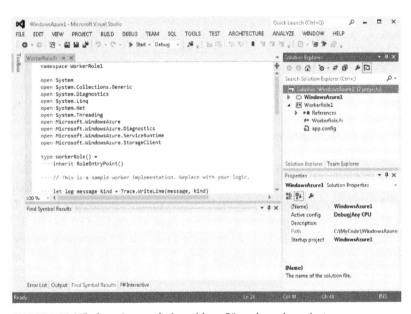

FIGURE 8-10 Windows Azure solution with an F# worker role project

The complete code for the worker-role processing logic is shown in Listing 8-1. The *WorkerRole* class inherits from *RoleEntryPoint* and overrides two methods. The *Run* method, like its name suggests, hosts the execution logic. Because the service is expected to run for an infinite amount of time, it is not surprising to see that the rudimentary code, found in the *Run* method, contains an infinite *while* loop. The *OnStart* method configures the service before it starts. The default code sets the connection limit to 12.

LISTING 8-1 Default F# worker role code

```
namespace WorkerRole1

open System
open System.Collections.Generic
open System.Diagnostics
open System.Linq
open System.Net
open System.Threading
open Microsoft.WindowsAzure
open Microsoft.WindowsAzure.Diagnostics
open Microsoft.WindowsAzure.ServiceRuntime
open Microsoft.WindowsAzure.StorageClient

type WorkerRole() =
    inherit RoleEntryPoint()

    // This is a sample worker implementation. Replace with your logic.
    let log message kind = Trace.WriteLine(message, kind)

    override wr.Run() =
        log "WorkerRole1 entry point called" "Information"
        while(true) do
            Thread.Sleep(10000)
            log "Working" "Information"

    override wr.OnStart() =
        // Set the maximum number of concurrent connections
        ServicePointManager.DefaultConnectionLimit <- 12

        // For information on handling configuration changes
        // see the MSDN topic at http://go.microsoft.com/fwlink/?LinkId=166357.
        base.OnStart()
```

You can hit F5 to run the application in the local Compute emulator. For a simple program like this, there is little effort needed for debugging.

You are now ready to deploy your application to the Windows Azure environment. Right-click on the WindowsAzure1 project, and select the menu item Publishing. You use this action to deploy the current solution to Azure. If this is the first time you have published an Azure application, you will need to download and import your credentials file. Figure 8-11 shows the Publish Windows Azure Application Wizard.

FIGURE 8-11 Publish Windows Azure Application Wizard

> **Note** Once an application is published to the Azure environment, the application is considered to be running and starts to be counted as computation time, even if the program does nothing. Therefore, it is recommended that you debug and fully test the application on your local computer before publishing.

Your HelloWorld-like application is ready. In the next section, you will go through several F# Azure examples.

Azure Cloud Queue

A *queue* is an abstract linear data structure. It is a first-in, first-out (FIFO) structure, in which the newest addition is inserted at the end of the queue and an item can be removed only at the beginning of the queue. The Azure Cloud Queue service is designed to store a large amount of data. The queue can be accessed from anywhere in the world (using an HTTP or HTTPS connection).

According to the MSDN documentation (*http://msdn.microsoft.com/en-us/library/windowsazure/hh767287.aspx*), the cloud queue should be used when any of the following scenarios apply to your application:

- You need to store messages of a combined size greater than or equal to 5 GB in a queue and the messages need to be kept in the queue for no more than one week.

- You need flexible leasing to process messages. This allows the worker process or processes to come back after an extended period of time to resume the processing of messages. This would not be possible with a short lease time. Additionally, worker processes can extend the lease time if the processing time is longer than expected.

- You need to track the progress of message processing. This enables other worker processes to resume message processing when another process is interrupted.

- You need server-side log information about all transaction activity on the queue.

In this section, I am going to implement a simple queue. The sample solution AzureQueueSample contains two projects in addition to the standard Azure configuration project. One is the worker project, which inserts a message into the queue, and the other is the consumer project named ConsumerProject, which takes the message from the queue. Because there is no UI work, two F# worker role projects are sufficient. I create two projects and call them WorkerRole project and ConsumerRole project. The project creation dialog box is shown in Figure 8-12.

FIGURE 8-12 Creating the WorkerRole and ConsumerRole projects

After you create these two projects, you can go to the AzureQueueSample Role folder to configure the queue connection strings. Right-click the WorkerRole node, and select Property to show the configuration menu. The queue connection string can be set in the Settings area. Create the connection string by clicking the Add Setting button. Figure 8-13 shows the default string that is created after you click this button. You can now rename the default string to **MyConnectionString** and set its type to Connection String.

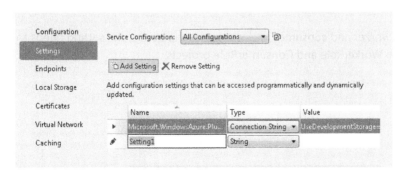

FIGURE 8-13 Adding a string to the project settings

You can click the button with the ellipsis (...) to set the connection string. You should first debug the program locally rather than initially targeting to the real Azure environment. Figure 8-14 shows the Storage Account Connection String dialog box. By default, the Azure project is set to use the Windows Azure storage emulator.

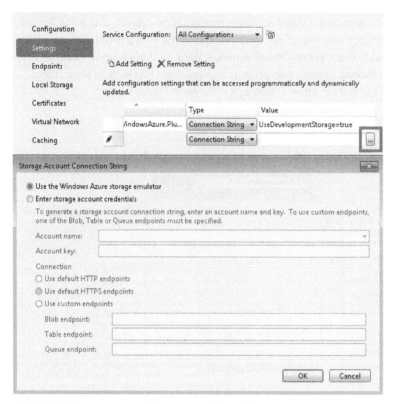

FIGURE 8-14 Storage Account Connection String dialog box

Accept this default setting by clicking OK and name the connection string as *MyConnectionString*. Figure 8-15 shows the WorkerRole project settings. The connection string is set to use development storage. The setting is stored in the .csdef files in the project in XML format. Although these XML files can be modified manually, beginners should use the Settings dialog box.

> **Note** Because both worker and consumer projects access the queue, the setting needs to be made on both the WorkerRole and ConsumerRole projects.

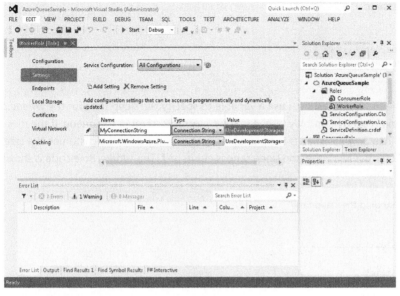

FIGURE 8-15 Project settings for the WorkerRole project

These are some of the Azure cloud queue operations used in the sample:

- Create a queue

```
let queueClient = storageAccount.CreateCloudQueueClient()
let queue = queueClient.GetQueueReference("myqueue")

queue.CreateIfNotExist()
```

- Add a message to the queue

```
let message = CloudQueueMessage("Hello, World")
queue.AddMessage(message)
```

- Peek at the message from the queue, and show the message as a string

```
let peekedMessage = queue.PeekMessage()
if (peekedMessage <> null) then
    let msg = queue.GetMessage()
    log msg.AsString "Information"
```

- Dequeue a message

```
let msg = queue.GetMessage()
queue.DeleteMessage(msg)
```

To make this sample more interesting, I use a variable to specify the sleep time for the *Thread.Sleep* function. The sleep time is set dynamically by the current message count in the queue. If the message count is greater than 3, which means there are plenty of messages for the customer, the sleep time is increased by 100 ms. Otherwise, the sleep time is cut in half. The WorkerRole code is shown in Listing 8-2.

LISTING 8-2 Code for changing the sleep time

```
namespace WorkerRole1

open System.Diagnostics
open System.Net
open System.Threading
open Microsoft.WindowsAzure
open Microsoft.WindowsAzure.ServiceRuntime
open Microsoft.WindowsAzure.StorageClient

type WorkerRole() =
    inherit RoleEntryPoint()

    // This is a sample worker implementation. Replace with your logic.
    let log message kind = Trace.WriteLine(message, kind)

    override wr.Run() =

        log "WorkerRole1 entry point called" "Information"

        let connectionStringName = "MyConnectionString"
        let storageAccount =
CloudStorageAccount.Parse(CloudConfigurationManager.GetSetting(connectionStringName))
        let queueClient = storageAccount.CreateCloudQueueClient()
        let queue = queueClient.GetQueueReference("myqueue")

        ignore <| queue.CreateIfNotExist()
        let mutable sleepTime = 1000
        while(true) do
            Thread.Sleep(sleepTime)

            let message = CloudQueueMessage("Hello, World")
            queue.AddMessage(message)
            log "add new message" "Information"
```

```
            let queueSize = queue.RetrieveApproximateMessageCount()
            sleepTime <- if queueSize > 3 then
                                 sleepTime + 100
                          else
                                 max (sleepTime / 2) 1

            let msg = sprintf "Current Sleep time is %A" sleepTime
            log msg "Information"

    override wr.OnStart() =

        // Set the maximum number of concurrent connections
        ServicePointManager.DefaultConnectionLimit <- 12

        // For information on handling configuration changes
        // see the MSDN topic at http://go.microsoft.com/fwlink/?LinkId=166357.
        base.OnStart()
```

 Note To prevent *sleepTime* from being set to *0*, a *max* function is used to make sure *sleepTime*'s minimum value is *1*.

Microsoft.WindowsAzure.Configuration.dll needs to be added to the project references.

Compared to the WorkerRole code, the ConsumerRole code is simpler. The consumer project's job is to check the message queue for messages every 200 milliseconds (ms). If there is a message, the consumer project will dequeue and print the message. The complete code for ConsumerRole is shown in Listing 8-3.

LISTING 8-3 ConsumerRole code

```
namespace ConsumerRole

open System.Diagnostics
open System.Net
open System.Threading
open Microsoft.WindowsAzure
open Microsoft.WindowsAzure.ServiceRuntime
open Microsoft.WindowsAzure.StorageClient

type WorkerRole() =
    inherit RoleEntryPoint()

    // This is a sample worker implementation. Replace with your logic.

    let log message kind = Trace.WriteLine(message, kind)

    override wr.Run() =
        log "ConsumerRole entry point called" "Information"
```

```
        let connectionStringName = "MyConnectionString"
        let storageAccount =
CloudStorageAccount.Parse(CloudConfigurationManager.GetSetting(connectionStringName))
        let queueClient = storageAccount.CreateCloudQueueClient()
        let queue = queueClient.GetQueueReference("myqueue")
        ignore <| queue.CreateIfNotExist()

        while(true) do
            Thread.Sleep(200)
            // Peek at the next message
            let peekedMessage = queue.PeekMessage()
            if (peekedMessage <> null) then
                let msg = queue.GetMessage()
                log msg.AsString "Information"
                queue.DeleteMessage(msg)
            else
                log "no message" "Information"
                ()

    override wr.OnStart() =
        // Set the maximum number of concurrent connections
        ServicePointManager.DefaultConnectionLimit <- 12

        // For information on handling configuration changes
        // see the MSDN topic at http://go.microsoft.com/fwlink/?LinkId=166357.
        base.OnStart()
```

Note *Microsoft.WindowsAzure.Configuration.dll* needs to be added to the project references.

Before executing the code, you need to set the instance number for ConsumerRole and WorkerRole in the Configuration area in the project settings. For test purposes, the ConsumerRole project instance count is set to *1*, so there is only one consumer removing the messages from the queue. The WorkerRole project instance count is set to *3*. Other deployment settings such as VM Size can also be set. For this sample, default values are used. Figure 8-16 shows the settings for the WorkerRole project.

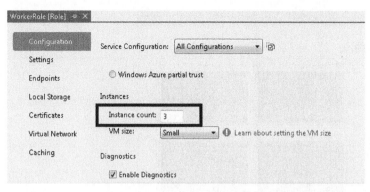

FIGURE 8-16 Setting the instance count number for the WorkerRole project

When the project is executed, the emulator is started first. You can display the emulator by clicking the blue emulator icon in the Windows system tray, which is shown in Figure 8-17.

FIGURE 8-17 Emulator icon

You can display the Compute Emulator UI and Storage Emulator UI options by right-clicking the emulator icon, as shown in Figure 8-18.

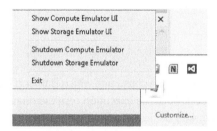

FIGURE 8-18 Displaying the emulator UIs

The Compute Emulator UI shows current running instances. You can see in the left panel in Figure 8-19 that there is 1 consumer role instance and 3 worker role instances. The right panel shows the output from these instances.

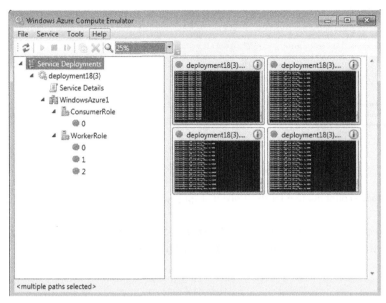

FIGURE 8-19 An example of the Compute Emulator UI

The Storage Emulator UI, shown in Figure 8-20, displays the blob, queue, and table status.

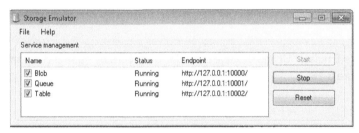

FIGURE 8-20 An example of the Storage Emulator UI

Because there are three workers generating messages and only one consumer, which is taking one message every 200 ms, I expect that the sleep time will be set to 600. The execution result verifies my expectation. After several iterations, the sleep time of the WorkerRole instances is changed to 622 on my computer. The WorkerRole activity information can be viewed in the console window output, which you saw in Figure 8-19.

Note The actual execution result, which is a number, will vary from execution to execution.

Azure WCF Service

Windows Communication Foundation (WCF) is a programming framework for building secure and reliable communication between applications. It is part of the Microsoft .NET Framework and is a unified programming model used to build service-oriented applications. In this section, I am going to present a mortgage calculator, which is a WCF service built to be hosted on the Azure cloud. The complete solution can be downloaded from the F# team sample archive, F# 3.0 Sample pack, at *http://fsharp3sample.codeplex.com/*.

You can access the project by clicking the Source Code tab, AzureSamples, and WcfInWorkerRole, as shown in Figure 8-21.

FIGURE 8-21 WcfInWorkerRole project in the F# 3.0 Sample Pack project on Codeplex

The solution structure is shown in Figure 8-22. There are four projects in the WcfInWorkerRole solution:

- The LoanCalculatorContracts project defines service contracts.

- The WCFWorker project is the F# worker role project that starts and hosts the WCF service.

- The WCFWorkerAzure project is the Azure configuration project.

- The WPFTestApplication project is a C# WPF application used to test the WCF service. This project is a client-side application.

FIGURE 8-22 WCF service sample solution structure

The LoanCalculatorContracts project contains the WCF service and data contract interfaces. Listing 8-4 defines the data contract and service contract interfaces by which the client and service exchange the loan and payment information and perform the computations.

LISTING 8-4 Mortgage calculator data contract and service contract interfaces

```
Data contract interfaces for loan and payment information

/// Record for LoanInformation
[<DataContract>]
type LoanInformation =
    { [<DataMember>] mutable Amount : double
      [<DataMember>] mutable InterestRateInPercent : double
      [<DataMember>] mutable TermInMonth : int }

/// Record for PaymentInformation
[<DataContract>]
type PaymentInformation =
    { [<DataMember>] mutable MonthlyPayment : double
      [<DataMember>] mutable TotalPayment : double }



Service contract interface

[<ServiceContract>]
type public ILoanCalculator =
    /// Use Record to send and receive data
    [<OperationContract>]
    abstract Calculate : a:LoanInformation -> PaymentInformation
```

Note All the interface methods must be given a parameter name—for example, *a:LoanInformation*. Otherwise, the service host will fail to start.

The F# worker role project named WCFWorker implements the *ILoanCalculator* interface. Listing 8-5 shows the implementation code.

LISTING 8-5 *ILoanCalculator* interface implementation

```
namespace WCFWorker

open System
open System.Collections.Generic
open System.Linq
open System.Text
open LoanCalculatorContracts
open System.ServiceModel
open System.Runtime.Serialization

[<ServiceBehavior(AddressFilterMode = AddressFilterMode.Any)>]
type public LoanCalculatorImplementation() =

    member this.Calculate(loan : LoanInformation) = (this :> ILoanCadulator).Calculate
loan

    interface ILoanCalculator with
        override this.Calculate(loan : LoanInformation) =
            let monthlyInterest = Math.Pow((1.0 + loan.InterestRateInPercent / 100.0), 1.0
/ 12.0)
 - 1.0
            let num = loan.Amount * monthlyInterest
            let den = 1.0 - (1.0 / (Math.Pow(1.0 + monthlyInterest, (double)loan.
TermInMonth)))
            let monthlyPayment = num / den

            let totalPayment = monthlyPayment * (double)loan.TermInMonth
            let paymentInformation  = {MonthlyPayment = monthlyPayment;
                                        TotalPayment = totalPayment}

        paymentInformation
```

The worker role execution code is relatively simple. It starts the WCF service and then executes an infinite loop. The WCF service will run and listen for an incoming request, calculate the loan payment, and return the result. The worker role code is shown in Listing 8-6.

LISTING 8-6 Worker role code that starts and hosts the WCF service

```
namespace WCFWorker

open System
open System.Collections.Generic
open System.Diagnostics
open System.Linq
open System.Net
```

```
open System.Threading
open Microsoft.WindowsAzure
open Microsoft.WindowsAzure.Diagnostics
open Microsoft.WindowsAzure.ServiceRuntime
open Microsoft.WindowsAzure.StorageClient
open System.ServiceModel
open System.Runtime.Serialization
open LoanCalculatorContracts

type WorkerRole() as this =
    inherit RoleEntryPoint()

    [<DefaultValue>]
    val mutable serviceHost : ServiceHost

    member private this.CreateServiceHost() =

        this.serviceHost <- new ServiceHost(typeof<LoanCalculatorImplementation>)
        let binding = new NetTcpBinding(SecurityMode.None)
        let externalEndPoint =
                RoleEnvironment.CurrentRoleInstance.InstanceEndpoints.["WCFEndpoint"]
        let endpoint = String.Format("net.tcp://{0}/LoanCalculator",
                                            externalEndPoint.IPEndpoint)
        this.serviceHost.AddServiceEndpoint(typeof<ILoanCadulator>, binding, endpoint)
        |> ignore

        this.serviceHost.Open()

    override wr.Run() =
        while (true) do
                Thread.Sleep(10000)
                Trace.WriteLine("Working", "Information")

    override wr.OnStart() =

        // Set the maximum number of concurrent connections
        ServicePointManager.DefaultConnectionLimit <- 12

        // For information on handling configuration changes
        // see the MSDN topic at http://go.microsoft.com/fwlink/?LinkId=166357.
        this.CreateServiceHost()
        base.OnStart()
```

Azure Blob Storage

The Azure blob storage service is used to store unstructured data whose size can be hundreds of gigabytes (GBs). A storage account can hold up to 100 TBs of blob data. The typical usage for blob storage is to store and share unstructured data such as image, video, and audio files. You can also use it as a way to back up your data. Like the Azure Cloud Queue service, it can be accessed anywhere by using HTTP or HTTPS.

The sample thumbnails in this section can be downloaded from *http://fsharp3sample.codeplex. com/.* You can access the project by clicking the Source Code tab, AzureSamples, and the Thumbnails_ Dev11 folder. Figure 8-23 shows the project.

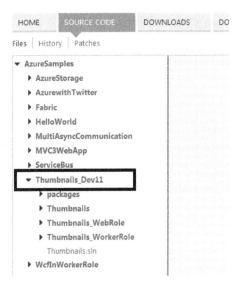

FIGURE 8-23 Thumbnails project in F# 3.0 Sample Pack on Codeplex

The project demonstrates how to use the Azure cloud queue and blob service. The queue is used to transfer the image file path. The blob is used to store the image data. The F# worker role gets the path from the queue, generates a thumbnail, and stores the thumbnail file on the blob. The solution structure is shown in Figure 8-24.

FIGURE 8-24 Thumbnails solution structure

The following basic blob operations are available:

- Create blob client

```
let storageAccount = CloudStorageAccount.Parse(RoleEnvironment.
GetConfigurationSettingValue(
                                   "DataConnectionString"))
let blobStorage = storageAccount.CreateCloudBlobClient()
```

- Create a container, and set permissions

```
let container = blobStorage.GetContainerReference("photogallery")
container.CreateIfNotExist() |> ignore
let mutable permissions = container.GetPermissions()
permissions.PublicAccess <- BlobContainerPublicAccessType.Container
container.SetPermissions(permissions)
```

- Upload blob to container

```
let thumbnail = container.GetBlockBlobReference("thumbnails/" + thumbnailName)
thumbnail.Properties.ContentType <- "image/jpeg"
thumbnail.UploadFromStream(this.CreateThumbnail(image))
```

- Download blob

```
let content = container.GetBlockBlobReference(path)
let image = new MemoryStream()
content.DownloadToStream(image)
```

The solution contains three projects. The Thumbnails project is he Azure configuration. The Thumbnails_WebRole project is a C# web role project for uploading and displaying thumbnails generated from the Thumbnails_WorkerRole project. Thumbnails_WorkerRole is an F# worker role project that does the heavy lifting of the thumbnail image-processing work.

Listing 8-7 shows the F# worker role code. When the role starts and executes the *OnStart* function, it sets up an event handler to process the configuration changes. The *OnRun* function first sets up the blob and queue before going into the infinite loop. Within the loop, the queue is repeatedly checked to see whether there is a message that needs to be processed. If there is a message in the queue, the message is taken and the image specified by the message is turned into a thumbnail image. The thumbnail image then will be uploaded to the blob storage, where a web role can take the thumbnail image and display it.

LISTING 8-7 F# worker role code

```fsharp
namespace Microsoft.Samples.ServiceHosting.Thumbnails

open System
open System.Collections.Generic
open System.Configuration
open System.Diagnostics
open System.Drawing
open System.IO
open System.Text
open System.Linq
open System.Net
open Microsoft.WindowsAzure
open Microsoft.WindowsAzure.Diagnostics
open Microsoft.WindowsAzure.ServiceRuntime
open Microsoft.WindowsAzure.StorageClient

type public WorkerRole() =
    inherit RoleEntryPoint()
    [<DefaultValue>]
    val mutable width : int

    [<DefaultValue>]
    val mutable height : int

    [<DefaultValue>]
    val mutable configSetter : string * bool -> unit

    // function to create thumbnail from a stream
    member private this.CreateThumbnail( input : Stream ) =
        let orig = new Bitmap(input)

        if (orig.Width > orig.Height) then
            this.width <- 128
            this.height <- 128 * orig.Height / orig.Width
        else
            this.height <- 128
            this.width <- 128 * orig.Width / orig.Height

        let thumb = new Bitmap(this.width,this.height)

        use graphic = Graphics.FromImage(thumb)
        graphic.InterpolationMode <-
            System.Drawing.Drawing2D.InterpolationMode.HighQualityBicubic
        graphic.SmoothingMode <- System.Drawing.Drawing2D.SmoothingMode.AntiAlias
        graphic.PixelOffsetMode <- System.Drawing.Drawing2D.PixelOffsetMode.HighQuality

        graphic.DrawImage(orig, 0, 0, this.width, this.height)

        let ms = new MemoryStream()
        thumb.Save(ms,System.Drawing.Imaging.ImageFormat.Jpeg)
        ms.Seek(0L,SeekOrigin.Begin) |> ignore
        ms
```

```
    override this.OnStart() =
        // This code sets up a handler to update CloudStorageAccount
        // instances when their corresponding
        // configuration settings change in the service configuration file.
        CloudStorageAccount.SetConfigurationSettingPublisher(
            new Action<string,Func<string,bool>>(
                fun (configName:string) (configSetter:Func<string,bool>) ->
                    // Provide the configSetter with the initial value
                    configSetter.Invoke(
                        RoleEnvironment.GetConfigurationSettingValue(configName)) |>
ignore
                    RoleEnvironment.Changed.Add(
                        fun (arg : RoleEnvironmentChangedEventArgs) ->
                            let c =
                                arg.Changes.OfType<RoleEnvironmentConfigurationSettingCha
nge>()
                            if (c.Any(fun n -> n.ConfigurationSettingName = configName))
then
                                let cN = RoleEnvironment.GetConfigurationSettingValue(con
figName)
                                if (not (configSetter.Invoke(cN))) then
                                    // In this case, the change to storage account
credentials in
                                    // service configuration is significant enough that
the role
                                    // needs to be recycled in order to use the latest
settings.
                                    // (for example, the endpoint has changed)
                                    RoleEnvironment.RequestRecycle()
                    )
        ))

        base.OnStart()

    override this.Run() =
        let storageAccount =
            CloudStorageAccount.Parse(
                RoleEnvironment.GetConfigurationSettingValue("DataConnectionString"))
        let blobStorage = storageAccount.CreateCloudBlobClient()
        let container = blobStorage.GetContainerReference("photogallery")

        let queueStorage = storageAccount.CreateCloudQueueClient()
        let queue = queueStorage.GetQueueReference("thumbnailmaker")

        Trace.TraceInformation("Creating container and queue...")

        // If the Start() method throws an exception, the role recycles.
        // If this sample is run locally and development storage tool has not been
started, this
        // can cause a number of exceptions to be thrown because roles are restarted
repeatedly.
        // Let's try to create the queue and the container and
        // check whether the storage services are running at all.
        let mutable containerAndQueueCreated = false
```

```
        while(not containerAndQueueCreated) do
            try
                container.CreateIfNotExist() |> ignore
                let mutable permissions = container.GetPermissions()
                permissions.PublicAccess <- BlobContainerPublicAccessType.Container

                container.SetPermissions(permissions)
                permissions <- container.GetPermissions()
                queue.CreateIfNotExist() |> ignore
                containerAndQueueCreated <- true

            with
            | :? StorageClientException as e ->
                    if (e.ErrorCode = StorageErrorCode.TransportError) then
                        Trace.TraceError(
                            String.Format(
                                "Connect failure! The most likely reason is that the local
"+
                                "Development Storage tool is not running or your storage
account
 configuration is incorrect. "+
                                "Message: '{0}'", e.Message))
                        System.Threading.Thread.Sleep(5000)

                    else
                        raise e

        Trace.TraceInformation("Listening for queue messages...")

        // Now that the queue and the container have been created
        // in the preceding initialization process, get messages
        // from the queue and process them individually.
        while (true) do
            try
                let msg = queue.GetMessage()
                if (box(msg) <> null) then
                    let path = msg.AsString
                    let thumbnailName = System.IO.Path.GetFileNameWithoutExtension(path) +
".jpg"

                    Trace.TraceInformation(String.Format("Dequeued '{0}'", path))
                    let content = container.GetBlockBlobReference(path)
                    let thumbnail = container.GetBlockBlobReference("thumbnails/" +
thumbnailName)

                    let image = new MemoryStream()

                    content.DownloadToStream(image)

                    image.Seek(0L, SeekOrigin.Begin) |> ignore
                    thumbnail.Properties.ContentType <- "image/jpeg"
                    thumbnail.UploadFromStream(this.CreateThumbnail(image))

                    Trace.TraceInformation(String.Format("Done with '{0}'", path))

                    queue.DeleteMessage(msg)
```

```
        else
            System.Threading.Thread.Sleep(1000)

        // Explicitly catch all exceptions of type StorageException here
        // because we should be able to
        // recover from these exceptions next time the queue message,
        // which caused this exception,
        // becomes visible again.
        with
        | _ as e ->
                        System.Threading.Thread.Sleep(5000)
                        Trace.TraceError(
                            String.Format(
                              "Exception when processing queue item. Message:
'{0}'",
                                e.Message))
```

Azure SQL Database

In addition to blob storage, Azure also provides SQL database support. You can create a database
from the management portal. On the management portal, you can select the SQL DATABASES tab.
After clicking one of the servers, you can click the New button in the lower-left portion of the page to
create a database on that server, as shown in Figure 8-25.

FIGURE 8-25 Creating a database on the Azure cloud

After you click the New button, the dialog box for creating a database is displayed, as shown in Figure 8-26. Click the Custom Create option to create the database.

FIGURE 8-26 Creating a database dialog box

Figure 8-27 shows the dialog box that is displayed when you click Custom Create. It contains options for specifying the database name and edition, as well as other settings. There are two editions: Web and Business. These two editions are identical except for their capacity. The Web edition scales from 1 GB to 5 GBs, while the business edition scales from 10 GBs to 50 GBs in 10-GB increments.

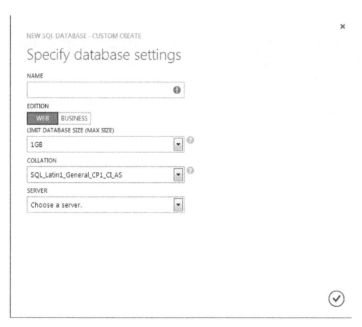

FIGURE 8-27 Creating a database dialog box with database parameters

After you click the button in the lower-right corner of the dialog box, your new database is created, as shown in Figure 8-28. All the created database are listed. The connection to the database is listed in the Connect To Your Database area.

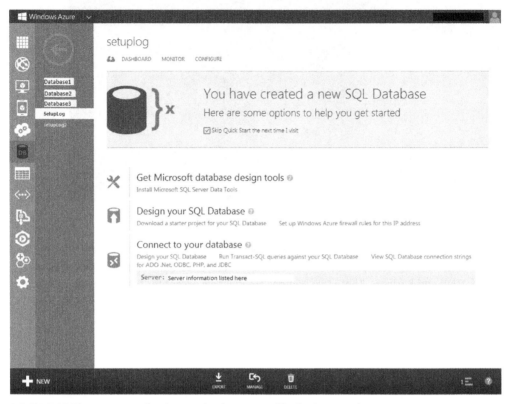

FIGURE 8-28 The setup page for the new database created in the Azure environment

After the database is created, you can log in to it to create a table. Figure 8-29 shows the database management UI. In the pane on the lower-right side of this UI, you can find information about the connection string. Listing 8-8 demonstrates how to create the Log table.

LISTING 8-8 Creating the Log table

```
create table Log (
    ID int not null primary key,
    Event varchar(50),
    Description varchar(2500))

insert into Log Values(1,'Info', 'starting...')
insert into Log Values(2,'Info', 'working...')
insert into Log Values(3,'Info', 'end')
```

FIGURE 8-29 UI for managing the database

It is easy for F# to access an Azure SQL database by using a type provider. Because the SQL Connection type provider works only for the SQL Server database, you can use only the Entity type provider to access an Azure SQL database. Listing 8-9 shows how to use the Entity type provider to connect to the database, query the database, and print out the query results.

LISTING 8-9 Connecting to and querying an Azure SQL database using the Entity type provider

```
#if INTERACTIVE
#r "System.Data"
#r "System.Data.Entity"
#r "FSharp.Data.TypeProviders"
#endif

open System.Data
open System.Data.Entity
open Microsoft.FSharp.Data.TypeProviders

[<Literal>]
let conString = """Server=tcp:<server name>.database.windows.
net,1433;Database=SetupLog;User
 ID=<user id>;Password=<password>;Trusted_Connection=False;Encrypt=True;Connection
Timeout=30"""

// You can use Server Explorer to build your ConnectionString.
type internal SqlConnection =
    Microsoft.FSharp.Data.TypeProviders.SqlEntityConnection<ConnectionString = conString>
let internal db = SqlConnection.GetDataContext()
```

```
// query the log table
let internal table = query {
    for r in db.Log do
    select r
    }

// print the log information
for p in table do
    printfn "[%d] %s: %s" p.ID p.Event p.Description
```

Execution result

```
[1] Info: starting...
[2] Info: working...
[3] Info: end
```

Code Snippet for Azure Development

You can find some Azure F# code snippets at *http://fsharpcodesnippet.codeplex.com/*. Table 8-1 lists the name and default code of these Azure code snippets.

TABLE 8-1 Code snippet for Azure development

Name	Default code

Create Azure cloud queue	`let connectionStringName = "MyConnectionString"`
	`let storageAccount =`
	`CloudStorageAccount.Parse(CloudConfigurationManager.GetSetting(connectionSt`
	`ringName))`
	`let queueClient = storageAccount.CreateCloudQueueClient()`
	`let queue = queueClient.GetQueueReference("myqueue")`
	`ignore <| queue.CreateIfNotExist()`

Create Azure Service Bus Queue	`let QueueName = "GAQueue";`
	`let dp = QueueDescription(QueueName)`
	`let connectionString =`
	`CloudConfigurationManager.GetSetting("Microsoft.ServiceBus.`
	`ConnectionString");`
	`let namespaceManager = NamespaceManager.CreateFromConnectionString(connecti`
	`onString);`
	`if not <| namespaceManager.QueueExists(QueueName) then`
	`    ignore <| namespaceManager.CreateQueue(dp)`

Create blob and set permission	`let container = blobStorage.GetContainerReference("ref")`
	`container.CreateIfNotExist() |> ignore`
	`let mutable permissions = container.GetPermissions()`
	`permissions.PublicAccess <- BlobContainerPublicAccessType.Container`
	`container.SetPermissions(permissions)`

Create blob storage	`let storageAccount =`
	`CloudStorageAccount.Parse(RoleEnvironment.GetConfigurationSettingValue(""))`
	`let blobStorage = storageAccount.CreateCloudBlobClient()]`

Name	Default code

Receive message from Azure Service Bus Queue	```let QueueName = "GAQueue";```
	```let dp = QueueDescription(QueueName)```
	```let connectionString =```
	```CloudConfigurationManager.GetSetting("Microsoft.ServiceBus.```
	```ConnectionString");```
	```let factory = MessagingFactory.CreateFromConnectionString(connectionStri```
	```ng);```
	
	```let receiver = factory.CreateMessageReceiver(QueueName);```
	```let msg = receiver.Receive()```
	```msg.Complete();```
	```let r = msg.Properties.["propertyName"]```

Send message to Azure Service Bus Queue	```let QueueName = "GAQueue";```
	```let dp = QueueDescription(QueueName)```
	```let connectionString =```
	```CloudConfigurationManager.GetSetting("Microsoft.ServiceBus.```
	```ConnectionString");```
	```let factory = MessagingFactory.CreateFromConnectionString(connectionStri```
	```ng);```
	```let sender = factory.CreateMessageSender(QueueName);```
	```let m = new BrokeredMessage(1)```
	```m.Properties.["propertyName"] <- 1```
	```sender.Send(m);```

MapReduce

From the definition on Wikipedia (*http://en.wikipedia.org/wiki/MapReduce*), MapReduce (which can also be written as *Map/Reduce*) is a programming model used to process large data sets. Google proposed it and applied it to processing large amounts of data, such as log files. *Large* means that the data set is so big that it has to be processed across thousands of machines in order to complete the process in a reasonable amount of time. MapReduce can process both unstructured data such as files or structured data such as a database. In most cases, the data is stored in a number of locations. The process happens at the location closest to the data, which saves the time associated with transferring data over the wire. In other words, the data is so vast, the computation is moved close to the data to improve the response time. The idea for MapReduce is derived from the functional programming paradigm; coincidently, F# is positioned to provide cloud programming support.

The MapReduce model is derived from functional programming concepts known as *map* and *reduce* combinators. As the name suggests, MapReduce has two steps: map and reduce. The map step starts at the master node, which takes the input and divides it into smaller problems; it then distributes these subsets to the worker nodes. The worker nodes could further divide the problem and pass down the data to its worker nodes, thus creating a multilevel tree. The process is shown in Figure 8-30. The master node at the top starts with a large amount of data (represented by the wide arrow). Then the data flows toward the bottom of the tree, and the data is distributed into smaller categories. When all of the worker nodes process the data simultaneously, the result can be returned much more quickly.

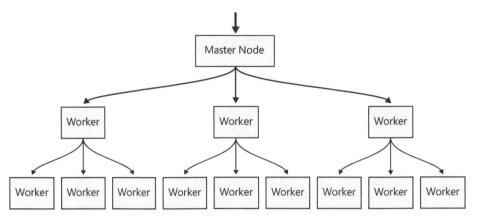

FIGURE 8-30 The map step in MapReduce

In the reduce step, the data flows the opposite way. The parent nodes start to collect the answers from their worker nodes. The master node collects all the results and combines them for the final output. The process is demonstrated in Figure 8-31. When the data is aggregated to the root node, a conclusion (represented by the light bulb) can be made.

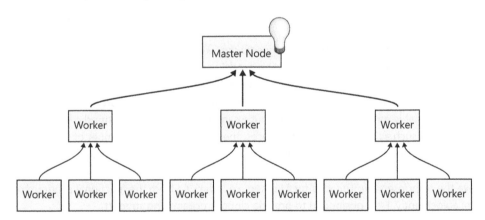

FIGURE 8-31 The reduce step in MapReduce

As an example, imagine that a 100-element array is passed to the master node and you want to know the sum of all the elements. The map step starts by splitting the data into small chunks, let's say 10 elements, and each chunk is passed to a child node. After adding up these 10 elements, the worker nodes return the result to the master node, which calculates the sum of all its child nodes and returns the final answer. Listing 8-10 shows how to simulate MapReduce on a local computer.

LISTING 8-10 Simulating MapReduce on a local computer

```
let data = [| 1..100 |]

let reduceFunction list =
    let r =
        list
        |> Seq.sum
    printfn "result = %A" r
    r

let map () =
    [0..9]
    |> Seq.map (fun i -> i * 10,(i + 1) * 10 - 1)
    |> Seq.map (fun (a,b) ->
                printf "from %A to %A: " a b
                async {
                    let! sum = async { return reduceFunction (data.[a..b]) } |> Async.
StartChild
                    return! sum
                })

let reduce seq =
    seq
    |> Seq.sumBy Async.RunSynchronously

let mapReduce =
    map()
    |> reduce

printfn "final result = %A" mapReduce




Execution result
from 0 to 9: result = 55
from 10 to 19: result = 155
from 20 to 29: result = 255
from 30 to 39: result = 355
from 40 to 49: result = 455
from 50 to 59: result = 555
from 60 to 69: result = 655
from 70 to 79: result = 755
from 80 to 89: result = 855
from 90 to 99: result = 955
final result = 5050
```

Another way to transfer the data is to pass in selection criteria, such as an index range or a database selection. Listing 8-11 shows how to pass an index range to the MapReduce process.

LISTING 8-11 MapReduce with an index range

```
let data = [| 1..100 |]

let reduceFunction a b =
    let r =
        data.[a..b]
        |> Seq.sum
    printfn "result = %A" r
    r

let map () =
    [0..9]
    |> Seq.map (fun i -> i * 10,(i + 1) * 10 - 1)
    |> Seq.map (fun (a, b) ->
                printf "from %A to %A: " a b
                async {
                    let! sum = async { return reduceFunction a b } |> Async.StartChild
                    return! sum
                })

let reduce seq =
    seq
    |> Seq.sumBy Async.RunSynchronously

let mapReduce =
    map()
    |> reduce

printfn "final result = %A" mapReduce
```

Execution result from MapReduce with an index range

```
from 0 to 9: result = 55
from 10 to 19: result = 155
from 20 to 29: result = 255
from 30 to 39: result = 355
from 40 to 49: result = 455
from 50 to 59: result = 555
from 60 to 69: result = 655
from 70 to 79: result = 755
from 80 to 89: result = 855
from 90 to 99: result = 955
final result = 5050
```

The simulation program shows how Map/Reduce works. Now you can implement it using Windows Azure. The master and worker nodes are both implemented as Azure F# worker role projects. The solution structure is shown in Figure 8-32.

FIGURE 8-32 MapReduce Azure sample solution structure

The master node takes the responsibility of splitting the big data set into small chunks and passing the chunks to the worker nodes. An Azure cloud queue is used to perform the communication between master and worker nodes. There are two queues: the parameter queue and the result queue. The parameter queue, which is named *queue1* as shown in Listing 8-12, is used to hold the small chunks of data. The result queue, which is named *queue2* as shown in Listing 8-12, is where the worker nodes insert the results. The master node gets all 10 elements from the result queue and then performs the reduce (sum) operation to get the final result, which is 5050.

LISTING 8-12 Master node code

```
namespace MasterNode

open System
open System.Diagnostics
open System.Net
open System.Threading
open Microsoft.WindowsAzure
open Microsoft.WindowsAzure.ServiceRuntime
open Microsoft.WindowsAzure.StorageClient

type WorkerRole() =
    inherit RoleEntryPoint()

    // This is a sample worker implementation. Replace with your logic.

    let log message kind = Trace.WriteLine(message, kind)
    let random = Random()

    override wr.Run() =

        let connectionStringName = "QueueConnectionString"
        let storageAccount =
CloudStorageAccount.Parse(CloudConfigurationManager.GetSetting(connectionStringName))
        let queueClient = storageAccount.CreateCloudQueueClient()
        let queue = queueClient.GetQueueReference("myqueue")
        let queue2 = queueClient.GetQueueReference("resultqueue")
```

```
ignore <| queue.CreateIfNotExist()
ignore <| queue2.CreateIfNotExist()

let data = [| 1..100 |]

// map step, split the data into small chunks
let chunk = 9
// insert 10 elements
[0..chunk]
|> Seq.map (fun i -> i * 10, (i + 1) * 10 - 1)
|> Seq.iter (fun (a,b) ->
                let l =
                    data.[a..b]
                    |> Array.map (fun i -> i.ToString())

                queue.AddMessage(CloudQueueMessage(String.Join(",", l))))

// reduce step, retrieve message and sum
let result =
    [0..chunk]
    |> Seq.map (fun _ ->
                while queue2.PeekMessage() = null do
                    Thread.Sleep(random.Next(5, 100))
                queue2.GetMessage().AsString |> Convert.ToInt32)
    |> Seq.sum

log (sprintf "final result = %A" result) "Information"

log "MasterNode entry point called" "Information"
while(true) do
    Thread.Sleep(10000)
    log "Working" "Information"

override wr.OnStart() =

// Set the maximum number of concurrent connections
ServicePointManager.DefaultConnectionLimit <- 12

// For information on handling configuration changes
// see the MSDN topic at http://go.microsoft.com/fwlink/?LinkId=166357

base.OnStart()
```

 Note The queue name cannot have uppercase characters.

The worker node code, which is relatively simple, is shown in Listing 8-13. It takes the data from the queue, which is queue1, and performs a *Seq.sum* operation. The summary result is inserted into the result queue, which is queue2.

LISTING 8-13 Worker node code

```
namespace WorkerNode

open System
open System.Diagnostics
open System.Net
open System.Threading
open Microsoft.WindowsAzure
open Microsoft.WindowsAzure.ServiceRuntime
open Microsoft.WindowsAzure.StorageClient

type WorkerRole() =
    inherit RoleEntryPoint()

    // This is a sample worker implementation. Replace with your logic.

    let log message kind = Trace.WriteLine(message, kind)
    let random = Random()

    override wr.Run() =

        let connectionStringName = "QueueConnectionString"
        let qs = CloudConfigurationManager.GetSetting(connectionStringName)
        let storageAccount = CloudStorageAccount.Parse(qs)
        let queueClient = storageAccount.CreateCloudQueueClient()
        let queue = queueClient.GetQueueReference("myqueue")
        let queue2 = queueClient.GetQueueReference("resultqueue")

        ignore <| queue.CreateIfNotExist()
        ignore <| queue2.CreateIfNotExist()

        let mutable msg = queue.GetMessage()
        while msg.DequeueCount <> 1 do
            Thread.Sleep(random.Next(5, 100))
            msg <- queue.GetMessage()

        queue.DeleteMessage(msg)

        let data =
            msg.AsString.Split([| "," |], StringSplitOptions.RemoveEmptyEntries)
            |> Array.map Convert.ToInt32

        let sum = data |> Seq.sum

        queue2.AddMessage(CloudQueueMessage(sum.ToString()))

        log "WorkerNode entry point called" "Information"
        while(true) do
            Thread.Sleep(10000)
            log "Working" "Information"

    override wr.OnStart() =
```

```
// Set the maximum number of concurrent connections
ServicePointManager.DefaultConnectionLimit <- 12

// For information on handling configuration changes
// see the MSDN topic at http://go.microsoft.com/fwlink/?LinkId=166357.

base.OnStart()
```

MapReduce Design Patterns

MapReduce is a powerful tool for processing data. This section introduces several MapReduce design patterns that can be used to solve common programming problems. There are several communication approaches that can be applied in addition to Azure cloud. In this section, I generalize these approaches as the *Emit* method. The *Emit* method sends a message containing the actual data as well as the key value to distinguish this message from others. Listing 8-12 and Listing 8-13 can be implemented as pseudo code, as shown in Listing 8-14.

LISTING 8-14 Summing using MapReduce

```
let map () =
    let chunks = split data
    for chunk in chunks do
        let sum = chunk |> Seq.sum
        emit(id, sum)

let reduce() =
    let sum =
        resultSet
        |> Seq.sum (fun (id, sum) -> sum)

    emit("final result", sum)
```

Another application is to count the occurrence of a term in a document. The key value is the term whose occurrence needs to be computed. The map step sends the term occurrence, and the reduce step aggregates the term occurrences. The pseudo code is shown in Listing 8-15.

LISTING 8-15 Counting using MapReduce

```
let map term =
    let sum =
        doc
        |> Seq.filter (fun word -> word = term)
        |> Seq.count

    emit(term, sum)
```

```
let reduce() =
    let hashTable = Hashtable<term, int>()
    resultSet
    |> Seq.iter (fun (term, count) -> hashTable.[term] <- hashTable.[term] + count

    emit("final result", hashTable)
```

MapReduce can also be used on a more complex structure. In the following new sample, a graph of the entity and its relationships is stored during each iteration. The map step sends one entity's state, which can be as simple as all reachable nodes. The reduce step goes through all messages, which contain the relationship information, and updates the state for each node. The state in one node quickly "infects" other nodes. The whole process is shown in Figure 8-33, Figure 8-34, and Figure 8-35.

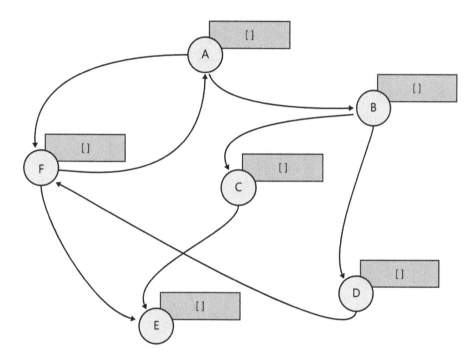

FIGURE 8-33 Graph processing initial state

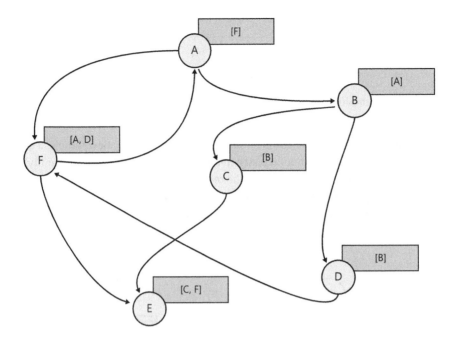

FIGURE 8-34 Graph processing after one iteration

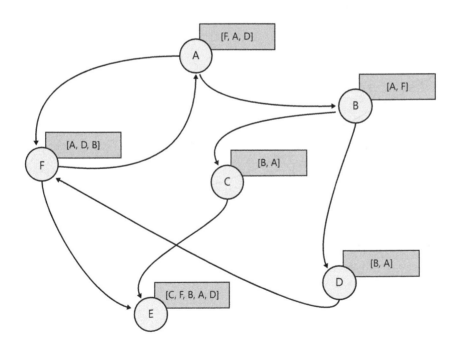

FIGURE 8-35 Graph processing after two iterations

The MapReduce pattern is a hot research topic. You can reference the following sites for more details:

- MapReduce Patterns, Algorithms, and Use Cases: *http://highlyscalable. wordpress.com/2012/02/01/mapreduce-patterns/*

- Design Patterns for Efficient Graph Algorithms in MapReduce: *http://www.umiacs.umd. edu/~jimmylin/publications/Lin_Schatz_MLG2010.pdf*

Genetic Algorithms on Cloud

A Genetic Algorithm (GA) deploys a large number of potential solutions, and these solutions are later filtered by the target function to decide if they are *close* to the optimal solution. The inferior solution, which is considered to be *far* from the optimum, will be abandoned. Those selected as *good* are used to generate new sets of potential solutions, and the whole process continues on. The selection process is usually performed with some randomization.

Unlike other computations, a GA does not stop by itself. The developer needs to set up how the computation process should be stopped. Because only the solutions close to optimum are selected, the whole process makes the majority of the solution converge at the optimum solution. Eventually, the optimum solution is found. The whole process simulates Darwin's natural selection theory, only the fit can survive and the survivor is the solution to the target problem. The GA is a perfect candidate for an NP-complete problem, such as the traveling salesman problem (TSP). It is often used in investment firms to find the best trading/investing strategies. One of the reasons that GA works so well is that it has implicit parallelism and error tolerance built in. It is a perfect candidate for a cloud computation sample, and this section demonstrates how to implement GA on the Azure cloud.

Understanding Genetic Algorithms

The group of potential solutions is called a *population*, and it contains individuals that are usually called *chromosomes*. The target function used to decide which chromosomes are fit and which are inferior is called the *fitness function*. The individual in the population is changed when experiences cross over with another individual or individuals, or when individuals mutate by themselves. The crossover and mutation process is also called *recombination*.

If the whole search space can be envisioned as a two-dimensional (2D) platform, the population is initially scattered everywhere on the platform. When the evaluation process starts, individuals far from the optimum die out and the whole population converges at the optimum area. The population can converge at a suboptimum area; therefore, the algorithm uses several parameters to maintain the diversity of the population with the hope that it does not prematurely converge. Note that the population does not necessarily converge on the optimum, but all the individuals are very close to optimum. If you are not all that familiar with GA, the whole evolutionary process is nothing more than chaos. But this population is disciplined by the target (fitness) function. This whole process wastes some search energy, but the problems that GA tries to attack are always NP-complete problems, in which you are interested only in finding a solution, regardless of whether that solution is optimum.

The GA pseudo code in Listing 8-16 shows how a simple GA (SGA) works. It first initializes a population of chromosomes. Each chromosome in the population is a potential solution to the target function, which is also the fitness function. The fitness function returns a value representing the quality of the solution (chromosome). The selection is then used to filter out inferior chromosomes. The selected chromosomes then perform a crossover and mutation operation. After these transformation operations, the chromosomes are put into a new population and the process is repeated. The process repeats for a certain number of iterations or until the best chromosome in the population is close enough to the optimum. The fitness function is used to determine how close a chromosome is to the optimum.

LISTING 8-16 GA pseudo code

```
initialize population
compute the chromosome fitness value from the fitness function

evolve the population for X times according to the following rule:

  step1: select a chromosome from the population and call it c0
  step2: select a chromosome from the population and call it c1
  step3: let c0 and c1 do the recombination and generate new chromosomes c0' and c1'
  step4: put c0 and c1 into new population
  step5: compute the fitness value from the fitness function

  repeat step1 to step5 until the new population size = the current population size

  current population = new population
```

The chromosome usually is represented as an array or list of integers or float numbers. The implementation in Listing 8-17 introduces an extra layer and makes a chromosome that has a geno-type layer and a pheno-type layer. The geno-type layer is where the actual data is located. If you take a single geno-type layer data item as input to a function, the result of the function is a data item in the pheno-type layer. You can use a function to transform the geno-type layer data to a pheno type, which can enable users to have more complex encoding for the chromosome. A user function needs to be passed in to initialize each building block, which is called *loci*. The mutation operation is going to be introduced later in the "Crossover and Mutation" section. The whole population initialization is shown in Listing 8-18.

LISTING 8-17 Chromosome definition

```
/// Chromosome type to represent the individual involved in the GAs
type ChromosomeType(f, size, ?converters) =
    let initialF = f
    let mutable genos = [for i in 1..size do yield f()]
    let mutable genoPhenoConverters = converters
```

```
    /// make a duplicate copy of this chromosome
    member this.Clone() =
        let newValue =
            match converters with
                | Some(converters) -> new ChromosomeType(initialF, size, converters)
                | None -> new ChromosomeType(initialF, size)
        newValue.Genos <- this.Genos
        newValue

    /// get fitness value with given fitness function
    member this.Fitness(fitnessFunction) = this.Pheno |> fitnessFunction

    /// gets and sets the Geno values
    member this.Genos
        with get() = genos
        and set(value) = genos <- value

    /// gets and sets the Pheno values
    member this.Pheno
        with get() =
            match genoPhenoConverters with
            | Some(genoPhenoConverters) -> List.zip genoPhenoConverters genos |> List.map
(fun
 (f,value) -> f value)
            | None -> this.Genos

    /// mutate the chromosome with given mutation function
    member this.Mutate(?mutationF) =
        let location = random.Next(Seq.length this.Genos)
        let F =
            match mutationF with
                | Some(mutationF) -> mutationF
                | None -> f
        let transform i v =
            match i with
                | _ when i = location -> F()
                | _ -> v
        this.Genos <- List.mapi transform this.Genos
```

LISTING 8-18 Population initialization

```
    /// generate a population for GAs
    let Population randomF populationSize chromosomeSize =
        [for i in 1..populationSize do yield (new
ChromosomeType(f = randomF, size = chromosomeSize))]
```

Selection

First, keep in mind that the selection can choose suboptimum individuals in order to keep the diversity in the population, and that is totally fine. There are two commonly used selection techniques:

- **Roulette wheel selection**   Imagine a roulette wheel that hosts all the individuals in the population. Each individual has its space according to its fitness value. The better the fitness value, the bigger space the individual has. The bigger space gives the individual a greater chance of being selected.

- **Rank selection**   The roulette wheel selection uses the fitness value to relocate the space, and rank selection uses the rank in the sorted list to do so. The worst individual is assigned to the first space, the second worst is assigned to the second space, and so on.

Rank selection gives more weight to the inferior individuals and can speed up the convergence process. It will be used as the default selection in the sample code, as shown in Listing 8-19.

LISTING 8-19 Rank selection

```
/// rank selection method
let RankSelection (population:ChromosomeType list) fitnessFunction=
    let populationSize = Seq.length population
    let r() = randomF() % populationSize
    let randomSelection() =
        let c0 = population.[r()]
        let c1 = population.[r()]
        let result = if (c0.Fitness(fitnessFunction) > c1.Fitness(fitnessFunction)) then
c0 else
c1
        result.Clone()
    Seq.init populationSize (fun _ -> randomSelection())
```

Crossover and Mutation

There are two typical recombination operations: crossover and mutation. These two operations are always performed on the selected individuals, and they transform the geno type layer data. The crossover rate and mutation rate control the execution of operations. The crossover needs two individuals, and they exchange the building blocks to generate offspring. Table 8-2 shows a simple crossover. The Chromosome 1 building blocks are exchanged with Chromosome 2. Because individuals going into the crossover are considered to be the good ones, the crossover hopes the offspring are better, or at least as good, as their parents—although in reality that might not always be the case. The crossover operation is defined in Listing 8-20.

TABLE 8-2 Crossover operation

Chromosome 1	0000 0000 0000 0000
Chromosome 2	1111 1111 1111 1111
Offspring 1	1000 1111 0001 0101
Offspring 2	0111 0000 1110 1010

LISTING 8-20 Shuffle crossover

```
/// shuffle crossover
let ShuffleCrossover (c0:ChromosomeType) (c1:ChromosomeType) =
    let crossover c0 c1 =
        let isEven n = n%2 = 0
        let randomSwitch (x, y) = if isEven (randomF()) then (x, y) else (y, x)
        List.zip c0 c1 |> List.map randomSwitch |> List.unzip
    let (first, second) = crossover (c0.Genos) (c1.Genos)
    c0.Genos <- first
    c1.Genos <- second
```

The mutation involves only one individual. The simplest mutation is to randomly change a building block on the chromosome to another valid value. Table 8-3 shows a one-location mutation.

TABLE 8-3 Mutation operation

Chromosome	0000 0000 0000 0000
Mutated chromosome	1000 0000 0000 0000

The crossover is considered to not introduce diversity, which means there is no new number introduced by the crossover. . The building block in the individual is just moving from one individual to another. The mutation, on the other hand, is considered to be a way to introduce diversity into the population. Depending on other evolutionary strategy settings, the crossover rate is usually set to a higher number, such as 90 percent, and the mutation rate is as low as 2 percent. This agrees with the real-world number. To maintain existence, species usually do not have a high mutation rate, but the crossover mate (mating) is high.

Elitism

Mother Nature does not necessarily give any favor to a good individual. The recombination operators, in most cases, generate new individuals by destroying their parents. Even though the best individual is selected every time, it can still be destroyed and the next generation will be downgraded. Most of the GA implementations add the concept of elitism to preserve the best individuals and allow them to go into the next generation without interruption from the recombination operation. The sample in this section uses elitism by default. The complete GA code is shown in Listing 8-21, and Listing 8-22 shows how to use the GA to find the maximum value for the formula $f(x_1, x_2 \ldots x_{10}) = \sum_{k=1}^{10} x_k$ where $x_i \in [0,9]$.

In Listing 8-16, you can see that the chromosome selection and transformation process can be executed in parallel. The GA computation can be parallel at the chromosome level as well as at the population level. The whole evolutionary process is perfect for a parallel programming model, and multiple populations can be executed simultaneously as long as these populations can exchange individuals. You might be surprised that the population does not need to be synchronized. When a population is initialized, chromosomes do not converge and are instead spread out in the search space. During the evolutionary process, chromosomes converge at the optimum area.

When the population converges, we say that the population's diversity is *low*. The diversity of the population is decreased during the evolutionary process. If the search space has several suboptimum areas, these areas can trap the population and cause convergence at a suboptimum area or areas. The only way to avoid premature convergence is to increase the diversity by introducing new chromosomes. The new chromosomes, with some probability, can help the population out of the suboptimum areas and eventually find a global optimum. If a population evolves slower than the others, the slow population can introduce diversity into the fast population when exchanging individuals. If the VM hosting the population crashes, the newly initialized population can provide more diversity to the whole system. Because of the large number of chromosomes in the population, missing a chromosome during the communication does not affect the evolutionary process. Because of these features, the GA is immune to crashes or communication errors, as long as it is spread among different virtual hosts in the Azure cloud.

LISTING 8-21 Genetic Algorithm code

```
/// Evolutionary computation module
/// this module is for Genetic Algorithm (GA) only
module EvolutionaryComputation

    /// random number generator
    let random = new System.Random((int)System.DateTime.Now.Ticks)

    /// random int generator
    let randomF() = random.Next()

    /// random float (double) generator
    let randomFloatF() = random.NextDouble()

    /// Chromesome type to represent the individual involves in the GAs
    type ChromosomeType(f, size, ?converters) =
        let initialF = f
        let mutable genos = [for i in 1..size do yield f()]
        let mutable genoPhenoConverters = converters

        /// make a duplicate copy of this chromosome
        member this.Clone() =
            let newValue =
                match converters with
                    | Some(converters) -> new ChromosomeType(initialF, size, converters)
                    | None -> new ChromosomeType(initialF, size)
```

```fsharp
            newValue.Genos <- this.Genos
            newValue

        /// get fitness value with given fitness function
        member this.Fitness(fitnessFunction) = this.Pheno |> fitnessFunction

        /// gets and sets the Geno values
        member this.Genos
            with get() = genos
            and set(value) = genos <- value

        /// gets and sets the Pheno values
        member this.Pheno
            with get() =
                match genoPhenoConverters with
                | Some(genoPhenoConverters) ->
                    List.zip genoPhenoConverters genos |> List.map (fun (f,value) -> f
value)
                | None -> this.Genos

        /// mutate the chromosome with given mutation function
        member this.Mutate(?mutationF) =
            let location = random.Next(Seq.length this.Genos)
            let F =
                match mutationF with
                    | Some(mutationF) -> mutationF
                    | None -> f
            let transform i v =
                match i with
                    | _ when i=location -> F()
                    | _ -> v
            this.Genos <- List.mapi transform this.Genos

    /// generate a population for GAs
    let Population randomF populationSize chromosomeSize =
        [for i in 1..populationSize do yield (new
ChromosomeType(f = randomF, size = chromosomeSize))]

    /// find the maximum fitness value from a population
    let maxFitness population fitnessF =
        let best = Seq.maxBy (fun (c:ChromosomeType) -> c.Fitness(fitnessF)) population
        best.Fitness(fitnessF)

    /// find the most fit individual
    let bestChromosome population fitnessF =
        let best = Seq.maxBy (fun (c:ChromosomeType) -> c.Fitness(fitnessF)) population
        best

    /// rank selection method
    let RankSelection (population:ChromosomeType list) fitnessFunction=
        let populationSize = Seq.length population
        let r() = randomF() % populationSize
        let randomSelection() =
            let c0 = population.[r()]
```

```
            let c1 = population.[r()]
            let result = if (c0.Fitness(fitnessFunction) > c1.Fitness(fitnessFunction))
then c0
else c1
            result.Clone();
        Seq.init populationSize (fun _ -> randomSelection())

    /// shuffle crossover
    let ShuffleCrossover (c0:ChromosomeType) (c1:ChromosomeType) =
        let crossover c0 c1 =
            let isEven n = n%2 = 0
            let randomSwitch (x,y) = if isEven (randomF()) then (x,y) else (y,x)
            List.zip c0 c1 |> List.map randomSwitch |> List.unzip
        let (first,second) = crossover (c0.Genos) (c1.Genos)
        c0.Genos <- first
        c1.Genos <- second


    /// evolve the whole population
    let Evolve (population:ChromosomeType list) selectionF crossoverF fitnessF
crossoverRate
mutationRate elitism =
        let populationSize = Seq.length population
        let r() = randomF() % populationSize
        let elites = selectionF population fitnessF |> Seq.toList
        let seq0 = elites |> Seq.mapi (fun i element->(i,element)) |> Seq.filter (fun
(i,_)->i%2=0) |> Seq.map (fun (_,b)->b)
        let seq1 = elites |> Seq.mapi (fun i element->(i,element)) |> Seq.filter (fun
(i,_)->i%2<>0) |> Seq.map (fun (_,b)->b)
        let xoverAndMutate (a:ChromosomeType) (b:ChromosomeType) =
            if (randomFloatF() < crossoverRate) then
                crossoverF a b
            if (randomFloatF() < mutationRate) then
                a.Mutate()
            if (randomFloatF() < mutationRate) then
                b.Mutate()
            [a] @ [b]

        if elitism then
            let seq0 = seq0
            let seq1 = seq1
            let r = Seq.map2 xoverAndMutate seq0 seq1 |> List.concat
            r.Tail @ [ bestChromosome population fitnessF ]
        else
            Seq.map2 xoverAndMutate seq0 seq1 |> List.concat

    /// composite function X times
    let rec composite f x =
        match x with
        | 1 -> f
        | n -> f >> (composite f (x-1))

    /// convert a function seq to function composition
    let compositeFunctions functions =
        Seq.fold ( >> ) id functions
```

LISTING 8-22 Invoking the GA code

```
open EvolutionaryComputation

// define the loci function to set each building block on the chromosome
let lociFunction() = box(random.Next(10))

// define the fitness (target) function
let fitnessF (items:obj list) =
    items |> Seq.map (System.Convert.ToInt32) |> Seq.sum

// initialize the population
let myPopulation = Population lociFunction 50 10

// evolve the population with rank selection, shuffle crossover (90%)
// mutation rate = 10% and elitism = true
let myEvolve population = Evolve population RankSelection ShuffleCrossover fitnessF 0.9
0.1
true

// evolve the population 75 times
let result = composite myEvolve 75 myPopulation

// print out the best fitness value which is the solution to the target function
printfn "%A" (maxFitness result fitnessF)
```

Azure Communication

Azure provides different ways to perform communications between hosts, such as AppFabric and Windows Azure Service Bus. In this section, the service bus is chosen to perform communication among the populations. The Service Bus mechanism provides both *relayed* and *brokered* messaging capabilities. The Service Bus Relay service supports direct one-way messaging, request/response messaging, and peer-to-peer messaging. One way that the Service Bus relay facilitates this is by enabling you to securely expose Windows Communication Foundation (WCF) services that reside within a corporate enterprise network to the public cloud, without having to open up a firewall connection or require intrusive changes to a corporate network infrastructure. Brokered messaging provides durable, asynchronous messaging components such as Queues, Topics, and Subscriptions, with features that support publish-subscribe and temporal decoupling: senders and receivers do not have to be online at the same time; the messaging infrastructure reliably stores messages until the receiving party is ready to receive them.

Setting Up the Service from Azure Management Portal

The service bus can be found in the management portal at the Azure website, as shown in Figure 8-36.

FIGURE 8-36 The Service Bus option in the Azure management portal

After you select the Service Bus option, you can create a service bus by clicking the Create button, which is shown in Figure 8-37.

FIGURE 8-37 Button for namespace and service bus queue

For the sample code in this chapter, a namespace named *testservicebus0* is required, as shown in Figure 8-38.

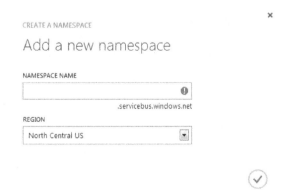

FIGURE 8-38 Creating sample namespace and service queue

Before the code is presented, you need to retrieve the default key by clicking the Access Key button at the bottom of the page, as shown in Figure 8-39.

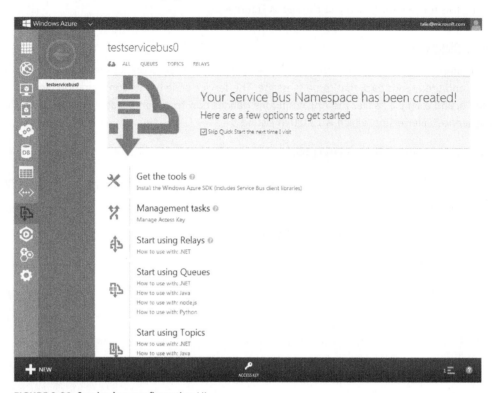

FIGURE 8-39 Service bus configuration UI

Figure 8-40 shows the default key.

ACCESS KEY

Connect to your namespace

CONNECTION STRING

<your connection string>

DEFAULT ISSUER

owner

DEFAULT KEY

<your default key>

Open ACS Management Portal →

FIGURE 8-40 Default key for the service

These setup steps provide the service bus namespace, service bus queue, and user secret. Creating a cloud queue structure is similar to the procedure for creating a service bus. It can be done using the Cloud Services menu item, which you can see in Figure 8-36.

Service-Side Code

The next sample code creates an echo service. The service listens for incoming messages, receives a message, and then sends back that same message. The service code has its configuration file, App.config, and a simple .fs file. The App.config file defines how to communicate with the Azure cloud and the service's file version, which is 1.7.0.0 in Listing 8-23.

LISTING 8-23 Configuration file for a service bus

```
<configuration>
  <system.serviceModel>
    <services>
      <service name="Microsoft.ServiceBus.Samples.EchoService">
        <endpoint contract="Microsoft.ServiceBus.Samples.IEchoContract"
binding="netTcpRelayBinding" />
      </service>
    </services>
    <extensions>
      <bindingExtensions>
        <add name="netTcpRelayBinding"
type="Microsoft.ServiceBus.Configuration.NetTcpRelayBindingCollectionElement, Microsoft.
ServiceBus,
Version=1.7.0.0, Culture=neutral, PublicKeyToken=31bf3856ad364e35" />
      </bindingExtensions>
    </extensions>
  </system.serviceModel>
  <startup>
    <supportedRuntime version="v4.0" sku=".NETFramework,Version=v4.0" />
  </startup>
</configuration>
```

The service code, shown in Listing 8-24, defines a contract interface named *IEchoContract* and a channel interface named *IEchoChannel*. The service namespace, service queue name, and *issuerSecret* are created during the setup step. You can use F5 to run the program.

LISTING 8-24 Echo service code using an Azure service bus

```
// Learn more about F# at http://fsharp.net
namespace Microsoft.ServiceBus.Samples

open System

open Microsoft.ServiceBus
open System.ServiceModel
```

```
[<ServiceContract(
    Name = "IEchoContract",
    Namespace = "http://samples.microsoft.com/ServiceModel/Relay/")>]
type IEchoContract = interface
    [<OperationContract>]
    abstract member Echo : msg:string -> string
end

type IEchoChannel = interface
    inherit IEchoContract
    inherit IClientChannel
end

[<ServiceBehavior(
    Name = "EchoService",
    Namespace = "http://samples.microsoft.com/ServiceModel/Relay/")>]
type EchoService() = class
    interface IEchoContract with
        member this.Echo(msg) =
            printfn "%s" msg
            msg
end

module Program =

    [<EntryPoint>]
    let Main(args) =
        let serviceNamespace = "testservicebus0"
        let issuerName = "owner"
        let issuerSecret = "<your account key>";

        // create the service credential
        let sharedSecretServiceBusCredential = TransportClientEndpointBehavior()
        sharedSecretServiceBusCredential.TokenProvider <-
            TokenProvider.CreateSharedSecretTokenProvider(issuerName, issuerSecret);

        // set up the service host
        let address = ServiceBusEnvironment.CreateServiceUri("sb",
                                                             serviceNamespace,
                                                             "EchoService");
        let host = new ServiceHost(typeof<EchoService>, address);
        let serviceRegistrySettings = new ServiceRegistrySettings(DiscoveryType.Public);

        // setup endpoints
        for endpoint in host.Description.Endpoints do
            endpoint.Behaviors.Add(serviceRegistrySettings);
            endpoint.Behaviors.Add(sharedSecretServiceBusCredential)

        // open the service host
        host.Open();
```

```
Console.WriteLine("Service address: " + address.ToString());
Console.WriteLine("Press [Enter] to exit");
Console.ReadLine() |> ignore

// close the host service
host.Close()

0
```

Note The *interface*, *class*, and *struct* keywords in the type definition are optional. The following two interface definition snippets are the same:

```
type IA =
    abstract F : int -> int

type IB = interface
    abstract F : int -> int
end
```

Client-Side Code

Like server-side code, the client-side code's configuration also is located in the App.config and has some simple .fs code. The configuration code is shown in Listing 8-25. The service bus DLL file is version 1.7.0.0. The client-side code is even simpler—it sends a string message to the service. In Listing 8-26, a service interface named *IEchoContract* and a channel interface named *IEchoChannel* are defined. The string message is sent via the created channel.

LISTING 8-25 Client-side configuration file

```
<?xml version="1.0" encoding="utf-8"?>
<configuration>
  <system.serviceModel>
    <client>
      <endpoint name="RelayEndpoint" contract="Microsoft.ServiceBus.Samples.IEchoContract"
binding="netTcpRelayBinding" />
    </client>
    <extensions>
      <bindingExtensions>
        <add name="netTcpRelayBinding"
type="Microsoft.ServiceBus.Configuration.NetTcpRelayBindingCollectionElement,
Microsoft.ServiceBus, Version=1.7.0.0, Culture=neutral, PublicKeyToken=31bf3856ad364e35"
/>
      </bindingExtensions>
    </extensions>
```

```
    </system.serviceModel>
    <startup>
      <supportedRuntime version="v4.0" sku=".NETFramework,Version=v4.0" />
    </startup>
</configuration>
```

LISTING 8-26 Client-side code for the service bus service

```fsharp
// Learn more about F# at http://fsharp.net

namespace Microsoft.ServiceBus.Samples

open System
open Microsoft.ServiceBus;
open System.ServiceModel;

[<ServiceContract(
    Name = "IEchoContract",
    Namespace = "http://samples.microsoft.com/ServiceModel/Relay/")>]
type IEchoContract = interface
    [<OperationContract>]
    abstract member Echo : msg:string -> string
end

type IEchoChannel = interface
    inherit IEchoContract
    inherit IClientChannel
end

module Program =

    [<EntryPoint>]
    let Main(args) =

        ServiceBusEnvironment.SystemConnectivity.Mode <- ConnectivityMode.AutoDetect;

        let serviceNamespace = "testServiceBus0"
        let issuerName = "owner"
        let issuerSecret = "<your account key>";

        let serviceUri = ServiceBusEnvironment.CreateServiceUri("sb",
serviceNamespace,
                                                                "EchoService");
        let sharedSecretServiceBusCredential = new TransportClientEndpointBehavior();
        sharedSecretServiceBusCredential.TokenProvider <-
            TokenProvider.CreateSharedSecretTokenProvider(issuerName, issuerSecret);

        let channelFactory = new ChannelFactory<IEchoChannel>(
                                    "RelayEndpoint",
                                    new EndpointAddress(serviceUri));
```

```
channelFactory.Endpoint.Behaviors.Add(sharedSecretServiceBusCredential);

let channel = channelFactory.CreateChannel();
channel.Open();

Console.WriteLine("Enter text to echo (or [Enter] to exit):");
let mutable input = Console.ReadLine();
while (input <> String.Empty) do
    try
        Console.WriteLine("Server echoed: {0}", channel.Echo(input));
    with
    | _ as e->
        Console.WriteLine("Error: " + e.Message);
    input <- Console.ReadLine();

channel.Close();
channelFactory.Close();

0
```

This simple communication mechanism is used to implement the cloud GA sample, which exchanges the best individuals among populations. The cloud GA sample is shown in next section.

Genetic Algorithms in the Cloud

When thinking about how to parallelize the GA in the cloud, there are two choices. One is to make the parallelization work on the chromosome level, and the other is to make it work on the population level. Because the communication cost in the cloud environment cannot be ignored, this implementation takes the population-level option, which means each virtual host on the cloud runs a population. The best chromosome in one population is selected and injected into another population or populations. After several iterations, all of the populations are supposed to converge at the same area and, we hope, that is where the optimum solution is located.

For the real implementation, cloud queue storage is used to store the best chromosomes from different populations. The population randomly enqueues its best chromosome and dequeues an element to replace the worst chromosome, if the queue is not empty. If the queue is empty, the population will just continue its evaluation, hoping that it can get some external information next time. There is another monitoring component that is used to make sure that the queue does not grow too fast. It deletes three items at once, trying to keep the queue length in control. The monitor component also hosts a service bus, which enables the client application to get the best result by querying the service bus service. Keep in mind that all the queue operations are randomly performed. It seems everything is in a chaos, but the fitness function, which is also the problem to solve, will guide the populations to the right spot. The whole architecture is shown in Figure 8-41.

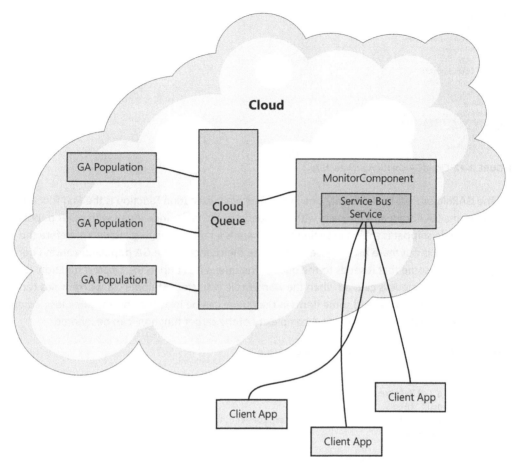

FIGURE 8-41 Cloud GA architecture

You can load the full solution from the F# 3.0 pack (*http://fsharp3sample.codeplex.com*). This sample is under the AzureSamples folder in the source tree. There are four projects in the solution, as shown in Figure 8-42:

- CloudGA is the configuration project, which every Azure project creates.

- FSharpComputationLibrary is the project that hosts the GA library and cloud-configuration parameters. It is a common F# library project.

- GARole is an F# worker role project created by the Azure cloud wizard. It runs the GA library and sends/receives the chromosomes from the cloud queue storage, which helps the current population evolve.

- MonitorRole is also an F# worker role project. It regularly cleans the queue and reports the solution to the problem by hosting a service bus service.

FIGURE 8-42 CloudGA solution architecture

The GARole project contains only one .fs file. The main execution function is the *Run* function. It invokes the GA library and interacts with the queue to exchange individuals with other populations. The code snippet is shown in Listing 8-27. There is a random waiting statement before the code snippet. It is put there on purpose to decrease the chance of the GA population always getting the chromosome that it sends to the queue. The queue is set up in the *OnStart* function. (See Listing 8-28.) The queue is cleared when the worker role is started. Multiple GA worker roles can be started at a different pace, and some items in the queue can be lost. The chromosome loss, compared to the whole GA evolutionary time and complexity of the target function, can be ignored.

LISTING 8-27 GA communicating with the cloud queue

```
let msg = q.GetMessage()
if msg <> null then
    worst.FromString(msg.AsString, System.Convert.ToInt32 >> box)
q.DeleteMessage(msg)

let bestStr = best.ToString()
q.AddMessage(CloudQueueMessage(bestStr))
```

LISTING 8-28 Setting up the cloud queue

```
override wr.OnStart() =

    // Set the maximum number of concurrent connections
    ServicePointManager.DefaultConnectionLimit <- 12

    // set up the queue
    let credential = StorageCredentialsAccountAndKey(
                        CloudConstant.storageAccount,
                        CloudConstant.accountKey)

    q <- CloudQueue(CloudConstant.queueUrl, credential)
    if q.Exists() then q.Clear()
    q.CreateIfNotExist() |> ignore

    base.OnStart()
```

The Monitor role is used to control the size of the cloud queue by deleting three items in a batch if the size of the queue is greater than a predefined number. In the sample, this predefined number is set to 3 as well. The code is shown in Listing 8-29. The queue setup code in the *OnStart* method for the Monitor role is not different from the GA role. The Monitor role interacts with the service bus service to enable it to answer the query from client applications regarding what the best solution for the target problem is. (See Listing 8-30.) The service bus code is similar to the one in Listing 8-23. The only difference is the extra field named *InstanceContextMode*. It is set to *InstanceContextMode.Single* in the *ServiceBehavior* on the service class. This field enables you to pass an instance of a service class instead of passing in the type.

LISTING 8-29 Monitor role *Run* function

```
override wr.Run() =

    log "MonitorRole entry point called" "Information"
    while(true) do
        Thread.Sleep 1000
        log "Monitor Working to clear" "Information"
        log (sprintf "queue length = %A" (q.RetrieveApproximateMessageCount()))
"Information"
        if (q.RetrieveApproximateMessageCount() > 3) then
            q.GetMessages(3) |> Seq.iter q.DeleteMessage

        let msg = q.GetMessage()
        if msg <> null then
            answerHost.Value <- msg.AsString
```

LISTING 8-30 Monitor role setting up the service bus service and cloud queue

```
override wr.OnStart() =
    // Set the maximum number of concurrent connections
    ServicePointManager.DefaultConnectionLimit <- 12

    // set up the queue
    let credential = StorageCredentialsAccountAndKey(CloudConstant.storageAccount,
CloudConstant.accountKey)

    q <- CloudQueue(CloudConstant.queueUrl, credential)
    q.CreateIfNotExist() |> ignore

    // start the service bus service
    let serviceNamespace = CloudConstant.serviceNamespace
    let issuerName = CloudConstant.issuerName
    let issuerSecret = CloudConstant.issuerSecret

    let sharedSecretServiceBusCredential = TransportClientEndpointBehavior()
    sharedSecretServiceBusCredential.TokenProvider <-
TokenProvider.CreateSharedSecretTokenProvider(issuerName, issuerSecret)
```

```
    let address = ServiceBusEnvironment.CreateServiceUri("sb", serviceNamespace,
CloudConstant.serviceName);
    host <- new ServiceHost(answerHost, address)
    let serviceRegistrySettings = ServiceRegistrySettings(DiscoveryType.Public)

    for endpoint in host.Description.Endpoints do
        endpoint.Behaviors.Add(serviceRegistrySettings)
        endpoint.Behaviors.Add(sharedSecretServiceBusCredential)

    host.Open()

    base.OnStart()
```

When the solution is executed, it can be viewed from the output windows in Visual Studio. Another approach is to use a service client to query the monitor role. Figure 8-43 shows the query result from the service bus client. As you monitor the results, you will see that the best solution is improving as time passes. Finally, the output will show the optimum, an all-9 string list. Because of the elitism concept that is used, once the population is converging at the optimum, it is very difficult for it to lose its focus.

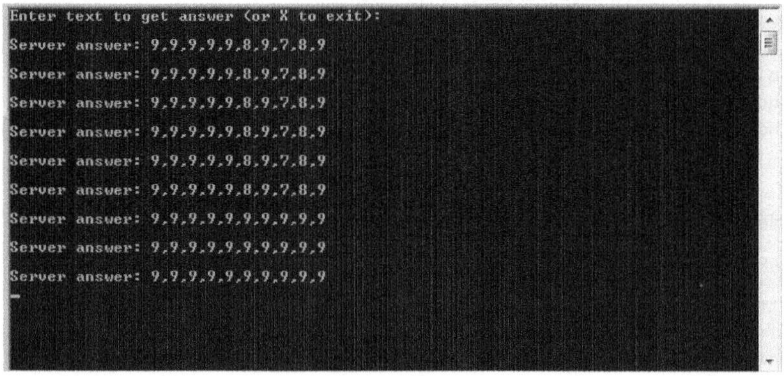

FIGURE 8-43 Query result from the GA execution

More sophisticated features, such as restart and acceptance of user input during the evolution, are beyond the scope of this book.

CHAPTER 9

GPGPU with F#

It's easy and natural to write a math formula in F#, and F# is widely used in scientific computation applications, such as those used by trading companies and investment banks. Applications can benefit greatly from being able to directly leverage the hardware, but providing this ability can be a challenge for many .NET languages. The common way for .NET to directly access hardware is by using .NET interop. F# has another weapon called *quotations*. A quotation shows the program structure and can be used to translate F# code. In this chapter, I will demonstrate how to use quotations to translate F# code to GPU code.

The *graphics processing unit (GPU)* chip on a graphics card can do something other than render an image for you. Most developers get excited when their machine has four or eight processors, but that is a drop in the bucket when compared to what the GPU offers. GPUs generally have tens and even hundreds of processors, which often sit in an idle state. A *general-purpose GPU (GPGPU)* takes advantage of these processors and extends them to more general-purpose applications. GPGPUs are not focused on rendering images; they are designed to use a large number of processors to perform parallel actions or computations.

In this chapter, I will describe how to use .NET interoperations and quotations to directly access hardware. F# does not have built-in support for GPU, so the F# library, which translates the quotations to code and can be executed on a GPU is needed. In addition to the F# translation library, some small samples are listed to show how to leverage the GPU to perform parallel computations.

Introducing GPU and GPGPU

One of the major F# application areas is financial services. A fundamental problem that financial businesses try to solve is how to perform mathematical computations in real time. From previous chapters, you know that F# is a perfect candidate for implementing mathematical functions, and GPGPUs include a mechanism to provide real-time computations. Adding a working knowledge of GPGPUs to your skill set can help you solve these kinds of real-world problems.

 Note This chapter is about how to use F# to leverage GPGPU to perform computations on the GPU. The code can be downloaded from the F# sample pack (*http://fsharp3sample. codeplex.com*). The code is located in the OtherSamples folder.

According to Wikipedia, the definition for GPU is the following.

> *A graphics processing unit (GPU), also occasionally called visual processing unit (VPU), is a specialized electronic circuit designed to rapidly manipulate and alter memory to accelerate the building of images in a frame buffer intended for output to a display. GPUs are used in embedded systems, mobile phones, personal computers, workstations, and game consoles. Modern GPUs are very efficient at manipulating computer graphics, and their highly parallel structure makes them more effective than general-purpose CPUs for algorithms where processing of large blocks of data is done in parallel. In a personal computer, a GPU can be present on a video card, or it can be on the motherboard or—in certain CPUs—on the CPU die. More than 90% of new desktop and notebook computers have integrated GPUs, which are usually far less powerful than those on a dedicated video card.*

For many people, the GPU is most relevant to computer games. However, the GPU has a number of other uses. Do you know that Amazon's GPU cluster (*http://aws.amazon.com/ec2/instance-types/*) can be used to enable high performance computations in the cloud? Maybe the application on your mobile phone or iPad is powered by the GPU running on a cloud cluster. Do you know that investment firms and brokerages are implementing GPU programming in their computation platforms to allow applications to quickly determine when to buy or sell stock? Any software developer working on these applications will have a lucrative career. Now might be a good time to take a second look at the small chip that has been ignored for a long time.

Wikipedia defines GPGPU as follows:

> *General-purpose computing on graphics processing units (GPGPU, GPGP or less often GP²U) is the means of using a graphics processing unit (GPU), which typically handles computation only for computer graphics, to perform computation in applications traditionally handled by the central processing unit (CPU). Any GPU providing a functionally complete set of operations performed on arbitrary bits can compute any computable value. Additionally, the use of multiple graphics cards in one computer, or large numbers of graphics chips, further parallelizes the already parallel nature of graphics processing.*

There are several GPU solutions on the market. OpenCL is the currently dominant open, general-purpose GPU computing language. The dominant proprietary framework is NVIDIA's CUDA. In this chapter, I use CUDA as the target framework.

CUDA

According to NVIDIA, the definition of CUDA is as follows:

> *CUDA is a parallel computing platform and programming model invented by NVIDIA. It enables dramatic increases in computing performance by harnessing the power of the graphics processing unit (GPU).*

CUDA provides a GPGPU platform including drivers, a development SDK, and an execution environment. In this chapter, CUDA is used for all samples. To run the samples from this chapter, you should install an NVIDIA graphic card and download the CUDA SDK from *http://developer.nvidia.com/cuda/cuda-downloads*. There are three installation packages:

- CUDA Toolkit

- Graphics drivers

- Development SDK

After you successfully install these three packages, the CUDA development environment is ready to use. The installation package creates several environment variables, as shown in Figure 9-1. And from the command line, you can execute the NVCC command, as shown in Figure 9-2.

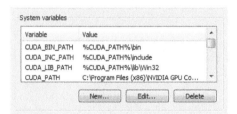

FIGURE 9-1 Environment variables created by the CUDA installation package

FIGURE 9-2 Executing NVCC from the command line

The first task is to retrieve the graphics card property using F# interop. You need to define the struct that holds the graphics card information. Listing 9-1 defines the CUDA structure in F#. *cudaError* is an enum structure that defines all CUDA error codes. *SizeT* is a struct wrapper for the *IntPtr* type. The *CUDADeviceProp* structure defines the graphics card properties. For this sample, there is a *Name* property that wraps the device property's name value.

LISTING 9-1 CUDA data structure definition

```
module CUDADataStructure

open System
open System.Runtime.InteropServices

// CUDA error enumeration
type cudaError =
    | cudaErrorAddressOfConstant = 22
    | cudaErrorApiFailureBase = 10000
    | cudaErrorCudartUnloading = 29
    | cudaErrorInitializationError = 3
    | cudaErrorInsufficientDriver = 35
    | cudaErrorInvalidChannelDescriptor = 20
    | cudaErrorInvalidConfiguration = 9
    | cudaErrorInvalidDevice = 10
    | cudaErrorInvalidDeviceFunction = 8
    | cudaErrorInvalidDevicePointer = 17
    | cudaErrorInvalidFilterSetting = 26
    | cudaErrorInvalidHostPointer = 16
    | cudaErrorInvalidMemcpyDirection = 21
    | cudaErrorInvalidNormSetting = 27
    | cudaErrorInvalidPitchValue = 12
    | cudaErrorInvalidResourceHandle = 33
    | cudaErrorInvalidSymbol = 13
    | cudaErrorInvalidTexture = 18
    | cudaErrorInvalidTextureBinding = 19
    | cudaErrorInvalidValue = 11
    | cudaErrorLaunchFailure = 4
    | cudaErrorLaunchOutOfResources = 7
    | cudaErrorLaunchTimeout = 6
    | cudaErrorMapBufferObjectFailed = 14
    | cudaErrorMemoryAllocation = 2
    | cudaErrorMemoryValueTooLarge = 32
    | cudaErrorMissingConfiguration = 1
    | cudaErrorMixedDeviceExecution = 28
    | cudaErrorNoDevice = 37
    | cudaErrorNotReady = 34
    | cudaErrorNotYetImplemented = 31
    | cudaErrorPriorLaunchFailure = 5
    | cudaErrorSetOnActiveProcess = 36
    | cudaErrorStartupFailure = 127
    | cudaErrorSynchronizationError = 25
    | cudaErrorTextureFetchFailed = 23
    | cudaErrorTextureNotBound = 24
    | cudaErrorUnknown = 30
    | cudaErrorUnmapBufferObjectFailed = 15
    | cudaErrorIncompatibleDriverContext = 49
    | cudaSuccess = 0
```

```fsharp
[<Struct>]
type SizeT =
    val value : IntPtr
    new (n:int) = { value = IntPtr(n) }
    new (n:int64) = { value = IntPtr(n) }

[<Struct>]
type CUDADeviceProp =
    [<MarshalAs(UnmanagedType.ByValArray, SizeConst = 256)>]
    val nameChar : char array
    val totalGlobalMem : SizeT
    val sharedMemPerBlock : SizeT
    val regsPerBlock : int
    val warpSize : int
    val memPitch : SizeT
    val maxThreadsPerBlock : int
    [<MarshalAs(UnmanagedType.ByValArray, SizeConst = 3)>]
    val maxThreadsDim : int array
    [<MarshalAs(UnmanagedType.ByValArray, SizeConst = 3)>]
    val maxGridSize : int array
    val clockRate : int
    val totalConstMem : SizeT
    val major : int
    val minor : int
    val textureAlignment: SizeT
    val deviceOverlap : int
    val multiProcessorCount : int
    val kernelExecTimeoutEnabled : int
    val integrated : int
    val canMapHostMemory : int
    val computeMode : int
    val maxTexture1D : int
    [<MarshalAs(UnmanagedType.ByValArray, SizeConst = 2)>]
    val maxTexture2D : int array
    [<MarshalAs(UnmanagedType.ByValArray, SizeConst = 3)>]
    val maxTexture3D : int array
    [<MarshalAs(UnmanagedType.ByValArray, SizeConst = 2)>]
    val maxTexture1DLayered : int array
    [<MarshalAs(UnmanagedType.ByValArray, SizeConst = 3)>]
    val maxTexture2DLayered : int array
    val surfaceAlignment : SizeT
    val concurrentKernels : int
    val ECCEnabled : int
    val pciBusID : int
    val pciDeviceID : int
    val pciDomainID : int
    val tccDriver : int
    val asyncEngineCount : int
    val unifiedAddressing : int
    val memoryClockRate : int
    val memoryBusWidth : int
    val l2CacheSize : int
    val maxThreadsPerMultiProcessor : int
    member this.Name = String(this.nameChar).Trim('\000')
```

Note In F#, the NULL character is represented as '\000', which is different from C#'s '\0'.

The interop code from the F# side is simple. The CUDA binary has 32-bit and 64-bit versions. Because of this, you define two modules, named CUDA32 and CUDA64. The CudaRT files are located under the CUDA installation folder. If the default installation path is used, the path should look like C:\ProgramData\NVIDIA Corporation\NVIDIA GPU Computing SDK 4.2\C\common\bin. The interop code is shown in Listing 9-2.

LISTING 9-2 F# CUDA interop code

```fsharp
open System
open System.Runtime.InteropServices
open CUDADataStructure

module CUDA32 =
    [<Literal>]
    let dllName = "cudart32_42_9"

    [<DllImport(dllName)>]
    extern cudaError cudaGetDeviceProperties(CUDADeviceProp& prop, int device)

    [<DllImport(dllName)>]
    extern cudaError cudaDeviceGetLimit(SizeT& pSize, cudaLimit limit)

module CUDA64 =
    [<Literal>]
    let dllName = "cudart64_42_9"

    [<DllImport(dllName)>]
    extern cudaError cudaGetDeviceProperties(CUDADeviceProp& prop, int device)

    [<DllImport(dllName)>]
    extern cudaError cudaDeviceGetLimit(SizeT& pSize, cudaLimit limit)

[<EntryPoint>]
let main argv =
    let mutable prop = CUDADeviceProp()

    // get the first graphic card by passing in 0
    let returnCode = CUDA32.cudaGetDeviceProperties (&prop, 0)

    printfn "%A - %A" returnCode prop.Name

    ignore <| System.Console.ReadKey()
    0 // return an integer exit code
```

Note The constant value *cudart64_42_9* could be different depending on the CUDA SDK installed on your computer. The file name shown in Listing 9-2 is based on CUDA 4.2. For the CUDA 4.0 SDK, the DLL file name is something like *cudart32_40_17*.

The F# *extern* method requires an ampersand (&) to pass a variable reference.

The execution result is shown in Figure 9-3.

FIGURE 9-3 Getting the device property execution result

The graphics card has some limitations, such as stack size. You need to know these limitations because your future coding needs to take these into consideration. The limitations are defined in our F# code as shown in Listing 9-3.

LISTING 9-3 *cudaLimit* enumeration

```
type cudaLimit =
    | cudaLimitStackSize = 0
    | cudaLimitPrintfFifoSize = 1
    | cudaLimitMallocHeapSize = 2
```

The interop code needed to get the device limitation information is shown in Listing 9-4, and the execution result is displayed in Figure 9-4. For most development activities, it is uncommon to have to query your hardware's limitations. This is because the operating system handles these limitations for you. However, this is not the case when programming against a GPU. For any code executed on the GPU, it is the developer's responsibility to understand and respect these limitations.

LISTING 9-4 Querying the limitations for the graphics device

```
let limitCategories = [
        cudaLimit.cudaLimitStackSize
        cudaLimit.cudaLimitPrintfFifoSize
        cudaLimit.cudaLimitMallocHeapSize ]

limitCategories |>
Seq.iter (fun category ->
                let mutable limit = SizeT()
                let returnCode = CUDA32.cudaDeviceGetLimit(&limit, category)
                printfn "%A: %A - %A" returnCode category limit.value)
```

```
cudaSuccess: cudaLimitStackSize - 1024n
cudaSuccess: cudaLimitPrintfFifoSize - 1048576n
cudaSuccess: cudaLimitMallocHeapSize - 8388608n
```

FIGURE 9-4 Getting the device limitations execution result

For device management, there are other commonly used functions (which are shown in Listing 9-5):

- **Reset device function** This function cleans up all resources on the current device associated with the current process. If there are multiple threads on the current process, it is the developer's responsibility to make sure the other thread or threads do not access this device.

- **Get device count function** This function returns the number of devices.

- **Set device flag function** This is useful for allowing you to set flags to configure how the GPU and CPU work together.

When the GPU is processing the data, there is a CPU thread waiting for the result to come back. The following flags configure how the CPU thread waits for the return value:

- *cudaDeviceScheduleAuto* is used as a default value. If the active CUDA context number is larger than the logical processor number, the thread can yield to other operating system threads. Otherwise, the CUDA will spin on the CPU processor and will not yield to other processors.

- *cudaDeviceScheduleSpin* instructs the CUDA thread on the CPU to never yield to other threads until it gets the result from the device. This can increase the CPU latency, but it can decrease the latency when waiting for results from the device.

- *cudaDeviceScheduleSpin* is the opposite of *cudaDeviceScheduleSpin*. It instructs the CUDA thread to yield to other operating system threads on the CPU when waiting for the result from the device.

- *cudaDeviceScheduleBlockingSync* instructs a CUDA thread on the CPU to block other CPU threads when waiting for the result from the device.

LISTING 9-5 Device flag definition

Code definition

```
type cudaDeviceFlag =
    | cudaDeviceScheduleAuto = 0
    | cudaDeviceScheduleSpin = 1
    | cudaDeviceScheduleYield = 2
    | cudaDeviceScheduleBlockingSync = 4

[<DllImport(dllName)>]
extern cudaError cudaDeviceReset()

[<DllImport(dllName)>]
extern cudaError cudaGetDeviceCount(int& count)
```

```
[<DllImport(dllName)>]
extern cudaError cudaSetDeviceFlags(cudaDeviceFlag count)
```

Invoking the code

```
let mutable deviceCount = 0
let returnCode = CUDA32.cudaGetDeviceCount(&deviceCount)
printfn "%A: %A" returnCode deviceCount

let returnCode = CUDA32.cudaSetDeviceFlags(cudaDeviceFlag.cudaDeviceScheduleAuto)
printfn "set flag return code %A" returnCode

let returnCode = CUDA32.cudaDeviceReset()
printfn "reset device %A" returnCode
```

In addition to the hardware information, the driver information is also important, because hardware functionalities are exposed by the device driver. Different hardware exposes different APIs and has different memory capacity. The managed language developer does not have to consider the memory because the operating system and .NET Framework take care of memory management. However, the developer does need to keep the hardware configuration in mind when programming for the GPU. Therefore, it is important to know the current driver version. Listing 9-6 shows how to get the driver version.

LISTING 9-6 Getting the driver version

```
type CUResult =
    | Success = 0
    | ErrorInvalidValue = 1
    | ErrorOutOfMemory = 2
    | ErrorNotInitialized = 3
    | ErrorDeinitialized = 4
    | ErrorNoDevice = 100
    | ErrorInvalidDevice = 101
    | ECCUncorrectable = 214
    | ErrorAlreadyAcquired = 210
    | ErrorAlreadyMapped = 208
    | ErrorArrayIsMapped = 207
    | ErrorContextAlreadyCurrent = 202
    | ErrorFileNotFound = 301
    | ErrorInvalidImage = 200
    | ErrorInvalidContext = 201
    | ErrorInvalidHandle = 400
    | ErrorInvalidSource = 300
    | ErrorLaunchFailed = 700
    | ErrorLaunchIncompatibleTexturing = 703
    | ErrorLaunchOutOfResources = 701
    | ErrorLaunchTimeout = 702
    | ErrorMapFailed = 205
```

```
        | ErrorNoBinaryForGPU = 209
        | ErrorNotFound = 500
        | ErrorNotMapped = 211
        | ErrorNotReady = 600
        | ErrorUnmapFailed = 206
        | NotMappedAsArray = 212
        | NotMappedAsPointer = 213
        | PointerIs64Bit = 800
        | SizeIs64Bit = 801
        | ErrorUnknown = 999

module InteropLibrary =
    [<DllImport("nvcuda")>]
    extern CUResult cuDriverGetVersion(int& driverVersion)

type CUDADriver() =
    member this.Version =
        let mutable version = 0
        (InteropLibrary.cuDriverGetVersion(&version), version)
```

 Note There is a *cudaError* structure defined in Listing 9-1. The *cuError* structure seems to serve the same purpose. However, *cuError* is defined as part of the CUDA driver API, while *cudaError* is part of the CUDA runtime API. The runtime API is based on the driver API. Programming runtime APIs is simpler, but driver APIs provide better control over the device. There is no performance difference between these two types of APIs. It is recommended that you refrain from combining these two kinds of APIs in one application. The function in the driver API is prefixed with *cu*, while the runtime API begins with *cuda*.

To make the GPU compute the data, the data should first be loaded into memory. The computations happen within the GPU's memory. You refer to the GPU as *device* and the CPU as *host*. The CPU memory is called the *host memory*, and the GPU memory is called the *device memory*. The memory-management function is defined in Listing 9-7. The enum type *CUDAMemcpyKind* defines four types of memory copy operations.

LISTING 9-7 CUDA device memory-management function

```
namespace CUDARuntime

open System
open System.Text
open System.Collections.Generic
open System.Runtime.InteropServices
open CUDADataStructure
```

```
type CUDAMemcpyKind =
    | cudaMemcpyHostToHost = 0
    | cudaMemcpyHostToDevice = 1
    | cudaMemcpyDeviceToHost = 2
    | cudaMemcpyDeviceToDevice = 3

module CUDARuntime64 =
    [<Literal>]
    let dllName = "cudart64_40_17"

    [<DllImport(dllName)>]
    extern cudaError cudaMemcpy(IntPtr dst, IntPtr src, SizeT count, CUDAMemcpyKind kind)

    [<DllImport(dllName)>]
    extern cudaError cudaMalloc(IntPtr& p, SizeT size)

    [<DllImport(dllName)>]
    extern cudaError cudaMemset(IntPtr& p, int value, int count)

module CUDARuntime32 =
    [<Literal>]
    let dllName = "cudart32_40_17"

    [<DllImport(dllName)>]
    extern cudaError cudaMemcpy(IntPtr dst, IntPtr src, SizeT count, CUDAMemcpyKind kind)

    [<DllImport(dllName)>]
    extern cudaError cudaMalloc(IntPtr& p, SizeT size)

    [<DllImport(dllName)>]
    extern cudaError cudaMemset(IntPtr& p, int value, int count)
```

Listing 9-8 shows how to copy data between the host and device memory, and its result is shown in Figure 9-5. Because memory copying is a bottleneck for GPGPU computations, it is not a good practice to copy data between host memory and device memory. The best practice is to keep the data in device memory as long as possible.

LISTING 9-8 Transferring data between device and host memory

```
open System.Runtime.InteropServices

let test5() =
    let getIntPtr arr =
        let nativeint = Marshal.UnsafeAddrOfPinnedArrayElement(arr, 0)
        let intptr = new System.IntPtr(nativeint.ToPointer())
        intptr

    let mutable ptr = IntPtr()
    let arr = [|1.f; 2.f; 3.f; 4.f; 5.f; 1.f; 2.f; 3.f; 4.f; 5.f;|]
    let arr2 = [|11.f; 12.f; 13.f; 14.f; 15.f; 11.f; 12.f; 13.f; 14.f; 15.f;|]
```

```
let intptr = getIntPtr arr
let intptr2 = getIntPtr arr2
let size = arr.Length * sizeof<float>
let error = CUDARuntime32.cudaMalloc(&ptr, SizeT(size))
let error = CUDARuntime32.cudaMemcpy(ptr,
                                     intptr,
                                     SizeT(10 * 4),
                                     CUDAMemcpyKind.cudaMemcpyHostToDevice)

let error = CUDA32.cudaMemcpy(intptr2,
                              ptr,
                              SizeT(size),
                              CUDAMemcpyKind.cudaMemcpyDeviceToHost)

printfn "%A - %A" arr arr2
```

```
[|1.0f; 2.0f; 3.0f; 4.0f; 5.0f; 1.0f; 2.0f; 3.0f; 4.0f; 5.0f|]
[|1.0f; 2.0f; 3.0f; 4.0f; 5.0f; 1.0f; 2.0f; 3.0f; 4.0f; 5.0f|]
```

FIGURE 9-5 Execution result from the code in Listing 9-8

This section demonstrated how to configure the device and copy data to or from the device. There are several CUDA libraries provided by NVIDIA. The CUDA runtime and CUDA driver API provide the basic ability to program against the GPU. In addition, CUDA provides a rich set of libraries to boost this development. In the next section, I am going to demonstrate how to use F# to invoke these libraries and perform basic computations on the GPU.

CUDA Toolkit

Some libraries, collectively known as the NVIDIA *CUDA Toolkit*, are provided with CUDA. According to the NVIDIA website (*http://developer.nvidia.com/cuda/cuda-toolkit*), the NVIDIA CUDA Toolkit provides a comprehensive development environment for C and C++ developers building GPU-accelerated applications. The CUDA Toolkit includes a compiler for NVIDIA GPUs, math libraries, and tools for debugging and optimizing the performance of your applications. You'll also find programming guides, user manuals, an API reference, and other documentation to help you get started with accelerating your application with the GPU.

In this section, two libraries—cuRAND and cuBLAS—are used to demonstrate how to use *PInvoke* to invoke CUDA functions from F#.

cuRAND Library

The first library presented is the NVIDIA CUDA Random Number Generation library (cuRAND). According to the NVIDIA website (*http://developer.nvidia.com/cuda/curand*), the cuRAND delivers high-performance, GPU-accelerated random number generation (RNG). The cuRAND library delivers high-quality random numbers using hundreds of processor cores available in the NVIDIA GPU. The random number generator is the basic building block for simulations such as the Monte Carlo simulation. The performance from the cuRAND library can improve the performance of the simulation.

There are several enumeration structures defined for the CUDA library. The *RanGenerator* structure, shown in Listing 9-9, is used to reference the random generator.

LISTING 9-9 cuRAND enumeration types

```
type curandStatus =
    | CURAND_SUCCESS = 0
    | CURAND_VERSION_MISMATCH = 100
    | CURAND_NOT_INITIALIZED = 101
    | CURAND_ALLOCATION_FAILED = 102
    | CURAND_TYPE_ERROR =103
    | CURAND_OUT_OF_RANGE = 104
    | CURAND_LENGTH_NOT_MULTIPLE = 105
    | CURAND_LAUNCH_FAILURE = 201
    | CURAND_PREEXISTING_FAILURE = 202
    | CURAND_INITIALIZATION_FAILED = 203
    | CURAND_ARCH_MISMATCH = 204
    | CURAND_INTERNAL_ERROR = 999

type CUDARandomRngType =
    | CURAND_TEST = 0
    | CURAND_PSEUDO_DEFAULT = 100
    | CURAND_PSEUDO_XORWOW = 101
    | CURAND_QUASI_DEFAULT = 200
    | CURAND_QUASI_SOBOL32 = 201
    | CURAND_QUASI_SCRAMBLED_SOBOL32 = 202
    | CURAND_QUASI_SOBOL64 = 203
    | CURAND_QUASI_SCRAMBLED_SOBOL64 = 204

type CUDARandomOrdering =
    | CURAND_PSEUDO_BEST = 100
    | CURAND_PSEUDO_DEFAULT = 101
    | CURAND_PSEUDO_SEEDED = 102
    | CURAND_QUASI_DEFAULT = 201

type CUDADirectionVectorSet =
    | CURAND_VECTORS_32_JOEKUO6 = 101
    | CURAND_DIRECTION_VECTORS_32_JOEKUO6 = 102
    | CURAND_VECTORS_64_JOEKUO6 = 103
    | CURAND_DIRECTION_VECTORS_64_JOEKUO6 = 104

[<Struct>]
type RandGenerator =
    val handle : uint32
```

Because the library has both an x86 and x64 flavor, the F# cuRAND library needs to provide two versions as well, as shown in Listing 9-10. The CUDAPointer struct wraps the pointer to the data stored in the GPU memory.

LISTING 9-10 cuRAND library code

```
open System
open System.Text
open System.Collections.Generic
open System.Runtime.InteropServices
open CUDADataStructure
open CUDARuntime

[<Struct>]
type CUDAPointer =
    val Pointer : IntPtr
    new(ptr) = { Pointer = ptr }
    new(cudaPointer:CUDAPointer) = { Pointer = cudaPointer.Pointer }
    member this.PointerSize with get() = IntPtr.Size

[<Struct>]
type RandDirectionVectors32 =
    [<MarshalAs(UnmanagedType.ByValArray, SizeConst = 32)>]
    val direction_vectors :  uint32[]

[<Struct>]
type RandDirectionVectors64 =
    [<MarshalAs(UnmanagedType.ByValArray, SizeConst = 64)>]
    val direction_vectors :  uint64[]

// CUDA random generator x86 version
module CUDARandomDriver32 =
    [<Literal>]
    let dllName =  "curand32_40_17"
    [<DllImport(dllName)>]
    extern curandStatus curandCreateGenerator(RandGenerator& generator,
                                               CUDARandomRngType rng_type)

    [<DllImport(dllName)>]
    extern curandStatus curandCreateGeneratorHost(RandGenerator& generator,
                                                   CUDARandomRngType rng_type)

    [<DllImport(dllName)>]
    extern curandStatus curandDestroyGenerator(RandGenerator generator)
    [<DllImport(dllName)>]
    extern curandStatus curandGenerate(RandGenerator generator,
                                       IntPtr outputPtr,
                                       SizeT num)

    [<DllImport(dllName)>]
    extern curandStatus curandGenerateLogNormal(RandGenerator generator,
                                                 IntPtr outputPtr,
                                                 SizeT n,
                                                 float mean,
                                                 float stddev)

    [<DllImport(dllName)>]
    extern curandStatus curandGenerateLogNormalDouble(RandGenerator generator,
                                                       IntPtr outputPtr,
                                                       SizeT n, double mean,
double stddev)
```

```fsharp
    [<DllImport(dllName)>]
    extern curandStatus curandGenerateLongLong(RandGenerator generator,
                                               IntPtr outputPtr,
                                               SizeT num)
    [<DllImport(dllName)>]
    extern curandStatus curandGenerateNormal(RandGenerator generator,
                                             IntPtr outputPtr,
                                             SizeT n, float mean, float stddev)
    [<DllImport(dllName)>]
    extern curandStatus curandGenerateNormalDouble(RandGenerator generator,
                                                   IntPtr outputPtr,
                                                   SizeT n, double mean, double
stddev)
    [<DllImport(dllName)>]
    extern curandStatus curandGenerateSeeds(RandGenerator generator)
    [<DllImport(dllName)>]
    extern curandStatus curandGenerateUniform(RandGenerator generator,
                                              IntPtr outputPtr, SizeT num)
    [<DllImport(dllName)>]
    extern curandStatus curandGenerateUniformDouble(RandGenerator generator,
                                                    IntPtr outputPtr, SizeT num)
    [<DllImport(dllName)>]
    extern curandStatus curandGetDirectionVectors32(RandDirectionVectors32& vectors,
                                                    CUDADirectionVectorSet set)
    [<DllImport(dllName)>]
    extern curandStatus curandGetDirectionVectors64(RandDirectionVectors64& vectors,
                                                    CUDADirectionVectorSet set)
    [<DllImport(dllName)>]
    extern curandStatus curandGetScrambleConstants32(IntPtr& constants)
    [<DllImport(dllName)>]
    extern curandStatus curandGetScrambleConstants64(IntPtr& constants)
    [<DllImport(dllName)>]
    extern curandStatus curandGetVersion(int& version)
    [<DllImport(dllName)>]
    extern curandStatus curandSetGeneratorOffset(RandGenerator generator, uint64 offset)
    [<DllImport(dllName)>]
    extern curandStatus curandSetGeneratorOrdering(RandGenerator generator,
                                                   CUDARandomOrdering order)
    [<DllImport(dllName)>]
    extern curandStatus curandSetPseudoRandomGeneratorSeed(RandGenerator generator,
                                                           uint64 seed)
    [<DllImport(dllName)>]
    extern curandStatus curandSetQuasiRandomGeneratorDimensions(RandGenerator generator,
                                                                uint32 num_
dimensions)
    [<DllImport(dllName)>]
    extern curandStatus curandSetStream(RandGenerator generator, CUDAStream stream)

    let CreateGenerator(rng_type) =
        let mutable generator = Unchecked.defaultof<RandGenerator>
        let r = curandCreateGenerator(&generator, rng_type)
        (r, generator)
```

```
let DestroyGenerator(generator) =
    curandDestroyGenerator(generator)

let SetPseudoRandomGeneratorSeed(generator, seed) =
    curandSetPseudoRandomGeneratorSeed(generator, seed)

let SetGeneratorOffset(generator, offset) =
    curandSetGeneratorOffset(generator, offset)

let SetGeneratorOrdering(generator, order) =
    curandSetGeneratorOrdering(generator, order)

let SetQuasiRandomGeneratorDimensions(generator, dimensions) =
    curandSetQuasiRandomGeneratorDimensions(generator, dimensions)

let CopyToHost(out:'T array, cudaPtr:CUDAPointer) =
    let devPtr = cudaPtr.Pointer
    let outputPtr = GCHandle.Alloc(out, GCHandleType.Pinned).AddrOfPinnedObject()
    let unitSize = Marshal.SizeOf(typeof<float32>)
    let n = out.Length
    let size = SizeT(n * unitSize)
    let r = CUDARuntime32.cudaMemcpy(outputPtr, devPtr, size,
                                    CUDAMemcpyKind.cudaMemcpyDeviceToHost)
    r

let GenerateUniform(generator, n:int) =
    let unitSize = Marshal.SizeOf(typeof<float32>)
    let size = SizeT(n * unitSize)
    let mutable devicePtr = Unchecked.defaultof<IntPtr>
    let r = CUDARuntime32.cudaMalloc(&devicePtr, size)
    let r = curandGenerateUniform(generator, devicePtr, size)
    (r, CUDAPointer(devicePtr))

let GenerateUniformDouble(generator, n:int) =
    let unitSize = Marshal.SizeOf(typeof<float>)
    let size = SizeT(n * unitSize)
    let mutable devicePtr = Unchecked.defaultof<IntPtr>
    let r = CUDARuntime32.cudaMalloc(&devicePtr, size)
    let r = curandGenerateUniform(generator, devicePtr, size)
    (r, CUDAPointer(devicePtr))

let GenerateNormal(generator, n:int, mean, stddev) =
    let unitSize = Marshal.SizeOf(typeof<float32>)
    let size = SizeT(n * unitSize)
    let mutable devicePtr = Unchecked.defaultof<IntPtr>
    let r = CUDARuntime32.cudaMalloc(&devicePtr, size)
    let r = curandGenerateNormal(generator, devicePtr, size, mean, stddev)
    (r, CUDAPointer(devicePtr))

let GenerateNormalDouble(generator, n:int, mean, stddev) =
    let unitSize = Marshal.SizeOf(typeof<float32>)
    let size = SizeT(n * unitSize)
    let mutable devicePtr = Unchecked.defaultof<IntPtr>
    let r = CUDARuntime32.cudaMalloc(&devicePtr, size)
```

```
            let r = curandGenerateNormalDouble(generator, devicePtr, size, mean, stddev)
            (r, CUDAPointer(devicePtr))

    let GenerateLogNormal(generator, n:int, mean, stddev) =
        let unitSize = Marshal.SizeOf(typeof<float32>)
        let size = SizeT(n * unitSize)
        let mutable devicePtr = Unchecked.defaultof<IntPtr>
        let r = CUDARuntime32.cudaMalloc(&devicePtr, size)
        let r = curandGenerateLogNormal(generator, devicePtr, size, mean, stddev)
        (r, CUDAPointer(devicePtr))

    let GenerateLogNormalDouble(generator, n:int, mean, stddev) =
        let unitSize = Marshal.SizeOf(typeof<float>)
        let size = SizeT(n * unitSize)
        let mutable devicePtr = Unchecked.defaultof<IntPtr>
        let r = CUDARuntime32.cudaMalloc(&devicePtr, size)
        let r = curandGenerateLogNormalDouble(generator, devicePtr, size, mean, stddev)
        (r, CUDAPointer(devicePtr))

// CUDA random generator x64 version
module CUDARandomDriver64 =
    [<Literal>]
    let dllName = "curand64_40_17"
    [<DllImport(dllName)>]
    extern curandStatus curandCreateGenerator(RandGenerator& generator,
                                              CUDARandomRngType rng_type)
    [<DllImport(dllName)>]
    extern curandStatus curandCreateGeneratorHost(RandGenerator& generator,
                                                  CUDARandomRngType rng_type)
    [<DllImport(dllName)>]
    extern curandStatus curandDestroyGenerator(RandGenerator generator)
    [<DllImport(dllName)>]
    extern curandStatus curandGenerate(RandGenerator generator, IntPtr outputPtr, SizeT
num)
    [<DllImport(dllName)>]
    extern curandStatus curandGenerateLogNormal(RandGenerator generator,
                                                IntPtr outputPtr,
                                                SizeT n, float mean, float
stddev)
    [<DllImport(dllName)>]
    extern curandStatus curandGenerateLogNormalDouble(RandGenerator generator,
                                                      IntPtr outputPtr,
                                                      SizeT n, double mean,
double stddev)
    [<DllImport(dllName)>]
    extern curandStatus curandGenerateLongLong(RandGenerator generator,
                                               IntPtr outputPtr, SizeT num)
    [<DllImport(dllName)>]
    extern curandStatus curandGenerateNormal(RandGenerator generator,
                                             IntPtr outputPtr,
                                             SizeT n, float mean, float stddev)
```

```
    [<DllImport(dllName)>]
    extern curandStatus curandGenerateNormalDouble(RandGenerator generator,
                                                   IntPtr outputPtr,
                                                   SizeT n, double mean, double
stddev)
    [<DllImport(dllName)>]
    extern curandStatus curandGenerateSeeds(RandGenerator generator)
    [<DllImport(dllName)>]
    extern curandStatus curandGenerateUniform(RandGenerator generator,
                                              IntPtr outputPtr, SizeT num)
    [<DllImport(dllName)>]
    extern curandStatus curandGenerateUniformDouble(RandGenerator generator,
                                                    IntPtr outputPtr, SizeT num)
    [<DllImport(dllName)>]
    extern curandStatus curandGetDirectionVectors32(RandDirectionVectors32& vectors,
                                                    CUDADirectionVectorSet set)
    [<DllImport(dllName)>]
    extern curandStatus curandGetDirectionVectors64(RandDirectionVectors64& vectors,
                                                    CUDADirectionVectorSet set)
    [<DllImport(dllName)>]
    extern curandStatus curandGetScrambleConstants32(IntPtr& constants)
    [<DllImport(dllName)>]
    extern curandStatus curandGetScrambleConstants64(IntPtr& constants)
    [<DllImport(dllName)>]
    extern curandStatus curandGetVersion(int& version)
    [<DllImport(dllName)>]
    extern curandStatus curandSetGeneratorOffset(RandGenerator generator, uint64 offset)
    [<DllImport(dllName)>]
    extern curandStatus curandSetGeneratorOrdering(RandGenerator generator,
                                                   CUDARandomOrdering order)
    [<DllImport(dllName)>]
    extern curandStatus curandSetPseudoRandomGeneratorSeed(RandGenerator generator,
                                                           uint64 seed);
    [<DllImport(dllName)>]
    extern curandStatus curandSetQuasiRandomGeneratorDimensions(RandGenerator generator,
                                                                uint32 num_
dimensions)
    [<DllImport(dllName)>]
    extern curandStatus curandSetStream(RandGenerator generator, CUDAStream stream)

    let CreateGenerator(rng_type) =
        let mutable generator = Unchecked.defaultof<RandGenerator>
        let r = curandCreateGenerator(&generator, rng_type)
        (r, generator)

    let DestroyGenerator(generator) =
        curandDestroyGenerator(generator)

    let SetPseudoRandomGeneratorSeed(generator, seed) =
        curandSetPseudoRandomGeneratorSeed(generator, seed)

    let SetGeneratorOffset(generator, offset) =
        curandSetGeneratorOffset(generator, offset)
```

```
let SetGeneratorOrdering(generator, order) =
    curandSetGeneratorOrdering(generator, order)

let SetQuasiRandomGeneratorDimensions(generator, dimensions) =
    curandSetQuasiRandomGeneratorDimensions(generator, dimensions)

let GenerateUniform(generator, n:int) =
    let unitSize = Marshal.SizeOf(typeof<float32>)
    let size = SizeT(n * unitSize)
    let mutable devicePtr = Unchecked.defaultof<IntPtr>
    let r = CUDARuntime64.cudaMalloc(&devicePtr, size)
    let r = curandGenerateUniform(generator, devicePtr, size)
    (r, CUDAPointer(devicePtr))

let GenerateUniformDouble(generator, n:int) =
    let unitSize = Marshal.SizeOf(typeof<float>)
    let size = SizeT(n * unitSize)
    let mutable devicePtr = Unchecked.defaultof<IntPtr>
    let r = CUDARuntime64.cudaMalloc(&devicePtr, size)
    let r = curandGenerateUniform(generator, devicePtr, size)
    (r, CUDAPointer(devicePtr))
let GenerateNormal(generator, n:int, mean, stddev) =
    let unitSize = Marshal.SizeOf(typeof<float32>)
    let size = SizeT(n * unitSize)
    let mutable devicePtr = Unchecked.defaultof<IntPtr>
    let r = CUDARuntime64.cudaMalloc(&devicePtr, size)
    let r = curandGenerateNormal(generator, devicePtr, size, mean, stddev)
    (r, CUDAPointer(devicePtr))

let GenerateNormalDouble(generator, n:int, mean, stddev) =
    let unitSize = Marshal.SizeOf(typeof<float32>)
    let size = SizeT(n * unitSize)
    let mutable devicePtr = Unchecked.defaultof<IntPtr>
    let r = CUDARuntime64.cudaMalloc(&devicePtr, size)
    let r = curandGenerateNormalDouble(generator, devicePtr, size, mean, stddev)
    (r, CUDAPointer(devicePtr))

let GenerateLogNormal(generator, n:int, mean, stddev) =
    let unitSize = Marshal.SizeOf(typeof<float32>)
    let size = SizeT(n * unitSize)
    let mutable devicePtr = Unchecked.defaultof<IntPtr>
    let r = CUDARuntime64.cudaMalloc(&devicePtr, size)
    let r = curandGenerateLogNormal(generator, devicePtr, size, mean, stddev)
    (r, CUDAPointer(devicePtr))

let GenerateLogNormalDouble(generator, n:int, mean, stddev) =
    let unitSize = Marshal.SizeOf(typeof<float>)
    let size = SizeT(n * unitSize)
    let mutable devicePtr = Unchecked.defaultof<IntPtr>
    let r = CUDARuntime64.cudaMalloc(&devicePtr, size)
    let r = curandGenerateLogNormalDouble(generator, devicePtr, size, mean, stddev)
    (r, CUDAPointer(devicePtr))
```

If you prefer to use a class, a class version of *CUDARandom* is defined in Listing 9-11.

LISTING 9-11 *CUDARandom* class definition

```
type CUDARandom() =

    let is64bit = IntPtr.Size = 8

    member this.CreateGenerator(rand_type) =
        if is64bit then
            CUDARandomDriver64.CreateGenerator(rand_type)
        else
            CUDARandomDriver32.CreateGenerator(rand_type)
    member this.DestroyGenerator(g) =
        if is64bit then
            CUDARandomDriver64.DestroyGenerator(g)
        else
            CUDARandomDriver32.DestroyGenerator(g)
    member this.SetPseudoRandomGeneratorSeed(g, obj) =
        if is64bit then
            CUDARandomDriver64.SetPseudoRandomGeneratorSeed(g, obj |> unbox |> uint64)
        else
            CUDARandomDriver32.SetPseudoRandomGeneratorSeed(g, obj |> unbox |> uint64)
    member this.SetGeneratorOffset(g, obj) =
        if is64bit then
            CUDARandomDriver64.SetGeneratorOffset(g, obj |> unbox |> uint64)
        else
            CUDARandomDriver32.SetGeneratorOffset(g, obj |> unbox |> uint64)
    member this.SetGeneratorOrdering(g, ordering) =
        if is64bit then
            CUDARandomDriver64.SetGeneratorOrdering(g, ordering)
        else
            CUDARandomDriver32.SetGeneratorOrdering(g, ordering)
    member this.SetQuasiRandomGeneratorDimensions(g, obj) =
        if is64bit then
            CUDARandomDriver64.SetQuasiRandomGeneratorDimensions(g, obj |> unbox |>
uint32)
        else
            CUDARandomDriver32.SetQuasiRandomGeneratorDimensions(g, obj |> unbox |>
uint32)
    member this.GenerateUniform(g, seed) =
        if is64bit then
            CUDARandomDriver64.GenerateUniform(g, seed)
        else
            CUDARandomDriver32.GenerateUniform(g, seed)
    member this.GenerateUniformDouble(g, seed) =
        if is64bit then
            CUDARandomDriver64.GenerateUniformDouble(g, seed)
        else
            CUDARandomDriver32.GenerateUniformDouble(g, seed)
    member this.GenerateNormal(g, seed, mean, variance) =
        if is64bit then
            CUDARandomDriver64.GenerateNormal(g, seed, mean, variance)
```

```
        else
            CUDARandomDriver32.GenerateNormal(g, seed, mean, variance)
    member this.GenerateNormalDouble(g, seed, mean, variance) =
        if is64bit then
            CUDARandomDriver64.GenerateNormalDouble(g, seed, mean, variance)
        else
            CUDARandomDriver32.GenerateNormalDouble(g, seed, mean, variance)
    member this.GenerateLogNormal(g, seed, mean, variance) =
        if is64bit then
            CUDARandomDriver64.GenerateLogNormal(g, seed, mean, variance)
        else
            CUDARandomDriver32.GenerateLogNormal(g, seed, mean, variance)
    member this.GenerateLogNormalDouble(g, seed, mean, variance) =
        if is64bit then
            CUDARandomDriver64.GenerateLogNormalDouble(g, seed, mean, variance)
        else
            CUDARandomDriver32.GenerateLogNormalDouble(g, seed, mean, variance)
```

The sample code needed to invoke the *CUDARandom* class is shown in Listing 9-12. The sample code generates 256 random numbers.

LISTING 9-12 Sample code to invoke the *CUDARandom* class

```
open System.Runtime.InteropServices

let test6() =
    let n = 256
    let r = CUDARandom()
    let status, g = r.CreateGenerator(CUDARandomRngType.CURAND_PSEUDO_DEFAULT)
    if status = curandStatus.CURAND_SUCCESS then
        let status, v = r.GenerateUniform(g, n)
        if status = curandStatus.CURAND_SUCCESS then
            let array : float32 array = Array.zeroCreate n
            let nativePtr = Marshal.UnsafeAddrOfPinnedArrayElement(array, 0)
            let p = System.IntPtr(nativePtr.ToPointer())
            CUDARuntime.CUDARuntime64.cudaMemcpy(
                p,
                v.Pointer,
                SizeT(n*Marshal.SizeOf(sizeof<float32>)),
                CUDAMemcpyKind.cudaMemcpyDeviceToHost)
            r.DestroyGenerator(g)
            array
            |> Seq.iter (printfn "%A")
        else
            printfn "generation failed. status = %A" status
            r.DestroyGenerator(g)
    else
        printfn "create generator failed. status = %A" status
        r.DestroyGenerator(g)
    ()
```

The generated random numbers result in a uniform distribution. If the random numbers need to be generated from a customized function, you can use an accept-rejection algorithm. This method is based on the observation that one can sample uniformly from the region under the graph of its density function. The algorithm works like this:

- Sample a point *x* from a distribution—for example, uniform distribution.

- Draw a vertical line from *x* to cut the target function's diagram.

- Sample uniformly along this vertical line starting from *x*. If the point is located outside the target function's distribution, reject it.

You can then use the filter to generate the agreed-to sample value with the formula f(x), as shown in Listing 9-13.

LISTING 9-13 Accept-reject algorithm

```
open System.Runtime.InteropServices

let test6_2() =
    let n = 256
    let r = CUDARandom()
    let status, g = r.CreateGenerator(CUDARandomRngType.CURAND_PSEUDO_DEFAULT)
    if status = curandStatus.CURAND_SUCCESS then
        let status, v = r.GenerateUniform(g, n)
        if status = curandStatus.CURAND_SUCCESS then
            let array : float32 array = Array.zeroCreate n
            let nativePtr = Marshal.UnsafeAddrOfPinnedArrayElement(array, 0)
            let p = System.IntPtr(nativePtr.ToPointer())
            CUDARuntime.CUDARuntime64.cudaMemcpy(
                p,
                v.Pointer,
                SizeT(n*Marshal.SizeOf(sizeof<float32>)),
                CUDAMemcpyKind.cudaMemcpyDeviceToHost)
            r.DestroyGenerator(g)
            array
        else
            r.DestroyGenerator(g)
            failwith "generation failed. status = %A" status
    else
        r.DestroyGenerator(g)
        failwith "create generator failed. status = %A" status

let test7() =
    let xArray = test6_2()
    let yArray = test6_2()

    Array.zip xArray yArray
    |> Array.filter (fun (x, y) -> x * x <= y)
    |> Seq.iter (fun (x, y) -> printfn "(%A, %A)" x y)
```

cuBLAS Library

The second library is the CUDA Basic Linear Algebra Subroutines library (cuBLAS). According to the NVIDIA website (*http://developer.nvidia.com/cuda/cublas*), the cuBLAS library is a GPU-accelerated version of the complete standard BLAS library that delivers performance that's 6 to 17 times faster than the latest MKL BLAS. The code that defines the data structure in F# is shown in Listing 9-14.

LISTING 9-14 cuBLAS data structures

```
[<Struct>]
type CUDABLASHandle =
    val handle : uint32

[<Struct>]
type CUDAStream =
    val Value : int

[<Struct>]
type CUDAFloatComplex =
    val real : float32
    val imag : float32

type CUBLASPointerMode =
    | Host = 0
    | Device = 1

type CUBLASStatus =
    | Success = 0
    | NotInitialized = 1
    | AllocFailed = 3
    | InvalidValue = 7
    | ArchMismatch = 8
    | MappingError = 11
    | ExecutionFailed = 13
    | InternalError = 14
```

The F# wrapper code for the cuBLAS library is shown in Listing 9-15. The 32-bit version does not list all of the functions. The only difference between the 32-bit version and the 64-bit version is the *dllName* variable. The 64-bit version is *cublas64_42_9*, and the 32-bit version is *cublas32_42_9*.

LISTING 9-15 cuBLAS library

```
module CUDABLASDriver64 =
    [<Literal>]
    let dllName =  "cublas64_42_9"
    [<DllImport(dllName)>]
    extern CUBLASStatus cublasInit()
    [<DllImport(dllName)>]
    extern CUBLASStatus cublasShutdown()
```

```
[<DllImport(dllName)>]
extern CUBLASStatus cublasGetError()
[<DllImport(dllName)>]
extern CUBLASStatus cublasFree(CUDAPointer devicePtr)
[<DllImport(dllName)>]
extern CUBLASStatus cublasCreate_v2(CUDABLASHandle& handle)
[<DllImport(dllName)>]
extern CUBLASStatus cublasSetStream_v2(CUDABLASHandle handle, CUDAStream streamId)
[<DllImport(dllName)>]
extern CUBLASStatus cublasGetStream_v2(CUDABLASHandle handle, CUDAStream& streamId)
[<DllImport(dllName)>]
extern CUBLASStatus cublasGetPointerMode_v2(CUDABLASHandle handle,
                                            CUBLASPointerMode& mode)
[<DllImport(dllName)>]
extern CUBLASStatus cublasSetPointerMode_v2(CUDABLASHandle handle,
                                            CUBLASPointerMode mode)
[<DllImport(dllName)>]
extern CUBLASStatus cublasIcamax_v2(CUDABLASHandle handle,
                                    int n, IntPtr x, int incx, int& result)
[<DllImport(dllName)>]
extern CUBLASStatus cublasIdamax_v2(CUDABLASHandle handle,
                                    int n, IntPtr x, int incx, int& result)
[<DllImport(dllName)>]
extern CUBLASStatus cublasIsamax_v2(CUDABLASHandle handle,
                                    int n, IntPtr x, int incx, int& result)
[<DllImport(dllName)>]
extern CUBLASStatus cublasIzamax_v2(CUDABLASHandle handle,
                                    int n, IntPtr x, int incx, int& result)
[<DllImport(dllName)>]
extern CUBLASStatus cublasIcamin_v2(CUDABLASHandle handle,
                                    int n, IntPtr x, int incx, int& result)
[<DllImport(dllName)>]
extern CUBLASStatus cublasIdamin_v2(CUDABLASHandle handle,
                                    int n, IntPtr x, int incx, int& result)
[<DllImport(dllName)>]
extern CUBLASStatus cublasIsamin_v2(CUDABLASHandle handle,
                                    int n, IntPtr x, int incx, int& result)
[<DllImport(dllName)>]
extern CUBLASStatus cublasIzamin_v2(CUDABLASHandle handle,
                                    int n, IntPtr x, int incx, int& result)
[<DllImport(dllName)>]
extern CUBLASStatus cublasSasum_v2(CUDABLASHandle handle,
                                   int n, IntPtr x, int incx, float32& result)
[<DllImport(dllName)>]
extern CUBLASStatus cublasDasum_v2(CUDABLASHandle handle,
                                   int n, IntPtr x, int incx, float& result)
[<DllImport(dllName)>]
extern CUBLASStatus cublasScasum_v2(CUDABLASHandle handle,
                                    int n, IntPtr x, int incx, float32& result)
[<DllImport(dllName)>]
extern CUBLASStatus cublasDzasum_v2(CUDABLASHandle handle,
                                    int n, IntPtr x, int incx, float& result)
```

```
    [<DllImport(dllName)>]
    extern CUBLASStatus cublasSaxpy_v2(CUDABLASHandle handle,
                                       int n, float32& alpha, IntPtr x,
                                       int incx, IntPtr y, int incy)
    [<DllImport(dllName)>]
    extern CUBLASStatus cublasDaxpy_v2(CUDABLASHandle handle,
                                       int n, float& alpha, IntPtr x,
                                       int incx, IntPtr y, int incy)
    [<DllImport(dllName)>]
    extern CUBLASStatus cublasCaxpy_v2(CUDABLASHandle handle, int n,
                                       CUDAFloatComplex& alpha, IntPtr x,
                                       int incx, IntPtr y, int incy)
    [<DllImport(dllName)>]
    extern CUBLASStatus cublasZaxpy_v2(CUDABLASHandle handle, int n,
                                       CUDAFloatComplex& alpha, IntPtr x,
                                       int incx, IntPtr y, int incy)
    [<DllImport(dllName)>]
    extern CUBLASStatus cublasScopy_v2(CUDABLASHandle handle,
                                       int n, IntPtr x, int incx, IntPtr y, int
incy)
    [<DllImport(dllName)>]
    extern CUBLASStatus cublasDcopy_v2(CUDABLASHandle handle,
                                       int n, IntPtr x, int incx, IntPtr y, int
incy)
    [<DllImport(dllName)>]
    extern CUBLASStatus cublasCcopy_v2(CUDABLASHandle handle,
                                       int n, IntPtr x, int incx, IntPtr y, int
incy)
    [<DllImport(dllName)>]
    extern CUBLASStatus cublasZcopy_v2(CUDABLASHandle handle,
                                       int n, IntPtr x, int incx, IntPtr y, int
incy)
    [<DllImport(dllName)>]
    extern CUBLASStatus cublasSdot_v2(CUDABLASHandle handle,
                                      int n, IntPtr x, int incx, IntPtr y,
                                      int incy, float32& result)
    [<DllImport(dllName)>]
    extern CUBLASStatus cublasDdot_v2(CUDABLASHandle handle,
                                      int n, IntPtr x, int incx,
                                      IntPtr y, int incy, float& result)
    [<DllImport(dllName)>]
    extern CUBLASStatus cublasCdotu_v2(CUDABLASHandle handle, int n,
                                       IntPtr x, int incx,
                                       IntPtr y, int incy, CUDAFloatComplex&
result)
    [<DllImport(dllName)>]
    extern CUBLASStatus cublasCdotc_v2(CUDABLASHandle handle, int n,
                                       IntPtr x, int incx,
                                       IntPtr y, int incy, CUDAFloatComplex&
result)
```

```
    [<DllImport(dllName)>]
    extern CUBLASStatus cublasZdotu_v2(CUDABLASHandle handle, int n,
                                    IntPtr x, int incx,
                                    IntPtr y, int incy, CUDAFloatComplex&
result)
    [<DllImport(dllName)>]
    extern CUBLASStatus cublasZdotc_v2(CUDABLASHandle handle, int n,
                                    IntPtr x, int incx,
                                    IntPtr y, int incy, CUDAFloatComplex&
result)
    [<DllImport(dllName)>]
    extern CUBLASStatus cublasSnrm2_v2(CUDABLASHandle handle, int n,
                                    IntPtr x, int incx, float32&result)
    [<DllImport(dllName)>]
    extern CUBLASStatus cublasDnrm2_v2(CUDABLASHandle handle, int n,
                                    IntPtr x, int incx, float& result)
    [<DllImport(dllName)>]
    extern CUBLASStatus cublasScnrm2_v2(CUDABLASHandle handle, int n,
                                    IntPtr x, int incx, float32&result)
    [<DllImport(dllName)>]
    extern CUBLASStatus cublasDznrm2_v2(CUDABLASHandle handle, int n,
                                    IntPtr x, int incx, float& result)
    [<DllImport(dllName)>]
    extern CUBLASStatus cublasSrot_v2(CUDABLASHandle handle, int n,
                                    IntPtr x, int incx,
                                    IntPtr y, int incy, IntPtr c, IntPtr s)
    [<DllImport(dllName)>]
    extern CUBLASStatus cublasDrot_v2(CUDABLASHandle handle, int n,
                                    IntPtr x, int incx,
                                    IntPtr y, int incy, IntPtr c, IntPtr s)
    [<DllImport(dllName)>]
    extern CUBLASStatus cublasCrot_v2(CUDABLASHandle handle, int n,
                                    IntPtr x, int incx,
                                    IntPtr y, int incy, IntPtr c, IntPtr s)
    [<DllImport(dllName)>]
    extern CUBLASStatus cublasCsrot_v2(CUDABLASHandle handle, int n,
                                    IntPtr x, int incx,
                                    IntPtr y, int incy, IntPtr c, IntPtr s)
    [<DllImport(dllName)>]
    extern CUBLASStatus cublasZrot_v2(CUDABLASHandle handle, int n,
                                    IntPtr x, int incx,
                                    IntPtr y, int incy, IntPtr c, IntPtr s)
    [<DllImport(dllName)>]
    extern CUBLASStatus cublasZdrot_v2(CUDABLASHandle handle, int n,
                                    IntPtr x, int incx,
                                    IntPtr y, int incy, IntPtr c, IntPtr s)
    [<DllImport(dllName)>]
    extern CUBLASStatus cublasSrotg_v2(CUDABLASHandle handle, IntPtr a, IntPtr b, IntPtr
c,
                                    IntPtr s)
    [<DllImport(dllName)>]
    extern CUBLASStatus cublasDrotg_v2(CUDABLASHandle handle, IntPtr a, IntPtr b, IntPtr
c,
                                    IntPtr s)
```

```
    [<DllImport(dllName)>]
    extern CUBLASStatus cublasCrotg_v2(CUDABLASHandle handle, IntPtr a, IntPtr b, IntPtr
c,
                                       IntPtr s)
    [<DllImport(dllName)>]
    extern CUBLASStatus cublasZrotg_v2(CUDABLASHandle handle, IntPtr a, IntPtr b, IntPtr
c,
                                       IntPtr s)
    [<DllImport(dllName)>]
    extern CUBLASStatus cublasSrotm_v2(CUDABLASHandle handle, int n,
                                       IntPtr x, int incx,
                                       IntPtr y, int incy, IntPtr param)
    [<DllImport(dllName)>]
    extern CUBLASStatus cublasDrotm_v2(CUDABLASHandle handle, int n,
                                       IntPtr x, int incx,
                                       IntPtr y, int incy, IntPtr param)
    [<DllImport(dllName)>]
    extern CUBLASStatus cublasSrotmg_v2(CUDABLASHandle handle, IntPtr d1,
                                        IntPtr d2, IntPtr x1, IntPtr y1, IntPtr
param)
    [<DllImport(dllName)>]
    extern CUBLASStatus cublasDrotmg_v2(CUDABLASHandle handle, IntPtr d1,
                                        IntPtr d2, IntPtr x1, IntPtr y1, IntPtr
param)
    [<DllImport(dllName)>]
    extern CUBLASStatus cublasSscal_v2(CUDABLASHandle handle, int n,
                                       IntPtr alpha, IntPtr x, int incx)
    [<DllImport(dllName)>]
    extern CUBLASStatus cublasDscal_v2(CUDABLASHandle handle, int n,
                                       IntPtr alpha, IntPtr x, int incx)
    [<DllImport(dllName)>]
    extern CUBLASStatus cublasCscal_v2(CUDABLASHandle handle, int n,
                                       IntPtr alpha, IntPtr x, int incx)
    [<DllImport(dllName)>]
    extern CUBLASStatus cublasCsscal_v2(CUDABLASHandle handle, int n,
                                        IntPtr alpha, IntPtr x, int incx)
    [<DllImport(dllName)>]
    extern CUBLASStatus cublasZscal_v2(CUDABLASHandle handle, int n,
                                       IntPtr alpha, IntPtr x, int incx)
    [<DllImport(dllName)>]
    extern CUBLASStatus cublasZdscal_v2(CUDABLASHandle handle, int n,
                                        IntPtr alpha, IntPtr x, int incx)
    [<DllImport(dllName)>]
    extern CUBLASStatus cublasSswap_v2(CUDABLASHandle handle, int n,
                                       IntPtr x, int incx, IntPtr y, int incy)
    [<DllImport(dllName)>]
    extern CUBLASStatus cublasDswap_v2(CUDABLASHandle handle, int n,
                                       IntPtr x, int incx, IntPtr y, int incy)
    [<DllImport(dllName)>]
    extern CUBLASStatus cublasCswap_v2(CUDABLASHandle handle, int n,
                                       IntPtr x, int incx, IntPtr y, int incy)
    [<DllImport(dllName)>]
    extern CUBLASStatus cublasZswap_v2(CUDABLASHandle handle, int n,
                                       IntPtr x, int incx, IntPtr y, int incy)
```

```
module CUDABLASDriver32 =
    [<Literal>]
    let dllName = "cublas32_42_9"
    [<DllImport(dllName)>]
    extern CUBLASStatus cublasInit()
    [<DllImport(dllName)>]
    extern CUBLASStatus cublasShutdown()
    ...
    // other functions are same as the 64-bit version
```

> **Note** dumpbin.exe is used to check the exported functions from the CUDA BLAS DLL.
> The *cublas64_<version>.DLL* is located in the directory <CUDA installation folder>\ C\
> common\bin. The result from dumpbin.exe shows that a function can have two versions.
> For example, the *cublasZdscal* and *cublasZdscal_2* functions are shown in the result list. It is
> recommended that you use the function with *_2* suffix.

There are some overloaded functions in the cuBLAS library. Because F# does not allow you to
define the function with the same name, another module is needed to declare the function with
the same name, as shown in Listing 9-16. Some of the 64-bit version functions are not listed. These
functions are the same as those in the 32-bit module.

LISTING 9-16 cuBLAS library in a different module

```
module CUDABLASDriver32_2 =
    [<Literal>]
    let dllName = "cublas32_42_9"

    [<DllImport(dllName)>]
    extern CUBLASStatus cublasSrotmg_v2(CUDABLASHandle handle,
                                        float32& d1, float32& d2,
                                        float32& x1, float32& y1,
                                        IntPtr param)
    [<DllImport(dllName)>]
    extern CUBLASStatus cublasDrotmg_v2(CUDABLASHandle handle,
                                        float& d1, float& d2,
                                        float& x1, float& y1,
                                        IntPtr param)
    [<DllImport(dllName)>]
    extern CUBLASStatus cublasZrotg_v2(CUDABLASHandle handle,
                                        CUDAFloatComplex& a,
                                        CUDAFloatComplex& b,
                                        float& c,
                                        CUDAFloatComplex& s)
    [<DllImport(dllName)>]
    extern CUBLASStatus cublasSrot_v2(CUDABLASHandle handle,
                                        int n,
                                        IntPtr x, int incx,
```

```
                                            IntPtr y, int incy,
                                            float32&c,
                                            float32&s)
[<DllImport(dllName)>]
extern CUBLASStatus cublasCrotg_v2(CUDABLASHandle handle,
                                    CUDAFloatComplex& a,
                                    CUDAFloatComplex& b,
                                    float32& c,
                                    CUDAFloatComplex& s)
[<DllImport(dllName)>]
extern CUBLASStatus cublasDrotg_v2(CUDABLASHandle handle,
                                    float& a, float& b, float& c,
                                    float& s)
[<DllImport(dllName)>]
extern CUBLASStatus cublasSrotg_v2(CUDABLASHandle handle,
                                    float32& a, float32& b, float32& c,
                                    float32& s)
[<DllImport(dllName)>]
extern CUBLASStatus cublasZdrot_v2(CUDABLASHandle handle,
                                    int n,
                                    IntPtr x, int incx,
                                    IntPtr y, int incy,
                                    float& c,
                                    float& s)
[<DllImport(dllName)>]
extern CUBLASStatus cublasSaxpy_v2(CUDABLASHandle handle,
                                    int n,
                                    IntPtr alpha,
                                    IntPtr x, int incx,
                                    IntPtr y, int incy)
[<DllImport(dllName)>]
extern CUBLASStatus cublasDaxpy_v2(CUDABLASHandle handle,
                                    int n,
                                    IntPtr alpha,
                                    IntPtr x, int incx,
                                    IntPtr y, int incy)
[<DllImport(dllName)>]
extern CUBLASStatus cublasCaxpy_v2(CUDABLASHandle handle,
                                    int n,
                                    IntPtr alpha,
                                    IntPtr x, int incx,
                                    IntPtr y, int incy)
[<DllImport(dllName)>]
extern CUBLASStatus cublasZaxpy_v2(CUDABLASHandle handle,
                                    int n,
                                    IntPtr alpha,
                                    IntPtr x, int incx,
                                    IntPtr y, int incy)
[<DllImport(dllName)>]
extern CUBLASStatus cublasDrot_v2(CUDABLASHandle handle,
                                    int n,
                                    IntPtr x, int incx,
                                    IntPtr y, int incy,
                                    float& c, float& s)
```

```
[<DllImport(dllName)>]
extern CUBLASStatus cublasCrot_v2(CUDABLASHandle handle,
                                  int n,
                                  IntPtr x, int incx,
                                  IntPtr y, int incy,
                                  float32&c,
                                  CUDAFloatComplex& s)
[<DllImport(dllName)>]
extern CUBLASStatus cublasCsrot_v2(CUDABLASHandle handle,
                                   int n,
                                   IntPtr x, int incx,
                                   IntPtr y, int incy,
                                   float32& c, float32& s)
[<DllImport(dllName)>]
extern CUBLASStatus cublasZrot_v2(CUDABLASHandle handle,
                                  int n,
                                  IntPtr x, int incx,
                                  IntPtr y, int incy,
                                  float& c,
                                  CUDAFloatComplex& s)

module CUDABLASDriver64_2 =
    [<Literal>]
    let dllName =  "cublas64_42_9"

    [<DllImport(dllName)>]
    extern CUBLASStatus cublasSrotmg_v2(CUDABLASHandle handle,
                                        float32& d1, float32& d2,
                                        float32& x1, float32& y1,
                                        IntPtr param)
    [<DllImport(dllName)>]
    extern CUBLASStatus cublasDrotmg_v2(CUDABLASHandle handle,
                                        float& d1, float& d2,
                                        float& x1, float& y1,
                                        IntPtr param)

    ...
    // other 64-bit version functions
```

The code to invoke the preceding API is listed in Listing 9-17. The variable a is a 100-element-length array, and all the elements in the array are set to *1*. The variable b is also a 100-element-length array, and all elements in the array are set to *2*. The dot product from a and b is *200*.

LISTING 9-17 Invoking the CUDA BLAS library

```
open System.Runtime.InteropServices

let test8() =
    let n = 100
    let a = Array.create n 2.f
    let b = Array.create n 1.f
```

```
let copyToDevice(array) =
    let nativePtr = Marshal.UnsafeAddrOfPinnedArrayElement(array, 0)
    let p = System.IntPtr(nativePtr.ToPointer())
    let mutable dst = IntPtr()
    let count = SizeT(Marshal.SizeOf(sizeof<float32>) * array.Length)
    let r = CUDARuntime.CUDARuntime64.cudaMalloc(&dst, count)

    if r = cudaError.cudaSuccess then
        let r = CUDARuntime.CUDARuntime64.cudaMemcpy(
                    dst,
                    p,
                    count,
                    CUDAMemcpyKind.cudaMemcpyHostToDevice)
        if r = cudaError.cudaSuccess then
            Some dst
        else
            None
    else
        None


let mutable handle = CUDABLASHandle()
let r = CUDABLASDriver64.cublasInit()
let r = CUDABLASDriver64.cublasCreate_v2(&handle)
let deviceA = copyToDevice(a)
let deviceB = copyToDevice(b)
let mutable result = 1.f

match deviceA, deviceB with
| Some(pA), Some(pB) ->
    let status = CUDABLASDriver64.cublasSdot_v2(
                    handle,
                    Marshal.SizeOf(sizeof<float32>) * n,
                    pA,
                    1,
                    pB,
                    1,
                    &result)
    printfn "result is %A" result
| _ -> failwith "computation error"
```

F# Quotation and Transform

The F# quotation is a tree structure that presents the current F# program structure. The
ReflectedDefinition attribute is the key attribute used to get an F# quotation. According to MSDN
(*http://msdn.microsoft.com/en-us/library/ee353643.aspx*), here is how you use it:

> *Add this attribute to the let-binding for the definition of a top-level value to make
> the quotation expression that implements the value available for use at runtime.*

Add this attribute to a type or module to make it apply recursively to all the values in the module or all the members of the type.

Listing 9-18 shows how to show the quotation expression for the function. The `<@@ ... @@>` is used to get the quotation from a function that is decorated with the *ReflectedDefinition* attribute.

LISTING 9-18 Getting a quotation from a function with the *ReflectedDefinition* attribute

```
[<ReflectedDefinition>]
let f() =
    let b = 99
    b*2

<@@ f @@>
```

Execution result

```
val f : unit -> int
val it : Quotations.Expr = Lambda (arg00@, Call (None, f, []))
```

There are several approaches to converting F# code to CUDA code. Figure 9-6 shows one of these approaches. The PTX file is an assembly-like language for the GPU. In this chapter, the path from quotation via C code to PTX file is chosen.

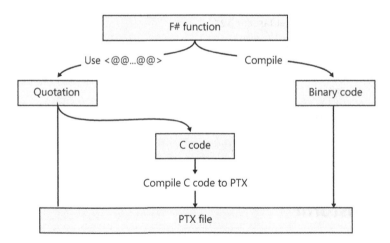

FIGURE 9-6 Converting code from F# to GPU code

After the quotation is ready, a translation function can be applied. Listing 9-20 shows how to traverse the tree structure and get the CUDA C code. There are several ways to generate code from a quotation tree. Listing 9-20 generates C code, which can make the quotation generation easy to understand; the listing traverses the parse tree structure emitting C code. To support the code generation, *CUDAPointer2* is defined, as shown in Listing 9-19.

LISTING 9-19 *CUDAPointer2* code for code generation

```
type CUDAPointer2<'T>(p:CUDAPointer) =
    new(ptr:IntPtr) = CUDAPointer2(CUDAPointer(ptr))
    member this.Pointer = p
    member this.PointerSize = p.PointerSize
    member this.Is64Bit = this.PointerSize = 8
    member this.Item
        with get (i:int) : float32 = failwith "for code generation only"
        and set (i:int) (v:float32) = failwith "for code generation only"
    member this.Set(x:float32, i:int) = failwith "for code generation only"
```

Note *CUDAPointer* is defined in Listing 9-10.

Listing 9-20 implements only part of the conversion and does not provide full support for an F# quotation conversion.

LISTING 9-20 Quotation tree traversal

```
open System
open System.Reflection
open Microsoft.FSharp.Quotations
open Microsoft.FSharp.Quotations.Patterns
open Microsoft.FSharp.Quotations.DerivedPatterns
open Microsoft.FSharp.Quotations.ExprShape

let accessExpr exp =

    let addSemiCol (str:string) =
            if str.EndsWith(";") ||
                String.IsNullOrEmpty(str) &&
                String.IsNullOrWhiteSpace(str) then str
            else str + ";"

    let rec iterate exp : string=

        let print x =
            let str = sprintf "%A" x
            str

        let matchExp expOption =
            match expOption with
            | Some(n) -> iterate n
            | None -> String.Empty
```

```
        let isCUDAPointerType (exp:Expr Option) =
            match exp with
            | Some(n) ->
                n.Type.IsAssignableFrom(
                    typeof<CUDAPointer2<float>>) ||
                    n.Type.IsAssignableFrom(typeof<CUDAPointer2<float32>>)
            | _ ->
                false

    match exp with
    | DerivedPatterns.Applications (e, ell) ->
        let str0 = iterate e
        let str1 =
            ell
            |> Seq.map (fun n -> n |> Seq.map (fun m -> iterate m ))
            |> Seq.map (fun n -> String.Join("\r\n", n |> Seq.toArray))
        str0 + String.Join("\r\n", str1 |> Seq.toArray)
    | DerivedPatterns.AndAlso (e0, e1) ->
        (iterate e0) + (iterate e1)
    | DerivedPatterns.Bool e ->
        print e
    | DerivedPatterns.Byte e ->
        print e
    | DerivedPatterns.Char e ->
        print e
    | DerivedPatterns.Double e ->
        print e
    | DerivedPatterns.Int16 e->
        print e
    | DerivedPatterns.Int32 e->
        print e
    | DerivedPatterns.Int64 e ->
        print e
    | DerivedPatterns.OrElse (e0, e1)->
        (iterate e0) + (iterate e1)
    | DerivedPatterns.SByte e ->
        print e
    | DerivedPatterns.Single e ->
        print e
    | DerivedPatterns.String e ->
        print e
    | DerivedPatterns.UInt16 e ->
        print e
    | DerivedPatterns.UInt32 e ->
        print e
    | DerivedPatterns.UInt64 e ->
        print e
    | DerivedPatterns.Unit e ->
        String.Empty //"void"
    | Patterns.AddressOf address ->
        iterate address
    | Patterns.AddressSet (exp0, exp1) ->
        (iterate exp0) + (iterate exp1)
```

```
| Patterns.Application (exp0, exp1) ->
    (iterate exp0) + (iterate exp1)
| Patterns.Call (expOption, mi, expList)  ->
    if isCUDAPointerType expOption && mi.Name = "Set" then
        let callObject = matchExp expOption
        let index = iterate expList.[1]
        let postfix =
            match mi with
            | DerivedPatterns.MethodWithReflectedDefinition n -> iterate n
            | _ -> iterate expList.[0]
        let s = sprintf "%s[%s] = %s;" callObject index postfix
        s
    else
        let callObject = matchExp expOption
        let returnType = translateFromNETType mi.ReturnType String.Empty
        let postfix =
            match mi with
            | DerivedPatterns.MethodWithReflectedDefinition n -> iterate n
            | _ -> translateFromNETOperator mi expList
        let s = sprintf "%s%s" callObject postfix
        s
| Patterns.Coerce (exp, t) ->
    let from = iterate exp
    //sprintf "coerce(%s, %s)" from t.Name
    sprintf "%s" from
| Patterns.DefaultValue exp ->
    print exp
| Patterns.FieldGet (expOption, fi) ->
    (matchExp expOption) + (print fi)
| Patterns.FieldSet (expOption, fi, e) ->
    let callObj = matchExp expOption
    let fi = print fi
    let str = iterate e
    callObj + fi + str
| Patterns.ForIntegerRangeLoop (v, e0, e1, e2) ->
    let from = iterate e0
    let toV = iterate e1
    let s = String.Format("for (int {0} = {1}; {0}<{2}; {0}++) {{ {3} }}",
                          v, from ,toV, iterate e2)
    s
| Patterns.IfThenElse (con, exp0, exp1) ->
    let condition = (iterate con)
    let ifClause = addSemiCol(iterate exp0)
    let elseClause = addSemiCol(iterate exp1)
    sprintf "if (%s) { %s }\r\nelse { %s }" condition ifClause elseClause
| Patterns.Lambda (var,body) ->
    //let a = print var
    //let b = iterate body
    match exp with
```

```
        | DerivedPatterns.Lambdas (vll, e) ->
            let s =
                vll
                |> List.map (fun n-> n
                                     |> List.map (fun m ->
                                                    sprintf "%s %s"
                                                    (translateFromNETType m.Type
"")
                                                    m.Name))
                |> List.fold (fun acc l -> acc@l) []
            let parameterNames = vll |> List.map (fun n -> sprintf "%s" n.Head.Name)
            let returnType = getCallReturnType e
            let returnTypeID = translateFromNETTypeToFunReturn returnType ""
            let fid = code.FunctionID;
            code.IncreaseFunctionID()
            let functionName = sprintf "ff_%d" fid
            let statement = iterate e
            let functionCode = sprintf "__device__ %s %s(%s) { %s } "
                                        returnTypeID
                                        functionName
                                        (String.Join(", ", s))
                                        (addSemiCol(statement))
            code.Add(functionCode)
            sprintf "%s(%s)" functionName (String.Join(", ", parameterNames))
        | _ -> failwith "not supported lambda format"
    | Patterns.Let (var, exp0, exp1) ->
        let a = print var
        let b = iterate exp0
        let t = var.Type
        let s =
            if t.Name = "FSharpFunc'2" then
                sprintf "__device__ %s; //function pointer" (translateFromNETType t a)
            else
                String.Empty
        code.Add(s)
        let c = iterate exp1
        let assignment =
            if t.Name = "FSharpFunc'2" then
                sprintf "%s;\r\n%s = %s;" (translateFromNETType t a) a b
            else
                sprintf "%s %s;\r\n%s = %s;" (translateFromNETType t a) a a b
        sprintf "%s\r\n%s" assignment c
    | Patterns.LetRecursive (tupList, exp) ->
        let strList = tupList |> Seq.map (fun (var, e) -> (print var) + (iterate e))
        String.Join("\r\n", strList |> Seq.toArray) + (iterate exp)
    | Patterns.NewArray (t, expList) ->
        let str0 = print t
        let str1 = expList |> Seq.map (fun e -> iterate e)
        str0 + String.Join("\r\n", str1)
    | Patterns.NewDelegate (t, varList, exp) ->
        (print t) + (print varList) + (iterate exp)
```

```
| Patterns.NewObject (t, expList) ->
    let str0 = print t
    let str1 = expList |> Seq.map (fun e -> iterate e)
    str0 + String.Join("\r\n", str1)
| Patterns.NewRecord (t, expList) ->
    let str0 = print t
    let str1 = expList |> Seq.map (fun e -> iterate e)
    str0 + String.Join("\r\n", str1)
| Patterns.NewObject (t, expList) ->
    let str0 = print t
    let str1 = expList |> Seq.map (fun e -> iterate e)
    str0 + String.Join("\r\n", str1)
| Patterns.NewRecord (t, expList) ->
    let str0 = print t
    let str1 = expList |> Seq.map (fun e -> iterate e)
    str0 + String.Join("\r\n", str1)
| Patterns.NewTuple expList ->
    let ty = translateFromNETType (expList.[0].Type) String.Empty
    let l = expList |> Seq.map (fun e -> iterate e)
    let l = String.Join(", ", l)
    sprintf "newTuple<%s>(%s)" ty l
| Patterns.NewUnionCase (t, expList) ->
    let str0 = print t
    let str1 = expList |> Seq.map (fun e -> iterate e)
    str0 + String.Join("\r\n", str1)
| Patterns.PropertyGet (expOption, pi, expList) ->
    let callObj = matchExp expOption
    let r = match pi with
            | DerivedPatterns.PropertyGetterWithReflectedDefinition e ->
                iterate e
            | _ -> pi.Name
    let l = expList |> List.map (fun n -> iterate n)
    if l.Length > 0 then
        if r = "Item" then
            sprintf "%s[%s]" callObj (String.Join(", ", l))
        else
            sprintf "%s.%s[%s]" callObj r (String.Join(", ", l))
    else
        if String.IsNullOrEmpty callObj then
            sprintf "%s" r
        else
            sprintf "%s.%s" callObj r
| Patterns.PropertySet (expOption, pi, expList, e) ->
    let callObj = matchExp expOption
    let r = match pi with
            | DerivedPatterns.PropertyGetterWithReflectedDefinition e ->
                iterate e
            | _ -> print pi
    let l = expList |> Seq.map (fun n -> iterate n)
    if r = "Item" then
        callObj + String.Join("\r\n", l) + (iterate e)
    else
        callObj + r + String.Join("\r\n", l) + (iterate e)
```

```
          | Patterns.Quote e ->
              iterate e
          | Patterns.Sequential (e0, e1) ->
              let statement0 = addSemiCol(iterate e0)
              let statement1 = addSemiCol(iterate e1)
              sprintf "%s\r\n%s" statement0 statement1
          | Patterns.TryFinally (e0, e1) ->
              (iterate e0) + (iterate e1)
          | Patterns.TryWith (e0, v0, e1, v1, e2) ->
              (iterate e0) + (print v0) + (iterate e1) + (print v1) + (iterate e2)
          | Patterns.TupleGet (e, i) ->
              (iterate e) + (print i)
          | Patterns.TypeTest (e, t) ->
              (iterate e) + (print t)
          | Patterns.UnionCaseTest (e, ui) ->
              (iterate e) + (print ui)
          | Patterns.Value (obj, t) ->
              (print obj) + (print t)
          | Patterns.Var v ->
              v.Name
          | Patterns.VarSet (v, e) ->
              let left = (print v)
              let right = (iterate e)
              sprintf "%s = %s" left right
          | Patterns.WhileLoop (e0, e1) ->
              let condition = iterate e0
              let body = iterate e1
              sprintf "while (%s) { \r\n %s \r\n}" condition (addSemiCol(body))
          | _ -> failwith "not supported pattern"

      and translateFromNETOperator (mi:MethodInfo) (exprList:Expr list) =
          let getList() = exprList |> List.map (fun n -> iterate n)
          let ty = translateFromNETType (exprList.[0].Type) String.Empty

          let generateFunction (mi:MethodInfo) (mappedMethodName:string) (parameters:Expr
list) =
              let result = sprintf "%s(%s)" mappedMethodName (String.Join(", ", getList()))
              result

          match mi.Name with
              | "op_Addition" ->
                  let l = getList()
                  sprintf "(%s) + (%s)" l.[0] l.[1]
              | "op_Subtraction" ->
                  let l = getList()
                  sprintf "(%s) - (%s)" l.[0] l.[1]
              | "op_Multiply" ->
                  let l = getList()
                  sprintf "(%s) * (%s)" l.[0] l.[1]
              | "op_Division" ->
                  let l = getList()
                  sprintf "(%s) / (%s)" l.[0] l.[1]
```

```
        | "op_LessThan" ->
            let l = getList()
            sprintf "(%s) < (%s)" l.[0] l.[1]
        | "op_LessThanOrEqual" ->
            let l = getList()
            sprintf "(%s) <= (%s)" l.[0] l.[1]
        | "op_GreaterThan" ->
            let l = getList()
            sprintf "(%s) > (%s)" l.[0] l.[1]
        | "op_GreaterThanOrEqual" ->
            let l = getList()
            sprintf "(%s) >= (%s)" l.[0] l.[1]
        | "op_Range" -> failwith "not support range on GPU"
        | "op_Equality" ->
            let l = getList()
            sprintf "(%s) == (%s)" l.[0] l.[1]
        | "GetArray" ->
            let l = getList()
            sprintf "%s[%s]" l.[0] l.[1]
        | "CreateSequence" -> failwith "not support createSeq on GPU"
        | "FailWith" -> failwith "not support exception on GPU"
        | "ToList" -> failwith "not support toList on GPU"
        | "Map" -> failwith "not support map on GPU"
        | "Delay" ->
            let l = getList()
            String.Join(", ", l)
        | "op_PipeRight" ->
            let l = getList()
            sprintf "%s ( %s )" l.[1] l.[0]
        | "ToSingle" ->
            let l = getList()
            sprintf "(float) (%s)" l.[0]
        | _ ->
            let l = getList()
            sprintf ".%s(%s)" (mi.Name) (String.Join(", ", l))

    let s = iterate exp
    addSemiCol(s)
```

Note Some functions in the preceding code are defined in the rest of the chapter.

The transform function does not list all of the possible conversions inside the match expression. We will demonstrate how to expand this function in later sections of this chapter.

Listing 9-21 shows how to convert .NET types to C.

LISTING 9-21 Translating .NET types to C type

```
type Type with
    member this.HasInterface(t:Type) =
        this.GetInterface(t.FullName) <> null

let rec translateFromNETType (t:Type) (a:string) =
    if t = typeof<int> then "int"
    elif t = typeof<float32> then "float"
    elif t = typeof<float> then "double"
    elif t = typeof<bool> then "bool"
    elif t.IsArray then
        let elementTypeString = translateFromNETType (t.GetElementType()) a
        sprintf "List<%s>" elementTypeString
    elif t.HasInterface(typeof<System.Collections.IEnumerable>) then
        let elementTypeString = translateFromNETType (t.GetGenericArguments().[0]) a
        sprintf "List<%s>" elementTypeString
    elif t = typeof< Microsoft.FSharp.Core.unit > then String.Empty
    elif t = typeof< CUDAPointer2<float> > then sprintf "%s*" "double"
    elif t = typeof< CUDAPointer2<float32>> then sprintf "%s*" "float"
    elif t.Name = "FSharpFunc'2" then
        let input = translateFromNETType (t.GetGenericArguments().[0]) a
        let out = translateFromNETType (t.GetGenericArguments().[1]) a
        sprintf "%s(*%s)(%s)" input a out
    elif t = typeof<System.Void> then
        String.Empty
    else failwith "not supported type"

let translateFromNETTypeToFunReturn (t:Type) (a:string) =
    let r = translateFromNETType t a
    if String.IsNullOrEmpty(r) then "void"
    else r

let translateFromNETTypeLength (t:Type) c =
    if t.IsArray then
        sprintf ", int %A_len" c
    else
        String.Empty

let isValueType (t:Type) =
    if t.IsValueType then true
    elif t.HasInterface(typeof<IEnumerable>) then false
    else failwith "is value type failed"
```

The code generation needs to generate a few intermediary functions. Listing 9-22 shows the code structure used to generate these functions.

LISTING 9-22 Code structure hosts intermediate functions

```
type Code() =
    inherit System.Collections.Generic.List<string>()
    let mutable functionID = 0
    let mutable variableID = 0
    member this.FunctionID
        with get () = functionID
        and set (v) = functionID <- v
    member this.VariableID
        with get () = variableID
        and set(v) = variableID <- v
    member this.IncreaseFunctionID() =
        functionID <- this.FunctionID + 1
    member this.IncreaseVariableID() =
        variableID <- this.VariableID + 1

    member this.ToCode() =
        "#include \"CUDALibrary.h\"\r\n" + String.Join("\r\n", this) + "\r\n\r\n\r\n"

let code = Code()
```

> **Note** The CUDALibrary.h file is a placeholder file. In this sample, the file content is empty. You can implement additional functions in this file to make the translation easier and the code more readable.

Listing 9-23 shows several functions used to handle the function definitions, including return type and function signatures, in F# and convert them to CUDA code.

LISTING 9-23 Functions for finding the return type and signature

```
open System
open System.Reflection
open Microsoft.FSharp.Quotations
open Microsoft.FSharp.Quotations.Patterns
open Microsoft.FSharp.Quotations.DerivedPatterns
open Microsoft.FSharp.Quotations.ExprShape

let rec getFunctionBody (exp:Expr) =
    match exp with
    | DerivedPatterns.Lambdas(c, callPattern) ->
        match callPattern with
        | Patterns.Call (e, mi, exprList) ->
            match mi with
                | DerivedPatterns.MethodWithReflectedDefinition n ->
                    callPattern
```

```
                    | _ ->
                            callPattern
            | Patterns.Sequential _ -> callPattern
            | _ -> callPattern
        | Patterns.Sequential _ -> exp
        | _ -> failwith "Argument must be of the form <@ foo @>!"


let getFunctionParameterAndReturn (exp:Expr) =
    match exp with
        | DerivedPatterns.Lambdas (c, Patterns.Call(a, mi, b)) ->
            Some(b, mi.ReturnType)
        | _ -> None


let getFunctionName (exp:Expr) =
    match exp with
        | DerivedPatterns.Lambdas(c, Patterns.Call(a, mi, b)) ->
            mi.Name
        | _ ->
            failwith "Argument must be of the form <@ foo @>!"


let getFunctionTypes (exp:Expr) =
    match getFunctionParameterAndReturn(exp) with
        | Some(exprList ,t) ->
            let out = exprList |> List.map (fun n -> (n, n.Type))
            Some(out, t)
        | None -> None


let getFunctionReturnType (exp:Expr) =
    match getFunctionTypes(exp) with
    | Some(_, t) -> t
    | _ -> failwith "cannot find return type"


let rec getCallReturnType (exp:Expr) =
    match exp with
    | Patterns.Call (_, mi, _) -> mi.ReturnType
    | Patterns.Var n -> n.Type
    | Patterns.Let (var, e0, e1) -> getCallReturnType e1
    | Patterns.Sequential (e0, e1) -> getCallReturnType e1
    | Patterns.Value(v) -> snd v
    | Patterns.WhileLoop(e0, e1) -> typeof<System.Void>
    | Patterns.ForIntegerRangeLoop(var, e0, e1, e2) -> getCallReturnType e2
    | Patterns.IfThenElse(e0, e1, e2) -> typeof<System.Void>
    | _ -> failwith "not supported expr type"


let getFunctionSignature (exp:Expr) =
    let template = @"extern ""C"" __global__ void {0} ({1}) "
    let functionName = getFunctionName(exp)
    let parameters = getFunctionParameterAndReturn(exp)
```

```
match parameters with
| Some(exprList, _) ->
    let parameterNames =
        exprList
        |> Seq.map (fun n ->
                match n with
                | _ when n.Type.IsAssignableFrom(typeof<CUDAPointer2<float>>) ->
                    sprintf "double* %s" (n.ToString())
                | _ when n.Type.IsAssignableFrom(typeof<CUDAPointer2<float32>>) ->
                    sprintf "float* %s" (n.ToString())
                | _ -> sprintf "%s %s" (n.Type.Name) (n.ToString()) )
    String.Format(template, functionName, String.Join(", ", parameterNames))
| None -> failwith "cannot get parameter and return type"
```

Some low-end GPU hardware can support only the *float32* data type. Listing 9-24 can be modified to make sure the data type is a convertible type. If the hardware you have does not support int or float, you can change the return to *false*.

LISTING 9-24 Functions for checking supported types

```
let isTypeGPUOK t =
    if t = typeof<int> ||
        t = typeof<float32> ||
        t = typeof<float> then true
    else false

let isValueGPUOK (v:obj) =
    match v with
    | :? Int | :? float32 -> true
    | :? float -> true     //if the hardware does not support this, you can make it false
    | _ -> false
```

Before you can proceed in the translation of the F# quotation, an attribute is needed, as shown in Listing 9-25. The attribute uses reflection to identify the GPU function in the assembly. This attribute is used to identify the function that needs to be converted.

LISTING 9-25 *GPUAttribute* definition

```
type GPUAttribute() =
    inherit Attribute()
```

F# Quotation on GPGPU

The goal for this section is to translate the F# code in Listing 9-26 to CUDA code. The sample function is used to add two arrays, named *a* and *b*, and set the result to array *c*. The *pascalTriangle* function is used to compute the Pascal Triangle values on a given line. The *sample2* function demonstrates how the *while* statement is used to translate the F# code to CUDA code.

CUDA uses an array of threads to process the data. So the code `output.[threadid] = input.[threadId]` is a transaction that will be executed by many threads. Because of these threads, you can process a number of elements in an array simultaneously. More detailed information can be found in the NVIDIA documentation at *http://www.nvidia.com/content/cudazone/download/Getting_Started_w_CUDA_Training_NVISION08.pdf.*

LISTING 9-26 F# code for the translation to CUDA code

```
[<ReflectedDefinition; GPU>]
let sample (a:CUDAPointer2<float>) (b:CUDAPointer2<float>) (c:CUDAPointer2<float>)=
    let x = blockIdx.x
    c.Set(a.[x] + b.[x], x) //c.[x] = a.[x] + b.[x]
    ()


[<ReflectedDefinition; GPU>]
let pascalTriangle (a:CUDAPointer2<float32>) (b:CUDAPointer2<float32>) =
    let x = blockIdx.x
    if x = 0 then
        b.Set(a.[x], x)
    else
        b.Set(a.[x] + a.[x - 1], x)
    ()


[<ReflectedDefinition; GPU>]
let sample2 (a:CUDAPointer2<float>) (b:CUDAPointer2<float>) (c:CUDAPointer2<float>)=
    let x = blockIdx.x
    for j = 0 to x do
        c.Set(a.[j] + b.[j], x)
    let mutable i = 3
    while i >= 8 do
        if i > 3 then
            c.Set(a.[i] + b.[i], x)
        else
            c.Set(a.[i] + b.[0], x)
        i <- i + 1
```

 Note To simplify the translation, the function must return *unit*.

To translate the code, you need to first define some basic data structures, which are defined in Listing 9-27. The GPU kernel can launch multiple threads simultaneously. *ThreadIdx* is the thread identifier. *BlockDim* is a way to segment the data. Their relationship is shown in Figure 9-7.

LISTING 9-27 CUDA data structures

```
type dim3 (x, y, z) =
    new() = dim3(0, 0, 0)
    new(x) = dim3(x, 0, 0)
    new(x, y) = dim3(x, y, 0)
    member this.x = x
    member this.y = y
    member this.z = z

type ThreadIdx() =
    inherit dim3()

type BlockDim() =
    inherit dim3()
```

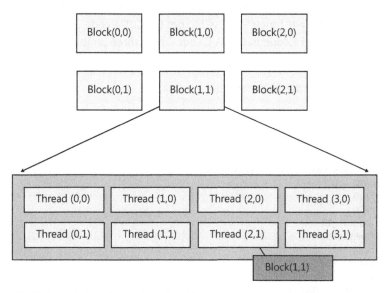

FIGURE 9-7 Block and thread relationship

The generated code has two sections: the function that starts with the __*device*__ keyword, and the function with the __*global*__ keyword. The function with the __*device*__ keyword cannot be invoked from the host. The __*global*__ function can be invoked from the host. If you need to access the functionality in the __*device*__ function, there must be a __*global*__ function. The generated code is in the following format:

```
#include "CUDALibrary.h"

__device__ void ff_0(float* a, float* b) {
   // some generated code
}

extern "C" __global__ void sample4 (float* a, float* b)  {
ff_0(a, b);
}
```

The code has three parts:

- Header file CUDALibrary.h

- Generated __*device*__ function (*ff_0* in the preceding code)

- Generated __*global*__ function, which will be invoked from the host and call into the __*device*__ function *ff0*

Listing 9-28 shows the function used to generate the CUDA code. The *Code* class is used to hold the generated functions. The *getCUDACode* function is used to get the CUDA code. The translation code translates three samples from F# code to CUDA C code. These three samples show how to translate WHILE and FOR structures.

LISTING 9-28 Code-generation function and the generated code

```
let tempFileName = "temp1.cu"

type Code() =
    inherit System.Collections.Generic.List<string>()
    let mutable functionID = 0
    let mutable variableID = 0
    member this.FunctionID
        with get () = functionID
        and set (v) = functionID <-v
    member this.VariableID
        with get () = variableID
        and set(v) = variableID <- v
    member this.IncreaseFunctionID() =
        functionID <- this.FunctionID + 1
    member this.IncreaseVariableID() =
        variableID <- this.VariableID + 1

    member this.ToCode() =
        "#include \"CUDALibrary.h\"\r\n" + String.Join("\r\n", this) + "\r\n\r\n\r\n"

let code = Code()
```

```fsharp
let getCUDACode f =
    let s = getFunctionSignature f
    let body = f |> getFunctionBody
    let functionStr = sprintf "%s {\r\n%s\r\n}\r\n\r\n" s (accessExpr body)
    sprintf "%s" functionStr

let getCommonCode() = code.ToCode()

[<ReflectedDefinition; GPU>]
let pascalTriangle (a:CUDAPointer2<float32>) (b:CUDAPointer2<float32>) =
    let x = blockIdx.x
    if x = 0 then
        b.Set(a.[x], x)
    else
        b.Set(a.[x] + a.[x-1], x)
    ()

[<ReflectedDefinition; GPU>]
let sample2 (a:CUDAPointer2<float>) (b:CUDAPointer2<float>) (c:CUDAPointer2<float>)=
    sample a b c
    let x = blockIdx.x
    for j = 0 to x do
        c.Set(a.[j] + b.[j], x)
    let mutable i = 3
    while i >= 8 do
        if i > 3 then
            c.Set(a.[i] + b.[i], x)
        else
            c.Set(a.[i] + b.[0], x)
        i <- i + 1

[<ReflectedDefinition; GPU>]
let sample (a:CUDAPointer2<float>) (b:CUDAPointer2<float>) (c:CUDAPointer2<float>)=
    let x = blockIdx.x
    c.Set(a.[x] + b.[x], x) //c.[x] = a.[x] + b.[x]
    ()

let WriteToFile() =
    let a1 = <@@ sample @@>
    let b = getCUDACode(a1)
    let a2 = <@@ sample2 @@>
    let b2 = getCUDACode(a2)
    let a3 = <@@ pascalTriangle @@>
    let b3 = getCUDACode(a3)
    let commonCode = getCommonCode()

    System.IO.File.WriteAllText(tempFileName, commonCode + b + b2 + b3)
    ()
```

Generated CUDA C code

```c
#include "CUDALibrary.h"

__device__ void ff_0(double* a, double* b, double* c) { int x;
x = blockIdx.x;
c[x] = (a[x]) + (b[x]);
; }


__device__ void ff_1(float* a, float* b) { int x;
x = blockIdx.x;
if ((x) == (0)) { b[x] = a[x]; }
else { b[x] = (a[x]) + (a[(x) - (1)]); };
; }


__device__ void ff_3(double* a, double* b, double* c) { int x;
x = blockIdx.x;
c[x] = (a[x]) + (b[x]);
; }



__device__ void ff_2(double* a, double* b, double* c) { ff_3(a, b, c);
int x;
x = blockIdx.x;
for (int j = 0; j < x; j++) { c[x] = (a[j]) + (b[j]); };
int i;
i = 3;
while ((i) >= (8)) {
 if ((i) > (3)) { c[x] = (a[i]) + (b[i]); }
else { c[x] = (a[i]) + (b[0]); };
i = (i) + (1);
}; }


extern "C" __global__ void sample (double* a, double* b, double* c)  {
 ff_0(a, b, c);
}
extern "C" __global__ void pascalTriangle (float* a, float* b)  {
 ff_1(a, b);
}
extern "C" __global__ void sample2 (double* a, double* b, double* c)  {
 ff_2(a, b, c);
}
```

> **Note** The CUDALibrary.h header file serves as a placeholder, which can hold some customized functions. In this sample, the file is empty.

It is not convenient to use <@@...@@> on each function that needs to be converted. The *GPUAttribute* enables you to automatically scan the assembly and generate CUDA code. Listing 9-29 shows how to scan the assembly and identify the function with the GPU attribute and generate code from these functions. The generated code is stored in the "temp1.cu" file, which is specified by the *tempFile* value.

LISTING 9-29 Generating code from functions decorated with the GPU attribute

```
let getCommonCode() = code.ToCode()

let getGPUFunctions() =
    let currentAssembly = Assembly.GetExecutingAssembly()
    let gpuMethods =
        currentAssembly.GetTypes()
        |> List.ofArray
        |> List.collect (fun t -> t.GetMethods() |> List.ofArray)
        |> List.filter (fun mi ->
                            mi.GetCustomAttributes(typeof<GPUAttribute>, true).Length >
0)

    gpuMethods
    |> List.map (fun mi -> (mi, (Quotations.Expr.TryGetReflectedDefinition mi)))
    |> List.map (fun (mi, Some(expr)) -> (mi, expr))
    |> List.map (fun (mi, expr) ->
                        sprintf "%s {\r\n %s \r\n}"
                            (getFunctionSignatureFromMethodInfo mi)
                            (accessExpr expr))

let tempFile = "temp1.cu"

let GenerateCodeToFile() =
    let gpuCode = getGPUFunctions()
    let commonCode = getCommonCode()
    let allCode = String.Join("\r\n", commonCode :: gpuCode)
    System.IO.File.Delete(tempFile)
    System.IO.File.WriteAllText(tempFile, allCode)
```

The generated C code will not be able to execute on the GPU. You can use NVCC.exe to compile the C code to a PTX file. The PTX file can be loaded and executed on the GPU. The PTX code is not an executable binary. Instead, the PTX file is compiled for a specific target GPU binary code at run time. It is more like the assembly language on the GPU. The generated PTX file is shown in Listing 9-30.

LISTING 9-30 Generated PTX file

```
    .version 1.4
    .target sm_10, map_f64_to_f32
    // compiled with C:\Program Files\NVIDIA GPU Computing Toolkit\CUDA\v4.0\bin\../
open64/lib//be.exe
    // nvopencc 4.0 built on 2011-05-13

    //-----------------------------------------------------------
    // Compiling C:/Users/taliu/AppData/Local/Temp/tmpxft_00000a84_00000000-11_temp.cpp3.i
(C:/Users/taliu/AppData/Local/Temp/ccBI#.a04920)
    //-----------------------------------------------------------
```

```
//-----------------------------------------------------------
// Options:
//-----------------------------------------------------------
//  Target:ptx, ISA:sm_10, Endian:little, Pointer Size:64
//  -O3     (Optimization level)
//  -g0     (Debug level)
//  -m2     (Report advisories)
//-----------------------------------------------------------


    .file    1     "C:/Users/taliu/AppData/Local/Temp/tmpxft_00000a84_00000000-10_temp.
cudafe2.gpu"
    .file    2     "c:\program files (x86)\microsoft visual studio
10.0\vc\include\codeanalysis\sourceannotations.h"
    .file    3     "C:\Program Files\NVIDIA GPU Computing Toolkit\CUDA\v4.0\bin/../include\
crt/device_runtime.h"
    .file    4     "C:\Program Files\NVIDIA GPU Computing Toolkit\CUDA\v4.0\bin/../include\
host_defines.h"
    .file    5     "C:\Program Files\NVIDIA GPU Computing Toolkit\CUDA\v4.0\bin/../include\
builtin_types.h"
    .file    6     "c:\program files\nvidia gpu computing toolkit\cuda\v4.0\include\device_
types.h"
    .file    7     "c:\program files\nvidia gpu computing toolkit\cuda\v4.0\include\driver_
types.h"
    .file    8     "c:\program files\nvidia gpu computing toolkit\cuda\v4.0\include\
surface_types.h"
    .file    9     "c:\program files\nvidia gpu computing toolkit\cuda\v4.0\include\
texture_types.h"
    .file    10    "c:\program files\nvidia gpu computing toolkit\cuda\v4.0\include\
vector_types.h"
    .file    11    "c:\program files\nvidia gpu computing toolkit\cuda\v4.0\include\
builtin_types.h"
    .file    12    "c:\program files\nvidia gpu computing toolkit\cuda\v4.0\include\host_
defines.h"
    .file    13    "C:\Program Files\NVIDIA GPU Computing
Toolkit\CUDA\v4.0\bin/../include\device_launch_parameters.h"
    .file    14    "c:\program files\nvidia gpu computing
toolkit\cuda\v4.0\include\crt\storage_class.h"
    .file    15    "C:\Program Files (x86)\Microsoft Visual Studio
10.0\VC\bin/../../VC/INCLUDE\time.h"
    .file    16    "temp.cu"
    .file    17    "c:\mycode\codecenter\f#\fsharpgpu\fsharpgpu\bin\debug\CUDALibrary.h"
    .file    18    "C:\Program Files\NVIDIA GPU Computing
Toolkit\CUDA\v4.0\bin/../include\common_functions.h"
    .file    19    "c:\program files\nvidia gpu computing toolkit\cuda\v4.0\include\math_
functions.h"
    .file    20    "c:\program files\nvidia gpu computing toolkit\cuda\v4.0\include\math_
constants.h"
    .file    21    "c:\program files\nvidia gpu computing
toolkit\cuda\v4.0\include\device_functions.h"
    .file    22    "c:\program files\nvidia gpu computing toolkit\cuda\v4.0\include\sm_11_
atomic_functions.h"
    .file    23    "c:\program files\nvidia gpu computing toolkit\cuda\v4.0\include\sm_12_
atomic_functions.h"
```

```
    .file    24    "c:\program files\nvidia gpu computing toolkit\cuda\v4.0\include\sm_13_
double_functions.h"
    .file    25    "c:\program files\nvidia gpu computing toolkit\cuda\v4.0\include\sm_20_
atomic_functions.h"
    .file    26    "c:\program files\nvidia gpu computing toolkit\cuda\v4.0\include\sm_20_
intrinsics.h"
    .file    27    "c:\program files\nvidia gpu computing toolkit\cuda\v4.0\include\
surface_functions.h"
    .file    28    "c:\program files\nvidia gpu computing toolkit\cuda\v4.0\include\
texture_fetch_functions.h"
    .file    29    "c:\program files\nvidia gpu computing toolkit\cuda\v4.0\include\math_
functions_dbl_ptx1.h"


    .entry sample (
        .param .u64 __cudaparm_sample_a,
        .param .u64 __cudaparm_sample_b,
        .param .u64 __cudaparm_sample_c)
    {
    .reg .u32 %r<3>;
    .reg .u64 %rd<10>;
    .reg .f64 %fd<5>;
    .loc    16    33    0
$LDWbegin_sample:
    .loc    16    5    0
    cvt.s32.u16    %r1, %ctaid.x;
    cvt.s64.s32    %rd1, %r1;
    mul.wide.s32    %rd2, %r1, 8;
    ld.param.u64    %rd3, [__cudaparm_sample_a];
    add.u64    %rd4, %rd3, %rd2;
    ld.global.f64    %fd1, [%rd4+0];
    ld.param.u64    %rd5, [__cudaparm_sample_b];
    add.u64    %rd6, %rd5, %rd2;
    ld.global.f64    %fd2, [%rd6+0];
    add.f64    %fd3, %fd1, %fd2;
    ld.param.u64    %rd7, [__cudaparm_sample_c];
    add.u64    %rd8, %rd7, %rd2;
    st.global.f64    [%rd8+0], %fd3;
    .loc    16    35    0
    exit;
$LDWend_sample:
    } // sample

    .entry sample2 (
        .param .u64 __cudaparm_sample2_a,
        .param .u64 __cudaparm_sample2_b,
        .param .u64 __cudaparm_sample2_c)
    {
    .reg .u32 %r<7>;
    .reg .u64 %rd<12>;
    .reg .f64 %fd<8>;
    .reg .pred %p<4>;
    .loc    16    36    0
```

```
$LDWbegin_sample2:
    .loc    16    10    0
    cvt.s32.u16      %r1, %ctaid.x;
    cvt.s64.s32      %rd1, %r1;
    mul.wide.s32     %rd2, %r1, 8;
    ld.param.u64     %rd3, [__cudaparm_sample2_c];
    add.u64     %rd4, %rd3, %rd2;
    ld.param.u64     %rd5, [__cudaparm_sample2_b];
    ld.param.u64     %rd6, [__cudaparm_sample2_a];
    add.u64     %rd7, %rd2, %rd5;
    ld.global.f64     %fd1, [%rd7+0];
    add.u64     %rd8, %rd2, %rd6;
    ld.global.f64     %fd2, [%rd8+0];
    add.f64     %fd3, %fd1, %fd2;
    st.global.f64     [%rd4+0], %fd3;
    .loc    16    14    0
    mov.u32     %r2, 0;
    setp.le.s32      %p1, %r1, %r2;
    @%p1 bra     $Lt_1_3074;
    mov.s32     %r3, %r1;
    .loc    16    10    0
    ld.param.u64     %rd6, [__cudaparm_sample2_a];
    .loc    16    14    0
    mov.s64     %rd9, %rd6;
    .loc    16    10    0
    ld.param.u64     %rd5, [__cudaparm_sample2_b];
    .loc    16    14    0
    mov.s64     %rd10, %rd5;
    mov.s32     %r4, 0;
    mov.s32     %r5, %r3;
$Lt_1_3586:
//<loop> Loop body line 14, nesting depth: 1, estimated iterations: unknown
    .loc    16    17    0
    ld.global.f64     %fd4, [%rd9+0];
    ld.global.f64     %fd5, [%rd10+0];
    add.f64     %fd6, %fd4, %fd5;
    st.global.f64     [%rd4+0], %fd6;
    add.s32     %r4, %r4, 1;
    add.u64     %rd10, %rd10, 8;
    add.u64     %rd9, %rd9, 8;
    setp.ne.s32      %p2, %r4, %r1;
    @%p2 bra     $Lt_1_3586;
$Lt_1_3074:
    .loc    16    38    0
    exit;
$LDWend_sample2:
    } // sample2

    .entry pascalTriangle (
        .param .u64 __cudaparm_pascalTriangle_a,
        .param .u64 __cudaparm_pascalTriangle_b)
    {
    .reg .u32 %r<4>;
```

```
        .reg    .u64  %rd<8>;
        .reg    .f32  %f<5>;
        .reg    .pred %p<3>;
        .loc    16    39    0
$LDWbegin_pascalTriangle:
        .loc    16    40    0
        cvt.s32.u16    %r1, %ctaid.x;
        cvt.s64.s32    %rd1, %r1;
        mul.wide.s32    %rd2, %r1, 4;
        ld.param.u64    %rd3, [__cudaparm_pascalTriangle_a];
        add.u64     %rd4, %rd3, %rd2;
        ld.param.u64    %rd5, [__cudaparm_pascalTriangle_b];
        add.u64     %rd6, %rd5, %rd2;
        ld.global.f32    %f1, [%rd4+0];
        mov.u32     %r2, 0;
        setp.ne.s32     %p1, %r1, %r2;
        @%p1 bra     $Lt_2_1282;
        .loc    16    28    0
        st.global.f32     [%rd6+0], %f1;
        bra.uni     $Lt_2_1026;
$Lt_2_1282:
        .loc    16    29    0
        ld.global.f32    %f2, [%rd4+-4];
        add.f32     %f3, %f2, %f1;
        st.global.f32     [%rd6+0], %f3;
$Lt_2_1026:
        .loc    16    41    0
        exit;
$LDWend_pascalTriangle:
        } // pascalTriangle
        .global .u32 error;
```

The *CUDARuntime* class is responsible for managing how to load and execute functions on the GPU. *GPUExecution* is a wrapper class that also includes the function to generate the PTX file. *GPUExecution* class uses nvcc.exe with a *–ptx* switch to generate the PTX file. In the *Init* function, *GPUExecution* calls the *CUDARuntime* method to load the PTX file into the GPU, as shown in Listing 9-31.

LISTING 9-31 *GPUExecution* and the *CUDARuntime* class

CUDA runtime and CUDA array class

```
open System
open System.Text
open System.Collections.Generic
open System.Runtime.InteropServices

type uint = uint32
```

```
[<Struct>]
type CUDAModule =
    val Pointer : IntPtr

[<Struct>]
type CUDADevice =
    val Pointer : int

[<Struct>]
type CUDAContext =
    val Pointer : IntPtr

[<Struct>]
type CUDAFunction =
    val Pointer : IntPtr

module CudaDataStructureExtensions =
    let is64Bit = IntPtr.Size = 8

module InteropLibrary2 =
    [<DllImport("nvcuda")>]
    extern CUResult cuParamSetv(CUDAFunction hfunc, int offset, IntPtr ptr, uint numbytes)

module InteropLibrary =
    [<DllImport("nvcuda")>]
    extern CUResult cuModuleLoad(CUDAModule& m, string fn)
    [<DllImport("nvcuda")>]
    extern CUResult cuDriverGetVersion(int& driverVersion)
    [<DllImport("nvcuda")>]
    extern CUResult cuInit(uint Flags)
    [<DllImport("nvcuda", EntryPoint = "cuCtxCreate_v2")>]
    extern CUResult cuCtxCreate(CUDAContext& pctx, uint flags, CUDADevice dev)
    [<DllImport("nvcuda")>]
    extern CUResult cuDeviceGet(CUDADevice& device, int ordinal)
    [<DllImport("nvcuda")>]
    extern CUResult cuModuleGetFunction(CUDAFunction& hfunc, CUDAModule hmod, string name)
    [<DllImport("nvcuda")>]
    extern CUResult cuFuncSetBlockShape(CUDAFunction hfunc, int x, int y, int z)
    [<DllImport("nvcuda")>]
    extern CUResult cuLaunch(CUDAFunction f)
    [<DllImport("nvcuda")>]
    extern CUResult cuLaunchGrid(CUDAFunction f, int grid_width, int grid_height)

    [<DllImport("nvcuda", EntryPoint = "cuMemAlloc_v2")>]
    extern CUResult cuMemAlloc(CUDAPointer& dptr, uint bytesize)
    [<DllImport("nvcuda", EntryPoint = "cuMemcpyDtoH_v2")>]
    extern CUResult cuMemcpyDtoH(IntPtr dstHost, CUDAPointer srcDevice, uint ByteCount)
    [<DllImport("nvcuda", EntryPoint = "cuMemcpyHtoD_v2")>]
    extern CUResult cuMemcpyHtoD(CUDAPointer dstDevice, IntPtr srcHost, uint ByteCount)
    [<DllImport("nvcuda", EntryPoint = "cuMemFree_v2")>]
    extern CUResult cuMemFree(CUDAPointer dptr)
```

```
    [<DllImport("nvcuda")>]
    extern CUResult cuParamSeti(CUDAFunction hfunc, int offset, uint value)
    [<DllImport("nvcuda")>]
    extern CUResult cuParamSetf(CUDAFunction hfunc, int offset, float32 value)
    [<DllImport("nvcuda")>]
    extern CUResult cuParamSetv(CUDAFunction hfunc, int offset, int64& value, uint
numbytes)
    [<DllImport("nvcuda")>]
    extern CUResult cuParamSetSize(CUDAFunction hfunc, uint numbytes)

    [<DllImport("nvcuda", EntryPoint = "cuMemsetD8_v2")>]
    extern CUResult cuMemsetD8(CUDAPointer dstDevice, byte uc, uint N)
    [<DllImport("nvcuda", EntryPoint = "cuMemsetD16_v2")>]
    extern CUResult cuMemsetD16(CUDAPointer dstDevice, uint16 us, uint N)

type CUDAArray<'T>(cudaPointer:CUDAPointer2<_>, size:uint, runtime:CUDARunTime) =
    let unitSize = uint32(sizeof<'T>)
    interface IDisposable with
        member this.Dispose() = runtime.Free(cudaPointer) |> ignore
    member this.Runtime with get() = runtime
    member this.SizeInByte with get() = size
    member this.Pointer with get() = cudaPointer
    member this.UnitSize with get() = unitSize
    member this.Size with get() = int( this.SizeInByte / this.UnitSize )
    member this.ToArray<'T>() =
        let out = Array.create (int(size)) Unchecked.defaultof<'T>
        this.Runtime.CopyDeviceToHost(this.Pointer, out)

and CUDARunTime(deviceID) =
    let mutable device = CUDADevice()
    let mutable deviceContext = CUDAContext()
    let mutable m = CUDAModule()

    let init() =
        let r = InteropLibrary.cuInit(deviceID)
        let r = InteropLibrary.cuDeviceGet(&device, int(deviceID))
        let r = InteropLibrary.cuCtxCreate(&deviceContext, deviceID, device)
        ()
    do init()

    let align(offset, alignment) = offset + alignment - 1 &&& ~~~(alignment - 1);
    new() = new CUDARunTime(0u)

    interface IDisposable with
        member this.Dispose() = ()

    member this.LoadModule(fn) =
        (InteropLibrary.cuModuleLoad(&m, fn), m)
    member this.Version
        with get() =
            let mutable a = 0
            (InteropLibrary.cuDriverGetVersion(&a), a)
    member this.Is64Bit with get() = CudaDataStructureExtensions.is64Bit
```

```
member this.GetFunction(fn) =
    let mutable f = CUDAFunction()
    (InteropLibrary.cuModuleGetFunction(&f, m, fn), f)
member this.ExecuteFunction(fn, x, y) =
    let r, f = this.GetFunction(fn)
    if r = CUResult.Success then
        InteropLibrary.cuLaunchGrid(f, x, y)
    else
        r
member this.ExecuteFunction(fn) =
    let r, f = this.GetFunction(fn)
    if r = CUResult.Success then
        InteropLibrary.cuLaunch(f)
    else
        r
member this.ExecuteFunction(fn, [<ParamArray>] parameters:obj list) =
    let func = this.GetFunctionPointer(fn)
    this.SetParameter(func, parameters)
    let r = InteropLibrary.cuLaunch(func)
    r
member this.ExecuteFunction(fn, parameters:obj list, x, y) =
    let func = this.GetFunctionPointer(fn)
    let paras =
        parameters
        |> List.map (fun n -> match n with
                              | :? CUDAPointer2<float> as p -> box(p.Pointer)
                              | :? CUDAPointer2<float32> as p -> box(p.Pointer)
                              | :? CUDAPointer2<_> as p -> box(p.Pointer)
                              | _ -> n)

    this.SetParameter(func, paras)
    InteropLibrary.cuLaunchGrid(func, x, y)
member private this.GetFunctionPointer(fn) =
    let r, p = this.GetFunction(fn)
    if r = CUResult.Success then p
    else failwith "cannot get function pointer"

// allocate
member this.Allocate(bytes:uint) =
    let mutable p = CUDAPointer()
    (InteropLibrary.cuMemAlloc(&p, bytes), CUDAPointer2(p))
member this.Allocate(array) =
    let size = this.GetSize(array) |> uint32
    this.Allocate(size)
member this.GetSize(data:'T array) =
    this.MSizeOf(typeof<'T>) * uint32(data.Length)
member this.GetUnitSize(data:'T array) =
    this.MSizeOf(typeof<'T>)
member private this.MSizeOf(t:Type) =
    if t = typeof<System.Char> then 2u
    else Marshal.SizeOf(t) |> uint32
member this.Free(p:CUDAPointer2<_>) : CUResult =
    InteropLibrary.cuMemFree(p.Pointer)
```

```fsharp
    member this.CopyHostToDevice(data: 'T array) =
        let gCHandle = GCHandle.Alloc(data, GCHandleType.Pinned)
        let size = this.GetSize(data)
        let r, p = this.Allocate(size)
        let r = (InteropLibrary.cuMemcpyHtoD(p.Pointer, gCHandle.AddrOfPinnedObject(),
size), p)
        gCHandle.Free()
        r
    member this.CopyDeviceToHost(p:CUDAPointer2<_>, data) =
        let gCHandle = GCHandle.Alloc(data, GCHandleType.Pinned)
        let r = (InteropLibrary.cuMemcpyDtoH(
                    gCHandle.AddrOfPinnedObject(),
                    p.Pointer,
                    this.GetSize(data)),
                    data)
        gCHandle.Free()
        r

    //parameter setting
    member private this.SetParameter<'T>(func, offset, vector:'T) =
        let gCHandle = GCHandle.Alloc(vector, GCHandleType.Pinned)
        let numbytes = uint32(Marshal.SizeOf(vector))
        let r = InteropLibrary2.cuParamSetv(func, offset, gCHandle.AddrOfPinnedObject(),
numbytes)
        gCHandle.Free()
        r
    member private this.SetParameterSize(func, size) =
        if InteropLibrary.cuParamSetSize(func, size) = CUResult.Success then ()
        else failwith "set parameter size failed"
    member this.SetParameter(func, parameters) =
        let mutable num = 0
        for para in parameters do
            match box(para) with
            | :? uint32 as n ->
                num <- align(num, 4)
                if InteropLibrary.cuParamSeti(func, num, n) = CUResult.Success then ()
                else failwith "set uint32 failed"
                num <- num + 4
            | :? float32 as f ->
                num <- align(num, 4)
                if InteropLibrary.cuParamSetf(func, num, f) = CUResult.Success then ()
                else failwith "set float failed"
                num <- num + 4
            | :? int64 as i64 ->
                num <- align(num, 8)
                let mutable i64Ref = i64
                if InteropLibrary.cuParamSetv(func, num, &i64Ref, 8u) = CUResult.Success
then ()
                else failwith "set int64 failed"
                num <- num + 8
            | :? char as ch ->
                num <- align(num, 2)
                let bytes = Encoding.Unicode.GetBytes([|ch|])
```

```
                    let v = BitConverter.ToUInt16(bytes, 0)
                    if this.SetParameter(func, num, v) = CUResult.Success then ()
                    else failwith "set char failed"
                    num <- num + 2
            | :? CUDAPointer as devPointer ->
                num <- align(num, devPointer.PointerSize)
                if devPointer.PointerSize = 8 then
                    if this.SetParameter(func,
                                        num,
                                        uint64(int64(devPointer.Pointer)))
                                    = CUResult.Success then ()
                    else failwith "set device pointer failed"
                else
                    if InteropLibrary.cuParamSeti(func,
                                                num,
                                                uint32(int(devPointer.Pointer)))
                                    = CUResult.Success then ()
                    else failwith "set device pointer failed"
                num <- num + devPointer.PointerSize
            | :? CUDAArray<float32> as devArray ->
                let devPointer:CUDAPointer2<_> = devArray.Pointer
                num <- align(num, devPointer.PointerSize)
                if devPointer.PointerSize = 8 then
                    if this.SetParameter(func,
                                        num,
                                        uint64(int64(devPointer.Pointer.Pointer)))
                                    = CUResult.Success then ()
                    else failwith "set device pointer failed"
                else
                    if InteropLibrary.cuParamSeti(func,
                                                num,
                                                uint32(int(devPointer.Pointer.
Pointer)))
                                    = CUResult.Success then ()
                    else failwith "set device pointer failed"
                num <- num + devPointer.PointerSize
            | _ when para.GetType().IsValueType ->
                let n = int(this.MSizeOf(para.GetType()))
                num <- align(num, n)
                if this.SetParameter(func, num, box(para)) = CUResult.Success then ()
                else failwith "set no-char object"
                num <- num + n
            | _ -> failwith "not supported"
        this.SetParameterSize( func, uint32(num) )
```

Execution class

```
namespace FSharp.Execution

open System
open System.Diagnostics
open System.IO
open Microsoft.FSharp.Quotations
```

```fsharp
open Microsoft.FSharp.Quotations.Patterns
open Microsoft.FSharp.Quotations.DerivedPatterns
open Microsoft.FSharp.Quotations.ExprShape

type BlockID() =
    inherit dim3()

type GPUExecution () as this =
    let runtime = new CUDARunTime()
    let nvcc = "nvcc.exe"
    do this.Init() |> ignore

    interface IDisposable with
        member this.Dispose() = ()

    member this.Runtime with get() = runtime

    // compile the code to PTX file
    member private this.CompileToPTX() : string =
        let fn = @".\temp.cu"
        this.CompileToPTX(fn)

    // compile the file to PTX file and return PTX file name
    member private this.CompileToPTX(fn) : string =
        use p = new Process()
        let para = sprintf "%s -ptx" fn
        p.StartInfo <- ProcessStartInfo(nvcc, para)
        p.StartInfo.UseShellExecute <- false
        p.StartInfo.WindowStyle <- ProcessWindowStyle.Hidden
        p.Start() |> ignore
        p.WaitForExit()
        System.IO.Path.GetFileNameWithoutExtension(fn) + ".ptx"

    // compile to PTX file and load the PTX file to GPU
    member this.Init() =
        let fn = this.CompileToPTX()
        let r, m = runtime.LoadModule(fn)
        if isSuccess r then m
        else failwith "cannot load module"

    member this.Init(fn:string) =
        let fn = this.CompileToPTX(fn)
        let r,m = runtime.LoadModule(fn)
        if isSuccess r then m
        else failwith "cannot load module"

    // execute function loaded on GPU with parameter list
    member this.Execute(fn:string, list:'T array list) =
        let unitSize = (sizeof<'T>) |> uint32
        let size = list.Head.Length |> uint32
        let results =
            list
            |> List.map (fun l -> this.Runtime.CopyHostToDevice(l))
            |> List.map (fun (r,p) -> (r, new CUDAArray<'T>(p, size, this.Runtime)))
```

```
        let success = results |> Seq.forall (fun (r, _) -> isSuccess(r))
        if success then
            let pointers = results |> List.map snd
            let head = List.head list
            let result = this.Runtime.ExecuteFunction(
                            fn,
                            pointers |> List.map box,
                            head.Length,
                            1)
            let out = Array.create head.Length 0.f
            let a = this.Runtime.CopyDeviceToHost(pointers.[0].Pointer, out)
            (result, pointers)
        else
            failwith "copy host failed"

    // copy data from host (CPU) memory to device (GPU) memory
    member this.CopyHostToDevice(data: 'T array) =
        let r, out = this.Runtime.CopyHostToDevice(data)
        if r = CUResult.Success then out
        else failwith "cannot copy host to device"

    // copy data from device (GPU) memory to host (CPU) memory
    member this.CopyDeviceToHost(p:CUDAPointer2<_>, data) =
        let r, out = this.Runtime.CopyDeviceToHost(p, data)
        if r = CUResult.Success then out
        else failwith "cannot copy device to host"

    // convert a list to CUDA array
    member this.ToCUDAArray(l) =
        let r, array = this.Runtime.CopyHostToDevice(l)
        if r = CUResult.Success then array
        else failwith "cannot copy host to device"

    // execute function loaded on GPU with cuda array list
    member this.ExecuteFunction(fn:string, cudaArray:CUDAPointer list) =
        let r = this.Runtime.ExecuteFunction(
                    fn,
                    cudaArray |> List.map box,
                    cudaArray.Length,
                    1)
        r
```

Pascal Triangle

With everything ready, you can create a few examples that use the GPU. Listing 9-32 compares
the CPU and GPU versions of the Pascal Triangle computation. The execution result shows that the
GPU can finish the computation more efficiently, even with the additional overhead of loading and
retrieving the data from the GPU. If the data set is large, the data load time is relatively small and
applying the GPU is worthwhile. If the data set is small, most of the time will be spent on loading data
to and unloading data from the GPU, causing the GPU version to be slower.

LISTING 9-32 Pascal Triangle computation on CPU and GPU

```
let len = 1000

let blockIdx = new BlockDim()
let threadIdx = new ThreadIdx()

[<ReflectedDefinition; GPU>]
let pascalTriangle (a:CUDAPointer2<float32>) (b:CUDAPointer2<float32>) =
    let x = blockIdx.x
    if x = 0 then
        b.Set(a.[x], x)
    else
        b.Set(a.[x] + a.[x - 1], x)
    ()

// GPU version
let test3() =
    WriteToFile()      // it is defined in Listing 9-29
    let execution = new GPUExecution()
    let m = execution.Init(tempFileName)

    let stopWatch =  System.Diagnostics.Stopwatch()
    stopWatch.Reset()
    stopWatch.Start()

    let l0 = Array.zeroCreate len
    let l1 = Array.zeroCreate len
    l0.[0] <- 1.f
    l1.[0] <- 0.f
    let r, p = execution.Runtime.CopyHostToDevice(l0)
    let r, p2 = execution.Runtime.CopyHostToDevice(l1)
    let rs =
        [1..len]
        |> Seq.map (fun i ->
                        if i % 2 = 1 then
                            let r = execution.Runtime.ExecuteFunction(
                                        "pascalTriangle",
                                        [p; p2],
                                        len,
                                        1)
                            r
                        else
                            let r = execution.Runtime.ExecuteFunction(
                                        "pascalTriangle",
                                        [p2; p],
                                        len,
                                        1)
                            r)
        |> Seq.toList

    let result1, o1 = execution.Runtime.CopyDeviceToHost(p, l0)
    let result2, o2 = execution.Runtime.CopyDeviceToHost(p2, l1)
```

```
        stopWatch.Stop()
        printfn "%A" stopWatch.Elapsed
        ()

let computePascal(p:float32 array, p2:float32 array) =
        let len = p.Length
        [0..len-1]
        |> Seq.iter (fun i ->
                        if i = 0 then p2.[i] <- 1.f
                        else p2.[i] <- p.[i-1] + p.[i])

        ()

// CPU version of Pascal Triangle
let test4() =
        let stopWatch = System.Diagnostics.Stopwatch()
        stopWatch.Reset()
        stopWatch.Start()

        let l0 = Array.zeroCreate len
        let l1 = Array.zeroCreate len
        l0.[0] <- 1.f
        l1.[0] <- 0.f

        [1..len]
        |> Seq.map (fun i ->
                        if i % 2 = 1 then
                                let r = computePascal(l0, l1)
                                r
                        else
                                let r = computePascal(l1, l0)
                                r)
        |> Seq.toList
        |> ignore

        stopWatch.Stop()
        printfn "%A" stopWatch.Elapsed

        ()
```

Execution result that runs the CPU version followed by the GPU version

00:00:00.1034888
```
temp.cu
c:\mycode\codecenter\f#\fsharpgpu\fsharpgpu\bin\debug\CUDALibrary.h(56): warning
: variable "sizeT" was declared but never referenced

temp.cu
tmpxft_00001558_00000000-3_temp.cudafe1.gpu
tmpxft_00001558_00000000-10_temp.cudafe2.gpu
temp.cu
c:\mycode\codecenter\f#\fsharpgpu\fsharpgpu\bin\debug\CUDALibrary.h(56): warning
: variable "sizeT" was declared but never referenced
```

```
temp.cu
tmpxft_00000790_00000000-3_temp.cudafe1.gpu
tmpxft_00000790_00000000-10_temp.cudafe2.gpu
00:00:00.0448262
```

 Note Some functions in the preceding listing were defined previously.

Using Binomial Trees and the BOPM

If you've ever wondered about a real-world application for the Pascal Triangle code in Listing 9-32, you'll enjoy this section. The Pascal Triangle shows how to code and represent a way to use the GPU to process a binomial-tree-like structure. The Pascal Triangle is generated as shown in Figure 9-8.

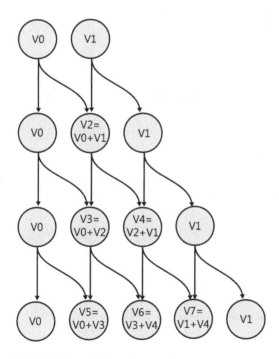

FIGURE 9-8 Pascal Triangle processing

In the financial sector in the United States, the binomial options pricing model (BOPM) uses a binomial tree to value options that are exercisable at any time in a given time interval. The pricing model generates a binomial tree like the one in Figure 9-9.

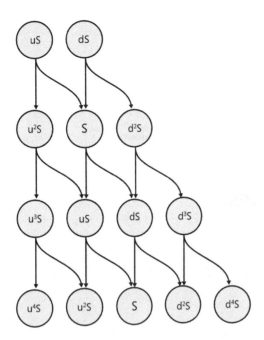

FIGURE 9-9 Binomial tree from BOPM

In the preceding diagram, you can find the following relationship:

$$A^{rowX}[i] = \begin{cases} A^{rowX-1}[i] \times u, & when\ i = 0 \\ A^{rowX-1}[i-1] \times d, & when\ i \neq 0 \end{cases}$$

You can easily change the Pascal Triangle function to the BOPM, as shown in Listing 9-33.

LISTING 9-33 The BOPM function

```
let blockIdx = new BlockDim()
let threadIdx = new ThreadIdx()

[<ReflectedDefinition; GPU>]
let bopm (a:CUDAPointer2<float32>) (b:CUDAPointer2<float32>) =
    let u = 0.2f
    let d = 1.f / u

    let x = blockIdx.x
    if x = 0 then
        b.Set(a.[x] * u, x)
    else
        b.Set(a.[x - 1] * d, x)
    ()
```

Maximum Values in Subarrays

Processing an array is one scenario where a GPU can be of help. Because the GPU has dozens of processors, it can process the elements simultaneously. In this section, you need to find the largest element in an array. The function takes the array and the search starting point and returns the largest element from the starting point.

Listing 9-34 shows a GPU version of the algorithm. For the GPU version, the code is straightforward. The starting point *x* will iterate to the end of the array. The maximum value is stored in the *max* variable and later will be assigned to another array. Some functions in Listing 9-34 are defined in code shown earlier in the chapter.

LISTING 9-34 Finding the maximum value in an array

```
let blockIdx = new BlockDim()
let threadIdx = new ThreadIdx()

let input = [1.f .. 15.f] |> Array.ofList

[<ReflectedDefinition; GPU>]
let sample4 (a:CUDAPointer2<float32>) (b:CUDAPointer2<float32>) : unit =
    let x = blockIdx.x
    let mutable max = 0.f
    for i = x to 15 do
        if max < a.[i] then
            max <- a.[i]
        else
            ()
    b.Set(max, x)

let WriteToFile2() =
    let a1 = <@@ sample4 @@>
    let b = getCUDACode(a1)      // defined in Listing 9-28
    let commonCode = getCommonCode()    // defined in Listing 9-28

    System.IO.File.Delete(tempFileName)  // defined in Listing 9-28
    System.IO.File.WriteAllText(tempFileName, commonCode + b);

let getMax() =
    let tempFileName = @".\temp.cu"
    WriteToFile2()
    let execution = new GPUExecution()
    let m = execution.Init(tempFileName)
    let output = Array.create input.Length 0.f
    let r, ps = execution.Execute("sample4", [input; output;])
    let results =
        ps
        |> List.map (fun p -> p.ToArray() |> snd)
    ()
```

Generated code in temp.cu

```
#include "CUDALibrary.h"


__device__ void ff_0(float* a, float* b) { int x;
x = blockIdx.x;
float max;
max = 0.0f;
for (int i = x; i<15; i++) { if ((max) < (a[i])) { max = a[i]; }
else { } };
b[x] = max; }


extern "C" __global__ void sample4 (float* a, float* b)  {
ff_0(a, b);
}
```

Using the Monte Carlo Simulation to Compute the π Value on a GPU

Other than using GPUs for array processing, you also can use them in simulations. In this section, you take a look at a small application designed to calculate the π using the Monte Carlo simulation. The algorithm is used to count the random generated number hit in two areas. The two areas are a square and, within it, a circle that touches each edge of the square. Figure 9-10 shows the positions of the circle and rectangle. If you know that the radius of the circle is r, the area of the circle is $circle\ area$ = πr^2. And the area of the square is $squareArea$ = $4r^2$. Imagine a large number of random hits in the rectangle area. The π value can be calculated from the number of hits in the circle area and the number of hits in the rectangle area.

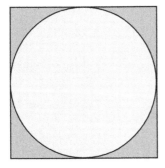

FIGURE 9-10 Position of the circle and rectangle in the Monte Carlo simulation for π

The cuRAND library provides functions used to generate uniform random numbers between 0 and 1. Instead of using the model shown in Figure 9-10, you can create a quarter of the circle whose area computation involves π. The diagram is shown in Figure 9-11. The formula to compute π value from *area1* and *area2* is listed here:

$$\frac{\frac{1}{4} \times \pi r^2}{r^2} = \frac{hit\ in\ area0}{hit\ in\ area1}$$

$$\frac{\pi}{4} = \frac{hit\ in\ area0}{hit\ in\ area1}$$

$$\pi = \frac{hit\ in\ area0}{hit\ in\ area1} \times 4$$

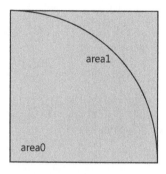

FIGURE 9-11 Monte Carlo computation for π using the cuRAND library

Before you can generate the code, the code translation function in Listing 9-35 is used to translate the *sqrt* function. The code then needs to be added to the *translateFromNETOperator* function shown in Listing 9-20.

LISTING 9-35 Translating the *sqrt* function

```
| "Sqrt" ->
    let l = getList()
    sprintf "sqrt(%s)" l.[0]
```

The GPU code is defined in the *sample3* function in Listing 9-36. The *WriteToFile2* function is used to get the function quotation and translate it to CUDA code. The computation result is passed back from the GPU to the CPU, allowing filtering and counting to happen on the CPU.

LISTING 9-36 Computing π using the GPU

```
let blockIdx = new BlockDim()
let threadIdx = new ThreadIdx()

[<ReflectedDefinition; GPU>]
let sample3 (a:CUDAPointer2<float32>) (b:CUDAPointer2<float32>) (c:CUDAPointer2<float32>)
=
    let x = blockIdx.x
    c.Set(sqrt(a.[x] * a.[x] + b.[x] * b.[x]), x)
    ()

let WriteToFile2() =
    let a1 = <@@ sample3 @@>
    let b = getCUDACode(a1)   // defined in Listing 9-28
    let commonCode = getCommonCode()   // defined in Listing 9-28

    System.IO.File.WriteAllText(tempFileName, commonCode + b);

let computePI() =
    let len = 1000
    WriteToFile2()
    let execution = new GPUExecution()
    let r = execution.Init(tempFileName)

    let r = CUDARandom()
    let status, g = r.CreateGenerator(CUDARandomRngType.CURAND_PSEUDO_DEFAULT)
    if status = curandStatus.CURAND_SUCCESS then
        let status, l0 = r.GenerateUniform(g, len)
        let status, l1 = r.GenerateUniform(g, len)

        let output = Array.create len 0.f
        let _ = execution.Runtime.CopyDeviceToHost(CUDAPointer2<_>(l0), output)
        let _ = execution.Runtime.CopyDeviceToHost(CUDAPointer2<_>(l1), output)
        let r, l2 = execution.Runtime.CopyHostToDevice(output)

        let r = execution.Runtime.ExecuteFunction("sample3", [l0; l1; l2], len, 1)
        let result, output = execution.Runtime.CopyDeviceToHost(l2, output)
        float ( output |> Seq.filter (fun n-> n<=1.f) |> Seq.length) / float len * 4.0
    else
        failwith "execution error"
```

> **Note** This program uses the cuRAND library; therefore, some types such as *curandStatus* are defined in Listing 9-9.

The generated code is shown in Listing 9-37.

LISTING 9-37 Generated code after running Listing 9-36

```
#include "CUDALibrary.h"

__device__ void ff_0(float* a, float* b, float* c) { int x;
x = blockIdx.x;
c[x] = sqrt(((a[x]) * (a[x])) + ((b[x]) * (b[x])));
; }


extern "C" __global__ void sample3 (float* a, float* b, float* c)  {
ff_0(a, b, c);
}
```

Generated PTX file after running the code from Listing 9-28

```
    .version 1.4
    .target sm_10, map_f64_to_f32
    // compiled with C:\Program Files\NVIDIA GPU Computing Toolkit\CUDA\v4.2\\bin/../
open64/lib//be.exe
    // nvopencc 4.1 built on 2012-04-07


    //-----------------------------------------------------------
    // Compiling C:/Users/taliu/AppData/Local/Temp/tmpxft_00000e3c_00000000-11_temp.cpp3.i
(C:/Users/taliu/AppData/Local/Temp/ccBI#.a02796)
    //-----------------------------------------------------------


    //-----------------------------------------------------------
    // Options:
    //-----------------------------------------------------------
    //  Target:ptx, ISA:sm_10, Endian:little, Pointer Size:64
    //  -O3    (Optimization level)
    //  -g0    (Debug level)
    //  -m2    (Report advisories)
    //-----------------------------------------------------------


    .file   1    "C:/Users/taliu/AppData/Local/Temp/tmpxft_00000e3c_00000000-10_temp.
cudafe2.gpu"
    .file   2    "c:\program files (x86)\microsoft visual studio
10.0\vc\include\codeanalysis\sourceannotations.h"
    .file   3    "C:\Program Files\NVIDIA GPU Computing Toolkit\CUDA\v4.2\bin/../include\
crt/device_runtime.h"
    .file   4    "C:\Program Files\NVIDIA GPU Computing Toolkit\CUDA\v4.2\bin/../include\
host_defines.h"
    .file   5    "C:\Program Files\NVIDIA GPU Computing Toolkit\CUDA\v4.2\bin/../include\
builtin_types.h"
    .file   6    "c:\program files\nvidia gpu computing toolkit\cuda\v4.2\include\device_
types.h"
    .file   7    "c:\program files\nvidia gpu computing toolkit\cuda\v4.2\include\host_
defines.h"
    .file   8    "c:\program files\nvidia gpu computing toolkit\cuda\v4.2\include\driver_
types.h"
```

```
    .file      9      "c:\program files\nvidia gpu computing toolkit\cuda\v4.2\include\
surface_types.h"
    .file     10      "c:\program files\nvidia gpu computing toolkit\cuda\v4.2\include\
texture_types.h"
    .file     11      "c:\program files\nvidia gpu computing toolkit\cuda\v4.2\include\
vector_types.h"
    .file     12      "c:\program files\nvidia gpu computing toolkit\cuda\v4.2\include\
builtin_types.h"
    .file     13      "C:\Program Files\NVIDIA GPU Computing
Toolkit\CUDA\v4.2\bin/../include\device_launch_parameters.h"
    .file     14      "c:\program files\nvidia gpu computing
toolkit\cuda\v4.2\include\crt\storage_class.h"
    .file     15      "temp.cu"
    .file     16      "c:\mycode\codecenter\f#\fsharpgpu\fsharpgpu\bin\debug\CUDALibrary.h"
    .file     17      "C:\Program Files\NVIDIA GPU Computing
Toolkit\CUDA\v4.2\bin/../include\common_functions.h"
    .file     18      "c:\program files\nvidia gpu computing toolkit\cuda\v4.2\include\math_
functions.h"
    .file     19      "c:\program files\nvidia gpu computing toolkit\cuda\v4.2\include\math_
constants.h"
    .file     20      "c:\program files\nvidia gpu computing
toolkit\cuda\v4.2\include\device_functions.h"
    .file     21      "c:\program files\nvidia gpu computing toolkit\cuda\v4.2\include\sm_11_
atomic_functions.h"
    .file     22      "c:\program files\nvidia gpu computing toolkit\cuda\v4.2\include\sm_12_
atomic_functions.h"
    .file     23      "c:\program files\nvidia gpu computing toolkit\cuda\v4.2\include\sm_13_
double_functions.h"
    .file     24      "c:\program files\nvidia gpu computing toolkit\cuda\v4.2\include\sm_20_
atomic_functions.h"
    .file     25      "c:\program files\nvidia gpu computing toolkit\cuda\v4.2\include\sm_20_
intrinsics.h"
    .file     26      "c:\program files\nvidia gpu computing toolkit\cuda\v4.2\include\sm_30_
intrinsics.h"
    .file     27      "c:\program files\nvidia gpu computing toolkit\cuda\v4.2\include\
surface_functions.h"
    .file     28      "c:\program files\nvidia gpu computing toolkit\cuda\v4.2\include\
texture_fetch_functions.h"
    .file     29      "c:\program files\nvidia gpu computing toolkit\cuda\v4.2\include\math_
functions_dbl_ptx1.h"


    .entry sample3 (
        .param .u64 __cudaparm_sample3_a,
        .param .u64 __cudaparm_sample3_b,
        .param .u64 __cudaparm_sample3_c)
    {
    .reg .u32 %r<3>;
    .reg .u64 %rd<10>;
    .reg .f32 %f<7>;
    .loc    15      9      0
$LDWbegin_sample3:
    .loc    15      5      0
    cvt.s32.u16    %r1, %ctaid.x;
```

```
        cvt.s64.s32      %rd1, %r1;
        mul.wide.s32     %rd2, %r1, 4;
        ld.param.u64     %rd3, [__cudaparm_sample3_b];
        add.u64     %rd4, %rd3, %rd2;
        ld.param.u64     %rd5, [__cudaparm_sample3_a];
        add.u64     %rd6, %rd5, %rd2;
        ld.global.f32     %f1, [%rd4+0];
        ld.global.f32     %f2, [%rd6+0];
        mul.f32     %f3, %f1, %f1;
        mad.f32     %f4, %f2, %f2, %f3;
        sqrt.approx.f32     %f5, %f4;
        ld.param.u64     %rd7, [__cudaparm_sample3_c];
        add.u64     %rd8, %rd7, %rd2;
        st.global.f32     [%rd8+0], %f5;
        .loc    15    11    0
        exit;
$LDWend_sample3:
        } // sample3
        .global .u32 error;
```

The filtering function can be moved from the CPU to the GPU, as shown in Listing 9-38. This new version performs the comparison inside the *sample3* function, which is executed on the GPU. The result is an array of 1 and 0, and the CPU side can simply add the array elements.

LISTING 9-38 GPU function that performs checks and related CPU functions

```
let blockIdx = new BlockDim()
let threadIdx = new ThreadIdx()


[<ReflectedDefinition; GPU>]
let sample3 (a:CUDAPointer2<float32>) (b:CUDAPointer2<float32>) (c:CUDAPointer2<float32>)=
    let x = blockIdx.x
    if sqrt(a.[x] * a.[x] + b.[x] * b.[x]) <= 1.f then
        c.Set(1.f, x)
    else
        c.Set(0.f, x)
    ()


computePI function

let computePI() =
    let len = 1000
    WriteToFile2()      // defined in Listing 9-34
    let execution = new GPUExecution()
    let r = execution.Init(tempFileName)

    let r = CUDARandom()
    let status, g = r.CreateGenerator(CUDARandomRngType.CURAND_PSEUDO_DEFAULT)
    if status = curandStatus.CURAND_SUCCESS then //defined in Listing 9-9
        let status, l0 = r.GenerateUniform(g, len)
```

```
        let status, l1 = r.GenerateUniform(g, len)

        let output = Array.create len 0.f
        let _ = execution.Runtime.CopyDeviceToHost(CUDAPointer2<_>(l0), output)
        let _ = execution.Runtime.CopyDeviceToHost(CUDAPointer2<_>(l1), output)
        let r, l2 = execution.Runtime.CopyHostToDevice(output)

        let r = execution.Runtime.ExecuteFunction("sample3", [l0; l1; l2], len, 1)
        let result, output = execution.Runtime.CopyDeviceToHost(l2, output)
        float ( output |> Seq.sum) / float len * 4.0
    else
        failwith "execution error"
```

Now let's examine the performance when the number of random data points increases. Listing 9-39 executes the function *computePI* with different array lengths. From the execution result, you can tell that the execution time does not increase significantly even when the array length increases exponentially, except for the first one, which performs a few one-time initialization operations.

LISTING 9-39 Measuring the GPU performance

```
let computePI() =
    WriteToFile2()      // defined in Listing 9-34
    let execution = new GPUExecution()
    let r = execution.Init(tempFileName)

    let r = CUDARandom()
    let status, g = r.CreateGenerator(CUDARandomRngType.CURAND_PSEUDO_DEFAULT)
    let sw = System.Diagnostics.Stopwatch()

    if status = curandStatus.CURAND_SUCCESS then // curandStatus is defined in Listing 9-9
        let compute(len) =
            sw.Reset()
            sw.Start()
            let status, l0 = r.GenerateUniform(g, len)
            let status, l1 = r.GenerateUniform(g, len)

            let output = Array.create len 0.f
            let _ = execution.Runtime.CopyDeviceToHost(CUDAPointer2<_>(l0), output)
            let _ = execution.Runtime.CopyDeviceToHost(CUDAPointer2<_>(l1), output)
            let r, l2 = execution.Runtime.CopyHostToDevice(output)

            let r = execution.Runtime.ExecuteFunction("sample3", [l0; l1; l2], len, 1)
            let result, output = execution.Runtime.CopyDeviceToHost(l2, output)
            let pi = float ( output |> Seq.sum) / float len * 4.0
            sw.Stop()
            pi, sw.ElapsedTicks

        [50; 100; 500; 1000; 5000; 10000]
        |> Seq.map compute
    else
        failwith "execution error"
```

Generated CUDA code

```
#include "CUDALibrary.h"

__device__ void ff_0(float* a, float* b) { int x;
x = blockIdx.x;
float max;
max = 0.0f;
for (int i = x; i < 15; i++) { if ((max) < (a[i])) { max = a[i]; }
else { } };
b[x] = max; }


extern "C" __global__ void sample4 (float* a, float* b)  {
ff_0(a, b);
}
```

Execution result

```
(3.04, 142194L)
(2.84, 1643L)
(3.152, 3595L)
(3.144, 3369L)
(3.1632, 4685L)
(3.1588, 3511L)
```

 Note Depending on your graphics card, you might run into errors when giving large numbers to the *computePI* function.

Useful Resources

If your requirements involve matrix manipulation or linear algebra, Statfactory's FCore numerical library: (http://www.statfactory.co.uk/) is a good choice. This library provides GPGPU-based matrix, linear algebra and random number generating functions.

Other than Statfactory library, the following websites are good resources for more information:

- General-Purpose Computation on Graphics Hardware (*http://gpgpu.org/developer/cuda*)

- CUDA Zone (*https://developer.nvidia.com/category/zone/cuda-zone*)

- OpenCL on NVIDIA (*https://developer.nvidia.com/opencl*)

- The Khronos Group (*http://www.khronos.org/opencl/*)

In Closing

For a C# developer, functional programming might not be a familiar concept. Chapter 1 to Chapter 3 introduced the imperative and object-oriented (OO) features. If you are planning to use F# in your project, you do not have to dedicate three months to learning a new language from scratch. Instead, you can start to implement some components from the material presented in Chapter 1 to Chapter 3. Chapter 4 to Chapter 6 introduced some F# unique features, such as type providers. Chapter 7 to Chapter 9 introduced a few F# applications. These chapters demonstrate how to solve complex problems using features introduced in previous chapters.

Functional programming is not a silver bullet. F# is a language that provides both functional and OO features. Having knowledge in these two areas is a perfect complementary skill set for the C# developer to solve daily programming tasks more efficiently. For example, the LINQ feature in C#, which is a functional programming concept, increasingly attracts developer interest and dramatically changes the way developers write code. A number of problems are solved more naturally by applying these functional programming concepts. If you are curious and motivated to explore a new way to talk to the computer, F# is a great candidate for further exploration.

Index

Symbols

About the Author

TAO LIU is a VP leading a team of .NET and Java developers in the Credit Technology group at Citi. He was a Software Design Engineer in Test (SDET) on the Microsoft F# team. A leader in the F# user community and organizer of the Seattle, Washington F# user group, Liu gives video talks on F# design patterns for Microsoft Channel 9 and he's the main contributor to the F# 3.0 sample package on Codeplex.

What do you think of this book?

We want to hear from you!
To participate in a brief online survey, please visit:

microsoft.com/learning/booksurvey

Tell us how well this book meets your needs—what works effectively, and what we can do better. Your feedback will help us continually improve our books and learning resources for you.

Thank you in advance for your input!